LET'S GO

VIETNAM

EDITORS
JULIE VODHANEL
JAKE SEGAL

RESEARCHER-WRITERS
ROSS ARBES
STEPHEN FAN
SARITHA KOMATIREDDY
ANNA ELSE PASTERNAK
JULIET SAMUEL

SHIYANG CAO MAP EDITOR
SILVIA GONZALEZ KILLINGSWORTH MANAGING EDITOR

ST. MARTIN'S PRESS ✶ NEW YORK

HELPING LET'S GO. If you want to share your discoveries, suggestions, or corrections, please drop us a line. We read every piece of correspondence, whether a postcard, a 10-page email, or a coconut. **Address mail to:**

> Let's Go: Vietnam
> 67 Mount Auburn St.
> Cambridge, MA 02138
> USA

Visit Let's Go at **http://www.letsgo.com,** or send email to:

> feedback@letsgo.com
> Subject: "Let's Go: Vietnam"

In addition to the invaluable travel advice our readers share with us, many are kind enough to offer their services as researchers or editors. Unfortunately, our charter enables us to employ only currently enrolled Harvard students.

Maps by David Lindroth copyright © 2007 by St. Martin's Press.

Distributed outside the USA and Canada by Macmillan.

Let's Go: Vietnam Copyright © 2007 by Let's Go, Inc. All rights reserved. Printed in the United States of America. No part of this book may be used or reproduced in any manner whatsoever without written permission except in the case of brief quotations embodied in critical articles or reviews. Let's Go is available for purchase in bulk by institutions and authorized resellers. For information, address St. Martin's Press, 175 Fifth Avenue, New York, NY 10010, USA.

ISBN-13: 978-0-312-36095-5
ISBN-10: 0-312-36095-9
Second edition
10 9 8 7 6 5 4 3 2 1

Let's Go: Vietnam s written by Let's Go Publications, 67 Mount Auburn St., Cambridge, MA 02138, USA.

Let's Go® and the LG logo are trademarks of Let's Go, Inc.

ADVERTISING DISCLAIMER. All advertisements appearing in Let's Go publications are sold by an independent agency not affiliated with the editorial production of the guides. Advertisers are never given preferential treatment, and the guides are researched, written, and published independent of advertising. Advertisements do not imply endorsement of products or services by Let's Go, and Let's Go does not vouch for the accuracy of information provided in advertisements.

If you are interested in purchasing advertising space in a Let's Go publication, contact: Let's Go Advertising Sales, 67 Mount Auburn St., Cambridge, MA 02138, USA.

LET'S GO

■ PAGES PACKED WITH ESSENTIAL INFORMATION

"Value-packed, unbeatable, accurate, and comprehensive."

—The Los Angeles Times

"The guides are aimed not only at young budget travelers but at the independent traveler; a sort of streetwise cookbook for traveling alone."

—The New York Times

"Unbeatable; good sight-seeing advice; up-to-date info on restaurants, hotels, and inns; a commitment to money-saving travel; and a wry style that brightens nearly every page."

—The Washington Post

■ THE BEST TRAVEL BARGAINS IN YOUR BUDGET

"All the dirt, dirt cheap."

—People

"Let's Go follows the creed that you don't have to toss your life's savings to the wind to travel—unless you want to."

—The Salt Lake Tribune

■ REAL ADVICE FOR REAL EXPERIENCES

"The writers seem to have experienced every rooster-packed bus and lunar-surfaced mattress about which they write."

—The New York Times

"[Let's Go's] devoted updaters really walk the walk (and thumb the ride, and trek the trail). Learn how to fish, haggle, find work—anywhere."

—Food & Wine

"A world-wise traveling companion—always ready with friendly advice and helpful hints, all sprinkled with a bit of wit."

—The Philadelphia Inquirer

■ A GUIDE WITH A SPIRIT AND A SOCIAL CONSCIENCE

"Lighthearted and sophisticated, informative and fun to read. [Let's Go] helps the novice traveler navigate like a knowledgeable old hand."

—Atlanta Journal-Constitution

"The serious mission at the book's core reveals itself in exhortations to respect the culture and the environment—and, if possible, to visit as a volunteer, a student, or a teacher rather than a tourist."

—San Francisco Chronicle

LET'S GO PUBLICATIONS

TRAVEL GUIDES

Australia 9th edition
Austria & Switzerland 12th edition
Brazil 1st edition
Britain 2007
California 10th edition
Central America 9th edition
Chile 2nd edition
China 5th edition
Costa Rica 3rd edition
Eastern Europe 12th edition
Ecuador 1st edition
Egypt 2nd edition
Europe 2007
France 2007
Germany 13th edition
Greece 8th edition
Hawaii 4th edition
India & Nepal 8th edition
Ireland 12th edition
Israel 4th edition
Italy 2007
Japan 1st edition
Mexico 21st edition
Middle East 4th edition
New Zealand 7th edition
Peru 1st edition
Puerto Rico 2nd edition
South Africa 5th edition
Southeast Asia 9th edition
Spain & Portugal 2007
Thailand 3rd edition
Turkey 5th edition
USA 23rd edition
Vietnam 2nd edition
Western Europe 2007

ROADTRIP GUIDE

Roadtripping USA 2nd edition

ADVENTURE GUIDES

Alaska 1st edition
Pacific Northwest 1st edition
Southwest USA 3rd edition

CITY GUIDES

Amsterdam 4th edition
Barcelona 3rd edition
Boston 4th edition
London 15th edition
New York City 16th edition
Paris 14th edition
Rome 12th edition
San Francisco 4th edition
Washington, D.C. 13th edition

POCKET CITY GUIDES

Amsterdam
Berlin
Boston
Chicago
London
New York City
Paris
San Francisco
Venice
Washington, D.C.

ABOUT LET'S GO

NOT YOUR PARENTS' TRAVEL GUIDE

At Let's Go, we see every trip as the chance of a lifetime. If your dream is to grab a machete and forge through the jungles of Brazil, we can take you there. If you'd rather bask in the Riviera sun at a beachside cafe, we'll set you a table. We write for readers who know that there's more to travel than sharing double deckers with tourists and who believe that travel can change both themselves and the world—whether they plan to spend six days in London or six months in Latin America. We'll show you just how far your money can go, and prove that the greatest limitation on your adventures is not your wallet, but your imagination.

BEYOND THE TOURIST EXPERIENCE

To help you gain a deeper connection with the places you travel, our fearless researchers scour the globe to give you the heads-up on both world-renowned and off-the-beaten-track attractions, sights, and destinations. They engage with the local culture, only to emerge with the freshest insights on everything from local festivals to regional cuisine. We've also opened our pages to respected writers and scholars to hear their takes on the countries and regions we cover, and asked travelers who have worked, studied, or volunteered abroad to contribute first-person accounts of their experiences. In addition, we increased our coverage of responsible travel and expanded each guide's Beyond Tourism chapter to share more ideas about how to give back while on the road.

FORTY-SEVEN YEARS OF WISDOM

Let's Go got its start in 1960, when a group of creative and well-traveled students compiled their experience and advice into a 20-page mimeographed pamphlet, which they gave to travelers on charter flights to Europe. Four and a half decades later, we've expanded to cover six continents and all kinds of travel—while retaining our founders' adventurous attitude toward the world. Laced with witty prose and total candor, our guides are still researched and written entirely by students on shoestring budgets, experienced travelers who know that train strikes, stolen luggage, food poisoning, and marriage proposals are all part of a day's work.

THE LET'S GO COMMUNITY

More than just a travel guide company, Let's Go is a community. Our small staff comes together because of our shared passion for travel and our desire to help other travelers see the world the way it was meant to be seen. We love it when our readers become part of the Let's Go community as well—when you travel, drop us a postcard (67 Mt. Auburn St., Cambridge, MA 02138, USA), send us an e-mail (feedback@letsgo.com), or post on our forum (http://www.letsgo.com/connect/forum) to tell us about your adventures and discoveries.

For more information, visit us online: www.letsgo.com.

HOW TO USE THIS BOOK

Before you go to Vietnam, this book will be your wise old mentor, purveying valuable advice. Once you're there, it will be your travel-savvy best friend, suggesting must-sees, giving you directions to them, and keeping you company on bus rides with entertaining, witty vignettes. And after you get back, this book will be a really, really good paperweight. Below, we tell you how to use it:

COVERING THE BASICS. Read this before you go. The first chapter, **Discover Vietnam** (p. 1), is meant to help you—ahem—discover Vietnam, with short overviews of travel there and **suggested itineraries** to help you plan yours. **Essentials** (p. 13) covers all things practical, like health and safety concerns, transport information, and more fun tips for safe travel. **Life And Times** (p. 55) provides valuable cultural and historical background that you can use to impress your friends. **Beyond Tourism** (p. 87) is just that—a chapter designed to point you to non-standard ways of experiencing Vietnam. Our delightful **Appendix** (p. 448) introduces you to the Vietnamese language, with a **pronunciation guide,** a **phrasebook,** and a **glossary.** The reader is invited to partake of sundry **conversion charts** as well.

COVERAGE LAYOUT. Read this as you go. We move from north to south; beautiful maps at the beginning of each chapter make it easy to navigate as you move from region to region. Coverage starts in Hà Nội, makes a sweep across the north, and then makes its way south to Hồ Chí Minh City (HCMC) and the Mekong Delta. There, having read everything else, you can re-read that gripping **appendix.**

TRANSPORTATION INFO. Each city and town includes **transportation** info in as exact a form as we can put it; bear in mind that departure/arrival times can be imprecise and may have changed after we researched them. Prepare to be flexible. If you want to get to Town X, but can't find it in the transportation section of the city you're in, you'll probably need to find an intermediate hub. Parenthetical bus/train info is divided like so: "(duration; departure time; price)."

SCHOLARLY ARTICLES, FEATURES, AND BOXES. This book stars four edifying scholarly articles on **helmets** (p. 91), the **economy** (p. 70), **phở** (p. 259), and **modernization** (p. 408). We've also prepared a mouthwatering panoply of **sidebars** and **boxes** by our researchers. Sidebars are insightful, entertaining supplements to the coverage, in the form of interviews with local notables, paeans to foods we like, travel stories, and so forth. Boxes are more practical and come in four flavors: warnings (**M**), helpful hints and resources (**⊠**), candid opinions (**⬛**), and cheap finds (**⬛**).

PRICE DIVERSITY. With each accommodation and food listing, you'll find an icon listing a price range; ranges are listed on p. xv. We rank establishments in order of quality, *not* price. Our favorites are indicated with a **⬛thumbs-up.**

PHONE CODES AND TELEPHONE NUMBERS. Area codes for each region appear opposite the name of the region and are denoted by the **☎** icon.

A NOTE TO OUR READERS. The information for this book was gathered by *Let's Go* researchers from May through August of 2006. Each listing is based on one researcher's opinion, formed during his or her visit at a particular time. Those traveling at other times may have different experiences since prices, dates, hours, and conditions are always subject to change. You are urged to check the facts presented in this book beforehand to avoid inconvenience and surprises.

CONTENTS

RESEARCHER-WRITERS

Ross Arbes *Southern Central Coast, Northern Central Vietnam*

O ROSS-TAIN! my Ross-tain! your fearful trip is done;
Your *xe ôm's* weather'd all setbacks, your literary prize is won;
The port is near, the bells we hear, the people all exulting,
While follow we your steady heels, your Georgian accent blaring:
But O heart! heart! heart!
   O the lovely things we've read!
We're grateful for the brilliant lines.
   And many laughs you've bred.

Stephen Fan *Northwest Highlands, Northern Vietnam, Northern Central Vietnam*

Two stilt houses in the Highlands stood,
And sorry he could not stay in both
And be one RW in the wood
He researched both as well he could
Before deciding to take an oath:

To research it all, just to be fair,
To get us the facts without pretense
To be the one who'd take the wear
Who'd trek through mountains without despair—
And that has made all the difference.

Saritha Komatireddy *Central Highlands, Southern Central Coast, Mekong Delta*

there's nowhere she has never traveled(entirely beyond
what third-world experience we needed—she jumped:
at the thought of VI ET
N AM['twixt mexico and rome.]
since revealing at first, her travel savvy
a *; never to disappoint. never; nevernever.
(we do not know what it is about her; but her chapters are unflawed)

Anna Pasternak *Hà Nội, Northern Coast, Northern Vietnam*

Once upon a shoreline breezy, while she researched, chic and cheery, / Many a quaint and curious aspect of restaurant decor, / As she finished, soon to start mapping, suddenly there came a flapping, / As of some food vendor unwrapping, unwrapping a sandwich of roasted boar. / "'I must be thorough,'" she muttered, "and eat this scary-looking boar; / I'll try this sandwich, and much, much more."
(...like cobra hearts and grilled scorpions.)

Juliet Samuel *Hồ Chí Minh City, Mekong Delta*

What happens to a Brit deterred?
Does her research crumble / Like a coffee cake?
Or get tough and dry / Like a well-done steak?
Does she shrink in the moment's heat?
Or turn cold and weary / Like London sleet?

Maybe she just quits / like a tired snail.

Or does she prevail?

CONTRIBUTING WRITERS

Sarah Rotman is a graduate of Harvard University and a former *Let's Go* researcher-writer, editor, and manager. An experienced traveler to Asia, she developed websites for local businesses in Hà Nội while living in Vietnam in 2003. Sarah is also an avid student of international business; she recently returned from Seoul, Korea, where she assisted in teaching a pre-MBA course at Korea University. She currently designs educational programs for businesses and schools in the US and Korea.

Matt Norcini is a high school US and World History teacher in Tampa, Florida, and a recipient of a Fulbright-Hays Fellowship to Thailand and Vietnam. He engages his students by making cutting remarks involving barnyard animals and his favorite historical character, Smedley Butler. His hobbies include traveling, writing, and challenging his intestinal fortitude by sampling open-market foods in developing nations.

Jeff Fortescue is a noodle soup enthusiast and reference librarian who regrets he can't get phở for breakfast in Pittsburgh.

ACKNOWLEDGMENTS

TEAM VIET THANKS: our awesomely epic and always hard-core RWs: agent arbes, sfan, anita, j, and phantom—this book is yours. silvia—wow. you taught us everything. sergio, for empowering us, and THAI for dealing with our ridiculousness. CORI, for laughs. shiyang—you rock our digital world. laura martin, for what we want to be when we grow up. jesse, for a good rough draft and endearing narcissism. jzac, for tons of good advice. matt norcini, for successfully pretending to be a scholar. and last but not least, Việt Nam—for amazingly delicious food and coffee, but probably for other things, too.

JULIE THANKS: jake, for keeping me sane and for absurd dedication; silvia, for signing up to be my therapist, and for all the emo music; sergio, for knowing; anne, bev, and helen, for giving me something to come home to; mrs. ford, for getting me here; and mom, dad, trina, and mark—for four giant sets of footsteps to follow in, and for always letting me go when i wanted to make my own.

JAKE THANKS: julie, for putting up with me, for an amazing work ethic, for great FM dancing. silvia, for crazy slash amazing slash best-ever. mrol, for funny. serg—you're great. shiyang—mapping god. The 'rents, for everything—rides and meals and fam fun. josh, for letting me ramble. cec, of course—most of all—too much to say. friends, phở, and fuz—and —make for one hell of a summer. who's coming to 'nam with me?

SHIYANG THANKS: Cliff, for bearing with me; Mapland, for the laughs; the RWs, for lots of numbers and colors; my roommate Howard, for doing the dishes; my girlfriend Yiying, for support; and my family—for everything.

Editors
Julie Vodhanel
Jake Segal
Managing Editor
Silvia Gonzalez Killingsworth
Map Editor
Shiyang Cao
Typesetter
Ariel Fox

LET'S GO

Publishing Director
Alexandra C. Stanek
Editor-in-Chief
Laura E. Martin
Production Manager
Richard Chohaney Lonsdorf
Cartography Manager
Clifford S. Emmanuel
Editorial Managers
August Dietrich, Samantha Gelfand, Silvia Gonzalez Killingsworth
Financial Manager
Jenny Wong
Publicity Manager
Anna A. Mattson-DiCecca
Personnel Manager
Sergio Ibarra
Production Associate
Chase Mohney
IT Director
Patrick Carroll
Director of E-Commerce
Jana Lepon
Office Coordinators
Adrienne Taylor Gerken, Sarah Goodin

Director of Advertising Sales
Mohammed J. Herzallah
Senior Advertising Associates
Kedamai Fisseha, Roumiana Ivanova

President
Brian Feinstein
General Manager
Robert B. Rombauer

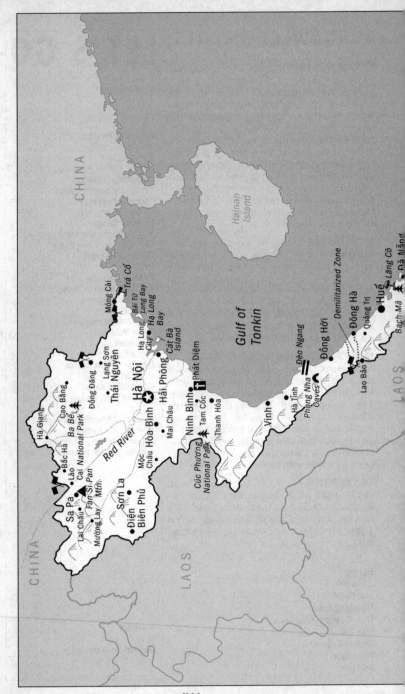

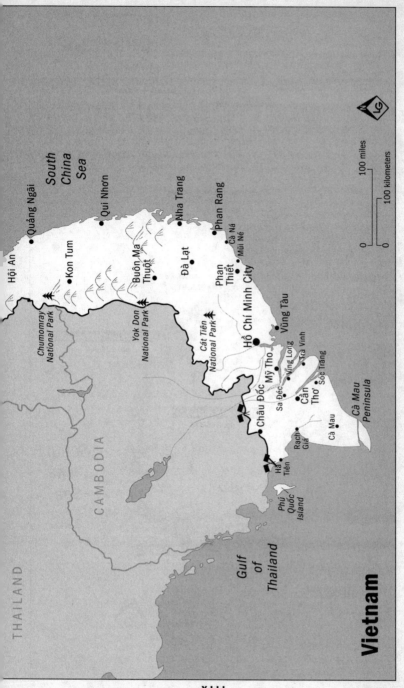

Vietnam

THAILAND

CAMBODIA

Gulf of Thailand

South China Sea

Hội An
Quảng Ngãi
Qui Nhơn
Kon Tum
Buôn Ma Thuột
Đà Lạt
Nha Trang
Phan Rang
Cà Ná
Mũi Né
Phan Thiết
Hồ Chí Minh City
Vũng Tàu
Châu Đốc
Mỹ Tho
Sa Đéc
Vĩnh Long
Trà Vinh
Cần Thơ
Sóc Trăng
Cà Mau
Rạch Giá
Hà Tiên
Cà Mau Peninsula
Phú Quốc Island

Chumomray National Park
Yok Don National Park
Cát Tiên National Park

0   100 miles
0   100 kilometers

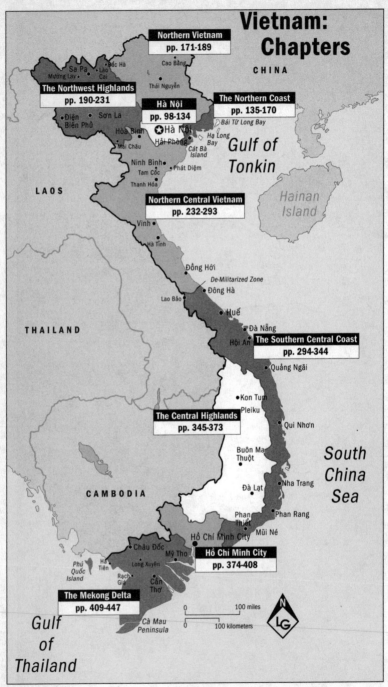

Vietnam: Chapters

Northern Vietnam
pp. 171-189

CHINA

Cao Bằng

Bắc Hà
Sa Pa
Lào Cai
Mường Lay
Thái Nguyên

The Northwest Highlands
pp. 190-231

The Northern Coast
pp. 135-170

Điện Biên Phủ
Sơn La

Hà Nội
pp. 98-134

Bái Tử Long Bay

Hòa Bình
Mai Châu

Hà Nội
Hải Phòng

Hạ Long Bay

Cát Bà Island

Gulf of Tonkin

LAOS

Ninh Bình
Tam Cốc
Phát Diệm
Thanh Hóa

Hainan Island

Northern Central Vietnam
pp. 232-293

Vinh

Hà Tĩnh

Đồng Hới

De-Militarized Zone

Đông Hà

Lao Bảo

Huế

THAILAND

Đà Nẵng

Hội An

The Southern Central Coast
pp. 294-344

Quảng Ngãi

Kon Tum
Pleiku

The Central Highlands
pp. 345-373

Qui Nhơn

Buôn Ma Thuột

South China Sea

Đà Lạt
Nha Trang

CAMBODIA

Phan Thiết
Phan Rang
Mũi Né

Hồ Chí Minh City

Châu Đốc
Mỹ Tho

Hồ Chí Minh City
pp. 374-408

Phú Quốc Island
Hà Tiên
Long Xuyên
Rạch Giá
Cần Thơ

The Mekong Delta
pp. 409-447

0   100 miles

0   100 kilometers

Cà Mau Peninsula

N

LG

Gulf of Thailand

PRICE RANGES>>VIETNAM

Our researchers list establishments in order of value from best to worst; our favorites are denoted by the Let's Go thumbs-up (🌟). Because the best value is not always the cheapest price, however, we have also incorporated a system of price ranges, based on a rough expectation of what you'll spend. For **accommodations,** we base our range on the cheapest price for which a single traveler can stay for one night. For **restaurants** and other dining establishments, we estimate the average amount a traveler will spend. The table tells you what you'll *typically* find in Vietnam at the corresponding price range; keep in mind that no system can allow for every individual establishment's quirks, and you'll typically get more for your money in larger cities. Expect anything. Even insect semen.

ACCOMMODATIONS	RANGE	WHAT YOU'RE *LIKELY* TO FIND
❶	under US$6 under 96,000Đ	A basic budget hotel, featuring running water, a bed, shared bath, and probably some six-legged visitors. The lucky few may be blessed with hot water, TV, private bath, or a fan.
❷	US$6-10 96,000-160,000Đ	Cleaner, and likely to be either a state-owned concrete block or in the middle of backpacker central. A/C and TV for the fortunate. Perhaps an insect, but it just wants to be your friend.
❸	US$10-16 160,000-255,000Đ	Similar to 2, with more amenities and usually in a quieter part of town. Often has A/C, TV, private bath, fridge, cleanliness, and tourist services. Hope for Internet and breakfast, too.
❹	US$16-30 255,000-480,000Đ	A resort, or maybe a business hotel. Usually has excellent service, all of the amenities, and prime location. Lots of tourist services, meant to prevent you from leaving. Ever.
❺	over US$30 over 480,000Đ	Can you say "really really really nice hotel or resort?" If it's a 5 and doesn't have everything you want, you paid too much.

FOOD	RANGE	WHAT YOU'RE *LIKELY* TO FIND
❶	under US$1.25 under 20,000Đ	Basic phở (noodle) and cơm (soup) shops, or bakeries and dessert venues. Don't expect a menu, or for that matter, seats.
❷	US$1.25-2.50 20,000-40,000Đ	Local joints, sometimes hole-in-the-wall establishments, but should have seating. Noodles with meat or veggies. The menu might be extensive and probably won't be in English.
❸	US$2.50-4.50 40,000-70,000Đ	All the expected dishes in a slightly more pleasant setting. No lack of new and exciting gastronomic options! Try the cat.
❹	US$4.50-6.25 70,000-100,000Đ	Often catered to tourists. Exotic dishes or Western comfort foods likely to be well prepared, or at least appear that way.
❺	over US$6.25 over 100,000Đ	The freshest meat and fish, cooked to perfection. Excellent service should be a part of the experience; ditto amazing location. It had better be worth writing home about.

WWW.LETSGO.COM
HERE TODAY, WHEREVER YOU'RE HEADED TOMORROW.

Whether you're planning your next adventure or are already far afield, letsgo.com will play companion to your wanderlust.

LET'S GO
COSTA RICA

NEXT 96 km

LET'S GO
AUSTRALIA

Peruse our articles and descriptions as you select the spots you're off to next. If we're making your decision harder, consult fellow travelers on our written and photo forums or search for anecdotal advice in our researchers' blogs.

If you're itching to leave, there's no need to shake that pesky travel bug. From embassy locations to passport laws, we keep track of all the essentials, so find out what you need to know fast, book that high-season hostel bed, and hit the road.

LET'S GO
THAILAND

READY. SET. LET'S GO

DISCOVER VIETNAM

Vietnam is tough. Vietnam is the country, after all, that swallows beating cobra hearts in rice whiskey to relax after-hours. It is a country whose will to live has been challenged since its inception by foreign armies without number—from impassive imperial China to the bloodthirsty Khmer Rouge, from colonial France to the napalm bombers of the Americans. Vietnam is hallucinogenic limestone landscapes and dense forests sprawling across chocolate river deltas, insane high-pitched motorbike traffic and 5-to-9 workdays. And travel here is subject to the same extremes. Expect endless, comically crowded bus rides blaring the same four Vietpop songs without cease; expect to spend hours a day negotiating the price of absolutely everything; expect to be pummeled by waves of mind-numbing heat and 48-hour batteries of rain; expect to be stared at; expect motorbike break-downs in deserted mountains. In short—expect adventure. Unparalleled, expectation-breaking, story-making, life-changing adventure.

FACTS AND FIGURES

POPULATION: 84.5 million.	**MEDIAN AGE:** 25.9 years.
NUMBER OF VIETNAMESE ETHNIC GROUPS: 54.	**AVERAGE HEIGHT OF A VIETNAMESE MAN IN HIS TWENTIES:** 162.5cm.
NUMBER OF POLITICAL PARTIES: 1.	**PRICE OF BIA HO'I (BEER):** 1500Đ.
TOTAL AREA: 329,560 sq. km.	**PRICE OF BOTTLED WATER:** 5000Đ.
TOTAL AREA UNDER NATIONAL PROTECTION: 21,949 sq. km.	**AVERAGE ANNUAL HUMIDITY:** 84%.
LENGTH FROM NORTH TO SOUTH: 1650km.	**TONS OF RICE PRODUCED ANNUALLY:** 38 million.
WIDTH OF THE COUNTRY AT QUẢNG BÌNH PROVINCE: 50km.	**NUMBER OF SECONDS A SNAKE'S HEART CONTINUES BEATING ONCE DROPPED INTO A SHOT OF WHISKEY:** Depends on how many seconds it takes for it to meet the human digestive tract.
HIGHEST ELEVATION: 3144m.	
TOTAL COASTLINE: 3444km, excluding islands.	**HIV INFECTION RATE:** 0.3% (2006).
TOTAL NUMBER OF ISLANDS IN HẠ LONG BAY: 1969.	**DISTANCE TO THE NEAREST ENGLISH-SPEAKING CONTINENT (AUSTRALIA):** 5100km.

What you pay in time, sweat, and energy in Vietnam, you get back a thousand-fold. The natural beauty of the country is legendary and spectacularly varied, with brilliant white beaches and lonely mountain passes that pierce the clouds. Jagged monoliths shoot up from mirror-bright bays in the far north; intricate lattices of canals run under mangrove canopies in the far south. The landscape resonates, too, with a history both chaotic and profound via faded, millennia-old relics of fallen dynasties and abandoned tanks and bunkers rusting under new grass. The country's architecture echoes the same contorted past, from eye-bending Chàm ruins and bucolic French villas to glass-and-steel monuments to globalization.

TOP 10 PLACES
TO GET LOST

There's a lot to be said for travel-ing to the middle of nowhere—especially when it's as naturally stunning as Vietnam. Parts of the country are overrun with travelers, but other parts are lonely, iso-lated, and absolutely breathtak-ing. Try getting lost here:

10. Phan Thiết (p. 337) and **Mũi Né** (p. 341). If you haven't heard of Vietnam's famous *nước mắm,* your olfactory glands will soon let you in on the secret. Wan-der through Phan Thiết's fish sauce refineries and be sure to leave time to visit the Sahara-style sand dunes and Red Canyon near Mũi Né. Oh, and did we mention there's a beach?

9. The Central Highlands (p. 345). Hang out with ethnic minor-ity villagers and drink coffee straight from the bush in small towns and villages between Đà Lạt and Kon Tum. Don't miss the pristine lakes, national parks, and giant concrete chicken (p. 357).

8. Floating Villages near Châu Đốc (p. 446). Take a canoe down the Mekong to visit these ingenious boathouse villages, and try to figure out how it is that they have electricity. Hint: no one really knows.

7. Củ Chi Tunnels (p. 403). Please don't actually get lost, though. The ingenious under-ground hideouts of the Việt Cộng are nice places to visit, but you wouldn't want to live there.

[Cont'd on next page...]

Inevitably, you will be blown away by Vietnam-ese cuisine. Masterfully subtle, in the debt of kitch-ens from Sichuan Province to Marseille, meals considered prosaic by everyday Vietnamese are nonetheless revered by epicures the world over. And no meal better expresses the country's culi-nary genius than phở—tender rice noodles under thin sheets of beef, floating in amber broth with ginger, star anise, mint, basil, and lime. It's the national food, the street food, the breakfast-lunch-and-dinner food of both the urban poor and the five-star kitchens. It's that good.

The people of Vietnam are stubborn, demanding, and intensely proud of their country. To travelers unused to constant bargaining and zero personal space, they can be extremely frustrating; they can also be what makes your visit more meaningful than you ever would have expected. The fundamen-tal good nature and sincere extraversion of the Vietnamese are overwhelming. You'll be invited to play pick-up football with kids in the street, cele-brate Tết in the living rooms of joyful families, and coach English at every available opportunity. But best of all is their contagious, undying optimism; in the face of warfare, poverty, and hunger, there per-sists in Vietnam the belief that things will get bet-ter—much better—fueled by the tireless will to make them so. Today's Vietnam is modernizing with a vengeance, and the atmosphere is thick with hope and breathless anticipation.

Yes, Vietnam is tough. But you didn't pick up this book for "easy." You chose Vietnam because you want travel to thrill and amaze you—because you want stories that will last you the rest of your life. You chose it for the dizzying diversity of landscapes, tastes, and ethnicities that make traveling to Viet-nam, dare we say, the greatest adventure on the planet. So go. And take us with you.

WHEN TO GO

When you go depends on where you go. The coun-try's climate is completely subject to the whims of tropical monsoons, which are unpredictable, espe-cially on the coast. Northwest and southeast mon-soons are seasonal; travelers will be delighted to know that additional, unscheduled tropical storms can wreak havoc at any time. Monsoons on the northern coast are most likely to occur between July and November, while from Huế south they hit earlier, in April and May. And it is always humid, almost everywhere in the country.

The timing and character of Vietnam's seasons vary substantially from north to south. In the south, temperatures remain reasonably constant, but precipitation is seasonal, with the dry season from November to March and the wet season from May to October. The farther north you go, the more the temperature varies between winter and summer, hitting punishing spikes in the northwestern highlands (40°C in the summer; the odd snowfall during January and February). Just to complicate matters, dry and wet seasons are inverted along the central coast, where the dry season occurs from March to August— but beware that on the coast, "dry season" is an admittedly optimistic term.

Thus, travelers destined for the **north** should time their visit between October and December or March and April, the months between the summer's heat and humidity and the cold, misty drizzle of the winter. During the summer, lower temperatures make Hà Nội somewhat more bearable than the rural areas of the Red River Delta. Along the **Northern Coast,** September through December and March through April are the most advisable periods during which to visit, as errant tropical storms are less likely after October. Farther down the coast, especially from Huế south, visits are most pleasant between February and May, due to the reversal of the wet season. The **Central Highlands** are best visited during the dry season between December and April, although the later you go, the hotter it gets; the same applies to **Hồ Chí Minh City (HCMC)** and the **Mekong Delta,** where summer torrents prove particularly disruptive to regional transportation. On the bright side, there's usually somewhere in the country that's sunny and dry at any given time. But if you're traveling throughout the country, do what everyone else does: bring a durable raincoat, and expect to get wet anyway.

WHAT TO DO

Vietnam's sheer range of landscapes and scope of history can keep you happily occupied for the rest of your natural life, and while that wouldn't necessarily be a bad thing, your visa might run out. To help you prioritize, Let's Go has compiled some of the country's best features and written its highlights into suggested itineraries. Don't forget to take plenty of detours.

TREK, PEDAL, AND ZOOM

Breathtaking vistas and hikes are a đồng a dozen in this country. Rural Vietnam is characterized by

6. Huế (p. 270). Vietnam has the best food in the world; Huế has the best food in Vietnam. Lose all self-restraint as you eat your way through the amazingly, mind-blowingly delicious cuisine of this old imperial capital.

5. Cao Bằng (p. 175). This province is remote and serene. Montagnard markets and virginal lakes are highlights; find out how four loosely associated bamboo logs can be technically classified as a "vehicle."

4. Chợ Lớn (p. 390). Even HCMC has a Chinatown. The chaotic markets at each end of this district make for some of the best people-watching sites in the city, and Chinese medicine shops and fabric stalls will lure both your interest and your đồng.

3. Bái Tử Long Bay (p. 159). Hạ Long Bay's untouristed alternative. Don't miss the untarnished splendor of Ba Mun Island's nature reserve or the perfect beaches of Quán Lạn. Electricity is optional. Lounging on the beach is not.

2. The road from Mường Lay to Tuần Giáo (p. 213). Only hardcore escapists need apply. Roads are dicey, towns are desolate and refreshingly amenity-free, and the rolling, mountainous landscape is simply unbelievable.

1. Ninh Bình Province (p. 232). So close to Hà Nội, yet so far from its madding crowd. Limestone monoliths shoot up from verdant rice fields, and ancient temples dot the hills. The natural beauty of this province defies words. Just go.

lovely and less-than-lovely towns surrounded on all sides by natural splendor; get a map or a guide, rent an old-fashioned bicycle or a speedy ■**motorbike,** and go exploring. Among the mountains and pristine lakes of the north, base yourself in **Cao Bằng** (p. 175), **Bắc Hà** (p. 202), **Sa Pa** (p. 194), or **Mai Châu** (p. 226). Ethnic minority homes and villages dot the mountainous landscape. While near Hà Nội, don't miss the jungles and beaches of **Cát Bà Island** (p. 142) and the isolated islands of **Bái Tử Long Bay** (p. 159). Northern central Vietnam's limestone karsts shoot up from the rice paddies near **Ninh Bình** (p. 232), while lonely mountain passes overlook the coast in **Hà Tĩnh Province** (p. 252) and the valleys and summits of **Bạch Mã National Park** (p. 290). **Yok Don** (p. 367) and **Cát Tiên** (p. 358), two national parks in the central highlands, make for laid-back forays into a wilderness filled with endangered species. Past HCMC, boats trump boats as a means of transportation in the Mekong Delta; nevertheless, **Phú Quốc Island** (p. 431) has some trek-worthy forests and shining white beaches for relaxing. For more national parks, flip a few pages to our suggested itinerary, **Park Avenue** (p. 10).

GET WET

Vietnam is a long, skinny country with 3444km of coastline, dominated by river deltas and rice paddies—if there weren't water activities galore, something would be seriously wrong. The natural place to start is the **Mekong Delta** (p. 409). Take boat tours to the floating villages near **Châu Đốc** (p. 444) and floating markets near **Cần Thơ** (p. 418) for proof that dry land is overrated. **Phú Quốc Island** (p. 431) features beautiful strips of sand, as well as snorkeling and scuba diving among the underwater denizens of the Gulf of Thailand. The cheerful seaside towns of **Hà Tiên** (p. 439) and **Rạch Giá** (p. 429) are also some of our Mekong favorites. Moving up from HCMC, life becomes one enormous beach along the southern central coast, starring Saigonese favorite **Vũng Tàu** (p. 404), resort-happy **Mũi Né** (p. 341), and beach party town **Nha Trang** (p. 323), filled with floating wine bars. Farther north, the shoreline becomes more popular with domestic vacationers and less so with foreign tourists, but the beaches remain first-class. We recommend **China Beach** (p. 303) near Đà Nẵng, **Cua Dai** (p. 314) next to Hội An, **Lăng Cô** (p. 293) under lofty Hai Van Pass, **Cửa Lò** (p. 251) near Vinh, **Sầm Sơn** (p. 245) near Thanh Hóa, and the distant, sun- and seashell-dappled **Trà Cổ** (p. 169) down the road from Móng Cái. In from the coast, the floating tours of **Kênh Gà** (p. 238) and of the caves near **Tam Cốc** (p. 237) are spectacular. For boat rides across lakes in the north, try the man-made duo of **Núi Cốc** (p. 189), and **Sông Đà** (p. 231). Finally, the 1969 islands and islets of **Hạ Long Bay** (p. 153) and **Bái Tử Long Bay** (p. 159) create a labyrinthine paradise; tour the grottoes, go for a swim, or relax on the sand. For a method to your beach-crazed madness, try our **Go Coastal** itinerary (p. 9).

EAT

Skipping out on some of the world's most revered cuisine would be the worst decision you have ever made. Ever. Vietnamese food is life-changing. It ranges from the delicate and exquisite to the more adventurous; we've all heard about meals featuring dog and cat, but snake penis and cock testicles have graced many a menu as well. For starters, street food—■**phở** (noodle soup) and **cơm** (rice dishes)—is ubiquitous, inexpensive, and delicious. The odoriferous and powerful **fish sauce** (*nước mắm*), made from huge volumes of fish fermenting in a vat, is the country's culinary alpha and omega, though it's admittedly an acquired taste. Don't knock it until you've tried it at least 10 or 15 times; much of what you eat will incorporate it so subtly that you won't know it's there. **Phú Quốc Island** (p. 431) and **Phan Thiết** (p. 337) are major producers of the amber goodness. **Hội An** (p. 304)—the culinary capital of the country—and **Huế** (p. 270) are famed for distinctive cuisines; Huế's crepes and omelettes will absolutely floor your taste buds. Vietnam's exotic **fruits** (p. 77) are also sources of constant joy for travelers. The country is a major exporter of coffee, with its plantations centered around **Buôn Ma Thuột** (p. 361). Try everything (and yes, street food is reasonably safe); eat things that will make your friends drool and your little sister cringe. For a food-themed journey, test-drive our tempting and delicious **Phở Real** itinerary (p. 11).

BURN INCENSE

Pagodas and temples without number stud the hills, fields, and streets of Vietnam. Vietnam's **triple religion** (p. 57) is largely structured around the ritual and practice of Mahayana Buddhism; one of its spiritual centers is the **Perfume Pagoda** (*Chùa Hương*; p. 131) near Hà Nội. The countryside around the Vietnamese capital is liberally blessed with an abundance of other pagodas as well. Ancient **Huế** (p. 270) is rich with religious architecture; take a bike and pedal from *chùa* to *chùa* in the city's tranquil suburbs. After visiting magnificently intricate **Giác Lâm Pagoda** (p. 397) and the other Buddhist places of worship in **Hồ Chí Minh City** (p. 374), you can switch faiths and check out the Vietnamese **Notre Dame Cathedral** (p. 396), along with sundry other churches, mosques, and Hindu temples—an interesting reflection of the city's religious diversity. North of the city, the enormous, eye-popping **Cao Đài Holy See** (p. 404) is the world center of Cao Đài, a syncretic greatest-hits religion in which Jesus Christ, Muhammad, the Buddha, Lao Tse, Joan of Arc, Shakespeare, and, needless to say, V.I. Lenin are all considered prophets or saints. Vietnam also brings its religion to the beach, in the form of the Buddha, Jesus, and Madonna statues at **Vũng Tàu** (p. 404). Literally every town in Vietnam has its own pagoda or six, and many are peaceful, intricate, and beautiful.

LIVE FOR THE CITY

Urban Vietnam explodes with energy and history. While the country's mountains and beaches get a lot of attention, the cities are absorbing in their own right. **Hồ Chí Minh City** (p. 374), the country's high-speed economic nerve center, features a pounding **nightlife** (p. 401), sprawling **markets** (p. 399), and chaotic but exhilarating motorbike traffic. Stately **Cần Thơ** (p. 418), a Vietnamese Venice of sorts in the Mekong, eases the burn. The quaint, winding streets of **Hội An** (p. 304), lined with old merchant houses and the most tantalizing cuisine in the country, recall the colonial, mercantile past of the cities on the coast; **Huế** (p. 270), capital under Vietnamese imperial dynasties, evokes more history with its storied **Citadel** (p. 281) and **royal tombs** (p. 287). **Hải Phòng** (p. 135) and **Đà Nẵng** (p. 294), the country's third- and fourth-largest cities, are economic behemoths brimming with gritty vitality. Finally, **Hà Nội** (p. 98) has a grace and sincere charm all its own; the lakeside capital is a city of parks and pagodas, as well as of **bars and clubs** (p. 113), ranging in tone from controlled mellowness to chaotic madness.

VIETNAM'S GREATEST HITS (2 MONTHS)

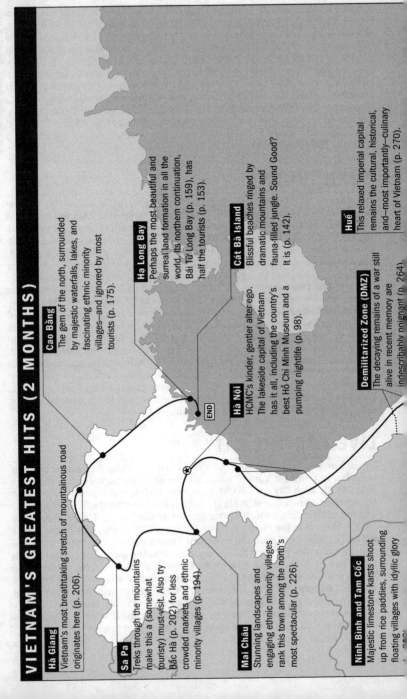

Hà Giang
Vietnam's most breathtaking stretch of mountainous road originates here (p. 206).

Cao Bằng
The gem of the north, surrounded by majestic waterfalls, lakes, and fascinating ethnic minority villages—and ignored by most tourists (p. 175).

Hạ Long Bay
Perhaps the most beautiful and surreal land formation in all the world. Its northern continuation, Bái Tử Long Bay (p. 159), has half the tourists (p. 153).

Cát Bà Island
Blissful beaches ringed by dramatic mountains and fauna-filled jungle. Sound Good? It is (p. 142).

Huế
This relaxed imperial capital remains the cultural, historical, and—most importantly—culinary heart of Vietnam (p. 270).

Hà Nội
HCMC's kinder, gentler alter ego. The lakeside capital of Vietnam has it all, including the country's best Hồ Chí Minh Museum and a pumping nightlife (p. 98).

Demilitarized Zone (DMZ)
The decaying remains of a war still alive in recent memory are indescribably poignant (p. 264).

Sa Pa
Treks through the mountains make this a (somewhat touristy) must-visit. Also try Bắc Hà (p. 202) for less crowded markets and ethnic minority villages (p. 194).

Mai Châu
Stunning landscapes and engaging ethnic minority villages rank this town among the north's most spectacular (p. 226).

Ninh Bình and Tam Cốc
Majestic limestone karsts shoot up from rice paddies, surrounding floating villages with idyllic glory

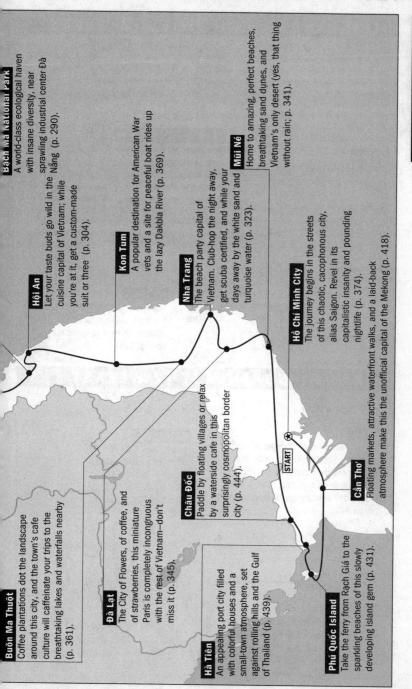

Bạch Mã National Park
A world-class ecological haven with insane diversity, near sprawling industrial center Đà Nẵng (p. 290).

Hội An
Let your taste buds go wild in the cuisine capital of Vietnam; while you're at it, get a custom-made suit or three (p. 304).

Kon Tum
A popular destination for American War vets and a site for peaceful boat rides up the lazy Dakbla River (p. 369).

Nha Trang
The beach party capital of Vietnam. Club-hop the night away, get scuba certified, and while your days away by the white sand and turquoise water (p. 323).

Mũi Né
Home to amazing, perfect beaches, breathtaking sand dunes, and Vietnam's only desert (yes, that thing without rain; p. 341).

Buôn Ma Thuột
Coffee plantations dot the landscape around this city, and the town's cafe culture will caffeinate your trips to the breathtaking lakes and waterfalls nearby (p. 361).

Đà Lạt
The City of Flowers, of coffee, and of strawberries, this miniature Paris is completely incongruous with the rest of Vietnam—don't miss it (p. 345).

Châu Đốc
Paddle by floating villages or relax by a waterside cafe in this surprisingly cosmopolitan border city (p. 444).

Hồ Chí Minh City
The journey begins in the streets of this chaotic, cacophonous city, alias Saigon. Revel in its capitalistic insanity and pounding nightlife (p. 374).

Cần Thơ
Floating markets, attractive waterfront walks, and a laid-back atmosphere make this the unofficial capital of the Mekong (p. 418).

Hà Tiên
An appealing port city filled with colorful houses and a small-town atmosphere, set against rolling hills and the Gulf of Thailand (p. 439).

Phú Quốc Island
Take the ferry from Rạch Giá to the sparkling beaches of this slowly developing island gem (p. 431).

START

DISCOVER

HIGH LANDS, HIGH TIMES (3 WEEKS)

Hà Giang
One of the most secluded and difficult-to-reach towns in the country, Hà Giang's rewards far outweigh its transportation challenges (p. 206).

Bắc Hà
During the week, this thriving market settles into a more inviting, less crowded role (p. 202).

Lai Châu
While the city is unremarkable, the villages and hikes in the nearby countryside are unsurpassed in the north. Be sure to leave via Route 6 (p. 209).

Ba Bể National Park
Homestays are the most popular way to enjoy this park's biologically diverse ecosystem (p. 182).

Cao Bằng
The odyssey continues in a town of Chinese temples and delicious food. Be sure to take in the sacred stillness of nearby Thắng Hen Lake (p. 175).

Thái Nguyên
Ease into Vietnam's northern territory in this town's relaxed beer gardens and cultural museums (p. 378).

Hà Nội
START

Điện Biên Phủ
A history-buff haven and a symbol of Vietnam's fiercely independent spirit (p. 216).

Tuần Giáo
Quieter, more scenic, and more authentic than other minority villages (if that's possible; p. 220).

END

Mai Châu
Move in with a White Thài family for a few days—unlike most ethnic minority villages, it's legal to spend the night here (p. 226).

NORTH BY NORTHEAST (2 WEEKS)

Hà Nội
Home of excellent restaurants, shops, and musuems. Shop the streets of the Old Quarter, see the embalmed remains of Uncle Ho, and take daytrips to the handicraft villages and ornate pagodas surrounding the city (p. 98).

Hạ Long City
This smoke-filled tourist city offers the most established access to beautiful Hạ Long Bay; head to the islands and be amazed (p. 153).

START

Cát Bà Island
Pristine beaches and national park make this a great launch point for exploring Hạ Long Bay. But come quickly—this island wonder is starting to develop in a big way (p. 142).

Ninh Bình
...is amazing. This is Hạ Long Bay all over again, replacing water with brilliantly green rice paddies and majestic limestone towers and some water, too (p. 232).

END

MEKONG HIGHLIGHTS(3 WEEKS)

Phú Quốc Island
Need we say more about the beach, jungle, and water of this island paradise? Just go (p. 431).

Hà Tiên
Gorgeous scenery, friendly locals, and a four-headed coconut tree make Hà Tiên a favorite Mekong destination (p. 439).

END

Châu Đốc
On the border with Cambodia, Châu Đốc captures the laid-back charm of the Mekong Delta (p. 444).

Hồ Chí Minh City
Almost as populous as New York City, this thriving metropolis is the capitalist epicenter of Vietnam (p. 374).

START

Mỹ Tho
The Tiên River and its islands are your first glimpse into the Delta's natural beauty (p. 409).

Rạch Giá
An enchanting waterfront and inviting streets make this seaport a charming stopover on your way through the Mekong (p. 429).

Sa Đéc
This picturesque French villa and its peaceful botanical gardens are easy to get to, but tough to leave (p. 416).

Trà Vinh
One of the only towns in the Mekong where the principal sights (Khmer pagodas) are all on dry land (p. 412).

Cần Thơ
Pleasant harbor strolls and a maze of canals offset the commercial importance of this bustling port city (p. 418).

GO COASTAL (2 WEEKS)

Lăng Cô Beach
Below historic Hai Van Pass, the shoreline's dramatic setting and idyllic calm are to-die-for (p. 293).

START

Cua Đại Beach
This calm, seafood-filled beach is just minutes from the markets and clothing of Hội An (p. 314).

Nha Trang
Fast-paced, tourist-filled Nha Trang is the epicenter of Vietnamese partying and the place to scuba dive. Expect perfect sand beaches under coconut trees, turquoise water, and hordes of fun-hungry tourists (p. 329).

China Beach
A quiet beach under the shadow of the Marble Mountains. Frequented by the Đà Nẵng crowd, and a famous landing spot for American GIs (p. 303).

Mũi Né
The most beautiful strip of sand in Vietnam—cheap options exist, but this is the place to get pampered to within an inch of your life (p. 341).

Phú Quốc Island
Vietnam's next tourist paradise, sparkling and (relatively) undeveloped in the waters of the Gulf of Thailand (p. 431).

Hồ Chí Minh City

END

Vũng Tàu
A Saigonese favorite; the panoply of beaches is complemented by statues of Jesus, the Madonna, and multiple renditions of the Buddha (p. 404).

PARK AVENUE (2 WEEKS)

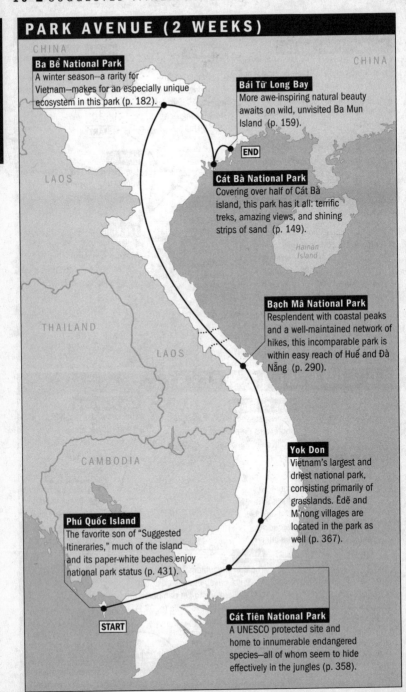

Ba Bể National Park
A winter season—a rarity for Vietnam—makes for an especially unique ecosystem in this park (p. 182).

Bái Tử Long Bay
More awe-inspiring natural beauty awaits on wild, unvisited Ba Mun Island (p. 159).

END

Cát Bà National Park
Covering over half of Cát Bà island, this park has it all: terrific treks, amazing views, and shining strips of sand (p. 149).

Bạch Mã National Park
Resplendent with coastal peaks and a well-maintained network of hikes, this incomparable park is within easy reach of Huế and Đà Nẵng (p. 290).

Yok Don
Vietnam's largest and driest national park, consisting primarily of grasslands. Êđê and M'nong villages are located in the park as well (p. 367).

Phú Quốc Island
The favorite son of "Suggested Itineraries," much of the island and its paper-white beaches enjoy national park status (p. 431).

START

Cát Tiên National Park
A UNESCO protected site and home to innumerable endangered species—all of whom seem to hide effectively in the jungles (p. 358).

CHINA

LAOS

THAILAND

LAOS

CAMBODIA

Hainan Island

PHỞ REAL (TEN DAYS)

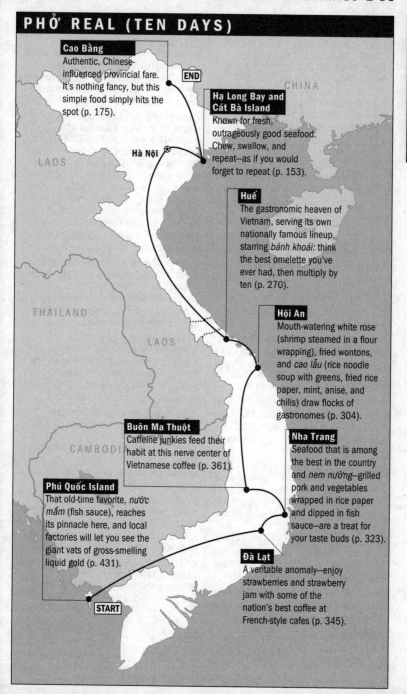

Cao Bằng
Authentic, Chinese-influenced provincial fare. It's nothing fancy, but this simple food simply hits the spot (p. 175).

END

CHINA

Hạ Long Bay and Cát Bà Island
Known for fresh, outrageously good seafood. Chew, swallow, and repeat—as if you would forget to repeat (p. 153).

Hà Nội

LAOS

Huế
The gastronomic heaven of Vietnam, serving its own nationally famous lineup, starring *bánh khoái:* think the best omelette you've ever had, then multiply by ten (p. 270).

THAILAND

LAOS

Hội An
Mouth-watering white rose (shrimp steamed in a flour wrapping), fried wontons, and *cao lầu* (rice noodle soup with greens, fried rice paper, mint, anise, and chilis) draw flocks of gastronomes (p. 304).

Buôn Ma Thuột
Caffeine junkies feed their habit at this nerve center of Vietnamese coffee (p. 361).

CAMBODIA

Nha Trang
Seafood that is among the best in the country and *nem nướng*—grilled pork and vegetables wrapped in rice paper and dipped in fish sauce—are a treat for your taste buds (p. 323).

Phú Quốc Island
That old-time favorite, *nước mắm* (fish sauce), reaches its pinnacle here, and local factories will let you see the giant vats of gross-smelling liquid gold (p. 431).

Đà Lạt
A veritable anomaly—enjoy strawberries and strawberry jam with some of the nation's best coffee at French-style cafes (p. 345).

START

DISCOVER

🔖 LET'S GO PICKS: VIETNAM

BEST PLACE TO SLEEP WITH THE STARS (OR AT LEAST CLOSER TO THEM THAN MOST): The stilt houses of **Ba Bể National Park** (p. 182) offer the perfect night's sleep. Be sure not to miss the sight-packed boat tour down the Nang River and the stalagmite that (kind of) resembles the Buddha.

BEST RIPOFF OF FAMOUS PARISIAN ARCHITECTURE: Escape Vietnam without ever having to leave its borders. **Đà Lạt's** (p. 345) alpine French feel extends to its cafes and its very own mini Eiffel Tower. Head to the hills for some great ecotourism, and don't miss the city's artistic community.

BEST PLACE TO DRINK AWAY YOUR HANGOVER: Nha Trang (p. 323) is Vietnam's collective party. It's the kind of tropical paradise you thought only existed on postcards—except crowded with fun wine bars and wine-filled tourists. Who ever thought Communism could be so much fun?

BEST PLACE TO SWALLOW A STILL-BEATING HEART: If you're gonna live the Vietnamese dream, you may as well do it with the pros in **Lê Mật** (p. 133), the snake village just outside of Hà Nội.

BEST PLACE TO GET WIRED: Any of the numerous **cafes** in **Buôn Ma Thuột** (p. 361), Vietnam's coffee capital, provides an ideal setting to savor unique, authentic blends.

BEST STARTING POINT FOR A WARDROBE OVERHAUL: The possibilities are endless at the **Mai stall** (p. 312) in Hội An. No tailoring skills necessary. Sense of style (and silk boxers) recommended.

BEST "DISNEYWORLD GONE WRONG": Near Thái Nguyên, **Lake Núi Cốc** (p. 189) flaunts a wonderfully tacky theme park. Bring the kids!

BEST INTERSECTION: Hà Nội's Lương Ngọc Quyền and Tạ Hiên meet to form **Bia Hơi Junction** (p. 113), where all four street corners house *bia hơi* bars.

BEST TWO-STORY CONCRETE CHICKEN: The residents of a **K'ho ethnic minority village** (p. 357), near Đà Lạt, have constructed what is probably the best two-story concrete chicken in Vietnam. Probably.

BEST PLACE TO LEARN HOW TO PROTECT MONKEYS (AND THEIR DELICIOUS, DELICIOUS BRAINS): The Endangered Primate Resource Center at **Cúc Phương National Park** (p. 240) provides a wealth of information on Vietnam's unique fauna. Contemplate the issue on one of the park's amazing hikes. However, if you're just interested in the monkeys for their nutritious brains, perhaps we can dissuade you (see **"Iniquitous Delicacies,"** p. 242).

BEST PLACE TO GO UNDERGROUND: The **Vĩnh Mốc tunnels** (p. 269) were home to more than 300 Vietnamese during the war with the US. The extensive subterranean abode is open for exploration—claustrophobes beware.

BEST NATURALLY OCCURING MUDBATH: We assume "Marvellous Hot Water Pot" is a loose translation of "Hot Springs." Just 45 minutes in the 37°C mud bath at **Bình Châu** (p. 407) is said to reduce your risk of skin cancer.

BEST PLACE TO ESCAPE MODERN TECHNOLOGY: No hot water, no A/C, and the town generator stops running at 11pm; welcome to the capital of **Quán Lạn Island** (p. 165), one of the remote outposts of Bái Tử Long Bay. A flashlight and some matches might not be a bad idea.

BEST PLACE TO ROCK THE NIGHT AWAY: The brand new boat-turned-bar-and-club in Hà Nội, **Titanic** (p. 113) will groove you, pending any untimely iceberg collisions.

BEST WAY TO (SORT OF) STAY AFLOAT: The water, four more-or-less-related bamboo logs, and thou; ladies and gentlemen, we give you **Thăng Hen Lake** (p. 179).

ESSENTIALS

PLANNING YOUR TRIP

BEFORE YOU GO

Passport (p. 14). Required for citizens of all countries.

Visa (p. 16). Visas are required of citizens of all countries, except those who have signed a bilateral visa exemption agreement (see p. 15 for a detailed list). Allow at least 2 weeks to process visas. In order to officially work or study in Vietnam, you'll need a sponsor to write a **letter of invitation** and obtain a business or student visa for you. You can also transfer the status of a tourist visa once in Vietnam.

Special Permits (p. 23). Travelers need special **travel permits** to visit certain politically or environmentally sensitive regions in the Central Highlands and Northwest Highlands. These are nearly impossible for casual travelers to obtain. Ask at your embassy or consulate.

Recommended Vaccinations (p. 27). Diphtheria, typhoid, hepatitis A and B, measles, and polio top the list—you'll need others if you will be staying for an extended period of time in rural areas, exposed to animals during your stay, or if you are traveling from South America or sub-Saharan Africa.

Vaccination Certificates (p. 27). You'll need a certificate of yellow fever vaccination if you are traveling from South America or sub-Saharan Africa.

Other Health Concerns: Malaria pills are recommended for those traveling to malaria risk areas (p. 29), including much of Vietnam. If your regular **medical insurance policy** (p. 27) does not cover travel abroad, you may wish to purchase additional coverage.

EMBASSIES AND CONSULATES

VIETNAMESE CONSULAR SERVICES ABROAD

Australia: 6 Timbarra Crescent, O'Malley, ACT 2606 (☎2 6286 6059 or 6290 1549; http://members.iinet.net.au/~vembassy). **Consulate:** Ste. 205, Level 2, Edgcliff Centre, 202-233 New South Head Rd., Edgcliff, NSW 2027 (☎2 9327 1912 or 9327 2539; fax 9328 1653).

Canada: 470 Wilbrod St., Ottawa, ON K1N 6M8, Canada (☎613-236-0772; fax 236-2702).

New Zealand: Level 21 Grand Plimmer Tower, 2-6 Gilmer Terrace, P.O. Box 8042, Wellington (☎473 5912; fax 473-5913; embassyvn@paradise.net.nz).

UK: 12-14 Victoria Road, London W8 5RD (☎20 7937 1912; www.vietnamembassy.org.uk).

US: 1233 20th St. NW, Ste. 400, Washington, D.C. 20036 (☎202-861-0737; www.vietnamembassy-usa.org). **Consulate:** 1700 California St., Ste. 430, San Francisco, CA 94109 (☎415-922-1707; www.vietnamconsulate-sf.org).

ESSENTIALS

CONSULAR SERVICES IN VIETNAM

Australia: 8 Đạo Tan, Ba Đình District, Hà Nội (☎4 831 7755; www.vietnam.embassy.gov.au). Open M-F 8:30am-noon and 1-4pm. **Consulate:** 5th fl. Landmark Bldg., 5B Tôn Đức Thắng, Dist. 1, Hồ Chí Minh City (☎8 829 6035; fax 829 6031). Open M-F 8:30am-noon and 1-5pm.

Cambodia: 71 Trần Hưng Đạo, Hà Nội (☎4 942 4788; arch@fpt.vn). Visa US$20, 1-day processing. Open M-F 8-11:30am and 2-4:30pm. **Consulate:** 45 Phùng Khắc Khoan, Hồ Chí Minh City (☎8 829 2751; fax 827 7696). Open M-F 8:30-11:30am and 2-5pm.

Canada: 31 Hùng Vương, Hà Nội (☎4 734 5000; www.dfait-maeci.gc.ca/vietnam). Open M-Th 8am-noon and 1-5pm, F 8am-1:30pm. Consular services M-Th 8:30-11am and 1:30-5pm, F 8:30-11:30am. **Consulate:** 10th fl., The Metropolitan, 235 Đồng Khởi, Dist. 1, Hồ Chí Minh City (☎8 827 9899; hochi@international.gc.ca). Open M-Th 8am-noon and 1-5pm, F 8am-1:30pm. Consular services M-Th 8:30-10:30am and 1:30-3:30pm, F 8:30-9:30am.

China: 46 Hoàng Diệu, Hà Nội (☎4 845 3736). For visas, go to the consulate (☎4 823 5569) on Trần Phú. Visas US$30, 4-day processing; US$47, 2-day processing. Open M-F 8:30-11am. **Consulate:** 39 Nguyễn Thị Minh Khai, Hồ Chí Minh City (☎8 829 2457; chinaconsul_hcm_vn@mfa.gov.cn). Open M-F 8-11am and 2-5pm.

Laos: 22 Trần Bình Trọng, Hà Nội (☎4 942 4576; fax 8 220 8414). Visas US$60, 1-day processing. Open M-F 8-11:30am and 1-4pm. **Consulate:** 93 Pasteur, Hồ Chí Minh City (☎8 829 7667; fax 829 9272). Open M-F 8:30-11:30am and 1:30-4:30pm.

New Zealand: Level 5, 63 Lý Thái Tổ, Hà Nội (☎4 824 1481; nzembhan@fpt.vn). Open M-F 8:30am-noon and 1-5pm. **Consulate:** 5th fl. YOCO Bldg., 41 Nguyễn Thị Minh Khai, Hồ Chí Minh City (☎8 822 6907; fax 822 6905). Open M-F 8:30am-5pm.

Thailand: Royal Thai Embassy, 63-65 Hoang Dieu, Hà Nội (☎4 823 5092; http://thaiembassy.org.vn). Open M-F 8:30am-noon and 1:30-5pm. **Consulate:** 77 Trần Quốc Thảo, District 3, Hồ Chí Minh City (☎8 932 7637). Open daily 8:30-11:30am and 1-4:30pm.

UK: Central Building, 31 Hai Bà Trưng, Hà Nội (☎4 936 0500; www.britishembassy.gov.uk). Open M-F 8:30am-12:30pm and 1:30-4:30pm. **Consulate:** 25 Lê Duẩn, Hồ Chí Minh City (☎8 829 8433; bcghcmc@hcm.vnn.vn). Open M-F 8:30am-noon and 1-3pm.

US: 7 Láng Hạ, Ba Đình District, Hà Nội (☎4 772 1500); consular section 2nd fl., Rose Garden Tower, 170 Ngoc Khanh, Hà Nội (☎4 831 4590). Consular section open M-F 8-11:30am. **Consulate:** 4 Lê Duẩn, District 1, Hồ Chí Minh City (☎8 822 9433; http://hochiminh.usconsulate.gov). Open M-F 7:30-11:30am and 1:30-5:30pm.

TOURIST OFFICES

The **Vietnam National Administration of Tourism,** 80 Quán Sứ, Hà Nội (☎4 942 3998), provides useful information about the country's history, people, and culture. Visit their website, www.vietnamtourism.com for news, upcoming events, travel deals, local weather, and links to just about everything else. Tourist offices are set to open in Australia, France, Germany, Japan, Singapore, and the US in the next five years.

DOCUMENTS AND FORMALITIES

PASSPORTS

REQUIREMENTS

Citizens of Australia, Canada, Ireland, New Zealand, the UK, and the US need valid passports to enter Vietnam and to re-enter their home countries. Returning home with an expired passport is illegal, and may result in a fine.

NEW PASSPORTS

Citizens of Australia, Canada, Ireland, New Zealand, the UK, and the US can apply for a passport at any passport office or at selected post offices and courts of law. Citizens of these countries may also download passport applications from the official website of their country's government or passport office. Any new passport or renewal applications must be filed well in advance of the departure date, though most passport offices offer rush services for a very steep fee. Note, however, that "rushed" passports can still take up to two weeks to arrive.

PASSPORT MAINTENANCE

Photocopy the page of your passport with your photo, as well as your visas, traveler's check serial numbers, and any other important documents. Carry one set of copies in a safe place, apart from the originals, and leave another set at home. Consulates also recommend that you carry an expired passport or an official copy of your birth certificate in a part of your baggage separate from other documents. Passports are required at many Vietnamese hotels when you check in (although some will accept photocopies instead), but don't forget to pick yours up as you leave.

If you lose your passport, immediately notify the local police and the nearest embassy or consulate of your home government. To expedite its replacement, you will need to have valid ID and proof of citizenship. In some cases, a replacement may take weeks to process and may be valid for only a limited time. They also tend to be expensive. Any visas stamped in your old passport will be irretrievably lost. For US citizens who lose passports, friends or relatives can call the Overseas Citizens Services at ☎ 202-647-5225 for help in relaying information to the consulate. In an emergency, ask for immediate temporary traveling papers that will permit you to re-enter your home country. If you lose your passport, you must obtain a new visa in order to exit the country, so be prepared for a few weeks of navigating bureaucracy.

VISAS

TOURIST VISAS

As of August 2006, citizens of Australia, Canada, Ireland, New Zealand, the UK, the US need a visa in addition to a valid passport for entrance into Vietnam. Citizens of Thailand, Philippines, Malaysia, Singapore, Indonesia, and Laos do not need visas if they are staying for less than a month; citizens of Japan, South Korea, Sweden, Norway, Denmark, and Finland can visit for up to 15 days without a visa. A one-month single-entry visa for a US citizen is US$65; an equivalent, multiple-entry visa is US$130; a three-month single-entry visa is US$110; the equivalent multiple-entry is US$150. You won't find this information at the Vietnamese tourism website, so call the embassy to ensure visa fees are up to date. Visa extensions (US$25-40) are available at most tourist cafes in Hà Nội and Hồ Chí Minh City. Visas can be purchased at embassies and consulates, or by mail through embassies or consulates. Allow up to two weeks for processing if you mail in your visa, though it's less if you go in person. Expedited service is usually available. Call the embassy of your home country to obtain an application and to find out requirements, or download the visa application online at your country's Vietnamese Embassy website. Verify the dates on your visa before leaving for Vietnam. It is best to be flexible with your dates and have a few extra days on either end, especially your arrival.

Double-check entrance requirements at the nearest embassy or consulate of Vietnam (see **Vietnam Consular Services Abroad,** p. 13) for up-to-date info before departure. US citizens can also consult www.pueblo.gsa.gov/cic_text/travel/foreign/foreignentryreqs.html.

ESSENTIALS

MONEY MATTERS

At the end of 2003, the Vietnamese central bank announced that it would begin issuing 500,000-đồng notes. Until a few years ago, the biggest denomination had been the 100,000 đồng note (first issued in 2000), but in the past few years people have been spending larger quantities of money. The new notes are an indication of the increasing wealth of many Vietnamese citizens.

The *đổi mới* ("open door") reforms, begun in 1986 to shift Vietnam from a centrally planned economy over to a market economy with socialist influences, have resulted in an economic boom for the country. The bilateral trade agreement between the US and Vietnam, signed in 2001, has benefited the latter significantly as well. These factors have led to the growing affluence of many Vietnamese citizens.

The central bank also recently reported that it will start minting coins again. Coins were used in the country until *đổi mới* began, at which point rapid inflation rendered them worthless; they have since been out of circulation. However, more Vietnamese now have the extra money to spend on small, non-essential items such as sodas and cigarettes, available via a small but growing number of vending machines. All these monetary modifications suggest the potential for increased economic prosperity in Vietnam's future.

BUSINESS AND STUDENT VISAS

Entering Vietnam to work or study requires a special visa. In order to obtain a business or student visa, a sponsor from an institution in Vietnam must apply for a visa for you. If you do not have a sponsor before departure but find a study program or a job while in Vietnam, you can get the organization to transfer your visa status from tourist to student or business.

IDENTIFICATION

When you travel, always carry at least two forms of identification on your person, including a photo ID; a passport and a driver's license or birth certificate is usually adequate. Never carry all of your IDs together; split them up in case of theft or loss, and keep photocopies of all of them in your luggage and at home. Remember that passports are usually required at guesthouses in Vietnam, so don't forget to pick them up when you leave. It is useful to bring extra passport-size photos (2" x 2") to affix to the visas and IDs you may acquire or in case you need replacements.

STUDENT, TEACHER, AND YOUTH IDENTIFICATION

The **International Student Identity Card (ISIC),** the most widely accepted form of student ID, provides discounts on some sights, accommodations, food, and transportation; access to a 24hr. emergency helpline; and insurance benefits for US cardholders (see **Insurance,** p. 27). Visit www.isicus.com/MyISIC/ to search for available discounts in Hà Nội, Hồ Chí Minh City, Biên Hòa, and Hội An. Applicants must be full-time secondary or post-secondary school students at least 12 years of age. Because of the proliferation of fake ISICs, some services (particularly airlines) require additional proof of student identity.

The **International Teacher Identity Card (ITIC)** offers teachers the same insurance coverage as the ISIC and similar but limited discounts. For travelers who are under 26 years old but are not students, the **International Youth Travel Card (IYTC)** also offers many of the same benefits as the ISIC.

Each of these identity cards costs US$22. ISICs, ITICS, and IYTCs are valid for one year from the date of issue. To learn more about ISICs, ITICs, and IYTCs, try www.myisic.com. Many student travel agencies issue the cards; for a list of issuing agencies or more information, see the **International Student Travel Confederation (ISTC)** website, www.istc.org.

CUSTOMS

Upon entering Vietnam, you must declare certain items from abroad and pay a duty on the value of those articles if they exceed the allowance established by Vietnam's customs service. Note that goods and gifts purchased at **duty-free** shops abroad are not exempt from duty or sales tax; "duty-free" merely means that you need not pay a tax in the country of purchase. Upon returning home, you must likewise declare all articles acquired abroad and pay a duty on the value of articles in excess of your home country's allowance. Vietnam places quotas on the amount of alcohol, tobacco, tea, and coffee that visitors are allowed to bring into the country. Visit www.customs.gov.vn at the official customs website for a detailed list (look for the "English" button at the top right). The total value of all items brought into Vietnam must not exceed 5,000,000Đ (about US$335). Items that you cannot bring into Vietnam include munitions, explosives and other flammable items, firecrackers of all kinds, opium and other assorted drugs, toxic chemicals, harmful children's toys, and cultural materials deemed unsuitable to Vietnamese society (pornographic or otherwise seditious publications, films, or photos). All videotapes will be confiscated and checked upon arrival and will be returned several days later. In order to expedite your return, make a list of any valuables brought from home and register them with customs before traveling abroad, and be sure to keep receipts for all goods acquired abroad.

Vietnam has a **value added tax** (**VAT**; see **Taxes,** p. 22) that can be claimed upon departure. You'll be taxed on goods and services as you go throughout the country, but in order to be refunded you must keep all your receipts until you leave the country. In general, expect a five percent tax on essential goods, including clean water, food, and medicine, and 10 percent on your accommodations and tradable goods (electronics, electricity, raw materials, and fuels).

MONEY

CURRENCY AND EXCHANGE

The currency chart below is based on August 2006 exchange rates between Vietnam's local currency, the đồng (Đ), and Australian dollars (AUS$), Canadian dollars (CDN$), European Union euros (EUR€), New Zealand dollars (NZ$), British pounds (UK£), and US dollars (US$). The đồng comes in denominations of 100; 200; 500; 1000; 2000; 5000; 10,000; 20,000; 50,000; 100,000; and 500,000. Coins are in circulation but not widely used. Check websites like www.xe.com or www.bloomberg.com or a large newspaper for the latest exchange rates.

CURRENCY (Đ)		
	AUS$1 = 12,245Đ	100,000Đ = AUS$8.17
	CDN$1 = 14,290Đ	100,000Đ = CDN$7.00
	EUR€1 = 20,622Đ	100,000Đ = EUR€4.85
	NZ$1 = 10,076Đ	100,000Đ = NZ$9.92
	UK£1 = 30,550Đ	100,000Đ = UK£3.27
	US$1 = 16,010Đ	100,000Đ = US$6.25

Many establishments in Vietnam take US$ along with (or even instead of) đồng; it's a good idea to have reserves of both. In this book, we usually list prices in đồng, and use US$ only when they're preferred or more common. In general, the cheaper the service, the more sense it makes to pay in đồng. US$ are preferable for things like tours, expensive rentals, and upscale hotels. Bear in mind that it's difficult to exchange đồng for dollars at any currency exchange; once banks have dollars, they are loath to give them up. **ATMs** tend to be the cheapest, most convenient way of getting money, but they only dispense đồng. Thus, it makes sense to bring enough dollars to last you through most of your trip.

TOP TEN LIST

P 10 WAYS TO SAVE IN VIETNAM

o most Western travelers, Vietnam is ...tremely cheap country to ...ourist traps abound, hough ... the Vietnamese are catching on to the beauty of the foreign dollar. Here are a few ways to stretch your đồng from coast to coast.

10. Hire motorbike drivers by the hour, not the kilometer. If you're doing a lot of intercity travel and are pressed for time, it can be far cheaper to hire xe ôm drivers by the hour than by the individual trip. This also allows you a great chance to get to know your motorbike driver—one of the easiest ways to get in touch with Vietnam's friendly people.

9. Buy all of your clothes in Hội An. Because, honestly, it's incredibly cheap and incredibly good ...ity. A silk suit of the same fabric would be five times more expensive at home and would take twice as long to make. You'd be a fool to buy any... se.

... **eer clear of cities' tourist centers.** Everything in the tourist center is more expensive: transportation, food, accommodations, shopping. If you must go to see some attraction, walk a few blocks from the main sights before hiring a xe ôm to take you home.

7. Buy food at local markets. For a taste of how the Vietnamese really eat, head to the markets
Cont'd on next page...]

If you do have to convert money, it's cheaper to do so in Vietnam than at home. If you're abroad, try to go to banks that have at most a 5% margin between their buy and sell prices. Since you lose money with every transaction, **convert large sums** (unless the currency is depreciating rapidly), **but no more than you'll need.**

If you use traveler's checks or bills, carry some in small denominations (the equivalent of US$50 or less) for times when you are forced to exchange money at disadvantageous rates, but bring a range of denominations, as charges may be levied per check cashed. Store your money in a variety of forms; ideally, at any given time you will be carrying some cash, some traveler's checks, and an ATM and/or credit card. Euros can be exchanged in Hà Nội and HCMC.

TRAVELER'S CHECKS

Traveler's checks are not widely accepted in Vietnam. Many banks and agencies sell them for a small commission. Check issuers provide refunds if the checks are lost or stolen, and many provide additional services, such as toll-free refund hotlines abroad, emergency message services, and stolen credit card assistance. However, the bureaucracy and time involved in exchanging the traveler's checks for money often renders them a burden rather than an intelligent, protective move. As a general rule, the less paperwork involved in Vietnam, the better. Ask about toll-free refund hotlines and the location of refund centers when purchasing checks, and always carry emergency cash. If you carry traveler's checks, it is advised to have them in US$ or euros. Some hotels may accept them in Hà Nội or HCMC.

American Express: Checks available with commission at select banks, at all AmEx offices, and online (www.americanexpress.com; US residents only). American Express cardholders can also purchase checks by phone (☎800-528-4800). Checks available in Australian, British, Canadian, European, Japanese, and US currencies, among others. American Express also offers the Travelers Cheque Card, a prepaid, rechargable card. Cheques for Two can be signed by either of two people traveling together. For purchase locations or more information, contact AmEx's service centers: in Australia ☎800 688 022, in New Zealand 050 855 5358, in the UK 0800 587 6023, in the US and Canada 800-221-7282; elsewhere, call the US collect at 801-964-6665.

Visa: Checks available (generally with commission) at banks worldwide. For the location of the nearest office, call the Visa Travelers Cheque Global Refund and Assistance Center: in the UK ☎0800 895 078, in the US 800-227-6811; elsewhere, call the UK collect at +44 2079 378 091. Checks available in British, Canadian,

European, Japanese, and US currencies, among others. Visa also offers TravelMoney, a prepaid debit card that can be reloaded online or by phone. For more information on Visa travel services, see http://usa.visa.com/personal/using_visa/travel_with_visa.html.

ATM, CREDIT, AND DEBIT CARDS

ATMs are widespread in Vietnam; your ATM card will prove extremely useful. Depending on the system that your home bank uses, you can most likely access your personal bank account from abroad. ATMs distribute money in đồng. They get the same wholesale exchange rate as credit cards, but there is often a limit on the amount of money you can withdraw per day (usually around US$500). There is typically also a surcharge of US$1-5 per withdrawal.

Where they are accepted, **credit cards** often offer superior exchange rates—up to 5% better than the retail rate used by banks and other currency exchange establishments. The two major international money networks are **Cirrus** (US ☎ 800-424-7787; www.mastercard.com) and **Visa/PLUS** (US ☎ 800-843-7587; www.visa.com). Credit cards may also offer services like insurance or emergency help, and they are sometimes required to reserve hotel rooms or rental cars, but they are not widely accepted outside of Hà Nội and HCMC. Mastercard and Visa are the most welcome; American Express cards work at a few ATMs, AmEx offices, and major airports. In the North, Visa is by far the most commonly taken. Cash advances on credit cards are not recommended, as they stick you with a high fee.

Debit cards are as convenient as credit cards but have a more immediate impact on your funds. A debit card can be used wherever its associated credit card company (usually Mastercard or Visa) is accepted, but the money is withdrawn directly from the holder's checking account. Debit cards often also function as ATM cards and can be used to withdraw cash from associated banks and ATMs throughout Vietnam. Ask your local bank about obtaining one.

GETTING MONEY FROM HOME

If you run out of money while traveling, the easiest and cheapest solution is to have someone back home make a deposit to your bank account. Failing that, consider one of the following options. The online **International Money Transfer Consumer Guide** (http://international-money-transfer-consumer-guide.info) may also help.

and buy your own food. This is also a great idea for picnic lunches and snacks for daytrips.

6. Agree on a price beforehand. Once you've finished bargaining with motorbike or bus drivers, make sure to write down the agreed-upon price. Never just hop on and haggle later—this leads to serious overcharging and arguments.

5. Bargain for EVERYthing. Unless you see set, tagged prices and witness locals paying without negotiating, assume that the given prices are flexible. For tips on bargaining, see **"The Art of the Deal,"** p. 21.

4. Skip Nha Trang. Though tourist agencies tout this beach city as a must-do on every open-tour route, other beaches on the Southern Central Coast are just as breathtaking and a lot less expensive.

3. Use public transportation. For long distances, public buses are the way to go (see **"The Kindness of Strangers,"** p. 414). Be prepared to wait, as schedules are erratic.

2. Walk everywhere else. The best way to get to know Vietnam is by spending time face-to-face with its people. Plus, walking is far less scary than motorbiking.

1. Eat on the street. Though they seem inherently shady to Westerners, streetside vendors offer some of the tastiest—and cheapest—eats in the city. Ironically, Vietnamese street food is less likely to get you sick than Western-style food in restaurants.

WIRING MONEY

It is possible to arrange a **bank money transfer,** which means asking a bank back home to wire money to a bank in Vietnam. This is the cheapest way to transfer cash, but it's also the slowest, usually taking several days or more. Note that some banks may only release your funds in đồng, potentially sticking you with a poor exchange rate; inquire about this in advance. Banks in Vietnam tend to have unreliable hours, so if you do wire money, try an international bank like the Hong Kong and Shanghai Banking Corporation, which has branches in Hà Nội and HCMC. Money transfer services like **Western Union** are faster and more convenient than bank transfers, but also much pricier. Western Union has many locations all over the country. To find one, visit www.westernunion.com, or in Australia call ☎1800 173 833, in Canada and the US 800-325-6000, and in the UK 0800 833 833. Money transfer services are also available at **American Express** in Hà Nội and HCMC. There is also Vietnamhost (www.vietnamhost.com), where one can pay by credit or debit to have money transferred to Vietnam.

US STATE DEPARTMENT (US CITIZENS ONLY)

In serious emergencies only, the US State Department will forward money within hours to the nearest consular office, which will then disburse it according to instructions for a US$30 fee. If you wish to use this service, you must contact the Overseas Citizens Service division of the US State Department (☎202-647-5225; toll-free 888-877-8339).

COSTS

The cost of your trip will vary considerably, depending on where you go, how you travel, and where you stay. The most significant expenses will probably be your round-trip **airfare** to Vietnam (see **Getting to Vietnam: By Plane,** p. 32). Before you go, spend some time calculating a reasonable daily budget.

STAYING ON A BUDGET

A bare-bones day in Vietnam (sleeping in the cheapest available guesthouses, buying food at supermarkets) would cost about US$6-9 (96,000-144,000Đ); a slightly more comfortable day (sleeping in hostels or guesthouses, eating one meal per day at a restaurant, going out at night) would cost US$10-17 (160,000-270,000Đ); and for a luxurious day, the sky's the limit. Don't forget to factor in emergency reserve funds (at least US$200) when planning how much money you'll need.

TIPS FOR SAVING MONEY

Some simple ways to save include searching out opportunities for free entertainment, splitting accommodation and food costs with trustworthy fellow travelers, and buying food in markets and supermarkets rather than eating out. You can also do your laundry in the sink (unless you're explicitly prohibited from doing so). If you are eligible, consider getting an ISIC or an IYTC; many sights and museums offer reduced admission to students and youth. For getting around quickly, bikes are the most economical option. Renting a bike is cheaper than renting a moped or scooter. Because bargaining is so widespread, it pays to know the lowest accepted prices for bus rides, rooms in guesthouses, and so forth. That said, don't go overboard. Though staying within your budget is important, don't do so at the expense of your health or a great travel experience.

TIPPING AND BARGAINING

Tipping is not generally practiced in Vietnam. Obviously, any gratuity will be greatly appreciated, but do not feel compelled to tip, and if you do, a small amount

THE ART OF THE DEAL. Bargaining in Vietnam is a given: no price is set in stone, and vendors and drivers will automatically quote you a price that is several times too high; it's up to you to get them down to a reasonable rate. With the following tips and some finesse, you might be able to impress even the most hardened hawkers:

1. Be cool. The most important rule of bargaining is that you not lose your temper; some Westerners come to feel as though everyone in Vietnam is out to gouge them out of their savings and react with visible, audible frustration. These Westerners are roundly hated by all Vietnamese. The truth is that bargaining is a way of market life in Vietnam, and losing your cool will do you no good. Raising your voice, looking angry, and making accusations will not only cause both you and the seller to lose face, but it also characterizes you as a rich, clueless, ungracious foreigner who deserves to be ripped off.

2. Use your poker face. The less your face betrays your interest in the item the better. If you touch an item to inspect it, the vendor will be sure to "encourage" you to name a price or make a purchase. Coming back again and again to admire a trinket is a good way of ensuring that you pay a ridiculously high price. Never get too enthusiastic about the object in question; point out flaws in workmanship and design (although do so respectfully).

3. Know when to bargain. In most cases, it's quite clear when it's appropriate to bargain. Most private transportation fares, things for sale in outdoor markets, and even hotel rooms are all fair game. Don't bargain on prepared or pre-packaged foods on the street or in restaurants. In some stores, signs will indicate whether "fixed prices" prevail. When in doubt, ask tactfully, "Is that your lowest price?" or whether discounts are given.

4. Never underestimate the power of peer pressure. Bargaining with more than one seller at a time always leads to lower prices. Alternatively, try having a friend discourage you from your purchase—if you seem to be reluctant, the merchant will want to drop the price to interest you again.

5. Know when to turn away. Feel free to refuse any vendor or driver who bargains rudely, and don't hesitate to move on to another vendor if one will not be reasonable about the final price he offers. However, to start bargaining without an intention to buy is a major *faux pas*. Agreeing on a price and declining it is also very, very gauche. Turn away slowly with a smile and "thank you" upon hearing a ridiculous price—the price may plummet.

6. Start low. Never feel guilty offering a ridiculously low price. Your starting price should be no more than one-third to one-half the asking price.

7. Get it in writing. If you're bargaining over transportation, or in any situation where you don't pay directly after settling on a price, make sure you write down the agreed-upon figure and keep it with you—it will be of use if your partner in capitalism conveniently forgets the sum. And be sure not to pay until you reach your destination.

ESSENTIALS

(such as US$1 or 16,000Đ) will suffice. If you hire a guide, you might want to consider tipping him or her at the end of the trip.

You can bargain for almost anything in Vietnam when a price isn't posted, and you can even try your luck with hotels that do post prices (see **"The Art of the Deal,"** above). Accommodations and transportation are more easily bargained down than restaurant food, although the prices of market food and goods prices aren't set. Ask elsewhere (such as at your hotel) about appropriate prices before bargaining to get a sense of how much things cost. When in the act, be firm, but maintain a pleasant demeanor and smile. Do not get angry—you'll only end up offending people and feeling like an idiot.

TAXES

Many international and domestic flights have an additional "airport tax" tacked onto the price of the seat. These are usually listed as extra charges. In other cases when you see a tax added to various services and bills, you are paying the 10% VAT tax (p. 16), for which you can be refunded when you leave.

PACKING

Pack lightly: Lay out only what you absolutely need, then take half the clothes and twice the money. The Travelite FAQ (www.travelite.org) is a good resource for tips on traveling light. The online **Universal Packing List** (http://upl.codeq.info) will generate a customized list of suggested items based on your trip length, the expected climate, your planned activities, and other factors. If you plan to do a lot of hiking, also consult **The Great Outdoors,** p. 46. **Plastic bags** are critical for keeping things dry and organized; do not underestimate their value.

Luggage: If you plan to cover most of your itinerary by foot, a sturdy **internal-frame backpack** is unbeatable. (For the basics on buying a pack, see p. 47.) Toting a **suitcase** is fine if you plan to live in one or two cities and explore from there, but not a great idea if you plan to move around often. In addition to your main piece of luggage, a **daypack** (a small backpack or courier bag) is useful. Courier or drawstring bags are better for crowded cities.

Clothing: No matter when you're traveling, it's a good idea to bring a warm jacket or wool sweater, a rain jacket (Gore-Tex® is both waterproof and breathable), sturdy shoes or hiking boots, and thick socks. Flip-flops or waterproof sandals are must-haves for grubby hostel showers. You may also want one outfit for going out and a nicer pair of shoes. Vietnam has two seasons—the cold, dry season (14-19°C in the north, 22-33°C in the south) lasts from mid-Oct. to mid-Mar. and the warm, rainy season (25-33°C throughout Vietnam) lasts from mid-May to mid-Sept.—so be sure to pack accordingly. Be prepared for monsoons and high amounts of rainfall throughout the country during the rainy season. If you plan to visit religious or cultural sites like traditional villages, remember that you will need modest and respectful dress. Shorts are almost never a good idea—no one wears them in Vietnam. Women should also consider wearing long sleeves, especially when visiting religious sites.

Sleepsack: Some hostels require that you either provide your own linens or rent sheets from them. Save cash by making your own sleepsack: fold a full-size sheet in half the long way, then sew it closed along the long side and one of the short sides. You'll definitely want something to separate you from the bed.

Converters and Adapters: In Vietnam, electricity is 220V AC, enough to fry any 120V North American appliance. 220/240V electrical appliances won't work with a 120V current, either. Americans and Canadians should buy an adapter (which changes the shape of the plug; US$5) and a converter (which changes the voltage; US$10-30). Don't make the mistake of using only an adapter (unless appliance instructions explicitly state otherwise). Australians and New Zealanders (who use 230V at home) won't need a converter, but will need a set of adapters to use anything electrical; travelers from the UK also need adapters. For more on all things adaptable, check out http://kropla.com/electric.htm.

Toiletries: Toothbrushes, towels, cold-water soap, talcum powder (to keep feet dry), deodorant, razors, tampons, and condoms are available in the big cities, but bring your own if you're devoted to specific brands. Condom dispersion is still minimal even in small or medium-size cities. Contact lenses are likely to be expensive and difficult to find, so bring enough extra pairs and solution for your entire trip. Also bring your glasses and a copy of your prescription in case you need emergency replacements. If you use heat-disinfection, either switch temporarily to a chemical disinfection system (check first to make sure it's safe with your brand of lenses), or buy a converter to 220/240V.

First-Aid Kit: For a basic first-aid kit, pack bandages, a pain reliever, antibiotic cream, a thermometer, a multifunction pocketknife, tweezers, moleskin, decongestant, motion-sickness remedy, diarrhea or upset-stomach medication (Pepto Bismol® or Imodium®), an antihistamine, sunscreen, insect repellent, burn ointment, and a syringe for emergencies (get an explanatory letter from your doctor).

Film: Film is not too expensive in Vietnam; be sure to check the expiration date before buying it, and try to buy from stores sheltered from the sun. You can develop film in Vietnam more cheaply than back at home, although quality varies. If you don't want to bother with film, consider using a digital camera. Although it requires a steep initial investment, a digital camera means you never have to buy film again. Just be sure to bring along a large enough memory card and extra (or rechargeable) batteries. For more info on digital cameras, visit www.shortcourses.com/choosing/contents.htm. Less serious photographers may want to bring a disposable camera or two. Despite disclaimers, airport security X-rays can fog film, so buy a lead-lined pouch at a camera store or ask security to hand-inspect it. Always pack film in your carry-on luggage in an easily accessible place, since higher-intensity X-rays are used on checked luggage.

Other Useful Items: For safety purposes, you should bring a **money belt** and a small **padlock**. Basic **outdoors equipment** (plastic water bottle, compass, waterproof matches, pocketknife, sunglasses, sunscreen, hat) may also prove useful. Quick repairs of torn garments can be done on the road with a **needle and thread;** also consider bringing **electrical tape** for patching tears. If you want to do laundry by hand, bring detergent, a small rubber ball to stop up the sink, and string for a makeshift clothes line. Other things you're liable to forget are an umbrella; sealable **plastic bags** (for damp clothes, soap, food, shampoo, and other spillables); an **alarm clock;** safety pins; rubber bands; a flashlight; earplugs; garbage bags; and a calculator. A **cell phone** can be a lifesaver; see p. 42 for information on acquiring one that will work in Vietnam.

Important Documents: Don't forget your passport, traveler's checks, ATM and/or credit cards, adequate ID, and photocopies of all of the aforementioned in case these documents are lost or stolen (p. 26). Also check that you have your travel insurance forms and ISIC (p. 16).

SAFETY AND HEALTH

GENERAL ADVICE

In any type of crisis situation, the most important thing to do is **stay calm.** Your country's embassy abroad (p. 14) is usually your best resource when things go wrong; registering with that embassy upon arrival in the country is often a good idea. The government offices listed in the **Travel Advisories** box (p. 25) can provide information on the services they offer their citizens in case of emergencies abroad.

LOCAL LAWS AND POLICE

While in Vietnam, you are subject to the laws of the country, regardless of your nationality. Discussions about government issues are strongly discouraged, especially if your opinion is negative or critical. Photographing military and government buildings is not permitted. In general, always ask permission before taking photographs, particularly in minority areas. Travel into some minority villages (especially in the Central Highlands) is difficult because it requires a "special permit," which often translates to "bribe." This can potentially lead to legal problems,

ESSENTIALS

so be sure to check out the situation thoroughly with locals and other tourists whenever possible. The phone numbers and locations of local police are included in each town heading, but you may not want to involve the police if you can avoid it. Be prepared to deal with inquisitive police who may want to check your pockets for no apparent reason. If you are harassed by the police, stay calm and be patient—they probably won't bother you beyond rifling through your belongings.

Police corruption has decreased over the past few years as a result of increased government pressure; police officers face severe penalties if convicted of extorting money from foreigners. However, officials and officers still sometimes look to supplement their income, and you might well be asked to pay a suspicious-sounding tax or fine at least once in Vietnam. It makes more sense to pay than to make a fuss and subject yourself to the time-draining caprice of Vietnam's maddening governmental bureaucracy. If you pay with alacrity, the amount probably won't come to much. That said, never assume you're being asked for a bribe unless specifically petitioned for money—offering an unsolicited bribe can get you in a lot of trouble.

DRUGS AND ALCOHOL

Penalties for the use, possession, or trafficking of illegal drugs are strict. Drugs are accessible and offered frequently to foreigners in much of urban Vietnam, but do not get involved. Be firm in saying "no" and walk away. Until 2005, the US State Department had considered Vietnam a center for drug trafficking, but the Vietnamese government has taken a series of actions in the last decade to virtually eliminate its opium production. Vietnam has been working to strengthen drug-related legislation and has therefore been hardening enforcement—including the arrest (and occasional execution) of foreigners smuggling drugs. Alcohol is legal, although driving while intoxicated is not legal and is highly punishable.

PROSTITUTION

If you are male, you will be approached and fawned over by prostitutes. A lot. Be prepared to say "no" many, many times, and never accept a ride from a female motorbike driver—she's not just offering the *xe ôm*. The sad fact is that prostitution, though illegal, is a major source of tourist revenue in Vietnam. This does not mean that a great number of people are in Vietnam for the prostitutes, but those who are can be drained of vast sums of money by the gangs of toughs that invariably come with the deal. In addition, the health risks involved and the simple illegality of prostitution persuade pretty eloquently against it.

SPECIFIC CONCERNS

NATURAL DISASTERS

Travelers should be aware of weather conditions whenever possible. Severe flooding during the rainy season (May to October everywhere but the central coast, where the "dry" season is March to August) can affect travel and safety conditions. Flooding is common in the Mekong Delta and along the Red River. Roads and bridges can be damaged to the point of prohibiting travel, particularly in central Vietnam during the rainy season. Visitors to the Northwest Highlands should be especially careful of traveling in bad weather due to dilapidated road conditions.

MONSOONS. Monsoons are severe tropical storms (equivalent to "hurricanes" in the Atlantic) with very high winds. They occur between April and May in the north and from June to November south of Hué, with the season peaking between August and October. If there is a monsoon, move inside, keep away from windows, and stay informed on the movement of the storm.

DEMONSTRATIONS AND PROTESTS

Recent protests and clashes between ethnic minorities and the government in the Central Highlands have rendered that area slightly unstable. Be sure to check the local news to stay updated on demonstrations and police action taking place if you plan on traveling there. Violence against foreigners is extremely rare—most conflicts are domestic. Still, foreign government officials are often prohibited from visiting these areas, so if anything goes wrong, you may be left stranded.

TERRORISM

Although there have been no incidents of terrorism in Vietnam recently, there has been an increase in terrorist activity in Southeast Asia, particularly in Bali and Jakarta, Indonesia. The governments of Australia, Canada, Ireland, New Zealand, the UK, and the US advise travelers to exercise caution in large public spaces like bars, major sights, and places of worship, particularly those frequented by tourists and expats. The box on **travel advisories** lists offices to contact and webpages to visit to get the most updated list of your home country's government advisories about travel.

TRAVEL ADVISORIES. The following government offices provide travel information and advisories by telephone, by fax, or via the web:

Australian Department of Foreign Affairs and Trade: ☎612 6261 1111; www.dfat.gov.au.

Canadian Department of Foreign Affairs and International Trade (DFAIT): Call ☎800-267-8376; www.dfait-maeci.gc.ca. Call for their free booklet, *Bon Voyage...But.*

New Zealand Ministry of Foreign Affairs: ☎044 398 000; www.mfat.govt.nz.

United Kingdom Foreign and Commonwealth Office: ☎020 7008 1500; www.fco.gov.uk.

US Department of State: ☎888-407-4747; http://travel.state.gov. Visit the website for the booklet *A Safe Trip Abroad.*

PERSONAL SAFETY

EXPLORING AND TRAVELING

To avoid unwanted attention, try to be as inconspicuous as possible. Respecting local customs (in many cases, dressing more conservatively than you would at home) may placate would-be hecklers. Never wear shorts, short skirts, or clothing with large, recognizable labels on them. Familiarize yourself with your surroundings before setting out, and carry yourself with confidence. Check maps in shops and restaurants, not on the street. If you are traveling alone, be sure someone at home knows your itinerary, and never tell anyone you meet that you're by yourself. When walking at night, stick to busy, well-lit streets and avoid dark alleyways. If you ever feel uncomfortable, leave the area as quickly and directly as you can.

There is no sure-fire way to avoid all the threatening situations you might encounter while traveling, but a good **self-defense course** will give you concrete ways to react to unwanted advances. **Impact, Prepare, and Model Mugging** can refer you to local self-defense courses in Australia, Canada, Switzerland, and the US. Visit the website at www.modelmugging.org for a list of nearby chapters. Workshops (2-4hr.) start at US$50; full courses (20hr.) run US$350-500.

ESSENTIALS

CRIME

Violent crime is extremely rare in Vietnam, but it's been on the rise for the past few years. There have been reports of armed robberies in Hồ Chí Minh City and even a few attacks on tourists on Cát Bà Island in recent years. The vast majority of tourist-related crime is limited to petty theft and pickpocketing, but tourists should be especially vigilant in urban areas. Travelers are advised not to resist theft attempts and to report all incidents to their home country's embassy.

POSSESSIONS AND VALUABLES

Never leave your belongings unattended; crime occurs in even the most demure-looking guesthouses and hotels. Don't ever store highly valuable items in a locker, and bring a **padlock** for storing other items in one. Vietnamese guesthouse and hotel owners take pride in the trustworthiness of their establishments, and are acutely aware of the impact an incidence of theft might have on their business. However, that does not protect you from other travelers and employees. Be particularly careful on **buses** and **trains;** horror stories abound about determined thieves who wait for travelers to fall asleep. Carry your bag or purse in front of you where you can see it. When traveling with others, sleep in shifts. When alone, use good judgment in selecting a train compartment: never stay in an empty one, and use a lock to secure your pack to the luggage rack. Use extra caution if traveling at night or on overnight trains. Try to sleep on top bunks with your luggage stored above you (if not in bed with you), and keep important documents and other valuables on you at all times.

There are a few steps you can take to minimize the financial risk associated with traveling. First, **bring as little with you as possible.** Second, buy a few combination **padlocks** to secure your belongings either in your pack or in a hostel or train station locker. Third, **carry as little cash as possible.** Keep your traveler's checks and ATM/credit cards in a **money belt**—not a "fanny pack"—along with your passport and ID cards. Fourth, **keep a small cash reserve separate from your primary stash.** This should be about US$50 sewn into or stored in the depths of your pack, along with your traveler's check numbers and photocopies of your passport, your birth certificate, and other important documents. But also check ahead as to the availability of banks and ATMs where you will be traveling to ensure you do not run out of cash.

THEFT

Pickpockets, petty crime, and con artistry top the list of crimes against travelers in urban Vietnam. Maintain a heightened sense of awareness, but don't be paralyzed by fear of criminal activity; most problems can be almost completely avoided with a few precautions and would cause only temporary setbacks. Use common sense and don't let culture shock and hassling throw you off guard.

Street crime is a big problem in Vietnam's increasingly crowded cities. Beware of **pickpockets** in city crowds. Women and children will often distract you with innocent appeals while someone else steals your wallet. Beware of certain classics: sob stories that require money, rolls of bills "found" on the street, spitting on or distracting you while they snatch your bag. Watch out for drive-by motorcycle theft—riders speeding by and grabbing loosely guarded bags and valuables out of your grasp. **Never let your passport and your bags out of your sight.** The best way to avoid misplaced documents is to keep your valuables in your money pouch or other hidden pockets. Most tourists will look inevitably out-of-place in Vietnam, but anyone who looks especially lost, confused, or helpless is a prime target for thievery.

More well-organized scams are ubiquitous and inventive, and frequently take the form of "hidden costs" that are difficult to prove or disprove. Tales of woe include locks sold by motorcycle rental owners whose friends have keys to them, forcing the renter to pay vast sums to replace the "stolen" bike, and motorboat drivers who claim higher-than-plausible fees for gas or alleged damage to their vehicle. Your intuition is probably your best ally here. Try to limit your transactions to more established outfits or ones that other travelers have vouched for, and be wary of recommendations from drivers and hotel owners you don't know well.

If you will be traveling with electronic devices, such as a laptop computer or a PDA, check whether your homeowner's insurance covers loss, theft, or damage when you travel. If not, you might consider purchasing a low-cost separate insurance policy. **Safeware** (US ☎ 800-800-1492; www.safeware.com) specializes in covering computers and charges US$90 for 90-day comprehensive international travel coverage up to US$4000. Let's Go does not recommend bringing large electronic devices unless strictly necessary. It is often difficult to find adequate power resources and, unless you are staying in one place for an extensive period of time, they are not worth the extra load and the hassle of heightened supervision. If you do bring a laptop, keep it in a backpack or drawstring bag, not a laptop case.

PRE-DEPARTURE HEALTH

In your **passport,** write the names of any people you wish to be contacted in case of a medical emergency, and list any allergies or medical conditions. Matching a prescription to a foreign equivalent is not always easy, safe, or possible, so if you take prescription drugs, consider carrying up-to-date prescriptions or a statement from your doctor listing the medication's trade name, manufacturer, chemical name, and dosage. While traveling, be sure to keep all medication with you in your carry-on luggage. For tips on packing a **first-aid kit** and other health essentials, see p. 23. Almost all Vietnamese pharmacies will recognize the generic names for common over-the-counter drugs but not the American brand names, so ask for acetaminophen or ibuprofen instead of Tylenol or Advil.

IMMUNIZATIONS AND PRECAUTIONS

All travelers over two years old should make sure that the following vaccines are up to date: MMR (for measles, mumps, and rubella); DTaP or Td (for diphtheria, tetanus, and pertussis); IPV (for polio); Hib (for *haemophilus* influenza B); and HepB (for Hepatitis B). Adults traveling to Vietnam or elsewhere in the developing world on trips longer than four weeks should consider the following additional immunizations: Hepatitis A vaccine and/or immune globulin (IG), an additional dose of polio vaccine, typhoid, cholera, and Japanese encephalitis vaccines, (particularly if traveling in rural areas), as well as a meningitis vaccine, a rabies vaccine, and yearly influenza vaccines. While yellow fever is only endemic to parts of South America and sub-Saharan Africa, the Vietnamese government may deny entrance to travelers arriving from these zones without a certificate of vaccination. For recommendations on immunizations and prophylaxis, consult the CDC (see below) in the US or the equivalent in your home country, and check with a doctor for guidance.

INSURANCE

Travel insurance covers four basic areas: medical/health problems, property loss, trip cancellation/interruption, and emergency evacuation. Though regular insurance policies may well extend to travel-related accidents, you may consider purchasing separate travel insurance if the cost of potential trip cancellation, interruption, or emergency medical evacuation is greater than you can absorb. Prices for travel insurance purchased separately generally run about US$50 per

> **INOCULATION RECOMMENDATIONS**
> The inoculations needed for travel in Vietnam vary with the length of your trip and the activities you plan to pursue. Visit your doctor at least 4-6 weeks prior to your departure to allow time for the shots to take effect. Be sure to keep your inoculation records with you as you travel—you may be required to show them to border officials.
>
> **Diphtheria and tetanus, measles, and polio:** booster doses recommended as needed for all travelers.
>
> **Typhoid:** strongly recommended because of *S. typhi* strains resistant to multiple antibiotics in Southeast Asia.
>
> **Hepatitis A** or **immune globulin (IG):** recommended for all travelers.
>
> **Hepatitis B:** if traveling for 6 months or more, or if needle-sharing, sexual contact, or exposure to others' blood is likely. Important for health care workers and those who might seek medical treatment abroad.
>
> **Japanese Encephalitis:** only if you will be in rural areas for 4 weeks or more, or if there are known outbreaks in the regions you plan to visit; elevated risk between May and October.
>
> **Rabies:** if you will be exposed to animals while you travel.
>
> **Yellow fever:** if you are traveling from South America or sub-Saharan Africa or other infected areas, a certificate of vaccination may be required for entry. There is no risk in Vietnam.

week for full coverage, while trip cancellation/interruption may be purchased separately at a rate of US$3-5 per day depending on length of stay.

Medical insurance (especially university policies) often covers costs incurred abroad; check with your provider. **US Medicare** does not cover foreign travel. **Canadian** provincial health insurance plans increasingly do not cover foreign travel; check with the provincial Ministry of Health or Health Plan Headquarters for details. **Homeowners' insurance** (or your family's coverage) often covers theft during travel and loss of travel documents (passport, plane ticket, etc.) up to US$500.

ISIC and **ITIC** (p. 16) provide basic insurance benefits to US cardholders, including US$100 per day of in-hospital sickness for up to 100 days and US$10,000 of accident-related medical reimbursement (see www.isicus.com for details). Cardholders can access a toll-free 24hr. helpline for medical, legal, and financial emergencies overseas. **American Express** (☎800-338-1670) grants most cardholders automatic collision and theft car rental insurance on rentals made with the card.

USEFUL ORGANIZATIONS AND PUBLICATIONS

The American **Centers for Disease Control and Prevention** (**CDC;** ☎877-FYI-TRIP/394-8747; www.cdc.gov/travel) maintains an international travelers' hotline and an informative website. Consult the appropriate government agency of your home country for consular information sheets on health, entry requirements, and other issues for various countries (see the listings in the box on **Travel Advisories,** p. 25). For quick information on health and other travel warnings, call the **Overseas Citizens Services** (M-F 8am-8pm from US ☎888-407-4747, from overseas 202-501-4444), or contact a passport agency, embassy, or consulate abroad. For information on medical evacuation services and travel insurance firms, see the US government's website at http://travel.state.gov/travel/abroad_health.html or the **British Foreign and Commonwealth Office** (www.fco.gov.uk). For general health info, contact the **American Red Cross** (☎202-303-4498; www.redcross.org).

STAYING HEALTHY

Common sense is the simplest prescription for good health while you travel. Drink lots of water to prevent dehydration and constipation, and wear sturdy, broken-in shoes and clean socks. Avoid tap water and ice throughout Vietnam, and use bottled water to brush your teeth.

ONCE IN VIETNAM

ENVIRONMENTAL HAZARDS

High Altitude: Allow your body a few days to adjust to lower oxygen levels before exerting yourself. Alcohol is more potent and UV rays are stronger at high elevations.

Heat exhaustion and dehydration: Vietnam can be oppressively hot between March and October; the southern half of the country is susceptible to extremely hot days at any time of year. Heat exhaustion leads to nausea, excessive thirst, headaches, and dizziness. Avoid it by drinking plenty of fluids, eating salty foods (e.g., crackers), abstaining from dehydrating beverages (e.g., alcohol and caffeinated beverages), and wearing sunscreen. Continuous heat stress can eventually lead to heatstroke, characterized by a rising temperature, severe headache, delirium, and cessation of sweating. Victims should be cooled off with wet towels and taken to a doctor. Rehydration powders (like Gatorade®) that have sodium and carbohydrates in the solution are good to have, especially if the water you'll be drinking from doesn't taste so good.

Hypothermia and frostbite: A rapid drop in body temperature is the clearest sign of overexposure to cold. Victims may also shiver, feel exhausted, have poor coordination or slurred speech, hallucinate, or suffer amnesia. *Do not let hypothermia victims fall asleep.* To avoid hypothermia, keep dry, wear layers, and stay out of the wind. When the temperature is below freezing, watch out for frostbite. If skin turns white or blue, waxy, and cold, do not rub the area. Drink warm beverages, stay dry, and slowly warm the area with dry fabric or steady body contact until a doctor can be found.

Sunburn: Always wear sunscreen (SPF 30 or higher) when spending excessive amounts of time outdoors. If you get sunburned, drink more fluids than usual and apply an aloe-based lotion once the burn has cooled. Severe sunburns can lead to sun poisoning, a condition that can cause fever, chills, nausea, and vomiting. Sun poisoning should always be treated by a doctor.

INSECT-BORNE DISEASES

Many diseases are transmitted by insects—mainly mosquitoes, fleas, ticks, and lice. Be aware of insects in wet or forested areas, especially while hiking and camping; wear long pants and long sleeves, tuck your pants into your socks, and use a mosquito net. Use insect repellents with DEET and soak or spray your gear with permethrin (licensed in the US only for use on clothing). **Mosquitoes**—responsible for malaria, dengue fever, yellow fever, and Japanese encephalitis, among others—can be particularly dangerous in wet, swampy, or wooded areas, which characterize the majority of rural Vietnam.

Dengue fever: An "urban viral infection" transmitted by *Aedes* mosquitoes, which bite during the day rather than at night. The incubation period can be as long as 14 days, but it's usually 4-7. Early symptoms include a high fever, severe headaches, swollen lymph nodes, and muscle aches. Many patients also suffer from nausea, vomiting, and a pink rash. If you experience these symptoms, see a doctor immediately, drink plenty of water, and take fever-reducing medication such as acetaminophen (Tylenol®). *Never take aspirin to treat dengue fever.* There is no vaccine available for dengue fever.

ESSENTIALS

ESSENTIALS

Japanese Encephalitis: Another mosquito-borne disease, most prevalent during the rainy season in rural, agricultural areas near rice fields and livestock pens. Aside from delirium, most symptoms are flu-like: chills, headache, fever, vomiting, muscle fatigue. As the disease has a high mortality rate, it's vital to go to a hospital as soon as any symptoms appear. While the JE-VAX vaccine, usually given in 3 shots over a 30-day period, is effective for a year, it has been associated with serious side effects. According to the CDC, there is little chance of being infected if proper precautions are taken, such as using mosquito repellents containing DEET and sleeping under mosquito nets.

Lymphatic filariasis: A roundworm infestation transmitted by mosquitoes. Infection causes enlargement of extremities and has no vaccine.

Malaria: Transmitted by *Anopheles* mosquitoes that bite at night. The incubation period varies anywhere between 10 days and 4 weeks. Early symptoms include fever, chills, aches, and fatigue, followed by high fever, sweating, and sometimes vomiting and diarrhea. See a doctor for any flu-like sickness that occurs after travel in a risk area. To reduce the risk of contracting malaria, use mosquito repellent, particularly in the evenings and when visiting forests. Make sure you see a doctor at least 4-6 weeks before a trip to a high-risk area to get up-to-date malaria prescriptions and recommendations. A doctor may prescribe oral prophylactics such as **mefloquine** or **doxycycline.** Mefloquine can have serious side effects, including paranoia, psychotic behavior, and nightmares.

FOOD- AND WATER-BORNE DISEASES

Prevention is the best cure: be sure that your food is properly cooked and your drinking water is clean. Peel fruits and vegetables before eating them and avoid tap water (including ice cubes and anything washed in tap water, like salad). Watch out for food from markets or street vendors that may have been cooked in unhygienic conditions. Other culprits are raw shellfish, unpasteurized milk, and sauces containing raw eggs. Buy bottled water (cheap and ubiquitous in Vietnam), or purify your own water by bringing it to a rolling boil or treating it with **iodine tablets;** note, however, that some parasites such as *giardia* have exteriors that resist iodine treatment, so boiling is more reliable. Always wash your hands before eating or bring a quick-drying purifying liquid hand cleaner. Street food in general should be safe, but use your common sense. Many travelers find that food poisoning is most common in Western dishes served at tourist-oriented restaurants rather than in recipes more familiar to Vietnamese cooks.

Cholera: An intestinal disease caused by bacteria in contaminated food. Symptoms include diarrhea, dehydration, vomiting, and muscle cramps. See a doctor immediately; if left untreated, cholera can be lethal within hours. Antibiotics are available, but the most important treatment is rehydration. No vaccine is available in the US.

Dysentery: Results from an intestinal infection caused by bacteria in contaminated food or water. Common symptoms include bloody diarrhea, fever, and abdominal pain and tenderness. The most common type of dysentery lasts for only a week, but it is highly contagious. Seek medical help immediately. Dysentery can be treated with the drugs norfloxacin or ciprofloxacin (commonly known as Cipro). If you are traveling in especially rural regions, consider obtaining a prescription before you leave home.

Giardia: Transmitted through parasites and acquired by drinking untreated water from streams or lakes. Symptoms include diarrhea, cramps, bloating, fatigue, weight loss, and nausea. If untreated it can lead to severe dehydration. Giardiasis occurs worldwide.

Hepatitis A: A viral infection of the liver acquired through contaminated water or shellfish. Symptoms include fatigue, fever, loss of appetite, nausea, dark urine, jaundice, vomiting, aches and pains, and light stools. The risk is highest in rural areas and the countryside, but it is also present in urban areas. Ask your doctor about the Hepatitis A vaccine or an injection of immune globulin (IG).

Leptospirosis: A bacterial disease caused by exposure to fresh water or soil contaminated by the urine of infected animals. Able to enter the human body through cut skin, mucus membranes, and by ingestion, it is most common in tropical climates, including some tropical areas in Vietnam. Symptoms include a high fever, chills, nausea, and vomiting. If left untreated, it can lead to liver failure and meningitis. There is no vaccine; consult a doctor for treatment.

Traveler's diarrhea: Results from drinking fecally-contaminated water or eating uncooked and contaminated foods. Symptoms include nausea, bloating, and urgency. Try quick-energy, non-sugary foods with protein and carbohydrates to keep your strength up. Over-the-counter anti-diarrheals (e.g., Imodium®) may counteract the problem. The most dangerous side effect is dehydration; drink 8 oz. of water with ½ tsp. of sugar or honey and a pinch of salt, try decaffeinated soft drinks, or eat salted crackers. If you develop a fever or your symptoms don't go away after 4-5 days, consult a doctor. Consult a doctor immediately for treatment of diarrhea in children.

Typhoid fever: Caused by the salmonella bacteria; **common in villages and rural areas in Vietnam.** While mostly transmitted through contaminated food and water, it may also be acquired by direct contact with another person. Early symptoms include high fever, headaches, fatigue, appetite loss, constipation, and a rash on the abdomen or chest. Antibiotics can treat typhoid, but a vaccination (70-90% effective) is recommended.

OTHER INFECTIOUS DISEASES

The following diseases exist in every part of the world. Travelers should know how to recognize them and what to do if they suspect they have been infected.

AIDS and HIV: Acquired Immune Deficiency Syndrome (AIDS), caused by Human Immunodeficiency Virus (HIV), attacks and eventually disables the immune system, making common colds and diseases fatal for virus carriers. AIDS has been on the rise throughout Asia in recent years. For information on AIDS/HIV in Vietnam, call the US Center for Disease Control's 24hr. hotline at ☎800-342-2437. Also see **The AIDS Crisis,** p. 72.

Avian Influenza (Bird flu): A virulent strain of flu largely restricted to birds; cases of bird-to-human transmission in Vietnam and Thailand in early 2004 led to international fears that a SARS-like outbreak was imminent, which fortunately was not the case (though 36 people have died in Vietnam since). There have been no recorded cases of human-to-human transmission, and travelers who avoid large-scale contact with poultry and their feces shouldn't be at any risk. See **The Bird Flu Outbreak,** p. 73, for more info.

Hepatitis B: A viral infection of the liver transmitted via blood or other bodily fluids. Symptoms, which may not surface until years after infection, include jaundice, appetite loss, fever, and joint pain. It is transmitted through unprotected sex and unclean needles. A 3-shot vaccination sequence begun 6 months before traveling is recommended for sexually active travelers and anyone planning to seek medical treatment abroad.

Rabies: Transmitted through the saliva of infected animals; fatal if untreated. By the time symptoms (thirst and muscle spasms) appear, the disease is in its terminal stage. If you are bitten, wash the wound, seek immediate medical care, and try to have the animal located. A rabies vaccine, which consists of 3 shots given over a 21-day period, is available and recommended for developing world travel, but is only semi-effective.

Sexually transmitted infections (STIs): Gonorrhea, chlamydia, genital warts, syphilis, herpes, and other STIs are easier to catch than HIV and can be just as serious. Though condoms may protect you from some STIs, oral or even tactile contact can lead to transmission. If you think you may have contracted an STD, see a doctor immediately.

ESSENTIALS

OTHER HEALTH CONCERNS

MEDICAL CARE ON THE ROAD

The radical disparity between Vietnam's haves and have-nots characterizes the country's hospitals, as with so many other things. Most hospitals are state-run and are in mediocre condition; their facilities don't have the kind of absolute hygiene to which Westerners seeking medical care might be accustomed (be wary of blood hygiene—this is yet another reason to make sure you get vaccinated for Hepatitis A and B). Their general state of disrepair can be disconcerting. Privately run hospitals are a different story; patients are treated with state-of-the-art technology and in completely sterile conditions. A single consultation at one will cost over US$50. Private hospitals primarily serve expats and tourists and can only be found in Vietnam's biggest and most popular cities, like Hà Nội, HCMC, and Nha Trang.

If you are concerned about obtaining medical assistance while traveling, you may wish to employ special support services. The *MedPass* from **GlobalCare, Inc.**, 6875 Shiloh Rd. East, Alpharetta, GA 30005, USA (☎800-860-1111; www.globalcare.net), provides 24hr. international medical assistance, support, and medical evacuation resources. The **International Association for Medical Assistance to Travelers (IAMAT;** Canada ☎519-836-0102, US 716-754-4883; www.iamat.org) has free membership, lists English-speaking doctors worldwide, and offers detailed info on immunization requirements and sanitation. If your regular **insurance** policy does not cover travel abroad, you may wish to purchase additional coverage (p. 27).

Those with medical conditions (such as diabetes, allergies to antibiotics, epilepsy, or heart conditions) may want to obtain a **MedicAlert** membership (first year US$35, annually thereafter US$20), which includes among other things a stainless steel ID tag and a 24hr. collect-call number. Contact the MedicAlert Foundation, 2323 Colorado Ave., Turlock, CA 95382, USA (US ☎888-633-4298, elsewhere 209-668-3333; www.medicalert.org).

WOMEN'S HEALTH

Women traveling in unsanitary conditions are vulnerable to **urinary tract (including bladder and kidney) infections (UTIs).** Over-the-counter medicines can sometimes alleviate symptoms, but if they persist, see a doctor. **Vaginal yeast infections** may flare up in hot and humid climates. Wearing loosely fitting trousers or a skirt and cotton underwear will help, as will over-the-counter remedies like Monistat® or Gynelotrimin. Bring supplies from home if you are prone to infection, as they may be difficult to find on the road. **Tampons, pads,** and **contraceptive devices** are widely available in Vietnam, but your favorite brand probably won't be stocked—bring extras of anything you can't live without. **Abortion** is legal in Vietnam; contact the Vietnam Family Planning Association (VINAPFPA; vinafpa@hn.vnn.vn).

GETTING TO VIETNAM

BY PLANE

When it comes to airfare, a little effort can save you a bundle. For those flexible enough to deal with the restrictions, courier fares are the cheapest. Tickets bought from consolidators and standby seating are also good deals, but last-minute specials, airfare wars, and charter flights often beat these fares. The key is to hunt around, to be flexible, and to ask persistently about discounts. Students, seniors, and those under 26 should never pay full price for a ticket.

AIRFARES

Airfare prices to Vietnam peak between June and August and between November and January; international holidays are also expensive. The cheapest times to travel are from September to early November and from February to April. Mid-week (M-Th morning) round-trip flights run US$40-50 cheaper than weekend flights, but they are generally more crowded and less likely to permit frequent-flyer upgrades. Not fixing a return date ("open return") or arriving in and departing from different cities ("open-jaw") can be pricier than round-trip flights. Patching one-way flights together is the most expensive way to travel. The two primary international airports are **Nội Bài International Airport** in Hà Nội and **Tân So'n International Airport** in HCMC, although there is a smaller airport in Đà Nẵng **(Đà Nẵng International Airport).** Flights between Vietnam's capitals or regional hubs—Hà Nội, HCMC, Đà Nẵng, and Huế—tend to be cheaper. It generally costs the same to fly into Hà Nội and out of HCMC or visa versa as it does to fly in and out of the same airport.

If Vietnam is only one stop on a more extensive globe-hop, consider a round-the-world (RTW) ticket. Tickets usually include at least five stops and are valid for about a year; prices range US$1200-5000. Try **Northwest Airlines/KLM** (US ☎ 800-447-4747; www.nwa.com) or **Star Alliance,** a consortium of 16 airlines including United Airlines (www.staralliance.com).

The lowest **fares** for round-trip flights to Hà Nội and HCMC from Australia should cost US$1100-1400; from the North American Atlantic Coast cost US$1100-1800; from the North American Pacific Coast US$900-1300; from New Zealand US$1000-1300; from the UK US$1000-1300, depending on the time of year. Tickets are a great deal more expensive during holidays. A handful of international flights into Đà Nẵng are available, although they tend to be more expensive since the air-port isn't as large or as popular of a destination. **Don't forget your entry/exit form**—you will need it when you leave. Also, remember there is a US$14 international departure tax you'll have to pay as you leave (in US$ or đồng).

BUDGET AND STUDENT TRAVEL AGENCIES

While knowledgeable agents specializing in flights to Vietnam can make your life easy and help you save, they may not spend the time to find you the lowest possi-ble fare—they get paid on commission. Travelers holding **ISICs** and **IYTCs cards** (p. 16) qualify for big discounts from student travel agencies. Most flights from budget agencies are on major airlines, but in peak season some may sell seats on less reli-able chartered aircraft.

STA Travel, 5900 Wilshire Blvd., Ste. 900, Los Angeles, CA 90036, USA (24hr. reserva-tions and info ☎800-781-4040; www.statravel.com). A student and youth travel organi-zation with over 150 offices worldwide (check their website for a listing of all their offices), including US offices in Boston, Chicago, L.A., New York, Seattle, San Francisco, and Washington, D.C. Ticket booking, travel insurance, railpasses, and more. Walk-in offices are located throughout Australia (☎03 9207 5900), New Zealand (☎09 309 9723), and the UK (☎08 701 630 026).

Travel CUTS (Canadian Universities Travel Services Limited), 187 College St., Toronto, ON M5T 1P7, Canada (☎866-246-9762; www.travelcuts.com). Offices across Canada and the US including Los Angeles, New York, Seattle, and San Francisco.

USIT, 19-21 Aston Quay, Dublin 2, Ireland (☎01 602 1904; www.usit.ie), Ireland's lead-ing student/budget travel agency has 20 offices throughout Northern Ireland and the Republic of Ireland. Offers programs to work, study, and volunteer worldwide.

ESSENTIALS

FLIGHT PLANNING ON THE INTERNET. The Internet may be the budget traveler's dream when it comes to finding and booking bargain fares, but the array of options can be overwhelming. Many airline sites offer special last-minute deals on the web.

STA (www.statravel.com) and **StudentUniverse** (www.studentuniverse.com) provide quotes on student tickets, while **Orbitz** (www.orbitz.com), **Expedia** (www.expedia.com), and **Travelocity** (www.travelocity.com) offer full travel services. Zuji (www.zuji.com) is their Pacific equivalent. **Priceline** (www.priceline.com) lets you specify a price, and obligates you to buy any ticket that meets or beats it; **Hotwire** (www.hotwire.com) offers bargain fares, but won't reveal the airline or flight times until you buy. Other sites that compile deals include www.bestfares.com, www.flights.com, www.lowestfare.com, www.onetravel.com, and www.travelzoo.com.

Increasingly, there are online tools available to help sift through multiple offers; **SideStep** (www.sidestep.com) and **Booking Buddy** (www.bookingbuddy.com) let you enter your trip information once and search multiple sites.

An indispensable resource on the Internet is the **Air Traveler's Handbook** (www.faqs.org/faqs/travel/air/handbook), a comprehensive listing of links to everything you need to know before you board a plane.

COMMERCIAL AIRLINES

The commercial airlines' lowest regular offer is the **APEX** (Advance Purchase Excursion) fare, which provides confirmed reservations and allows "open-jaw" tickets. Generally, reservations must be made seven to 21 days ahead of departure, with a seven- to 14-day minimum stay and up to 90-day maximum stay restrictions. These fares carry hefty cancellation and change penalties (fees rise in summer). Book high-season APEX fares early. Use **Expedia** (www.expedia.com) or **Travelocity** (www.travelocity.com) to get an idea of the lowest published fares, then use the resources outlined here to try and beat those fares. Low-season fares should be cheaper than the high-season (June-Aug. and Nov.-Jan.) ones listed here.

Standard commercial carriers like American (for Canada and the US) or Qantas (for Australia and New Zealand) will probably offer the most convenient flights, but they won't be the cheapest, unless you manage to grab a special promotion or airfare war ticket. You will probably find flying one of the following airlines a better deal, if any of their limited departure points is convenient for you. Let's Go does not endorse any of these airlines; they're just suggestions to get you started.

Cathay Pacific Airways, AUS ☎ 131 747; NZ 379 0861; UK 8834 8888; US 800-233-2742; www.cathaypacific.com. Call for reservations.

China Airlines, www.china-airlines.com/en/index.htm. Check online for regional reservation contact numbers.

Japan Airlines, IRE ☎ 408 3757; UK 845 774 7700; Canada and the US 800-JAL-FONE/800-525-3663; www.jal.com/en. Call for reservations. AUS and NZ: Check online for regional offices.

JetStarAsia, www.jetstarasia.com. A regional offshoot of Australia's Qantas, it offers good deals on travel in Asia. Based out of Singapore.

Korean Air, AUS ☎ 9262 6000; IRE 799-7990; UK 800 0656 2001; Canada and the US 800-438-5000; www.koreanair.com. Call for reservations.

Thai Airways International, AUS ☎ 130 065 1960; UK 807 907 9532; US 800-426-5204; www.thaiair.com. Call for reservations.

Tiger Airways, www.tigerairways.com. A budget airline for the Asia-Pacific region offering flights from Singapore Changi Airport.

Vietnam Airlines, AUS ☎29 283 1355; Canada 416 599 6555; UK 870 220 2318; US 415-677-0888; www.vietnamair.com.vn

FROM SOUTHEAST ASIA

Compared to other ways of getting around Southeast Asia, plane is relatively more convenient. Vietnam Airlines is a logical choice for getting around the area. Some other popular airlines include Thai Airways International, Bangkok Airways, Malaysian Airlines, and Pacific Airlines. In the **Practical Information** section of each large city introduction, you can find out about travel agencies that offer the cheapest and most up-to-date information on plane travel in Southeast Asia.

 AIRCRAFT SAFETY. The airlines of developing world nations do not always meet safety standards. The *Official Airline Guide* (www.oag.com) and many travel agencies can tell you the type and age of aircraft on a particular route. The **International Airline Passengers Association** (UK ☎020 8681 6555, US 800-821-4272; www.iapa.com) provides region-specific safety information to its members. The **Federal Aviation Administration** (www.faa.gov/passengers/international_travel) reviews the airline authorities for countries whose airlines enter the US. **US State Department** travel advisories (☎202-647-5225; www.travel.state.gov) sometimes involve foreign carriers, especially when terrorist bombings or hijackings may be a threat.

STANDBY FLIGHTS

Traveling standby requires considerable flexibility in arrival and departure dates and cities. Companies dealing in standby flights sell vouchers rather than tickets, along with the promise to get you to your destination (or near your destination) within a certain window of time (typically 1-5 days). You call in before your specific window of time to hear your flight options and the probability that you will be able to board each flight. You can then decide which flights you want to try to make, show up at the appropriate airport at the appropriate time, present your voucher, and board if space is available. Vouchers can usually be bought for both one-way and round-trip travel. You may receive a monetary refund only if every available flight within your date range is full; if you opt not to take an available flight, you can only get credit toward future travel. Carefully read agreements with any company offering standby flights, as tricky fine print can leave you in the lurch. Be careful in Vietnam—scams are uncommon but do occur. To check a company's service record, call the Better Business Bureau (US ☎703-276-0100).

TICKET CONSOLIDATORS

Ticket consolidators, or **"bucket shops,"** buy unsold tickets in bulk from commercial airlines and sell them at discounted rates. The best place to look is in the Sunday travel section of any major newspaper (such as *The New York Times*), where many bucket shops place tiny ads. Call quickly, as availability is typically extremely limited. Not all bucket shops are reliable, so insist on a receipt that gives full details of restrictions, refunds, and tickets, and pay by credit card (in spite of the 2-5% fee) so you can stop payment if you never receive your tickets. For more info, see www.travel-library.com/air-travel/consolidators.html.

Fare.net (www.fare.net) is an Asia-specific site that compares airfares from many different airlines. **Travel Avenue** (☎800-333-3335; www.travelavenue.com) searches for the best available published fares and then uses several consolidators to attempt to beat that fare. **NOW Voyager,** 315 W. 49th St. Plaza Arcade, New York, NY 10019 (US ☎212-459-1616; www.nowvoyagertravel.com) arranges discounted flights, mostly from New York, to destinations in Europe—but you might have luck finding a Southeast Asian destination. Other consolidators worth trying are **Rebel** (US ☎800-732-3588; www.rebeltours.com) and **Cheap Tickets** (US ☎800-652-4327; www.cheaptickets.com). Yet more consolidators on the web include **Flights.com** (www.flights.com) and **TravelHUB** (www.travelhub.com). Keep in mind that these are just suggestions to get you started in your research; Let's Go does not endorse any of these agencies. As always, be cautious, and research companies before you hand over your credit card number.

TRAVELING FROM AUS, NZ, AND THE UK

In London, the **Air Travel Advisory Bureau** (UK ☎020 7636 5000; www.atab.co.uk) provides names of reliable consolidators and discount flight specialists. In Australia and New Zealand, look for consolidator ads in the travel section of the *Sydney Morning Herald* and other major papers.

SPECIALTY CONSOLIDATORS

A limited number of travel agencies deal in unconventional arrangements of flights. **Circle Pacific** (www.airtimetable.com/circle_pacific_airfares.htm) and **Circle of Asia** (www.circleofasia.com) tickets provide one-way flights to, from, and around Southeast Asia, especially Thailand. These tickets are best for extended trips; most have flexible dates, and are valid up to one year from the commencement of travel. For more complicated itineraries, RTW and other unconventional tickets are often a better deal. Try **Air Treks** (US ☎877-350-0612 or 415-912-5600; www.airtreks.com) or **Circle the Planet** (US ☎800-799-8888; www.circletheplanet.com), and leave at least a month to book tickets.

CHARTER FLIGHTS

Tour operators contract charter flights with airlines in order to fly extra loads of passengers during peak season. These flights are far from hassle-free. They occur less frequently than major airlines, make refunds particularly difficult, and are almost always fully booked. Their scheduled times may change and they may be cancelled at the last moment (as late as 48 hours before the trip, and without a full refund). And check-in, boarding, and baggage claim for them are often much slower. They can, however, be much cheaper.

Discount clubs and fare brokers offer members savings on last-minute charter and tour deals. Study contracts closely; you don't want to end up with an unwanted overnight layover.

BY LAND AND WATER

There are only a few ways of entering Vietnam other than by plane. If you're going over land, you'll be going through one of the **border crossings** (p. 37).

FERRY FROM CAMBODIA

A few Cambodian tourist companies offer daily transport by boat from Phnom Penh to Châu Đốc in the Mekong Delta (p. 447). The trip costs US$7-15 one way.

TRAIN FROM CHINA

There is one train route into Vietnam that goes from Beijing to Hà Nội once daily. You can book a place on the overnight sleeper car at www.china-train-ticket.com.

BORDER CROSSINGS

You are free to travel in and out of Vietnam overland at any of the 12 border crossings as long as you have a **tourist visa.** In most cases, it is necessary to have one before arriving at the border, save two exceptions when entering Cambodia. There are four crossings into Cambodia, five into Laos, and three into China. Before you go, be sure to check whether or not the borders are open.

Although bribes and border police corruption are not typical, be prepared to unpack your gear to show the border police. Be sure to have US dollars on you to avoid problems with exchanging local currencies, though most border crossings have currency exchanges nearby.

The primary border crossing into **Cambodia** is at **Mộc Bài** in the Tây Ninh Province, 70km northwest of HCMC. Buses that leave HCMC at 6am and head to Phnom Penh cost about US$12. Otherwise, you can take a cab or minibus to the border, walk across, and pick up another in Cambodia. In the same province is also the **Sa Mát** border gate, on Highway 22B. Down south, there are two border crossings in the An Giang province. **Tịnh Biên** is 25km southwest of Châu Đốc, along Highway 91. But the ferry that departs from **Châu Đốc,** crossing the border at Vĩnh Xương, is well worth the US$7-8 for a trip through the Mekong Delta. You can get a Cambodian visa on arrival from the Mộc Bài and Châu Đốc border crossing for US$26; one passport photo is required. Don't expect visas at either Sa Mát of Tịnh Biên. A new border crossing in the Mekong is expected to open soon.

The most popular border crossing into **China** is the **Friendship Pass,** known as Hữu Nghị Quan (Youyi Guan in Chinese), through the town of Đồng Đăng, about 18km north of Lạng Sơn. The fastest means of getting to Đồng Đăng from Lạng Sơn is by motorbike, although you can also take a minibus and then hire a taxi to the Chinese town of Piang Xiang. You can also take the train that goes through the Friendship Pass. A second border crossing option can be found at **Lào Cai,** which crosses over the Ho Kieu bridge into the Yunnan Province. A third crossing is at **Móng Cái** in northeastern Vietnam. You can get there by hydrofoil direct from Hải Phòng or Hạ Long City, 178km south. The Chinese border town is Dongxing. Be sure to have a tourist visa before arriving at any of these border crossings.

Be sure to obtain a traveler's visa before heading into Laos, where the border police are slightly more thorough in their search policies. The **Kẹo Nưa** (Cầu Treo) **Pass** is 80km southwest of Vinh on Highway 8, near Tây Sơn. There are direct overnight buses from Hà Nội to Vientiane available through travel agents in Hà Nội. Local buses approach the border from either side but do not cross. The same is true of the **Lao Bảo** border crossing, 80km west of Đông Hà on Highway 9. The Lao town for arrivals and departures is Savannakhet. You can walk the mile-long border or else rent a motorbike if you choose not to take a tourist bus. A third and less frequented border crossing into Laos is from **Na Mèo,** 213km northwest of Thanh Hóa. To get there, take Road 45 to the Vĩnh Loc District onto Highway 217 to the Na Mèo-Nam Xoi border. There are also crossings at **Nậm Cắn,** in the Nghệ An province, and **Cha Lo,** in Quảng Bình province.

GETTING AROUND VIETNAM

There are numerous ways of getting around Vietnam over land and by plane. Many tourists utilize the open-tour buses operated by tourist agencies in HCMC and Hà Nội. Motorbikes—often with hired drivers—are also a popular method of transportation, and they are sometimes the only option in more rural or less-traveled areas. The public bus system is by far the cheapest option, although for safety and comfort reasons, few tourists choose the public transportation system.

BY PLANE

For those who can afford it, travel by plane is by far the most efficient and comfortable means of covering large distances in Vietnam. There are airports in Buôn Ma Thuột, Đà Lạt, Đà Nẵng, Điện Biên Phủ, Hải Phòng, Hà Nội, Hồ Chí Minh City, Huế, Nha Trang, Phú Quốc, Pleiku, Qui Nhơn, Rạch Giá, Sơn La, and Vinh. The airports at Đà Nẵng, Hà Nội, and Hồ Chí Minh City also have international service. **Vietnam Airlines** (Hà Nội ☎4 832 0320, HCMC 8 832 0320, Đà Nẵng 51 811 111; www.vietnamairlines.com) is the main airline for domestic flights, although **Pacific Airlines** (www.pacificairlines.com.vn) operates a few routes. Domestic flights can run anywhere from 400,000-4,000,000Đ, and prices will vary with class and seating type. It's easiest to book a flight through one of the primary travel agencies in HCMC or Hà Nội, although you can book flights online ahead of time if you so desire. See **Aircraft Safety** (p. 35) for information regarding domestic flight safety.

BY TRAIN OR BUS

Trains exist in Vietnam, but solely for the joy of existing. They are slow, but also tend to be more comfortable and far less crowded than the public bus. Keep your ticket or you'll be charged again to disembark. Tracks that once extended throughout the country were destroyed during the war, and now the only rail routes run from HCMC to Hà Nội (with plenty of stops in between) or Hà Nội to a handful of northern destinations. A journey on the **Reunification Express** route from Hà Nội to HCMC or vice versa is a scenic way to visit most of Vietnam's major cities and offers more contact with local culture than travel by minibus.

Train fares depend both on the length of the route and the class of travel. There are two types of trains in Vietnam: the newer, air-conditioned SE trains (numbered one to six) have soft seats, hard sleepers, and soft sleepers; older TN trains (numbered three to 10) include hard seats, soft seats, soft sleepers, and hard sleepers, with or without air-conditioning. Sleepers are two- or three-tiered; bottom sleepers are the most expensive. If you'll be traveling a long distance, be sure to use an express train. Regular trains on the Reunification Express line stop frequently, making the 36-hour journey from Hà Nội to HCMC days longer. For more information about train travel in Vietnam, visit **Vietnam Railways** online at www.vr.com.vn.

Most tourists use **open-tour buses** operated by budget travel cafes based in HCMC and Hà Nội. Open-tour buses cost more than public buses (below), but run more regularly, boast air-conditioning and more comfortable seating, and don't require haggling. The downside is that you will see most of Vietnam through a window and your fellow riders will all be travelers, so you're less likely to share your journey with loads of fruit or gigantic bags of grain—but you'll miss out on the opportunity to meet Vietnamese locals. Your choice of destinations is also limited to those along the open-tour bus path from HCMC to Hà Nội, passing over many out-of-the-way destinations that Let's Go recommends. You can, however, hop on and off any of these buses according to your schedule, as long as you reserve your seat a day in advance with a tourist company. Open-tour buses will pick you up right at your hotel and shuttle you to the affiliated hotel in your destination city.

If you're looking for a more adventurous and interesting way to travel between cities, take the **public bus.** Few foreigners use it, but those that do can claim a legitimately authentic Vietnamese experience: improbable numbers of riders, bags, items of fruit, and bikes get packed in tight in a sweaty, joyous tribute to makeshift bus engineering and the human ability to overcome claustrophobia. If there's no bus station at your city of origin, you'll have to wait on the highway and flag down the next bus (they run extremely frequently). Tell the driver where you'd like to go and start negotiating for a fare immediately, or you'll be tricked into paying an inflated tourist rate. Learn Vietnamese numbers and phrases like "How much is it to..." and "too expensive" (see **Phrasebook,** p. 450), but bring a pen and pencil so your "6000" doesn't sound mysteriously like "60,000" to the driver. Rides on public buses are hot and long and you might be dropped off on the outskirts of town rather than in the center, but they will take you to most out-of-the-way locations that open-tour buses won't. Note that drivers don't exactly follow traffic and safety laws, but then again, these don't really exist in Vietnam to begin with.

You'll notice both regular buses and **minibuses** on the highways in Vietnam. Regular buses usually stop running mid-afternoon but are more comfortable. Minibuses are slightly more expensive, travel more quickly (and dangerously), make more stops, and run all day long. They often have air-conditioning as well.

BY CAR, MOTORBIKE, OR BICYCLE

Individual means of transportation in Vietnam are a popular but undeniably risky options, particularly in big cities. The streets are overcrowded and drivers typically take little heed of transportation rules that barely exist. Road conditions outside of cities and sometimes in the cities themselves are not very reliable, and roads in rural areas are especially dangerous. However you chose to get around within the cities and between cities and towns, be extremely cautious. Always demand to use a **helmet** if you ride on a motorcycle or even a bicycle; your driver may refuse initially to get you one, but it pays to be insistent (see **"Promote Helmets, Prevent Death,"** p. 91). Consider bringing one with you or buying one there.

Settle on prices for transportation before you hop on for a ride, unless there is a visibly functioning meter. Never pay until you reach your destination. Bring a notebook and pen to write down the agreed price (in plain view of your driver).

BY CAR

The only option if you wish to travel by car is to rent a car and a driver for US$30-50 per day, as foreigners are prohibited from renting cars themselves in Vietnam. International Driving Permits (IDP) are not valid. If you wish to drive, you must obtain a Vietnamese driver's license by calling the **Vietnamese Road Administration** in Hà Nội (☎4 857 1444; www.vra.gov.vn). This, of course, applies only to those people who will be spending a long period of time in Vietnam.

Taxis are also an option in the big cities, but this is one of the most expensive ways to travel in Vietnam. Prices depend on the city—check the essentials information section at the beginning of the city chapters. Make sure the driver turns on the meter; don't get stuck haggling over prices after the drive.

BY MOTORBIKE

Motorbike taxis, or *xe ôm*s ("hugging bike"; the passenger hugs the driver to stay on), are an extremely popular means of transportation in Vietnam. They are also extremely dangerous, due to the blatant disregard for or ignorance of traffic laws and overcrowded streets, but are often your only option when you're traveling outside of urban areas. Let's Go strongly recommends using a **helmet** whenever you ride a *xe ôm*. Prices are negotiable—never accept the first price the driver gives you. Don't pay until you've reached your destination, whether traveling around a city or long distances. Ask around to get an idea of reasonable prices between two locations or per km; 2000-3000Đ per km is a reasonable rate in cities, less for longer distances through the countryside. Renting a motorcycle *(xe máy)* for yourself will run about US$5-10 per day, but they can be very dangerous for inexperienced drivers. Rental shops abound; prioritize reputable over cheap, because

ESSENTIALS

cheap rentals frequently end up costing you more when the motorcycle breaks down or miraculously runs out of gas two blocks down the road.

BY BICYCLE

There are several different means of traveling by bicycle in Vietnam, as there are several different types of bicycle. In the cities, you can get carted around in a **cyclo,** a three-wheeled bicycle rickshaw with a driver in front, but it's slower and more expensive than a *xe ôm*. As with any sort of transportation in Vietnam, be sure to bargain and settle on a price beforehand, and bring along a city map to avoid getting lost. The drivers typically know their way around, but communication can sometimes be difficult. Drivers who speak English tend to be a bit pricier than those who don't. Prices run lower for cyclos than for taxis.

Regular bicycles are a popular means of transportation in the big cities. You can rent bikes in the cities, but be forewarned—Vietnamese traffic is not for the faint of heart. Western-style mountain bikes are becoming more popular means of transportation in Vietnam. A growing number of tourist agencies are offering tours of Vietnam by bike. There aren't really specialty stores in Vietnam, so it is best to bring your own gear. Rentals in major cities run about US$1 per day.

BY THUMB

 Let's Go never recommends hitchhiking as a safe means of transportation, and none of the information presented here is intended to do so.

Though hitchhiking is nearly ubiquitous in Vietnam, Let's Go strongly urges you to consider the risks before you choose to hitchhike. Hitching means entrusting your life to a stranger and risking assault, sexual harassment, theft, and unsafe driving. For women traveling alone (or even in pairs), hitching is just too dangerous. A man and a woman are a less dangerous combination; two men will have a harder time getting a lift, while three men will go nowhere.

Flagging down a bus is similar enough to hitchhiking that some travelers find themselves hitching a ride by accident; travelers standing by the side of the road are fair game for bus drivers and motorists alike. Many drivers who pick up hitchhikers expect some compensation, and may try to scam you once you've been driven to your destination, demanding money for gas, wear on the car, etc.

KEEPING IN TOUCH

BY EMAIL AND INTERNET

Vietnam likes the Internet. **Cybercafes** are truly everywhere in larger cities, and your odds of finding somewhere to get online—even in more out-of-the-way towns—are pretty good. Consequently, pricing is very competitive and you're unlikely to save money by shopping around, as long as you're not looking for Internet access in relatively expensive tourist-heavy districts (though these places tend to have more features like USB connections and CD burning). The average range you'll pay in any major urban area is 100-500Đ per minute. It is also worth noting that the Vietnamese government requires cybercafe owners to restrict access to sites containing "bad and poisonous information," licensing them to fairly arbitrary acts of surveillance and censorship (see **Don't Read This,** p. 73).

Though in some places it's possible to forge a remote link with your home server, in most cases this is a much slower (and thus more expensive) option than taking advantage of free **web-based email accounts** (e.g., www.hotmail.com and www.yahoo.com). **Internet cafes** are listed in the **Practical Information** sections of major cities, but in Hà Nội and Hồ Chí Minh City they pop up about every other building. Keep an eye out for wireless access in big cities; many Internet cafes often provide free wireless access for customers.

BY TELEPHONE

ESSENTIALS

>
> **PLACING INTERNATIONAL CALLS.** To call Vietnam from home or to call home from Vietnam, dial:
>
> 1. The **international dialing prefix.** To call from **Australia**, dial 0011; **Canada** or the **US**, 011; **Ireland, New Zealand**, the **UK**, or **Vietnam** 00.
> 2. The **country code** of the country you want to call. To call **Australia**, dial 61; **Canada** or the **US**, 1; **Ireland**, 353; **New Zealand**, 64; the **UK**, 44; **Vietnam**, 84.
> 3. The **city/area code.** Let's Go lists the city/area codes for cities and towns in Vietnam opposite the city or town name, next to the symbol ☎. If the first digit is a zero (e.g., 020 for London), omit the zero when calling from abroad (e.g., dial 20 from Canada to reach London).
> 4. The **local number.**

CALLING HOME FROM VIETNAM

You have three options: the international phone at the local post office, your cell phone (p. 42), or an ■**Internet phone**, available at nearly all Internet cafes. This last option is by far the cheapest, and gets even cheaper if you buy an Internet phone card (available at cell phone stores and convenience stores; 1000-5000Đ per min.). Because these cards eliminate the profit made by cybercafes themselves, however, their staff will occasionally refuse to allow you to use them

A **calling card** is the way to go if calling from the post office. Calls are billed collect or to your account. You can frequently call collect without even possessing a company's calling card just by calling their access number and following the instructions. **To obtain a calling card** from your national telecommunications service before leaving home, contact the appropriate company listed below (using the numbers in the first column). **To call home with a calling card**, contact the operator for your service provider in Vietnam by dialing the appropriate toll-free access number (listed below in the third column). You can also buy international "1717" or "1719" calling cards at any post office for 100,000Đ per 15 minutes.

COMPANY	TO OBTAIN A CARD:	TO CALL ABROAD:
AT&T (US)	800-364-9292 or www.att.com	1 201 2088
Canada Direct	800-561-8868 or www.infocanadadirect.com	1201 1010
MCI (US)	800-777-5000 or www.minutepass.com	1201 1022
Telstra Australia	1800 676 638 or www.telstra.com	120 061 111

You can usually also make **direct international calls** from the post office, but if you aren't using a calling card, the cost per minute will probably be prohibitively high, and the staffer at the post office desk may get worried and, humorously, cut you off. Prepaid phone cards and occasionally major credit cards can be used for direct international calls, but they are generally less cost-efficient. Placing a **collect call** through an international operator is even more expensive, but may be necessary in case of emergency. You can place collect calls through the service providers listed above even if you don't have one of their phone cards. Before settling on a calling card plan, be

ESSENTIALS

sure to research your options in order to pick the one that best fits both your needs and your destination.

CALLING WITHIN VIETNAM

There are no public-access payphones in Vietnam. The most convenient way to call within the country is to use the call centers in post offices, as most Vietnamese do; give the number to the desk attendant, who puts the call through, then pay afterward based on the length of the call. Your hotel may also allow you to use the phone at their desk. The other cheap, easy option is to use a cell phone if you have one (see below).

CELLULAR PHONES

If you have an international cell phone, it can make calling from and within Vietnam simple and cost-effective; buying a phone in Vietnam is only worth it if you're staying for a while or planning to use the phone in other countries after you leave. Phones are available for purchase everywhere in major urban areas and start at around 800,000Đ; use common sense and buy from reputable distributors, not street vendors. Prices vary greatly depending on model and plan.

The international standard for cell phones is **GSM,** a system that began in Europe and has spread to much of the rest of the world. To make and receive calls in Vietnam you will need a **GSM-compatible phone** and a **SIM (subscriber identity module) card,** a country-specific, thumbnail-sized chip that gives you a local phone number and plugs you into the local network. Many SIM cards are **prepaid,** meaning that they come with calling time included and you don't need to sign up for a monthly service plan. Incoming calls are frequently free. When you use up the prepaid time, you can buy additional cards or vouchers (usually available at convenience stores) to get more. For more information on GSM phones, check out www.telestial.com, www.orange.co.uk, www.roadpost.com, or www.planetomni.com. Companies like **Cellular Abroad** (www.cellularabroad.com) rent cell phones that work in a variety of destinations around the world, providing a simpler option than picking up a phone in-country.

The most popular network providers in Vietnam are **Mobifone** and **Vinaphone.** Both sell SIM cards that charge a small, flat rate per day regardless of usage. International call rates vary by country, but there is a 30% discount on calls made during off-peak hours (11pm-7am, Sundays, and holidays).

 GSM PHONES. Just having a GSM phone doesn't mean you're necessarily good to go when you travel abroad. The majority of GSM phones sold in the United States operate on a different **frequency** (1900) than international phones (900/1800) and will not work abroad. Tri-band phones work on all three frequencies (900/1800/1900) and will operate through most of the world. As well, some GSM phones are **SIM-locked** and will only accept SIM cards from a single carrier. You'll need a **SIM-unlocked** phone to use a SIM card from a local carrier when you travel.

TIME DIFFERENCES

Vietnam does not observe Daylight Saving Time. Between the last Sunday in October and the last Sunday in March, Vietnam is 7 hours ahead of **Greenwich Mean Time (GMT);** from April through October, the country is 8 hours ahead of GMT. Similarly, depending on the time of year, Vietnam is 11-12 hours ahead of New York City, 14-15 hours ahead of Vancouver and San Francisco, 3-4 hours behind Sydney (three between March and October, four between October and March), and 5-6 hours behind Auckland.

The following table applies from late October to early April.

4AM	5AM	6AM	7AM	8AM	NOON	7PM
Vancouver Seattle San Francisco Los Angeles	Denver	Chicago	New York Toronto	New Brunswick	London	Hà Nội HCMC

BY MAIL

SENDING MAIL HOME FROM VIETNAM

Airmail is the best way to send mail home from Vietnam. Be advised that officials may check through your package to make sure it doesn't have any offending items like contraband, pirated CDs, etc. Aerogrammes, printed sheets that fold into envelopes and travel via airmail, are available at post offices. Write "airmail" and "par avion" all over the front; if you want to send it express, choose a special EMS (Express Mail Service) envelope and refrain from writing "airmail" on it. Most post offices will charge exorbitant fees or simply refuse to send aerogrammes with enclosures. EMS is available for parcels, as well, and costs about three times as much as airmail, but gets there in half as much time (or less). Surface mail is by far the cheapest and slowest way to send mail. It takes one to two months to cross the Atlantic and one to three to cross the Pacific—good for heavy items you won't need for a while, like souvenirs or other articles you've acquired along the way that are weighing down your pack. You can send a postcard anywhere in the world for 9000Đ. For sending parcels via airmail, the first kilogram costs around US$10, and then it's about US$3.50 per kg thereafter to ship to the US. For other overseas countries, shipping costs between US$10-20 for the first kg, and US$1-5 for every kg afterwards. The standard rates for airmail from Vietnam to the following destinations are:

Australia: Allow 7-10 days delivery. Small letters 14,000Đ; packages up to 0.5kg US$5.

Canada: Allow 10-14 days delivery. Packages up to 0.5kg US$8.

Ireland: Allow 7-10 days delivery. Packages up to 0.5kg US$6.

New Zealand: Allow 7-10 days delivery. Packages up to 0.5kg US$5.

UK: Allow 7-10 days delivery. Packages up to 0.5kg US$6.

US: Allow 7-14 days delivery. Small letters 19,000Đ; packages up to 0.5kg US$8.

SENDING MAIL TO VIETNAM

To ensure timely delivery, mark envelopes "airmail" and "par avion." In addition to the standard postage system, whose rates are listed below, **Federal Express** (www.fedex.com; Australia ☎ 132 610; Canada and the US 800-463-3339; Ireland 1800 535 800; New Zealand 0800 733 339; UK 08456 070 803) handles express mail services from most countries to Vietnam. They can get a letter from New York or London to Vietnam in 1-2 days for US$48. Sending a postcard within Vietnam costs 800Đ, as does sending a letter (up to 20g) domestically. Nearly all cities and towns in Vietnam have a post office.

Australia: Allow 4-5 days for regular airmail to Vietnam. Postcards and letters up to 50g cost AUS$1.25; packages up to 0.5kg AUS$11.50, up to 2kg AUS$37. Express Courier International (ECI) can get a letter to Vietnam in 3-4 days for AUS$33. www.auspost.com.au/pac.

Canada: Allow 6-10 days for regular airmail to Vietnam. Postcards and letters up to 30g cost CDN$1.50; packages up to 0.5kg CDN$12, up to 2kg CDN$43. Purolator International can get a letter to Vietnam in 4-6 days for CDN$54. www.canadapost.ca/personal/rates/default-e.asp.

Ireland: Allow 7 days for regular airmail to Vietnam. Postcards and letters up to 50g cost €0.75; packages up to 0.5kg €20, up to 2kg €34. Courier Post can get a letter to Vietnam in 1 business day for €18. www.letterpost.ie.

New Zealand: Allow 1-2 weeks days for regular airmail to Vietnam. Postcards and letters up to 10g cost NZ$1.50, packages up to 0.5kg NZ$15.80, up to 2kg NZ$49.60. International Express can get a letter to Vietnam in 2-4 days for NZ$36.20. www.nzpost.co.nz.

UK: Allow 5 days for regular airmail to Vietnam. Letters up to 20g cost UK£0.72; packages up to 0.5kg UK£9.85, up to 2kg UK£37.60. www.royalmail.co.uk/calculator.

US: Allow 4-7 days for regular airmail to Vietnam. Letters up to 1 oz. cost US$0.85; packages up to 1 lb. US$15.25, up to 5 lb. US$34.50. Global Express Mail can get a letter to Vietnam in 2-3 days for US$33.75. http://ircalc.usps.gov.

RECEIVING MAIL IN VIETNAM

There are several ways to arrange pickup of letters sent to you by friends and relatives while you are in Vietnam. Mail can be sent via **Poste Restante** (General Delivery) to almost any city or town in Vietnam with a post office, and is reliable by developing-world standards; however, you may be required to provide extensive documentation to prove your identity. Address *Poste Restante* letters like so:

Firstname LASTNAME

Poste Restante

City, Việt Nam

The mail will go to a special desk in the central post office, unless you specify a post office by street address. It's best to use the largest post office, since mail may be sent there regardless. It is usually safer and quicker, though more expensive, to send express or registered mail. Bring your passport (or other photo ID) for pickup; there may be a small fee. If the clerks insist that there is nothing for you, have them check under your first name as well. Let's Go lists post offices in the **Practical Information** section for each city and most towns.

ACCOMMODATIONS

HOTELS AND GUESTHOUSES

Most of Vietnam's lodging comes in the form of hotels and guesthouses, which are run similarly; the major distinction between the two tends to be in price. At the high end of the price spectrum are Western-style hotels with perks (like pools) and a comprehensive range of amenities. At the lower end are guesthouses run by live-in owners and hotels without private bathrooms, air-conditioning, and the like. Traveling in numbers is cost-effective; the prices of guesthouse rooms usually stay fixed regardless of how many people are staying in them. A couple might spend US$8 on a room that would cost an individual traveler US$7.

Small splurges tend to be worth it—quality can increase dramatically by the dollar. Generally speaking, the cheapest rooms will cost US$3-6 (50,000-95,000Đ) and have a bed, shared bath, and little else. US$6-10 (95,000-160,000Đ) can get you air-conditioning, breakfast, and a higher standard of cleanliness. TVs, private bath, and other guilty pleasures are yours for US$10 and up. Except for more upscale hotels, **reservations** are hardly ever necessary (and not often accepted). Call ahead the day of your arrival to make sure your chosen guesthouse has vacancies; in the unlikely event that it doesn't, other similar options will.

BOOKING CHEAP HOTELS ONLINE. One of the easiest ways to ensure you've got a bed for the night is by reserving online. Click to the **Hostelworld** booking engine through **www.letsgo.com,** and you'll have access to bargain accommodations from Argentina to Zimbabwe with no added commission.

HOSPITALITY CLUBS

Hospitality clubs link their members with individuals or families abroad who are willing to host travelers for free or for a small fee to promote cultural exchange and general good karma. In exchange, members usually must be willing to host travelers in their own homes; a small membership fee may also be required. **The Hospitality Club** (www.hospitalityclub.org) is a good place to start. An Internet search will find many similar organizations, some of which cater to special interests (e.g., women, gay and lesbian travelers, members of certain professions). As always, use common sense when planning to stay with someone you do not know.

LONG-TERM ACCOMMODATIONS

Renting an **apartment** in Vietnam is the way to go for travelers planning on extended stays. US$160-200 per month can get you a decent room in someone's house, and US$400-600 is good for a well-located, multiple-room suite in Hà Nội or HCMC. Cheaper options exist for the less exacting. Reputable realtors with sufficient English abilities are not difficult to find in bigger cities. However, exercise caution—don't agree on an apartment until you've visited it, and be sure you understand all the requirements of the lease agreement. **Asia Xpat** (http://vietnam.asiaxpat.com) is one place to start looking; the classifieds in *Việt Nam News* and the boards of expat bars in major cities are also littered with apartment offers. Also search through www.hanoirealestate.com and www.hochiminhcityrealestate.com.

CAMPING

Camping is generally only sanctioned in national parks, and then often only with the permission and accompaniment of local officials. Campgrounds do not really exist outside of protected areas. Travelers who try to camp elsewhere in Vietnam without official sanction will be arrested by the police when found doing so. RVing in Vietnam is virtually unknown.

LEAVE NO TRACE. Let's Go encourages travelers to embrace the "Leave No Trace" ethic, minimizing their impact on natural environments and protecting them for future generations. Trekkers and wilderness enthusiasts should set up camp on durable surfaces, use cookstoves instead of campfires, bury human waste away from water supplies, bag trash and carry it out with them, and respect wildlife and natural objects. For more detailed information, contact the **Leave No Trace Center for Outdoor Ethics,** P.O. Box 997, Boulder, CO 80306, USA (☎800-332-4100 or 303-442-8222; www.lnt.org).

THE GREAT OUTDOORS

The **Great Outdoor Recreation Pages** (www.gorp.com) provides excellent general information for travelers planning on camping or spending time in the outdoors.

USEFUL RESOURCES

A variety of publishing companies offer hiking guidebooks to meet the educational needs of novice or expert. For information about camping, hiking, and biking, write or call the publishers listed below to receive a free catalog.

Great Outdoor Recreation Pages (www.gorp.com). This website provides excellent general information for travelers planning on camping or spending time in the outdoors. It also has info on a few Vietnam-specific trips.

Sierra Club Books, 85 Second St., 2nd fl., San Francisco, CA 94105, USA (☎415-977-5500; www.sierraclub.org). Publishes general resource books on hiking and camping.

The Mountaineers Books, 1001 SW Klickitat Way, Ste. 201, Seattle, WA 98134, USA (☎206-223-6303; www.mountaineersbooks.org). Boasts over 600 titles on hiking, biking, mountaineering, natural history, and conservation. At least 1 is on Vietnam.

NATIONAL PARKS

Vietnam's national parks, despite a rudimentary tourist infrastructure, are for the most part well designed for visits and encompass a gorgeous array of landscapes, from peaks in the lofty Hoàng Liên Sơn Range to the limestone islands and coral reefs of Cát Bà. Accommodations include campgrounds, guesthouses, and rooms in administrative buildings.

Most national parks and nature preserves charge an entrance fee; some require additional fees to tour the area; some parks don't allow any excursions without the accompaniment of a ranger (and another fee). The protection of endangered species may make some areas off-limits to casual visitors. Travelers should consider visiting with a tour group if they have a particular interest in a park's wildlife—organized tours frequently have access to restricted parts of the park. Our park writeups note in which places this is systematic. Also look in the **Environmental Conservation** section (p. 92) of our **Beyond Tourism** chapter for opportunities to work with park scientists.

WILDERNESS SAFETY

Staying **warm, dry,** and **well hydrated** is key to a happy and safe wilderness experience. For any hike, prepare yourself for an emergency by packing a first-aid kit, a reflector, a whistle, high-energy food, extra water, ■raingear, a hat, mittens, and extra socks. Paying a little extra for the best raingear is a worthwhile investment in Vietnam. For warmth, wear wool or insulating synthetic materials designed for the outdoors. Cotton is a bad choice since it dries painfully slowly.

Check **weather forecasts** often and pay attention to the skies when hiking, as weather patterns can change suddenly. Always let someone—a friend, your hostel, a park ranger, or a local hiking organization—know when and where you are going. Know your physical limits, and do not attempt a hike beyond your ability. See **Safety and Health,** p. 23, for information on outdoor medical concerns.

WILDLIFE

MOSQUITOES. Mosquitoes are your biggest wildlife concern in Vietnam. They are aggressive, and they are everywhere in the countryside. First and foremost, take your **malaria medication** daily and make sure you are vaccinated against other mosquito-borne diseases (dengue fever and Japanese encephalitis are the big ones; p.

29). Insect repellent with **DEET** is recommended; more effective, and indispensable if you plan to sleep outdoors, are **mosquito nets,** ubiquitously available in cities. Wearing long shirts and pants can also help deter these ravenous pests. As a rule of thumb, wetter areas have more mosquitoes—if you go to the Mekong between May and November, make sure you have adequate mosquito deterrents.

LEECHES. Sound gross? They are. Leeches are suave and quiet predators. They live in the shallow bottoms of ponds and lakes, and they're most prevalent in the summer. Buy leech guards and cover every inch of flesh, and check yourself after any period of time spent wading through water or swimming. For that matter, do not swim anywhere unless explicitly told that the water is safe.

SNAKES. US soldiers in the American War used to say that there are 100 types of snakes in Vietnam—99 were poisonous, and the last one could crush you to death. The real numbers are more like 140 species, around 30 of which are poisonous, including the famous King Cobra. The danger for tourists is low, but nearly 30,000 Vietnamese rice farmers get bitten every year, mostly by stepping on hidden snakes. If you're walking through national parks or rice paddies, make sure to wear long pants and appropriate shoes; if you see a snake, maintain a respectful distance. If it has a triangular head (as many poisonous snakes do), simply leave the area. Snake bites, even poisonous ones, aren't usually life-threatening if treated quickly and properly. Don't bother snakes, and they shouldn't bother you.

CAMPING AND HIKING EQUIPMENT

WHAT TO BUY

Good camping equipment is both sturdy and light. North American suppliers tend to offer the most competitive prices.

Sleeping Bags: Most sleeping bags are rated by season; "summer" means 30-40°F (around 0°C) at night; "four-season" or "winter" often means below 0°F (-17°C). Bags are made of **down** (warm and light, but expensive; miserable when wet) or of **synthetic** material (heavy, durable, and warm when wet). Prices range US$50-250 for a summer synthetic to US$200-300 for a good down winter bag. **Sleeping bag pads** include foam pads (US$10-30), air mattresses (US$15-50), and self-inflating mats (US$30-120). Bring a **stuff sack** to store your bag and keep it dry.

Tents: The best tents are free-standing (with their own frames and suspension systems), set up quickly, and only require staking in high winds. Low-profile dome tents are the best all-around. Good 2-person tents start at US$100; 4-person tents at US$160. Make sure your tent has a rain fly, and seal its seams with waterproofer. Other useful accessories include a **battery-operated lantern,** a plastic **groundcloth,** and a nylon **tarp.**

Backpacks: Internal-frame packs mold well to your back, keep a lower center of gravity, and flex adequately to allow you to hike difficult trails, while **external-frame packs** are more comfortable for long hikes over even terrain, as they carry weight higher and distribute it more evenly. Make sure your pack has a strong, padded hip-belt to transfer weight to your legs. There are models designed specifically for women. Any serious backpacking requires a pack of at least 4000 cu. in. (16,000cc), plus 500 cu. in. for sleeping bags in internal-frame packs. Sturdy backpacks cost anywhere from US$125 to 420—your pack is an area where it doesn't pay to economize. On your hunt for the perfect pack, fill up prospective models with something heavy, strap it on correctly, and walk around the store to get a sense of how the model distributes weight. Either buy a **rain cover** (US$10-20) or store all of your belongings in plastic bags inside your pack.

Boots: Be sure to wear hiking boots with good **ankle support.** They should fit snugly and comfortably over 1-2 pairs of **wool socks** and a pair of thin **liner socks.** Break in boots over several weeks before you go to spare yourself blisters.

Experts in adventure and cultural tours
Offering tours, day trips, extensions
hotels and domestic travel

Hanoi: 9-13 Hang Muoi St.
Tel: (04) 828 0702
HCMC: 56 Dong Khoi St. Suite 302
Ph: (08) 827 9170

Be inspired
by travel again

Buffalo
tours
www.buffalotours.com

Other Necessities: Synthetic layers, like those made of polypropylene or polyester, and a pile jacket will keep you warm even when wet. A **space blanket** (US$5-15) will help you to retain body heat and doubles as a groundcloth. Plastic **water bottles** are vital; look for shatter- and leak-resistant models. Carry **water-purification tablets** for when you can't boil water. Although most campgrounds provide campfire sites, you may want to bring a small **metal grate** or grill. For those places that forbid fires or the gathering of firewood, you'll need a **camp stove** (the classic Coleman starts at US$50) and a propane-filled **fuel bottle** to operate it. Also bring a **first-aid kit, pocketknife, insect repellent,** and **waterproof matches** or a **lighter.** And we know we're getting repetitive, but bring a **raincoat.** A really, really good raincoat.

WHERE TO BUY IT

The online and mail-order companies listed below offer lower prices than many retail stores. A visit to a local camping or outdoors store will give you a good sense of the look and weight of certain items before you buy.

Campmor, 28 Parkway, P.O. Box 700, Upper Saddle River, NJ 07458, USA (☎800-525-4784; www.campmor.com).

Cotswold Outdoor, Unit 11 Kemble Business Park, Crudwell, Malmesbury Wiltshire, SN16 9SH, UK (☎08704 427 755; www.cotswoldoutdoor.com).

Discount Camping, 880 Main North Rd., Pooraka, South Australia 5095, Australia (☎08 8262 3399; www.discountcamping.com.au).

Eastern Mountain Sports (EMS), 1 Vose Farm Rd., Peterborough, NH 03458, USA (☎888-463-6367; www.ems.com).

Gear-Zone, 8 Burnet Rd., Sweetbriar Rd. Industrial Estate, Norwich, NR3 2BS, UK (☎1603 410 108; www.gear-zone.co.uk).

L.L. Bean, Freeport, ME 04033, USA (US and Canada ☎800-441-5713; UK 0800 891 297; www.llbean.com).

Mountain Designs, 443a Nudgee Rd., Hendra, Queensland 4011, Australia (☎7 3856 2344; www.mountaindesigns.com).

Recreational Equipment, Inc. (REI), Sumner, WA 98352, USA (Canada and the US ☎800-426-4840, elsewhere 253-891-2500; www.rei.com).

ORGANIZED ADVENTURE TRIPS

Organized adventure tours offer another way of exploring the wild. Activities include hiking, biking, canoeing, kayaking, rafting, climbing, photo safaris, and archaeological digs. Tourism bureaus often can suggest parks, trails, and outfit-ters. Organizations that specialize in camping and outdoor equipment like REI and EMS (see above) also are good sources for info.

Specialty Travel Index, 305 San Anselmo Ave., Ste. 309, San Anselmo, CA 94960 (US ☎800-624-4030, elsewhere 415-455-1643; www.specialtytravel.com). Links to numerous adventure tour organizers all over the world.

Vietnam Adventurer, 15 Ho Quynh, Hà Nội (☎844 625 0315; fax 844 625 0316; www.vietnamadventurer.com). Offers hiking, kayaking, bicycling, jeep, and motorcycle tours. Operates throughout the country, with bases in most major cities.

SPECIFIC CONCERNS

SUSTAINABLE TRAVEL

As the number of travelers on the road continues to rise, the detrimental effect they can have on natural environments becomes an increasing concern. With this in mind, Let's Go promotes the philosophy of **sustainable travel.** Through a sensitivity to issues of ecology and sustainability, today's travelers can be a powerful force in preserving and restoring the places they visit.

Ecotourism, a rising trend in sustainable travel, focuses on the conservation of natural habitats and using them to build up the economy without exploitation or overdevelopment. Travelers can make a difference by doing advance research and by supporting organizations and establishments that pay attention to their impact on their natural surroundings and strive to be environmentally friendly. The increase in popularity of ecotourism hasn't escaped the attention of tourist cafes in Hà Nội and HCMC, and many unscrupulous tour organizers will claim to be environmentally responsible, when in fact they aren't; do your homework, talk to other travelers, and choose accordingly. Ecotourism in Vietnam is still in its nascent stages; it's at its most developed in Đà Lạt (p. 345), where environmentally conscious tours abound. Ecotours range from boat trips up the Mekong Delta to hiking trips through national parks and Chàm ruins to snorkeling and scuba diving off the pristine coasts of Nha Trang.

 ECOTOURISM RESOURCES. For more information on environmentally responsible tourism, contact one of the organizations below:
Conservation International, 1919 M St. NW, Ste. 600, Washington, D.C. 20036, USA (☎800-406-2306 or 202-912-1000; www.conservation.org).
Green Globe 21 (☎61 2 6257 9102; www.greenglobe.com).
International Ecotourism Society, 733 15th St. NW, Ste. 1000, Washington, D.C. 20005, USA (☎202-347-9203; www.ecotourism.org).
United Nations Environment Program (UNEP), 39-43 Quai André Citroën, 75739 Paris Cedex 15, France (☎33 1 44 37 14 50; www.uneptie.org/pc/tourism).

RESPONSIBLE TRAVEL

The impact of tourist đồng on the destinations you visit should not be underestimated. The choices you make during your trip can have potent effects on local communities—for better or for worse. Travelers who care about the destinations and environments they explore should become aware of the social and cultural implications of the choices they make when they travel. Simple decisions such as buying local products instead of globally available ones, paying fair prices for products or services, and attempting to say a few words in the local language can have a strong, positive effect on the community.

LONELY LADY

Women traveling alone in Vietnam are unlikely to encounter any special danger. Violent crimes against foreigners, women included, are relatively rare here. The biggest hassles most single foreign women face from the local men are stares and catcalls. Occasionally, men will also suck at their teeth, which seems to be the Vietnamese version of whistling, although it feels slightly more offensive—if only because it's different.

What may be more challenging for some single women is everyone's sheer pity concerning their solo status. Vietnamese cultural norms emphasize couplehood and marriage, so a woman traveling alone appears rather pathetic, like someone who has a birthday party but no guests. The question about one's relationship status comes up early on in conversations, and women who say they're alone are usually met with sorrowful looks and statements like, "It's very sad for you," or "But where is your friend?" Even the most independent woman may feel a bit lonely after this treatment. Try not to let it get you down; instead, let people know that you're happy to be alone, and explain that you chose to travel that way. If that doesn't work, you can always create a wonderful (albeit imaginary) boyfriend or husband who is waiting for you in your home country.

—*Marianne Cook*

Community-based tourism aims to channel tourist đồng into the local economy by emphasizing tours and cultural programs that are run by members of the host community and that often benefit disadvantaged groups; unfortunately, few such organizations exist. The majority of tours in Vietnam herd you off the bus, encourage you to take photos of everything in sight, and then herd you back on the bus. New programs, though, spurred by recent interest in ecotourism and international backing, have crept slowly onto the tourist radar. The Netherlands Development Organization (SNV), teamed with The World Conservation Union (IUCN), support the pilot project "Support to Sustainable Tourism in Sa Pa," which works with tourist agencies to share more equitably the benefits from and control of tourism in Sa Pa with its inhabitants. In general, these kinds of programs are small and underfunded, and their impact has yet to be felt on a national level. Look in our **Beyond Tourism** chapter to find some opportunities for both community service and responsible travel (see **Social Activism,** p. 89). An excellent resource for general information on community-based travel is *The Ethical Travel Guide* (UK£10), a project of **Tourism Concern** (☎ 020 7133 3330; www.tourismconcern.org.uk).

You can still be a responsible traveler without joining an organized tour. Visiting rural communities on your own, or with the aid of a private driver, is much less disruptive than arriving as part of a crowd, provided you behave respectfully and observe local customs. Hotel attendants and other locals will be glad to tell you the appropriate way to act. While it's tempting to give **handouts** to begging children, don't do it—it just encourages more begging. Your money is far better put to use contributing to international charity organizations. As for flora and fauna, your best bet is to do as the locals do. Endangered species, including some primate and snake species, are eaten mostly as cocktail delicacies. Rare plants can grow only in areas that see few humans. By eating typical foods and staying on the path, you can avoid adding to the destruction of Vietnam's amazingly diverse wildlife.

TRAVELING ALONE

There are many benefits to traveling alone, including independence and a greater opportunity to connect with locals. On the other hand, solo travelers are more vulnerable targets of harassment and theft. If you're traveling alone, look confident, try to blend in, and be careful in deserted or very crowded areas. Stay away from poorly-lit areas. Never admit that you are traveling alone. Maintain regular contact with someone at home who knows your itinerary, and always research your destination before traveling. For more tips, pick up *Traveling Solo* by Eleanor Berman (Globe Pequot Press, US$18), visit www.travelaloneandloveit.com, or subscribe to **Connecting: Solo Travel Network,** 689 Park Rd., Unit 6, Gibsons, BC V0N 1V7, Canada (☎604-886-9099; www.cstn.org; membership US$30-48).

WOMEN TRAVELERS

Personal space and privacy are not mainstays of Vietnamese culture; this may make female travelers particularly uncomfortable. Catcalls, often in the form of a teeth-sucking noise, are inevitable but harmless when ignored. Again, physical violence against foreigners in Vietnam is extremely rare. Verbal harassment is irritating but very rarely leads to anything threatening.

Your best answer to verbal harassment is none at all; feigning deafness, sitting motionless, and staring straight ahead at nothing in particular will do a world of good that reactions usually don't achieve. The extremely persistent can sometimes be dissuaded by a firm, loud, and very public "Go away!" in Vietnamese; "I have a husband" is also useful (see **Phrasebook,** p. 450). Don't hesitate to seek out a sympathetic passerby if you are being harassed—it's worth stressing again that Vietnam is hyper-aware of the detrimental effect instances of crime and harassment can have on tourism and the money they get from it, and bystanders will act accordingly. Memorize the emergency numbers in places you visit, and consider carrying a whistle on your keychain. A self-defense course will both prepare you for a potential attack and raise your level of awareness of your surroundings (see **Self Defense,** p. 26). Also be aware of the health concerns that women face when traveling (p. 32).

Finally, certain precautions are common sense. Stick to centrally located accommodations and avoid solitary late-night excursions. Always carry extra money for a phone call, bus, or taxi. Hitchhiking is never safe for lone women, or even for two women traveling together, and Let's Go never recommends it. Look as if you know where you're going and approach older women or couples for directions if you're lost or uncomfortable. The less you look like a tourist, the better off you'll be. Dress conservatively, especially in rural areas. Wearing a conspicuous **wedding band** sometimes helps to prevent unwanted overtures.

GLBT TRAVELERS

There are no laws expressly prohibiting homosexuality in Vietnam, but gay, lesbian, bisexual, and transgendered (GLBT) travelers should bear in mind that the country's cultural adherence to conservative, traditional family values leaves little place for them to openly demonstrate their sexuality. Displays of affection are more likely to be met with discomfort than with outright hostility, but in either event, we recommend a high degree of discretion.

To avoid hassles at airports and border crossings, transgendered travelers should make sure that all of their travel documents consistently report the same sex. Many countries (including Australia, Canada, Ireland, New Zealand, the UK, and the US) will amend the passports of post-operative transsexuals to reflect their true sex, although governments are generally less willing to amend documents for pre-operative transsexuals and other transgendered individuals.

Listed below are contact organizations, mail-order bookstores, and publishers that offer materials addressing some specific concerns. **Out and About** (www.planetout.com) offers a weekly newsletter and a comprehensive site addressing gay travel concerns. The online newspaper **365gay.com** also has a travel section (www.365gay.com/travel/travelchannel.htm).

ESSENTIALS

ESSENTIALS

Utopia (www.utopia-asia.com). A great website with articles on GLBT issues in both Southeast Asia generally and Vietnam specifically, plus listings, scam warnings, and other useful posts from travelers.

Gay's the Word, 66 Marchmont St., London WC1N 1AB, UK (☎07 278 7654; www.gaystheword.co.uk). The largest gay and lesbian bookshop in the UK, with both fiction and non-fiction titles. Mail-order service available.

Giovanni's Room, 345 South 12th St., Philadelphia, PA 19107, USA (☎215-923-2960; www.queerbooks.com). An international lesbian and gay bookstore with mail-order service (carries many of the publications listed below).

International Lesbian and Gay Association (ILGA), 81 rue Marché-au-Charbon, B-1000 Brussels, Belgium (☎32 2 502 2471; www.ilga.org). Provides political information, such as homosexuality laws of individual countries.

> **ADDITIONAL RESOURCES: GLBT**
> *Spartacus 2005-2006: International Gay Guide.* Bruno Gmunder Verlag (US$33).
> *The Gay Vacation Guide: The Best Trips and How to Plan Them,* Mark Chesnut. Kensington Books (US$15).

TRAVELERS WITH DISABILITIES

It is extremely difficult to be physically disabled in Vietnam. Budget travel is all but out of the question; cheaper guesthouses and hotels simply don't have the facilities to accommodate the needs of travelers with disabilities, and everyday forms of transportation (buses, taxis, cyclos) are similarly ill-equipped. Check out the Disability Forum for Vietnam at http://forum.wso.net for tips. Those with disabilities should inform airlines and hotels of their disabilities when making reservations; some time may be needed to prepare special accommodations. Call ahead to restaurants, museums, and other facilities to find out if they are wheelchair-accessible. **Guide dog owners** should inquire as to quarantine policies.

USEFUL ORGANIZATIONS

Accessible Journeys, 35 West Sellers Ave., Ridley Park, PA 19078, USA (☎800-846-4537; www.disabilitytravel.com). Designs tours for wheelchair users and slow walkers. The site has tips and forums for all travelers.

Mobility International USA (MIUSA), P.O. Box 10767, Eugene, OR 97440, USA (☎541-343-1284; www.miusa.org). Provides a variety of books and other publications containing information for travelers with disabilities.

Society for Accessible Travel & Hospitality (SATH), 347 Fifth Ave., #610, New York, NY 10016, USA (☎212-447-7284; www.sath.org). An advocacy group that publishes free online travel information and the travel magazine *OPEN WORLD* (annual subscription US$13, free for members). Annual membership US$45, students and seniors US$30.

MINORITY TRAVELERS

All non-Asian travelers are minority travelers in Vietnam. People will stare at you, unblinking, for the duration of five-hour bus rides; children will point at you and giggle; aspiring English speakers will test their "hello" on you ad nauseam. Non-white travelers may actually attract less attention, for better or for worse. Instances of harassment or refusal of service based on race are extremely rare. Being of Asian descent, though, doesn't mean you won't stand out; especially in more rural areas, any outsider at all will attract substantial attention. Don't feel threatened by the stares or the laughter—in tourist-sensitive Vietnam, being an outsider with đồng usually results in extra safety and courtesy, not hostility. Then again, don't go out of your way to identify yourself as a tourist. Following local customs and dressing conservatively are always good ideas, helping you to integrate with local communities and helping local communities accept you.

DIETARY CONCERNS

Predominantly Buddhist Vietnam is vegetarian- and even vegan-friendly, at least in the broad sweep of things. In practice, vegetarians and vegans may have to be vocal about their eating preferences, especially in smaller cities. Often due simply to misunderstanding, roadside stall owners and restaurant servers will occasionally provide faulty reassurance that a dish contains no animal fat, or (for example) that a huge chunk of beef is actually a vegetable in disguise. Be patient, be persistent, and always double-check. Try writing *tôi không ăn thịt* ("I don't eat meat") on a notecard and showing it to food vendors. All of Vietnam's staple dishes have vegetarian and vegan counterparts, which are delightfully inexpensive.

The travel section of the The Vegetarian Resource Group's website, at www.vrg.org/travel, has a comprehensive list of organizations and websites that are geared toward helping vegetarians and vegans traveling abroad. For more information, visit your local bookstore or health-food store, and consult *The Vegetarian Traveler: Where to Stay if You're Vegetarian, Vegan, Environmentally Sensitive*, by Jed and Susan Civic (Larson Publications; US$16). There are also resources on the web, such as www.vegdining.com and www.happycow.net.

Travelers who keep kosher should contact synagogues in larger cities for information on kosher restaurants. Your own synagogue or college Hillel should have access to lists of Jewish institutions across the nation. If you are strict in your observance, you may have to prepare your own food on the road. A good resource is the *Jewish Travel Guide*, edited by Michael Zaidner (Vallentine Mitchell; US$18). Travelers looking for halal restaurants may find www.zabihah.com a useful resource.

OTHER RESOURCES

Let's Go tries to cover all aspects of budget travel, but we can't put *everything* in our guides. Listed below are books and websites that can serve as jumping-off points for your own research.

PUBLICATIONS AND PUBLISHERS

Hippocrene Books, Inc., 171 Madison Ave., New York, NY 10016, USA (☎212-685-4371; orders 718-454-2366; www.hippocrenebooks.com). Free catalog. Publishes foreign-language dictionaries and language learning guides.

Rand McNally, 8255 N. Central Park, Skokie, IL 60076, USA (☎847-329-8100; www.randmcnally.com). Publishes road atlases.

Adventurous Traveler Bookstore, P.O. Box 2221, Williston, VT 05495, USA (☎800-282-3963 or 802-860-6776; www.adventuroustraveler.com). Focus on adventure travel.

WORLD WIDE WEB

Almost every aspect of budget travel is accessible via the web. In 10 minutes at the keyboard, you can make a hostel reservation, get advice on travel hotspots from other travelers, or find out how much a train from Hà Nội to Hải Phòng costs.

ESSENTIALS

Listed here are some regional and travel-related sites to start off your surfing; other relevant web sites are listed throughout the book. Because website turnover is high, use search engines (such as www.google.com) to strike out on your own.

www.letsgo.com. Let's Go's website features a wealth of information and valuable advice at your fingertips. It offers excerpts from all our guides as well as monthly features on new hot spots in the most popular destinations. In addition to our online bookstore, we have great deals on everything from airfares to cell phones. Our resources section is full of information you'll need before you hit the road, and our forums are buzzing with advice from other travelers. Check back often to see constant updates, exciting new tips, and prize giveaways. See you soon!

THE ART OF TRAVEL

How to See the World: www.artoftravel.com. A compendium of great travel tips, from cheap flights to self defense to interacting with local culture.

Travel Library: www.travel-library.com. A fantastic set of links for general information and personal travelogues.

Travel Intelligence: www.travelintelligence.net. A large collection of travel writing by distinguished travel writers.

World Hum: www.worldhum.com. An independently produced collection of "travel dispatches from a shrinking planet."

BootsnAll.com: www.bootsnall.com. Numerous resources for independent travelers, from planning your trip to reporting on it when you get back.

INFORMATION ON VIETNAM

Vietnam National Administration of Tourism: www.vietnamtourism.com. Snazzy government-affiliated website in English and French. Logistical facts on specific destinations and descriptions of upcoming events.

Things Asian: www.thingsasian.com. Compilations of articles on Vietnam (and other Asian countries) ranging from architecture to adoption.

Việt Nam News: http://vietnamnews.vnagency.com.vn. The national English-language daily newspaper.

BBC and CNN: http://news.bbc.co.uk/2/hi/asia-pacific/default.stm and http://edition.cnn.com/ASIA. British and American news services with major Vietnam news stories; updated constantly.

Cornell University Southeast Asia Program: www.einaudi.cornell.edu/southeastasia. Links to hundreds of Vietnam-related sites.

CIA World Factbook: http://www.odci.gov/cia/publications/factbook/geos/vm.html. Tons of vital statistics on Vietnam's geography, government, economy, and people.

Geographia: www.geographia.com. Highlights, culture, and people of Vietnam.

PlanetRider: www.planetrider.com. A subjective list of links to the "best" websites covering the culture and tourist attractions of Vietnam.

Time Asia: www.time.com/time/asia. Asia's version of popular *Time* magazine. Current events, cultural information, and technology news throughout Asia.

Atevo Travel: www.atevo.com/guides/destinations. Detailed introductions, travel tips, and suggested itineraries.

World Travel Guide: www.travel-guides.com. Helpful practical info.

LIFE AND TIMES

Vietnam prides itself on its unique heritage and strong survival instinct; after centuries of invasion and influence by the Chinese, French, and Japanese, Vietnamese culture is anything but simple. The country's history of struggle against imperialism and desire for independence has created a culture unique from that of its Southeast Asian neighbors—the nuances can be hard for visitors to grasp. Tourist cafes whisk most travelers around on sputtering minibuses, providing spoon-fed doses of "authentic" local practice. A truer taste of contemporary Vietnam hides in alleyway eateries, *bia hơi* stalls, and amid the plastic furniture of street-side cafes.

LAND

For a country with so much waterfront real estate—over 3250km of coastline—Vietnam is surprisingly hilly: roughly 80% of the country is composed of hills and mountains. In the northwest, the Hoàng Liên Sơn Range—home to Vietnam's highest peak, **Fan Si Pan** (3143m)—dominates the landscape. Farther east, the hills give way to the fertile lowlands of the **Red River Delta,** culminating in the land's disintegration into thousands of islands and islets in Hạ Long Bay and Bái Tử Long Bay. Much of the inland north, too, is dotted with towering ▓limestone cliffs and monoliths (called karsts). Central Vietnam north of Huế sees the Trường Sơn Range, blanketed in forest, descend steeply from the Lao border into the sea. Around Huế, winter ceases to exist; the stretch of amazing coastline you see on tourist brochures begins here and reaches almost all the way to Hồ Chí Minh City. Inland, the Central Highlands aren't as high as the northwest, but they're just as striking, carved by rivers and waterfalls and scattered with dense forests. Here, limestone gives way to basalt, and the ground becomes more fertile, supporting the coffee plantations of Buôn Ma Thuột and the strawberry fields of Đà Lạt. Approaching HCMC from the northeast, the landscape flattens out; southwest of HCMC, the land sinks into the swamps and mangrove jungle of the **Mekong Delta,** an area kept arable by the delta's industrious denizens.

PEOPLE

DEMOGRAPHICS

Ethnic Vietnamese, or **Kinh,** make up roughly 90% of the country's 84.4 million people; the remaining population is split between 53 minority groups. Often called **Montagnards** or **hill tribes,** these people tend to live in the highlands and mountainous regions of Vietnam, almost always adhering to conservative, agrarian ways of life. Most speak traditional Vietnamese as either their primary or secondary language, but a few rely solely on the dozen or so dialects spoken throughout the country, and some even have their own systems of writing. Vietnamese ethnic minorities are often classified according to their language groups and somewhat less frequently by their primary location or population size.

Concentrated largely in the northwest and Central Highlands, Montagnards are most easily recognized by their colorful traditional clothing, which often involves complex headdresses, large jewelry, and elaborate dresses and costumes. Tourism among Montagnard communities in the northwest largely targets their bright and engaging markets, which usually sell a wide variety of goods, from clothing to fresh fruit to live animals. The relaxing pace of daily life in the villages is another highlight of trekking through the northwest, and most often foreign visitors' and polite tourists' presence is met with a bit of surprise, a great deal of curiosity, and an overwhelming sense of welcome.

With a population over two million, the largest minority group in Vietnam is the **Hoa,** descendent from the Han Chinese. They are concentrated in urban and lowland areas and remain isolated from Vietnamese society, instead maintaining their ties to China and Chinese culture. Other large groups in the north include the **Tày, Mường,** and **Thài,** part of the Malay ethnolinguistic group, as well as the **H'mông, Dao,** and **Nùng,** who have roots in southern China and may have migrated to Vietnam as recently as the 19th century. The Dao have a distinctive and remarkable dress, resplendent with jangling coins and sweeping headdresses. In the Central Highlands, the largest groups are the **M'nong, Êdê,** and **Bahnar,** who usually live in houses built on stilts and are perhaps Vietnam's most disenfranchised minorities.

The **Khmer** and **Chàm** make up another class of minority groups. Khmer are ethnic Cambodians indigenous to Vietnam's Mekong Delta region, which they controlled until the late 19th century. Chàm are native to the central coast of Vietnam descendants of the Champa kingdom conquered by Kinh from the north in the 15th century. The Khmer practice an adaptation of Theravada Buddhism, while the Chàm practice a mix of Hinduism and Islam.

Not surprisingly, Vietnam's track record with its ethnic minorities has been less than ideal. Montagnards are often viewed as backward and uneducated, and some have been subjected to government-sponsored harassment and discrimination. Protestant minorities in the Central Highlands have historically been the most mistreated group, robbed of their land by the Diệm administration and persecuted by the Communist government for creating underground churches. Since then the Communist Party of Vietnam has made efforts to bring the hill tribes up to date with modern agricultural technology, education, and medicine. However, the economic divide between Kinh and minority groups continues to widen, reflecting the growing urban-rural disparity in Vietnam today.

Another important sector of Vietnamese demography is the people called **Việt Kiều,** or "overseas Vietnamese," who were born outside of the country or left as refugees after national reunification in 1975. Around three million ethnic Vietnamese live in other parts of the world, about 1.2 million of them in the US. The largest concentration of Việt Kiều resides in Orange County, California, in one of many communities commonly called **Little Saigon.** The Vietnamese government's trend toward a more open economy and the official policy of reconciliation with refugee Việt Kiều have attracted many of these people back to Vietnam, though few intend to stay there for good.

Since the American War, Vietnam has been home to a remarkably young population: the war's death toll dramatically shifted the country's demographics, and today over 60% of the population is under 25 years old. This new generation has developed a greater sense of independence, which their elders often disapprovingly refer to as *mất gốc,* or "losing roots." Though the new trend has downplayed the importance of family and respect for one's elders, the independent spirit of the new generation is a natural continuation of the stubborn national urge not to be colonized—even by their parents.

LANGUAGE

Vietnamese is the only official language of Vietnam and is spoken by the great majority (around 90%) of the population; those who don't speak it are largely ethnic minorities in the rural highlands. About half of all Vietnamese words are descended from Chinese, but there is evidence of Thai, Khmer, and Mường influence as well. Vietnamese was originally written in Chinese characters, called *chữ* *nôm*, which were adapted to fit the indigenous vocabulary. Seventeenth-century French Jesuit missionary **Alexandre de Rhodes** adapted Vietnamese to the Latin alphabet, using an ingenious system of diacriticals to transcribe the tonal qualities of words. The result was called *quốc ngữ* ("national language"), and today it is the exclusive written form of Vietnamese. With the establishment of the independent Democratic Republic of Vietnam in 1945, government workers and intellectuals expanded the vocabulary of the Vietnamese language to help it address the nuances of advanced scientific and political discussion

The language appears to be monosyllabic, but in fact multiple syllables, separated by spaces, can still belong to the same word, as, for example, with "tourism" *(du lịch)*. For foreigners, the most difficult part of learning Vietnamese is the pronunciation. The language is tonal, meaning that the pitch at which a word is said helps to determine its meaning. Vietnamese has six separate tones, and Western speakers need substantial practice before they can speak in a way that sounds natural to native speakers. Additionally, certain distinctions among vowels are difficult for the Western ear to discern. Vocabulary and grammar, however, are significantly easier. Lengthier words have a modular quality, making compounds easy to remember: *xe máy*, meaning "motorcycle," decomposes into *xe* ("vehicle") and *máy* ("machine"). Grammatically, words themselves do not change to reflect changes in tense or case; instead, additional particles are added. For a tantalizingly cursory Vietnamese primer, flip to our Appendix and peruse the **Vietnamese Pronunciation Guide** (p. 449) and the **Phrasebook** (p. 450).

RELIGION

Religion in Vietnam is a confusing affair. It tends to be a rough amalgamation of Buddhism, Taoism, and Confucianism, with a sprinkling of animism, astrology, and local superstition thrown in for good measure. No church or organization wields any profound nation-wide influence, thanks in large part to governmental suppression, and observance is mostly an individual or family affair. The constitution guarantees freedom of religion, albeit with the unsettling caveat that religion may not be used "to violate state laws or policies," which has translated to arbitrary restrictions on organized religious practice. Today, religious persecution is uncommon, except in the central highlands, and particularly the provinces of Đắk Lắk and Gia Lai, where minority Protestants are still harassed by local police.

THE TRIPLE RELIGION

Vietnam's home-grown "triple religion" derives from Mahayana Buddhism, Taoism, and Confucianism, but the extent to which each informs one's spiritual life-style varies wildly from person to person.

BUDDHISM. Most adherents of the Triple Religion classify themselves as Buddhists, but some refer to themselves as non-religious, though they all make offerings at Buddhist pagodas and engage in ancestor worship. Buddhism was born in the 6th century BC with the enlightenment of **Prince Siddhartha "the Buddha" Gautama,** a prince-turned-ascetic-turned-sage. Buddhists seek to attain **nirvana,** the state of enlightenment wherein one is free of all desire and pain. This can only be achieved by following the **Eightfold Path**—Right Understanding, Right Thought, Right Speech, Right Action, Right Livelihood, Right Effort, Right Mindfulness, and Right Concentration. Tough luck, lefties.

Mahayana ("Great Vehicle") Buddhism is Vietnam's favorite flavor; the older **Theravada** ("Way of the Elders") school, popular in the rest of Southeast Asia, is practiced mainly in the Mekong Delta by ethnic Khmer. Mahayana, unlike Theravada, teaches that anyone, not just the clergy, can attain nirvana.

LIFE AND TIMES

TAOISM. On a basic level, Taoism is a means of understanding the role of man in the natural and metaphysical order, relating everything to the all-powerful **Dao** ("the Way"). Simplicity, balance, and the unified nature of everything are hallmarks of the Taoist philosophy. It also propounds the harmony between **yin** (stillness/contraction) and **yang** (movement/dilation). The indigenous spirits and demons of ancient Vietnamese spirituality are accounted for in the triple religion via Taoist cosmology. Consequently, Taoism was the subject of government censure after 1975 and until recently, as socialist Vietnam cracked down on what it perceived as antiquated superstition.

CONFUCIANISM. Where Taoism and Buddhism have clear religious characteristics, Confucianism inhabits a more secular, philosophical area of Vietnamese popular thought. **Confucius,** born in 551 BC south of latter-day Beijing, stressed the importance of sacred rituals and hierarchies of respect: sons should obey fathers, wives should obey husbands, and subjects should obey rulers. Social harmony is more important than the needs of the individual, and **filial piety,** everyone's favorite Confucian catchphrase, is of great significance. The individual is judged by his self-cultivation, benevolence, and loyalty, and noble birth does not ensure noble worth. The importance assigned to family resonates deeply within the Vietnamese psyche, and is an essential component of Vietnamese culture—even for those who don't practice the Triple Religion.

OTHER RELIGIONS

Catholicism, Hòa Hảo Buddhism, Cao Đài, and Protestantism are Vietnam's major minor religions; each has a following of over one million and a stormy relationship with the Communist government. Islam, Hinduism, Baha'i, and the Church of Jesus Christ of Latter-Day Saints have smaller followings.

CATHOLICISM. The Roman Catholic Church enjoys official recognition by the Vietnamese government and roughly six million followers (about 8% of the population). It was introduced to Vietnam by the **French** in the 17th century, and though the Church's members were harassed by the Communist government after reunification, Catholicism was finally accepted as "a positive force" in recent government statements. Demographically, the balance remains skewed to the south, where Catholics fled to after the country split in 1954, although Hà Nội and Hải Phòng are witnessing a mild Catholic renaissance of sorts.

HÒA HẢO. Established in 1939 by **Huỳnh Phú Sổ,** Hòa Hảo ("Harmony") Buddhism is extremely low-profile; official estimates place its following at anywhere between 1.5 and three million. This quiet religion has no clergy and rejects most ceremony, emphasizing spiritual over material wealth. Value is placed on individual acts of worship and service to others, as manifest in the **Four Debts of Gratitude**—one's allegiance to family, homeland, mankind, and the Buddha. Not until 1999 did the government give official sanction to one branch of Hòa Hảo; the rest are still seen as dissident political groups. The religion's devotees are concentrated in the Mekong Delta, where Huỳnh Phú Sổ did the majority of his teaching.

CAO ĐÀI. Cao Đài ("High Palace"), another Mekong Delta creation, was founded in 1926, seven years after founder **Ngô Văn Chiêu** was visited by **an enormous floating eye** (see **"Someone to Watch Over You,"** p. 431). In Cao Đài iconology, the eye is the symbol of the Supreme Being; among the religion's recognized prophets are the Buddha, Jesus Christ, and Muhammad. According to the nearly two million Caodaists, all religions share the same origin and recognize the same Supreme Being in some way. The purpose of Cao Đài as a whole is to unite all worshippers by demonstrating their fundamental sameness, while each practicer's goal is to unite him or herself with the Supreme Being.

PROTESTANTISM. Protestants are the most persecuted religious group in Vietnam. Some have been summarily hunted down and executed, their churches torn down and their leaders beaten or sent to prison. Though repression has slackened somewhat, reports of harassment persist, and the government has restricted travel to the Central Highlands, preventing outsiders from getting accurate confirmation of either persecution or the state's reassurances to the contrary.

OTHER MINOR RELIGIONS. Vietnam's 65,000 **Muslims** tend to be comprised of ethnic Chàm and immigrant communities; many Chàm practice **Bani Islam,** which is made distinctive by a 20-page Qur'an and prayers to Chàm and Hindu divinities. Roughly 50,000 **Hindus,** mostly ethnic Chàm and Indian-Vietnamese, reside along the southern central coast and in HCMC. **Baha'i** and the **Church of Jesus Christ of Latter-Day Saints** are both mainly confined to expat communities in the cities of HCMC and Hà Nội.

FLORA AND FAUNA

Despite Vietnam's impressive biodiversity and natural wealth, plants and animals get both positive and negative attention. The smuggling of coveted exotic plants is only one of the many issues facing this country, and according to a 1996 World Wildlife Fund report, 10% of Vietnam's wildlife is in danger of **extinction.** Deforestation, overfishing, unchecked tourism, and habitat infringement brought on by population growth are also taking their toll. On the other hand, the extensive and still-expanding national park system, conservation groups, and several centers for endangered animals and research, are taking steps to reduce the negative impacts of the human population on Vietnam's environment.

WHERE THE WILD THINGS ARE (FAUNA)

Vietnam is considered one of the top 25 biodiversity locales in the world. Over 800 species of bird decorate the skies of the country. And that's not even touching on the thriving marine life that feeds the country and its economy—Vietnam is home to more than 1200 species of fish and shellfish. But according to the International Union for the Conservation of Nature and Natural Resources, 273 species mammal, bird, reptile, and fish species hold **threatened** status, including five of the world's 25 most threatened primates. **Endangered species** include the Asian elephant, the otter civet, the particolored flying squirrel, the leaf-nosed bat, the tiger, and the only Javan rhinoceros population outside of Java. As for animals that roam the country without fear of extinction, the list is quite extensive. The **water buffalo** is a popular domesticated mammal; among more common wild animal species are deer, bears, leopards, foxes, mongeese, wildcats, crocodiles, lizards, iguanas, cobras, and pythons.

PRIMATES. Singing monkeys are only the beginning of Vietnam's alluring primate kingdom. The pleasingly vocal species of monkey in question, the **black-crested gibbon,** has recently been discovered near Hà Nội. Its future is uncertain, due in part to the nation's taste for primate meat, considered a delicacy and a source of male virility (see **"Iniquitous Delicacies,"** p. 242). Today there are four other endangered primates in Vietnam: the Tonkin snub-nose, Delacour's langur, the douc langur, and the **golden-headed langur**—the world's most endangered primate, found in Cát Bà National Park. Other primate species, like the rhesus monkey and pygmy loris, eke out a living elsewhere in the country. The Endangered Primate Resource Center in Cúc Phương National Park provides an environmentally safe means of viewing the monkeys.

LIFE AND TIMES

WHERE THE MILD THINGS ARE (FLORA)

Technically speaking, there are two principal types of vegetation in Vietnam: evergreen and deciduous forests. In practice, the variations are endless: more than two-thirds of the country is covered in forest, and almost 14,000 plant species have been discovered. These statistics are rendered even more impressive by the fact that during the American War, over 10% of southern Vietnam was sprayed with 70 million liters of herbicides (like Agent Orange) intended solely for the purpose of clearing vegetation. The damage is still apparent in some areas, but the plant life has proven resilient. Today, though, **logging and resettlement** continue to threaten Vietnam's reviving wildlife.

Thick **mangrove forests** line the coast and most of the waterways in the southern half of the country. **Swamplands** also abound in the rich, wet Mekong Delta, the largest rice-producing region in the country. Herbs, vegetables, and fruits are also more abundant in this area. The mountainous central region is covered in **evergreen** and **semi-evergreen forests;** the areas that aren't are primarily estuaries and sand dunes dotted with small deciduous trees like the **eucalyptus.** The region's lowlands are also important to rice cultivation. The soil in the north isn't as rich as in the south, but all is forgiven in the presence of the **limestone mountains** in the northwest and the Hạ Long Bay area. **Pine trees** grow in the mountains of the north, while **bamboo** and **brushwood** share the soil in areas more affected by population growth and logging. Despite the tropical monsoon climate, rainforests are not particularly common, though they do pop up in some of the national parks, like Bạch Mã (p. 290) and Cát Bà (p. 142). **Savannahs** now remain in the areas that have suffered at the hands of deforestation.

With 174 catalogued species in Southeast Asia, the **orchid** and its diverse color palette floods the floral scene in Vietnam. The thin-petaled flower thrives in mountainous areas and on the plains. Although not indigenous to the country, **chrysanthemums,** with their tiny manifold white-and-yellow blossoms, are widely cultivated for decorative purposes and for teas. The **white tuberose,** a sweet-smelling daffodil species, also grows in abundance. In the south, the **yellow plum blossom** is popular among artists for its highly pliable branches and trunk. In the north, the red flowers of the **peach blossom** adorn streets and homes during the Tết celebration, bringing joy and good luck. Dried and crushed leaves are used as a natural skin rejuvenator. In wetter locales, the **lotus** is plentiful and particularly valuable: the beautiful and delectable leaves are used to wrap rice and flavor tea, and the seeds are used for medicinal purposes. **Waterlilies,** whose stems are edible, also grow in the ponds and lakes throughout the country. The romantic city of **Đà Lạt,** known as the "City of Flowers," is famous for its gardens and is well worth a trip.

HISTORY

A FAIRY-TALE BEGINNING

Vietnam's history is largely one of foreign domination interspersed with brief periods of national independence. The nation's 54 ethnic groups speak to the complexity of Vietnam's cultural makeup and reflect the long-standing ambiguity of what it means to be "Vietnamese." The earliest history of the country remains contested, but the ethnic Vietnamese (Kinh) people generally refer to the **legend of ◪Lạc Long Quân** ("Dragon King of Lac") to explain the beginnings of their nation.

According to the legend, about 5000 years ago Lạc Long Quân and his immortal fairy wife, **Âu Cò,** gave birth to 100 sons, who all hatched from eggs. It wasn't until after the army of little Long Quâns came to be, of course, that the Dragon King declared natural incompatibility with Âu Cò and filed for Vietnam's very first divorce. After they separated, Lạc Long Quân moved to the seaside with 50 sons, and Âu Cò returned in to her home in the mountains with the other half of the crew. In 2879 BC Âu Cò's eldest son, **Hùng Vương**, became the first king of Âu Lạc—the country that would centuries later become Vietnam. The **Hùng Dynasty** that followed ruled the nation until 258 BC. The mythical lovers' split is said to be the reason for the variety of the Vietnamese people that is still apparent today.

In 258 BC the Hùng were supplanted by Thục Phản; he, in turn, was overthrown in 207 BC by Triệu Đà. This former Chinese general then established the kingdom of **Nam Việt.** The Chinese **Han Dynasty** conquered the new nation in 111 BC, and Vietnam entered recorded history for the first time, in the annals of Chinese history books. It then spent a millennium rebelling against foreign Chinese rule.

FOREIGN RULE BECOMES TRADITION

During the first few centuries of Chinese rule, Vietnam (called **Giao Chi** at the time) remained a fairly independent protectorate, though they were forced to accept Chinese culture. Despite the efforts of the Chinese to quell their subjects' independent streak, however, the Vietnamese retained more than a sense of autonomy. Ideological differences between the two groups—specifically, the Vietnamese aversion to adopting a strict patriarchal society—ended in bloodshed when **two sisters** instigated the first rebellion against the Chinese in AD 40. That year **Trưng Trắc** and **Trưng Nhị,** along with their army of women-warriors, successfully overthrew the Chinese, but enjoyed independence from them for only three years. Nearly two centuries later, in 248, the Chinese again faced feminine wrath in the form of **Lady Triệu** (Triệu Thi Trịnh), who led an insurrection and temporarily established an independent state, which collapsed with her premature death only a few years later. After this point, the Chinese tightened their grip over the rebellious state.

The Vietnamese quietly accepted Chinese rule for a few centuries, but in the sixth century, a new wave of resistance began, effectively continuing until Vietnam's final independence from China in 1418. During those years, the Vietnamese played a centuries-long game of tug-of-war with the Hán for control of their land; they learned as they went along how to unite their ethnically diverse people into one nation against foreign imperialists. The Chinese were their last foreign invaders—if you ignore two Mongol invasions, a skirmish with the Ming Chinese, friendly visits from the Portuguese, Dutch, and several other European countries, a century or so of French colonization, and a short but productive "conflict" with the Americans in the 1960s. But perhaps we are getting ahead of ourselves.

In 1009, Lý Thái Tổ ascended to the throne and established the **Lý Dynasty** (1009-1225), the first long-lasting, non-mythological Vietnamese dynasty. Meanwhile, the aristocracy managed to master relevant political lessons from their Chinese rulers

2879 BC
Hùng Vương establishes the Hùng Dynasty.

207 BC
Former Chinese general Triệu Da creates Kingdom of Nam Việt.

111 BC
Han Dynasty conquers Nam Việt and begins a millennium of Chinese domination.

AD 40
The Trưng sisters instigate the first rebellion against the Chinese.

AD 248
Lady Triệu leads... another rebellion.

AD 544
Lý Bon leads a rebellion and establishes the Early Lý Dynasty.

AD 939
Ngô Quyền names himself king of an independent Vietnam.

1009
Lý Thái Thổ comes to power and establishes the Lý Dynasty.

LIFE AND TIMES

without losing touch with the lower classes—a vital skill that came to characterize successful Vietnamese rulers. Thus, the Lý Dynasty began doing some conquering of its own, turning its gaze southward to the Hindu-Islamic kingdom of **Champa,** which extended into the Mekong Delta.

As the nation of Vietnam grew geographically, the aristocracy integrated Buddhism into the country's political structure, established a **national educational system,** and promoted Vietnamese **nationalism.** Ultimately, the Lý Dynasty tumbled into oblivion in a complex scandal, ending with an eight-year-old girl giving up her rule to the first king of what became the **Trần Dynasty** (1225-1400). Under this family's leadership, the Vietnamese resolutely (and somewhat miraculously) prevented **Kublai Khan and the Mongols** from overtaking them. In 1407, the country fell once again into the hands of the Chinese, but just 11 years later—in the vaunted national tradition of bucking foreign rule—the nobleman Lê Lợi led another rebellion, culminating in the establishment of a third dynasty, the **Lê.** This one lasted.

1407
The Chinese Ming Dynasty regains temporary control.

1418
Lê Lợi defeats the Chinese and establishes the Later Lê Dynasty.

FAMILY AFFAIRS

The most famous of the Lê rulers, **Lê Thánh Tôn,** who ruled from 1460-1497, had a prolific influence on the national culture. He ordered the writing of a national history and introduced a new legal code, the Hồng Đức Code, which was (as usual) based on the Chinese legal code. Lê's version, however, was more amenable to women's rights, granting equal inheritance rights to daughters and sons. The Later Lê Dynasty managed to bring Champa under its control during the 16th century, and by 1757, Vietnam as we know it—geographically—officially existed.

But the geographical unity of Vietnam masked a great deal of animosity between the north and south. In 1545, the Lê rulers were forced to partition the nation into three areas, ceding the north to the Mạc family, the central area to the Trịnh family, and the south to the Nguyễn family. The Trịnh defeated the Mạc family soon after coming to power, thus bringing the northern third of the territory into their realm. Meanwhile, the Nguyễn family aggressively continued their policy of expansion into the south, expelling large portions of the Khmer population. Both the Nguyễn and Trịnh rulers faced a series of peasant rebellions. During this relatively unstable time, the Europeans conveniently appeared on the scene, although they went relatively unnoticed during their first two centuries in the region.

1545
Vietnam is partitioned into three family-owned kingdoms.

THE EUROPEANS, INEVITABLY, ARRIVE

The first Europeans to establish prolonged contact with Vietnam were the **Portuguese,** who set up a port in present-day Hội An. Though most of the trading posts set up by the Europeans had disappeared by 1700, due to clashes with the Vietnamese locals and government, some ever-passionate **missionaries** persisted. European missionaries began their religious conquest in the mid-17th century. One notable French Jesuit missionary by the name of **Alexandre de Rhodes** managed to leave quite a mark

1627-44
French Jesuit missionary Alexandre de Rhodes creates the Latin-based *quốc ngữ* script.

by inventing *quốc ngữ* ("national language"), the Latin-alphabet script that came to supplant Chinese characters in written Vietnamese. It was originally utilized only by missionaries, but the Vietnamese eventually adopted it, and they continue to use it today. Aside from de Rhodes, the Europeans didn't exercise much influence over the existing nation until the end of the 18th century, when political unrest erupted into a civil war, beginning with the Tây Sơn Rebellion.

REBEL RULERS

In 1772, Vietnam—like most dynastic and once-feudal hierarchical societies—experienced a **massive peasant revolt.** Everything came tumbling down when three brothers from the tiny village of **Tây Sơn,** somewhat piqued by economic disaster and complete social immobility, decided to wreak a bit of havoc. The brothers, who lived by the Robin Hood-style motto "seize the property of the rich and distribute it to the poor," first gained control of Saigon then moved north to conquer Hà Nội. Adept as they were at battle, effective rule wasn't particularly their specialty. Consequently, the kingdom became vulnerable to attacks from **Nguyễn Anh**—the one member of the previous ruling dynasty who had escaped the mass murder of his family at the hands of the Tây brothers—and his Chinese and French supporters. Nguyễn Anh turned to the French missionary Pigneau de Behaine and his buddy Louis XVI, who promised to send troops and supplies in exchange for control of the trading post at Tourane (present-day Đà Nẵng). Shockingly, the troops and supplies never came. Nevertheless, Nguyễn Anh ascended the throne in 1882 and adopted the Chinese name **Gia Long,** along with Confucianism and the Chinese practice of isolationism. Around the same time, the Chinese formally changed the country's name to **Việt Nam.** Gia Long's new but retrogressive national policies set the country up for (another) imperialist disaster: after establishing relations with the French, he found it difficult to terminate them.

COLONIALISM (SIGH)

In typical colonial manner, the French took little time to assert their influence in Vietnam once they realized its potential. In 1847, the French blew up five Vietnamese ships under the pretense of reclaiming a hostage missionary, who had in fact already been released. But it wasn't until 10 years later, when **Napoleon III** invaded the country, that the French conquest of Vietnam became a reality. By 1862, the French had officially eliminated the name Việt Nam and signed the **Treaty of Saigon** with Emperor Tử Đức, giving them control of three provinces around the city of **Gia Định**—renamed **Saigon** by the French. The ease with which the French gained control of the south was remarkable given the nation's history; it is most often attributed to the lack of national cohesion that dated back to the Later Lê Dynasty. By 1874, under the military leadership of Francis Garnier, the French had added **Hà Nội** to their aegis, bringing the whole country (and parts of Cambodia) under their power.

1772
Three brothers instigate the Tây Sơn Rebellion and seize control.

1802
Nguyễn Anh crushes the rebellion and comes to power.

LIFE AND TIMES

1857
Napoleon III attacks Vietnam.

1862
Emperor Tử Đức signs the Treaty of Saigon, handing southern Vietnam to the French.

1883
Treaty of Protectorate signed, formally ending Vietnamese independence.

Vietnam's independence formally ended in 1883, when the **Treaty of Protectorate** integrated the country with Cambodia and Laos into the French protectorate *Indochine*. In the direct aftermath of the transfer of power, the ex-emperor Hàm Nghi instigated the Cân Vương Rebellion ("Loyalty to the King"), but the uprising was quickly repressed, and the fragmented Vietnamese people quietly—and uncharacteristically—began to cooperate with their foreign rulers.

After securing control, the French began their *mission civilatrice*, or "civilizing mission." Shockingly, the noble and well-intentioned colonists seemed to do more harm than good to the Vietnamese people. A restructured social hierarchy left half of the Vietnamese landless by WWII and a new elitist education system lowered the literacy rate to 20%. Slowly, periodic peasant uprisings grew fiercer, more frequent, and increasingly difficult to ignore.

1904
Phan Bội Châu founds the first revolutionary society.

THE RISE OF NATIONALISM AND WORLD WAR I

Around the turn of the 20th century, a new generation of ambitious Vietnamese began bucking colonial oppression once more. The first person to do so was **Phan Bội Châu,** who traveled to Japan in 1905 to rally Vietnamese expatriates and to enlist the aid of China and Japan. Châu championed Western intellectual and scientific practices in addition to the complete expulsion of the French, but he was unsuccessful in Japan, and he never managed to produce a widespread revolt. He did, however, plant rebellious ideas in the minds of Vietnamese intellectuals, who later spread the notion of independence to a wider audience.

WWI
Several small-scale revolts fail to remove the French from power.

A lack of focused leadership and a disconnect between the nationalist leaders and the peasants robbed the Vietnamese of the opportunity to stage a full-scale rebellion during **WWI**, when the French were otherwise distracted. The one planned revolt spearheaded by **King Duy Tân** was betrayed before it grabbed the attention of the masses. The city of Thái Nguyên was momentarily liberated in 1917, but the momentum didn't last. A variety of underground societies were founded, including one led by **Phan Xích Long,** which featured primitive weapons and small-scale, old-fashioned tactics of warfare. The tricky French colonists, however, caught on quickly and ended up transplanting Vietnamese guerillas to fight on the front lines in Europe. Upwards of 50,000 Vietnamese soldiers and an equal number of workers were sent to the battlefields to aid the French war effort.

HỒ CHÍ MINH, COMMUNISM, AND THE "DEMOCRATIC REPUBLIC"

Things really started to change after WWI, as Vietnamese scholars and revolutionaries reacted strongly to tightening post-war French rule. In the 1920s, a young Vietnamese man named **Nguyễn Tat Thánh,** alias Nguyễn Ái Quốc, but most fondly remembered as ▓**Hồ Chí Minh** ("Uncle Ho"), entered the scene. After witnessing persecution around the world and reading Marx, he joined the **French Communist Party** in Paris and traveled to Russia and China to study communism. Upon his return to Vietnam in 1924, he organized a series of pretty unsuccessful uprisings in central Vietnam, and then founded the formidable **Indochinese Communist Party.**

Unlike the Europeans, Vietnam actually learned a lesson or two from "the war to end all wars" and took advantage of France's relative disinterest in its Asian colonies during WWII. Their efforts were soon thwarted, however, by (surprise!) foreign invaders—this time by fascist Japan. In 1940, the Japanese gained control of the country and wreaked havoc, causing widespread famine.Only a year later, the Indochinese Communist Party founded the **Revolutionary League for the Independence of Vietnam,** better known as the **Việt Minh,** led politically by Hồ Chí Minh and militarily by mastermind **General Võ Nguyễn Giáp.** Interestingly, both the Soviets and the US supported the Việt Minh's guerrilla campaign against the Japanese.

On August 16, 1945, immediately after Japan's surrender to the US, the Việt Minh seized control of the country in the **August Revolution.** Three days later, they conquered Hà Nội; by the end of August they had taken control of the entire country. On **Sept. 2, 1945,** Hồ Chí Minh celebrated the creation of the **Democratic Republic of Vietnam (DRV)** in a famous speech, ironically recalling the American Declaration of Independence and applying the lovable notions of life, liberty, and the pursuit of happiness to the newly founded Vietnamese state. And for the next 30 years the Vietnamese fought once more to hold onto their dream of actual autonomy.

THE LONG HAUL TOWARD INDEPENDENCE

Hồ Chí Minh's first obstacle to de facto sovereignty was the French, who refused to recognize the independent state of Vietnam. Fighting ensued. The **First Indochina War,** or the War of Resistance, as the Vietnamese called it, lasted for nine years, beginning in December 1945. With some help from Britain, France was able to regain control of most of the country, but when **Mao Zedong** took control of China in 1949 and began aiding the Vietnamese, a full-fledged modern war broke out. Though General Giap knew the Vietnamese could not compete with France's advanced war technology, he relied on the country's nationalist fervor and guerrilla warfare. In the end, a homefield advantage and the country's dense jungle terrain helped Giap's unremitting men to surround the crucial northern town of **Điện Biên Phủ,** which they attacked on March 13, 1954. Fifty-six days and 7000 casualties later, the demoralized French surrendered, announcing their intention to withdraw from the country. One month later, France, the Soviet Union, the UK, and the US found themselves in Geneva, dictating the fate of Vietnam, which had little say in the matter. As a result of the **Geneva Convention,** Vietnam found itself divided along the 17th parallel for two years; it was intended that the period would end in elections and unified independence in 1956. In the interim Hồ Chí Minh and the Vietnam Workers' Party were

1930
Hồ Chí Minh founds the Indochinese Communist Party.

1940
Vichy government takes over in France; Japan gains control of Vietnam.

1943
Hồ Chí Minh and General Võ Nguyễn Giáp form the Việt Minh Front.

Sept. 2, 1945
Hồ Chí Minh declares the Democratic Republic of Vietnam and proclaims himself President.

Dec. 1945
The First Indochina War breaks out with France.

1954
The French fall to General Giáp's forces at the historic battle at Điện Biên Phủ.

June 1954
Geneva Convention divides Vietnam in two and forces the French troops to withdraw.

LIFE AND TIMES

granted control of the northern area of Vietnam known as the Democratic Republic of Vietnam, or **North Vietnam,** and the capital of that region, Hà Nội. In the south, the anti-Communist, pro-Western **Ngô Đình Diệm** was placed in power in the **Republic of Vietnam (South Vietnam).** French troops withdrew from all of Vietnam, and the Việt Minh pulled out of the south.

Problems soon developed in the south under Diệm, who ended up enjoying power much more than the Western leaders had anticipated. Diệm refused to allow the elections outlined at the Geneva Convention and supported flagrant **human rights violations** during his rule. In 1959 alone, he murdered in excess of 1000 of his own government officials to secure his power, claiming that his victims were Communists. Buddhist monks turned to **self-immolation** as a means of protest, and security forces, responding to the growing crowds they inspired, opened fire into a crowd of Buddhist protestors on the 2527th birthday of the Buddha.

A DISASTER CALLED "THE AMERICAN WAR"

The unrest in the south did not go unnoticed. The US, who had been supplying aid to the southern regime in an effort to counter the growing strength of northern forces, helped organize a coup in 1963. The Kennedy administration allegedly intended only to have Diệm exiled, but one way or another, the Vietnamese president was murdered by his generals. His successor was **General Nguyễn Văn Thiệu.** Meanwhile, the northern forces of Hồ Chí Minh's party were mobilizing. Angered by the violent and excessive actions of Diệm, Hồ Chí Minh agreed in 1960 to support a newly founded guerrilla force, the **National Front for the Liberation of South Vietnam (NLF),** or **Việt Cộng.** The NLF was organized into small groups that worked to rally the support of peasants while carrying out small-scale attacks in strongholds throughout southern Vietnam. In just a few years, the NLF gained notoriety throughout the south as a powerful and cunning force. It soon became apparent that the happenings in Vietnam were of major importance on the American political scene, and the early 1960s witnessed an escalation of US and Vietnamese naval activity in the **Gulf of Tonkin.** On August 2, 1964, Hồ Chí Minh's government launched a supposedly unprovoked attack on the *USS Maddox* and then the *USS Turner Joy* in retaliation for the aid the US was giving the south; it was later discovered that the *Maddox* had been involved in coastal reconnaissance and that the reported attack on the second ship never actually occurred. Nonetheless, the US government found the incident sufficient reason to draw the **Gulf of Tonkin Resolution,** essentially a carte blanche for aggressive American military generals to begin bombing in North Vietnam.

After the US Congress passed President Lyndon B. Johnson's resolution almost unanimously, the Americans launched **Operation Rolling Thunder.** Disguised as an eight-week plan to cut off North Vietnam's economic support and destroy aid to the NLF, this operation entailed a great deal of guesswork and, yes,

1960
Hồ Chí Minh backs the resistance army's new guerrilla force, the Việt Cộng.

Aug. 2, 1964
The *USS Maddox* is torpedoed in the Gulf of Tonkin, setting into motion the American War.

bombing. One of the greatest difficulties for the US military was targeting the **Hồ Chí Minh Trail,** which cut through dense jungles to connect North Vietnam with their Việt Cộng supporters in the south. Because the forest cover made the trail invisible from the air, the US sprayed large areas of the country with harmful exfoliants, including the infamous **Agent Orange** and **napalm,** designed to expose the hidden NLF forces. Unfortunately for the Vietnamese civilians, the toxic chemicals did much more than just destroy forests; they killed crops, too, and caused appallingly high rates of cancer and birth defects. The US government is still battling a number of **lawsuits** from the victims of these chemical attacks.

The first American combat troops entered Vietnam in 1965 and began a campaign of **Search and Destroy operations,** intended to obliterate Việt Cộng forces (and any civilian men, women, and children who happened to inhabit the surrounding villages). In early 1968, hoping to demoralize the Americans, the NLF launched the Tết Offensive, attacking more than 100 cities in the south over the course of the Vietnamese New Year in February. The NLF even managed to penetrate Saigon briefly and occupy the US Embassy. The psychological effect on the south is difficult to exaggerate; the NLF had made it clear that nowhere in Vietnam was safe and that they were willing to sustain mind-numbing numbers of casualties to inflict harm on their adversaries. The offensive marked a major turning point in US public opinion about the war; a few months later details and photographs of the infamous **Mỹ Lai massacre,** one of the most tragic and devastating of the Search and Destroy missions, found their way into newspapers across the globe. US President Johnson decided not to run for re-election, and the newly elected President Richard Nixon pursued secret peace talks with the northern forces.

In 1969, Hồ Chí Minh died, but the Communists didn't let the loss of their ideological leader weaken their spirits. Indeed, the drive toward independence only intensified. The US continued fighting, but to little avail and to the growing anger of the American population. To appease his own country's malaise, US President Nixon pursued a policy he dubbed **"Vietnamization,"** stepping up aerial bombings and gradually putting the ground war completely in the hands of the South Vietnamese—essentially a retreat in disguise. In the fall of 1972, US Secretary of State **Henry Kissinger** and two representatives of the northern republic, Xuan Thuy and Lê Đức, met to discuss an initial peace treaty. The southern forces refused to agree. American aggression culminated in the **Christmas Bombing** of 1972, an attempt to force the peace negotiations along.

Finally, in January 1973, both Vietnamese governments and the US signed the **Paris Peace Accords,** which called for a ceasefire and allowed for the withdrawal of US troops. By the end of 1973, the last of the US combat troops had left Vietnam; only a few soldiers remained in Saigon. With the US forces out of the picture, the North Vietnamese managed to rebuild their forces and began a concerted effort to penetrate the south, despite the ceasefire. The US failed to react

LIFE AND TIMES

Mar. 16, 1968
An entire civilian village is slaughtered in what came to be known as the Mỹ Lai Massacre.

Sept. 2, 1969
Hồ Chí Minh dies on the 24th anniversary of his declaration of the Democratic Republic of Vietnam.

Jan. 1973
The US and Vietnam sign the Paris Peace Accords, ending the American War.

to this violation of the peace accord, instead remaining on the sidelines as the NLF began capturing cities in the south. During March of 1975, the northern forces launched a full-scale attack on the Central Highlands and larger coastal cities like Đà Nẵng and Huế, causing thousands of civilians and members of the southern army to flee toward Saigon, many dying en route either at the hands of the northern forces or from starvation. By early April, the southern forces (**Army of the Republic of Vietnam,** or **ARVN**) had lost nearly a third of its forces; over eight million people in 12 provinces were under northern control. The US again decided to take action, organizing two airlift evacuations: **Operation Babylift** and **Operation Frequent Wind.** The last 1000 US troops and over 7000 Vietnamese were evacuated during this 11th-hour undertaking in the face of certain defeat at the hands of North Vietnam.

On **April 30, 1975,** the northern forces stormed into Saigon, crashing through the walls of the Imperial Palace, overthrowing the southern government, and renaming Saigon **Hồ Chí Minh City.** Vietnam was reunited. Just under one year later, on April 25, 1976, the Democratic Republic of Vietnam was renamed the **Socialist Republic of Vietnam,** and elections for the National Assembly were held as part of an initial effort to promote unity. In 1977, the country joined the United Nations.

Apr. 1975
Northern military forces overthrow the southern government and rename Saigon Hồ Chí Minh City.

Apr. 1976
Vietnam changes its name to the Socialist Republic of Vietnam.

REUNIFICATION AND REBUILDING

Following reunification, the newly independent nation found itself faced with the devastation of nearly a century of exploitation and several decades of warfare. Close to three million soldiers and civilians had died. Many southerners lived in terror of governmental reprisal for opposition to the NLF. Regional conflicts over the following decades continued to take their toll on Vietnam: an invasion of Cambodia, motivated by the systematic killing of Vietnamese living in Cambodia by the communist **Khmer Rouge,** led to an influx of refugees, and both China and several western nations reacted strongly against the Vietnamese government. The brief but bloody **Third Indochina War** with China remained unresolved until recently; the trade embargo Western Europe and the US placed on the country in reaction to the invasion caused economic problems and mass starvation. The Soviet Union was essentially the only substantial power providing aid to the country, which of course only increased tension with Western Europe and the US.

1978
Vietnam invades Cambodia to overthrow Pol Pot, leading to an economic embargo from the West and the Third Indochina War.

Beyond international woes, the Southern Vietnamese were subject to the paranoia and vengeance of the socialist government. The US agreed to evacuate over 150,000 Vietnamese who had supported the southern government upon withdrawing from Vietnam, but never acted on their word. Out of fear of government retaliation, over a million Vietnamese fled the country illegally, often on fishing boats, earning themselves the nickname **"boat people."** Over the two and a half decades following the war, thousands of Vietnamese refugees died attempting to escape the country, either at the hands of the new government or at sea from natural catastrophes or pirate attacks. They

LIFE AND TIMES

landed all over Southeast Asia and were placed in sprawling refugee camps, subject to disease and abuse; the lucky ones made it to Canada and the US, where they started new lives at the very bottom of the social ladder. The Vietnamese who achieved refuge in other countries, known as **Việt Kiều**, ("overseas Vietnamese"), often remained closely connected to their relatives and sometimes provided vital economic support.

By 1986, the **inflation rate** in Vietnam had reached an astonishing **774%**. The same year, the country had to import 1.5 million tons of rice to alleviate mass famine caused by government-organized collectivization of agriculture in the south. Fortunately, that was also the year that the Sixth National Congress of Vietnam voted to abolish the Marxist market planning and instead begin the implementation of **đổi mới** ("renovation"), a complete restructuring of the economy that involved shifting from collectivization to free markets. *Đổi mới* did not promote radical economic change; instead, it prescribed a gradual shift that allowed for the maintenance of political stability. Among other things, the new policy permitted foreign direct investment, the transferal of large portions of state-owned land to the population, fewer restrictions on private enterprise, self-determined finance, and anti-inflationary measures including the devaluation of the đồng. The nation faced higher taxes in exchange for increased economic freedom, but the changes have helped the economy. By 1990, the inflation rate had decreased to 67%, and it was below 10% by the end of the decade. Throughout most of the 90s, the country experienced relatively high economic growth rates, reaching 8% in 1996.

Despite the shift away from a centralized government, Vietnam has been slow to move fully to a **free-market** economy. By the end of the 20th century, Vietnam had become the largest rice exporter in the world, the second-largest cashew nut exporter, and the third-largest coffee exporter. But this did not prevent a downturn in growth. Never considered one of the "Asian Tigers," Vietnam was nonetheless affected by the economic crisis that hit Southeast Asia in 1997, suffering from a recession that wasn't particularly helped by widespread government corruption.

The 1990s witnessed political changes as well. In 1992, Vietnam voted in a new constitution more devoted to the full transition to socialism than the previous drafts. Vietnam and the US agreed in 1991 to the establishment of an office in Hà Nội to help determine the fate of American soldiers missing in action. At this point, trade relations began to change with the US, and by 1994 the economic embargo was officially lifted. In 1995, the country joined the Association of Southeast Asian Nations (ASEAN), an organization devoted to economic, cultural, and political stability throughout the region. And in 2000, President Clinton traveled to Vietnam, making it the first trip by an American president to the country since Nixon's trip in 1969. Relations with the US were fully normalized in the following year with the signing of a trade agreement. The trend of historic reunions continues: in 2003, Russian President Vladimir Putin visited, making it the first meeting between leaders of the two countries since the collapse of the Soviet Union.

1986
Vietnamese government launches *đổi mới*, a series of economic reforms.

1997
Vietnam feels the effects of the Southeast Asian economic crisis. Trần Đức Lương is elected.

2001
The US embargo is officially lifted and the two countries sign a bilateral trade agreement.

Jan. 2004
Avian influenza breaks out in Vietnam and kills 42 people over the next 2 years.

Jun. 2004
Vietnam's first condom machine is installed in Hà Nội.

Oct. 2005
Lương Cao Khải, the government's anti-corruption taskforce leader, is arrested for, um, corruption.

LIFE AND TIMES

When the Vietnamese government enacted the *đổi mới* ("open door") economic reform policies in the mid-1980s, it was in part a reaction to the miserable failure of collectivized agriculture in the south in the 1970s and early 1980s. With the country near starvation and its major trading partner, the Soviet Union, near collapse, Vietnam found itself economically isolated and in dire need of reform. After successful experimentation with semi-privatized farming in the north, the government instituted nationwide reforms in 1986. These reforms centered around policies that relied more heavily on the private sector for economic growth. Private entities were allowed to deal directly with foreign companies for importing and exporting. Exchange and interest rates were allowed to respond to the market. Internally, state economic management was decentralized to give state industries some local autonomy. All of these policies added up to big changes for Vietnam: for the first time since before the war, Vietnam was opened to the world markets, and economists dreamed of Vietnam as the next "tiger" economy.

The transition from a centrally planned agricultural economy to a socialist market economy hasn't been easy. Unquestionably, development is taking place in Vietnam that would have been unthinkable before *đổi mới*. There are no Starbucks—yet—but local entrepreneurs are taking advantage of a more open market with their own successful franchises. Trung Nguyên, the Vietnamese-owned coffee chain, now speckles Vietnam's urban centers with over 100 stores, serving *cá phê sữa* made with locally grown beans (Vietnam is the world's second-biggest coffee exporter, after Brazil), and has recently opened branches in Japan, Singapore, Thailand, and Cambodia. But a closer look at coffee production reveals the challenges of participating in a free market. When coffee became a hot commodity in the 90s, many Vietnamese farmers jumped on the bandwagon and started growing coffee, flooding the world markets. The coffee glut caused prices to plummet. Small farmers especially had difficulty absorbing the fall in prices, which fell from over US$2000 per ton in 1996 to a low of US$450 per ton in 2002. The farmers' plight was complicated by the sticky fingers of local officials: Oxfam estimates that coffee producers in Vietnam's central highlands, where most of the nation's coffee is grown, only ever see about 60% of the proceeds from their crop sales. Much of the profits find their way into the pockets of local officials through excessive taxation.

The coffee situation is just one example of how the rural poor are feeling the sting of Vietnam's economic reforms, while urban centers are growing increasingly cosmopolitan, educated, and wealthy.

Certainly, the Vietnamese population overall is better off now than before *đổi mới:* a 1999 study by the World Bank reported that only 35-40% of the Vietnamese population of 80 million people are currently living below the poverty line, compared to 70% in the mid-1980s. But nearly 90% of the poor live in rural areas, where the average monthly income is only US$94, compared with US$220 in urban areas. Now that individuals have greater control over how and where they work, the countryside reports a "brain drain" of the educated from the country to the city. There they find more job opportunities with foreign investor-funded companies, and more opportunities to start their own businesses.

The face of Vietnam's economy is changing: over half the population is under 25, and one of Vietnam's strongest appeals to foreign investors is its young, educated workforce. More single women are entering the workforce, and staying longer too. The peak marrying age is now 25-30, whereas a few years ago it was 18-23, according to General Statistics Office reports. A prime example of what's possible in the new Vietnamese economy is 27-year-old Pham Thi Thu Hang, an unmarried former translator who now owns her own fashion design company and retail store, Celebrity Style. Ms. Pham has quickly carved out a name for herself in the Vietnamese fashion world with her asymmetric hemlines and innovative fabrics, and she acknowledges that her designs are a dramatic departure from what most of her neighbors do. Tailors who specialize in copies surround her store on Mai Hac De, near Hà Nội's largest fabric market; copying is such a norm in Vietnamese fashion (not to mention books, CDs, and DVDs, other pirated commodities) that originality is truly an anomaly. Ms. Pham recognizes, however, that circumstances are changing rapidly, and she benefits from the ever-growing number of foreign travelers to Vietnam who are elated to "discover" something original (and still reasonably priced). After only one year in business, she is opening branches in several provinces, and she hopes someday to export her designs to foreign markets.

While possibilities abound for new business and new investment, the government still has a long way to go in fully implementing its reforms, and in implementing reforms more radical than the first phase of *đổi mới*. Motivated by its acceptance into ASEAN (Association of Southeast Asian Nations) in 1995 and its participation in AFTA (Asian Free Trade Agreement), Vietnam continues to work toward making accounting practices more transparent, curbing corruption, and reducing import tariffs to encourage foreign investment. With the support of the government and the international community, perhaps this tiger may yet roar.

Sarah Rotman is a former Let's Go researcher-writer, editor, and manager. An experienced and avid traveler to Asia, she developed websites for local businesses while living in Hà Nội. She currently designs educational programs for businesses and schools in the US and Korea.

VIETNAM TODAY

LAW AND ORDER

Known to most as simply Vietnam, the **Socialist Republic of Vietnam** is a Communist state, seasoned with a delightful splash of French civil law. The current president, **Trần Đức Lương,** was elected from among several candidates within the single party in the country—the **Communist Party of Vietnam**—first in September 1997 and then again in 2002 to serve a second five-year term. The cabinet is appointed by the president, and the members of the judicial branch, the Supreme People's Court, are voted upon by the 448 members of the National Assembly. The real power, though, is held by the secretary-general of the Communist Party, **Nông Dừc Mạnh,** who was originally appointed in 2001 and re-elected in April 2006. The current president and his Prime Minister, **Phan Văn Khải,** are also both economically liberal, supporting the continuation of economic reform. However, the **Politburo**—the chief committee of the Communist Party—has worked (relatively unsuccessfully) to slow this process. Though there is no major organized political opposition group in the country, a few small groups, including the **Free Vietnam Movement (FVM),** have become increasingly active in promoting the move toward democracy.

Political organizations are not the only voice of dissent these days. Anti-government demonstrations erupted among the hill tribes in the Central Highlands in 2001 and have continued sporadically since. The problem is further complicated by the unjust treatment of Protestant minorities in the region (see **Religion,** p. 59). A November 2005 report to the United States Senate declared that ethnic Christians in the Northwest and Central Highlands "have continued to be beaten, detained, and pressured by local authorities to renounce their religion and cease religious gatherings." These smaller religious groups are seen by the government as political dissenters, and, true to the socialist legacy, have been harshly suppressed. In general, **human rights** have not ranked among the current government's priorities, and in 2002, several journalists came under attack for being a little too explicit in their disapproval of the administration.

But these issues are not going unnoticed. A series of **protests** in the Thái Bình and Đồng Nai provinces over local government corruption has prompted a call for the elimination of reprobate officials. The response is part of a nationwide effort to reduce corruption, widespread in the government and businesses. Large-scale prisoner absolution in 1998—including the early release of **Professor Doan Viêt Hoat,** a prominent pro-democracy demonstrator—was another positive step toward human rights protection in Vietnam. But the same laws under which Doan Viêt Hoat and other peaceful political protestors were arrested continue to exist, and full-scale democracy and freedom of speech have yet to be realized in Vietnam. Human rights groups remain intent on keeping out foreign powers, carrying on a deep tradition of independence.

The education system in Vietnam provides free schooling to all children between the ages of six and sixteen, and the country currently boasts a 90.2% literacy rate for women and a 95% rate for men. The government also provides free health care through an extensive social security plan, but insufficient funds have rendered the nature of that health care occasionally less than ideal.

THE ECONOMY

Vietnam's economy is growing quickly, and prospects for the future are bright. The economic crisis in Southeast Asia in the late 1990s led to a dip in the growth rate to 4%, but by 2003 it was back up to around 7%, and in 2006 it was above 8%. Because of both government corruption and globalization, the benefits of the recent growth have not reached the entire country, and the class divide has become more pronounced in recent years. The current **GDP per capita** remains around **US$2800,** and the **unemployment rate,** which reached a devastating **25%** in 1995, had dropped to 5.75% by 2005.

A 2001 bilateral trade agreement between Vietnam and the US was a landmark for the Vietnamese economy. A year later, the country had the second-fastest growing economy in Asia, second only to China. Vietnam's dominance of international **rice markets** provides some measure of economic stability: along with Thailand and India, it was one of the primary planners of the Council on Rice Trade Cooperation, which is designed to monitor international market prices.

Vietnam's primary exports, aside from seafood and rice, are coffee, rubber, tea, clothing, and a bit of crude oil. **Agriculture** remains the largest sector of the economy, leaving industry and services to account for 37% of activity.

After a series of talks with the United States, Vietnam stands at the brink of acceptance into the **World Trade Organization (WTO).** WTO membership promises the full integration of Vietnam into the global economy, as well as specific benefits that could help Vietnamese textile and clothing industries. It also opens the country to foreign investment, promising increased economic growth, though perhaps ensuring an even greater permeation of Vietnamese society by Western culture.

TOURISM

Vietnam's tourist infrastructure is young, but it's growing quickly. Dramatic mountains, world-class beaches, and mind-blowing food brought in 3.5 million tourists in 2005—18% more than in 2004. Vietnam recently opened tourist offices in **France** and **Japan,** and expanded those in China, Germany, and the US in order to broaden its tourist audience. As the number of annual visitors rises, so too does the need to improve Vietnam's ailing infrastructure, but the country has been slow to respond. The next several years should see vast improvement in road conditions and transportation safety, electrical and drainage systems, and medical facility conditions.

Western tourists are generally well treated in Vietnam; the police leave them alone, and locals welcome their money. More tourism means a greater exposure for and knowledge of Vietnamese society, and it provides an income for many Vietnamese families. It also invites commercialism, which threatens to degrade the authenticity of Vietnam's culture. Resort towns littering the country and shoreline, with open-tour buses to connect them, have helped to create a tourist-centered subculture that glosses over what's real and what's fascinating about Vietnam—its people. So by all means, go to Vietnam (it's too good to pass up) but don't miss out on the country's most impressive resource.

THE AIDS CRISIS

Until the summer of 2004, it was widely believed that the AIDS epidemic in Asia was relatively under control. But the infection rate has greatly increased in the past few years. Between 2002 and 2003, the infection rate increased 11% in Vietnam, though in June 2004, the US named Vietnam as the first Asian nation to receive part of its proposed five-year US$15 billion AIDS relief plan. Experts estimate that up to 265,000 people in Vietnam live with HIV.

This alarming number has almost everything to do with Vietnam's **prostitution** and **drug use** problems. According to UNAIDS, the joint United Nations program on AIDS, HIV infection rates of 40% are "not unusual" among drug injectors in larger cities, and drug-injecting sex workers are less than half as likely to use condoms as their substance-free coworkers. Tragically, campaigns aimed against these "social evils" tend to drive them further underground and away from government regulation, making these problems even more difficult to solve.

With 5000-10,000 new cases each year, AIDS poses a major threat to Vietnam for a number of reasons, and silence on the issue remains a troubling trend. Two major sources of the problem are the widespread misconceptions about the disease and the dearth of **educational programs** to combat them. Use of condoms in Vietnam remains very uncommon. A strong stigma is attached to purchasing condoms in pharmacies, and a common belief prevails that condoms reduce virility. Moreover, the open discussion of sexuality is **taboo,** even within some of the more progressive families. Although official warnings against the dangers of HIV/AIDS are posted throughout Vietnam, the dangerous notion that the epidemic is a foreign, African, or homosexual problem has not yet waned. Traditionally, women have little say in sexual relationships, and with men scorning the use of precautionary measures like condoms, women are at a higher risk. Fortunately, the government has begun to implement new education programs, and in June 2004, Hà Nội christened its first ⬛condom machine (see **"A Big Red Step in Preventing HIV,"** p. 109), a positive step toward effective proactive measures.

THE BIRD FLU OUTBREAK

In January 2004, Vietnam suffered an outbreak of **avian influenza** (more commonly known as bird flu) that killed six people, four of whom were children. Since then, Vietnam has lost several dozen more to one of the world's most frightening new diseases. Though it generally afflicts only birds, avian influenza was first discovered as communicable to humans in 1997 in **Hong Kong.** Although transmission of the disease has so far required **direct contact** with infected birds or their droppings, there remains a frightening possibility of a human pandemic. For this to happen, though, one person would have to pick up both human and avian strains, and the two viruses would have to **mutate** into a form communicable to humans—a fairly unlikely but conceivable possibility.

Vietnam's substantial poultry stock is a different story: many of the country's farms have been subjected to mass culling to prevent the spread of the disease. Bird flu drugs like **Tamiflu** and **Relenza** exist in very limited supply, and scientists are still scrambling to understand exactly how avian flu effects the body as well as how to fight a potential outbreak.

DON'T READ THIS

Government **censorship** is one of the last old-fashioned Communist policies of the modern Vietnamese state, and Vietnamese press remains one of the most controlled in the world. In the advent of the uncontrollable, all-powerful ⬛Internet, this practice has begun to face a daunting test—one that many hope will once and for all bring an end to restrictions on free speech. **The Internet Center of Vietnam** was founded by the government in 2003 to ensure that the Communist state is not undermined online, and the first batch of "cyber dissidents" are now receiving jail terms.

In May 2006, **Amnesty International** responded, launching a drive to end Internet censorship. Ironically, most Vietnamese won't be able to access their site; human rights and politically dissident sites are off-limits, and Internet cafes are required to keep records of their clients' web-surfing. This **public Internet access,** however, is taking the country by storm, and connection speeds and the number of online Vietnamese continue to skyrocket. Many predict that the government will soon be unable to control communications as thoroughly as in the past, unless it decides to risk a major international relations setback, should online restrictions make the country appear backward to the rest of the world.

But censorship does not end with the Internet. In 2004, responding to the increasingly eccentric physical appearances of Vietnamese performing artists, the government banned **outlandish hairdos**—including shaved heads and uncombed hair—that allegedly detract from a more conventional artistic tradition. The new rule appears not to be strictly enforced: in June 2004, a 67-year-old Vietnamese man made international headlines with his record-setting 20 feet of hair, which hadn't been cut in 31 years. He claims that his last haircut made him ill.

LAND HO!

Boasting a healthy supply of natural gas, oil, and fish, the resource-rich **Spratly Islands**—a small archipelago of 100 islands in the South China Sea—have miraculously been claimed at least in part by most countries in the region. China, Taiwan, and Vietnam allege to own them in full, while the Philippines, Brunei, and Malaysia lay claim to several of the islands. Controversy has persisted since the 1930s, and military clashes even erupted in 1974. One of the aims of the formation of the **Association of Southeast Asian Nations (ASEAN)** in 1992 was to resolve the issue through joint ownership and exploration, but relations remain strained, largely due to reports from Philippine authorities regarding Chinese military and economic activity in the area. Though Taiwan holds no official ownership rights to any of the islands, its government, too, has contributed to the chaos with the construction of a supposed **bird-watching facility** on one of Vietnam's authorized islands in early 2004. Vietnam reacted by sending a tourist cruise ship out to the archipelago—a move that Malaysia had attempted a few years before—much to the anger and dismay of other countries. In 2005, however, national oil companies in Vietnam, China, and the Philippines signed a treaty that would allow for **joint research** of the area, and for now, at least, the tensions seem to have cooled.

CULTURE

CUSTOMS AND ETIQUETTE

No matter where you are traveling, common sense begs that you be polite, considerate, and patient. But in Vietnam this is especially important, and even a simple smile goes a long way. In a country where price tags rarely exist and bargaining is a way of life, the only way to get by is to enjoy the process. Be persistent, as even a firm "no" will not always signify that the discussion is closed. At the same time be both courteous and patient—if you expect promptness, you will almost certainly be disappointed. If you must criticize, try to find a way to express your complaint as a joke. Displays of anger are frowned upon—they will cause your conversation partner to **lose face,** which shames him in front of his peers and plays a large role in Vietnamese social interactions.

SMILE AND THE WHOLE WORLD SMILES WITH YOU. It's difficult to exaggerate how important the smile is to the Vietnamese people. They often think that foreigners do not smile enough, especially during business deals. Most Westerners are accustomed to a relatively negative way of negotiating—we frown and fuss until we get what we want. But in Vietnam, bargaining is traditionally a friendly affair, and it will proceed much more smoothly if you accompany it with a smile. In fact, the Vietnamese consider it extremely rude to show frustration or disapproval, as it causes others to lose face. Losing your cool will only render your transactions more difficult.

DRESS NICELY. Be sure to **remove your shoes** before entering a temple, and when invited into someone's home, note whether your host takes off his shoes, then do the same. **Dress modestly** throughout the country, as Vietnamese styles of dress differ greatly from standards in Western countries, and be especially careful of your clothes when visiting religious sites. When you're unsure, follow the locals, not fellow tourists. **Women** should be especially conscious of their dress, particularly in the countryside, where conservative clothing is the best way to go. Vietnamese women prefer light skin to a tan, so most wear long-sleeved clothing as much out of vanity as respect for tradition—follow the trend. **Shorts** are worn only by Westerners, and in any context they're either inappropriate or awkward-looking; wear trousers instead. Nude or topless sunbathing is out of the question.

CONDUCT. As a gesture of respect, **take off your hat** and **bow your head slightly** when addressing elders or monks. In Vietnam, anyone older than you gets extra-special treatment, so be sure to follow local customs of addressing your elders and superiors. The Vietnamese also tend to be a humble people; don't be surprised when compliments are met only with modest recognition or even self-effacement.

TABOOS. The **feet** are regarded as the least holy part of the body. Don't point the bottoms of your feet at any person or Buddhist image, as this is considered rude. Conversely, Vietnamese regard the **head** as the most sacred part of the body, so never touch a person's head, even a small child's.

TABLE MANNERS. Don't leave **chopsticks** sticking out of a rice bowl; it is thought to resemble the incense burned for the dead, and is considered bad luck. Most locals wipe their chopsticks off before use—a special napkin is usually provided for this purpose. If you take a Vietnamese friend out for a meal or drink, be sure to count their bill on yours—your company likely will, especially since your money likely goes much farther than theirs. Don't be stingy with **toasts** when dining with Vietnamese; prepare to hear a lot of *"chúc"* (cheers). As a general rule, refrain from being the first to dig into the delicious meal in front of you, no matter how tempting it may be.

GIFTS. Give or receive objects or gifts with **both hands.** Wrap gifts in lucky green or red paper; never black and white. **Money** is discussed very openly in Vietnam, so don't be put off if people are **frank** and **inquisitive** about your earnings. If you prefer to keep your financial life private, just smile and politely evade a direct answer.

FAMILY MATTERS. Because of Confucian influence, the Vietnamese value **family** tremendously; in conversation with locals, be attentive to family details. Don't be surprised if stares and shock abound should you mention that you are unmarried. If you are of marriageable age (in Vietnamese terms), just be sure to assure your friends that settling down is not far in your future, and unnecessary worry will be averted. Women may find it useful to wear a simple ring on their wedding finger.

 ONE FOR THE AGES. In Vietnam, people are addressed in relation to their age, but it is difficult for many Vietnamese to guess how old Westerners are. Don't be offended if you are constantly asked your age—people simply want to know how to address you.

SPACE ISSUES. Personal space doesn't exist, per se, in Vietnamese society. Try not to be offended; pushiness is a way of life. Physical contact is usually the result of intense curiosity and is not intended as an offense. Even pointing and calls of "Westerner"—*ông tay* for men and *bà tay* for women—very rarely denotes anything ulterior or sinister, particularly in areas less frequented by tourists.

GLBT TRAVELERS. Homosexuality is not openly discussed or accepted in Vietnam, though major cities like Hồ Chí Minh City and Hà Nội have a small but growing gay nightlife. Most gay men remain closeted, and the gay community stays mostly underground. **Public displays of affection** between both heterosexual and homosexual couples are considered distasteful. At the same time, people of the same sex often hold hands while walking. If you see it, don't be surprised, and perhaps more importantly, don't assume the couple is homosexual. *The Men of Vietnam,* by Douglas Thompson (Floating Lotus, 1998), is the first comprehensive

guide to Vietnamese gay culture. **Utopia-Asia** (www.utopia-asia.com) also offers
tips for gay travelers in Vietnam.

FOOD AND DRINK

Trendy kitchens from Los Angeles to London have recently gone Vietnamese in a
major way. One wonders what took them so long. A tantalizing fusion of different
ethnic cuisines, Vietnamese food has it all—the stir-fries and chopsticks of China
alongside the *consommés* of France. **Rice,** a major national export, gets plenty of
face-time on Vietnamese tables—incarnations include fried rice, steamed rice, rice
noodles, and rice paper. A mouthwatering range of flavors and seasonings is a
national hallmark. Delicious spices and sauces, running the gamut from subtle to
overpowering, annihilate all rice-induced monotony.

 AGE BEFORE BEAUTY. In a Vietnamese family, the youngest person typically invites the oldest person to eat—it is considered impolite to pick up your
chopsticks before this ritual takes place. The invitation is often followed by a
chúc (toast), and then it's time to dine. The food will inevitably be good, but try
to resist the urge to wolf it all down, since dinner often runs slowly, and eating
fast is considered impolite.

If you enjoy the point-and-eat method of choosing your food, Vietnam was
made for you. Meals are often comprised of a number of smaller dishes served
together, from which you can **pick and choose;** even though you may not know
the name or even the primary ingredients, it's difficult to go wrong. **Vegetarians,** of course, may need to do additional research, as meats and fish are more
often than not a part of the preparation. Learn the phrase *"Tôi ăn chay"* ("I'm
a vegetarian") and be persistent. Buddhist influence renders the country relatively amenable to meatless alternatives, particularly during religious festivals
on the first or 15th of each month, and especially in the center of the country.
But even meat-lovers should beware that they may encounter some unusual
meats on the market—**bear, camel, cat, dog, monkey, snake, swan,** and **tiger** are
among the options available. And we promise not to mention some of Vietnam's more unusual ingredients that often find their way into some of the
country's more specialized dishes, including **mole blood, cock and goat testicles,
insect semen,** and **snake penis.** We promise.

TRADITIONAL DISHES

You haven't had Vietnamese food until you've had **phở.** You also won't have any
problem finding it within a few hours of landing in Vietnam—the streets are practically paved with fast-food phở shops and street vendors. **Morning** is the most
common time to have the wildly popular noodle soup, but the dish is eaten nationally all day long. Typically, it's served with beef, and the broth is flavored with a
multitude of mouth-watering herbs and animal bones, but you can find any number of renditions, from chicken to seafood to tofu.

Though it is widely considered a national icon, phở has actually been around
only for the past 100 years or so. The exact history of this tasty noodle soup is
uncertain, but the most popular belief is that phở originated in the northern part of
the country, probably somewhere on the outskirts of **Hà Nội.** Phở was probably
influenced by the French culinary tradition—the soup's light broth is particularly
similar to their *consommé,* and the use of beef itself may have been borrowed
from the European tradition. Traditional phở in the north was simple—just rice
noodles and a few bits of beef. After the 1954 Geneva Accords split the country in

two, many northerners headed south to escape communism and brought with them their phở, which then met up with the flair and extravagance of southern cooking. In its new, rebellious incarnation, phở was spiced up with cilantro, basil, lime, chiles, and hoisin sauce; and new meats like chicken, meatballs, and tripe, were sometimes used in place of beef. While the northern purists may have been be horrified, both north and south agree on the importance of phở, a meal that has taken on meaning far beyond its soupy nature. Some argue that phở symbolizes Vietnam's adoption of French and Chinese culture to form something entirely their own, something respected and enjoyed the world over. It's one of the world's few such symbols that's both edible and delicious.

The up-and-coming fast-food option of choice in Vietnam today is **cơm,** a rice-based dish. Cơm, like phở, is prepared in a number of fashions and with a number of ingredients, although the primary characteristic tends to be the grease dripping from the fried rice. Steamed rice-paper **gỏi cuốn,** or **summer rolls** (sometimes falsely, and confusingly, labeled "spring rolls") await those who oppose the practice of frying. In some restaurants, you can even exercise your culinary prerogative and wrap your own summer rolls from a medley of meat, veggies, and herbs; elsewhere, the masters take care of it for you. If you want the fried version (the *real* spring rolls, alias egg rolls), just ask for **chả giò** in the south or **nem rán** in the north; though you can also find it all wrapped up in lettuce *(cuốn diệp)*. It will satisfy regardless.

Most homes don't serve either phở or cơm—they can generally be found only on the streets. Usually, families share a large communal bowl of rice and a bowl of some kind of broth or soup. Meat and a few vegetables are piled on top of the rice. Soy and fish sauce are within reach. None of the more exotic meats, such as cat, dog, or snake, would typically be served in a home; those are mostly reserved for fancier restaurants, where they are still slightly uncommon.

On the other hand, there's no set culinary protocol in Vietnam. What you eat depends on where you are, unless of course you're far enough off the tourist track that phở may be the only option—which, admittedly, isn't a terrible fate. In the north, a history of Chinese influence makes **stir-fry** a popular cooking technique and **soy sauce** a popular additive. As you move south, you'll encounter a wider variety of herbs (thanks to the resource-rich Mekong Delta) and spicier, chili-based curries similar to those in Thailand, as well as the famous and odorous ◼**fish sauce** *(nước mắm)*. Central Vietnamese cooking is spicier, and perhaps more authentic, as it is less influenced by the Chinese and French. In the center of it all (both literally and figuratively) is **Huế,** the culinary capital of the country, which draws foreign and Vietnamese gastronomes alike with its unique fusion of traditional and contemporary tastes. As an important Buddhist hub, the city also happens to be a **vegetarian nirvana.** The "Huế pancake" *(bánh khoái)* is a blissful combination of pork or shrimp, mushrooms, bean sprouts and onions enveloped by a batter of egg, corn, and rice flour. Other pork-based delicacies include *bánh nam* (shrimp and pork with sticky rice in a banana leaf) and *nem lụi* (grilled pork and greens in rice paper with peanut sauce). The spicy **bún bò,** a noodle soup thicker than phở, is made with vermicelli, beef, lemongrass, and chili, and it also reigns supreme in the imperial capital. While the cuisine in Huế is hands-down the best in Vietnam, it's hard to go wrong anywhere in the country, even in the markets and on the street corners; sometimes these the best and most authentic meals you'll find. And always remember this: in Vietnam, the most unassuming stall or corner shop may serve a meal that changes your life. Seriously—it's that good.

FRUITACULAR

Huế may be a particular nirvana for vegetarians, but the fruit in Vietnam is magical to one and all. A wealth of indigenous fruits graces the country's varied landscapes, particularly in the rich soils of the **Mekong Delta,** where you'll likely encounter opportunities to sample more exotic varieties fresh off the tree. More famous fruits, including **banana, mango,** and **pineapple** are far better here than anywhere else, but don't be afraid to venture into the unknown. Below is a comprehensive list of the bliss that awaits you.

LIFE AND TIMES

NAME	SIZE AND LOOKS	TASTE	EVERYTHING NICE
Banana *chuối*	Yellow. Can be green.	You know. You've had it.	Taste and looks differ across regions. Young tree trunks can be eaten. Whoa.
Custard Apple *mãng cầ xiêm*	Green, easy-to-peel skin, despite thorns. A big green pinecone.	Seeds galore in the sour, yellow pulp inside. Guess what? Tastes like custard.	Head south for this non-traditional apple. Thorns are black when ripe. Also called sweetsop or soursop. Go figure.
Durian *sầu riêng* "one's own sorrows"	Massively huge. Up to several kilos. Green, thick-skinned, and thorny.	Heavenly taste; hellish scent. The custard-like pulp is dreamy, as long as you don't breathe in.	Considered the King of Fruits. Legend and modern literature have been obsessed with this unique fruit indigenous to Southeast Asia.
Green Dragon *thanh long*	Color: bright red. (Obviously.) Shape: like a blowfish. (Seriously.) Weight: up to 500g. Millions of seeds in a white, gelatinous pulp.	The seeds, which supposedly taste like cactus, can't be removed—just delight in the sweet-and-sour appeal. Best in Oct.-Nov. and Apr.-May.	Tough, pink outer skin, but peels like a banana. It's a bit like a large, gray kiwi, minus the citrus flavor. New on the market; harvested in the south. Best eaten chilled. As one source said: "Green dragon is whack." We agree.
Guava *ổi*	Size of an apple. Green skin that yellows as it ripens.	Yep—it's sweet. It's got seeds. It's pulpy. It's a fruit! Hooray.	100 different species. Sometimes eaten when it's not yet ripe, usually with salt.
Jackfuit *mít*	Legendary: the largest fruit in the world. Can be up to 35kg and 1m long. Yellow inside.	An extremely sugary, banana-like taste. Harder skin means crunchier; softer means more juice.	You can pluck it from anywhere: branch, trunk, or root. They're most prevalent in the Mekong. Eat around the core. Watch for thorns on the rind.
Longan *long nhãn*	Absolutely tiny. Light brown in color with not much of a skin.	The white pulp inside is as sweet in taste as the outside is in looks. Juicy.	Also called Dragon Eye. More abundant up north. If you like dried fruit, try this. Or try it in soup!
Lychee *vải*	Rough red, skin. Oval or even heart-shaped.	Sweet, with juicy, white pulp. Seeds are edible.	A larger version of the longan.
Mango *xoài*	Oval-like. Yellow, orange, and/or green.	Sweet, sugary, juicy, and simply delicious.	The skin is inedible. Don't try it. Bring dental floss—fibers abound.
Mangosteen *măng cụt*	Dark, purple, and thick skin. Small and round. White flesh.	The perfect balance of sweet and sour.	Cut through the skin to the juicy pulp at the center.
Papaya *đu đủ*	Yellow and pear-like in shape. Look inside: the flesh is pink or orange.	Sweet; almost so sweet that it doesn't have much of a taste.	They say it helps with digestion. If it's green, don't eat it raw, although you can cook and eat it.
Persimmon *hồng xiêm*	Like an orange, but heart-shaped—so much more enticing.	Sweet and sour versions; the sour one becomes sweet as it ripens.	All the vitamin C you could ever need or want. Again, like an orange. Again, better because the skin isn't bitter.
Pineapple *khóm/dứa*	Scary-looking the world over. Spiky.	Juicy, delicious, and (guess what) sweet.	Most delicious during the summertime, when the smell is unmistakable.
Pomelo *bưởi*	Round. A refreshing smell you won't forget.	Sweet but citrusy; much like a grapefruit.	So many types that each region has its own name for it.
Rambutan *chôm chôm*	Bright red when ripe. Rough, hairy skin.	Sweet and refreshing white pulp inside.	Harvested in the Mekong Delta May-Oct. Alias the "Hairy Cherry." Delicious.
Sapodilla *xa bô chê*	Orange or yellow pulp versions. Brown skin.	Excessively sweet and juicy. Like many fruits.	It grows on evergreen trees, so you must try it for variety's sake. Originally from South America.
▨ **Starfruit** *khế*	Shaped like a square (psych!). Yellow.	Tart and inspirational. It'll change your opinion of nature.	What could be cooler than a fruit in the shape of a star? Slice it up or just bite in. Let's Go's favorite.
Waterapple *roi or mận*	5cm in diameter. Varies from green to bright red.	Can be acidic, and sometimes really sour. But cool color!	Often used as an alter offering, because of the coloring. Hollow on the inside.

HERBALICIOUS

Vietnamese think of herbs as vegetables, so there's always a healthy array of spices and the like from which to choose at every meal. This practice is not borne of a lack of vegetables—most Vietnamese dishes are less meat-intensive than those of other Southeast Asian countries. The real reason for the emphasis on the enticing herbs is simply the need for variety. Although the average tourist will undoubtedly encounter a plethora of appealing dishes piled high with veggies and meats, many Vietnamese live primarily on rice and noodles, which necessitate the wide employment of herbs and spices for meals to be at all interesting. Herbs grow rampantly on the edges of rice fields, allowing for heavy usage with each meal. Some of the more popular flavorings include **black pepper, chili, coriander, ginger, lemongrass, mint,** and **star anise.** Beyond spicing up the palettes of Vietnamese dishes, herbs are believed to provide **medicinal benefits** both specific (aiding digestion and blood circulation) and general (overall well-being). And of course there's the ancient philosophy that they balance out the oft-excessive amount of starch (the *yang* of *yin-yang*) in the traditional daily diet, serving as an ideal and accessible source of *yin*.

SPECIAL SAUCES

Herbs and spices can only do so much before the Vietnamese chef arrives at the problem of making a rice- and grain-based diet exciting. Inevitably, one asks: why not try salting a lot of fish, fermenting them in a vat, and using their fluid leavings as a sauce? That's the innovative solution in much of Southeast Asia, but no one does it better than the Vietnamese. **Nước mắm** is quite potent, in terms of both taste and smell. Made from fermented anchovies, salt, and water, it is the most popular condiment in Vietnam—you won't have to go out of your way to find the opportunity for a taste. The biggest producers are in southern Vietnam, in **Phan Thiết** and on **Phú Quốc Island,** where the fish roam free and in abundance. If you find yourself becoming a connoisseur of the powerful liquid, be aware of false labels, as most businessmen in the country are more than willing to slap on the esteemed Phú Quốc label to conceal lower-quality products. To make the sauce, fresh anchovies and salt are layered in large wooden barrels, which are drained after three months. The liquid is then poured back into the barrel to ferment for another six months. It's easy to become a *nước mắm* expert: clearer sauce indicates more distillment and better quality. Less distilled (darker, more amber) *nước mắm* is used in cooking, while higher-end stuff goes on the table.

But even the most overpowering *nước mắm* can't compete with *mắm tôm*, a purple shrimp paste with an unbelievably noxious odor. Some travelers swear by it in soup; certain daring Vietnamese even eat it directly on dog meat. Let's Go claims no responsibility for the welfare of travelers who voluntarily ingest what is perhaps the worst-smelling thing in the entire world.

BEVERAGES

Even though the dehydrating powers of alcohol may not be the best way to beat the heat, the price is most definitely right. **Bia ho'i,** the Vietnamese brew of choice, flows more freely and cheaply than water on the streets of Vietnam. You can also find a variety of name-brand international brews and higher-quality Vietnamese ones. **Bottled water** is also cheap; avoid drinking anything that comes from a tap and hasn't been treated. Be wary of **ice,** as well, which is frequently just frozen tap water and can sneak easily into your smoothie or shake.

Other popular, non-alcoholic drinks abound. **Fruit shakes** of all sorts were a part of street fare in Vietnam long before they became a world-wide phenomenon. **Sugarcane juice** pressed fresh from the stalks is also a refreshing option; vendors often mix it with fruit and milk to create the heavenly liquid delight that is **chè** (see "**The**

LIFE AND TIMES

Wonders of Chè," p. 279). Iced green tea, **trà đá,** also world-famous, is served with most meals when it's not being shipped to various international destinations. When bought on the street, all of the above may be served in a plastic bag, with a straw—just go with it. Finally, mornings are the domain of Vietnam's almighty **coffee,** which is purported to be some of the best in the world, particularly when served ice-cold and mixed with sweetened condensed milk. You would be insane to miss out on it while actually in the country.

THE ARTS

LITERATURE

HISTORY. Vietnam's greatest writer is universally recognized as **Nguyễn Du,** who wrote *Truyện Kiều (Tale of Kieu)*, an epic in verse. *Truyện Kiều* is about the tragic life of an aristocratic woman, and it openly criticizes imperial society and describes the hardships of the peasants' life. Vietnamese of all ages and social classes can recite passages from the epic. Though this and all other early Vietnamese literature was written in the Chinese *chữ nôm* script, when the French occupied Vietnam, they sought to curtail Chinese influence by banning Chinese and instituting the Latin-based *quốc ngữ* script. Literature written in the vernacular flourished by the 1920s and 30s and played a significant role in the nationalist struggle against colonial power.

THE CURRENT SCENE. Vietnamese author **Bảo Ninh's** *The Sorrow of War* (1996) is exceedingly powerful and one of the few well-known Vietnamese books written about the American War. The 2002 novel *Catfish and Mandala,* by Vietnamese-American **Andrew X. Pham,** tells of the author's bike adventure through the country and his subsequent reconciliation with his country of birth. American author **Karin Muller's** *Hitchhiking Vietnam* is written in the same vein. Poetry remains a popular literary form, though today's poems are mostly written in reaction to the false Socialist patriotism that preceded it.

VISUAL ARTS

HISTORY. Pre-modern Vietnamese art was a reflection of traditional Chinese styles. **Painting,** never as popular in Vietnam as in other Asian countries, usually involved landscapes as well as figural themes such as ▲dragons and unicorns. Portrait painting was popular among wealthier families for the purpose of ancestor worship. **Lacquer painting** was first introduced during the 15th century and involves applying up to 12 layers of paint extracted from tree sap to a wooden background; while time-consuming, the practice's results are visually stunning. The method was traditionally used to decorate pagodas and palaces.

Early **sculpture** focused on figure-carvings of the Buddha, although the lotus flower was also a hit theme. The Hindu kingdom of Champa produced great sculpture, much of which is on display at the Chàm Museum in Đà Nẵng (p. 294). During the colonial period, painting and sculpture were heavily influenced by **French Impressionism.** During the 1930s and 40s, Vietnamese modernist artists reawakened national interest in art. Styles diverged during the war-torn decades following WWII. In the south, the style was more romantic, with the occasional violent, realist streak; in the Democratic Republic of Vietnam, inspirational and occasionally ludicrous propaganda scenes abounded. Unsurprisingly, themes other than Socialist Realist ones were "discouraged" by the state. In fact, they still are—though to a much lesser extent.

THE CURRENT SCENE. Today, Vietnam's artistic scene is centered in **Hà Nội,** but traditional **folk art** (including weaving, musical instrument construction, and wood figure carving) is found in all regions. The handicraft villages surrounding Hà Nội (p. 133) provide an opportunity to witness artists busy at ancient practices of metal work, embroidery, and paper-making. Every other year, **Huế** celebrates the arts with a large festival. The commercialization of the visual arts—often sold en masse in the streets—has led to a rebirth of traditional art forms, including lacquer- and silk-frame-painting. Since the opening of the economy to foreign influences, the government's hand in the art scene has diminished, allowing for the creation of more controversial and individualistic works. Many new galleries are popping up in Hà Nội and HCMC as a new generation of young painters and sculptors—many graduates of the **Fine Arts University** in Hà Nội—draws both national and international attention. The artistic community near Đà Lạt (p. 356) is an ideal place to catch up on the latest national trends.

ARCHITECTURE. Traditional Vietnamese architecture, which stresses **line symmetry** and **harmony**, is largely influenced by the Chinese. Although some have been destroyed or have weathered over time, many pagodas, temples, and palaces have been preserved and still stand today. The **Imperial Palace** in Huế remains an impressive monument to intricate but simple style. In the south, the Chàm influence is more apparent and is markedly distinct from the northern style, with more blocky, meticulously carved surfaces and an emphasis on Hindu religious figures.

DANCE AND DRAMA

HISTORY. Indigenous Vietnamese dances differ greatly across regions, as each minority group traditionally performs rituals specific to its own village. Every year during the Tết Celebrations, men and women celebrate the new year with a ritual dance (called the Unicorn Dance in the south and the Dragon or Lion Dance in the north) that signifies peace, complete with elaborate choreography and costumes.

All theatrical productions involve some sort of musical accompaniment. *Hát tuồng* and *cải lương* (reformed opera) are popular in Central and Southern Vietnam. *Tuồng* was influenced by Chinese opera in plot, costumes, and instrumentation, while *cải lương* combines elements of *tuồng* with Western musical traditions. A third popular genre, *múa rối nước* (water puppetry), originated in the north. Wooden puppets cavort across the surface of a shallow pool, acting out fairy tales. Puppeteers, standing knee-deep in water behind a screen, manipulate the puppets with rods.

THE CURRENT SCENE. The best way to catch a glimpse of the rich traditions of dance and drama at work today is to schedule your trip around a festival—try for Tết if at all possible. Water puppetry is still big; the best place to admire it is the **Thăng Long Water Puppet Theater** in Hà Nội (p. 111). The biannual Huế festival is also dazzling, with its international performing artists.

MUSIC

HISTORY. Folk songs *(dân ca)* originated in the countryside and were sung at festivals and in the fields. Musical theater is also characterized by regional variation. Most famous is the northern *hát chèo*, which combines singing, acting, and dancing. Đông Sơn drums, dating back to the earliest dynasties, are still used today, as are the *đàn bầu* (monochord) and bamboo flute. During the American War, Western-style music became popular, particularly in the south. Lyrics were often politically charged and served as a means of resistance, although the government restricted complete freedom of expression.

THE CURRENT SCENE. Today, traditional music troupes sometimes stage performances in Hà Nội theaters, and, more rarely, in HCMC. The **Opera House** in Hà Nội holds regular performances, although the Western tradition prevails in this performing space (p. 112). Popular Western music floods **karaoke bars** throughout the country. Vietnam even has its own **pop idol contest** on television, called *Morning Star—A Destination.* The government has expressed concern over the lyrics and dress embraced by popular artists, but the show remains a hit.

FILM

Vietnamese film does not have a particularly prolific history, although Vietnam itself is the subject of many American and French films. Most of the films coming out of **Vietnamese Feature Film Studies** in North Vietnam, until the market reforms of 1986, were essentially **political propaganda.** The focus turned to reunification after the war, and the films were largely the work of directors from the **College of Stage Arts and Cinematography** in Hà Nội. Today, however, a few Vietnamese directors are emerging on the international scene, with their aesthetically stunning work that centers on the challenges of daily life in Vietnam. The most famous director is Tran Anh Hung, known for his award-winning *The Scent of Green Papaya* (1993), in addition to *Cyclo* (1995) and *The Vertical Ray of the Sun* (2000). Vietnamese-American directors Tony and Timothy Bui have added to this theme with their respective films **Three Seasons** (1999) and **Green Dragon** (2001). **Daughter from Danang** (2002), directed by Gail Dolgin, chronicles a Vietnamese-American woman's journey to her country of birth to find her mother. Every other year since 2003, the Vietnamese International Film Festival has celebrated Vietnamese cinema in Irvine, CA.

As for films about Vietnam, the options are endless. American War films abound; some are of legendary status, like Francis Ford Coppola's **Apocalypse Now** (1979), based on Joseph Conrad's novel *Heart of Darkness*, and Stanley Kubrick's **Full Metal Jacket** (1987). For a more detailed list, please refer to **Additional Resources** (p. 86). The French film **Indochine,** directed by Regis Wargnier, addresses the colonial period in the most romanticized of manners.

SPORTS AND RECREATION

It may be hot, but nothing can keep the Vietnamese from upholding Hồ Chí Minh's high standard of physical fitness. Uncle Ho was a major advocate of exercise and sports, and ever since he came to power in 1945 and initiated **mandatory exercise** in high schools, the country has maintained an active national routine. Recently, international teams in sports such as **swimming, table tennis,** and **karate** have become increasingly more important to national pride. **Martial arts** are particularly popular. Vietnam has become a power in the Southeast Asia (SEA) Games: they hosted the event in 2003 and won the third most medals out of 11 participating countries in 2005 (behind only host the Philippines and rival Thailand).

Football (or soccer, in the US) is wildly popular all over the country, and the Vietnamese team is regarded as an up-and-coming power in Southeast Asia. The team won silver in the 2003 and 2005 SEA Games; irritatingly, it was the Thailand who beat them both times. Luckily, the women's team redeemed them, winning the 2005 gold. The Vietnamese have never qualified for a World Cup, however. Another extremely popular street sport is **shuttlecock,** or *da cau*, a game in which the participants juggle a shuttlecock over a net with the feet and knees—something like badminton without the rackets.

HOLIDAYS AND FESTIVALS

Whether they're burning incense for souls of the deceased, reenacting the military prowess of historic heroes and heroines, praying to spirits on high, or simply embracing life and one another, the Vietnamese know how to celebrate. Festivals are marked by thrilling, electric colors and intense dress that reflects a joyous national spirit. Celebrations include the traditional—dragon dances, wrestling, cock fights, and elephant races—as well contemporary offerings like performance art. Many festivals are rooted in history and tradition, but today, new ones seem to be popping up left and right as the Vietnamese government strives to promote tourism and cultural awareness.

FESTIVAL CHART

This chart lists dates for 2007 (unless otherwise specified); since many Vietnamese holidays are based on the lunar calendar (see **Lunar Calendar,** p. 448), the dates will change in following years. Most dates aren't set in stone, and may be subject to change.

DATE	NAME AND LOCATION	DESCRIPTION
Jan. 1	New Year's Day	International holiday.
Feb. 18-21	Tết Nguyễn Festival, everywhere	By far the most famous holiday of the year, Tết is a celebration of the Lunar New Year. Festivities include dancing, song, and plenty of deliciously prepared foods. Celebrations are everywhere (see below).
Feb. 21-Apr. 19	Nui Ba (Den) Mountain Festival, Tây Ninh Province	Pilgrims travel to a pagoda on Nui Mountain to remember the virtue of a devout nun, Den, from the village.
Feb. 23-Apr. 4	Hương (Perfume) Pagoda Festival, Hà Tây Province (near Hà Nội)	The longest festival in Vietnam, this famous celebration at the Perfume Pagoda provides the perfect opportunity to immerse yourself in the culture and stunning landscape and seek out good luck in the process.
Mar. 19-22	Dong Nhan Festival, Hà Nội	Young women dance their praise for the Trưng sisters, leaders of the earliest and most renowned peasant revolt.
Mar. 28-Apr. 1	Chu Dong Tu Temple Festival, near Hà Nội	Dances and prayers are offered to one of the Four Immortal Heroes of the country, Chu Dong Tu, who influenced agricultural practices and trade.
Apr. 18-26	Phu Giay Temple Festival, Nam Định Province	Cock fights, chess matches, and wrestling are in abundance at this festival honoring Queen Lieu Hanh.
Apr. 21-23	Thầy Pagoda Festival, Hà Tây Province (near Hà Nội)	Water puppet master and Buddhist monk Tu Hoa Danh is the focus of festivities.
Apr. 22	Tây Phương Pagoda Festival, Hà Tây Province (near Hà Nội)	The Tây Phương Pagoda, dedicated to the Buddha himself, bestows good luck during this holiday.
Apr. 24-26	Truong Yen Festival, Ninh Bình Province	Color and theatrical renditions abound at this festival honoring early rulers set in the ancient capital of Hoa Lư.
Apr. 24-May 6	Elephant Race Festival, Đắk Lắk Province	Beware of stray contestants in the races, which constitute the largest festival in the central highlands. Unreal.
Apr. 29	Do Tem Festival, Bắc Ninh Province	This extravagant festival and procession commemorate the eight kings of the Lý Dynasty.
May 6-10	Ba-Po Nagar Temple Festival, Khánh Hòa Province	Rice and its cultivating father, Po Nagar, are the object of praise at this yearly celebration.
Apr. 30	Saigon Liberation Day, everywhere	As the name suggests, this is a national holiday honoring the freeing of Saigon from the southern army.
May 1	Labor Day	Another international holiday you may know.
mid-June, 2008	Huế Festival, Huế	Held every 2 years, this festival of the arts features performers and artists from all over the country and world.
June 27-30	Chem Temple Festival, Hà Nội	Drums beat and processions flow through the streets and waters of the county's capital in tribute to the Hùng kings and their defeat of early invaders.
July 24-Aug. 3 (officially Aug. 1)	Quán Lạn Communal House Festival, Quán Lạn Island	On the opening day of ceremonies honoring the defeat of the Mongols in the 13th century, inhabitants are not allowed to leave the island. Visitors are welcome to watch the rowing contests and battle reenactments.
late July	Đà Nẵng Cultural Festival, Đà Nẵng	This week-long festival designed to promote tourism features boat performances, a variety of other artistically inclined celebrations, and games.
late July-early Aug.	Hội An Summer Festival, Hội An	Designed to awaken tourists to the historical and cultural wealth of the World Heritage Site, the festival features a range of performances, games, and much more.

DATE	NAME AND LOCATION	DESCRIPTION
Aug. 23	Nhuong Ban Festival, Hà Tĩnh	Honors Lady Hoang Can, imperial concubine of 14th-century ruler King Trần Tron. Burn incense for the seductress.
Sept. 7	Tết Trưng Nguyễn Festival, pagodas the country over	Families cook feasts and pray for the forgiveness of the souls of the deceased who strayed during their lives.
Aug. 30	Long Chu Festival, Hội An and surrounding villages	The *long chu* (dragon boat) is paraded through town and pushed out to sea, taking with it the threat of harmful insects and plagues.
Sept. 2	National Day of the Socialist Republic of Vietnam	This national holiday commemorates the birth of the independent nation of Vietnam as declared by Hồ Chí Minh.
Sept. 17-18	Đồ Sơn Buffalo Fighting Festival, Hải Phòng	It's bullfighting without the matador, and with buffaloes. Thousands gather to catch the action and savor the meat during this high-energy festival.
Sept. 25	Mid-Autumn Festival, everywhere	The whole country pauses to delight in pastries, drumbeats, and children's dances during this national holiday.
Sept. 24-29	Kiep Bac Temple Festival, Hải Dương Province	The military exploits of the famous general Trần Hưng Đạo are recalled and reenacted during this traditional festival.
Oct. 8-20	Kate Festival, Ninh Thuận and Bình Thuận Provinces	Chàm people from all around the southern region of the country gather at several famous towers and temples to celebrate their unique history during this simple holiday.
Oct. 17-18	Don Ta Festival, Bay Nui (An Giang)	Oxracing is what it's all about at this traditional Khmer festival.
Oct. 23-25	Keo Pagoda Festival, Thái Bình Province	Traditional religious rituals and performances are dedicated to Duong Lo, a famous Buddhist luminary.

TẾT

Spring fever is contagious during the advent of the Lunar New Year when Vietnam celebrates its most important yearly festival: Tết. Offically called **Tết Nguyên Đán** ("Feast of the First Morning"), this festival's traditions draw heavily on those of the Chinese New Year. Life outside of family, friends, and food goes on hold during this four-day national holiday (which actually lasts much longer in many places). Traditional dishes differ from region to region, but always involve *bánh chưng* (pork and rice cakes), and are always masterfully prepared in abundance. The colorful, artistic presentations are as appealing as the food is satisfying.

If you're flying through the country, pause in each place to observe the different traditions. What you witness and experience depends on where you are, as each village and community treats the holiday differently. Some villages hold more official and well-established celebrations than others. In **Hà Nội,** you can duck the flames of the dancing ◪**Thăng Long Fire Dragon,** the civic symbol, on the fifth day of the lunar month. In **Cửa Lò,** just outside the capital, the smell of rice from cooking competitions and the sounds of opera waft through the air for 10 festive days. If you're in the mood for human chess, head to the **Va Temple** in the Hà Tây Province; the less-tame **Sinh Wrestling Festival** outside of Huế begins a few days after Tết does and pulsates with youthful energy, as does the **Lieu Doi Wrestling Festival** in Ha Nam province in the north. Finally, if you'd like to purchase materials for your own personal holiday shrine, the **Gia Lac Spring Fair** in Huế is well-timed with the festivities.

ADDITIONAL RESOURCES

GENERAL HISTORY

Hell In a Very Small Place: The Siege of Dien Bien Phu, by Bernard Fall (Da Capo Press, 2002). A compelling account of the famous battle, based on thousands of interviews and declassified government documents.

Ho Chi Minh: The Missing Years, by Sophie Quinn-Judge (University of California Press, 2003). A focus on the early years—1919-1940—of Vietnam's favorite leader.

Postcolonial Vietnam: New Histories of a National Past, by Patricia Pelley (Duke University Press, 2002). A postmodern critical perspective on a well-known past.

Postwar Vietnam: Dynamics of a Transforming Society, by Hy V. Luong (Rowman & Littlefield Publishers, 2003). An historical perspective of the country in the aftermath of war.

AMERICAN WAR LITERATURE

Dispatches, by Michael Herr (Vintage, 1991). Vivid, mind-numbing stories from the front as recorded by *Esquire* correspondent Herr render this one of the must-reads on the subject of the American War. This book served as the inspiration for a number of movies, including *Apocalypse Now.*

A People's History of the Vietnam War, by Howard Zinn (New Press, 2004). The story of the American War, as told by the people who fought it, opposed it, and lived it.

Requiem: By the Photographers Who Died in Vietnam and Indochina, by Horst Faas, David Halberstam, Tim Page (Random House, 1997). A harrowing photographic account of the two Indochina Wars in Vietnam and other areas of the conflict.

The Sorrow of War, by Bảo Ninh (Riverhead Trade, 1994). A moving novel about love and war in the North; a must-read for anyone familiar with American War literature. Written by a North Vietnamese veteran.

The Things They Carried, by Tim O'Brien (Penguin, 1998). A fictional account of the harrowing effects of the war on the human mind and soul.

Vietnam: A History, by Stanley Karnow (Penguin, 1983). A Pulitzer Prize-winning, straightforward and journalistic history of the American War.

NON-FICTION

Catfish and Mandala, by Andrew X. Pham (Picador, 2000). A Vietnamese-American returns to his homeland many years after leaving for California and takes on the country by bike. A poignant, insightful account of contemporary Vietnam.

Culture and Customs of Vietnam, by Mark W. McLeod and Nguyen Thi Dieu (Greenwood Press, 2001). A comprehensive guide to the Vietnamese people and customs. Refreshingly little emphasis on the war with the United States.

Shadows and Wind: A View of Modern Vietnam, by Robert Templar (Penguin, 1999). Analyzes Vietnam's position in today's globalized world through interviews and analysis.

Vietnam, Now, by David Lamb (PublicAffairs, 2003). A comprehensive look at modern Vietnam, written by a wartime reporter upon his return to the country years later.

FICTION

The General Retires and Other Stories, by Nguyen Huy Thiep (Oxford University Press, 1987, trans. 1993). A collection of short stories focusing on the difficulty of everyday life after the American War.

The Lover, by Marguerite Duras (Pantheon, 1984). A wild young French girl's tale of growing up in colonial Vietnam.

The Quiet American, by Graham Greene (Penguin Classics, 1955). One of the best works of one of the 20th century's greatest authors. A British correspondent watches as the French blunder and struggle for control in Vietnam. Brilliantly anticipates the Americans' tragic involvement a decade later.

FILM

VIETNAMESE FILMS

Cyclo, dir. Tran Anh Hung (1995). A look into the world of crime and drugs in HCMC through the eyes of a struggling cyclo driver.

Green Dragon, dir. Timothy Bui (2001). Two young Vietnamese refugees deal with the realities of a new life in America.

The Scent of Green Papaya, dir. Tran Anh Hung (1993). An aesthetically masterful, molasses-slow romance between a servant and her employer. Oscar winner for Best Foreign Film in 1994.

Three Seasons, dir. Tony Bui (1999). A film detailing the crazy wanderings of an American vet who has returned to HCMC.

The Vertical Ray of the Sun, dir. Tran Anh Hung (2000). A beautiful film depicting the lives of three sisters in modern Vietnam.

AMERICAN WAR FILMS

Apocalypse Now, dir. Francis Ford Coppola (1979). The unforgettable Coppola masterpiece, considered one of the greatest war films ever made. It depicts the hopelessness and insanity on the American side during the war, in the form of tortured Captain Willard (Martin Sheen) and crazed Colonel Kurtz (Marlon Brando).

The Deer Hunter, dir. Michael Camino (1978). Robert de Niro, Christopher Walken, John Savage, and Meryl Streep star in this emotional tale of the war's effect on a young American generation.

Full Metal Jacket, dir. Stanley Kubrick (1987). A tense psychological analysis of the war through the eyes of soldiers in training and in combat.

Good Morning, Vietnam, dir. Barry Levinson (1987). A US Armed Forces Radio DJ (Robin Williams) humors the troops but tells them a little more than the military would like them to know.

Platoon, dir. Oliver Stone (1986). Two young officers deal with the harrows of war in the first in Stone's Vietnam War trilogy.

OTHER FILMS

Daughter from Da Nang, dir. Gail Dolgin (2002). Winner of the Sundance Film Festival Award for Best Documentary; story of a Vietnamese-American woman who returns to Vietnam in search of her mother.

Indochine, dir. Regis Wargnier (1992). The legendary French actress Catherine DeNeuve is a rich rubber plantation owner dealing with personal and political scandal in colonial Vietnam.

The Quiet American, dir. Philip Noyce, with Brendan Fraser and Michael Caine (2002). A remake of the 1958 film directed by Joseph Mankiewicz, based on Graham Greene's novel.

COOKBOOKS

Authentic Vietnamese Cooking: Food from a Family Table, by Corinne Trang (Simon & Schuster, 1999). The author shares her family recipes and the history behind Vietnam's traditional dishes.

Pleasures of the Vietnamese Table, by Mai Pham (Morrow Cookbooks, 2001). A Vietnamese expat living in America returns and weaves a delectable tale of her adventure through Vietnamese cuisine.

The Foods of Vietnam, by Routhier (Stewart, Tabori and Chang, 1999). Vietnamese-born New York City chef Routhier shares her secret recipes.

The Vietnamese Cookbook, by Diana My Tran (Capital Books, 2003). All of the classics and some rarer dishes fill the pages.

BEYOND TOURISM

A PHILOSOPHY FOR TRAVELERS

HIGHLIGHTS OF BEYOND TOURISM IN VIETNAM

VOLUNTEER at ▨Thảo Đàn Orphanage in Hồ Chí Minh City working with and teaching street children (p. 92).

STUDY BUTTERFLY DIVERSITY at Tam Đảo National Park, amid the most diverse snake population in the world (p. 93).

TEACH ENGLISH to eager and enthusiastic children, teenagers, or adults nearly anywhere in the country (p. 97).

LEARN BY IMMERSION while studying the Vietnamese language at Vietnam National University in Hà Nội (p. 96).

BULK UP after learning to cook (and eat) like the Vietnamese in Hôi An (p. 96).

Let's Go believes that the connection between travelers and their destinations is an important one. Over the years, we've watched the growth of the "ignorant tourist" stereotype with dismay, knowing that many travelers care passionately about the cultures they visit and environments they explore, but also knowing that even conscientious tourists can inadvertently do harm to natural wonders and local communities. With this chapter, Let's Go hopes to promote a better understanding of Vietnam and provide suggestions for a more meaningful experience there.

In Vietnam, there are several different options for Beyond Tourism activities. Structured opportunities for **volunteering** abound, both with local and international organizations; casual volunteering is less common and easiest to find in urban centers. **Studying** can also be fulfilling, either in the form of direct enrollment in a local university or via an independent research project. In most cases, Let's Go discourages **working** in the developing world due to high unemployment rates and weak economies; certain jobs in Vietnam, however, such as teaching English, translating or editing for publications, or low-paying development work, help more than they hurt. Indeed, you might find it easier to find a job than a volunteer position if you head overseas without a plan: Vietnam already has a number of local volunteer organizations of its own, many of which are closed to foreigners or prevent them from truly meaningful volunteering by restricting the time frame of their commitment or the degree to which they can participate. A great general online resource for programs in Vietnam is **www.goabroad.com.**

Much of Vietnam suffers from severe poverty. Although the economy is currently looking up, the country is still recovering from decades of warfare and economic hardship. As a volunteer in Vietnam, you can participate in projects from building local schools to teaching English to working in an orphanage, either on a short-term basis or as the primary purpose of your trip. There are also a variety of programs that incorporate travel and exploration into service projects. Later in this chapter, we recommend organizations that can help you find the opportunities that best suit your interests, whether you're looking to pitch in for a day or a year. Regardless of your personal goals, there should be a program, charity, or venue that can help you along your way. We recommend organizing a volunteer project ahead of time; such jobs are difficult to find after you touch down in the country, given the predominant Vietnamese attitude toward letting foreigners volunteer. But we've heard enough stories of foreigners waltzing into a local orphanage and finding a volunteer position that we do not discourage trying. You might be lucky enough to arrange to stay and help out for more than just an afternoon.

Studying at a college or language program is also a worthwhile option. Regardless of your age, a long-term stay in a foreign country will undoubtedly have a profound influence on your life and your perspective. Study abroad programs typically provide a relatively easy transition into a foreign culture through extensive orientation, and are thus a convenient means of immersing yourself. A number of programs which focus on issues related to economic development are offered through various international institutions, but if you're looking for something a little different, you might want to try experimenting with your culinary skills (see **Cooking Schools,** p. 96).

Although there aren't many jobs available to expatriates in Vietnam, a few opportunities exist in the non-profit, tourism, and information technology industries. As a general rule, the only jobs on offer are ones that wouldn't be available to Vietnamese anyway—where local firms can hire Vietnamese instead of foreigners, they nearly always will. Americans can research potential employment avenues via **InterAction: American Council for Voluntary International Action** (www.InterAction.org). Most available positions are directed toward those willing to stick around for at least a year. It is best to have Vietnamese language skills if you're in the market for a job that isn't teaching English, and plan ahead—don't count on arriving and finding a non-teaching job waiting for you. At the same time, you shouldn't have too difficult a time finding job teaching English once there, and it might save you time dealing with bureaucratic red tape. You might also keep an eye out for editing jobs, which are often paid under the table. If you do land a job after arriving, you'll have to leave the country (head into Cambodia or Laos) and return a few days later in order to transfer the status of your visa.

As far as accommodations are concerned, most programs that you register for beforehand will take care of housing. Some programs coordinate homestays, which provide a unique opportunity for a more comprehensive immersion in the local culture; others help in the apartment search process or house students in their own facilities. If you take on a job or volunteering position after you arrive, no need to worry—housing is typically pretty easy to find and refreshingly inexpensive in Vietnam (p. 45). While apartment searching in the bigger cities, you need not worry about racking up inordinate expenses; there are plenty of budget hotels and hostels available listed in the book you're holding right now.

Of course, you're welcome to zip through the country admiring all of the diverse marvels it has to offer, but if you really want to get to know the culture, it's best to stay a while and engage with it. We've listed here plenty of alternatives to tourism to suit a range of interests and goals, but it's up to you, the independent traveler, to take the initiative to see Vietnam for all it really has to offer.

 Start your search at ■ **www.beyondtourism.com,** Let's Go's brand-new searchable database of alternatives to tourism, where you can find exciting feature articles and helpful program listings by country, continent, and program type.

VOLUNTEERING

Volunteering can be one of the most fulfilling experiences in your life, especially when combined with the thrill of traveling in a new place. Read up before heading out, and be aware of the diversity of experiences on offer; putting in time at a daycare in HCMC will expose you to different cultural norms than you will find when working to improve health care in northern Tày villages. The best way to find opportunities that match up with your interests and schedule may be to check with any of the broad-based organizations listed under the **Social Activism** section (p. 89). You might want to check out **www.idealist.org, www.volunteerabroad.org,** and **www.volunteerinternational.org** for listings of volunteer opportunities. To find out more about what to expect living in the developing world, be sure to read our **Essentials** chapter (p. 13).

WHY PAY MONEY TO VOLUNTEER? Many volunteers are surprised to learn that some organizations require large fees or "donations." While this may seem ridiculous at first glance, such fees often keep the organization afloat, in addition to covering airfare, room, board, and administrative expenses for the volunteers. (Other organizations must rely on private donations and government subsidies.) If you're concerned about how a program spends its fees, request an annual report or finance account. A reputable organization won't refuse to inform you of how volunteer money is spent.

Pay-to-volunteer programs might be a good idea for young travelers who are looking for more support and structure (such as pre-arranged transportation and housing), or anyone who would rather not deal with the uncertainty implicit in creating a volunteer experience from scratch.

Vietnamese volunteer organizations tend to enlist the aid of Vietnamese citizens (or might be subsumed within exclusive local administrations, like Communist youth leagues), so you might have difficulty showing up and finding a position. Your best bet would be at an orphanage or similar institution in a larger city—it can be a bit tough to organize a project of your own in a village, given the lack of accommodations and infrastructure. People who volunteer in Vietnam without signing up for a program beforehand often do so on a short-term basis at organizations that make use of drop-in or once-a-week volunteers; long-term volunteer opportunities nearly always require some prior research. Be sure to get in touch with other expatriates in your city or town to find out about options.

Many volunteer services charge a participation fee. These costs can be surprisingly hefty (although they frequently cover most, if not all, living expenses). Most people choose to go through a parent organization that takes care of logistical details and frequently provides a group environment and support system. This is probably the most convenient approach for those interested in staying in Vietnam long enough to get a sense of the culture. Be aware that many organizations rotate destinations from year to year and may not have one in Vietnam at the time you apply even if it is listed, so be prepared to spend time searching.

SOCIAL ACTIVISM

Broad-based volunteer organizations offer opportunities in a variety of areas. Some programs charge discouragingly high fees, but in most cases you get what you pay for. Some organizations can connect you with alumni of their programs.

CHOICE Humanitarian, 7879 S 1530 W. Ste. 200, West Jordan, UT 84088, USA (☎888-474-1937; www.choicehumanitarian.org). 1- to 2-week programs building schools, refurbishing bicycles, or creating rain-harvesting systems in a rural community. Min. age 12. US$1800.

Global Humanitarian Expeditions, 602 South Ogden St., Denver, CO 80209, USA (☎800-543-1171; www.humanitariantours.com/home.htm). Volunteers help to operate mobile dental clinics around Đà Nẵng. Experience in dental work is appreciated but not necessary. Most programs 2-3 weeks.

Global Routes, 1 Short St., Northampton, MA 01060, USA (☎413-585-8895; www.globalroutes.org/student-travel.html). 5-week programs for high school students to travel through Southeast Asia, including 10 days in Vietnam. Participants live for a few weeks with families and engage in various volunteer projects.

Globe Aware Adventures in Service, 7232 Fisher Rd., Dallas, TX 75214, USA (☎877-588-4562; www.globeaware.org/content/vietnamprogram.htm). Offers 1-week programs near Hội An (US$1400) for teaching English, building playgrounds, restoring houses, and refurbishing schools.

i-to-i Vietnam (www.i-to-i.com), Woodside House, 261 Low Ln., Leeds LS18 5NY UK (☎870 333 2332); 190 East 9th Ave., Ste. 350, Denver, CO 80203, USA (☎800-985-4864). Teach English in Hà Nội, build homes in the Mekong, or work at a soup kitchen in HCMC. Most programs 2-12 weeks. Program fees run several thousand dollars plus airfare and food.

The Network, based in Hồ Chí Minh City. An organization of charitable opportunities all across the city, ranging from volunteering in homeless shelters and hospitals to building schools for street children. Volunteers are needed to help with fundraising, teach English, or help care for disabled children. Short- and long-term placements available. Contact Elizabeth Copley (☎9292 0100; elizabethcopley@hotmail.com).

United Nations Volunteer Program, 25-29 Phan Bội Châu, Hà Nội, Vietnam (☎4 925 2267; www.un.org.vn/unv). Hosts occasional programs for UN Volunteers. The website includes links to local volunteer-seeking organizations. The United Nations Development Program also offers highly competitive internships open to graduate students in development fields.

VentureCo, The Ironyard, 64-66 The Market Place, Warwick CV34 4SD, UK (☎192 641 1122; www.ventureco-worldwide.com). VentureCo offers gap year (year off before university), career break, summer venture, or custom group trips. These 16-week ventures pass through China, Cambodia, Laos, and Vietnam. The program cultural immersion and language courses, and a series of volunteer projects in the destinations included on the route.

🏶 **Volunteers for Peace,** 1034 Tiffany Rd., Belmont, VT 05730, USA (☎802-259-2759; www.vfp.org). The most comprehensive, affordable volunteer organization around. A huge variety of program types and lengths, and thousands of dollars cheaper than most similar organizations. Programs in Vietnam include working with children, environmental conservation, and HIV/AIDS prevention. Food and housing, but not airfare, included. 2- to 3-week programs are US$270.

VUFO-NGO Resource Centre, Building L at the back of the La Thành Hotel on 218 Đội Cấn, Hà Nội (☎4 832 8570; www.ngocentre.org.vn). The first and best place to find volunteering opportunities in Vietnam, this office of the Vietnam Union of Friendship Organizations and affiliated NGOs functions as a platform and liaison between volunteers and numerous aid and development organizations, complete with a large library of past and present NGO projects. The office is under the guidance of the governmental People's Aid Coordinating Committee (PACCOM). Open daily 8am-noon and 1:30-5pm.

Youth International, 232 Wright Ave., Toronto, Ontario M6R 1L3, Canada (☎416-538-0152; www.youthinternational.org). Three-month backpacking programs for those between 15 and 25 that combine travel, cultural immersion, and some volunteering in local communities in Vietnam, Thailand, and India. The program costs about US$7500.

YOUTH AND COMMUNITY

The easiest option for short-term, unplanned volunteering is to work in an orphanage or youth community center. Options abound in urban areas, where countless children would otherwise be forced to make a living selling postcards on the street. Volunteering for such organizations almost always means teaching English.

Blue Dragon Children's Foundation (www.bdcf.org). This Australian-based charity has opened two chapters in Vietnam, both of which are aimed at sending street children to Blue Dragon schools. The program in Hà Nội also organizes a football team and provides kids with bright blue uniforms, while the chapter in Hội An has students run their own restaurant (46 Bạch Dằng). Volunteers are always needed to work at these schools teaching English, math, art, and even yoga. Alternatively, you can sponsor a child for USụ75 per year, enough money to send him to school.

COMMUNITY INVOLVEMENT
Promote Helmets, Prevent Death

Riding home at night from the popular Le Maquis bar in Hà Nội, I tightly grip the seat of the Honda motorbike as we zoom past Hoàn Kiếm Lake. I glance at my friend riding next to me. She is on a bicycle; unlike everyone else on the road, we are both wearing helmets. In a flash, I see her topple to the side of the road. A drunk motorist, thinking it would be funny to kick her bike tire *while she is in motion,* has succeeded in making her fall. Four stitches and an unpleasant evening in the hospital follow; my friend emerges shaken but fine.

Visitors to Vietnam quickly realize where the risk lies in their travels. With low rates of violent crime but shockingly high rates of traffic-related injuries and deaths, the peace of mind Vietnam offers to travelers does not extend to those on motorbikes. On a daily basis, 37 people are killed in traffic accidents in Vietnam, and many more suffer serious injury. That's 13,000 road fatalities per year—and yet fewer than 3% of Vietnamese wear helmets. It's not uncommon to see a family of four or five on one motorbike, with Dad in front and Mom in back and the kids in between—not one of them wearing a helmet.

While the government remains passive about enforcing the existing helmet laws (even police officers don't wear them), it is the non-profit sector that has taken up the battle cry to armor road warriors with head protection. The Asia Injury Prevention Foundation (AIPF; www.asiainjury.org) spearheads public awareness programs, publicizing the dangers of road accidents and promoting helmets as "cool" protection. Part of their effort includes the establishment of the first non-profit helmet manufacturer in Asia, Protec Helmets, to make helmets that are safe, comfortable, and stylish.

Protec has developed a lightweight helmet that is both suitable for tropical climates and specially designed for motorbike drivers like the ones that crowd Vietnamese cities. Unlike the conventional heavy motorcycle helmets that reduce peripheral vision and threaten to melt your face under the hot Hà Nội sun, Protec helmets are ventilated and allow full peripheral perspective. Adhering to international certification standards, these helmets can increase a child's road- accident survival rate by 78%. Expats in the know already sport the brightly colored helmets as a must-have accessory, but AIPF has to work hard to promote helmet-wearing among Vietnamese adults and children. Through its Helmets for Kids program, AIPF has given more than 50,000 helmets away for free to schoolchildren through corporate sponsorships. They also sponsor school education programs and launch legislative advocacy campaigns to encourage the government to enforce helmet laws.

The stakes for these initiatives are high: the fatalities and serious injuries caused by road accidents have already put urban hospitals in crisis mode. Despite government initiatives to install traffic lights and enforce traffic laws, the roads continue to resemble something closer to an anarchic war-zone than a peaceful Communist state. Since the economy opened to foreign investment in 1987, many more Vietnamese have been able to afford motorbikes (the number of bikes on the road increases annually by 10%, according to the National Traffic Safety Committee). The sheer number of vehicles on the road, combined with the continued willingness to ignore traffic laws makes accidents increasingly likely. Helmets provide a workable solution to protect riders at risk from head injury and death.

AIPF accepts a limited number of volunteer workers to assist the Vietnamese staff in written English communication, public relations, and research and project development. Volunteers should be able to commit to working for at least three months. For more information, see the AIPF website or contact Office Manager Tran Giang Huong (huong.tran@aipf-vietnam.org).

If volunteering is not a possibility for you, you can spread road safety awareness by wearing a helmet every time you get on a *xe ôm.*

Sarah Rotman is a former Let's Go researcher-writer, editor, and manager. An experienced and avid traveler to Asia, she developed websites for local businesses while living in Hà Nội. She currently designs educational programs for businesses and schools in the US and Korea.

Cosmic Volunteers, Cosmic Volunteers, Inc., P.O. Box 11738, Philadelphia, PA 19101, USA (☎610-279-2052; www.cosmicvolunteers.org/vietnam.html). Work in an orphanage in HCMC teaching English, basic math, arts and crafts, music, and sports. The 1-week to 3-month programs include stays in guesthouses or with host families.

Đà Nẵng Orphanage, 283 Lê Van Hiên, south of Đà Nẵng on the way to the Marble Mountains. A small but welcoming orphanage of about 30 children where little English is spoken. Visiting hours daily 9-11am and 3-5pm.

Global Volunteer Network, Global Volunteer Network Ltd., P.O. Box 2231, Wellington, New Zealand (AUS ☎800 203 012, NZ 644 569 9080, UK 800 032 5035, US 800-963-1198; www.volunteer.org.nz). Current programs include teaching English and working in an orphanage. Programs 1-5 months, US$500-700 per month (plus airfare).

Nguyễn Đình Chiểu (Hà Nội's School for the Blind), 21 Lac Trung St, Hà Nội. A massage center operated by blind masseurs trained at Saint Paul's hospital, Bạch Mai hospital, and Tue Tinh school for traditional medicine. Volunteers welcome. Open daily 8:30am-11pm.

Hội An Orphanage, 4 Nguyễn Trường Tô, next to the church. All visitors are welcome to come by and sit, play, or chat with the children. Some are learning English and are looking to practice; all appreciate a visit. Open to visitors 8-10am and 2-4pm. Please dress conservatively.

SOS Village, 67 Hùng Vương. Volunteer, mentor, and teach English at a branch of the international SOS orphanage network. The village originally housed the orphaned children of American soldiers and Vietnamese women. When US soldiers left after the American war, many Vietnamese women were left with children, some of whom ended up in the SOS Village. The village is located in a villa-style complex on the south side of the lake, hidden among pines. Volunteers should dress conservatively and arrange for their own food and accommodations. Open daily 7am-5pm.

Sozo, 176 Bùi Viện and 844 Sư Hanh Hồ Chí Minh City, Vietnam (☎838 8825). These nonprofit cafes provide jobs to children who would otherwise be on the streets selling gum and postcards. Through Sozo, volunteers can find short-term placements at other charities in HCMC, most likely teaching English. Also runs "Friday Night School," a discussion group for Vietnamese students to improve their English. Seeks English-speaking volunteers. Call or inquire at either cafe.

Thảo Đàn, 451/1 Hai Bà Trưng, Hồ Chí Minh City, Vietnam(☎8 846 5410; thaodan@hcmc.netnam.vn), in the alley off 451 Hai Bà Trưng. Thảo Đàn is a welcoming organization that is home to about 40 former street children ages 5-22. The charity provides them with education in English, French, Japanese, Vietnamese and math, and it often organizes daytrips and games to celebrate festivals. Visitors and volunteers welcome, especially to teach. It is recommended that you call before visiting.

Từ Đàm Pagoda, just south of Huế, doubles as a religious school where monks pass on their knowledge of languages to the local children; French and English classes are popular parts of the lesson plan. Foreigners interested in joining these monks as teachers would be warmly welcomed. For details contact Thuh Phap Tri, 1 Lieu Quan (cell ☎ 0914 190 109; dha_wisdom@yahoo.com).

ENVIRONMENTAL CONSERVATION

Natural beauty abounds in Vietnam and the government is starting to take action to preserve it. Most conservation programs are still young but growing. Spend time on the Internet researching, and you're bound to find some kind of project.

Ba Bể National Park (☎281 894 027; thedien@hn.vnn.vn). As a student or a scientist, it is possible to obtain a permit for the Biodiversity Research Station in Ba Bể National Park. Visitors will receive a home stay, office, and equipment. For more information, contact Nông Thế Diên, Vice Director of Ba Bể National Park.

Butterflies of Vietnam (AUS ☎613 9682 6828, JPN 813 3511 3360, UK 186 531 8831, US 800-776-1088; www.earthwatch.org/expeditions/vu.html). Work for 9 days with entomologists to compile information regarding butterfly diversity in Tam Đảo National Park. From US$2000.

Frontier, 50-52 Rivington St., London EC2A 3QP, UK (☎207 613 2422; www.frontier-projects.ac.uk/). 10-week research and conservation programs carried out across Southeast Asia aim to provide scientific documentation on natural resources. Most of the actual conservation takes place in Cambodia. Expedition training included in payment for 4-week program. Around US$5000.

Restoring Vietnam's Forests, run by the same organization as Butterflies of Vietnam. Help Dr. Nguyen Van Sinh research the optimal life cycles of almost 2000 plant species in his effort to restore natural forests. 9-day trips in Cúc Phương National Park go for around US$2100. Guesthouse accommodations included.

The Tam Đảo Project (office.tdmp@gtz-vietnam.com.vnpark) is an organization that is struggling to address the issues of uncontrolled hunting and deforestation. Local resident farmers and the logging industry pose serious threats to the park and to the country's wildlife in general. Email the group if you're interested in helping out.

EDUCATION PROGRAMS

Most of the education programs below are English-teaching programs, but differ from those listed in the **Teaching English** section (p. 97) in that they do not require previous experience or teaching certification.

Cung Thiếu Nhi Hà Nội (The Children's Palace of Hà Nội), around the corner from the post office on 15 Trần Nguyên Han (☎091 350 0582; honghoarose@yahoo.com) is supported by the Vietnamese government as an after-school and summer-school program for teaching children ages 5-12. Hiring volunteers and paid teachers. Open daily 8am-5pm.

Project Trust, The Hebridean Centre, Isle of Coll, Argyll PA78 6TE, UK (☎187 923 0444; www.projecttrust.org.uk). Open to EU citizens ages 17-19. Spend a year teaching English at a high school or university. £4190 program fee covers almost all expenses.

Travel to Teach, 535 Rim Khong Road, Th-43 000 Nongkhai, Thailand (☎66 06 239 5481; www.travel-to-teach.org). Spend 1-6 months teaching English at a primary school and organizing afterschool activities in Hà Nội, Nha Trang, or HCMC. Also hosts environmental and youth programs. €200-600 per month plus travel costs.

Volunteers in Asia, P.O. Box 20266, Stanford, CA 94309, USA (☎650-723-3228; www.viaprograms.org). 1- to 2-year university teaching programs open to college graduates. Undergrads can spend 6 weeks running workshops on American culture with the Teach-in-Huế program. Airfare, housing, and training covered in cost of program (USų1500-3000). Scholarships available.

STUDYING

Study-abroad programs range from basic language and culture courses to college-level classes, often for credit. In order to choose a program that best fits your needs, research as much as you can before making your decision—determine costs and duration, as well as what kinds of students participate in the program, what sort of accommodations are provided, and any academic or age requirements that might be a part of the program. There are many programs out there, so be sure to take your time in finding the program that best fits your interests. Anyone studying economic development, particularly, will find a number of programs in Vietnam that fit his or her field of study.

VISA INFORMATION. You'll need more than just a tourist visa to study for a long period of time in Vietnam. Luckily, **student visas** are rather easy to obtain. You can arrange for one ahead of time by having your host institution write a letter to obtain the visa for you, or they can transfer your visa once you're there (but you'll have to leave the country and come back in order for the status of your visa to change). Student visas generally last for one year but can be extended, and you'll be required to attend a minimum number of hours of class per week. Visit the website of your country's embassy (see **Embassies,** p. 13) to download an application form.

Decide carefully about enrolling in a study-abroad program where most of the other students speak your home language. You may feel more comfortable in the community, but you will not have the same opportunity to practice a foreign language or to befriend other international students. For accommodations, dorm life provides a better opportunity to mingle with fellow students, but there is less of a chance to experience the local scene. Living with a family, one has the potential to build lifelong friendships with Vietnamese citizens and to experience day-to-day life in more depth, but conditions can vary greatly from family to family. Most organizations are usually more than willing to work with you to find the right fit.

Most of the programs are located in larger cities, where there are universities or other pre-existing institutions. Some of the programs offer their own study centers, whereas others offer courses through Vietnamese institutions such as Vietnam National University. You will have a better chance to interact with Vietnamese students if you chose the latter. The programs range in length from a few weeks to a year, so you shouldn't have any problems finding something that fits your ideal commitment.

UNIVERSITIES

Most university-level study-abroad programs are conducted in Vietnamese, although many programs offer classes in English and beginner- and lower-level language courses. Those relatively fluent in Vietnamese may find it cheaper to enroll directly in a university abroad, although getting college credit may be more difficult. You can search **www.studyabroad.com** for various study abroad programs that meet your criteria, including your desired location and focus of study. The following is a list of organizations that can help place students in university programs abroad, or have their own branch in Vietnam.

AMERICAN PROGRAMS

The programs listed below are open to students enrolled in American universities. Some of the programs are open to adults in addition to students. Check the website for information about your eligibility. Also, check with the study abroad office at your home institution and see what sort of advice they have to offer.

Center for Study Abroad, 325 Washington Ave. S #93, Kent, WA 98032, USA (☎206-726-1498; www.centerforstudyabroad.com/vietnam.html). Summer-, semester-, and year-long language-intensive study-abroad programs open to students and adults (min. age 18). Classes at Vietnam National University in HCMC.

CET Vietnamese Immersion Program, 1920 N St. NW, Ste. 200, Washington, D.C. 20036, USA (☎800-225-4262; www.cetacademicprograms.com). Semester and summer study programs open to students. Fall and spring programs involve language immersion in Hà Nội and classes in HCMC; summer program based in HCMC. Volunteer internship opportunities included in program.

City College of San Francisco, Study Abroad Coordinator, 50 Phelan Ave., Box C212 San Francisco, CA 94112, USA (☎415-239-3778; studyabroad@ccsf.edu). Undergraduate, graduate students, and teachers are all welcome on this 2- to 4-week winter program. US$3000 fee includes airfare.

Council on International Educational Exchange (CIEE), 7 Custom House St., Portland, ME 04101, USA (☎800-40-STUDY/800-407-8839; www.ciee.org/study). Offers semester- and year-long programs in Hà Nội at Vietnam National University. Vietnamese language instruction included in study plan, as well as optional internship, work, and volunteer opportunities.

International Association for the Exchange of Students for Technical Experience (IAESTE), 10400 Little Patuxent Pkwy. Ste. 250, Columbia, MD 21044, USA (☎410-997-2200; www.aipt.org/subpages/iaeste_us/index.php). Offers 8- to 12-week internships in Vietnam for college students who have completed 2 years of technical study. US$50 application fee.

School for International Training, College Semester Abroad, Admissions, Kipling Rd., P.O. Box 676, Brattleboro, VT 05302, USA (☎888-272-7881 or 802-258-3212; www.sit.edu/studyabroad/asia/vietnam.html). Semester-long program in Vietnam (US$13,000-16,000) focuses on culture and development and involves combination of travel and homestays. Open to undergraduates.

SUNY Brockport Vietnam Program (☎800-298-SUNY/800-298-7869; www.brockport-abroad.com/thirdlvl/vietnam_3rd.html). Summer-, semester-, and year-long programs in Đà Nẵng open to undergraduate and graduate students enrolled in American universities. Classes at Đà Nẵng University, Duy Tân University, and the government-run School of Politics. Program includes community service projects.

INTERNATIONAL PROGRAMS

The following programs are not limited to students at American universities, although some are limited to students at universities in other countries. Some exclude adults, so check the websites to find out more.

Australian National University: Year-in-Vietnam, Level 2 Baldessin Precinct Building, Faculty of Asian Studies Entrance, Australian National University campus, Acton, Canberra, ACT 0200 Australia (☎616 125 0006; www.anu.edu.au/asianstudies/contacts.html). Year-long study-abroad program involving intensive language and multidisciplinary study. Open to students enrolled in Australian universities.

IBike Tours, 4887 Columbia Dr. South, Seattle, WA 98108, USA (☎/fax 206-767-0848; www.ibike.org/ibike/vietnam/index.htm). 2-week bike tours for well-conditioned beginners and more advanced cyclists. US$1500 includes a support van as well as 2 meals and 60-120km of biking per day.

Kulturstudier, Markveien 35B, 0554 Oslo, Norway (☎22 85 80 22; mail@kulturstudier.no). Semester-long development studies program in Hội An. Open to undergraduates, graduates, and professionals. Previous knowledge of the subject not required. Open to people of all nationalities.

Pacific Challenge, P.O. Box 3151, Eugene, OR 97403, USA (☎800-655-3513; hq@pacificchallenge.org). A 2-month study and excursion through Thailand, Laos, Vietnam, and Cambodia; can be used for college credit. Non-students ages 18-30 are welcome, too.

HIGH-SCHOOL PROGRAMS

Pacific International Exchange, 8880 Rio San Diego, Suite 1045, San Diego, CA 92108, USA (☎619-238-6767; www.pieusa.org). Summer-, semester-, and year-long homestay programs in Hà Nội and HCMC for students ages 15-19.

Where There Be Dragons, P.O. Box 4651, Boulder, CO 80306, USA (☎800-982-9203; www.wheretherebedragons.com). A 6-week summer study and service program for students aged 16-19 involving homestays and travel throughout the country, in addition to language classes. The US$6700 fee includes airfare from Los Angeles, CA.

LANGUAGE SCHOOLS

Language schools can be independently run international or local organizations or divisions of foreign universities. They rarely offer college credit, but they're a good alternative to university study, providing a deeper focus on the language and a slightly less rigorous courseload. These programs are also good for high school students who might not feel comfortable in a university program.

Vietnamese Advanced Summer Institute (VASI; www.streamingmedia.org/vasi). A program administered through the 12-member Group of Universities for the Advancement of Vietnamese Abroad (GUAVA). Offers a 2-month advanced language program during the summer at the Hà Nội University of Foreign Study and the Saigon Vietnamese Language School for Foreigners. Offered to 12 individuals selected nationally; proficiency in Vietnamese required. Coursework is the equivalent of a year's worth of academic work.

COOKING SCHOOLS

Vietnamese food is popular right now, and the local masters are more than aware of this. For the most part, your best bet is to simply inquire at your favorite restaurant to see if there are any opportunities to take a class or watch a demonstration—most chefs at least provide the latter. You'll probably see signs offering evening or afternoon classes, so keep your eyes peeled. If you have some extra cash and are extremely interested in Vietnamese fare, you can also check out culinary-focused trips online, but they're not recommended unless you're pressed for time and not for money. The few options listed below may not be the cheapest, so do your own research once in Vietnam.

Hai's Scout Cafe, 98 Nguyễn Thái Học, Hội An, Vietnam (☎ 863 210; info@visithoian.com). Offers nightly Vietnamese cooking classes. During the 2hr. class (starting at 6pm), students make grilled fish in banana leaves, spring rolls, and squid salad, and then they eat their own dishes along with other Hội An specialities. 125,000Đ covers enrollment and the meal. The teacher speaks great English and is very funny. There is also a 235,000Đ morning class, starting at 8:15am, given by the same teacher, which involves a visit to the market and a boat trip down the river. Make rice paper, pancakes, and eggplant, and learn how to decorate your food. Inquire at the cafe for more details.

Ms. Vy's Cooking School, The Cargo Club, 107-109 Nguyễn Thái Học, Hội An, Vietnam (☎ 510 910 489). Learn the family secrets from a master.

Red Bridge Cooking School, 4 Cam Thanh, Hội An, Vietnam (☎ 510 933 222, mobile 913 457 029). Half-day courses include a trip to the market and the opportunity to prepare and delight in a delicious lunch.

Thánh Hôi Phu Nứ Women's Group, 11 Ly Thưởng Kiệt, Huế, Vietnam (☎ 823 231). Teaches nightly classes to men and women in English M-Sa.

Vietnamese Cookery School, 117 Diện Biên Phủ, Hồ Chí Minh City, Vietnam (☎ 823 5872; www.vietnamcookery.com). Offers day-long courses in traditional Vietnamese cooking for amateurs and professionals.

WORKING

The Vietnamese government is wary of giving jobs to foreigners and generally restricts foreign employment to jobs requiring skills not readily available in the country. Teaching English is the most commonly available job, though some foreigners can find local editing and publishing jobs. If you want to work in Vietnam, you'll need to secure a business visa.

VISA INFORMATION. You'll need to obtain a **business visa** to be employed in Vietnam, which requires your sponsor organization in Vietnam to apply for one for you (in addition to the normal visa requirements, listed on p. 15). If you land in Vietnam and find a job afterward, you'll have to ask the organization to transfer the status of your visa and leave the country for a few days (probably just to head into Cambodia or Laos). Check the website or call your country's embassy for details.

TEACHING ENGLISH

Teaching professionally in Vietnam almost always requires official certification such as **TEFL (Teaching English as a Foreign Language), TESOL (Teach English to Speakers of Other Languages),** or **CERTA (Cambridge Certificate in English Speaking to Adults).** Certification programs are surprisingly expensive, but they often guarantee placement into paid positions in the country, and some program fees include airfare and housing costs. Most programs require applicants to have a B.A. or higher; teaching experience is not usually necessary but often ensures better placement and a higher-paying position after certification. Undergraduates can sometimes get summer positions teaching or tutoring in Vietnam, but these jobs are relatively hard to come by and generally pay very little.

English speakers working in private schools are most often hired for English-immersion classrooms where no Vietnamese is spoken. Those volunteering or teaching in poorer public schools are more likely to be working in both languages.

Placement agencies or university fellowship programs are the best resources for finding teaching jobs. Alternatively, you can make contact directly with schools or just try your luck once you get there. The best time to look once in Vietnam is several weeks before the start of the school year.

Experimental Learning International (ELI), P.O. Box 9282, Denver, CO 80209, USA (☎303-321-8278; www.eliabroad.org/volunteer/vietnam). Teach English or French in Hà Nội or a nearby town. Summer-school and school-year positions available. US$700, not including accommodations.

ILA Vietnam, 402 Nguyễn Thị Minh Khai, District 3, Hồ Chí Minh City, Vietnam (☎8 929 0100; www.ilavietnam.com). All applicants must have a B.A. and TEFL qualifications. A few summer positions, in addition to year- and semester-long positions, are available.

International Schools Services (ISS), 15 Roszel Rd., Box 5910, Princeton, NJ 08543-5910, USA (☎609-452-0990; www.iss.edu). Hires teachers for more than 200 overseas schools, including one in HCMC. Candidates must have a college degree, 2 years of teaching experience, and usually teacher certification. 2-year commitment expected.

LanguageCorps, 101 Longfellow Rd., Sudbury, MA 01776, USA (☎877-216-3267; www.languagecorps.com). Flagship program (US$4395) includes 4-week TESOL certification course, cultural and Vietnamese-language training, excursions throughout Vietnam, and guaranteed job placement. LanguageCorps also hosts TESOL-only and short-term programs (US$1690-2595).

TEFL International, 72 Pentyla Baglan Rd., Port Talbot, SA12 8AD, UK (☎709 216 5424; www.teflcourse.com/locations/vietnam.htm). Offers 1-month English-language CELTA (US$1500) course in Vietnam, then helps find you a paid teaching job in Vietnam.

Trung Tâm Anh Ngữ Sydney (Sydney Center of English), 26 Lương Ngọc Quyến, Hà Nội (☎926 0762; sydneycentre@fpt.vn). This and many other English-language schools hire mostly native speakers to teach English to Vietnamese locals. Wages and hours will vary significantly for each teacher and each week, but hours usually include weekends and evenings.

BEYOND TOURISM

HÀ NỘI

Hà Nội evokes images of a stern, austere bastion of Vietnamese Communism, ravaged by war and closed to the world. Visitors to the capital, however, will be surprised to find themselves in one of Southeast Asia's most charming cities. With its Chinese architecture, majestic French colonial buildings, and tree-lined lanes, this ancient city of lakes extends a reserved but genuine welcome. Less cosmopolitan than Hồ Chí Minh City, less touristy than Hội An, less industrial than Đà Nẵng, Hà Nội is kinder and gentler than its southern rivals. The hard-core Communist era is on the wane; the almost overnight transformation of the infamous "Hà Nội Hilton" prison into the Hà Nội Tower Commercial Center was an omen of things to come. Hammers and sickles still adorn the cityscape, but the *đổi mới* policies are rapidly reshaping the face of the city. Construction is rampant throughout the city, as the ever-growing economy begins to sculpt the country's capital.

Tourism has been on the rise in Hà Nội in recent years. The Old Quarter has stepped up as the city's tourist enclave, with hotels geared toward foreigners, travel cafes, and Western restaurants popping up left and right. The rest of Hà Nội hasn't yet caught on, but the construction of hotels along the shores of romantic West Lake and the rise of souvenir shops in the handicraft villages surrounding Hà Nội confirm that the city is still changing. For now, plenty of hidden gems remain, revealing a different Hà Nội to the curious and open-minded.

To most backpackers, Hà Nội is a gateway in or out of Vietnam or a haven of luxury and infrastructure on their journey through less-accommodating northern Vietnam. Either way, it would be a pity to pass through this beautiful ancient city without establishing at least a brief acquaintance with its unique ambience, turbulent history, savory cuisine, and cozy cafes.

HIGHLIGHTS OF HÀ NỘI

PAY YOUR RESPECTS at the **Hồ Chí Minh Mausoleum** (p. 126), where the man's body is preserved à la Lenin in an huge, climate-controlled edifice. Ah, communism.

PAY YOUR RESPECTS, AGAIN, this time to the Buddha at the otherworldly ■ **Perfume Pagoda** (p. 131). This epicenter of Buddhism in northern Vietnam is located against a magical backdrop of cliffs and verdant rice paddies.

PAY MONEY INSTEAD OF YOUR RESPECTS for the herbs and silks of the Old Quarter's **specialty trade streets** (p. 113), a labyrinthine, centuries-old market zone. Old-fashioned goods are also sold at the handicraft villages (p. 133) outside the city.

BELIEVE IN A JUST AND WONDERFUL GOD at Tây Hồ's ■ **Kem Bảo Oanh** (p. 129), purveyor of frozen coconut ecstasy; a walk by the nearby **lakes** (p. 129) showcases Hà Nội at its most beautiful.

STUFF YOURSELF all over the city. From **streetside bowls of phở** to **black-tie French fusion restaurants,** Hà Nội is an epicurean's delight.

GET EDUCATED at the excellent ■ **Museum of Ethnology** (p. 130), devoted to Vietnam's ethnic minority groups. The informative displays are a great precursor to trips to Montagnard villages in the Northwest Highlands.

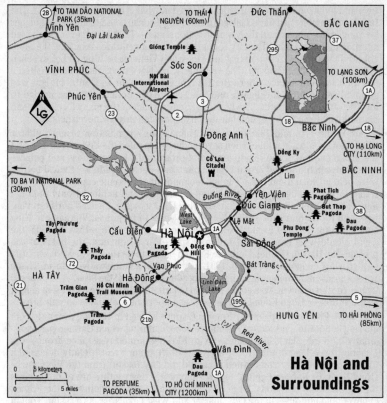

Hà Nội and Surroundings

HISTORY

Due to its location in the middle of the Red River delta, Hà Nội has always been a social and commercial center. Archaeological discoveries indicate that the area was inhabited by the end of the Paleolithic Period, some 20,000 years ago. However, about three millennia later, the Gulf of Tonkin flooded the delta, forcing the inhabitants to flee to the mountains. The area was uninhabited during the Neolithic period, and it wasn't until the beginning of the Bronze Age that settlements sprung up again in the Hà Nội area.

The first recorded history of Hà Nội concerns the resistance of the **Hùng Dynasty** against the invading Qin Chinese in 258 BC. Thực Phán established his capital in Cổ Loa, about 15km north of what is now Hà Nội, where he constructed a spiral citadel. However, he and his capital fell in 207 BC when he was defeated by Triệu Đà, general of the Chinese Hán Dynasty. During the ensuing millennium of Chinese occupation, Hà Nội lost its import as a geographical hub.

In AD 1010, King Lý Thái Tổ of the **Lý Dynasty,** believing he saw a dragon rise from Hoàn Kiếm Lake, moved his capital there and named it Thăng Long, **"City of the Soaring Dragon."** In Vietnamese culture, ◢dragons bring rain, and therefore good luck. It comes as no surprise, then, that during the centuries that followed, Thăng Long flourished. Its markets attracted merchants and artisans from as far as

Java and India, and a true bourgeoisie formed in what is now the Old Quarter. The **Temple of Literature and Royal College** (p. 130) were constructed to encourage higher learning, while poetry and the visual arts flourished—Thăng Long even developed a trendy nightlife scene. The city spent the next four centuries rebuffing the Mongols and the Chinese, culminating in 1418, when Vietnamese King Lê Lợi expelled the occupying Ming Dynasty. The **Lê Dynasty,** Hà Nội's next rulers, constructed a fortified forbidden city where the Hà Nội Citadel is now. Confucianism was adopted as the official religion, and the Temple of Literature was expanded to include official doctorates. The Lê kings tried to kick out the many foreigners and unemployed from their capital, but the city's population grew nevertheless.

During the 17th and 18th centuries, Thăng Long's population reached almost 20,000 households, in a time when several dynasties ruled the Red River Delta and the urban centers of the region grew and prospered. Many pagodas and palaces were constructed in and around the capital, and demonstrations of naval battles were held in Hoàn Kiếm Lake. Though an important economic center, the city still relied largely on agriculture and small merchants and achieved only regional importance. Then, in 1788, the Chinese Qing Dynasty again invaded northern Vietnam and took control of Thăng Long for a year. In response, Vietnamese King Quang Trưng decided to move the capital to the more secure Huế. In 1805, the royal citadel was demolished to make space for a new one, the basis of the present-day Hà Nội Citadel. Until the French occupation, the city served primarily as a growing economic center. In 1831, as part of an administrative reform, Thăng Long was given the name Hà Nội, meaning **"City in a Bend of the River."** The imperial magic, for the moment, was gone. The Old Quarter began to take its present shape, as the shores of Hoàn Kiếm Lake become an important civil and economic area.

In 1873, French troops under Francis Garnier arrived in Hà Nội, promptly conquering it. Sporadic periods of resistance ensued, during which Garnier was assassinated and the Black Butterflies (an anti-French armed resistance group) was formed; these lasted until 1884, when all of Vietnam was officially declared a French protectorate. The French renamed the city **Tonkin** (from the Vietnamese Đông Kinh, or **Eastern Capital**) and reshaped it, constructing broad boulevards through its neighborhoods, large colonial administrative buildings in the French Quarter, and churches in the Old Quarter and West Lake area. As a result, Tonkin lost much of its Chinese character and became distinctly French. In 1902, it became capital of French Indochina.

In September 1940, the Japanese invaded Tonkin, beginning a five-year period of exploitation and starvation all over Vietnam. When they withdrew in 1945, French authority was weak, enabling the Communists to exert their influence. That same year, **Hồ Chí Minh** proclaimed an independent Vietnam on the spot where he now rests, and in 1946 the Communists began armed resistance against the French. Tonkin was not much affected, as most of the combat took place in the mountains, but when the French surrendered in 1954, Hồ Chí Minh's Communists were enthusiastically received in the new country's capital—once again renamed Hà Nội.

During the **American War,** US planes bombed Hà Nội repeatedly, but relative to the rest of the country, the northern capital was practically unscathed. With the aid of foreign powers like the Soviet Union, the northern government managed to keep the capital and the military functioning. The Long Biên Bridge was reconstructed after each bombing (which stopped when rumors spread that POWs were forced to rebuild it), and Đường Thanh Niên was constructed by young volunteers to facilitate military transport. Although much of the offensive action of the NLF took place in southern Vietnam and a fair amount of organization took place secretly in HCMC, Hà Nội served as the government capital from which Hồ Chí Minh and his Communist party controlled the action.

Following the war, aid from the Soviet Union decreased and the Chinese attacked (and we repelled yet again), leading to the expulsion of all Chinese from Hà Nội. In response to dire economic and diplomatic straits, the government implemented the *đổi mới* market reforms in 1986. The trade and influx of cash that followed benefited Hà Nội greatly, especially after US President Clinton lifted the American trade embargo in 1994. The Asian **financial crisis** of the late 1990s, however, curbed the city's prosperity. Subsequently, the government lifted a number of restrictions on tourism, and the economy has turned around. The future, at least for now, seems bright for the charming lakeside capital.

▐ INTERCITY TRANSPORTATION

BY PLANE

Flights into Hà Nội land at **Nội Bài International Airport,** 35km north of the city (about a 45min. drive). There's a 25,000Đ domestic departure tax and a US$14 tax for international flights. The white Nội Bài Transport Co-op booth right outside the airport runs **taxis** to (US$10) and from (US$8.50) town. Most travelers split the fare with one or two others, so ask around. **Minibus** tickets purchased on board run for 25,000Đ, though they're mostly reserved for locals. Be careful with airport transportation: sometimes travelers are misled by the fact that multiple guest-houses have the same name (see **"The Sincerest Form of Flattery,"** p. 106), so make sure you know the address. The cheapest and slowest way to and from the airport is public bus #7 (5000Đ), which stops in front of the airport and heads downtown. **Vietnam Airlines minibuses** (☎ 886 5054) also run between the airport and city every 30min. (45-60min., US$2), stopping at the Vietnam Airlines office on Quang Trưng. To head back to the airport, call Nội Bài Airport Taxis (☎ 886 5615) or Vietnam Airlines Airport Taxis (☎ 883 3333) to arrange for pickup.

 Keep your baggage tags or you won't be allowed to claim your bags. **Keep your stamped immigration card with your passport at all times;** you'll need it to leave the country.

Several airlines operate domestic and international flights from Hà Nội: **Cathay Pacific Airways,** 49 Hai Bà Trưng (☎ 826 7298); **China Airlines,** 18 Trần Hưng Đạo (☎ 824 2688); **Lao Aviation,** 269 Kim Mã (☎ 846 4873); **Malaysia Airlines,** 15 Ngô Quyền (☎ 826 8820); **Pacific Airlines,** 100 Lê Duẩn (☎ 733 2162); **Singapore Airlines,** 17 Ngô Quyền (☎ 826 8888); **Thai Airways,** 44B Lý Thường Kiệt (☎ 826 6893); **Vietnam Airlines,** 1 Quang Trưng, at the intersection with Tràng Thi (☎ 825 0888; open M-F 7am-6:30pm, Sa-Su 8-11:30am and 1:30-5pm). Sometimes two airlines will share one plane leaving from Hà Nội. In that case, purchase your ticket from Vietnam Airlines, as it is usually US$20 cheaper. Be aware that the prices listed in the chart above vary with the season—they're usually cheapest March through May and September through November. Make sure you also check up on discount airlines online: **www.tigerairways.com** and **www.jetstarasia.com** can provide cheap tickets, and **www.fare.net** compares prices from different airlines. Remember too that many accommodations will book your flights for you, if you prefer.

DESTINATION	FREQUENCY	PRICE	DESTINATION	FREQUENCY	PRICE
Đà Nẵng	3 per day	825,000Đ	Hong Kong	1-2 per day	US$272
Hồ Chí Minh City	6-8 per day	1,525,000Đ	Kuala Lumpur	2-3 per day	US$250
Huế	3 per day	825,000Đ	Manila	1 per day	US$280
Nha Trang	1 per day	1,325,000Đ	Singapore	1-2 per day	US$310
Bangkok	3 per day	US$155	Vientiane	2 per day	US$100

BY TRAIN

Trains are the safest, most comfortable mode of domestic transport in Vietnam. Reserving a sleeper is well worth the extra cost, as the seating compartments sometimes get quite crowded.

Hà Nội Railway Station (Gà Hà Nội), 120 Lê Duẩn (☎825 3949), at the west end of Trần Hưng Đạo, a 10min. cyclo ride (10,000-15,000Đ) from the city center. Travelers arriving in Hà Nội from Lạng Sơn, Lào Cai, and southern Vietnam disembark here. Purchase tickets for southern destinations at Counter 1, the booking window for foreigners in the main building (open daily 7am-12:30pm and 1-8:45pm). Counter 2, beside the tourist window, exchanges currency. Always buy tickets at least 1 day in advance to get the seat or sleeper you want. **Save your ticket** or you will have to pay again upon arrival. Fares vary by train speed. Prices listed reflect the full range of amenities. To: **Đà Nẵng** (15-19hr.; 3, 7, 11pm; 410,000-580,000Đ); **Hải Phòng** (3hr.; 7, 9am, 2, 6pm; 33,000Đ); **Hồ Chí Minh City** (32-41hr.; 3, 7, 11pm; 410,000-1,200,000Đ); **Huế** (12-16hr.; 3, 7, 11pm; 220,000-500,000Đ); **Nha Trang** (24-32hr.; 3, 7, 11pm; 410,000-950,000Đ); **Ninh Bình** (2½-3hr.; 3, 7, 11pm; 33,000-45,000Đ); **Sa Pa** via **Lào Cai** (9hr.; 6:15am, 9:20pm; 72,000-260,000Đ); **Vinh** (5-7hr.; 11pm; 85,000-165,000Đ).

Other Departure Points: Buy tickets for **Hải Phòng, Lạng Sơn,** and **Lào Cai** at Hà Nội Railway Station, at the booth near Gate 5 (open daily 7am-12:30pm and 1-7pm), up to 2hr. before departure; otherwise buy them at the station. On the opposite side of the tracks from the main station (accessible via Trần Quý Cáp), daily trains run to **Lạng Sơn** (5:40am, 10pm; 78,000Đ). Trains to **Hải Phòng** (2hr.; 29,000Đ) leave from **Long Biên Station (Ga Long Biên)** near Đồng Xuân Market. Trains also leave from **Gia Lâm Station (Gà Gia Lâm)** across the Red River (2 blocks north of the **Gia Lâm** bus station) and head to: **Hải Phòng** (12:40, 3:35pm; 23,000Đ); **Lạng Sơn** (6½hr.; 6:10, 7:10am, 1:50pm; 28,000Đ); **Lào Cai** (6:35am, 10:30pm; 60,000-70,000Đ).

BY BUS

Using public buses requires patience for overcrowded, jostling rides that leave only when full, regardless of quoted departure time. In true Vietnamese style, the prices below are approximations, but don't be overcharged: current prices are usually clearly listed in the bigger stations. Try to buy your ticket at the station. On board, the collector may demand an inflated fare.

Gia Lâm Bus Station, 3km across the Red River on the left. To: **Hải Phòng** (2½hr.; 9-12 per day 6am-4:30pm; 25,000Đ); **Hạ Long City** (3hr.; every hr. 6am-3pm; 35,000Đ); **Lạng Sơn** (5hr.; every hr. from 7am; 30,000Đ). Motorbike to the station 15,000Đ.

Southern Bus Station (Bến Xe Nam Hà Nội), on Đường Giải Phóng, the extension of Lê Duẩn, 5km south of the train station. For all destinations south of Hà Nội. To **Điện Biên Phủ** (16-20hr.; 4, 9am, 1pm; 130,000Đ); **HCMC** (1-2 days; 10am-3pm; 310,000Đ); **Ninh Bình** (2½hr.; every 2hr.; 32,000Đ).

Há Đông Bus Station, down Tôn Đức Thắng, a 20min. cyclo ride from the city center (15,000-25,000Đ), in the suburb of Há Đông. To **Lào Cai** (20hr.; 5am; 86,000Đ) and **Sơn La** (8hr.; 5:30am; 68,000Đ). To get to **Mai Châu,** head toward Sơn La and ask to get off at **Tòng Đâu.**

Tourist buses: More comfortable and reliable, but also more expensive. An established bus line departs daily at 7pm from **Sinh Cafe,** 18 Lương Văn Can (☎828 7552 or 928 6631; www.tosercohanoi.com) to: **Đông Hà** (12½hr.; US$11); **Huế** (14½hr.; US$12) via **Ninh Bình** (2hr.; US$5); **Quang Bình** (10hr.; US$10); **Vinh** (6hr.; US$11). A popular **open-tour ticket** to **HCMC** (US$27) via **Đà Nẵng, Hội An,** and **Nha Trang** lets you get off at any of these towns and then jump back on the bus to the next destination southward at your leisure. Those who want to get off at **Đà Lạt** can buy the special US$29 open ticket. There are innumerable other tourist cafes in Hà Nội, many by the name of "Sinh Cafe," so beware of frauds.

ORIENTATION

Hà Nội is divided into seven districts *(quận)*: **Hoàn Kiếm** (the **Old Quarter** to the north, p. 114, and the **French Quarter** to the south, p. 123), **Ba Đình** (p. 125), **Hai Bà Trưng** to the south (p. 128), **Tây Hồ** (p. 128) to the north, **Đống Đa** (p. 130) and **Cầu Giấy** (p. 130) to the west, and **Thanh Xuân** to the far southwest. Most streets in Vietnam are called *đường*, though Hà Nội still sometimes uses the word *phố* and, in the Old Quarter, *hàng*. Downtown Hà Nội is small but disorganized, with streets changing names almost every block; a good map is essential. Large color maps (10,000-30,000Đ) are available from guesthouses, bookstores, the international post office, and hawkers around **Hoàn Kiếm Lake,** the heart of central Hà Nội.

The Old Quarter, enclosed between the **Hà Nội Citadel Military Complex,** the **Red River** (Sông Hồng), and Hoàn Kiếm Lake, is divided in two by twin one-way streets going north from Hoàn Kiếm Lake (starting as **Lương Văn Can** and **Hàng Đào**) which form good points of reference in the district's confusing labyrinth. The Old Quarter is made up of small alleys named after the goods sold (or once sold) there. A backpacker's heaven of small shops, restaurants, bars, tourist cafes, and hotels, this area north of and around Hoàn Kiếm Lake is also the oldest and most interesting district. Nightlife, cuisine, and accommodations in the area south of Hoàn Kiếm Lake and even west of the Citadel, though, are beginning to attract more and more visitors. From the Citadel, **Đường Lê Duẩn** leads south to **Bảy Mẫu Lake** in the more residential Hai Bà Trưng district, and west (down Khâm Tiên) to Đống Đa's pagodas and small lakes. Farther north, up **Đường Hùng Vương,** the Ba Đình district overlooking **West Lake** (Hồ Tây) hosts the **Hồ Chí Minh Mausoleum,** the **Temple of Literature,** most embassies, and the majority of Hà Nội's expats.

> **HOW TO USE THIS CHAPTER.** Hà Nội is best experienced one *quận* at a time. Listings for accommodations, food, sights, museums, and nightlife are grouped together by neighborhood. More general information on these aspects of Hà Nội, as well as shopping and specific listings for entertainment, is located after the practical information below.

LOCAL TRANSPORTATION

Taxis: Everywhere in Hà Nội. Lines form outside the Vietnam Airlines office, the train station, and major hotels. **Hanoi Taxi** (☎853 5252) or **Huong Lua Taxi** (☎825 2525) will pick you up curbside (8000Đ per km). Insist that the driver use the meter. **Airport Taxi** (☎873 3333) runs to and from the airport (160,000Đ).

Cyclos and Motorbike Taxis (xe ôm): Abundant and cheap 3-wheeled **cyclos** (a.k.a. pedicabs) are the bastard children of rickshaws and tricycles. Banned from most major thoroughfares, they are nonetheless a fun must-try for any traveler. Perfect for 1 person, perhaps a little cramped for 2. Agree on a price beforehand (15,000-30,000Đ per hr.; usually 5000Đ is a fair rate within town). Ask hotel employees for a ballpark figure if you're unsure about a reasonable fare, or just ask around and haggle until you find a driver willing to take you where you want to go for your price. Hire **motorcycle taxis** for longer rides (2000-3000Đ per km; 15,000Đ around town). Few people wear helmets around town, but Let's Go recommends it. Be persistent in asking for one. Also keep in mind that to many of your fellow road users, traffic rules are more of a suggestion than anything else—if they even know them in the first place. Never let the

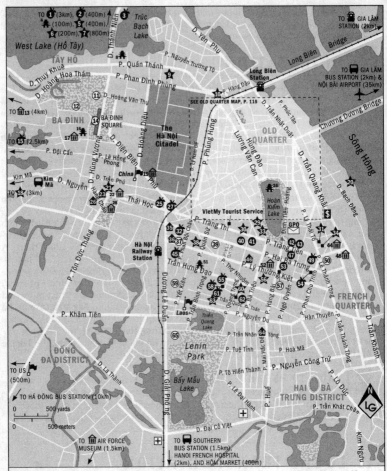

HÀ NỘI

Greater Hà Nội

♠ ACCOMMODATIONS
An Dong Hotel, **35**
Hoang Ngoc Hotel, **23**
Lotus Guest House, **46**
Polonez Hotel, **64**
Thương Hất Hotel, **36**
Tràng An Hotel, **26**

❀ FOOD
Brother's Cafe, **25**
Cơm Chay Nàng Tấm
    Vegetarian Restaurant, **55**
Đẹp Restaurant and Bar, **15**
Hải Phòng, **61**
Hoa Sữa Restaurant
    d'Application, **58**
Indochine Vietnamese
    Restaurant, **32**
Luna d'Autumno, **27**

Nhà Hàng Bánh Tôm, **3**
Nhà Nổi Hồ Tây, **2**
Pane e Vino, **49**
Phương Nguyên Quán, **1**
Qun ân Ngun, **45**
Thu Ngu, **54**

★ NIGHTLIFE
25°J Club, **60**
BoBoChaCha, **9**
Càfé 75, **63**
Café Dàn Loan Quán, **10**
Cổ Ngư Trà Lầu, **7**
Diva Art Cafe, **31**
Gốc Đa Quán, **6**
Hơ Guom Xanh, **33**
Hoa Giấy Cafe, **21**
Kem Bảo Oanh, **5**
Liễu Giai Café, **18**
Minh Minh, **29**
New Century Night Club, **30**

Press Club, **34**
Thư Giãn Bar, **38**
Titanic, **20**
Tuyết Café, **56**

● SERVICES
The Bookworm, **62**
Foreign Book Center, **43**
International SOS
    Clinic and UK Embassy, **53**
National Library, **40**
Ngoại Văn Foreign Language
    Bookshop, **42**
Thăng Long Bookshop, **47**
Vietnam Airlines Office, **41**

○ 🏛 ♣ SIGHTS
Alliance Française, **59**
Army Museum, **19**
August Cinema, **57**
Fansland Cinema, **37**

History Museum, **48**
Hồ Chí Minh Mausoleum, **14**
Hồ Chí Minh Museum, **17**
Hồ Chí Minh's
    Stilted House, **12**
Hoa Lo Prison/Hanoi
    Towers, **39**
Museum of Ethnology, **13**
Museum of Fine Arts, **22**
Museum of the Vietnamese
    Revolution, **44**
National Circus, **65**
Ngoc Sơn Temple, **24**
One Pillar Pagoda, **16**
Opera House, **50**
Presidential Palace, **11**
Quan Sư Pagoda, **51**
Quán Thánh Pagoda, **8**
Temple of Literature/
    Royal College, **28**
Trần Quốc Pagoda, **4**
Women's Museum, **52**

scenery distract you too much from the traffic situation. **Hùng Motorcycles,** 5 Đinh Liệt (☎926 0938; www.vietnamadventuretour.com). Open daily 7am-7pm. Rents both modern Honda motorbikes and (for those nostalgic for Soviet technology) Minsks for $6-25 per day or US$50 per month. They also provide helmets and raincoats and do motorcycle repair.

 ZEN AND THE ART OF MOTORCYCLE HAGGLING. Haggling with *xe ôm* drivers is indeed an art. Though it may seem cheap to haggle over a 1000Đ difference, you'll soon discover the fun of it—and your driver may reward skillful haggling with an admiring smile.
Here are some of the basics for success:
1. Don't look for a motorbike close to a museum, station, or other touristy area. Walk a few blocks and prices will fall drastically.
2. Don't seem in dire need of transport. The best approach is to respond to their "Motobai?" beckoning with some feigned doubt and then walk on a little, letting the motorbike rider come after you. This will also separate him from his buddies, making your job easier.
3. Never let your driver know that you don't know exactly where your destination is. Show him a business card of your destination and point in its direction if you know it. Always be sure, however, that he does understand exactly where you want to go.
4. Never get on the bike without first agreeing on a price. The best way is to use a notepad—"thirteen" may sound like a lot like "thirty" in the driver's ears.
5. Unless you're in the Old Quarter, never be the first to name a price. Wait for his offer, divide it by three and name that as your price. Be firm in your haggling and never concede to more than half their original price. Within the Old Quarter, immediately propose 5000Đ and don't concede a single đồng.
6. Don't be afraid to walk out of negotiations, even if there are no other motorbikes around. Chances are the driver will follow you and give in with a smile.
7. Don't lose your cool. Remain respectful even when firm.
8. Be wary of accepting rides from female bikers. If you're male, they may want to offer you a whole different service.

Bicycles (xe đạp) and Motorbike Rentals (xe máy): In spite of Hà Nội's hectic and challenging traffic, driving a motorcycle is a convenience that many think is worth the trouble. Most hotels, guesthouses, and rental shops in the Old Quarter, north of Hoàn Kiếm Lake, rent **motorbikes** (US$7-8 per day). Check out the rental shops on **Hàng Bạc** and **Ta Hiền** (US$5-6). Be warned, though, that Vietnamese traffic is not for the timid or the inexperienced. **Bicycles** can be rented from most lodging or rental shops for around 15,000Đ per day. If you plan to ride a bike or motorbike for a long time, wear something to cover your face and eyes from insects and exhaust. Helmets are usually available to rent for 5000Đ. Be prepared to fork over 1000-2000Đ when you park your bike or motorbike in busy areas: a parking guard will write a number on your seat with chalk and give you the corresponding ticket when you pay. To avoid confusion or a chalky behind, wipe off the number when you take leave.

⁊ PRACTICAL INFORMATION

TOURIST AND FINANCIAL SERVICES

TOURIST SERVICES

Tourist cafes and most hotels and guesthouses organize cheap **package tours,** which provide a hassle-free opportunity to see Northern Vietnam. For the less adventurous and time-constrained tourist, such short tours are definitely the best way to explore Vietnam's more authentic regions. Services and prices vary only slightly, but quality can vary considerably, even from one week to the next. The best and only way of verifying the quality of a tour provider is to approach tourists returning from it.

Though most hotels and guesthouses use the services of established tourist cafes, it's a good idea to approach the tour provider directly. Flags on the shop window don't imply that the corresponding language is spoken, and logos on the window don't guarantee the tourist cafe is an official representative or dealer—consider both mere decoration. Be aware of exactly what is included and what isn't, since some tourist cafes cut corners to lower costs. Small-group tours are more expensive, but they enable a more personalized and flexible experience; those few extra đồng could prevent a lot of frustration and annoyance. It's often better to spend a little extra rather than less; with each đồng or dollar you save, the quality of your tour will plummet. Check whether your guides or drivers speak at least a little English, even if just for emergencies. At the end, it is expected that you **tip your guide** a small amount if you are satisfied. Most tourist cafes also arrange **visas** to China (1 month US$25-35) and Laos (1 month US$33-50) and 30-day Vietnam **visa extensions** (US$25-40). Allow three to four days for processing, even if they tell you it's two. Some standard packages are listed below.

Hạ Long Bay: 1 night US$20-39; 2 nights, including **Cát Bà Island,** US$27-80.

Hoa Lư-Tam Cốc: daytrip US$15-20.

Mai Châu: Take either an expensive private tour or take a bus in the direction of Hòa Bình. 1 night US$20-25.

Perfume Pagoda: daytrip US$9-16.

Sa Pa: 3 nights including **Bắc Hà** US$50-70.

THE SINCEREST FORM OF FLATTERY. As more travelers head to Hà Nội, hotels, tourist agencies, and restaurants are facing an increasingly competitive market, and some have resorted to deceitful measures to snap up that foreign buck. Many establishments take on the name of other, more popular businesses in order to trick travelers into thinking they're getting the real thing. Make sure to know the exact address and telephone number of the establishment you are looking for, so you too don't fall victim to the scams of these imitators.

Some established tourist cafes include:

Green Bamboo Cafe, 24 Đương Thành (☎828 6504).

Hanoi Tour, 23 Yên Thái (☎928 7978).

ODC Travel, 63 Trúc Bạch (☎715 0789; www.odctravel.com.vn). Smaller branch at 43 Hàng Bạc (☎824 3024).

Ocean Tours, 51 Hàng Bè (☎926 0463).

Kangaroo Cafe, 18 Bảo Khánh (☎828 1996).

Queen Cafe, 50 Hàng Bè, 13 and 65 Hàng Bạc (☎826 0860; www.queencafe.com.vn).

TF Handspan Cafe, 116 Hàng Bạc (☎828 1996). Smaller branch at 18 Bảo Khánh (☎828 9931).

Wide Eyed Travel, 40 Lương Ngọc Quyến, near Bia Hơi Corner. Offers an adventurous alternative to the traditional package tour.

EMBASSIES AND FINANCIAL SERVICES

Embassies: Argentina, 360 Kim Mã (☎831 5262). Open M-F 8:30-noon and 1-4:30pm. **Australia,** 8 Đạo Tan (☎831 7755), behind Hanoi-Daewoo Hotel. Open M-F 8:30am-noon and 1-4pm. **Cambodia,** 71 Trần Hưng Đạo (☎942 4788). Visa US$20, 1-day processing; bring a photo. Open M-F 8-11:30am and 2-4:30pm. **Canada,** 31 Hùng Vương (☎734 5000). Open M-F 8am-noon and 1-5pm. **China,** 46 Hoàng Diệu (☎845 3736). For visas, go to the consulate (☎823 5569) on Trần Phú. Visa US$30, 4-day processing; US$47, 2-day processing. Bring 2 photos. Open M-F 8:30-11am. **Indonesia,** 50 Ngộc Quyền (☎825 3353). **Brazil,** T72 14 Thuy Khe (☎843 2544). Open 8:30am-noon and 1-4pm. **Laos,** 22 Trần Bình Trọng (☎942 4576). Visa US$60, 1-day processing. Bring a photo. Open M-F 8-11:30am and 1-4pm. **Malaysia,** Fortuna Hotel, GB Lang Ha (☎831 3400). Open M-F 8am-4:30pm. **Myanmar,** Block A3 Vạn Phúc, on Kim Mã (☎845 3369). Open M-F 8:30am-noon and 1:30-5pm. **New Zealand,** Level 5, 63 Lý Thái Tố (☎824 1481). Open M-F 8:30am-noon and 1-5pm. **Philippines,** 27B Trần Hưng Đạo (☎943 7873). **Singapore,** 41-43 Trần Phú (☎823 3965). **Thailand,** 63-65 Hoàng Diệu (☎823 5092). Open M-F 8:30am-noon and 1:30-5pm. **UK,** 31 Hai Bà Trưng (☎936 0500). Open daily 8:30am-4:30pm. Visa applications 8:30-11:30am only. **US,** 7 Láng Hạ (☎772 1500). Open daily 8am-noon and 1-5pm. Visa services to Cambodia, Laos, and Thailand are also available in tourist cafes.

Currency Exchange: Vietcombank (☎824 0880), on the corner of Trần Quang Khải and Lê Lai. Best exchange rates in Hà Nội. Open M-F 8-11:30am and 1-3:30pm. **ANZ Bank,** 14 Lê Thái Tố (☎825 8190), on the west bank of Hoàn Kiếm Lake, has a 24hr. **ATM.** Bank open M-F 8:30am-4pm. **Sacombank,** 87 Phố Hàng Bạc (☎926 1392), north of Hoàn Kiếm Lake, also has a 24hr. **ATM.** Bank open M-F 8am-8pm, Sa 8am-5pm, Su 8am-4pm. All of these banks exchange currency, issue traveler's checks, and offer MC/V cash advances. For currency exchange with half the hassle, change your đồng to dollars at a **jewelry shop,** and then head to the bank to get traveler's checks if you need them. The shop at 5 Hàng Trong has an authorized Vietcombank exchange bureau.

LOCAL SERVICES

Local Publications: All publications are available at most Western restaurants and guesthouses.

The Guide, published monthly with the *Vietnam Economic Times,* provides useful information on events, hotels, shops, and local services (15,000Đ).

Hà Nội Pathfinder, has a similar monthly listing with a map, although it only lists businesses that advertise.

International Women's Group, puts out one of the best guides to Hà Nội.

Timeout, lists the week's nightlife (www.vir.com.vn).

Việt Nam News, the English daily (5000Đ).

Wazzup, has free Internet publications which comes out every W (www.wazzup.com.vn).

English-Language Bookstores:

The Bookworm, 15A Ngo Van So (☎943 7226; bookworm@fpt.vn), 1 block south of Trần Hưng Đạo. Hà Nội's only English-language bookstore with a second-hand section. Buys paperbacks. Open Tu-Su 10am-7pm.

Foreign Book Center, 44 Tráng Tiền, 2nd fl. in the Tráng Tiền Bookstores complex (☎826 0313, ext. 228). Chinese, English, French, Japanese, Korean, Lao, and Russian books; specializes in a variety of "learn English" books. Open M-F 8am-9pm, Sa-Su 8am-10pm.

Ngoại Văn Foreign Language Bookshop, 64 Tráng Tiền (☎825 7376). Carries books and paperbacks. Open daily summer 8am-9:30pm; winter 8am-7:30pm.

HÀ NỘI

Thăng Long Bookshop, 55 Tráng Tiền (☎825 7043), across the road from Ngoại Văn. Sells paperbacks and phrasebooks. Open daily 8am-7pm.

Library: National Library of Vietnam (Thư Viện Quốc Gia), 31 Tràng Thi (☎825 5397). Enter across from 39 Hai Bà Trưng. A limited mix of English magazines on the 2nd fl. Dress modestly and bring a valid ID. You'll have to check your bags before entering. Open daily 8am-8pm.

Beyond Tourism:

Trung Tâm Anh Ngữ Sydney (Sydney Center of English), 26 Lương Ngọc Quyến (☎926 0762; sydneycentre@fpt.vn). This and many other English-language schools hire mostly native speakers to teach English to Vietnamese locals. Wages and hours will vary significantly for each teacher and each week, but hours usually include weekends and evenings.

VUFO-NGO Resource Center, Building L at the back of the La Thành Hotel on 218 Đội Cấn (☎832 85 70; www.ngocentre.netnam.vn). The first and best place to find volunteering opportunities in Vietnam. See **Beyond Tourism,** p. 90. Open daily 8am-noon and 1:30-5pm.

Cung Thiệu Nhi Hà Nội (The Children's Palace of Hà Nội), around the corner from the post office on 15 Trần Nguyên Han (☎091 350 0582; honghoarose@yahoo.com) is supported by the Vietnamese government as an after-school and summer-school program for teaching children ages 5-12. Hiring volunteers and paid teachers. Open daily 8am-5pm.

Nguyễn Đình Chiểu (Hà Nội's School for the Blind), 21 Lac Trung St. A massage center operated by blind masseurs trained at Saint Paul's hospital, Bạch Mai hospital, and Tue Tinh school for traditional medicine. Volunteers welcome. Open daily 8:30am-11pm.

EMERGENCY AND COMMUNICATIONS

Emergency: ☎115.

Police: ☎113. Hoàn Kiếm District Headquarters, 2 Lê Thái Tổ (☎824 4141), in the booth on the northwest corner of Hoàn Kiếm Lake. Don't expect knights in shining armor to come to your rescue.

Pharmacy: A strip of pharmacies lines Quán Sú near the intersection with Tràng Thi southwest of Hoàn Kiếm Lake. The **24hr. pharmacy** at 14 Phu Doan (☎825 5934) is small but well stocked.

Medical Services: Vietnam's national hospitals are sometimes severely overcrowded, and physicians and nurses usually speak very little English, so contact one of the organizations listed below first.

Hà Nội Family Medical Practice, 1A Van Phuc 109-112 Kim Mã (☎843 0748, emergency 09 040 1919).

Hà Nội French Hospital, 1 Phuong Mai (☎570 0740). Expat doctors provide 24hr. emergency care. US$25-30 per consultation.

International SOS Clinic, 31 Hai Bà Trưng (☎934 0555; www.internationalsos.com/countries/vietnam). From south of Hoàn Kiếm Lake, walk 1 block down Bà Triệu until you see their large office signpost. A reliable medical service for expats, with doctors who speak Dutch, English, French, Japanese, and Mandarin Chinese. 24hr. emergency care. US$75 per consultation (US$65 for a Vietnamese physician), US$58 for dental, US$33 for vaccine (US$52 for families). Medivac service (from anywhere in Vietnam to Bangkok or Singapore) available for members, but exceptions can be made for serious cases and, of course, an extra fee.

Telephones: Telephone office, 75B Đinh Tiên Hoàng (☎826 0977), next to the international post office. International calls 15,000Đ per min. Fax and phone card calls are free but don't always work. English spoken. Open daily summer 6am-10pm; winter 6am-9:30pm. **Branch office,** 66 Lương Văn Can (☎826 2999). English spoken. Open daily 6am-9pm. **Information** and **Directory** ☎1080. **International Operator (collect calls)** ☎110. Available only from post office. It can be hard to get through.

Internet Access: Most cybercafes, especially those concentrated near Hàng Bạc, offer Internet access for 50-100Đ per min. Cybercafes near Bảo Khánh are more expensive, but sometimes they're negotiable. Printing usually costs around 1000Đ. The smaller Internet cafes—usually squeezed between other stores—are 3000Đ per hr., but they're cramped and hot during the summer months. In the evenings (especially on the weekend), crowds of young Hanoians head to cybercafes for instant messaging, which slows the service, so try to fulfill your online needs during the morning or early afternoon.

Queen Salute Cafe Travel, 50 Hàng Bè (☎826 7356), has a very fast connection and plenty of computers. 4000Đ per hr.

Diểm Truy Cập Internet, 45 Lương Ngọc Quyến (☎824 7250) offers a good connection for only 3000Đ per hr.

Thanh Tùng Internet, 71 Thàng Điếu (☎828 9172). 4000Đ per hr. for a decent connection.

Nhip Sống, 72 Mã Mây (☎926 1432), near the corner of Mã Mây and Lương Ngọc Quyến. Modern computers and a good connection. You can also use your own laptop. Usually open until 1:30am.

Post Offices: International Post Center, 6 Đinh Tiên Hoàng, on the corner with Đinh Le. A large Stalinist-looking building east of Hoàn Kiếm Lake. The post office is in the main entrance. *Poste Restante* available. Sells international phone cards (to be used at public phones) for 150,000Đ, but they're about the same price as using a booth and paying per min. English spoken. Open daily summer 7am-9pm; winter 7am-8:30pm.

Express Mail: FedEx, 6 Đinh Le (☎826 4925). **DHL,** 1 Bà Triệu (☎826 5389; ctsc@fpt.vn). English spoken.

▄ MORNINGS IN HÀ NỘI

In contrast to the average pub-crawling backpacker, many Hanoians enjoy being early risers: the city wakes up around 5am and bustles with life soon after. Starting around 6am, masses of scooters swarm the streets, housewives raid the markets for the freshest fruit and vegetables, and sidewalk vendors begin to cook breakfast. But it is Hà Nội's collective **morning gymnastics,** in Lenin Park and in the park around Hoàn Kiếm Lake, that are a sight especially worth getting up before dawn. Dating back to the 1950s when Hồ Chí Minh instituted mandatory daily exercise for all Vietnamese, Hanoians have long kept up the tradition of starting their day with a workout. Men stretch, meditate, and practice martial arts; hundreds of women collectively practice aerobics to energetic techno music; youngsters play badminton and var-

IN RECENT NEWS

A BIG RED STEP IN PREVENTING HIV

The HIV/AIDS epidemic is a worldwide problem to which Vietnam isn't immune, despite common misconceptions (see **The AIDS Crisis,** p. 72). Of its 84.5 million inhabitants (Vietnam is the world's 13th most populous country), roughly 96,000 people are HIV-positive, according to official reports. However, some foreign experts estimate that the infection count is over 300,000 and is growing rapidly due to prostitution and drug use.

In June 2004, however, the Vietnamese government made a surprising, taboo-breaking move forward in preventing HIV/AIDS when Vietnam's Committee for Population, Family, and Children allowed Vietnam's first condom vending machine to be opened in the men's room of Lan Chin Beer Garden, one block away from Hà Nội's opera building. The red metal vending box (selling "OK" brand condoms for 200Đ) is the first step in a campaign to install 40 more such red dispensers in public places around the city, including railway stations, public toilets, and karaoke bars. This unusually progressive project is sponsored by the World Bank and DKT International, a non-governmental organization that sells subsidized condoms. So far, most men haven't befriended their new red pal, and condom machines are still rare, but hopefully this initiative will be a vital step to help arrest the spread of HIV in Hà Nội.

ious local sports; even elderly men and women calmly and carefully exercise in their pajamas. Hà Nội energetically greets the new day, as well as the occasional bedraggled, red-eyed tourist. The breathtaking view of the timeless Ngọc Sơn temple reflected in Hoàn Kiếm Lake in the dim light of the rising sun is a sight well worth setting your alarm clock to a painfully early hour.

EVENINGS IN HÀ NỘI

Not a morning person? Hà Nội park life regains some of its early-morning energy in the evenings. Lovers gather along the banks of the West River to cuddle on the seats of their motor bikes while families picnic outside of the Hồ Chí Minh Mausoleum. The young and single stroll through the night market open daily in the Old Quarter before heading out to local dance clubs. To get the most out of this city, it's best to wake up early, beat the heat with a midday nap, and then go out again.

ACCOMMODATIONS

ACCOMMODATIONS BY PRICE

UNDER US$6/UNDER 96,000Đ (❶)		US$10-16/160,000-255,000Đ (❸)	
Apple Hotel (117)	OQ	Anh Đào Hotel (117)	OQ
▨ Lotus Guest House (123)	FQ	An Dong Hotel (123)	FQ
Mạnh Dung Internet Guest House (116)	OQ	Long Hung Hotel (117)	OQ
Queen Salute Cafe Travel (116)	OQ	Paradise Hotel (117)	OQ
Real Darling Cafe (116)	OQ	Thanh An Hotel (117)	OQ
		Thương Hàt Hotel (123)	FQ
US$6-10/96,000-160,000Đ (❷)			
Cát Tường Hotel (116)	OQ		
Phú Hoa Hotel (117)	OQ	**US$16-30/255,000-480,000Đ (❹)**	
Sinh Travel Hotel (117)	OQ	Hoang Ngoc Hotel (126)	BĐ
▨ Thu Giang Guesthouse (116)	OQ	Polonez Hotel (128)	TH
Tràng An Hotel (126)	BĐ		
Youth Hotel (117)	OQ		
▨ Van Xuan II Hotel (116)	OQ		

BĐ Ba Đình **FQ** French Quarter **OQ** Old Quarter **TH** Tây Hồ

Because of its central location, the **Old Quarter** (p. 114) is where the great majority of tourists stay in Hà Nội; to be fair, there's no real need to stay anywhere else. Long-term apartment rentals are also available (US$125-145 per month, plus roughly 100,000Đ for electricity, and about 40,000Đ for water). Rooms near West Lake, a popular neighborhood for expats, are pricier. The *Việt Nam News* (a newspaper in English) runs advertisements for apartments for rent. **Viet My,** 4A Tràng Thi (☎826 3915), provides information about housing. Some hotels also rent long-term rooms with kitchens; they require less paperwork than apartments do.

The landlord will need to obtain a special license from the authorities to rent to a foreigner, for which a copy of your passport is required; do not accept a contract if the landlord doesn't first ask you for a copy of your passport. Contracts usually begin on the 1st or 15th of every month, but allow extra time for the paperwork.

🗋 FOOD

FOOD BY TYPE

BAKERY/SNACKS		STREET FOOD	
Baguette & Chocolat (118)	OQ ❶	Hải Tý (119)	OQ ❶
Bánh Gối Bánh Rán (118)	OQ ❶	Mrs. Lan (118)	OQ ❶
Paris Deli (118)	OQ ❷		
Tẩy Đô (118)	OQ ❶	**VEGETARIAN**	
		Cơm Chay Nàng Tấm Restaurant (124)	FQ ❸
FRENCH		The Whole Earth (119)	OQ ❷
Cyclo Bar and Restaurant (118)	OQ ❸		
� Hoa Sữa Rest. d'Application (123)	FQ ❹	**VIETNAMESE**	
		69 (117)	OQ ❸
GERMAN		Bảo Khánh (118)	OQ ❷
Kaiser Kaffee (118)	OQ ❷	BoBoChaCha (126)	BĐ ❶
		Brother's Cafe (126)	BĐ ❺
INDIAN		Bún Bò Nam Bộ (119)	OQ ❶
Tandoor Restaurant (118)	OQ ❸	Cafe Linh Phụng (118)	OQ ❷
		🔳 Cơm Việt (117)	OQ ❷
ITALIAN		Đep Restaurant & Bar (126)	BĐ ❸
Luna d'Autumno (126)	BĐ ❹	Indochine Vietnamese (124)	FQ ❹
Pane e Vino (124)	FQ ❺	La Place Cafe (119)	OQ ❸
		Lay Bac (119)	OQ ❸
NORTHWESTERN		Green Papaya Salad Vendor (119)	OQ ❶
Highway 4 (117)	OQ ❷	🔳 Little Hà Nội Restaurant (117)	OQ ❷
		Nhà Hàng Đắc Kim (119)	OQ ❷
SANDWICHES		🔳 Phương Nguyên Quán (129)	TH ❸
Bánh Mỳ (119)	OQ ❶	🔳 Qun ăn Ngon (123)	FQ ❷
No Noodles (118)	OQ ❷	Thach Chè Lộc Tái (119)	OQ ❶
		Thu Nga (124)	FQ ❶
SEAFOOD			
Hải Phong (124)	FQ ❹	**WESTERN**	
Nhà Hàng Bánh Tôm (129)	TH ❸	Pepperoni's Pizza & Cafe (119)	OQ ❸
Nhà Nổi Hồ Tây (129)	TH ❹		

BĐ Ba Đình **FQ** French Quarter **OQ** Old Quarter **TH** Tây Hồ

🎵 ENTERTAINMENT

WATER PUPPETS

You can't come to Hà Nội without visiting the **Thăng Long Water Puppet Theater,** 57 Đinh Tiên Hoàng (☎ 824 9494). This ancient art form, unique to northern Vietnam, traces its origins from rice-farmer folk culture through the court entertainment of the Lý and Trần dynasties. The puppets move and dance in a shallow pool of murky water (to hide the mechanisms operating them) and are accompanied by the voices and instruments of traditional Vietnamese musicians. Because the puppets wear out after a few months of working their magic, you can buy the used ones in souvenir shops all over the Old Quarter. The puppets display northern Vietnam's agricultural practices and act out Vietnam's history and mythology—though the show is entirely in Vietnamese, you will probably recognize the mystical turtle of Hoàn Kiếm Lake and the bright-colored flags of Vietnam's dynasties. The theater offers both close-up first-class seats (40,000Đ) and the farther back

HÀ NỘI

second-class seats (20,000Đ). Shows are daily at 5:15, 6:30, and 8pm, and last roughly one hour, beginning with a short introduction to Vietnamese folk music.

OPERA

Looming over Phố Tráng Tiên, the **Nhà Hát Lớn,** or **French Opera House,** is a majestic reminder of Hà Nội's years under French rule. Constructed in 1911 and modeled after its big brother, the Opéra de Paris, the building's Napoleonic architectural style was meant to reflect the colonial grandeur of the French Empire. Today, it is home to the Vietnam National Symphony Orchestra and hosts national celebrations. The Opera House has two main rooms: a 400-seat, three-tier theater for ballet, symphonies, and, of course, opera; and the Mirror Hall at the front, where 100 seats offer a more intimate setting. The marble interior, complete with chandeliers, mirrors, mosaics, and red carpet, has a distinctive 19th-century touch. The balcony offers a great view over the French district, and the primly manicured courtyards complete the outward appearance of this impressive anachronism. The only way to see this beautiful building from the inside, though, is to attend a performance. The calendar of events is displayed on the stairs, though some of the most exciting events come last-minute for special festivals. (59 Ngō Trúc. ☎736 6172. Tickets 80,000-180,000Đ. Free delivery available.)

CINEMA

Hà Nội has no shortage of movie theaters, but most movies are dubbed into Vietnamese. Check with the ticket counters for screenings of subtitled films.

August Cinema, 45 Phố Hàng Bai (☎825 3911). The cinema shows primarily subtitled Western movies, but check before buying your ticket. Ticket booth open daily 9am-8:30pm. Tickets 20,000-25,000Đ.

Fansland Cinema, 84 Lý Thường Kiệt (☎924 4484), next to the Saigon Hotel. Similar offerings and set-up as August Cinema. Ticket booth open daily 9am-8:30pm. Tickets 20,000-25,000Đ.

Alliance Français, 42 Phố Yết Kiêu (☎942 2970), near the Hà Nội Railway Station. French movies are shown most nights (except M) at this French governmental organization, which also provides cultural resources for Vietnamese, expats, and tourists.

Vincom City Tower, 191 Bà Triêu (☎974 3335), located on the 6th fl. of the shopping mall. This new, sleek cinema shows a large selection of blockbusters in English. A classy kind of atmosphere—high heels and button-down shirts prevail. Tickets 30,000-50,000Đ. Open daily 9am-10:30pm.

SPAS

Hà Nội is home to many spas and pampering services for the weary traveler. Establishments that provide massages, facials, manicures, and haircuts (which include a head massage) line the streets, and services usually run for under US$10. Some Western-style places offer Swedish massages, but locals tend to splurge on the more expensive Thai massage. Try them all—the same service can cost hundreds at home. For foot massages, look for the neon foot in the window.

Nguyễn Đình Chiểu, at 21 Lac Trung, a massage center operated by Hà Nội's School for the Blind (see **Beyond Tourism,** p. 108). 50,000Đ per hr. Open daily 8:30am-11pm.

Van Xuân, 59B Đương Thành (☎828 6779), across the street from the Cyclo Bar and Restaurant. Frequented by Vietnamese, this sanctuary from the bustling streets offers foot and body massages—feet soak in a tea concoction while a masseuse kneads your back. Foot massage 60,000Đ per hr.; 75,000Đ per 1½hr. Body massage 80,000Đ per hr. Special body and foot massage 120,000Đ. Open daily 10am-11pm.

DermaCare, 27 Lý Thái Tố (☎934 7438), uses a high-quality European product line, Dermatalogica, for all its services. Facials US$14-90 for 60-90mins. Also offers full-body treatments and waxing in a clean and relaxing setting. Open daily 9am-7:30pm.

🗋 SHOPPING

Years ago, each of the Old Quarter's 36 streets had its own specialty trade. Today, the legacy continues on some streets, although many stores carry a larger variety of goods. Hàng Dầu specializes in cheap **shoes** (though many of them are exported to Europe, so larger sizes are hard to find) while **funeral stones** are made on its continuation, Hàng Bè. **Electronics** manufacture is concentrated on Lý Nam Dê, though cheaper pawn shops also sell electronics on Dăng Dung. Also popular are the **silk shops** on Hàng Gai and Lương Văn Can, which sell ready-made and tailored clothing of varying quality. Phùng Khắc Khoan, a few blocks south from Hoàn Kiếm Lake, sells much cheaper fabric and has several tailors, but don't expect Hội An prices or one-day service. Hà Trung sells **leather** products; Hàng Quạt peddles colorful **funeral flags** and **religious objects;** Hàng Mã specializes in **paper products,** including votive candles burned for ancestors; Lãn Ông exudes the sweet scent of **medicinal herbs;** Hàng Bạc is home to **silver jewelry;** Hàng Đào features **clothing;** and Hàng Ngang has a huge selection of **watches. Chợ Đồng Xuân** (Đồng Xuân Market) is a night marketplace in the northern part of the Old Quarter, off the extension of Hàng Đào, selling a variety of wholesale goods including inexpensive cotton and linen fabric in the daytime and fruits, vegetables, and flowers from midnight onwards, when the market moves east onto Trần Nhật Duật. North of the market, on Hàng Khoai, are many small eating stands—the perfect place for a late-night snack. On the western side of Đồng Xuân market (on Hàng Đào), stands open up after 10pm for ◼**glitter drawing,** a favorite for Vietnamese couples. Shower bright-colored glitter over sticky paper to fill in cute (if somewhat cheesy) drawings. Sticky paper drawings go for 5000-10,000Đ—be sure to ask for a plastic cover afterward. After you've shopped till you dropped, recover with a coffee in one of Hà Nội's **coffee shops** on Hàng Hanh or Nhà Thờ (also known as Church Street, east of St. Joseph Cathedral), or have ice cream either on Phố Tráng Tiên or at the evening street vendors on the northern shore of Hoàn Kiếm Lake.

LOCALS ONLY. Leave early-morning shopping to the locals. The first sale of the day is extremely important to shop owners in Vietnam, as they believe it determines how the rest of the sales for the day will be. Foreigners are known to window shop, ask prices, and decline from buying. Morning is not the time to do this. If you go to the market in the morning, buy, or do not just ask for prices.

Keep in mind that prices in the touristy Old Quarter tend to be higher than those in other districts. For those trying to find real bargains, venture out into the shops and markets of the Hai Bà Trưng and Ba Đình districts. The help of a friendly local can make finding the right products for the right prices a lot easier, as tourists are likely to get tourist prices even outside the Old Quarter. Locals will rarely bargain for you, but they should be able to tell you which places charge fair prices.

🜂 NIGHTLIFE

BARS AND CAFES

Hà Nội's bar and cafe scene is huge, but often a little dull. Some establishments cater exclusively to foreigners; others would be surprised to see a non-Vietnamese guest; most are somewhere in between. Travelers will have no problem finding a bar to quench their thirst: every other street corner has a *bia hơi* streetbar, selling cheap, watered-down beer for as little as 2000Đ. At the corner of Lương Ngọc Quyền and Tạ Hiên is ◼**Bia Hơi Junction,** a busy and popular crossroad with four *bia hơi* bars on each of the four corners. The Old Quarter's many bars and cafes also lure in tourists and their dollars. The coffee and tea cafes that line the city's streets, perhaps the most positive vestiges of French culture, are perfect for weary travelers and leisurely evenings. Expect delicious drinks, bamboo floor seating, and sleek leather cushions imported straight from the Latin Quarter in Paris.

THE BLISS OF BIA HƠI. It's nothing fancy. It's not even that good. But this light amber homebrew is the only way to get through a sweltering, hot and humid summer day in Vietnam. Some complain of *bia hơi's* watery taste. It's a fair complaint. But the watery aspect of *bia hơi* is Vietnam's genius solution to alcohol's dehydrating ability. Don't be fooled—if you drink enough, it'll still dry you up, and despite its taste, it's still pretty alcoholic. But oh, is it *good*. The next time that local street joint tries to offer you a bottled beer, just remember that one you can get 10 *bia hơi*s for the same 15,000Đ price tag. *-Anna Pasternak*

KARAOKE

Karaoke is one of Hà Nội's favorite pastimes and an amazing way to begin a night on the town. Karaoke bars offer living room-like spaces with several TV screens and microphones, allowing small groups to practice their singing talents while enjoying a drink. You'll spot plenty of neon karaoke signs in the Old and French Quarters, especially on and around Nguyễn Hữu Huân (northwest of Hoàn Kiếm Lake) and in the alleys on Lý Quốc Sư (north of St. Joseph's Cathedral). New bars are also opening on Lò Sũ, to the east of the Water Puppet Theater. All have a similar selection of songs in English, French, and Vietnamese, but it's a good idea to check the song list first if you're looking for something in particular. Expect to pay 50,000-80,000Đ, but feel free to negotiate. Most karaoke bars open in the late afternoon and close at midnight. You may find men with hired girls in some places, but the bars themselves have no affiliation with prostitution.

MASSAGE

Each evening, **street masseurs** offer their services on sidewalk mats and mattresses near the crossing of Điện Biên Phủ and Đường Lê Duẩn, just south of the Citadel and west of the railway tracks. Usually the fixed cost per massage (regardless of duration) is 10,000Đ. Expect a little pain. Street masseurs are always male and their services are for men only. Women have other options for massages (p. 112).

OLD QUARTER

Hoàn Kiếm district is divided up into two parts: the Old Quarter and the French Quarter. Enclosed by the **Hà Nội Citadel, Hoàn Kiếm Lake,** and the **Red River,** the Old Quarter used to be a fortified part of the Emperor's Citadel and was inhabited by artisans from all over the Red River Delta. With its complex patchwork of narrow tree-shaded streets that have different names with every block, the Old Quarter can be a daunting maze. Due to the recent flourishing of the tourism industry in this area, however, you'll easily find a hotel, cafe, restaurant, *bia hơi*, and karaoke bar on almost any street. The Old Quarter's small streets are named after the goods sold (or once sold) there, so don't be surprised to find that silk products, bamboo, or mechanic shops have taken over a given area. The Old Quarter has managed to maintain a fine balance between tradition and modernization: the new hotels and tourist cafes could not crowd out the many temples that adorn these streets, the homey coffeehouses and bars, and the numerous street eateries. All in all, the Old Quarter has the best food, accommodations, and shopping.

ACCOMMODATIONS

Scattered (and sometimes hidden) throughout the Old Quarter is a variety of mini-hotels, guesthouses, and hostels; the list below is just the tip of the iceberg. Most are located north of the Hoàn Kiếm Lake and also function as tourist and Internet

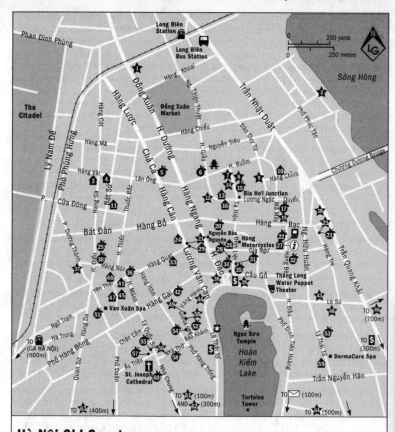

Hà Nội Old Quarter

ACCOMMODATIONS

Anh Đào Hotel, **10**
Apple Hotel, **16**
Cat Tuong Hotel, **26**
Long Hung Hotel, **59**
Mạnh Dung Internet
 Guest House, **47**
Paradise Hotel, **41**
Phú Hoa Hotel, **24**
Queen Salute Travel
 Cafe, **27**
Real Darling Cafe, **33**
Sinh Travel Hotel, **11**
Tạm Tương
 Guesthouse, **40**
Thanh An Hotel, **3**
Thu Giang
 Guesthouse, **45**
Van Xuan II Hotel, **13**
Youth Hotel, **29**
Youth Hotel, **4**

FOOD

69, **17**
Baguette & Chocolat, **5**
Bánh Gối Bánh Rán, **55**
Bánh Mỳ, **34**
Bảo Khánh, **52**
Bún Bò Nam Bộ, **30**
Cafe Linh Phụng, **31**
Com Việt, **53**
Cyclo Bar and
 Restaurant, **51**
Hải Tý, **6**
Highway 4, **21**
Kaiser Kaffee, **32**
La Place Café, **57**
Lay Bac, **20**
Little Hanoi Restaurant, **15**
Mrs. Lan, **42**
Nhà Hàng Đắc Kim, **36**
No Noodles, **60**
Paris Deli, **58**

Pepperoni's Pizza
 & Cafe, **54**
Tandoor Restaurant, **22**
Tẩy Đô, **28**
Thạch Chè lộc Tái, **25**
The Whole Earth, **35**

NIGHTLIFE

½ Man, ½ Noodle, **9**
Barracuda Bar, **2**
Cafe Giang, **38**
City View Cafe, **39**
Dêm Hà Nội, **18**
Finnegan's Irish Pub, **37**
Flagon Cafe, **43**
Funky Monkey Bar, **44**
Golden Cock Bar, **49**
Highway 4, **21**

Hơ Guom Xanh, **62**
Jazz Club by Quyen Van
 Minh, **23**
Labyrinth Bar, **8**
Le Maquis Bar, **7**
Minh Minh, **61**
Moca Cafe, **56**
New Century, **63**
Polite Pub, **50**
Press Club, **64**
R&R, **48**
Red Beer, **19**
Red Mask Bar, **14**
Sao Băng, **12**
Super Star Club, **1**
Titanic, **46**

HÀ NỘI

cafes with laundry and visa services. Most offer 30min. of free Internet. Be aware, however, that restaurant recommendations from the front desk do not ensure good quality; more likely, the recommendation is based on a commission for the guesthouse owner. Always ask to see the room first and check whether there is enough water pressure for showering. During summer, those few extra đồng for **air-conditioning** may prevent the room from becoming a sauna. And though most hostels will kindly look after your key while you explore town, it may be safer in your pocket than on their desk. It's a good idea to carry the business card of your hostel on you so that you can show it to the motorbike driver on your way home. Prices tend to be negotiable in smaller establishments.

Thu Giang Guesthouse, 5A Tạm Thương (☎828 5734; thugiangn@hotmail.com), down a small alley off Hàng Bông near Hàng Đào Market. The family-run guesthouses in this cozy and quiet alley are popular with backpackers. The owners are friendly and helpful, and for a small price you can have fruit and other foods from the market for breakfast. The rooms tend to be very small but quiet. Some have balconies and in-suite showers. Can arrange airport pickup. Doubles US$5-10, with A/C US$7-12. Their second-class sister on 35A Hang Điếu (☎923 2078) is similar, but lacks the same fun hangout culture. ❷

Van Xuan II Hotel, 46 Lương Ngọc Quyến (☎825 6948; vanxuan2@yahoo.com), 30m from the intersection with Ta Hiền, across from Apple Hotel (see below). A great deal—luxurious, but not terribly pricey. Beautiful rooms with fresh flowers. Breakfast included. Singles and doubles with A/C and TV US$8-15; triple with large balcony US$15. ❷

Paradise Hotel, 1 Yên Thái (☎928 6139). A classy, newly renovated hotel with well-furnished rooms, including fridge, private bath, A/C, and TV. Rooms at the back have no window but are quieter. Reasonable prices. Doubles US$12-30. ❸

Cát Tương Hotel, 10D Đinh Liệt (☎826 6054; www.bigbentour.com), conveniently located next to the outdoor food market. Very accommodating staff. Rooms are large and include TVs, fridges, spacious private bathrooms (some with bath), closets, and couches. Doubles without window US$7, with balcony US$8. With A/C US$2 extra. ❷

Real Darling Cafe, 33 Hàng Quạt (☎826 9386). Casual backpackers hostel with quiet, sober rooms. Helpful owner speaks perfect English and makes scrumptious banana pancakes. The rooms without the larger windows or balconies may feel like a squeeze. Dorms US$3; singles without window US$5; doubles without window US$7, with balcony US$8. With A/C US$2 extra. ❶

Queen Salute Cafe Travel, 50 Hàng Bè (☎826 7356). From Đinh Tiên Hoàng on the eastern shore of Hoàn Kiếm Lake, walk up Hàng Dầu, which becomes Hàng Bè; it's on the left. Queen Salute is Hà Nội's premier backpacker haunt. Offering tours, visas, Western food (pizza 40,000-45,000Đ; breakfast 10,000Đ), pool table, dart board, cybercafe (5000Đ per hr.), and laundry service (US₫1 per kg). Dorms 50,000Đ; singles US$6; doubles US$8, with A/C US$9. ❶

Mạnh Dung Internet Guest House, 2 Tam Thương (☎826 7201; tranmanh-dungvn@yahoo.com). A small and quiet guesthouse run by a friendly English-speaking household. Cozy rooms with private bath. Doubles US$5; with A/C US$1 extra. ❶

Youth Hotel, 33 Lương Văn Can (☎828 5822; trekking-travel@hn.vnn.vn). Centrally located. Popular with younger crowds. Internet 12,000Đ per hr. Rooms aren't anything special, but you do get a buzzing backpacker environment. Connected to Sinh Cafe for tour booking. Doubles US$8-17. ❷

Tạm Tương Guesthouse, 10A1 Yên Thái (☎828 6296; three_men_on_business @yahoo.com). A small establishment in a more serene part of the Old Quarter. Managers are laid-back and pleasant. Rooms are small but clean, and those in the back are quieter. Doubles US$6, with A/C US$8-10. ❷

Long Hung Hotel, 32 Lý Thái Tổ (☎824 2794; fax 825 3145), 1 block from Hoàn Kiếm Lake. Large rooms have fridge, A/C, satellite TV, bath and desk. Clean, comfortable singles $15; doubles US$17. MC/V. ❸

Thanh An Hotel, 46 Hàng Gà (☎826 7191), in a nice neighborhood in the northwest of the Old Quarter. Rooms are immaculate, though the ones in the rear can be dark and those on the street side can be noisy. Doubles with A/C and satellite TV US$11-13. ❸

Anh Đào Hotel, 37 Mã Mây (☎826 7151; anhdao@camellia-hotels.com). 31 spotless, newly remodeled rooms. Includes breakfast buffet (7-10am). Rooms have A/C and satellite TV. Free laundry service. Doubles US$12-15, with balcony US$2 extra. MC/V. ❸

Sinh Travel Hotel, 45 Bát Sứ (☎923 2111; hanoisinhcafe45@yahoo.co.uk), in the northwest Old Quarter. Well-furnished rooms with big bathrooms, satellite TVs, and fridges, but no windows. Doubles US$8, with balcony US$10; large rooms US$12. ❷

Youth Hotel, 14 Bát Sứ (☎824 5732; hangcot_30@yahoo.com), out in the northwest corner of the Old Quarter. 6 spacious but plain rooms. Free unlimited Internet. Doubles US$7; nicer deluxe rooms US$15. A/C US$2 extra. ❷

Apple Hotel, 53B Lương Ngọc Quyến (☎928 1403; applehotel53@hotmail.com), 30m from the intersection with Ta Hiền. Steep stairs lead to cheap, quiet rooms in a good location, with TVs. Some rooms are much nicer than others; check yours before agreeing to stay. Singles and doubles US$4, with A/C US$8. ❶

Phú Hoa Hotel, 16 Lương Văn Can (☎828 5173), down a narrow alleyway. A decent budget option in the center of town. Rooms are acceptable but lack personality. Doubles US$7, with A/C US$10. ❷

🍴 FOOD

Backpackers can easily find the Western spaghetti-and-pancake fare in the Old Quarter, but the most rewarding dining experiences are found on the street. Street stalls around the markets dish up delectable phở or cơm and plenty of vegetarian options. Get up early to beat the heat and try some typical breakfast foods: *xôi gà* (sticky rice with chicken), french bread with *pâté*, or the omnipresent phở. Vendors are set up all day long on the streets near the **Đồng Xuân Market** north of the Old Quarter, and each street tends to serve one type of dish. It is helpful to know that most restaurants have an air-conditioned space upstairs.

🍴 **Cơm Việt,** 14 Lý Thái Tổ (☎824 0637 www.comvietrestaurant.com), on the street behind the post office. The menu is amazingly diverse and the 3 dining rooms are elegant and comfortable. Entrees 20,000-120,000Đ. Live music. Open 10am-10pm. MC/V. ❷

🍴 **Little Hà Nội Restaurant,** 9 and 14 Ta Hiền (☎926 0168). A hospitable Vietnamese restaurant with the motto "A strange visitor will be an accustomed one, an accustomed visitor will be a good friend." Quite popular with tourists, and for good reason: service is friendly, the food is great, and prices are fair. Roll your own spring roll for 30,000Đ. Most dishes 28,000-39,000Đ. Open daily 11am-11pm. MC/V. ❷

69, 69 Mã Mây (☎926 1720; www.69vn.com). A few meters from the corner of Mã Mây and Lương Ngọc Quyến. In a restored 19th-century house, this restaurant evokes the ambience of Hà Nội's past. Traditional Vietnamese dishes around 45,000Đ. Well-stocked bar. Open daily 9am-11pm. ❸

Highway 4, 5 Hàng Tre (☎926 0639; www.highway4.com). This laid-back bar-restaurant specializes in the traditional liquor (Son Tinh; see **Nightlife,** p. 120) and cuisine of the northwest hill tribes. 3 floors beautifully decorated with traditional clothing and artifacts. The top floor is outdoors, with a thatched roof, giving the appearance of a house on stilts. Bamboo mats are arranged around low tables. Scorpion 24,000Đ; fresh pig's ear spring rolls 28,000Đ; other specialties from 20,000Đ-100,000Đ. Open daily 9am-2am. ❷

Paris Deli, 13 Nhà Thờ (☎928 6697), 50m east of St. Joseph Cathedral. Deliciously fresh croissants (9000Đ) and tasty desserts (25,000Đ). Take your pastries and coffee to go or sit in any one of the 3 beautifully decorated levels of the large cafe. Sandwiches 29,000-49,000Đ. Cake 22,000Đ. Open daily 7am-11pm. ❷

Bảo Khánh, 10 Bảo Khánh (☎828 7762), on the corner and just 1 block from the lake. A small restaurant where locals and visitors line up for a wide variety of authentic Vietnamese food at killer prices. Try anything from pigeon or frog to tortoise or cock testicles, or cure an illness by ordering an entree cooked with traditional medicine. Meals 35,000-50,000Đ. Open daily 9:30am-9pm. ❷

Mrs. Lan, 103 Hàng Gai. This street vendor is a symbol of all that is good and right in the world. She makes delicious sandwiches (4000-7000Đ), mostly for hungry clubbers and early-rising salesmen. Open daily 6pm-4am. After 10pm she'll be out on the street. ❶

Cyclo Bar and Restaurant, 38 Dường Thành (☎828 6844). Dường Thành intersects Hàng Gai as it becomes Hàng Bông; the restaurant is 100m down on the left from this crossing. Serving both Vietnamese and French cuisine in an elegant setting, Cyclo Bar revives Hà Nội's French heritage. Cyclo chairs and pleasant garden seating add to the ambience. Set lunch menu 75,000Đ from 11am-2pm. A la carte 45,000-75,000Đ. French dishes around 100,000Đ. Open daily 9am-11pm. MC/V. ❸

Cafe Linh Phụng, 7 Đinh Liệt (☎926 0592), right next to The Whole Earth. An inconspicuous budget eatery with Christmas baubles on the bamboo ceiling. Great value. Breakfast 6000-15,000Đ; pasta 24,000-29,000Đ; Vietnamese dishes 20,000-25,000Đ. Try the cream pumpkin soup (10,000Đ) or the baguette sandwiches (15,000Đ). Open Su-Th 7am-10pm, F-Sa 7am-11pm. ❷

Tandoor Restaurant, 24 Hàng Bè (☎824 5359 or 824 2252; tandoor@hn.vnn.vn). From Đinh Tiên Hoàng on the eastern shore of Hoàn Kiếm Lake, walk up Hàng Dầu, which becomes Hàng Bè; it's on the left past the intersection with Gia Ngư. Authentic Indian cuisine with delicious *naan* and vegetarian selections galore. Entrees 40,000-50,000Đ. Lunch special 42,000Đ. Free delivery. Halal food available. Ask about their sister vegetarian restaurant nearby. Open daily 11am-2:30pm and 6-10:30pm. ❸

Bánh Gối Bánh Rán, 52 Lý Quốc Sư (☎828 5922). A small makeshift eatery serving delicious fried Vietnamese snacks. Try the impressively greasy but oh-so-tasty "pillow pie" (stuffed with sweet rice and red beans; 1000-3500Đ). Friendly owner and quiet setting. Open daily 10am-10pm. ❶

Tẩy Đô, 36 Đinh Liệt (☎825 5802), right next to Bánh Mỳ. A small 24hr. bakery. Prepares a wide variety of fresh pastries (1000-3000Đ) every morning, adding bean paste pizzazz to European tradition. Pastries are freshest around 5am. ❶

Kaiser Kaffee, 33 Hàng Bè (☎926 0404; kaiserkaffee@hotmail.com). From Đinh Tiên Hoàng on the eastern shore of Hoàn Kiếm Lake, walk up Hàng Dầu, which becomes Hàng Bè; it's on your right where Hàng Bè meets Gia Ngư. Discover your inner German in this friendly eatery. Bratwurst is 15,000Đ, and that wonderfully named German staple, wiener schnitzel, is 29,500Đ. German dishes 20,000Đ-35,000Đ; Vietnamese entrees 20,000Đ-30,000Đ. Organizes tours. German spoken. Open daily 7:30am-10pm. ❷

No Noodles, 20 Nhà Chung (☎928 5969), about 50m down the street from St. Joseph's cathedral. As the name implies, this is not the place for Vietnamese cuisine: No Noodles serves good sub sandwiches with fresh ingredients, as well as breakfast food and salads, all around 30,000Đ. Delivery and takeout available. Open daily 9am-9pm. ❷

Baguette & Chocolat, 11 Chả Cá (☎923 1500; www.hoasuaschool.com). This stylish French bakery and cafe is part of the Hoa Sữa training school, where youngsters from disadvantaged backgrounds get practical training. Order downstairs and sit in the stylish room upstairs, but don't forget to take off your shoes. Delicious pastries 3000-8000Đ; coffee 12,000-22,000Đ; martinis 35,000Đ. Open daily 7am-10pm. ❶

Pepperoni's Pizza & Cafe, 31 Bảo Khánh (☎928 7030). Serves a variety of burgers (around 55,000Đ) and—you guessed it—pizza (from 40,000Đ). The best reason to come here, though, is the all-you-can-eat pasta and salad bar (28,000Đ) and the all-you-can-eat ice cream bar (10,000Đ, only with meals). Takeout and delivery available. Open daily 10am-11pm. MC/V. ❸

Bún Bò Nam Bộ, 67 Hàng Điểu (☎923 0701). A simple but popular food stop. Bowls of delicious, perfect beef noodles for a mere 16,000Đ; vegetarian noodles 10,000Đ. Open daily 7am-10:30pm. ❶

La Place Cafe, 4 Ấu Triệu (☎928 5859), right next to St. Joseph's Cathedral. A very hip cafe-restaurant with an orange, red and pink interior. Caters to the tourist and expat crowd. "West Side" cuisine 39,000-45,000Đ; "East Side" cuisine 29,000-55,000Đ. The soup is to die for. Sit upstairs on the private terrace if possible. Mixed drinks around 50,000Đ. Open daily 7:30am-11pm. ❸

Nhà Hàng Đắc Kim, 1 Hàng Mành, just a few steps from the corner of Hàng Mành and Hàng Quạt. Heaping servings of delicious *bún chả* (grilled pork over cold rice noodles; 20,000Đ) keep locals coming back. Served with crab rolls. Open daily 7am-7pm. ❷

Hải Tý, 20 Hàng Giầy (☎824 5101), on the corner of Hàng Giầy and Hàng Buồm. One of the Old Quarter's most popular street-eating joints, it's always crowded. At night, you can see the fire from the skillets blocks away. Serves your basic phở and cơm for 10,000-12,000Đ. Open daily 5-11pm. ❶

Bánh Mỳ, 38 Đinh Liệt (☎926 0493), 50m from the fountain, just around the corner of Đinh Liệt and Cầu Gỗ. A small Vietnamese restaurant that's almost always open. Good sandwiches only 5000Đ. *Hông doý* (pork- and vermicelli-stuffed buns) go for 3000Đ. Open daily 6:30am-1:30am. ❶

The Whole Earth, 7 Đinh Liệt (☎926 0696), inside Handspan Adventure Travel Cafe. A simple Vietnamese eatery that specializes in vegetarian dishes with imitation meat, a Buddhist specialty. Set menus 30,000Đ; with meat 35,000Đ. Some Western meals also available. Most dishes 18,000-25,000Đ. Open 8am-11pm. ❷

Lay Bac, 135 Hàng Bạc (☎826 6901). A pleasant eatery with laid-back service, as befits the name. Popular with tourists. Enormous Western and Vietnamese menu, including a good selection of pizzas. Entrees 38,000-70,000Đ. Baguette sandwiches 25,000-45,000Đ. Open daily 9am-11pm. ❸

Thạch Chè Lộc Tài, 63 Hàng Điếu, near the alley full of guesthouses (Tạm Thương). A dessert and snack shop with eel soup (6000Đ), smoothies, and colorful jelly drinks (6000Đ). Popular with Vietnamese students. Open daily 8:30am-10:30pm. ❶

Local Green Papaya Salad Vendor, everywhere you need him. The sound of clashing scissors means a cart of green papaya salad with dried beef *(nôm thịt bò)* is coming your way. Consider it the ice-cream truck of the Vietnamese streets. Those same scissors are used to cut the beef into small pieces and then mix up the wonderfully refreshing salad (6000Đ). Perfect for the hot summertime months. ❶

HÀ NỘI

🔵 SIGHTS

HOÀN KIẾM LAKE (HỒ HOÀN KIẾM). The lake takes its name ("Lake of the Restored Sword") from a 15th-century legend of a giant magic turtle who lent a sacred sword to Lê Lợi, the nobleman who led the Vietnamese against the invading Ming army. Paddling in the lake following the victory, the newly crowned emperor encountered the turtle, who demanded the sword back. The **Tortoise Tower** on a tiny island in the lake's center commemorates the event. Several mammoth turtles still live in the lake and occasionally surface, an event that locals believe is a sign of the impending death of one of the country's leaders. Strolls here are relaxing and enjoyable, but are often interrupted by the entreaties of persistent children who sell postcards and T-shirts on the north side of the lake.

NGỌC SƠN TEMPLE (ĐỀN NGỌC SƠN). Generations have added more and more frills to this shrine since its construction during the Trần Dynasty (AD 1225-1400). Most recently renovated in 1865, this Chinese-style temple is dedicated primarily to **Văn Xương,** the god of literature. Thirteenth-century hero Trần Hưng Đạo and physician La To are also honored. The entrance to the temple is through Tam Quan (Three Passage) gate on the northeast shore on Đinh Tiên Hoàng. Cross on the red wooden bridge, and behind the Hall of the Cult, the sanctuary to Văn Xương offers a beautiful view of the lake. *(Open daily 8am-6pm. 5,000Đ. Located on a wooded island in the middle of Hoàn Kiếm Lake)*

ST. JOSEPH CATHEDRAL. This cathedral is two blocks west from Hoàm Kiêm Lake, where Lý Quốc Sư becomes Nhà Chung. Though not the only Catholic church in Hà Nội, this French-built (or at least French-commissioned) neo-gothic cathedral and its statue dedicated to the "Queen of Peace" is a true landmark in the maze of the Old Quarter. Mass (in Vietnamese) at 6pm on Sunday is particularly impressive, as people overflow onto the street. *(Main gate open daily during mass 5-7am and 7-9pm. Su has 3 additional masses. At other times of the day, enter on the left side of the main entrance. Open daily 5am-noon and 2-7:30pm.)*

MOTOBAI, MADAME? Motorbike drivers can be cheaper by the hour. You can usually hire a motorbike driver for around US$2 per hour, whereas a single 10-minute ride around the Old Quarter costs about US$0.80. Hire by the hour and you'll not only save money, but you'll also likely get to know your friendly motorbike driver.

▧ NIGHTLIFE

BARS

When it comes to nightlife, bars dominate the Hà Nội scene. From medicinal liquor to small breweries to the ubiquitous *bia hơi* joints, the city is host to a multitude of watering holes catering to all kinds of drinkers.

▨ **Highway 4,** 5 Hàng Tre (☎926 0639; www.highway4.com). Named after the highway along the Chinese-Vietnamese border, this laid-back bar-restaurant specializes in the medicinal Son Tinh liquor of the northwest hill tribes. The bartender will help match a drink to your ailment or taste. Doses run 6000Đ-25,000Đ. Or try a sampler (16,000Đ) to wash down your crunchy grilled scorpion appetizer (24,000Đ). Open daily 9am-2am.

½ **Man,** ½ **Noodle,** 52 Đào Duy Từ (☎926 1943), on Ta Hiển. Walk into the alley next to Labyrinth Bar; it's on your right. The poster on the door says it all: "Drink here or we shoot the puppy!" You can win a shirt with that slogan if you spend more than 150,000Đ in a night. A small pub popular with backpackers. Beer 15,000Đ; mixed drinks 35,000-50,000Đ; big bowl 60,000Đ. Open daily 6pm until the puppy gets it.

Polite Pub, 5 Bảo Khánh (☎825 0959), right next to the **Golden Cock Bar** (see below). Frequented by expatriates for after-hour drinks. Lively music. Darts, pool table, and sports on TV. Happy hour 5-8pm (most beers for 15,000Đ). Otherwise 20,000Đ. Open daily 5pm-2am.

Golden Cock Bar, 5A Bảo Khánh (☎825 0499). Commonly referred to as the GC, this is one of the most comfortable and popular drinking holes in the city. Happy hour until 9pm (most beers 15,000Đ; otherwise 19,000Đ). Open daily 5:30pm-whenever.

Labyrinth Bar, 7 Ta Hiển (☎926 0788), on the corner across from Red Mask. A cozy and comfortable cocktail bar with a piano. Popular with expats, but not the easiest place to meet new people. Mixed drinks 45,000-55,000Đ. Open daily 6pm-3am.

Minh Minh (a.k.a. **I-Box**), 32 Lê Thái Tổ (☎828 8820), right on Hoàn Kiếm Lake. A stylish bar-cafe and expat meeting place. Happy hour 5-7pm. Beer 35,000Đ. Open daily 8am-midnight.

Dêm Hà Nội, 136B Trần Nhật Duật (☎926 1382), on the street next to the Cầu Chương Dương Hwy. A small, traditional parlor with low tables and woven mats for seating. Serves medicinal liquors (*liệu hồn rưử*; USụ4.50) in small jars. Open daily 10am-2am.

Red Beer, 97 Mã Mây (☎826 0247). Sick of *bia hơi?* You're not alone. The red walls of this big brewery match their Belgian Red Lager. Also try their less famous Pilsner for 16,000Đ. A selection of uninspired Vietnamese and Western food is available for 40,000-50,000Đ. Open daily 10am-11pm.

Le Maquis Bar, 2A Ta Hiền (☎828 2598), near the end of Ta Hiền. A tiny grotto-like bar with metal chairs, a pool table, and dart board. Cocktails US$1. Open daily 5pm-late.

Red Mask Bar, 2D Ta Hiền (☎928 2299), just down the street from Le Maquis. A fun and popular bar, though sometimes seating can be scarce. Happy hour 5-8pm (for every 3 mixed drinks, get 1 free; some beers 10,000Đ). Hà Nội cocktail (rice wine mixed with fruit juices and sometimes beer) US$1. Open daily 5pm-late.

Super Star Club, 41 Hàng Giầy (☎927 1427), after Đồng Xuân Market and just before the railway bridge on the right. A great snooker and billiards bar where local youngsters come to compete. Tables 20,000Đ per hr. Open daily 8am-midnight.

Funky Monkey Bar, 15B Hàng Hành (☎928 6113). Neon colors, flashing lights, and monkeys on the walls make this an interesting (even…"funky") bar. DJs spin a wide variety of electronic music every night, but there isn't much dancing. 2 Happy hours: 4-7pm (some beers 19,000Đ) and 7-9pm (3rd mixed drink is free). Open daily 4pm-2am.

CAFES

Cafes, too, play a significant role in nighttime recreation. Though Hà Nội is by no means a center for Vietnamese coffee producers or drinkers, the country's fabled beverage is as good here as anywhere, and the people-watching is better. Cafes attract a different, more relaxed crowd; they can be a good place to meet people, and a great place for a leisurely streetside drink.

Flagon Cafe, 36 Lò Sũ (☎824 8205). From the corner of Lò Sũ and Lý Thái Tổ, go 20m toward the highway; it's on the left. Go down the hallway and (quietly!) up 2 flights of stairs. Students and locals gather here to play on the acoustic guitars lying around. Sit outside on the roof terrace or inside on woven mats. Cages with tropical birds decorate the walls. Friendly service. All drinks 5000Đ or less. Open daily 8:30am-11pm.

Moca Cafe, 14-16 Nhà Thờ (☎825 6334), 50m east of St. Joseph Cathedral. The kind of coffeehouse you'd expect to find in Europe. 2 spacious floors with white walls and A/C, filled with chatter and the smell of fresh coffee. A small selection of novels in English are available for US$5 each. Breakfast 12,000-38,000Đ; huge selection of entrees, including Western, Vietnamese, and Indian dishes (around 80,000Đ). International coffees 12,000-26,000Đ. Open daily 8am-10:30pm. AmEx/MC/V.

City View Cafe, 7 Phố Đinh Tiên Hoàng (☎934 7911), 10m from the corner. Go upstairs to the 5th fl. An elegant cafe with a rooftop terrace. The superb panorama of the city, and especially of Hoàn Kiếm Lake, makes it worth the 5-story climb. Coffee 12,000-20,000Đ; tea 7000-10,000Đ; fruit shakes 14,000-20,000Đ. Open daily 7am-11pm.

Sao Băng, 46 Hàng Giầy (☎926 0443), right where Lương Ngọc Quyến meets Hàng Giầy. A 24hr. billiards cafe. Great for early-morning pool buffs. 3000Đ per table per hr.

Cafe Giang, 7 Hàng Gai. Open since 1945, this is a famous local coffee shop, and for good reason. The unique *nâu trung sữa nóng* (a shot of espresso with sugar and a beaten egg; 4000Đ), is a can't-miss. Open daily 6am-noon and 3-9:30pm.

LIVE MUSIC

Hà Nội used to be a barren land when it came to live music, but recently more bars have included live acts to attract music lovers. Local newspapers regularly include concert schedules.

HÀ NỘI

FROM THE ROAD

PROBLEMS OF THE HEART

One late Saturday night, I was playing pool with a Nordic friend of mine in a bar on the outskirts of Hà Nội. An attractive Vietnamese girl approached us and asked if we could teach her to shoot. My friend demonstrated the basics of the game to her; she proceeded to wipe him off the table with incredible skill. We gave up after a few humbling defeats and went dancing instead. My friend and the girl got close; I decided to let them be and headed home.

The next evening, he told me over dinner that she had invited him over for lunch with her family that day. When they got to her home, he was taken aback by how impoverished her family was. Worse, her mother was in bed with a heart affliction and probably didn't have another month to live if she didn't get surgery soon. "I was touched and overwhelmed by their misery," said my friend. "I withdrew six million đồng and quietly gave it to the girl to pay for her mother's surgery." I was touched by his generosity, but an old Vietnamese man who had overheard the story laughed, saying he had heard it many times before. "Her real affliction wasn't her heart, but her poverty."

Had my friend been tricked into giving up half a week's salary, or had he really saved somebody's life? Sometimes scams are scams; sometimes need is need. You can never know.

—Rick Slettenhaar

R & R, 47 Lò Sũ (☎ 934 4109), just 2 blocks east of Hoàn Kiếm Lake. Pictures of Uncle Ho and George Washington hang on both sides of the entrance in this Viet-American tavern. Live music every night, from classical to funk to rock'n'roll. On Sa locals and foreigners show their skills at open mike. Serves big portions of Tex-Mex fare for 20,000-85,000Đ. Beer 18,000Đ; mixed drinks 45,000-50,000Đ. Open 10am until very late.

Jazz Club by Quyen Van Minh, 31 Lương Văn Can (☎ 828 7890; jazzminh@hn.vnn.vn). Saxophonist Minh and his students drop anything from swing to hard bop every night (from 8:30pm on) in this laid-back yet classy club. Entrees 29,000-98,000Đ; mixed drinks 40,000-50,000Đ. 15% discount during Hà Nội's longest Happy hour (9:30am-5pm). Open daily 9am-midnight.

Ho' Guom Xanh, 32 Lê Thái Tổ (☎ 828 8820). Right next to Minh Minh, recognizable by the flashing neon lights. A popular Vietnamese cabaret establishment that draws crowds each night. Performances on the rotating stage include singing, dancing and simple acrobatics. Some shows are better than others; check out the program beforehand. Beer 35,000Đ; soda 25,000Đ. Open daily 6pm-late; 8-9pm is the highlight of the show.

Finnegan's Irish Pub, 16A Đường Thành (☎ 828 9065), a few steps from where Dương Thanh meets Háng Nón. Every city in the world seems to have an Irish pub; Hà Nội is no exception. Small and friendly, with bands on the weekends. Popular with expats. Beer 22,000Đ; steaks US$8-14; Asian entrees around US$5. Open daily 10am until everyone leaves.

CLUBS

Vietnam is not known for its dance floors. Fortunately, Hà Nội is home to a few of the country's true hotspots, clubs where flashing lights, blaring techno music, and all-night dancing are alive and well.

Barracuda Bar, Số 49-Tổ 4A (☎ 932 3244), in Phúc Tân. This club on the bank of the Red River is certainly worth the quest. Get on the dike road (parallel to the highway) between the Long Biên and Chương Dương bridges, and pass through the dike entrance. Turn left at the end of the alley; it's on your right after 100m. Motorbike and taxi drivers will likely know it. A European-flavored club where locals and foreigners mix on a great dance floor, at a bar area with a pool table, and on an enormous terrace overlooking the Red River. A prized DJ keeps the music going until all stumble home. W-Th are backpacker nights, featuring the bar's own "wheel of fortune." Beer 18,000-20,000Đ; mixed drinks 35,000-50,000Đ. Open daily 7pm until very late.

New Century, 10 Tràng Thi (☎ 928 5285). New Century has been the hottest disco in town for years. Sip a cocktail at one of the many tables spread out over the club's 2 fls., or go crazy on the packed dance floor under a ceiling covered with flags. DJs spin non-stop Euro-techno. Cover 45,000Đ; includes 1 drink. Open daily 8:30pm-3am.

Titanic, 42 Chương Dường Độ. One of Hà Nội's newest clubs. On the Red River, Titanic keeps rocking the boat until the early morning. The DJ spins mostly dance music and R&B, while clubbers blow off steam on the outside terrace. Occasional live music. Happy hour 5-9pm, every beer 15,000Đ; otherwise, 22,000Đ. French wine 25,000Đ per glass. Open daily 5pm-5am.

Press Club, 59A Lý Thái Tổ (☎934 0888; www.hanoi-pressclub.com), next to the Metropole Hotel. Take the elevator to this elegant 3rd fl. rooftop club where expats meet up and DJs blast great dance music. Buy drink tickets (12,000Đ) at the door. Beers 2-3 tickets; mixed drinks 4-5. Open daily 9pm-late; arrive early to find a table.

FRENCH QUARTER

The French Quarter, once a chaotic and swampy suburb of Hà Nội, was developed by French colonialists during their occupation in an attempt to recreate Parisian grandeur. Walking through the streets of this neighborhood, you'll find that much of that ambience remains. In terms of tourism, the French Quarter hasn't been as successful as the Old Quarter. Stately and resplendent with monumental buildings and broad boulevards, it has attracted more embassies than hotels. Still, it's got a lot to offer to visitors: the Opera, the diagonal Thợ Nhuộm (almost a direct extension of Điện Biên Phủ), and the alleys in the south are some of Hoàn Kiếm district's most happening areas.

ACCOMMODATIONS

Lotus Guest House, 42V Lý Thường Kiệt (☎/fax 826 8642). Walking south from the lake on Bà Triệu, turn right at the intersection with Lý Thường Kiệt and walk 2 blocks down. Enter the Safari Bar and go through the camouflaged door in the back wall. Idiosyncratic and inexpensive. Meals (27,000-45,000Đ) and wonderfully thick smoothies (10,000-18,000Đ) served at a little bar in front until midnight. 4-bed dorms US$4; singles US$6-7; doubles with fan US$8, with A/C US$10-18. Apartments are also available for long-term stays. ❶

Thương Hàt Hotel, 31 Nam Ngư (☎942 3142), 2 blocks from Hà Nội Railway Station. Simple but spacious rooms, each with A/C, satellite TV, fridge and a small private bathroom. Comfortable, but not particularly sociable. Doubles US$12-15. ❸

An Dong Hotel, 23 Nam Ngư (☎942 1019), down the quiet street from the Thương Hàt Hotel. Rooms with large windows, grand balconies, and all the amenities. Singles US$15; doubles US$25. ❸

FOOD

Hoa Sửa Restaurant d'Application, 28A Phố Ha Hoi (☎942 4448; www.hoasu-aschool.com). The Hoa Sửa training school is a stylish French restaurant where kids from underprivileged backgrounds get practical training. The students provide top-quality service, and the food is exceptional. Set 2-course menu 75,000Đ, 3-courses 85,000Đ. Su brunch with French and Vietnamese options. Open daily 11am-10pm. ❹

Qun ăn Ngon, 18 Phan Bội Châu (☎942 8162; ngonhanoi@vnn.vn), down the street from the Fansland Cinema. This large and extremely popular restaurant brings in both locals and tourists with its fantastic food. The huge menu lists an impressive collection of glorified and upscale Vietnamese street food. The quick staff will bring Hà Nội crispy shrimp and potato pancakes (18,000Đ) to your table in record time, unless you want to roll your own spring rolls with shrimp on sugarcane (35,000Đ). Outdoor seating available. Open daily 6:30am-10pm. AmEx/MC/V. ❷

HÀ NỘI

Indochine Vietnamese Restaurant, 16 Nam Ngư (☎942 4097). High-quality local specialties with impeccable service. The traditionally dressed and highly attentive staff serves creative seafood entrees and elegant French fusion dishes ($7). Entrees from US$3. Open daily 11:30am-2pm and 5-10pm. Reservations recommended. ❹

Cơm Chay Nàng Tấm Vegetarian Restaurant, 79A Trần Hưng Đạo (☎942 4140), between Quang Trưng and Quán Sứ intersections. Go into the little alley and follow the signs. Small Buddhist eatery named after a Vietnamese fairy tale. Come early for lunch—it gets crowded. Entrees 30,000-50,000Đ; set menus, which can include pâté, soup, entree and rice, 20,000-50,000Đ. Open daily 11am-1:30pm and 5-10pm. ❸

Pane e Vino, 3 Nguyễn Khắc Can (☎826 9080). Walk down Phố Tráng Tiên from Hoàn Kiếm Lake to the Opera, and take a right 1 block before the roundabout. It's on the corner on your left 1 block later. This beautifully decorated Italian restaurant serves good Italian cuisine. Try their famously thick and delicious smoothies (10,000-18,000Đ). F night buffet with live music (US$7). Get there early. Try their creamy risotto, made with everything from mushrooms to meat (US$9.50-12). Delivery available. Open daily 9am-11pm. ❺

Hải Phòng, 74 Trần Quốc Toản (☎942 5064), on the corner of Trần Quốc Toản and Liên Trì. A seafood restaurant with a garden in the back. Crab is their speciality. Soft shell crab 47,000Đ; hard shell 180,000-200,000Đ per kg. Open daily 9am-11pm. ❹

Thu Nga, Hai Bà Trưng (☎825 3916), at the cross street with Phan Chu Trinh. The perfect place to escape the summer heat. Try the house speciality, *kem xôi* (sticky rice with ice cream) for 5,000Đ at the little tables set up outside. Cold drinks with jelly or fruit 3000-8000Đ. Open daily 6:30am-11pm. ❶

KNOW YOUR DOUGH. In Vietnam, locals often pay one price and foreigners another. But if you've already seen a local pay his price, don't ask how much something costs—just hand that same amount over. Otherwise the vendor will undoubtedly name a higher price, which could lead to arguing, frustration, and losing face on both sides. But hand over the local price with a smile and he'll think you're in the know—which you are. *-Anna Pasternak*

◉ SIGHTS

HISTORY MUSEUM (BẢO TÀNG LỊCH SỬ). Housed in a stately French-designed building, this museum details Vietnam's past from ancient times to the birth of Communism. The almost incessant foreign aggression that the Vietnamese have withstood over the centuries makes for an impressive read. Don't miss the Đông Sơn bronze drums and ceramics or the Khmer and Chàm artifacts. *(1 block behind the Opera, across from the Museum of the Vietnamese Revolution on Phố Tráng Tiên. Enter through the gates on Tráng Tiên. Open Tu-Su 8-11:45am and 1:30-4:30pm. Admission 15,000Đ, students 8000Đ, children 2000Đ. Cameras an additional 15,000Đ, camcorders 30,000Đ.)*

MUSEUM OF THE VIETNAMESE REVOLUTION. Also housed in a former French governmental building, the Museum of the Vietnamese Revolution presents the communist struggles against the French, Japanese and Americans as a powerful shaping force of modern Vietnam. The 29 halls explore the events of modern Vietnamese history through visual displays and pictures, and include English commentary. *(1 block behind the Opera, across Phố Tráng Tiên from the History Museum. Enter off Trần Quang Khải. Open Tu-Su 8-11:45am and 1:30-4:15pm. 15,000Đ, students 8000Đ, children 2000Đ. Cameras an additional 15,000Đ, camcorders 30,000Đ.)*

QUAN SỨ PAGODA (AMBASSADOR'S PAGODA). In the old days, foreign delegates—mostly monks—would stay here. Quan Sứ is the center of Buddhist culture in Vietnam; many monks live and study here in Hà Nội's most bustling religious center. Enter through the gate on Quan Sứ, but try not to visit during ceremonies. *(73 Quan Sứ. Open daily 7:30-11:30am and 1:30-5:30pm.)*

HOA LÒ PRISON. Hoa Lò Prison has a long history of stern punishment. When it was built by the French in 1896, it was the largest prison in Indochina. It was soon packed full of political prisoners. Later, the Vietnamese imprisoned American POWs here—among them US Air Force Captain Pete Peterson and US Senator John McCain—until their release in 1973. These days, however, little remains of the notorious prison, nicknamed the "Hà Nội Hilton." The Hà Nội Towers, and the small museum they contain, are prominent reminders of the French colonial period. Most information is in Vietnamese. (*1 Phố Hoa Lò, on the corner with Hai Bà Trưng. Open Tu-Su 8-11:30am and 1:30-4:30pm. 5000Đ.*)

WOMEN'S MUSEUM. The Museum of Vietnamese Women is dedicated to Vietnam's mothers, wives, workers, teachers, and heroines and their roles in the country's history, defense, and society. The imperfect English translations range from admiring to belittling. (*36 Lý Thường Kiệt. Open Tu-Su 8am-4pm. 10,000Đ.*)

▣ NIGHTLIFE

Thư Giãn Bar (Relax Bar), 60 Lý Thường Kiệt and 68 Quan Sư (☎942 4409), on the corner of Lý Thường Kiệt and Quan Sư, across from the Quan Sư Pagoda. Despite heavy traffic, Thư Giãn Bar manages to create a relaxing tiki-bar feel, complete with a goldfish pond in the middle of the bar. Frequented by diplomats from the nearby UN buildings—check out the signed flags on the ceiling. Beer 13,000-18,000Đ; mixed drinks 37,000-49,000Đ; snack food, including hot dogs, around 22,000Đ. Open daily 9am-11pm.

Càfé 75, 75 Trần Quốc Toản (☎942 4919), close to the crossing of Trần Quốc Toản and Liên Trì. A quirky cafe: the terrace has a waterfall with a nativity scene under it, and the tables are covered with posters of boy bands and football stars. Try the kudzu juice (7000Đ); all other drinks 10,000-25,000Đ. Open daily 7am-10:30pm.

Tuyết Cafe, 39A Lý Thường Kiệt, across from the Women's Museum. A smoky little cafe with an unimpressive waterfall in the back. Coffee 5000-7000Đ; Italian sodas 15,000Đ; hamburgers 60,000Đ; cigarettes 2000-18,000Đ. Open daily 7am-11pm.

Diva Art Cafe, 39A Lý Thái Tổ (☎934 4088), 1 block from the Opera, on the same block as the Revolutionary Museum. A trendy cafe-bar with a terrace overlooking the streets and a little park. Great for people-watching. Live music: M-F piano, Sa jazz, Su flamenco. Happy hour 3-7pm (beer 12,000Đ). Otherwise, beer 18,000Đ; mixed drinks 38,000-42,000Đ. Open daily 7am-11:30pm.

25°J Club, 25 Ngo Van So (☎943 8099). Walk down a colorful tunnel into this brand new nightclub. Tables and crowds of locals fill up the dance floor and the VIP room upstairs. Best on the weekends. The DJ spins dance music with a techno tint. Beers 45,000-60,000Đ; full bottles of booze 500,000-25,000,000Đ. Open daily noon-late.

BA ĐÌNH DISTRICT

Ba Đình district, the area west of the Old Quarter and south of West Lake, is home to some of Hà Nội's most visited sights, including the Hồ Chí Minh Mausoleum, the Presidential Palace, and the Hà Nội Citadel. Best of all, the fruit hawkers and motorbike drivers keep a lower profile here, so a sidewalk stroll can be peaceful and refreshing. But the best way to travel the long boulevards of this district is by motorbike, unless you are heading to the Mausoleum, which is a nice morning walk from the Old Quarter. For accommodations, food, and entertainment, though, go elsewhere. Also, a word to animal lovers: skip the zoo.

▌ ACCOMMODATIONS

Hostels and hotels in Ba Đình, like in Hai Bà Trưng, have not yet succeeded in attracting many backpackers, who tend to favor the cheaper, more touristy Hoàn

Kiếm district (for good reason). However, the good deals on apartments in Ba Đình are quite popular for long-term stays.

Tràng An Hotel, 46 Phố Hàng Cháo (☎/fax 823 2837; tranganhotel@yahoo.com). Take a right onto Hàng Cháo after passing the Temple of Literature. Quiet rooms, some without windows, some with private bath. Rooms with twin beds, A/C, and TV 150,000Đ. ❷

Hoang Ngoc Hotel, 19 Phố Hàng Cháo (☎823 2660; fax 823 2605). An upscale alternative to Tràng An Hotel. Spacious, well-furnished rooms with bath, TV, phone, A/C, fridge, and big windows. Some rooms have a couch and a street view. Doubles USự17-25, with sitting area and desk USự30. MC/V. ❹

🍴 FOOD

Đep Restaurant & Bar, 38 Liễu Giai (☎832 5379). Head west on Phố Kim Mã and turn right just before the Daewoo Hotel onto Liễu Giai. It's on your left after about 250m. Owned by Vietnam's trendy Đep fashion magazine, this restaurant has remained in style for years. Private dining rooms available. Oysters in chili sauce 50,000Đ. Mullet fish 50,000Đ. Most other entrees 40,000-80,000Đ. Open daily 7am-11pm. MC/V. ❸

Brother's Cafe, 26 Phố Nguyễn Thái Học (☎733 3866; www.brothercafe.com). This popular cafe started in 1997, when 2 brothers renovated a century-old family temple into a fashionable restaurant. Generous portions make it worth the journey to this otherwise dull street. All-you-can-eat buffets of Vietnamese and Western cuisine. Lunch served M-Sa 11:30am-2pm (96,000Đ). Dinner, including a seafood-and-meat-BBQ, served daily 6:30-10pm (184,000Đ). AmEx/MC/V. ❺

Luna d'Autumno, 11B Điện Biên Phủ (☎823 7338). This classy Italian restaurant with a relaxed lounge upstairs completely escapes the street sounds of motorbikes and hawkers. Popular with expats. Occasional live piano music. Wood-fired pizza 55,000-115,000Đ. Pasta 86,000-105,000Đ. Open daily 11am-11pm. MC/V. ❹

BoBoChaCha, 5 Trần Quang Minh (☎733 5556). From Phố Phan Đình Phùng (a one-way street north of the Citadel), take the 2nd left after the Catholic church. After about 100m, take another left into the alley and follow the BoBoChaCha signs to the small patio. A friendly family hosts mostly students for their after-school appetites. The menu features sweet bean, jelly, and coco soup for 2000Đ, as well as a sausage and fruit platter for 7000Đ. Open daily 2-6pm. ❶

👁 SIGHTS

The area around Ba Đình Square is where Hồ Chí Minh delivered Vietnam's Declaration of Independence speech in 1945. It also contains most of the city's principal sights west of the Old Quarter. The most convenient way to reach this district is via Điện Biên Phủ. Along the way, on the left, is a small park with a huge and impressive statue of Vladimir Lenin.

HÀ NỘI CITADEL. Vietnam's Ministry of Defense occupies this restricted area, once called the Thăng Long Citadel and home to the imperial city. Inside its gates is the Army Museum (Bảo Tàng Quân Đội), which details the exploits of the People's Army of Vietnam. Highlights include a light-and-sound diorama of Điện Biên Phủ Valley and the tank that crashed through the gates of Saigon's Presidential Palace in April 1975. Next door is the 31m Hà Nội Flag Pillar, a former guard tower built in 1812 under the Nguyễn Dynasty. *(Museum: 28A Điện Biên Phủ. Open Tu-Th and Sa-Su 8-11:30am and 1-4:30pm. 10,000Đ; cameras 2000Đ.)*

HỒ CHÍ MINH MAUSOLEUM (LĂNG HỒ CHÍ MINH). Despite his wish to be cremated and have his ashes dispersed around the country, Hồ Chí Minh couldn't escape his well-preserved fate. Completed in 1975, this sober granite structure serves as a receiving stand for officials and party leaders, upholding the slightly macabre Communist tradition of constructing glass sarcophagi for their idols. Almost every morning, a procession of pilgrims and curious visitors solemnly passes under the Communist and Vietnamese symbols that adorn the mausoleum. You, too, can join them, braving the building's sanitized air and the uniformed soldiers guarding his earthly remains—and keeping you quietly in line—for a few glory-filled seconds with the late president's corpse. It would have made any pharaoh jealous. Make sure to swing by the palace, stilted house, and museum located on the same compound. *(In Ba Đình Sq. Open Apr.-Oct. Tu-Th 7:30-10:30am, Sa-Su 7:30-11am; Nov.-Mar. Tu-Th 8-11am, Sa-Su 8-11:30am. Get there early to avoid lines, especially on May 19th, Hồ Chí Minh's birthday, and Sept. 2nd, Vietnam's independence day. Closed briefly every Nov. for maintenance. Dress and act conservatively. Free; brochures 5000Đ.)*

PRESIDENTIAL PALACE AND HỒ CHÍ MINH'S STILTED HOUSE. The former residence of the Governor-General of French Indochina, this presidential palace has served as a state guesthouse since 1954, when the Việt Minh defeated the French. Unfortunately, no one but close friends of the Vietnamese government is allowed inside. Hồ Chí Minh believed the building should belong to the people and chose to live in an electrician's hut on the grounds, which remains exactly as he left it. In 1958, he moved into a simple stilted house near a carp pond, which remained his residence until his death in 1969. Note the picture of Vladimir Lenin on his desk and the military helmet next to the phone—a silent reminder that American bombers were still active when Vietnam's leader died. Hồ Chí Minh summoned fish from the nearby carp pond for feeding by clapping his hands. Tourists can still do so today, attracting hordes of hawkers along with the fish. *(North of the mausoleum, across from its exit. Open daily 8-11:30am, Tu-Th and Sa-Su also 2-4pm. Guided tour of the palace, electrician's hut, and stilted house 5000Đ. Wait for a tour guide at the entrance.)*

HỒ CHÍ MINH MUSEUM (BẢO TÀNG HỒ CHÍ MINH). You can learn a little more about this revolutionary leader and his achievements in this large, oppressive gray building. The museum chronicles the life and times of Hồ Chí Minh through a series of bizarre visual displays that blend socialist realism and postmodernism. The exhibit on the uppermost floor tops the others, so be sure to make the climb. Also take a minute for the musicians in the concert hall, who play traditional Vietnamese music. *(From the mausoleum, head south on Hùng Vương and make the first right. It's 200m beyond the One Pillar pagoda. Open Tu-Th and Sa-Su 8-11am and 1:30-4pm. 5000Đ.)*

ONE PILLAR PAGODA (CHÙA MỘT CỘT). Emperor Lý Thánh Tông built this pagoda after dreaming that Quan Âm, the goddess of mercy, gave him a son. Soon after, the son was born to him. The pagoda, built to resemble a lotus plant, was destroyed by the French on their way out of Hà Nội in 1954, but the government has since rebuilt it. *(Between the mausoleum and Hồ Chí Minh Museum. Dress conservatively. Open daily 6-11:30am and 2-6:30pm.)*

MUSEUM OF FINE ARTS (BẢO TÀNG MỸ THUẬT). North of the Temple of Literature, this museum features Vietnamese art from the Stone Age through the 1980s, including Vietnamese stone sculpture and woodwork, socialist realist sculpture, and a series of "combat art" lacquer paintings. Designed for real art enthusiasts. *(66 Nguyễn Thái Học. Open Tu, Th-F, Su 8:30am-5pm. W and Sa 8:30am-9pm. 15,000Đ.)*

⬛ NIGHTLIFE

Cafe Dài Loan Quán, 3 Phan Dình Phùng (☎ 747 2139), just outside of the Old Quarter. A crowded nightspot for well-dressed Vietnamese twentysomethings. Open pretty much around the clock to fulfill your kumquat or pearl banana tea (15,000Đ) cravings. Porridge 20,000Đ. Open daily 5am until very late.

Hoa Giấy Cafe, 21 Chu Văn An (☎843 7928), one block north of the Temple of Literature. A miniature Garden of Eden in a bamboo hut, serving mostly locals and diplomats.
Fruit juices 8000-10,000Đ. Beer 10,000-14,000Đ. Open daily 7am-11pm.

Liễu Giai Cafe, 28 Liễu Giai (☎ 762 6909). Take Phố Kim Mã away from the inner city
and turn right, just before the Daewoo Hotel, onto Liễu Giai. It's on your left after about
300m. A with-it joint for Hà Nội's jet-set crew. Tables set up on the patio and around the
bar. Mixed drinks 40,000-60,000Đ. Ice cream 15,000-30,000Đ. Ice cream with liquor
15,000Đ. Open daily 7am-late.

HAI BÀ TRƯNG DISTRICT

All the way in the south of the city, Hai Bá Trưng district is a mostly residential
area untouched by tourism. Small street restaurants dot the principal avenues, but
its main attraction is still the beautiful Lenin Park. The south of the district is
home to Hà Nội's polytechnical university. With its newly built student village, the
university has brought a few lounging afternoon cafes to an otherwise dull region.

◪ ACCOMMODATIONS

Polonez Hotel, 6A Trấn Nhân Tông (☎822 5715), 1km east of Lenin Park. Although the
hotel itself is nice enough, the area surrounding it is uninteresting. Breakfast included.
Beautifully furnished doubles with satellite TV (and extensive channels) US$22-35. ❹

◉ SIGHTS

LENIN PARK. Beautiful and peaceful Lenin Park (Công Viên Lenin), the largest
park in Hà Nội, is 1km south of the train station on Lê Duẩn. This well-manicured
getaway, starring Bảy Mẫu Lake (bigger than Hoàn Kiếm Lake), attracts joggers,
exercisers, and couples at all hours of the day and late into the evening. Despite
the annoying fee, this park is worth a visit and a relaxed afternoon. *(Enter off Trần
Nhân. Open daily 7am-11pm. 3000Đ, children 1000Đ.)*

AIR FORCE MUSEUM. The most interesting part of this vast museum is outside:
MiGs, helicopters, and other aircraft are on display for up-close and personal
inspection. Inside, all kinds of information and propaganda posters about air war-
fare decorate the walls. A great stop for war buffs. *(Go 1km south from Lenin Park on Lê
Duẩn, take a right on Trường Chinh, and walk down another km; the museum is on your left. Open
Tu-Sa 8-11am and 1-4:30pm. 10,000Đ.)*

NATIONAL CIRCUS. If you want to see amazing human contortions and dancing
animals—and let's be honest, who doesn't?—spend an evening at the Vietnam
National Circus, in a modern circular building on the north side of Lenin Park.
Enter off Phố Trần Nhân Tông, 50m right from the entrance of the park. *(☎822
0277. Shows W-Su 8pm. Tickets available 8am-8pm. Make sure the circus is in town—the acrobats go on tours regularly.)*

TÂY HỒ DISTRICT

Tây Hồ district is centered around West Lake, a 5-square-kilometer deposit of
green-brown water. The lake area, whose marshy shores used to be adorned only
by pagodas, trees, and the occasional house, has developed into a nice spot for a
stroll, meal, or drink, and a posh place to live. It is now also the most popular place
for young couples to meet in the evenings and watch the sunset from a swan paddle boat or from the seat of a motorbike. Tây Hồ district also houses Hà Nội's most
chic hotels and apartment buildings, as well as some large mansions owned by the
nation's economic and political elite.

FOOD

Phương Nguyên Quán, 51-53 Đương Tô Ngọc Vâ (☎823 9948), right on the northeastern shore of West Lake. Go north on Đường Nghi Tám until it splits and take a left onto Đương Xuân Diệu. Then take the 4th right (Đương Tô Ngọc Vâ) and continue until the end. The amazing view over West Lake from this enormous stilted bamboo house attracts Vietnamese from far and wide. Most entrees 45,000-66,000Đ. Menu has many interesting options—try the bean banana turtle for 39,000Đ. Open daily 9am-10pm. ❸

Nhà Nổi Hồ Tây (Floating House; ☎829 3884), usually anchored just north of the Trần Quốc Pagoda, on the West Lake side of Đường Thánh Niên. For a small surcharge (and when enough guests are onboard), it will leave its mooring and float around the lake. Fondue starting at 100,000Đ; seafood 55,000-80,000Đ. Open daily 9am-10pm. ❹

Nhà Hàng Bánh Tôm (☎823 8914), on the Trúc Bạch Lake side of Đường Thánh Niên, just south of the Trần Quốc Pagoda. A huge seafood restaurant with great terraces right on the lake, in the shade of the trees. Large circular tables and private dining areas make this a great place for a party. Try the signature dish, *bánh tôm* (small shrimp doughnuts; 5000Đ). Seafood entrees starting at 40,000Đ. Open daily 9am-11pm. ❸

SIGHTS

The two lakes—**West Lake** (Hồ Tây) and smaller but scenic **Trúc Bạch Lake**—form a pleasant neighborhood for a scenic walk or evening stroll. Be sure to save at least an hour for this route, as Tây Hồ's pagodas and terraces may very well lure you in. To get from the Old Quarter to West Lake, go to the roundabout where Phố Hàng Đậu and Phố Phùng Hưng meet and walk down the beautiful tree-lined Phố Phan Đình Phùng, which runs west, parallel to the north wall of the Citadel. Two blocks after the Catholic church, at the intersection of Phố Quán Thánh and Đường Thánh Niên, is the beautiful **Quán Thánh Pagoda** (Đền Quán Thánh), built by Emperor Lo Thái Tổ during the 11th century. (Open daily 8am-5:30pm. 2000Đ.)

Take a right onto Đường Thánh Niên, the road that separates West Lake from Trúc Bạch Lake. This beautiful lane is a venue for fruit and drink vendors as well as a romantic hangout spot for young lovers, who often rent swan paddle boats for the kind of privacy a shoreside bamboo mat can't provide. (Rent from the southern shore of either lake. 40,000Đ for as long as you like.) On the right, a statue on the shore of Trúc Bạch Lake commemorates the site where future US Senator John McCain's fighter plane was gunned down during the American War. On a small peninsula jutting into West Lake near the north end of Đường Thánh Niên is **Trần Quốc Pagoda** (Chùa Trần Quốc), built during the Lê Dynasty and recently renovated. It's a favorite among locals for its beautiful location among the lake's lilypads. (Open daily 8am-5:30pm.)

The extension of Đường Thánh Niên on the northern shore of Trúc Bạch Lake is a popular picnic location, with street vendors providing ice cream, drinks, and snacks. Shoreline bamboo mats are available for rent. The shore continues across the bridge on Chinh Nam Tràng, on the eastern shore of Trúc Bạch Lake. The little park in front of Ngũ Xá Temple is a nice place to sit down for a while and admire the trees that line the shore before heading back to the bustle of the Old Quarter.

NIGHTLIFE

Kem Bảo Oanh, 7 Đường Thánh Niên (☎823 9688), on the corner across the road from the Hà Nội Lake View apartment building, on the northern shore of Trúc Bạch Lake. A very popular ice cream joint. Four floors provide a majestic view of both lakes and Hà

HÀ NỘI

Nội's skyline. Order the house specialty (coconuts filled with fruit and homemade coconut ice cream; 19,000Đ)—everyone else will. Be prepared for intense pleasure. All kinds of fruit juices 10,000-15,000Đ. Open daily 8am-midnight.

Cổ Ngư Trà Lầu (Tửu Quán), 8 Đường Thánh Niên (☎823 9992). As hard to find as it is to pronounce, great views and prices make this bar well worth the extra effort. Follow Đường Thánh Niên in between the 2 lakes, taking the first left after the Lake View Hotel. It's on your left after about 200m. Head up 2 flights of stairs to find a majestic view of Hà Nội from a hidden rooftop terrace. A great place for watching the sunset. Welcoming service and approachable clientele. Drinks 6000-13,000Đ. Open daily 9am-10:30pm.

Gốc Đa Quán, 1 Đường Thánh Niên (☎829 3005), across the road from Trần Quốc Pagoda, in between the lakes. Nice terrace overlooking Trúc Bạch Lake. Ice cream 15,000Đ. Open daily 9am-midnight.

ĐỐNG ĐA DISTRICT

Đống Đa district encompasses Hà Nội's southwestern region. Like Hai Bá Trưng, this residential area doesn't have much of a tourist scene, but it does offer a few attractions worth checking out, most notably the Temple of Literature in the north end of the district. This district is also home to several nice restaurants and bars.

👁 SIGHTS

TEMPLE OF LITERATURE AND ROYAL COLLEGE. Dedicated to Confucius, the Temple of Literature (Văn Miếu) was allegedly built in 1070 during the reign of Emperor Lý Thánh Tông to honor scholars and literary men. Six years later, he built the adjacent Royal College (Quốc Tử Giám), Vietnam's first university, in order to educate the children of court mandarins. It remained in use until 1802, when the national university was moved to the new capital, Huế. The buildings remain in pristine condition. To enter, pass through the Four Pillars on Quốc Tử Giám. The first set of gates—meant to symbolize the academic experience—are those of Talent and Virtue. The next set leads to the 82 Tortoise Stelae, all erected between 1442 and 1778, on which the names, places of birth, and achievements of 1306 successful triennial examination scholars are inscribed. At the end of the path, the Gates of Synthesis lead to the sanctuary, which houses statues of Confucius and his four greatest disciples. *(At the intersection of Tôn Đức Thắng and Nguyễn Thái Học, 2km west of Hoàn Kiếm Lake. Enter off Quốc Tử Giám on the southern side. Open daily 7:30am-5:30pm. 5000Đ, students 2500Đ.)*

CẦU GIẤY DISTRICT

Cầu Giấy district has only recently been officially added to the city of Hà Nội. Construction is rampant in this mostly residential region, though some open spaces remain. Consistent with Hà Nội's image, small parks and lakes are scattered throughout the district, and the boulevards (including the highway to the airport) are broad, straight, and tree-lined. These days, boys can still be found playing football in the middle of the district's crossroads, but that may soon become an image of the past, when traffic picks up here, too.

🏛 MUSEUMS

▣ MUSEUM OF ETHNOLOGY. If you visit one museum in Hà Nội, this should be it. As one traveler put it, "When in Hà Nội, one must take in the trees, the lake, and the Museum of Ethnology." Though a bit out of the way, the museum is definitely worth a full morning or afternoon. Inaugurated in 1997, the building was designed to enhance visitors' understanding of Vietnam's 54 ethnic groups and diverse culture. The signs in English, French, and Vietnamese give ample information about the daily lives and traditions of the country's peoples. The best part, though, is the enormous backyard, where eight traditional houses from different ethnic groups have been reconstructed. You can explore them on your own. There is also a replica of a traditional gravesite (check out the wood carving), a puppet theater, a pottery workshop, and hydraulic rice pestles. *(Go west from Quán Thánh Pagoda down Đường Hoàng Hoa Thám. At its end, take a left, and 50m later a right onto Đường Hoàng Quốc Việt. Then, take the 4th left onto Đường Nguyễn Văn Nguyên, where the museum is located. It's a 15min. motorbike ride, but there are few motorbike taxis waiting by the museum to take you back to the city center. You can also take bus #14 from the fountain north of Hoàn Kiếm Lake in the direction of Cầu Giấy, get off at Nghĩa Tân, and walk east down Đường Hoàng Quốc Việt, taking a right onto Đường Nguyễn Văn Nguyên. ☎ 756 2193. Open Tu-Su 8:30am-5:30pm. 15,000Đ, students with ID 5000Đ. Motorbike parking 2000Đ, bicycle 1000Đ.)*

⊠ DAYTRIPS FROM HÀ NỘI

PAGODAS

◪ PERFUME PAGODA

The Perfume Pagoda is located 60km south of Hà Nội. The best way to see it is by organized tour. Typically, these tours include transport to Yên Vô village, a boat ride across the winding river, and a 4km hike to the main temple. US$13-18 includes transport, lunch, and admission. Alternatively, travelers can take a public bus south to Hà Đông (30min.; 5000-7000Đ) and catch another bus to Yên Vô village, or rent a motorbike for the day in Hà Nội (US$4-6). Renting a boat and rower costs 30,000-50,000Đ per person (depending on how many people are in the group). Lunch at one of the many stands along the path up the mountain can also be quite pricey. Dress conservatively. 35,000Đ.

Set in lush rice paddies studded with monstrous, jagged limestone karsts, Chùa Hương—the Perfume Pagoda—is a main destination of Buddhist pilgrims in Vietnam and a must-see for travelers. As with most pilgrimages, the journey is as important as the destination. It begins at Yên Vô village, where lotus sculptures adorn the shores of a long channel. A narrow red boat takes you on an amazingly beautiful 1hr. ride through a long, meandering waterway surrounded by cliffs, shrines, and jungle, eventually ending at the foot of a mountain. The second part of the journey is a steep hike on a twisty, stony trail. Don't let physical exhaustion or the many souvenir and snack stands distract you from the surrounding beauty. It's a good idea to bring hiking boots—the trail is very steep at times and can be dangerously slippery when wet. There's also an expensive cable car that goes to the pagoda for US$2 each way, but the hike is well worth the effort. After at least 1hr., you should see a staircase to the Perfume Pagoda. The pagoda derives its name from the huge grotto in the Hương Tích Mountains (Mountains of the Fragrant Traces) in which it resides. At the bottom of the cave is a tiny sanctuary with statues, a waterfall, and a cloud of incense. Bring a flashlight to see the shrine more clearly, and don't miss the statue of a million hands and eyes.

Aside from the Perfume Pagoda itself, the complex of temples at the bottom of the mountain, known as the **Thiên Trù Pagodas,** is also serene and beautiful. **Thiên Chù** and **Giải Oau Chù** are especially worth a small detour. The pagoda area, where over 100 temples once stood, was destroyed during the First Indochina War. Although it was partly rebuilt in 1968, only seven temples remain today.

For a month after the Lunar New Year, Buddhists flock to the temple during the **Perfume Pagoda Festival** (Lễ Hội Chùa Hương). To avoid shuffling shoulder-to-shoulder up the mountain, check out the pagoda Monday through Wednesday during this month. The crowds are smaller on odd dates of the lunar calendar.

TÂY PHƯƠNG AND THẦY PAGODAS

Only about 6km apart, a joint visit to these two pagodas makes for a pleasant trip from Hà Nội. The easiest way to get there is either on an organized tour or by hiring a motorbike

HÀ NỘI

ON THE MENU

SNAKES AND BLADDERS

Although all restaurants in Lệ Mật list serpent at the top of the menu (US$6-10), the preparation and accompanying show depend on where you go. Snake is traditionally eaten by men in order to increase their virility, but female guests will be served as well.

Usually the cook presents a live cobra at the table, either tied to a stick or held by an assistant. First he cuts the snake's neck, allowing the warm blood to gush out and fill a glass. Then he slices its stomach and removes a small green balloon-like venom sac, pouring it into another glass. The heart is next: the cook makes an incision a little higher, carefully cuts out the snake's still-beating heart, and presents the tiny organ on a plate or in a glass of rice whiskey. The brave can down the glass and its living content "100 percent." The snake's venom is blended with its urine and rice whiskey, which makes for quite a cocktail. The rest of the snake is then cut into three or four pieces and taken back to the kitchen to be fried, boiled, or grilled. Your late table guest will soon return as part of a rice dish, stir-fry, or any course of your liking.

If properly bred and prepared, snake can be a real delicacy for the more culinarily cultured palate. The cooks at Hà Nội's top restaurants, among others, are regular visitors in Lệ Mật. But beware, lest endangered species make the cut.

driver (about 70,000Đ). Riding over there yourself is also possible. Dress conservatively.

Tây Phương Pagoda (Pagoda of the West), is, not surprisingly, the westernmost pagoda around Hà Nội, situated on a steep limestone cliff. Walk up the 200 stone steps to arrive at the main pagoda. Inside its walls, you'll find a small monastery and several shrines (and the usual flock of hawkers). Enter through the small wooden doors on the left of the main building to discover the pagoda's treasure: a group of huge, antique, wood-carved figures representing all the emotional states of man—some in an almost caricature-like fashion. Don't miss the 80 monk statues, either. Next, pass through the small gate in the right pagoda wall and follow the big white arrows down a winding path on the cliff's side, passing by two smaller and simpler pagodas. When you reach the bottom of the cliff, take a right onto the concrete path that crosses the settlement. You'll find yourself back at the entrance, surrounded by snack stands. The walk takes about 45min. (About 37km from Hà Nội. Look for the big sign on your left on Hwy. 72. Open daily 7am-6pm. 10,000Đ.)

Thầy Pagoda (Master's Pagoda) lies practically on the next cliff over, in the direction of Hà Nội. Like its neighbor, Thầy Pagoda is actually a complex of pagodas and shrines, but unlike Tây Phương, its main structure is at the foot of the cliff. From the ticket booth, walk past a few stands and small shrines until you reach the chief pagoda, in front of a big pond filled with lotus flowers. This pond is used for water-puppet performances during religious festivals. In fact, many claim that water puppetry was invented here. Take off your shoes and enter the pagoda to see the many statues and shrines inside. Be sure not to miss the impressive central altar. The pagoda is also used as a classroom for the young monks who reside behind it. Past the main structure, a steep path ascends the cliff, leading to the other pagodas and shrines in the complex; the forest, caves, and natural rock formations along the meandering path are quite a sight. The top of the cliff can be reached in about 15min., but plan some extra time to walk around and see the entire site. Guides will flock eagerly to all visitors; it may be a good idea to hire an English speaker for 5000-20,000Đ, depending on the duration of the tour. From the fifth to the seventh of the third lunar month, there's a festival to honor Tu Dao Hanh, the monk who became king, so expect to present an offering or stand in line to pray. (About 30km from Hà Nội. Take a right on Hwy. 72 at the sign, and go down 1km of unpaved road. Open daily 7am-6pm. 10,000Đ.)

OTHER PAGODAS. There are tons of pagodas in the area around Hà Nội (see **Hà Nội and Surroundings** map, p. 99). Down nearly every major road, these old buildings give character to the surrounding landscape. While we certainly don't recommend "pagoda-hopping"—after all, we already cover the most spectacular pagodas in the area—stopping by one of these relics on the way into or out of the city can be a fun detour and provide a great spot for a picnic.

HANDICRAFT VILLAGES

The immediate area around Hà Nội contains many artisan villages, each of which specializes in a particular craft. Comprehensive tours are available for all of these villages, but with a good map you can also visit them by yourself.

■ **LỆ MẬT (SNAKE VILLAGE).** Every restaurant in this neighborhood specializes in serpent cuisine. You only get to see the serpent's "preparation" if you purchase a meal. Due to cutthroat (ha ha!) competition, any foreigner coming into the village will be approached by a flock of hawkers on motorbikes trying to lure you into their restaurants. Almost all restaurants have a 150,000Đ fixed price, but there are huge discrepancies in quality, cleanliness, and the amount of food and liquor included, so don't stop at the first place you come to. Keep your eyes open for that old-time favorite—snake-penis liquor. Would you rather not actually *eat* snake? Instead, participate in the snake dance held at an annual festival on the 23rd day of the 3rd lunar month. See **"Snakes and Bladders,"** p. 132. *(7km across the Red River from Hà Nội, just off Highway 1A. Take a motorbike there for 35,000Đ round-trip, including wait.)*

VAN PHÚC (SILK VILLAGE). Probably the most accessible village without a tour guide. Almost all of the silk in the tourist shops of the Old Quarter is woven here; walk into any alley and see the looms in operation. The silk made here is famous for its light weight and smooth texture. There is also a row of shops offering silk products (mainly pajamas) at prices that would wipe all of Hàng Gai out of business. If you ask nicely, they might even custom-make silk products for you. Before leaving, peek at the small shrine built for the ancestor who taught weaving to the village. *(Just southwest of Hà Nội in Hà Đông, 1km from Hwy. 6. Take a right after the bridge.)*

BÁT TRÀNG (POTTERY VILLAGE). The pottery made in this village is famous throughout Vietnam. The process has not changed much since the 11th century, during the Lý Dynasty, when royal blue enamel was introduced to the village. You can see the whole pottery and ceramic production process, or make your own. There are also many stores selling a wide selection of Vietnamese- and Western-style products. *(13km down the Red River from Hà Nội, off Hwy. 195.)*

OTHER DAYTRIPS

BA VI NATIONAL PARK

About 65km west of Hà Nội, 1½hr. by motorbike. Go down Hwy. 32 and take a left at the sign. Admission 10,000Đ per person, 5000Đ per motorbike. Rooms in local guesthouses about 150,000Đ.

Due west from Hà Nội in Hà Tây Province lies Ba Vi, a 1276m mountain shrouded in dense forest. The chilly peak and the national park around it together form a popular weekend getaway for Hanoians. However, as far as Vietnam's parks go, Ba Vi is not very exciting. The 90-minute drive alone is a turn-off, and there are really only two trails to hike and a small snack shop located at their base. The half-hour trail to the left leads to a pagoda dedicated to Hồ Chí Minh, while the trail to the right leads to a smaller, closer pagoda. The surrounding area, luckily, is quite famous for its dairy production. Off the side of the highway yogurt, milk, and even artisan cheese (a rare commodity in Vietnam) can be bought.

Near Ba Vi National Park lie several holiday **resorts** that Hanoians (especially couples) frequent on the weekends. They offer nearly identical packages of karaoke, swimming pools, massage salons, hotels, and restaurants, all wrapped up in a strange, Disney-like atmosphere and surrounded by impressive natural beauty. Travelers can spend the night or just enjoy the amenities during the day. Find out what Hanoians do for fun, but don't expect anyone to speak English.

Khoang Xanh (☎034 881 206), around a natural swimming pool. The least cheesy and gaudy of the resorts. Luxurious hotel rooms around 180,000Đ per night. Admission 30,000Đ. Open daily 7am-10pm.

Thác Đa (☎034 846 272), 1km from Khoang Xanh in a quiet valley. Includes tennis courts and swimming pool. Check out the 10m statues of random characters, including a breast-feeding woman standing next to a sword-carrying warrior. Admission 30,000Đ.

Hồ Snôi Há, about 10km south of Thác Đa. A vast lake surrounded by hills on a busy road. The island in the middle offers paddle boats, canoes, and bungalows.

Đồi Cẩm Đồng Mô (☎034 834 700). A popular massage salon that also includes a cafe-restaurant and karaoke bar. Open daily 8am-11pm.

TAM ĐẢO NATIONAL PARK

About 70km from Hà Nội. Take Hwy. 23 to the northwest, then take a right onto road 2B just before Vĩnh Yên. The gate to Tam Đảo National Park will appear in front of you; Tam Đảo Hill Station is another 11km up a steep 1-lane road. It's recommended that you drive a car or Minsk motorbike up this slope rather than a regular motorbike. On the way back, you won't need to start your engine until after you leave the park.

In the mountains northwest of Hà Nội lies Tam Đảo National Park, a stretch of 369 square kilometers of forest and rainforest on and around Tam Đảo Mountain (927m) that's perfect for hiking and wildlife observation. The park boasts a wide variety of endangered species, some impressive birds, 904 species of flora, and some of the most amazing views in the region. Those who want to hike or spot Tam Đảo's wildlife shouldn't venture out by themselves; hire a guide instead for about 60,000-80,000Đ at one of the bigger hotels.

In the middle of this beautiful area lies Tam Đảo Hill Station, a former French colonial resort whose once-charming face was later scarred by Soviet architecture. Only some small vineyards along the creek and a few remaining buildings recall French days. Tam Đảo's cool climate makes its unspoiled forest especially appealing to sweaty urbanites. Consequently, the small hill station has developed into a summer weekend getaway for Hanoians, composed almost exclusively of generic hotels, small *bia hơi* joints, and karaoke bars that fill the valley with raucous music day and night. Most guesthouses charge 100,000-120,000Đ a night. Come during the week to avoid the weekend's rowdy crowds.

The park officials at Tam Đảo are struggling to address the issues of uncontrolled hunting and deforestation. Local resident farmers and the logging industry pose serious threats to the park and to the country's wildlife in general. If you're interested in helping with conservation efforts, email **The Tam Đảo Project** at office.tdmp@gtz-vietnam.com.vn.

HỒ CHÍ MINH TRAIL MUSEUM. The Hồ Chí Minh Trail Museum, about 15km south of Hà Nội, is dedicated to guerrilla warfare in South Vietnam during the American War. The museum displays pictures, scenes, and artifacts of the jungle war. Though it's probably not worth a trip by itself, the museum is on the road to the Perfume Pagoda and has some fun exhibits. Don't miss the visual display on the American bombardments, a dark, black-and-gray room with papier-mâché bombs suspended from the ceiling. Outside, just to the right of the entrance, a series of military vehicles is on display. Behind the museum is a shrine to those who fell during the war. All information is in Vietnamese, and the museum seems to be a bit past its prime. (*Take Hwy. 6 southwest out of city toward the Perfume Pagoda; after 14km, take a right at the crossing. The museum will be on your right, 100m from the road, next to a military compound. Open Tu-Su 7:30-11am and 1:30-4pm. 10,000Đ.*)

THE NORTHERN COAST

With a rich history influenced by centuries of international trade, Vietnam's northern seaboard is the picture of serenity, laced with ancient temples and pagodas overlooking popular beaches. From the powder-fine beach of Móng Cái, littered with hundreds of curly, conical seashells, to the isolated white-sand wonders spread across Bái Tử Long Bay, to the fractured golden shores of Cát Bà Island crowded with Vietnamese vacationers, the Northern Coast has bloomed into a popular destination for domestic and foreign travelers alike. Most beloved in tourist circles is the coast's world-renowned Hạ Long Bay, populated by fishing villages of floating blue-gray houses inhabited by families, dogs, and the occasional pool table. Visitors to this area are charmed by the poetic grandeur of limestone treasures that protrude from the bay's frothing, foam-capped waters washing picturesquely against the shore.

HIGHLIGHTS OF THE NORTHERN COAST

DRIFT AMONG LIMESTONE MAJESTY in Vietnam's most famous natural attraction, **Hạ Long Bay** (p. 153). Despite heavy waves of tourism, travelers can't help but be blown away by the endless, surreal silhouettes of stony monoliths rising from the sea.

DRIFT AMONG LESS-TOURISTED LIMESTONE MAJESTY on bucolic **Quán Lạn Island** (p. 165) in **Bái Tử Long Bay** (p. 159). Isolated, amazing beaches await.

DRIFT AMONG FOREIGN BEACHGOERS on seashell-dotted **Trá Cổ Beach** (p. 169), one of the far north's most beautiful strips of sand.

DRIFT AMONG LIMESTONE MAJESTY AND FOREIGN BEACHGOERS on lovely **Cát Bà Island** (p. 142). The national park's stark mountains and the shining beaches on the coast attract tourists in droves—and for good reason.

HẢI PHÒNG ☏31

A quiet city of wide, shady avenues, big plazas, and crumbling colonial buildings, Hải Phòng, Vietnam's third-largest city, offers little other than a stopover point for travelers en route to Cát Bà Island and Hạ Long Bay. Pool halls, cafes, and cell phone stores line the city's wide streets, but travelers tend to just pass through Hải Phòng—after all, you can only buy so many cell phone accessories. Built by the French in the early 1900s, it was meant to imitate the quiet towns in the south of France, and some areas do indeed retain that tranquility. However, the city also has a darker history. Because of its key role as a conduit for Soviet aid to North Vietnam during the American War, Hải Phòng suffered severe US bombing; in some places, it seems as though the city has yet to recover. Fledgling industries have also changed the face of the Hải Phòng that the French designed, making it a commercial center that drives most travelers toward the beaches and parks of nearby Cát Bà Island. Remnants of the city's old pace still remain, though, in its food-laden alleyways, away from the inevitable forces of change.

NORTHERN COAST

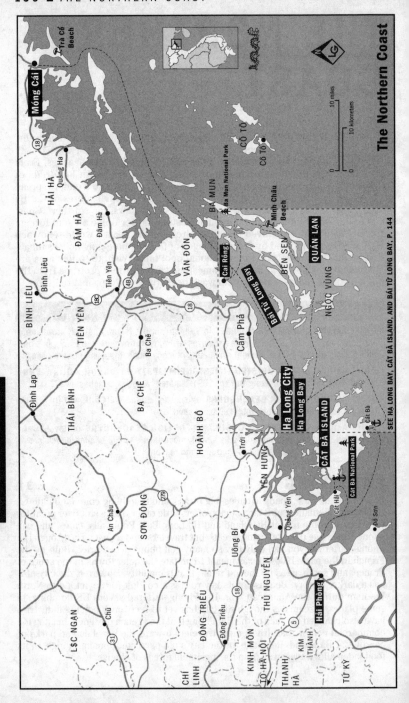

The Northern Coast

Trà Cổ Beach

Móng Cái

(18)

HẢI HÀ
Quảng Hà

ĐẦM HÀ
Đầm Hà

BÌNH LIÊU
Bình Liêu

TIÊN YÊN
Tiên Yên

(4B)

(18B)

(18)

THÁI BÌNH
Đình Lập

BA CHẼ
Ba Chẽ

HOÀNH BỒ

Trới

(279)

SƠN ĐỘNG
An Châu

LỤC NGẠN
Chũ

(31)

CHÍ LINH

ĐÔNG TRIỀU
Đồng Triều

(18)

Uông Bí

YÊN HƯNG

THỦY NGUYÊN

KINH MÔN

KIM THÀNH

THANH HÀ

TỪ KỲ

(5)

Hải Phòng

TỪ HÀ NỘI

Quảng Yên

Cát Hải

Đồ Sơn

CÁT BÀ ISLAND

Cát Bà National Park

Cát Bà

VÂN ĐỒN

Cẩm Phả

Cái Rồng

Bái Tử Long Bay

Hạ Long City

Hạ Long Bay

BÁI SEN

NGỌC VỪNG

QUÁN LẠN

Minh Châu Beach

BA MÙN
Ba Mùn National Park

CÔ TÔ
Cô Tô

LG

10 miles

10 kilometers

SEE HẠ LONG BAY, CÁT BÀ ISLAND, AND BÁI TỪ LONG BAY, P. 144

TRANSPORTATION

Flights: Cát Bà Airport (☎728 209), 7km southwest of the town center. Take a taxi (40,000Đ), motorcycle taxi (US$3), or cyclo (15,000-20,000Đ) from the town center. **Vietnam Airlines,** 30 Trần Phú (☎921 242; open M-Sa 8-11:30am and 1:30-6pm) offers flights to **HCMC** (1hr.; 8pm; 1,525,000Đ).

Trains: Haiphong Railway Station, 75 Lương Khánh Thiện (☎846 433), at the end of Phạm Ngũ Lão. Trains to: **Hải Dương** (1hr.; 7:40pm; hard seat 13,000Đ, soft seat 14,000Đ, soft seat with A/C 15,000Đ); **Hà Nội Central Station** (2-2½hr.; 8:50am, 6:40pm; hard seat 24,000Đ, soft seat 26,000Đ, soft seat with A/C 28,000Đ); **Hà Nội Gia Lâm Station** (2-2½hr.; 8pm; hard seat 23,000Đ, soft seat 24,000Đ); **Hà Nội Long Biên Station** (2-3hr.; 6, 8:50am, 2:35, 5:05pm; same prices as above).

Buses: Tam Bạc Bus Station, opposite the steel market. Buses to Hà Nội's **Gia Lâm station** (2-3hr.; every 15min. 5:30am-7pm, every 30min. after 7pm; 30,000Đ) and **Hạ Long City** (2¾hr.; 6am-4pm; 50,000Đ).

Ferries: The pier is on Bến Bính on the Cấm River. From the west end of Điện Biên Phủ, head north toward the port. Competing companies typically run a morning slow boat and hydrofoil as well as early afternoon slow boats to Cát Bà. Exact times vary; prices don't, and be prepared to pay the inflated tourist price. To: **Cát Bà** (slow boat 2-3hr.; 6:20am, 12:30pm; 80,000Đ; hydrofoil 45-60min.; 8:20, 8:40am; 100,000Đ); **Hạ Long City** (slow boat 3hr.; 11am; 60,000Đ); and **Móng Cái** (6pm; 90,000Đ). In the summer and on weekends boats fill up, so purchase tickets 1 day in advance.

Local Transportation: Cyclos should get you anywhere in the city for 5000-10,000Đ. **Motorbikes** cost only a little more. **Haiphong Taxi** (☎641 641) charges 6300Đ per km, with a base fare of 9000Đ; ask the driver to use the meter. There's a cab stand near the flower stalls on Hoàng Văn Thụ, and cabs can be flagged down on Điện Biên Phủ.

ORIENTATION

On the Red River Delta 103km east of Hà Nội on Highway 5, Hải Phòng has a compact, densely populated center flanked by huge, sprawling industrial zones and suburbs. After crossing the Lạc Long Bridge, Hwy. 5 becomes **Điện Biên Phủ,** Hải Phòng's main drag, and runs past a number of hotels. Two blocks east of the bridge, Điện Biên Phủ intersects **Hoàng Văn Thụ,** the second-largest street in town. This general area, called the "Center," is home to the train station, a park, and **Tam Bạc Lake. Trần Hưng Đạo, Trần Phú,** and **Lương Khánh Thiện** run diagonally between Điện Biên Phủ and Hoàng Văn Thụ. From the Municipal Theater, at the intersection of Trần Hưng Đạo and Hoàng Văn Thụ, **Quang Trưng** runs along Tam Bạc Lake before ending at the Tam Bạc Bus Station and **steel market.**

PRACTICAL INFORMATION

Tourist Office: Haiphong Tourist Company, 57 Điện Biên Phủ (☎747 216), in the Tháng Năm Hotel. Open M-Sa 7-11:30am and 2-5pm. Tours, boat rental, and car rental available. Caters to national tourists, so don't expect assistance in English.

Currency Exchange: Vietcombank, 11 Hoàng Diệu (☎842 658). Heading east on Điện Biên Phủ, turn left onto Minh Khai; it's at the end on the left. Open M-F 7:30-11:30am and 1:30-4pm. One of the few international **ATMs** in town is just within its gates, on the left. Open 24hr. Other Vietcombanks are around, but the central location of Hoàng Diệu is unbeatable.

Emergency: Police: ☎113. **Ambulance:** ☎115.

NORTHERN COAST

JUL 17

FROM THE ROAD

CULTURE SURFING

In today's media-saturated world, one of the best ways to understand a foreign culture is to watch its television programs. While the black-and-white documentaries of Hồ Chí Minh only reinforced the slightly dated ideas I had of Vietnam, I found that familiar images were only a few clicks away: the flashing mobile number of their pop-idol contest; eager contestants on *Hãy Chọn Giá Đúng* ("Is the Right Price?"); Martin Sheen playing the US president in a Vietnamese *West Wing*.

Flipping through channels is like cutting a cross-section of Vietnam. American war movies speak to a generation that once saw America as the enemy, while MTV music videos speak to one that embraces the US's consumer culture. Today, questions concerning the next National Party Congress no longer dominate the screens at home, having been replaced by *Ai Là Triệu Phú?* ("Who is the Millionaire?"). Perhaps today both questions are the same.

Of course, all Vietnamese television is filtered through the government-run broadcaster, which aims to "play an active role in the nation's ideological and cultural forefront." And while there's no longer a single ideological or cultural message coming from the government, the country's television is both an accurate reflection of contemporary Vietnam and a valid prediction as to where it is heading tomorrow.

-Stephen Fan

Pharmacy: Hoàng Lê Pharmacy, 63 Điện Biên Phủ (☎841 605). Reasonably stocked. Open M-Sa 8am-7pm, Su 8am-2pm. There are also many pharmacies lining Điện Biên Phủ. A few smaller ones, open until 9pm, are on Trần Quang Khải, east from the intersection with Hoàng Văn Thụ.

Medical Services: Việt-Tiệp Friendship Hospital, 1 Nhà Thương (☎700 514 or 832 721), 100m south of Tam Bạc Bus Station. Few doctors and nurses speak any English at all. A better option may be to contact the **International SOS Clinic** (p. 108) in Hà Nội, which can transport you to Hà Nội or Bangkok to be treated.

Telephones: Inside the GPO (see below). International phone and fax.

Internet: Hải Phòng has a good number of somewhat cramped cyber cafes. **135 Điện Biên Phủ** (☎746 168) charges 3000Đ per hr. for Internet use and computer games. The computers in the front are newer. In the back are 2 phone booths for Internet phone calls (3000Đ per min.). Open daily 8am-11pm. **Internet & Game,** 36 Minh Khai (☎745 598), charges the same rates. Open daily 8am-11pm.

Post Office: GPO, 5 Nguyễn Tri Phương (☎842 563). A big colonial building at the intersection with Hoàng Văn Thụ. *Poste Restante* and DHL. Open daily 6:30am-9pm.

■ ACCOMMODATIONS

Hải Phòng has not yet developed a hotel market for budget travelers. Almost all of the city's hotels are either on or 50m from Điện Biên Phủ and cater mostly to businessmen. They tend to be mediocre, and English is not widely spoken, so don't expect much navigational help from your hotel staff.

Quang Minh Hotel, 20 Minh Khai (☎823 404), the tall building halfway down the block from the intersection with Điện Biên Phủ. Rooms with big windows, A/C, TV, fridge, private bath, and phone. The best part is the included breakfast, ranging from Western omelettes to 10 different varieties of Vietnamese soups. Twins or doubles US$15. ❸

50 Điện Biên, 50 Điện Biên Phủ (☎842 409), down an alley. Adequate rooms away from traffic, overlooking a small courtyard. Rooms include A/C, TV, fridge, private bath, and phone. Singles 160,000Đ; doubles with double or twin beds 170,000Đ. ❸

Bến Bính Hotel, 6 Đương Bến Bính (☎842 260), east of the ferry dock. Standard rooms with nice views in a convenient location. Doubles with A/C, TV, and bath US$25. ❹

Hải Phòng

🏠 ACCOMMODATIONS
50 Điện Biên, **3**
Bến Bính Hotel, **1**
Minh Khai Hotel, **12**
Quang Minh Hotel, **9**
Tháng Năm Hotel, **6**

🍴 FOOD
Bia Rau Hải Phòng, **5**
Chie, **11**
Dại Thậưng, **8**
Haiphong Club, **15**
La Villa Blanche, **13**

**⭐ NIGHTLIFE &
ENTERTAINMENT**
Biện Goi Disco, **7**
Carmen Billiards Club, **14**
Dất Cảng, **18**
New Story, **2**
Fanny Ice Cream, **16**
Hà Trang, **10**
Philey's Lounge Bar, **17**
Star Billiards Club, **4**

NORTHERN COAST

Minh Khai Hotel, 23 Minh Khai (☎841 430). Spotless, simple rooms with A/C, TV, phone, and a private shower. Though the owner speaks no English, he is friendly and cheerful. Rooms 150,000Đ. ❷

Tháng Năm Hotel, 55-57 Điện Biên Phủ (☎747 216). Decent-size rooms with A/C, TV, phone, and balcony. The whole building could use a facelift, and rooms can be noisy due to Điện Biên Phủ traffic. Rooms with double or twin beds US$15-18. ❸

🍴 FOOD

In Hải Phòng, the street is the place to eat. Streets transform into open-air diners at night, filled with welcoming people whose English is usually limited to an enthusiastic "hello." Điện Biên Phủ, Trần Quang Khải, and the alleys in between them are especially good for streetside eats, offering many different kinds of phở, cơm, and other specialties for 5000-20,000Đ. Haggling is encouraged. Restaurants tend to be generic, kitschy, and overpriced.

Chie, 18 Trần Quang Khải (☎821 018). A Japanese restaurant with a very Japanese interior, accentuated by artwork and paper walls. Diners are separated with screens, giving them privacy to enjoy a rare (ha!) meal in Vietnam—sushi. Soup USụ2. Small sushi platters USụ2-11. Tempura USụ4. Open daily 10am-2pm and 4:30-10:30pm. ❸

Dại Thộng, 19 Lê Dại Hành (☎822 298). Walk down the long driveway and up the stairs into the first dining room. With a diverse menu, large portions, and helpful staff, Dại Thộng is a safe bet among the mediocre restaurants in the area. Serves typical beef and pork dishes as well as the more exotic frog and snail. Entrees 20,000-60,000Đ. Open daily 7:30am-2:30pm and 5-10pm. MC/V. ❸

Haiphong Club, 17 Trần Quang Khải (☎822 603), close to the intersection of Trần Quang Khải and Lê Dại Hành. A popular Vietnamese restaurant-bar with live Vietnamese music. Turtle sold at market price and served by Hawaiian-shirted staff members. Most other entrees 30,000-60,000Đ. Huge cocktail menu. Open daily 10am-midnight. ❸

La Villa Blanche, 5 Trần Hưng Đạo (☎810 275), 1 block from the funfair. Situated in a spacious but dilapidated French villa. During the summer, most guests sit on the blue plastic furniture in the garden terrace. Western breakfast around 10,000Đ; seafood from 50,000Đ. Open daily 8am-11pm. ❷

Bia Rau Hải Phòng, 123 Điện Biên Phủ (☎402 243), 50m from the intersection of Điện Biên Phủ and Hoàng Văn Thụ. This restaurant and its terrace feel more like a street eatery. Popular with ferry workers; women are a rare sight here. Phở 10,000Đ. The coldest *bia hơi* in town 2000Đ. Open daily 7am-11pm. ❶

👁 SIGHTS

MUNICIPAL THEATER (CITY SQUARE THEATER). The recently renovated Municipal Theater testifies to Hải Phòng's French architectural influence. It was built using materials imported from France, in the style of the Hà Nội Opera House. The Vietnamese, not to be outdone, have added a splash of their own culture: an enormous poster of Hồ Chí Minh hangs from its front door. The square in front of the theater was the site of a bloody four-day standoff between French forces and Việt Minh revolutionaries in November 1946. *(At the intersection of Trần Hưng Đạo and Hoàng Văn Thụ. Ticket prices vary according to the performance.)*

HẢI PHÒNG MUSEUM. The Hải Phòng Museum (Bảo Tàng Hải Phòng) presents the history of the city in a fading red colonial building. After another smiling Uncle Ho greets you, the museum covers Hải Phòng's origins and roles in the French and American Wars. Most information is in Vietnamese. The *bia hơi* in the garden seems to attract more visitors than the museum. *(On the corner of Điện Biên Phủ and Hoàng Văn Thụ. Open Tu and Th 8am-10:30pm, W and Su 7:30am-9:30pm. 10,000Đ.)*

NAVY MUSEUM. The big yellow modernist building on Điện Biên Phủ houses the Hải Phòng Navy Museum, which contains some poignant remnants of the city's battles with foreigners. This politicized display caters especially to those interested in the American War or Vietnam's general struggle for existence over the last century. *(38 Điện Biên Phủ. Open Tu-Su 8am-5pm. 10,000Đ.)*

NGHÈ TEMPLE. The many little compartments and the large courtyard of this red-and-gold temple commemorate Lê Chân, a female leader in the Trưng sisters' insurrection against the Chinese. The Vietnamese celebrate the heroine's birth and death at the temple on the eighth day of the second lunar month and the 25th day of the 12th lunar month, respectively. Special offerings are made at the shrine, and there seems to be an incense-burning contest in front of the stone elephant and horse statues outside. Check out the ornate bronze sedan chair to the right of the entrance. *(55 Lê Chân. Best reached by cyclo. Open daily 6am-9pm.)*

DƯ HÀNG PAGODA. Dư Hàng Pagoda (Chùa Hàng), has a beautiful Chinese-style garden with a multitude of small inner courtyards. Built during the Lê Dynasty and restored during the 20th century, this pagoda was used as a revolutionary base for the Communist Party in the 1930s. *(Open daily 5-11:30am and 1:30-6pm.)*

NORTHERN COAST

HÀNG KÊNH COMMUNAL HOUSE. History buffs should stop by the Hàng Kênh Communal House (Đình Hàng Kênh), built in 1719. Remnants of Imperial Vietnam adorn all objects and surfaces within this Chinese-style compound. On an altar stands a statue of Ngô Quyền, the liberator and king. An impressive gong is sounded daily at 6pm. *(The house is 1.5km south of the city square, just off Hàng Kênh on Nguyễn Cong Tru. Open M-Sa 8am-5pm. 10,000Đ.)*

ST. PETER'S CATHEDRAL. A big concrete-gray cathedral, dedicated to Christianity's first Pope, stands tall in the center of Hải Phòng. Lion heads defend its exterior, while its sober interior is adorned with paintings of saints and a purple-gold altar. The bell tower is detached from the cathedral itself and bedecked with a big neon cross. Two big sparkling-white statues of St. Peter and St. Paul stand in the churchyard. *(One block down Hoàng Văn Thụ from its intersection with Điện Biên Phủ. Services 7am and 6pm. Women and men sit separately.)*

ĐỒ SƠN BEACH. This beach attracts tourists from all over Vietnam and is cleaned regularly in a government-led effort to boost the local economy. In summer, get there early to find a good spot. Though the water is somewhat murky, vendors on the beach sell fresh and cheap seafood. Đồ Sơn also boasts Vietnam's sole casino, which serves mainly foreigners from China, Japan, and Korea. *(22km southeast of Hải Phòng. A 40,000Đ motorcycle taxi is the best way to get there. Buses depart to Đồ Sơn daily from Hải Phòng's bus stations when full and cost 5000Đ. To reach the beach and casino, make a right at the ocean and continue 4km.)*

OTHER SIGHTS. Pagoda-like **flower stalls**, built in 1944, imbue the squares near Tam Bạc Lake with vibrant colors. Farther west, hawker shops flank Quang Trưng and its side streets. At the end of this road by the bus station, on the site of old rice markets, is the modern behemoth known as **Chợ Sắt (Steel Market)**. On Điện Biên Phủ, a block from the Navy Museum and across from the funfair, are some fish aquariums, where vendors sell colorful tropical fish. An extensive street and indoor **market**, selling a strange assortment of fruit, squid, and undergarments, is on the corner of Phan Chu Trinh and Nguyễn Khu Yên.

🎭 ENTERTAINMENT

During summers, Hải Phòng's **funfair**, Vườn Hoa Kim Đồng, opens at the crossing of Điện Biên Phủ and Trần Hưng Đạo in the east side of town. The attractions that draw in children and young couples alike include a rollerskating course with built-in trees, a rollercoaster, and pool tables. Enter through the 🐉**dragon's mouth** into a popular house of wacky mirrors, and then end the fun times by weighing and measuring yourself on scales (confusingly) set up all over the park. (Open daily 8am-11pm. Free admission; rides and attractions 1000-3000Đ. Enter off Điện Biên Phủ.)

Cinema 1, 53 Hoàng Văn Thụ (☎ 810 294), plays Vietnamese movies. None of the movies are in English, so its a good way to brush up on (or acquire) those language skills you wish you had. Movies 15,000-25,000Đ, depending on the time of day.

Pool is quite popular in Hải Phòng, with numerous parlors to accommodate pool shark and pool bait alike. Young locals are quite willing to step up to the challenge (and beat you), if you ask politely. Listed are just a couple of options among the millions that seem to inhabit every corner and alleyway.

Carmen Billiards Club, 25 Trần Quang Khải (☎ 822 603), near the intersection with Đinh Tiên Hoàng. Probably the most popular pool bar in town, with 10 tables on both floors. Mainly male customers, with a few females providing moral support from the sidelines. Tables 25,000Đ per hr. Beer 12,000-15,000Đ. Open daily 9am-11pm.

Star Billiards Club, 135 Điện Biên Phủ (☎ 747 689), in the middle of a little courtyard off Điện Biên Phủ. One of Hải Phòng's smallest pool bars. Get there early to find an available table. Tables 25,000Đ per hr. Beer 12,000-15,000Đ. Open daily 9am-11pm.

NORTHERN COAST

🎵 NIGHTLIFE

Despite being a port city, Hải Phòng has a pretty quiet nightlife. Cafes are very popular, especially those on Minh Khai and Đinh Tiên Hoàng, which become street terraces on weekend nights. Karaoke and Thai massages are favorite pastimes, but they sometimes have associations with prostitution. Karaoke bars are popular, but usually have rather limited selections of English songs. Most people head home around 10pm, and the streets are deserted well before midnight.

New Story, 84 Điện Biên Phủ (☎ 821 821), near the corner of Điện Biên Phủ and Hoàng Văn Thụ. Wireless Internet and loud pop music make New Story popular with a student crowd. The television takes center stage to conversation. Juices 12,000-15,000Đ. Beer 15,000Đ. Cocktails made with ice cream 35,000Đ. Open daily 6:30am-11pm.

Dất Cảng, 28 Quang Trưng (☎ 839 668), across from the flower stalls. Waiters in white button-down shirts with red bow ties open the glass doors for you and seat you in a club packed with Vietnamese couples. Live music performances are illuminated by lively disco lights, but—like many clubs in Vietnam—nobody dances. Mixed drinks around 40,000Đ. Open nightly 7:30pm-midnight.

Philey's Lounge Bar, 115 Đinh Tiên Hoàng (☎ 810 871; www.phileysgroup.com.vn). The most wonderfully random and out-of-place establishment in town. A tunnel of red plush walls and seating is a comfortable place to watch European runway shows on the two plasma television screens. This bar-restaurant, brainchild of a Belgian designer, serves the hipster crowd. Wine US$17-23 per bottle. Shots US$2. Coffee US$1. Lunch entrees US$1.50-2.50. Open daily 7am-11pm.

Hà Trang, 31 Minh Khai (☎ 745 742). One of the most popular coffeehouses on this street, its terrace fills up rapidly on weekend nights. Great service with a French touch. Wide variety of coffees 5000-10,000Đ. Beer 13,000Đ. Open daily 6:30am-11:30pm.

Fanny Ice Cream, 152 Hoàng Văn Thụ (☎ 530 475). Despite the odd name, Fanny is one of Vietnam's best ice cream chains and the classiest ice cream parlor in Hải Phòng, with French ice cream served in a Mediterranean interior. Choose from the traditional chocolate to durian, jackfruit and other such exotic flavors. Ice cream 8000-12,000Đ per scoop, 40,000-72,000Đ per 500mL. With alcohol 23,000Đ. Open daily 8am-11pm.

Biện Goi Disco, 31 Điện Biên Phủ (☎ 823 314), through a narrow entry, up a small staircase. The only place in town to dance, if you don't mind the overbearing Vietnamese music and kitschy interior. On Sa nights, a bright spotlight pointed at the sky makes it easy to find, but you will only be let in once the bouncers pat you down. Cover 30,000-40,000Đ. Beer 20,000-23,000Đ. Mixed drinks from 45,000Đ. Open daily 8am-2am.

CÁT BÀ ISLAND ☎ 31

Home of Cát Bà Island National Park (p. 149), this island is a tourist trap with charm. Backpackers, families, and Vietnamese vacationers alike have descended in increasing numbers on its 350 sq. km of natural splendor. During winter, the island turns into a construction site as more and more restaurants and hotels go up for the next tourist season. Fortunately, the area between the bay and the mountains is small enough to curb this growth, and Cát Bà town may be able to maintain its small-town feel. In any case, the natural splendor of the island keeps bringing in visitors, and for good reason. Guides and locals are quick to point out that Cát Bà is not just a larger version of Hạ Long Bay. The island has an impressive array of limestone mountains, overgrown with jungle and ringed by fine-sand beaches. Its fertile, rolling hills make it ideal for the cultivation of rice, maize, and lychee. Despite the hordes of Vietnamese and foreign tourists wandering through the streets, especially in July and August, Cát Bà is the ideal place for rigorous hikes and boat excursions into Hạ Long Bay, or simply for relaxing on the beach.

☐ TRANSPORTATION

Though some tour companies will tell you otherwise, this little island paradise can be reached independently from Hà Nội, as well as through organized tours. Independent travelers can take a ferry from Hải Phòng (100,000Đ) or an inexpensive bus-and-boat deal from **Hoang Long Bus Company** in Hà Nội (leaves from Luong Yen Bus Station; 4½hr.; 120,000Đ). Another option is to hop on a tour from Hà Nội through Hạ Long Bay and then jump ship once on Cát Bà island (usually on the third day of the tour). On the island, motorbikes and organized tours are the easiest and often only option for getting around.

Ferries: Public ferries from Cát Bà run to Hạ Long City and Hải Phòng.

To **Hạ Long City:** The public ferry leaves from the main harbor (2½hr.; 7am; 70,000Đ). Alternatively, hitch a ride with an organized tour heading for Hà Nội (US$3-4). The tour boats arrive at and leave from the dock in the old harbor, past **Cát Cò Beaches I** and **II**. Head up the road past the GPO and veer left at the top of the hill. The road winds 1km to the old harbor and tour dock.

To **Hải Phòng:** In Cát Bà, purchase tickets at the **Sông Biển Hotel** to the left of Sun Flower One, on the last street on the left before the road heads to the beach (☎888 671; fax 888 671; open daily 6am-8pm). Alternatively, head to the office on the main stretch, just past the corner of the last northward branch of the road. All offices have stable prices for both slow boats (2½hr.; 5:45am, 1pm; 80,000Đ) and hydrofoils (1hr.; 3:15pm; 100,000Đ).

To **Hải Phòng** via **Cát Hải:** Hải Phòng can also be reached via **Cát Hải** (another island, closer to the mainland) by hopping onto a ferry from **Phù Long,** on the opposite side of the island from Cát Bà town. **Ferries** from Phù Long run daily to Cát Hải (15min.; every 90min. 7am-5pm; 8000Đ per person with motorbike, 2000Đ per extra passenger). Smaller ferries make the run as often as they fill up, which is about every 15-30min. Ferries from Cát Hải to Hải Phòng leave about 30min. after the arrival of those from Cát Bà and go to **Ding Vuu,** 6km from Hải Phòng (45min; 14,000Đ per person with motorbike, 2000Đ per extra passenger). To reach the pier on the island, go toward the national park, passing the entrance and then keeping left as the road forks. Continue along the main highway, circling around a mountain. Phù Long is 15km from the park entrance. Buses from Cát Bà town make the journey daily.

Buses: To reach the national park, catch a tour bus (US$6-10), which usually leaves only when full. Otherwise, scope out the public buses that run from Cát Bà town to the park entrance. Bus drivers assume foreigners to be part of an organized tour and usually don't charge anything. The official fare starts at 5000Đ.

Motorcycle: Due to accidents, motorcycles on the island are no longer rented to foreigners. A motorbike with a driver is probably your best bet to get to the park (US$5 per day; US$3 per half-day; 40,000-50,000Đ round-trip to the park).

Boats: Chartering a boat runs US$30-40 per day. You can inquire about speedboats at any hotel, but the **Noble House** is the best place to design your own tour.

☐ ORIENTATION

Cát Bà island is 50km east of Hải Phòng and 60km southwest of Hạ Long City. Cát Bà town lies at the southern tip of the island. The town's beaches run along the eastern coast, while the old harbor and tourist-boat dock is still farther east (and then north) along the shore. Nearly 17km directly north of the town is the entrance to **Cát Bà National Park.** Fifteen kilometers west of the park is the town and port of **Phù Long.** Small villages are scattered throughout the island. Though Cát Bà's roads sometimes have names, they are seldom used and are rarely known even by islanders. Instead, landmarks serve as the primary means of orientation. In Cát Bà, the **main ferry dock** is the center of the small city's universe. Three roads branch perpendicularly off the main street. The central street houses the GPO on its eastern corner and a slew of restaurants and hotels near its southern edge. The street farther east is home to the Prince and Sunflower One Hotels, along with other housing and food options. The street that runs along the western edge of town,

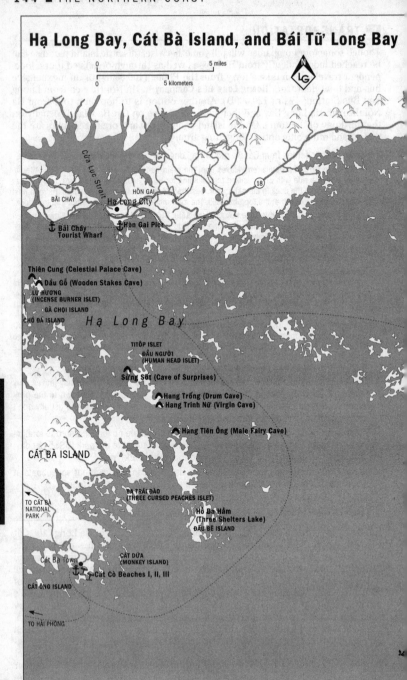

Hạ Long Bay, Cát Bà Island, and Bái Tử Long Bay

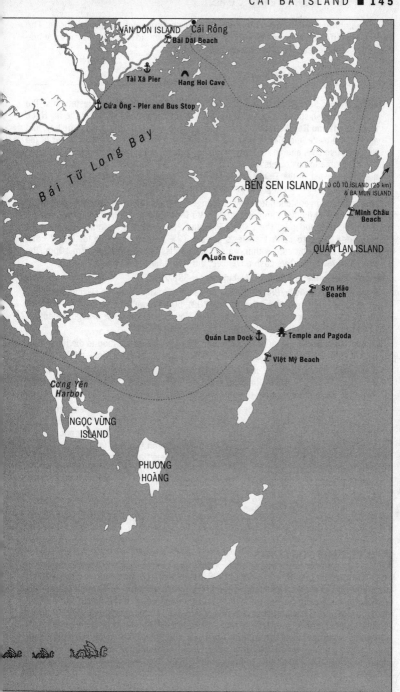

VÂN ĐỒN ISLAND · Cái Rồng
⚓ Bãi Dài Beach
⚓ Tài Xá Pier   ∧ Hang Hoi Cave
⚓ Cửa Ông - Pier and Bus Stop

Bái Tử Long Bay

BẾN SEN ISLAND (TÔ CÔ TÔ ISLAND (25 km)
& BA MUN ISLAND

⚓ Minh Châu Beach

QUÁN LẠN ISLAND

∧ Luồn Cave

⚓ Sơn Hào Beach

Quán Lạn Dock ⚓ ⚓ Temple and Pagoda

⚓ Việt Mỹ Beach

Cơ̆ng Yên Harbor

NGỌC VỪNG ISLAND

PHƯƠNG HOÀNG

near the fishing dock, houses the town market and currency exchange shops. The harbor beachfront stretches for about 400m on either side of the ferry pier, while the town's three beaches start about 300m east.

🛈 PRACTICAL INFORMATION

Tourist Office: Similar tourist services are offered at most hotels and restaurants. The excellent English-speaking owner at **Hoang Anh restaurant** and Mr. Lo' at the **Mỹ Ngọc Restaurant and Hotel** are both locals who organize and lead tours around the bay, and each can provide information about the surrounding area. The Australian owner of the **Noble House** sells alternative tours of the bay (led by an English-speaking captain) that are adaptable to customers' wishes. Tour lengths can range from a few hours to overnight. The owner of the **Thắng Loi Hotel** is informative and organized; his tours, however, generally have no English speakers on board.

Currency Exchange: Most hotels will exchange dollars for đồng, but at damaging rates. There is no ATM on the island. Head to the **Vũ Bình Gold and Silver Exchange** (☎ 888 641), on the road past the Fishing Pier and across from the market, for the best exchange rates to cash traveler's checks (2% commission) or for MC/V cash advances and debit card withdrawals (3% commission). Open daily 7am-10pm. The **Prince Hotel** also offers cash advances, but with a hefty 5% charge.

Emergency: Police: ☎ 888 239. **Ambulance:** ☎ 888 239.

Pharmacy: Hiệu Thốc (☎ 888 896) is in the center of town, next to the Flightless Bird bar. Open daily 6am-11pm. **Vang Bac** (☎ 888 308), 500m down the National Park Highway, doubles as a foreign exchange center. Open daily 9am-11pm. For a larger selection, head to the stalls in the town market.

Medical Services: The town **hospital** (☎ 888 239) is 1km up the road to the right of the beach, right after the ferry dock. When the road splits past the hill, hook a left.

Telephones: Inside the GPO, and in smaller offices scattered around town. Open M-F 7am-1pm, Sa-Su 9:30am-9pm. International calls are least expensive at **Phu'o'ng Phu'o'ng**, located across from the port (around 5000Đ per min.).

Internet Access: There are pricey Internet parlors along both the main beachfront road and its main artery, which shoots off from across the dock next to the GPO. Most shops charge 200-300Đ per min. for a slow dial-up connection. For slightly lower prices, head to the town market. A yellow sign points toward **Thành Đạt Net** (☎ 0912 732 489), near the edge of the market, and about 7m from where the road starts to climb. (Open daily 8am-midnight. 15,000Đ per hr.) Up the road from the post office, the **Prince Hotel** (☎ 688 150) has the same rate and is open 24hr.

Post Office: GPO (☎ 888 566), across the street from the ferry dock and on the corner of the main road that flows from the beach into the island. M-Sa calls to Canada, the UK, and the US cost US$0.70 per min. for the first 6min., then US$0.07 per second; Su and holidays US$0.55/0.05. Open daily 7am-10pm.

🏠 ACCOMMODATIONS

Since the introduction of electricity in 1998, hotels have sprung up all over town, filling the main road along the beach and spreading into the side-streets. Though options are numerous, especially during the winter and the beginning of the week, Vietnamese tourists take over the island on weekends. Independent travelers should reserve ahead on these nights and be prepared to pay a hefty price. Though some hotels and guesthouses standardize costs throughout the week and sometimes even throughout the year, others triple or quadruple their prices for the summer weekends. Nonetheless, plenty of affordable and quality options remain open from Sunday until Wednesday or Thursday. But beware—while some hotels and guesthouses are happy to accommodate budget travelers during summer weeks, others expect such visitors to vacate their rooms for high-paying or pre-booked customers. Ask ahead to avoid unpleasant surprises. Keep in mind that most rooms are spacious enough for three people.

The Noble House (☎888 363; fax 888 570), next door to the GPO. Run by a friendly Australian and Vietnamese couple, this hotel, restaurant, and bar has enormous doubles with balconies overlooking the bay. Rooms have A/C, satellite TV, fridge, homemade furniture, and new private baths. With great food and drink and a friendly staff, it's tempting not to leave. Summer rooms US$15; winter US$10. ❸

Giang So'n Hotel (☎888 214; giangsonhotelcb@hp.vnn.vn), opposite the fishing dock. There are 2 kinds of rooms, both with snow-white twin beds, dark wooden frames, satellite TV, and clean but cramped bathrooms with shower. Front rooms have great balconies overlooking the bay, but their neighbors, which cost about the same, lack windows. Summer weekdays rooms US$10-12, weekend US$15-20; winter US$8-10. ❸

Thắng Loi Hotel (☎888 531), directly across from the dock. A great deal with great views. Clean, comfortable rooms in a newly renovated building. The English-speaking owner provides information about the island and books tours of the island and bay. Summer rooms M-Th US$10, F-Su US$17; winter US$6-7. ❸

Hotel Nam Phương (☎888 561), past the Flightless Bird Bar. Refreshingly steady prices for plain and slightly aged rooms, all with a bay view. A bit cheaper than other hotels, at almost the same quality. Summer rooms US$8; winter US$5. ❷

Đức Toàn Guest House (☎887 694; fax 295 489), at the end of the road that houses the market. A family-run guesthouse featuring large and homey rooms with A/C, TV, fan, and small private bath. Summer rooms US$12; winter US$9. ❸

Trà My Hotel (☎888 650), a few doors down from The Noble House. Yet another solid deal. Two beds, balcony, and even a vanity set for reasonable prices. Rooms have A/C, TV, and phones. Summer rooms US$12-25; winter $7-10. ❸

Princess Hotel (☎888 899; www.princeshotel-catba.com). Towering 200m from the water, this is the closest lodging to Cát Cò Beach. A typical Western-style hotel with generic rooms and a uniformed staff. Shiny furniture battles the dark interior of some rooms. Rents bicycles for 20,000Đ per hr. Smaller standard rooms US$16; deluxe rooms with double and twin beds, tub, and satellite TV US$25; suites with fridge, bathtub, and balcony US$30. MC/V. ❹

⬛ FOOD

Since most visitors eat inferior hotel food as part of a tour package, Cát Bà's restaurants see fewer foreigners than most Vietnamese tourist hot spots. Still, seafood restaurants (all with surprisingly good banana and mango pancakes) populate the island, offering the freshest fare. As always, a good rule of thumb is to follow the locals—just make sure that the restaurant is not part of a hotel. Try exploring one of the floating restaurants near the dock, though eating at one requires negotiating for a boat trip. Boatmen on the pier are willing to make the journey—you should be able to bargain their asking price down to 15,000-20,000Đ. Otherwise, head farther down the pier along the railing. Two restaurants sit in the water and allow customers to grace their swishing floor by making the short seaexcursion on a floating walkway. More options with floating sidewalks are available at the old harbor, where tour boats dock. Keep in mind that you are paying for the ambience; you can get the same quality dishes for less along the town strip.

⬛ Green Mango (☎887 151; greenmangocatba@yahoo.com), on the waterfront next to Phương Phương. Organic fine dining has arrived on Cát Bà. Vegetarian snacks, huge salads, and great pasta for great prices (30,000-100,000Đ). Open 6:30am until the last bit of Egyptian *shisha* (60,000Đ) is smoked. ❸

Đức Tuân (☎ 888 783), on the main stretch, just down from the Family Hotel. Popular with Vietnamese weekend tourists. Friendly service and reasonable prices. The seafood is good and fresh—just point at the fish or crab you want from a big tank, and it'll be ready in minutes. Check out the terrace seating upstairs (where most guests dine). Spring rolls 15,000Đ. Fish 30,000Đ. Crab 50,000Đ. Open daily 6am-midnight. ❸

Hoàng Ý Restaurant, on the waterfront strip past the Quang Đuc Family Hotel, has tasty seafood dishes (30,000-60,000Đ) and large soups (8000-15,000Đ). Same menu, same great food as everywhere else. The pineapple and banana pancakes (8000Đ, with chocolate 10,000Đ) easily seduces any sweet tooth. Open daily 6am-midnight. ❸

Cát Tiên (☎ 887 855), the second restaurant on the walk from town to the beach. Fair prices and flavorful seafood dishes. Soup 16,000-17,000Đ. Crab 150,000-220,000Đ per kg. Fish 160,000-170,000Đ per kg. Tiger Beer 15,000Đ. Open daily 6am-midnight. ❹

The Noble House Restaurant (☎ 888 363; fax 888 570), right next to the GPO. Praised by visitors in search of a splash of variety. The fresh fish is highly recommended over the beef. The homemade pizza is absolutely fantastic—try it with seafood toppings (40,000Đ). The bar and terrace upstairs can make for a quiet evening or a rowdy night if a tour group stumbles in. The free pool table is an added bonus. Entrees 15,000-45,000Đ. Breakfast all day 15,000Đ. Fruit shakes and Tiger Beer 16,000Đ. Open daily 6:30am-11pm or until the last customer leaves (even if that means dawn). ❷

Hữu Dũng Restaurant (☎ 888 407), 100m past the Princess Hotel. Pleasant ambience—like a French colonial estate transplanted to the jungle. Good seafood dishes (25,000-50,000Đ) and Western omelette breakfasts. Open daily 6am-11pm. ❸

◉ SIGHTS

In order to visit the island at your own pace, rent a motorbike with a driver (US$5-6 per day) from a hotel or restaurant. Make sure to have a specific plan of attack in mind. For a picturesque view of the ocean and waves crashing against the steep limestone shores, ask to make one leg of the journey along the coast. Otherwise, join up with a tour and ride around in their minibus (US$5-6). Apart from the bay itself, Cát Bà's main attraction is its lush national park (p. 149).

HOSPITAL CAVE. The "Army Hospital Cave" (Hoang Sòn) is 4km before Trung Trang Cave (p. 151) and 5km before the entrance to the national park. Built in the early 1960s, the chambers of the cave were used by the North Vietnamese during the war. A bunker door is left unlocked to allow visitors to pass into the 17 concrete chambers; they once served as wards, operating rooms, and even recreation rooms. Small steps lead to a large enclosure that could fit 100 people and served as the army's cinema on weekends during the war. A small rectangular hole in the back functioned as a tiny swimming pool. Though the corridors are empty, they fill with the booming voice of the cave-keeper. Dressed in army attire, he enthusiastically imparts the area's history to willing listeners in Vietnamese. Lucky guests may get to hear a Vietnamese folk song reverberate off the cave walls. Then again—many Vietnamese will tell you that the war ended before the hospital was ever used. We won't tell you who to believe. (Open daily 8am-5pm. 20,000Đ.)

CÁT CÒ BEACHES. Deserted on most weekdays, Cát Bà's beaches become crowded in the evenings—so the locals can avoid getting a tan—and are overrun with Vietnamese vacationers on weekends. However, the beaches remain quiet in the earlier and hotter hours of the day. Heading east along the main road leads to a fork. Turning left will carry you up a hill to **Cát Cò I** and **II**, while staying flat leads to the more resort-like **Cát Cò III**. The beaches themselves have great views, but they're small and occasionally dirty.

A favorite spot of most Vietnamese, Cát Cò I lies closest to the town and receives the most visitors, who jostle for space on the small and oft-crowded shore. A fairly popular waterpark has recently been built on its shores. To escape the crowds of the waterpark and first beach, sneak up the stairs at the back or follow the red-and-white walkway, which winds about 700m around a limestone precipice and leads to Cát Cò II. Accessible only by foot and the farthest beach from the town, beautiful Cát Cò II remains the quietest of the three, even when crowds rush in for a swim on weekends. A walk under the rocky overhang leads to the other half of the beach, where a partly hidden entrance leaves it the best-protected of the town shores. Though there are no guesthouses on the beaches, you can ask the beach staff for permission to set up camp. *(Prices are standardized on Cát Cò I and II: lounge chairs 20,000Đ per day; bathroom use 1000Đ per day; changing rooms 2000Đ; showers 5000Đ; small lockers 5000Đ. Available for rent are various sizes of inflatable inner tubes 10,000Đ with 50,000 deposit; beds 30,000Đ with 100,000Đ deposit; kayaks 50,000Đ. Prices are listed by the hr. Camping on Cát Cò II 120,000Đ per 24hr. Open daily during the summer 6am-7pm.)*

Set in front of an overpriced beach resort lies Cát Cò III, a small beach whose natural beauty has been marred by its transformation into a tropical resort with bamboo bars and giant cocktail-drink umbrellas. This party beach is a bit more expensive than Cát Cò I and II. *(To reach Cát Cò III, keep right as the road from the town heads east along the mountainside. From Cát Cò I, follow the gray walkway west toward Cát Bà town, opposite the red-and-white walk that connects the Cát Cò beaches, for 15min. Bathroom use 2000Đ; showers 5000Đ; beach chairs with umbrellas 15,000Đ per hr.)*

NIGHTLIFE

Nightlife can be found on the main drag that runs along the water. Beer and refreshment stalls on the dock offer outdoor seating and an almost Riviera-like ambience, as long as you can ignore the numerous outdoor TVs.

Flightless Bird Cafe (☎888 517), past Hoàng Ý Restaurant toward the park. Backpackers and foreign tourists gravitate to this tiny, laid-back Vietnamese- and Kiwi-owned bar. Inside, darts, games, and a book exchange provide welcome low-key entertainment after a day of outdoor adventures. Spy on the bay and the people below from the balcony upstairs. Book exchange US$1. Orange juice 15,000Đ. Tiger Beer 16,000Đ. Mixed drinks 55,000Đ. Open daily 6:30-11:30pm.

Blue Note Bar (☎888 967). Go up the street from the GPO and hook the first right; this plush bar is around the corner. Keyboards and a guitar wait on the stage for spontaneous performances, while the menu sports recipes for many mixed drinks (40,000-50,000Đ). The "Lady in Red," with raw egg yolk, is an interesting experiment. Happy hour 5-6pm and 8-9pm (buy 2 get 1 free). Open daily 6am-midnight.

CÁT BÀ NATIONAL PARK

Established in 1986, the park encompasses an area of 152 sq. km—over 50% of Cát Bà Island. Its terrain is composed of limestone mountains which average 150m in height, with its highest peak, Cao Vong, measuring in at 322m. The waters of the park range from 15 to 20m in depth and take up 54 sq. km of its total area.

The park is also home to a botanical garden, fields of lychee trees, and over 120 animal species. Of these, over 69 species of birds, 20 reptiles, and 32 terrestrial mammals have so far been identified. As these mammals live in the remote areas of the park, visitors probably won't see much more than small snakes slithering along the trails. Other fauna include the python and numerous animals on the endangered list, among which are the golden-faced langur and the leopard cat. While the climate of the rest of the country may fluctuate substantially from season to season, the temperature of the park remains largely comfortable, ranging from 16-17°C in January to 28-29°C in July, with a yearly average of 23-24°C. While it is a little warmer from May to October, these months are also the rainiest.

At the **Environmental Education Center** directly behind park headquarters, visitors can watch movies about the park in Vietnamese or read about the climate, flora, and fauna of the preserve. Boards highlight a few of the park's natural species. Across the street from the Education Center is a **Specimen Exhibit.** A stuffed wild-cat, monkeys, and a few reptiles fill one case, while others are lined with sea creatures and butterflies. (Open daily 7am-5pm. Fee included in park entrance.)

CÁT BÀ AT A GLANCE

AREA: 152 sq. km.

CLIMATE: Average temperatures 23-24°C, although they reach 29°C in July and drop to 16°C in Jan. Rainy season May-Oct.

HIGHLIGHTS: A totally unique array of landscapes—from beaches to mangroves to evergreen forests to coral reefs—render this island-centered national park a true gem. Also home to very rare langurs.

FEATURES: Limestone mountains and tropical rainforests; coral reefs; caves; beaches.

GATEWAYS: About 30km east of Hải Phòng and just west of Hạ Long Bay.

ACCOMMODATIONS: Guesthouses and camping in the park headquarters.

FEES AND RESERVATIONS: Entrance fee 15,000Đ. Guides recommended but not necessary for hikes.

 ACCOMMODATIONS AND FOOD. Spending the night at the park is highly feasible and facilitates day hiking. Musty but clean **guesthouses** ❷ at the park head-quarters have large rooms with twin beds and private baths with hot water. (☎888 741; fax 821 249. Rooms 120,000Đ.) **Camping** at the park is only allowed at the ranger's station; bring your own equipment (25,000Đ per person per day). Those staying at the park can order **meals** ❷ through the park service. (Breakfast 10,000Đ; lunch and dinner 20,000-50,000Đ.) Those going on long hikes or planning to spend the day in the park are advised to bring along food and water, though there are a few vendors along the path into the forest.

> **WHEN TO GO.** The park is best visited during the dry season (Nov.-Apr.), when the temperatures drop to around 16-17°C. During the rainy season (May-Oct.), temperatures can reach 29°C in July, and monsoons and tropical rain-storms are frequent. Bring foul-weather gear, hiking shoes, and a flashlight, as there are numerous walking-heavy adventures that await in the mountains and caves that decorate the impressive scenery. Bringing your own meals if you want to avoid the overpriced food at the guesthouse in the park headquarters.

■ **HIKES.** Though the park provides numerous hikes, both relaxed and rigorous, two trails—Ngự Lâm and Việt Hải Village—have been adopted by tourist compa-nies and enjoy the most popularity. Other, less touristed routes allow visitors to walk through the forest on the way to caves or simply to wander through the park. Though guides (20,000-100,000Đ depending on the trail) are not required, they are available and recommended for longer and more arduous hikes.

A more relaxed hike open to visitors is a half-hour walk to the timber forest of **Kim Giao** (1km). From the park headquarters, head straight along the cement path until you reach the steps that mark the beginning of the mountain hike. Climb up into the forest. At the intersection, a sign points you left to Ngự Lâm Peak (turning right leads to the Trung Trang Cave).**Ngự Lâm** (1.5km; 2hr.), also known as the **Kim**

Giao Peak, is often referred to as the "short trail." From the park entrance, head straight along the road, passing the botanical gardens and the park zoo. The paved road turns into steps, which are made from small tiles. Farther up, the trek becomes more intense, and the end of the ascent requires a short rock climb. An old and rusty observation deck stands atop the mountain. From both the mountain and the tower (used as a fire watch), there is a spectacular panorama of the island.

 INTO THE WOODS. To bypass the entrance fee at Cát Bà National Park, some tour companies take their groups to surrounding towns that also have hikes and views, but aren't protected and lack wildlife. Watch for National Park signs and the ranger station to make sure you're getting the real thing.

To hike to **Trung Trang Cave** (1½-2hr.), follow the path toward Ngự Lâm, turning onto the trail just before the climb up to the peak. The 3.5km walk on a tile-laden path through the forest has a few ladder climbs. The cave is at the end of the path. You can also get there by walking down the road from the park entrance toward Cát Bà town. One kilometer down the road, a sign directs travelers to steer right. Similar to the caves of Hạ Long Bay, the 400m long Trung Trang Cave has an array of stalactites and is inhabited by bats. Don't forget to bring a flashlight. During the summer, guides are available on site; in the winter, arrange a tour at the park entrance (open daily 7am-5pm; 15,000Đ).

The trail to **Ao Éch Lake** and **Việt Hải Village** starts from behind park headquarters and passes over hills and through forest and grasslands. The 5km trek to the lake takes 2½hr. Past the lake, visitors can continue another 1½-2hr. along the main path for 3km, eventually reaching Việt Hải Village. Here, they can eat lunch before heading off on the remaining 5km hike toward **Lan Ha Bay** or stay overnight at a small **guesthouse** ❶ for 60,000Đ. A local boat heads back to Cát Bà town (1½-2hr; 15,000Đ). Due to the length of the trail and the ease with which hikers lose their way, it is advisable for day hikers to go with a group or hire a guide and arrange for a boat to pick them up from the bay. Most hotels arrange for independent travelers to join groups that leave for the trail at 8 or 8:30am and return to the town by 5pm. The trek usually costs US$8-10 per person and comes with bus, guide, boat, and lunch. For more homestay opportunities, try **Hiên Hà** village, 5km past the park.

HẠ LONG CITY ☎ 33

The gross and unbridled commercialism of this grimy city acts as a serious turn-off to travelers looking for the quiet beauty of Hạ Long Bay. Though 15-story neon hotels and an entire artificial beach testify to the city's tourist boom, the vulgar ostentation of this port city serves to dampen the appeal of its tourist infrastructure. It's a shame that the nearby polluting coal mine, chorus of honking trucks and megaphones, and pushy *xe ôm* drivers ruin what is otherwise a wonderful location in the middle of the world's most amazing land formation. Hạ Long City should be used only as a transportation hub to reach the more appealing towns along the northern coast. Tours from Hà Nội run through the city, but for the independent traveler, Cát Bà might be a better bet.

▐ **TRANSPORTATION. Buses** depart from **Bãi Chảy Bus Station,** 600m south of the Hòn Gai pier on Hạ Long Rd. Buy tickets from the station itself; drivers are tough to bargain with. Buses go to: Đà Nẵng (24hr.; 7am; 152,000Đ); Hải Phòng (2¾hr.; every 30min. 6am-5pm; 25,000Đ); Hà Nội (3-4hr.; every 15min. 5:30am-6pm; 40,000Đ); HCMC (48hr.; W, Th, Su 7am; 280,000Đ); Vinh (7-8hr.; 6:30am; 80,000Đ). **Minibuses** leave from across the street and can be flagged down along Hạ Long Rd., especially in front of the GPO. They head to: Hải Phòng (2½hr.; 6am-5pm; 20,000Đ), Hà Nội (4hr.; 6am-5pm; 38,000Đ), and Móng Cái (6hr.; every 30 min.;

42,000Đ). Foreigners may be charged up to three times these rates; bargain hard. **Ferries** leave from Bãi Cháy to Hòn Gai (every 10min. until 10pm, then every 30min.; 500Đ). A new bridge is under construction which should make the journey much faster by motorbike. The Hòn Gai pier (Bến Tàu Hòn Gai), 1.5km down Lê Thánh Tông from the bridge, at the end of the road to the right at the first small roundabout, has ferries to: Cát Bà Island (2½hr.; times vary; around 80,000Đ); Cát Hái (2hr.; 11:30am; 35,000Đ); Đân Tiện (5hr.; 6am; 28,000Đ); Hải Phòng (2½hr.; 6am, 1pm; 60,000Đ); Móng Cái (3hr.; 8am, 1pm; US$14); Quán Lạn (4hr.; 9am, 2pm; 80,000Đ). Since many companies offer ferry services at Hòn Gai pier, it may be confusing to find the right boat and the right time; check in advance. Also, be prepared to wait until the boat fills up. The more convenient **Tourist Hydrofoil** runs to Cát Bà (40min.; 7:30am, return 4:15pm; US$8) and to Móng Cái (3hr.; 8am, 1pm; US$13). Get tickets at the counter 100m down Hạ Long Road from the bus station (away from the center of Bãi Cháy) and catch the boat at the dock 400m back toward town. If you stay near the post office, the market and cafes are at your fingertips. However, getting anywhere else (including the ferry) is possible only with a **motorbike** driver. A *xe ôm* should take you anywhere for 6000-7000Đ, but drivers in Hạ Long City are notorious for trying to charge US$2 for a 3-block ride.

■ **ORIENTATION.** Hạ Long City lies 165km east of Hà Nội and 55km northeast of Hải Phòng. The city is divided up the **Cửa Lục Strait** into two districts: the more tourist-oriented **Bãi Cháy** on its western shore, and the more industrial **Hòn Gai** on its eastern shore. A new bridge, under construction at publication, should soon alleviate ferry congestion between the two. Bãi Cháy stretches out along the coast of Hạ Long Bay and is basically composed of two roads. Its main road is **Đường Hạ Long (Hạ Long Rd.)**, which runs along the entire bay from the **tourist boat pier** in the west to **ferry pier**, 4km east. All chartered boats to the grottoes leave from the tourist boat piers, all the way in the west. In the center of Bãi Cháy, **"Restaurant Row"** and the **GPO** crowd the intersection of **Vườn Đào ("Hotel Alley")** with **Hạ Long Rd.**, which continues 2km farther northeast to the bus station and local ferry.

■ **PRACTICAL INFORMATION.** The **Hạ Long Tourist Company** (☎846 272), at the tourist pier, organizes boat trips (4hr.; US$30-35) and gives useful information. (Open M-Sa 7:30-11:30am and 1-5pm.) **Vietcombank** (☎825 297), on Hạ Long Rd. down the road from the tourist pier, changes major currencies and traveler's checks. An **ATM** is accessible during banking hours. (Open M-F 8-11am and 1-5pm.) Call ☎825 486 for local **emergency** assistance; the national numbers are slower. **Quảng Ninh Provincial Hospital**, 651 Lê Thánh Tông (☎825 494), is 1km beyond the Hòn Gai GPO on the road that forks to the right. The director of the hospital, Mr. Hanh, speaks English. (US$53 per visit.) **Internet** access is available at **Emotion Cyber Cafe**, 500m from the GPO (☎847 354; 300Đ per min.), **Dilmah Cong Đoán** (see **Nightlife**, p. 153; US$1 per hr.), and various cybercafes (3000-4000Đ per hr.) on **Anh Đào** (up Vườn Đào; take a right just before Restaurant Asia). Internet phone is also available on this street. The **Hạ Long City Post Office** or **GPO** (☎846 201), at Vườn Đào intersection has telephones, but you must purchase a phone card (150,000Đ) first. Internet access is also available. (3000Đ per hr. Open daily 6:30am-9:30pm.)

■ **ACCOMMODATIONS AND FOOD.** To catch a sight like no other, veer off to the left from the GPO and walk 400m up the hill on Vườn Đào, the notorious **"Hotel Alley."** Mini-hotels line this street with a vengeance—there are over 75 on this small hill alone, none of which ever fill up. Be aware that the nicer your view of the bay, the noisier your room will be. All ask US$7-18 depending on amenities, and rooms include two beds, hot showers, and air-conditioning. Few owners speak English. **Anh Duy ❷**, across from the ferry dock, has private balconies and the best views in town, but is near the noisy bay. Walk under the sign saying "Vân Anh," and then veer right at the crest of the hill. (☎ 847 817. Rooms 120,000Đ, with A/C 140,000Đ.) **Hương Trầm Hotel ❷** is a comfortable mini-hotel overlooking the bay, probably run by the local military police. From the GPO, walk down Hạ Long Rd. and take the 3rd left, where a dirt path leads up the bluff. (☎ 846 365. Doubles 120,000-150,000Đ.) **Hồng Minh Hotel ❷** has clean rooms in a great central location. Rooms include air-conditioning, TV, fridge, and phone. (☎ 847 643. Doubles 150,000Đ, with balcony 180,000Đ.) **Bồ Lai Hotel ❸** is 100m down the dirt path from Hương Trầm Hotel but offers a slightly better view—and more noise. Pretty rooms include TV, phone, and balcony. (☎ 846 378. Doubles US$10.)

Seafood is the specialty in Hạ Long Bay, but it doesn't come cheap. "**Restaurant Row**," around the GPO, is the culinary hub for tourists. Live lobsters, crabs, fish, and clams await customers in water tanks outside each eatery. (Seafood entrees 35,000Đ.) Basic Western fare is also available. Keep in mind that the farther you walk away from the row, the cheaper the food becomes. Street stall **Phường Oanh** is recommended for its cheap prices. A small **market** hides in the shadow of the hotels. From the GPO, head up Vườn Đào; the first road branching right ends at the market. As with urban markets all over the country, this one has various street eateries, offering seafood dishes alongside the usual phở and cơm. The market is also great for an afternoon glass of *chè*. A third alternative is the small **Restaurant Asia ❸**, 24 Vườn Đào, featuring a mean phở (15,000-25,000Đ) and many simple seafood dishes (45,000-60,000Đ). The operation is run by Quang Vinh, a friendly former Berliner who speaks fluent German. (☎ 846 927. Up Hotel Alley, on your right. Open daily 7am-11pm.)

🎵 🎭 **ENTERTAINMENT AND NIGHTLIFE.** The beachfront is the place to go for entertainment. At the artificial "beach," there are wooden chairs under palm trees and stands every few meters offering sodas (10,000Đ), beer (15,000-20,000Đ), and snacks from 8am to 11pm. Though the beach itself is small and a little dirty in places (due to the nearby port), Hạ Long City tries to compensate: on the beachfront, travelers can rent jet skis (US$17-20 per 15min.), parasailing gear (US$100 per hr.), speedboats (US$100 per hr.), and a variety of other aquatic paraphernalia.

All nightlife in Hạ Long City centers around the beachfront and along Hạ Long Road. Don't expect too happening a scene, as tourists are scattered and locals wake up early. **Dilmah Cong Đoán,** about 500m west of the GPO is a small cafe-bar with an Internet corner and a relaxed terrace overlooking the bay. (☎ 848 309. Beer 15,000Đ; soda 7000Đ. Open daily 7am-11pm.) **Trung Nguyên,** up a few stairs from Hạ Long Rd., is a popular bar under a bamboo ceiling and fake grapes. (☎ 844 338. Coffee US$1; juices US$1; ice cream US$2. Open daily 7am-11pm.) **Oh La La Bar** is a huge bar on the beachfront blasting music from Tchaikovsky to the *Titanic* theme song in bamboo-decorated bliss. (Beer 17,000-20,000Đ. Open daily 3-11pm.)

HẠ LONG BAY   ☎ 33

With its 1969 limestone islands and 23 grottoes, this natural marvel has twice been proclaimed a national heritage site and remains under the watchful eye of UNESCO. In 1994, the international committee first considered the bay a natural wonder, simply for its overwhelming beauty. Then, in 1998, a British geologist found that the bay had rare and precious geological features. Following his report, UNESCO once more placed Hạ Long under consideration, and in July 1999 they recognized the site for its geological value, as well.

NORTHERN COAST

The legends of the origins of the bay's name are as numerous as the guides and locals who tell them. Literally, Hạ Long means ▨ **"Dragon Descending,"** a name Let's Go thinks is pretty awesome. As one story goes, the inhabitants of Hạ Long once lived in peace with a family of dragons. The mother and her children would descend over the bay to play in the waters. When a drought came, the dragons would spit rainwater to fill the bay. One day, according to the legend, a group of pirates pillaged the village and attacked its inhabitants. Hearing the cries of the villagers, the dragons rushed to their rescue, spitting fire into the bay to ward off the invaders. When the fire hit the water, it turned into the gray limestone rocks that now fill the bay. Another story claims that the bay was formed when a dragon spat out divine pearls, forming a barrier against an invading Chinese fleet. Once the enemy had been turned back, the dragon settled in the bay and its scales turned into rocky islets. A third version of the story describes a clumsier and less heroic dragon: the mother is fabled to have fallen into the sea, her body and tail carving out holes in the land during her descent. These later filled with water, surrounding the untouched land and transforming it into a network of separate islands.

Located in a tropical monsoon zone, Hạ Long is at its most beautiful in the early summer and autumn, when temperatures hover around the mid-twenties and blue skies are the norm. Though summers bring heat waves, late July and August also bring heavy rain and winds. It is easiest to reach the bay by tour from Hà Nội. However, these tours herd visitors around to major sites, allowing for little freedom, and many guides don't speak English. It's also possible to skip Hạ Long City altogether and explore the bay from Cát Bà Island via Hải Phòng. Large-group private tours from Cát Bà cost the same and allow for much more flexibility.

▣ TRANSPORTATION

There are three ways to explore the bay. The cheapest way as a solo traveler is to go via tour from Hà Nội. A more thorough and independent adventure embarks from either Hạ Long City or Cát Bà. Either way, you'll have to rent a boat at some point. Tourists can arrange their own plans (though such ventures are often costly without a big group) or pay for a package deal. Below are the tour options:

FROM HÀ NỘI

Agencies in Hà Nội sell packages with pre-arranged hotels, meals (not including drinks), and set schedules. Options run from one to three days in the bay. One-day tours include transportation, food, and a boat tour of Hạ Long that stops at two caves. Two-day trips allow visitors to stay overnight on Cát Bà Island or on the boat. Three-day tours usually include a trek into the national park. Prices of tours vary widely. The most expensive and reputable agencies are **TF Hanspan,** 84 Mã Mây (☎ 828 1996), its sister organization **Kangaroo Cafe,** 18 Bảo Khánh (☎ 828 9931), **ODC Travel,** 63 Trúc Bạch (☎ 715 0789; www.odc-travel.com.vn), with a smaller branch at 43 Hàng Bạc (☎ 824 3024), and **Hà Nội Tour,** 23 Yên Thái (☎ 928 7978). Three-day trips, including Cát Bà, cost around US$45-55. (All-inclusive. Max. group size 16.) Cheaper tours, often in larger groups and with lower-quality transportation, are run by **Queen** and **Sinh Cafes** (p. 106; US$30-40 for 3-day trips). More expensive trips can include a night or two on the boat, single rather than shared hotel rooms, and a long trek through Cát Bà national park. The large volume of travel agencies and frequent trips make it easy to book as little as a day in advance, but these reservations are not always reliable, and long treks are often cancelled for weather or if the tour doesn't fill up. If your plans are changed on you, you should be entitled to a partial refund. More expensive trips tend to be more reliable and get fewer complaints.

FROM CÁT BÀ

One-day tours from Cát Bà island are usually run by locals instead of tourist companies and tend to visit the smaller but less touristed sights in the bay. Trips run US$37-40, but the fixed price is divided among the number of passengers on board (up to 5). Most slow-boat tours begin at 8am and end around 5pm, visit two to three caves, deserted beaches, and Monkey Island. Ask around the restaurants and hotels along the beach and the main road that houses the GPO to see who offers such tours. The **Hoang Hoang Restaurant,** near the Flightless Bird Bar, is home to a local named Zoom, who offers various tour options and is an excellent source of information about the bay. The same goes for the Australian who runs **The Noble House** and has been living on the island for 12 years. Beware of flashy sales pitches that fail to deliver informed, English-speaking guides.

FROM HẠ LONG CITY

Due to the amount of foot traffic going through Hạ Long City each day, booking a private tour from the wharf can be quite stressful. You can avoid package tours by renting boats at the **Bãi Cháy Tourist Wharf.** (☎846 592. Boats priced by length of tour, desired destination, and the number of passengers onboard. 4hr. tour with 10-15 passengers 300,000Đ per boat or 40,000Đ per person; 6hr. 410,000/45,000Đ; 8hr. 520,000/60,000Đ. Entrance tickets are another 30,000Đ. Open daily 6am-6:30pm.) Local boats can be rented at the pier, but often for higher prices (85,000-115,000Đ per hr.). Overnight excursions can be arranged for around US$115, including all meals and entrance tickets.

▚ ORIENTATION

The limestone islands of Hạ Long are littered around the bay like divine pearls from a dragon's mouth, or perhaps like the scattered scales of a clumsy dragon. The major landmarks in Hạ Long Bay span from the northern point of Bãi Cháy to Cát Bà island. Four kilometers south of the tourist wharf in Hạ Long City, **Thiên Cung** (Celestial Palace) is the northernmost cave of the UNESCO Heritage Site. Situated slightly south of the Celestial Palace is **Đầu Gỗ**, the formation's second cave. **Lư Hương Islet**, which resembles a teapot, is just a hop southwest of the second grotto. West of the teapot is the image of the stone dog, **Chó Đá**. The famous **Gà Chọi** (Fighting Cocks) lie 3km farther south. A longer journey toward **Sửng Sốt** (Cave of Surprises) passes **Đần Bên Island** on its western edge and **Đầu Người**, the "man's head," before reaching the southernmost of the Bay's three most popular caves. The "lovers' grottoes"—**Hang Trinh Nữ** (Virgin Cave) and **Hang Trống** (Drum Cave)—are a few kilometers farther south. From the Virgin Cave, a short 2km float leads to the **Hang Tiên Ông** and the crystalline falls that lie inside. Five kilometers southwest is **Ba Trái Đào** (Three Cursed Peaches), 4km east of which is **Ba Hầm**. Back to the southeast are the restful shores of **Monkey Island.** From here, it is a 45min. slow curve, passing the southeastern tip of Cát Bà Island, to abandoned **Cát Ông** beach. From the beach a hop northeast lands at the boat pier in **Cát Bà** town.

▞ PRACTICAL INFORMATION

During the stormy season, boats and tours can be canceled. Visitors are advised to check with the **tourist center** at Bãi Cháy Tourist Wharf before heading out. The tourist center also provides free maps, as well as information about the bay and the various tours that are available. (☎847 481. Open daily 7am-4pm.) The **souvenir shop** near the dock sells information books (50,000Đ) about the bay. Most hotels and shops carry a hand-drawn picture map of the bay and some of its nearby attractions (10,000Đ). Detailed World Heritage Maps (12,000-15,000Đ) are available at the caves. All tourist boats will also have huge maps in their cabins.

👁 SIGHTS

Without a good guide or map, it is difficult to distinguish between the various rocks and islands of the bay. However, even the least-informed traveler can marvel at the sheer rock faces that protrude from the waters. The towering rock formations in the distance form a panoramic range of faded mountaintops, making the bay seem like an enormous lake. Breaking up the calm horizon, they shelter the bay from turbulent waters. Passing closer to remote islets, visitors can hear the low hum of insects singing in bush-topped cliffs. While some islands rise only slightly above sea level, others jump straight into the sky, towering 25m above the water. Near the mainland, the waters remain calm as boats slowly meander through Hạ Long's labyrinth. A trip farther out in the bay reveals aggressive waves that crash into the islands, spitting foam onto the white sands. Popular for its splendid views, the bay is never free of the tourist-packed brown boats that chug through. In the evening, these boats race in and out of the bay, some passing into the burning sun as it sets behind the cliffs, while others speed away from the growing silhouettes of the rocky horizon. Within the nearly 2000 stone giants jutting out from the sea, over 20 grottoes have been discovered. Some have been "improved" with multi-colored lights for the benefit of tourists, but these tend to make for an annoyingly artificial feel. Private boats are necessary to explore the obscure grottoes, because package boat tours only stop at a select neon-lit few.

GROTTOES

There are over 20 caves in the bay, but only a few are easily accessible to visitors. The largest and most popular caves are illuminated with colorful lights and have restricted visitation hours and entrance fees. Others have been left in unaltered beauty and can be visited at leisure for free. The first three listed see hordes of tourists daily, while the others, though just as striking, are usually empty.

THIÊN CUNG (CELESTIAL PALACE). Located 4km from the mainland and near the Đầu Gỗ island and cave, this grotto, only 30 minutes from Hạ Long City, is one of the most popular. The cave mouth, hovering 25m above sea level, is reachable by wooden stairs. Though the cave has been around for millions of years, its interior has been trod upon by eager tourists only for the past seven. Hidden behind overgrown plant life, the cave entrance remained secret until a local fisherman stumbled upon the majestic wonder in 1993. Tour guides proclaim that the lucky fisherman is now a very wealthy man and urge visitors to keep a keen eye out for other secret caves so that they, too, may strike it rich. Today, the cave is illuminated with red, blue, yellow, and green lights, which unfortunately detract from the cave's natural beauty. Inside, the spacious chambers are filled with impressive stalactites and stalagmites. One of the more attention-grabbing sights is the large Buddha meditating in the middle of the grotto. Behind the Buddha there is a tiny enclosure with a miniature waterfall. On the left side of the cave wall, lights illuminate a shadow that looks like the face of a watchful man. The enclosure is named for heavenly women who are fabled to descend into the cave to shower in the gently sprinkling waters. Past the heavenly shower is a small gate. To its side is a large stone that resembles a cherry-topped scoop of ice cream to some, a woman's breast to others. *(Open daily summer 7:30am-5pm, winter 8am-4:30pm. 30,000Đ.)*

ĐẦU GỖ GROTTO (CAVE OF THE WOODEN STAKES). Hidden next to the Celestial Palace, the Đầu Gỗ Grotto covers an impressive 8000 square meters and is composed of three chambers. Locals believe that the cave's name comes from its function during the 13th century, when Vietnamese fighters are said to have used it to store timber. The stakes created in the cave would then be hidden in nearby river beds at low tide. When they advanced at high tide, Mongolian invaders were left with ruined boats and captured soldiers. The cave was renamed "Grotto of

Marvels" during French colonial rule. Open since 1999, the gigantic cave, with its moss-covered stones and large stalactites, is now known by both names. Yellow lights illuminate the natural grandeur of the cave's interior. *(Open daily summer 7:30am-5pm, winter 8am-4:30pm. Entrance included in the Celestial Palace ticket.)*

SỬNG SỐT (CAVE OF SURPRISES). Another popular cave in the bay, Sửng Sốt was discovered in 1901 by the French and given its present name. Lying 25m above sea-level, the cave's entrance is accessible only by a network of stairs. Inside, it is composed of three distinct chambers, all connected by narrow passages. Guides will point out a resemblance between every rock and some known object, including a turtle, lovers, and a brightly lit red canon, which others see as a phallus. Cave of surprises, indeed. *(Open daily summer 8am-5pm, winter 8:30am-4:30pm. 30,000Đ.)*

HANG TRINH NỮ (VIRGIN CAVE). Three kilometers southeast of Sửng Sốt, this popular cave is easily visited from Cát Bà. It is one of the most spectacular wonders of the bay, left almost unmarked by the visitors who venture into its empty belly. A smaller raft is necessary to approach the cave entrance. A short climb allows visitors to enter the protrusion, which is more like a tunnel than a cave. A second mouth flows into the opposite side of the small limestone mountain and provides a stalactite-decorated panorama of the limestone-topped waters. The cave gets its name from a rock shaped like a young woman stretching one arm into the sea, in the direction of the Trống Cave, but its lack of artificial lights and painting help to keep the name a reality. *(Free.)*

HANG TRỐNG (DRUM CAVE). Seven hundred meters from the Virgin Cave, this grotto is named for the drum-like sound that the wind makes when blowing into the cave. The Trống grotto contains a stone column in the likeness of a young man. Paired with the Virgin Cave, regional interpretation holds that the two caves contain lovers reaching out to each other. The caves are not only united by the figures of the two lovers but also by the echo that travels from one to the other. Both caves remain free of artificial fixtures. *(Free.)*

HANG TIÊN ÔNG (MALE FAIRY CAVE). Two kilometers southeast of the Virgin Cave, the Male Fairy Cave gets its name from a local legend that male fairies would frequent the cave, which served as a secret enclosure where they could play chess and sometimes try on women's clothing without fear of reprisal from a repressive, heteronormative society. It is now the best-kept secret in the bay. To visit, you must bring own flashlight, and as there is no dock, a raft is also necessary. Inside are several chambers with a few stalactites. From the main cave, two smaller ones branch inward: the passage to the left leads to empty stone formations that, when hit, make drumming sounds; the passage to the right leads to a cave wall whose sparkling material is like a waterfall of a million diamond droplets frozen in time. With a size rivaling that of Sửng Sốt, this is a worthwhile cave to visit. *(Free.)*

MÊ CUNG. Just south of Sửng Sốt, this smaller cave is equally amazing. A walk through the dark, damp interior of the cave leads to a lush mountainside. Following the narrow path farther up presents yet another inspiring view of the bay—but then again, you can never have enough amazing views. *(Free.)*

ISLETS

Of the 1969 islets that span Hạ Long Bay, 980 have been named. The islands with the most distinct shapes have elicited consistent images in the minds of local fishermen; those images are the source of their names today. Many of those shapes are tough to spot, but their amusing diversity—from cannon to cat to fisherman—is entertaining nonetheless. Feel free to make up your own images and names.

LƯ HƯƠNG (INCENSE BURNER). One of the first distinct islets when traversing the bay from the north, this stone extends from the ocean and resembles a Vietnamese incense burner, used in worship and wish-making. Look for two rectangular isles that appear to be splitting, but remain connected by their sides. A small tunnel runs under the schism.

CHÓ ĐÁ (STONE DOG). West of the Incense Burner and the Đầu Gỗ Cave, the silhouette of a dog appears to be leaning against a rocky shore, trying to climb out of the water. His back paws climb the rock and his front ones are hidden among the brush; his head stares forward, and his posture also evokes images of a seal perched on a rock or a mermaid carefully emerging from the sea.

GÀ CHỌI (FIGHTING COCKS). Three kilometers south of the Incense Burner, small twin peaks protrude from the water. Locally, they are known to resemble two roosters with touching beaks, fabled to be fighting. Other visitors have also seen the islet as two monkeys, one crouching and one hunched over, both leaning in to grace the other with a kiss. It's weird, we know.

ĐẦU NGƯỜI (HUMAN HEAD). Near Sửng Sốt Cave, a side view of this islet resembles a man's face, albeit with feline ears surrounded by a thin layer of green bushes; extending behind that face is an awkward lump. The back of the islet can elicit images of a ponytail, blown back by the wind, the hair spreading to the shore, or can alternatively look like a ▨**huge mutant fish.**

CÁM ẤM (TEAPOT). Though locals have christened it "teapot," this islet, composed of two limestone rocks, has also struck viewers as a swan with an arched back or a peacock flashing its tail.

RÙA (TORTOISE). Even a completely unimaginative visitor would be hard-pressed not to notice the tortoise floating in the bay. A small round islet is attached to a larger and more oval rock and greets all visitors as they traverse Hạ Long Bay on their way south toward Cát Bà town.

YÊN NGỰA (SADDLE). One of the more aptly named islets, the limestone is composed of two humps, one slightly lower than the other, rolling over the water and clearly resembling a saddle. Literature connoisseurs might also be graced with a lighthearted image of a French classic—the famed hat of The Little Prince.

MẸ BỒNG CON (CHILD-CARRYING MOTHER). A large base supports two distinct stone towers, mimicking a cubist interpretation of a mother, perhaps reclined in a chair, holding her child in her lap. Each figure is made distinct by a triangular protrusion. You might need to use some imagination for this one.

BA TRÁI ĐÀO (THREE CURSED PEACHES). These three small islets, located near the shores of Cát Bà town, resemble—what else?—small peaches. They're home to one of Vietnam's few remaining coral reefs, which makes for great snorkeling. Legend claims that a fairy who fell in love with a local fisherman stole three magical peaches that would render her lover immortal. When the Jade Emperor learned of the theft, he turned the peaches into three islands and condemned the lovers never to see each other again. Oh, that wrathful Jade Emperor.

ISLANDS

While islets remain attractions to be admired from afar, group or private tours of the bay allow travelers to visit islands, often graced with small secluded beaches.

TITÔP. Though smaller than the rest, a quick climb to Titôp's peak is well worth the stop, offering a spectacular panoramic view. Don't bother with the beach.

CÁT DỨA (MONKEY ISLAND). A popular destination for tours from Cát Bà, this island is located east of the town and is only a 45min. boat ride away. A soft yellow beach greets tourists to the mountainous island, but the major attraction of the island lies at the top of one of its smaller peaks. To the right of the guardhouse, a 60m trail runs up the mountain. At the top, visitors can spot monkeys (brought to the island as a tourist attraction years ago) who come to greet their spectators. Though locals might urge tourists to bring some snacks for the friendly animals, feeding them is strictly prohibited. Viewers should keep their distance anyway; some monkeys have been known to bite, mistaking people for food or perhaps just angry about the illegal consumption of their brains (see **"Iniquitous Delicacies,"** p. 242). You can't really blame them. *(Open daily 7am-5pm. 7000Đ.)*

CÁT ÔNG ISLAND. Directly across from the harbor at Cát Bà town, this tiny island sports a small and deserted beach. Due to its recent popularity surge, a huge resort is under construction, and its waters are becoming increasingly polluted. You can rent a room in one of the **guesthouses ❸** at the Quang Đuc Family Hotel in Cát Bà. The rooms have twin beds, electricity, fans, and bathrooms with showers. However, there is no air-conditioning or hot water. The hotel also provides transportation to the island. *(20min. boat ride; 165,000Đ one-way, 250,000Đ round-trip. Local boatmen can also be hired to make the journey; settle on a price before heading out. Either way, arrange pickup in advance. Rooms US$10. For meals, bring your own food or pick your meals at the Family Hotel in advance. Breakfast 10,000-15,000Đ; lunch and dinner 30,000-50,000Đ.)*

ĐẦN BÊ ISLAND. The major attraction of this island is a pagoda perched on its golden beach. Most visitors marvel at the strange juxtaposition of man-made treasure and natural grandeur from a passing tour boat, but local fishermen continue to venture to the island to worship at the pagoda. There is also an annual boat race around the island on January 20th.

FLOATING VILLAGE. Close to the Hang Tiên Ông Cave floats a community of 400 people spread out among 150 houseboats. The village supports a floating school which allows visitors as show-and-tell guests during normal school hours. You will be amazed at the writing skills of these children on the rocking boats. Seafood is for sale, but try to get there just as the catch comes in or the majority will already be packaged for export to China. Before floating away, make a quick stop at the one-room museum, which provides photos and a history of the community.

OTHER FORMATIONS

BA HẦM (THREE SHELTERS) LAKE. This is not a sight to be missed. Ba Hầm is a large ocean lake surrounded by limestone mountains, and it's accessible from the bay only via a boat ride through three caves. The limestone itself is populated by orchids and bamboo trees that provide food for local monkeys. Inside the magnificent formation, the waters are clear and allow visitors to peek at the sea urchins and mussels that hide in the innermost enclosure. A tour of the caves and enclosed lake takes about 45min. and requires the use of a smaller rowboat or kayak that can pass into the caves. *(25km from the mainland, close to Cát Bà Town.)*

BÁI TỬ LONG BAY   ☎ 33

Passing from Hạ Long Bay to neighboring Bái Tử Long Bay takes visitors out of UNESCO-protected World Heritage territory, but not away from the region's overwhelming majesty. As in Hạ Long Bay, the waters near the mainland are spotted with stone towers projecting from the calm bay waters. A passage into the heart of the bay slithers out of the angular and bold rocks and travels between flatter islands, which roll gently out of the water and are covered with rich forests. The floating fishing villages of Hạ Long carry over to the sea of Bái Tử Long, as do more stationary and colorful houses perched on the shores of the green islands. Few of these natural formations have any sort of tourist infrastructure, but a steady flow of public ferries, running once or twice per day between the islands, makes them suitable for one-day excursions. Some locals disembark at isolated islands to catch dinner straight from the sea; we recommend that you do the same.

▐ TRANSPORTATION

One way of exploring Bái Tử Long Bay is to arrange a two- or three-day tour through a hotel or restaurant on Cát Bà Island or in Cái Rồng. Most can arrange an excursion into Hạ Long's sibling on a **sailboat,** including one overnight on the boat and one on Quán Lạn Island, in a bungalow on the gorgeous white-sand beach. However, chartering your own boat can be pretty expensive if you're traveling alone (usually US$40 per day). **The Noble House** (p. 147) books three-day, two-night tours (US$350 for as many people as can fit on board). All tours include transportation, room, and board. While touring the bay and its tiny islands might be easiest with a pre-arranged tour, travelers wishing to explore the area on their own can island-hop with the help of **public ferries,** which make infrequent but inexpensive and largely reliable trips between Bái Tử Long's populated islands. Daily ferries traverse the southern part of the bay on their way to and from Hạ Long City and Quán Lạn. Those wishing to spend a few days on the bay's beaches can easily reach the inhabited islands, where guesthouses stand ready to shelter tourists.

✦ ORIENTATION

Situated 10km northeast of **Cửa Ông** (on the mainland), **Cái Rồng** is on **Vân Đồn Island,** and it's the closest port in Bái Tử Long Bay to the rest of Vietnam. It's also the most developed and populated city in the bay. With the Tài Xã ferry running west to the mainland and inter-island ferries heading to the rest of the bay, Vân Đồn serves as the transportation hub of Bái Tử Long Bay. While virtually uninhabited limestone islands are scattered throughout the bay, the closest populated island east of Cái Rồng is **Bến Sen,** which takes about 1½hr. to reach by boat. Twenty kilometers from Cái Rồng and slightly northeast of Bến Sen is Ba Mun National Park. Heading straight east into the sea takes boats out of the cluster of islands and into the open ocean. A 3hr. ferry ride zigzagging around the islands eventually shoots straight out to **Cô Tô,** the farthest-out inhabited island. Closer to the mainland and farther south is peaceful **Quán Lạn** island. Around and in between are hundreds of smaller, untouched islands, all very much worth exploring.

✿ ISLANDS OF BÁI TỬ LONG BAY

BA MUN ISLAND. What the national park on Cát Bà Island is to Hạ Long Bay, Ba Mun Island is to Bái Tử Long—minus the flocks of tourists (or any sign of humanity whatsoever). The entire island, which is 18km in length but only 1km in width, is classified as a nature reserve. On its shores, visitors can spot a lowland evergreen forest and 400 plant species, three of which are listed in the 1997 IUCN Red List of Threatened Plants. Deep crimson and bright yellow flowers blanket the island. Along the slippery, rocky shores, patient visitors can see tiny crabs, while those who dare to walk into the forest can spot huge spiderwebs and their owners, whose rich red bodies and legs can span a 10-year-old's palm. Unlike the preserve on Cát Bà, however, this island remains as yet untouched by tourism—and there are no plans for development. As such, the landscape is entirely wild—no paths to guide visitors in and out, no landing docks that avoid the slippery shores and steep hills on the coast, and no ranger station or guided tours. Those willing to step into the vine-covered vegetation should arrive dressed in long sleeves and pants, armed with a compass, water, and a serious sense of adventure. There are no public ferries to the island, so you'll have to rent a boat in Cái Rồng (20km; 1½-2hr.)

NORTHERN COAST

NGỌC VỪNG (PEARL HALO). Characterized by small villages and soft sand beaches, Ngọc Vừng is home to Cống Yên, a commercial harbor that boomed with trade in the 11th century, and contains ruined citadels erected during the Mạc (16th century) and Nguyễn (19th century) dynasties. The tiny village of Cống Yên rests peacefully on the island's shore. Its deep orange and blue houses have palm trees scattered along their sides. The island derives its name from the ancient occupation of its inhabitants, who harvested bright pearls along the island's shores. A local fable whispers that pearls hidden in the water around the island would cover it in a halo of light visible to far-away ships. Ngọc Vừng can be reached by the public ferry that runs daily from Hòn Gai to Quán Lạn and back (about 2hr.; 45,000Đ). It departs both those cities at 7am and 1pm, allowing visitors to see the island between the arrival of the morning boat and the departure of the afternoon one, or as a half-day trip from either direction.

CÔ TÔ. The farthest inhabited island of Bái Tử Long Bay is also one of the three islands that currently allows visitors to spend the night on its shores. The journey to Cô Tô requires braving the rough waters of the exposed ocean, no longer protected by the islands that shield the inner bay. But Cô Tô has managed to keep huge tour boats from landing on its shores, making its deserted beaches all the better. Daily ferries returning from the island make it possible to visit these soft-sand shores without spending the night—though the allure of crashing waves and absolute seclusion is hard to ignore. Daily ferries run from Cái Rồng at 7am and return there at 2pm (3½hr.; 45,000Đ each way).

CÁI RỒNG ☎ 33

Though it is the most developed city in the Bái Tử Long archipelago, Cái Rồng has none of the tourist spectacle of Hạ Long's Cát Bà town or the grime of Hạ Long City. Removed even from the ambitions of Vietnamese tourist officials, Cái Rồng is a standard Vietnamese town. This sense of normalcy lends itself to a relaxed island atmosphere, which for some travelers can turn Cái Rồng into Cái oh-so-Right. The town is a true transportation hub, with boat service that connects Bái Tử Long's scattered islands. With its relaxed atmosphere, fresh seafood, and fantastic daytrips, Cái Rồng is a great base from which to explore the bay.

▌ TRANSPORTATION

Ferries: A **hydrofoil** runs daily to and from **Hạ Long City** (2hr.; 3:50pm; US$7). In Cái Rồng, purchase tickets at the Tourist Information and Hydrofoil Desk 30m from the pier. You can also catch a bus from Hạ Long City to Cửa Ông, on the mainland, where public ferries run to **Phà Tài Xã Pier,** about 8km from Cái Rồng town on Vân Đồn. The car and motorbike ferry runs every hr., and the passenger ferry every 30min. (15min.; 4:30am-9pm; 2000Đ). Public ferries connect Cái Rồng to the outlying islands with service to: **Cô Tô** (2½hr.; 7am, 2pm; 45,000Đ); **Móng Cái** (2½hr.; 8:30am; US$7); **Quán Lạn** (2½-3hr.; 7am, 2pm; 20,000Đ for Vietnamese, 40,000-60,000Đ for foreigners). Don't be surprised if the invented price for foreigners becomes up to 4 times the local price—so keep your cool and bargain hard.

Buses: Buses run every 15min. from Cái Rồng across a bridge to Cửa Ông (5000Đ). **Bến Xe Khách,** the island's bus station (☎874 074), is left from the market. Buses to: **Hạ Long City** (45min.; 5, 7am; 30,000Đ); **Hà Nội** via **Hà Đông** (4, 4:45am; 60,000Đ); **Hải Phòng** (45min.; 4:45am; 35,000Đ); **Móng Cái** (every hr.; 40,000Đ) via **Cửa Ông.**

Boats: You can charter boats near the town pier, about 15m from which is the hydrofoil ticket booth. The owners charter a small tourist boat to go along the bay or to visit specific destinations for 80,000-90,000Đ per hr. Inquire at the **Duy Khánh Guesthouse** (p. 163) about the **Thành Đá Tourist company.** New 2-story tourist boats with English-speaking guide can be rented for US$12 per hr. Public ferries are easier, though less reliable. Some of the women lined up along the dock are willing to take passengers in **rowboats** to a nearby cave and beach (20,000Đ round-trip, including wait).

Taxis: ☎874 874.

■ ORIENTATION

Even though it lacks street names and addresses, the town is easy to maneuver. All of Cái Rồng's attractions and services can be found along one of the town's two main roads. Their intersection marks the lively center of town. The **ferry dock** marks the beginning of one of Cái Rồng's main arteries, and the steps of the **post office** mark the street's end. While hotels and cơm shops cluster near the dock, a walk from the pier to the post office passes shops, the market, restaurants, and other services. A left at the road's end leads to Internet cafes, the hospital, and the **Phà Tài Xã** pier, while a right runs to the **Bãi Bài** beach.

■ PRACTICAL INFORMATION

Tourist Office: As the tourism bug has not yet spread to Bái Tử Long Bay, it is difficult to find any tourist information without a command of Vietnamese. One agency with rudimentary English skills operates in the **Duy Khánh Guesthouse,** which provides boat tours of the bay. Bring your own itinerary or risk floating around in circles.

Currency Exchange: Though there is no bank and no ATM in town, you can exchange currency at the **Tiêm Vàng Thắng Rồng** jewelry store (☎874 236), directly to the right of the town market. Open daily 6:30am-8pm.

Emergency: ☎874 255.

Pharmacy: There are pharmacy stalls in the town market.

Medical Services: The town hospital (☎874 255) lies 90m to the left of the GPO. Basic facilities.

Internet Access: Cái Rồng's proximity to the mainland has allowed it to plug into the Internet while its outlying neighbors, including the more developed Cát Bà town, lag behind. Internet parlors with DSL access, all charging 3000Đ per hr., clutter the intersection that leads from the dock to the center of town. Heading from the dock, steer left when the road ends at the GPO. Continue for about 100m. The first Internet cafe on the left has new equipment and friendly staff. (☎874 419. Open daily 7:30am-11pm.) Internet cafes are identifiable by "chat" or "yahoo" signs outside—or by the loud gunshots coming from computer games inside.

Post Office: Follow the road from the dock to the town center for about 1.5-2km; the road comes to a stop at the steps of the **GPO** (☎874 290). International mail and parcel services, as well as telephones. Open daily 7am-9pm.

■ ACCOMMODATIONS

While there are some guesthouses in the center of Cái Rồng, most accommodations are clustered near the dock, suggesting that the majority of visitors just spend the night and move on in the morning. An eerie similarity in quality and price characterizes the town's accommodations.

Sỹ Long Hotel (☎874 854), right at the edge of the dock. The best deal in town. A friendly owner will show you to a clean white room overlooking the bay. All rooms have TVs and 3 beds. Rooms 80,000Đ, with A/C 120,000Đ. ❷

Việt Linh Hotel (☎ 793 898), about 400m from the dock. The nicest and freshest rooms in Cái Rồng, with pleasant wooden decor, large windows, and a comparatively steep price tag. Back rooms have a view of the distant beach; all have A/C, satellite TV, refrigerator, and private bath. Rooms with double bed 180,000Đ. ❸

Hùng Cường Guesthouse (☎874 001), on the left side of the road on the way to the post office. The friendly locals hanging out at its restaurant will insist you join them for a beer, and the lively environment makes up for the small rooms (80,000Đ). ❶

Duy Khánh Guesthouse (☎874 316). Large, clean doubles with fresh furniture. Sparkling private bathrooms, but no tubs. Summer rooms 120,000Đ; winter 100,000Đ. ❷

Thu Hằng Guesthouse (☎874 623). The blue hotel on the right as you leave the dock. Large rooms with TV; some have a view of the bay. The top rooms are the cleanest and most pleasant. Reception rents bicycles for 20,000Đ per day and tourist boats for 100,000Đ per hr. Rooms with double bed 100,000Đ; with 2 twins 120,000Đ. ❷

🍴 FOOD

Cơm shops cluster around the pier and the town center. All are run by locals and serve delicious and inexpensive seafood. The few restaurants that dare to go by the title cater to Vietnamese passersby and don't provide English menus.

🍴 **Tuyết Tuyết** (☎874 256), next door to Hùng Cường Guesthouse. A wonderful array of seafood and wild boar, the local specialty, will keep you coming back. The *sam* (king crab sauteed with chili, ginger, and pineapple) is fantastic, as are the snails. There is no English menu, but the owners' daughter speaks perfect English and is eager to help with tourist information. Entrees 10,000-50,000Đ. Open daily 8am-11pm. ❷

Sỹ Long Cơm, in the hotel of the same name, right next to the pier. The shrimp is praised as the best in Vietnam. If you come after the pre-cooked meal is over, design your own dish and price. Cơm 4000Đ. Phở 9000Đ. Open daily 6am-11pm. ❶

Cơm and Phở (☎ 795 332). A friendly and popular shop 20m before the post office with a large selection of meat and seafood. Vegetarian soup available upon request. Cơm 4000Đ. Phở 5000Đ. Open daily 6am-4:30pm and 6-11pm. ❶

👁 SIGHTS

Cái Rồng has enough to see and do for at least a couple of days. Travelers can head to the island's "Long Beach" for a swim or to admire the waters, or find respite in an old and rarely visited temple hidden in the busy town. Nearby villages offer a glimpse (and taste) of island life. After a few hours of admiring and eating fresh jackfruit, there is, of course, Bái Tử Long Bay itself, which spans over 150 square kilometers of sea and islands. An excursion to discover the smaller islands and to get a close-up of the bay's beauty is, for now, best launched from Cái Rồng. Visitors can hire tourist boats and cruise the area around the island, discover the deserted beaches and caves of the limestone islands in the surrounding area, or admire from afar the islands inaccessible to public transportation—although private boats are for hire to reach them.

TOURS OF THE BAY. Launching a trip from Cái Rồng, visitors pass the floating villages and the fish farms near the port; those who want to check out the farms and merchandise can ask to stop. Passing out of the town harbor, the keen-eyed can spot tiny temples squatting upon the rocks of two islands, one on each side of the harbor entrance. A lonely house built on a tiny beach resides to the left of exiting boats, adjacent to a pink temple. While floating around the bay, visitors are surrounded by towering stone **islets** like those of Hạ Long Bay. Distinctively rounded, worn islands convey that Bái Tử Long is older than the more angular Hạ Long: worn by erosion, the stones are topped with forests and vines. Some offer yellow-sand **beaches** and small hidden **lakes** encircled by hard gray pillars. The landscapes of Bái Tử Long are much calmer than elsewhere on the northern coast. Lacking the legends of its neighboring bay, the scenery of Bái Tử Long Bay is open to fresh interpretation. Ironically, though it is Hạ Long which is named after descending dragons, the round islands scattered throughout Bái Tử Long Bay and the rolling formations on the eastern horizon do manage to elicit images of a dragon's back and tail.

VAN YÊN COMMUNE. About 20 minutes past Bãi Dài Beach lies a small village of farmers and their water buffalo. The town is interesting; getting to it is amazing. The bay lets out into a small estuary near a bridge leading to lush green pastures. Scattered around the fields are smaller versions of the bay's stone towers. After passing through a leaky hillside tunnel, you'll finally arrive at Van Yên, where children ride water buffaloes and throw sticks at jackfruit trees hoping for an afternoon snack. The small community lives pushed up against the mountainside. They congregate every morning at the Forestry building for government-sponsored classes about sustainable farming. Sneak in for a bit of the class, or head to the hillside to do some exploring. *(30,000Đ one way from Cái Rồng by motorbike.)*

VÂN ĐỒN CAVE. The island just opposite the port of Cái Rồng houses this enormous and generally unknown cave. The cave is huge in every direction and there are large sections of the cave that remain completely unexplored. Though young kids are willing to show you around, bring your own flashlight—there are some big plunges into the depths of nowheresville. *(A round-trip rowboat ride should be 20,000Đ.)*

BÁI SEN (TRÀ BÀN). This inhabited island, 20km from Cái Rồng, is easy to visit by rented boat or public ferry. Tourists can climb the dirt road into the deep green forest and trek up the hill for a view of the bay. There is a small village where they can get a sense of the island's quiet lifestyle. North of the island lies a distinct islet, whose larger and more circular body, with a small protrusion on its side and a beach at its feet, sort of resembles a flounder. *(1-1½hr. by boat.)*

BÁI DÀI BEACH. Stretching along the southeastern shore of Vân Đồn, the beach's proximity to populated cities and busy ports makes it a less-than-enticing place for a swim. Its sandy shores do, however, make for pleasant walks and have been known to produce severe relaxation. There is a refreshment stand near the entrance to the beach's bathing area and small resort; farther out, a garden, complete with gazebos, has been constructed along the shore. A wooden pier stretches out into the bay, and mountainous islands lining the horizon make the bay's calm waters appear more like a lake. **Hotel Tạ Thị Phương ❸** sits across from the beach resort entrance. Head 12km down the road toward Bái Dài beach; you won't be able to miss its domed roof. (☎ 793 188. Spacious, well-lit doubles with satellite TV and private baths but no A/C. Front rooms have balconies and a view of the resort and waters below. 300,000Đ.) Those who stay on the beach can dine at the **resort restaurant ❸**. The portions are large, but the menu is uninteresting. *(To reach the beach, head toward the post office from the pier. Go right as the road splits and continue straight through the island's villages. About 12km down the road is a giant yellow hotel with domes like a Russian Orthodox church. The entrance to the beach is right across from the hotel. Open daily 8am-5pm. Bathroom 500Đ. Shower 2000Đ. A motorbike ride from the pier will cost 15,000Đ.)*

CÁI RỒNG TEMPLE. Hiding behind a pond on the main road in Cái Rồng is an ancient-looking white gate adorned with carvings of red dragons. Old steps lead to a quiet nook that overlooks the boat-packed harbor and two temples. In the evening, older residents gather on these steps to play traditional music. The temple, small garden, and musicians seem strangely out of place in this port town. At the same time, the juxtaposition of urban and traditional noises makes this small site, imbued with history and a soothing calm, all the more appealing as a hidden getaway.

HANG HOI CAVE. The cave is 5km from Cái Rồng and 30min. from town by boat. Since the waters are shallow during the morning, it is best to visit in the afternoon, as you return to Cái Rồng from a tour of the bay. Fairly unspectacular, the once-natural cave is now home to a small cement shelter. Inside, visitors can spot a few stalactites and stalagmites, as well as bats hiding in the cave's dark corners. In the back, a small ladder leads to a fenced-off exit that goes to the island's other side. However, the rusted gate does not prevent some visitors from climbing their way to the island's back side for a picturesque view of the bay. Travelers who have tried this have done so at their own risk.

QUÁN LẠN

Near the eastern side of Bái Tử Long's network of inhabited islands, the beautiful island of Quán Lạn still remains largely unexplored. With no more than 7000 inhabitants spread throughout a few small villages, Quán Lạn is an unspoiled paradise. The undeveloped island and its gorgeous white-sand beaches have been tagged for major investments aimed at expanding its shaky tourist infrastructure. For now, though, visitors can stay in bungalows on the beach or live among locals in a village without a constant stream of motorbikes. Some day soon, tourists are bound to discover the gorgeous shores of this island paradise, and its unsullied beaches won't be isolated for much longer. So go now—and don't tell a soul about it.

▐ TRANSPORTATION

You can only reach the island by boat. Though you can bring along a motorbike, public transportation on the island is relatively easy, if sometimes overpriced.

To the island: If your primary destination is Quán Lạn, take the 4hr. public boat (80,000Đ) that runs from the Hòn Gai pier in Hạ Long City (p. 151) at 9am and 2pm. Look for a boat with a sign over the main cabin that reads "Quán Lạn." The boat will stop at **Thắng Lợi** (1½-2hr.; 40,000Đ) and **Cống Yên** (2-2½hr.; 50,000Đ) islands before getting to **Quán Lạn** (4hr.; 9am, 2pm;.) The boat usually lounges around until it is full, and it drops off 2km from the town center. Motorbikes into town cost 5000Đ.

From the island: Boats headed north and south depart from the dock 1.5km down the main road from Quán Lạn town and go **Hạ Long City** (4hr.; 9am, 2pm; 80,000Đ) and **Cái Rồng** (2½-3hr.; daily departures scheduled for 7am and 2pm, but boats leave when full; the official fare for Vietnamese is 20,000Đ, but foreign travelers are charged 40,000-60,000Đ). You can try to negotiate your fare in advance, but the lack of alternatives weighs heavily on the boatman's side.

On the island: You can get around the island on foot or by hiring a relatively expensive motorbike driver. To rent your own transportation, head to **Nhà Nghỉ Huyền Trang** (bicycles 20,000Đ per day; motorbikes 100,000Đ per day), or ask your hotel receptionist.

✦ ORIENTATION

Located near its northwestern tip, Quán Lạn town is the largest settlement on the island and is located about 2km from the pier. A paved road leads from the dock through a small rice- and fish-farming community into the heart of town. A few guesthouses, concentrated in the village center, line the road. The beaches line the other side of the thin island and are located east of the village.

▐ PRACTICAL INFORMATION

There is no bank or currency exchange on the island, but hotel owners will gladly exchange US dollars for đồng, though with a hefty commission. Across the street and a few doors away from the dock and post office is the Tram Y Tế, the village

doctor's office. (Open daily 8am-noon and 1-4pm.) The **post office** is on the left side of the main street in the heart of the village. International telephones are inside. (☎877 309. Open daily 7-11:30am and 1-4:30pm.)

🔳🔲 ACCOMMODATIONS AND FOOD

There are two types of accommodations options in Quán Lạn: guesthouses in town and bungalows on the beach. Be warned that the village is blissfully unaware of the luxuries of hot water and air-conditioning. The village generator runs from nightfall until midnight, when the town—and the fan in your room—falls completely asleep. With that in mind, rooms are overly expensive. There isn't much in the way of restaurants in town, but a few of the hotels double as restaurants.

Nhà Nghỉ Huyền Trang (☎877 351 or 877 505), on the main street, a few meters from the post office and across from the village doctor. Run by a friendly young mother and her numerous lively youngsters. Immaculate, well-lit rooms with pristine shared baths. Some have views of the bay. Motorbikes for rent 80,000Đ per day; bicycles 20,000Đ. Tasty fried noodles with vegetables 10,000Đ. Cơm with rice, veggies, soup, and eggs or meat for two 30,000Đ. All rooms 150,000Đ. ❷

Hotel Phưởng Hoàng (☎877 345), just past the post office on the way to the village center. A new hotel with sparkling private baths and views of the undeveloped fields leading to the ocean. Rooms with double or 2 twin beds 160,000Đ. ❸

Ngân Hà Hotel (☎877 296), across the street from the post office, on Quán Lạn's main drag. Spacious and clean rooms with private baths, some of which have balconies. Top rooms are much more pleasant. The restaurant downstairs is extremely popular (soup 6000Đ). Doubles 150,000Đ; triples 250,000Đ. ❷

Guesthouse Robinson (☎877 439; robinsonislandw2003@yahoo.com). On the streets shooting off from the corner of the Ngân Hà Hotel. Old rooms with private baths. Not the best, but certainly the cheapest rooms in town. Rooms 100,000-150,000Đ. ❷

🔵🔳 SIGHTS AND BEACHES

PAGODA AND TEMPLE. Constructed in the 12th century under the Lý Dynasty, the pagoda and its neighboring temple stand as reminders of the island's history as a center for international trade. Though the temple's interior is interesting in its own right, its main attractions are the two red wooden structures themselves. The pagoda to the right of the temple is less run-down and more majestic in appearance. The gate that leads to its doors is adorned with carvings of elephants, a tiger, and the ever-popular ⬛dragon. Local fishermen come here to worship, and from the 10th to the 18th of July (on the Chinese Calendar), the pagoda hosts a series of religious festivities. Between the temples are two stone tablets engraved with the names of warriors who fought to protect the island.

VIỆT MỸ. Located about 1km from Quán Lạn village, Việt Mỹ is the most frequented—though not the most beautiful—of the island's beaches. Its fine white sand stretches between two distant mountain edges. The western tip of the beach remains mostly isolated, but a walk toward its eastern edge reveals tree-stump chairs and refreshment stands. (From Quán Lạn village, head along the main road and toward the dock. About 600m from the post office is the town generator, a yellow bunker-like house surrounded by rice fields. Turn left onto the wooden path which leads to the beach.) Near the beach's edge there is a **Culture Ecological Tourism resort ❹**, providing beachside accommodations in private bungalows. The gorgeous wooden houses are sprinkled around a forest and are connected by red-brick paths; waves roll gently against the shore at night. (About 800m from the dock there is a blue sign that welcomes visitors to Quán Lạn. Follow the red-brick road into the forest—on the other side you'll stumble onto

NORTHERN COAST

the network of wooden bungalows. The reception desk is in the beach restaurant. www.baitu-long.com. Electricity daily 6-8am, 11am-noon, 6pm-midnight. Bungalows with clean private baths US$25. 25-person dorm US$150. The resort reception also allows visitors to camp in the forest on the nearby mountain. M-Th 100,000Đ per 24hr. F-Su 150,000Đ per 24hr.) The resort **restaurant ❷** is open 24hr. *(☎877 257. Fried egg and bread 5000Đ; soup 10,000Đ; fish 25,000-45,000Đ; set menu 40,000Đ.)*

SƠN HÂO BEACH. Though you'll have to pass through construction sights and mining pits to get to this beach, the trip is well worth it—most call Sơn Hâo the most beautiful of the island's beaches. White sand dunes streaked with small streams and lakes border the narrow tropical stretch that marks the edge of the stunning shore. Storming waves crash on the uncrowded sand. Resort-free and 7km from Quán Lạn, the beach sees more cows lounging or promenading on the beach than visitors or villagers. *(Follow the road that runs from the corner of the Ngân Hà Hotel and passes the Robinson Guesthouse. When you pass a pink cement fence about 5km from Quán Lạn, hook a left into the dunes. Motorbikes 10,000-15,000Đ each way.)*

MINH CHÂU BEACH. Lying 12km from Quán Lạn town, Minh Châu Beach is another strong contender for "best beach." At one end of the crescent-shaped beach are towering mountains, while a small cement road at the other leads 2km to the old port, once used for trade with China. During the day, the beach is largely deserted, save for a rowboat or two heading out to sea or returning to shore. The water is refreshingly cool and almost entirely waveless. Though there are no hotels or restaurants nearby, locals will often be willing to make you up a plate. *(Head in the direction of Sơn Hâo but bypass the right turn to the closer beach. At the road's end, turn left onto the paved walk and hook a quick right onto a worn dirt path. The road leads through Minh Châu village and ends at the beach. Motorbikes 20,000-25,000Đ each way.)*

NIGHTLIFE

The dearth of post-midnight electricity makes nightlife a wee bit difficult to sustain in this town. During the evening hours, locals and a few vacationers stroll along the village's main street, where **nước mía** (sugarcane juice) vendors and a few cafes stay open. The only sounds that dare to disturb the island are the melodic vibrations of karaoke bursting from living rooms and local karaoke cafes.

MÓNG CÁI ☎ 33

Móng Cái's bustling atmosphere seems to revolve around its border crossing into China, with hotel signs protruding from every corner and motorbike drivers crowding the streets, ready to sweep Chinese and Vietnamese businessmen to their desired destination. A small smattering of tourists—mostly bound for Trá Cổ (p. 169)—wander the streets and buy cheap Chinese goods, but the overwhelming theme of this city is international business, both legal and illegal. Surprisingly, Móng Cái lacks the sleaze and grime common of border towns. A day in Móng Cái en route to the bays of the south or the hills of the northwest is well spent, given the city's internationally flavored nightlife. Since few other foreigners make it to Móng Cái, there is little demand for English and therefore a limited supply of Anglophones. If you speak Mandarin or Cantonese—or even if you just really like Chinese food—you'll have no problem.

TRANSPORTATION

Ferries: Fast-paced **hydrofoils** connect Móng Cái to Vân Đồn Island and Hạ Long City. To **Hạ Long** (3hr.; 9am, 2pm; US$14), **Hải Phòng** (9½hr.; daily 6:30pm), and **Vân Đồn** (2½hr.; daily 2pm; US$7). Buy tickets at the **hydrofoil office,** 1 Trần Phú (☎883 988), at the intersection past the bridge, to the left of the post office. Open daily 6am-5pm.

Buses: The **bus station** is on the southwestern edge of town, over the bridge and about 1km from the town center (open daily 4am-5pm). Frequent buses go to **Hải Phòng** (7-9hr.; 18 per day; 45,000-55,000Đ), **Hạ Long City** (5-6hr.; every 30min. 4:30am-5pm; 60,000Đ), and **Hà Nội** (8-10hr.; every 30min. 4:30am-7:30pm; 60,000-80,000Đ).

◄▌ 🛈 ORIENTATION AND PRACTICAL INFORMATION

The main street, **Hùng Vương,** lopsidedly bisects Móng Cái. The bus station lies on the southwestern outskirts of the city. A walk or drive from the bus stop up Hùng Vương passes over the bridge and hits the first major intersection at a roundabout, then heads east through the city and out onto the coast. **Trần Phú,** the second major street, runs its course from the town's major intersection, passes the market, and heads north toward the Chinese border.

The **hydrofoil office** is on the corner to the left of the GPO. To cash traveler's checks, get MC/V cash advances, or to change American, Australian, British, or Canadian currency, go to the **Vietcombank,** 2 Vân Đồn. There is a **24hr. ATM** outside. Turn left onto Trần Phú at the main intersection and then take the next left onto Vân Đồn. The bank is at the end of the street on your right. (☎881 211; fax 881 676. Open M-F 7-11:30am and 1-4:30pm. 25,000Đ fee for cash advances.) There is a large **pharmacy** on 7 Trần Phú, to the left of the hydrofoil office. (☎770 536. Open daily 7am-11pm.) There are plenty of **Internet** parlors around the city, all charging 3000Đ per hr. There are a few cafes right by the **post office,** which sits across from the bridge at the intersection with Trần Phú. (☎881 101. International phones, ATM, and international mail and telegrams inside. Open daily 7am-9pm.)

📍 ACCOMMODATIONS

Accommodations in Móng Cái are scattered throughout the city, with distinct clusters near the bus station and around the market in the center of town. Rooms are plentiful but expensive. Some hotels promise luxurious quarters but fail to deliver; others are run out of houses, stores, and pharmacies, sometimes luring visitors with a nonexistent discounted price. Bargain especially hard in Móng Cái. The prices below are written as stated by their establishment owners. Some of the better options are found near the bus station.

Thanh Đạt, 49B Hùng Vương (☎887 013). Thanh Đạt is the name written on the awning above this makeshift hotel, but this place is run out of a shop selling plastic shoes. A small guesthouse with cheap beds. Small, uninteresting rooms 80,000Đ. ❶

Hoàng Tiến Hotel, 105 Trần Phú (☎887 916), near the town market. Though the friendly staff speaks no English, they can hunt down someone who can. Rooms are pleasant and clean, with A/C and neat private baths. Small, windowless rooms with double bed and TV 100,000Đ; larger rooms 150,000Đ. ❷

Bình Minh Hotel, 1 Vân Đồn (☎881 185; fax 881 014), across from Vietcombank. The surrounding area, close to the market, is quite lively, but it's a long walk from the bus station. Large rooms with clean baths and twin beds. Doubles 140,000Đ, with A/C 160,000Đ; triples 160,000-170,000Đ. ❷

Nha Nghỉ Hải Đường, 66 Đường Lê Hữu Trác (☎887 547). From the bus station, turn right and hook the first left. A middle-of-the-road guesthouse with well-maintained rooms. All rooms are 120,000Đ, but quality varies. Check your room before paying. ❷

🍴 FOOD

Móng Cái's Vietnamese food is unexciting, but it has some tasty Chinese food. Standard phở and cơm shops can be found all over town. There is a cluster of them next to the town market and around the bus station. One popular cơm restaurant can be found near the town market, at **99 Triều Đường ❶.** Turn right off

NORTHERN COAST

Trần Phú before the main square market; the restaurant is about 15m down the street on the right. There is no menu—just point at the raw materials you want included. (Tasty cơm with seafood, meat, or veggies 15,000-20,000Đ. Open daily 10:30am-8:30pm.) **Nhà Hành Trang Nguyễn ❷** is the best Cantonese restaurant in town. Heading away from the bus station, turn right on the street before the bridge and the restaurant is one block down. Run by a friendly English-speaking Hong Kong native, Nhà Hành Trang Nguyễn serves everything from seafood to dim sum. Although the prices are listed in Chinese currency, đồng and US dollars are also accepted. (☎884 205. Entrees US$1-3. Open daily 10am-midnight.)

🃟 MARKETS

After the border crossing, the markets just might be the town's biggest attraction. Stalls upon stalls of vendors sell fruit, food, and imported Chinese goods. Vietnamese flock to Móng Cái to buy everything from toilets to CD players at cheap Chinese prices. On the southern edge of the main market square, booths of tailors make for a warped imitation of Hội An. Electronic and appliance stores fill the streets near the market and line the way to the border crossing. To reach the market from the bus station, head toward the post office and hook a left onto Trần Phú. Continue straight until you see the three roof-covered markets on the left. Some stalls spread into nearby streets and alleys, so hunt around. The market is open daily 6:30am-6pm. The large stadium-like building near the post office is actually a clothing wholesaler (open 6am-noon).

🃟 NIGHTLIFE

Móng Cái has a surprisingly lively nightlife. Families and tourists meander along the bridge and through the streets that branch off from the intersection in the center of town. The cafes along the river offer a more romantic setting, and a younger crowd tends to gather along Hùng Vương and in the two pulsating clubs. The town's five-star hotel has a 24hr. casino, too, but local Vietnamese are not allowed into the hotel, so the only gamblers are Chinese.

Phòng Biểu Diễn Disco (☎770 557), in the Chinese store complex just across the bridge from the GPO, on the way to the bus station. A bar and lounge share the floor with a karaoke and disco bar. On karaoke nights, locals and Chinese patrons of all ages gather to admire singers. Soda 15,000Đ. Beer 20,000-22,000Đ. Cover only on nights with guest performers. Open nightly 8pm-midnight.

Kinh Đô Club, 10 Hùng Vương (☎887 557). Tables filled with Vietnamese youth mesmerized by the daring few who brave the dance floor. Coke 12,000-15,000Đ; liquor 30,000Đ. White Russian 35,000Đ. Cover 50,000Đ only on nights with musical guests. Open daily 7:30-11:30pm.

Cafe Trung Nguyễn, 2 Hồ Xuân Hương (☎884 336), at the major intersection to the right of the post office. Frequented by locals throughout the day and packed with a mix of Vietnamese and Chinese at night. Cute terraced seating upstairs is a major draw. Coffee 7000-9000Đ, with ice 7000-11,000Đ. Open daily 6am-midnight.

Đội Bởi Cafe, 26 Nguyễn Du (☎772 029), to the right of the post office. Home to the only Russian (or blond) you are likely to see in town—Natasha makes some mean *sinh tố* (fruit juice with milk or yogurt) for 10,000Đ. Mangosteen and mango are especially delicious. Open daily 6:30am-11pm.

TRÁ CỔ BEACH

Stretching for 17km along the Vietnamese coast, Trá Cổ is a tiny, laid-back fishing village that doubles as a hot spot for Chinese and Vietnamese vacationers. Sometimes called Northern Vietnam's best sand, the beach itself doesn't quite fit the bill—it's really only worth a trip on the way to or from China. Its major selling points include millions of spiral, cone-shaped shells scattered along the shore and high swells perfect for bodysurfing. Close to the beach is a French gothic church and Kilometer Zero, marking the northernmost point of Vietnam.

F TRANSPORTATION Trá Cổ lies about 10km from the Móng Cái bus station, from which it is easily reachable by **motorbike**. Drivers are willing to whisk you away for 15,000-20,000Đ. To reach the beach on your own, follow Hùng Vương over the bridge and into town. Continue straight until the road flows out of town and heads straight for the beach. A taxi ride from Móng Cái costs around 50,000Đ.

ORIENTATION AND PRACTICAL INFORMATION The village that controls Trá Cổ's shore is a rural version of a beach resort, with practically every sign along the town road advertising lodging or food. The main road that leads to the beach from Móng Cái traverses the town parallel to the shore. Smaller roads branch off into the sand and sea. The drive from Móng Cái is fairly straight, but curves right when the road reaches the town. About 700m from the curve, a right turn leads to the resort entrance. The Trá Cổ **post office** stands 5m from the main road. (☎ 780 008. Open daily 7am-9pm.) Also along the main road are a couple of **Internet** cafes, all charging 3000Đ per hour. (Most open daily 9am-10pm.) Farther down is the official **resort**, with a seaside cafe and a swimming pool (10,000Đ to take a dip). There are showers ("Nha Trang Nước Ngot") on the beach walkway, at the street entrance whose corner is marked by a sign reading "Nhà Nghi Loan Phương." (Open 7am-6pm. 3000Đ.)

ACCOMMODATIONS AND FOOD There are a few hotels and many guest-houses along the main road that runs through the town. Most have high prices, but the quality varies, so shop around. A few beachside lodging options cut the 10m walk from your room to the beach in half. **Hotel Toàn Truyền ❷,** across from the resort entrance, is the best option in town, offering high quality rooms at fair prices. (☎ 780 187. Clean triples with TV, large private bath, and balconies in some rooms 140,000Đ, with A/C 170,000Đ.) To get to **Hotel Trà Long ❷,** follow the sign about 550m from the turn in the road. Just a few steps from the boardwalk and beach, this old hotel is the closest to the action. The rooms are well-kept, though clearly aging. (☎ 780 131. Doubles 120,000Đ; triples 140,000Đ.) **Thanh Thao ❷,** right next to Hotel Toàn Truyền, offers some of the cheapest rooms in town, but the drop in price is accompanied by a drop in quality. The doubles (with fan) are small and the bathrooms are old. (☎ 780 393. Rooms 150,000Đ.)

While phở and cơm shops populate the village road that runs parallel to the beach, the boardwalk is lined with seafood restaurants. The food itself is undoubt-edly fresh, but the restaurant menus here are identical and uninspired. **Sâm Lợi ❷** is a fancy restaurant right on the beach in front of Hotel Trà Long. There are no menus, but the staff has a listing of prices by kilogram, and some of the younger workers speak some English. (☎ 883 081. Soup 10,000Đ; steamed fish 20,000Đ; rice 5000Đ; beer 12,000Đ. Open daily 7am-11pm.)

SIGHTS. The main road away from Móng Cái passes by a **French church** built more than one hundred years ago. Jesus greets you with his arms spread wide, as do the youngsters climbing the rocks on which he is standing. Although the church is open infrequently for special services, you can catch a glimpse of the interior through the open windows. Continuing down the road brings you to a dead-end with a marker **"Km 0."** This marks Vietnam's northernmost point, from which you can see China across the water. Supposedly, due to lax border patrol, this is also a popular point for smuggling goods in from the north.

NORTHERN VIETNAM

Smooth-riding tourist buses go as far as Hà Nội; to the surprise of many backpackers, Vietnam keeps on going. Even in Vietnam, it has become increasingly difficult to find places untouched by foreign tourists, but those willing to step onto cramped rigs, brave local "roads," and head north will soon discover that the journey is worthwhile. The provinces east of the famous Northwest Highlands are the least-touristed in Vietnam, and travel there is at its least directed—a curse to those seeking an effortless travel experience, but a blessing to travelers with the time and energy to explore uncharted territory and meet its inhabitants. Indeed, the people of Northern Vietnam are probably its best feature; they are remarkable for their cheerful, hard-working perseverance in the face of poverty and adversity.

Signs throughout the country read: "A Destination for the New Millennium." Nowhere do the Vietnamese believe that more than in the North. It has all the necessary ingredients—natural attractions, historical relics, and an ethnic diversity that lends the region its distinct flavor. Perhaps the tourist cafes will extend their coverage here one day, but for now it remains a destination for those in search of anything but a traditional vacation.

HIGHLIGHTS OF NORTHERN VIETNAM

DELIGHT IN THE SMORGASBORD that is ■**Cao Bằng province** (p. 175); the city itself is quiet and charming, but the real attractions are the area's **lakes** (p. 179), **waterfalls** (p. 180), **caves** (p. 180), and ethnic minority **markets** (p. 181).

SLEEP ON STILTS, or more accurately, in ■**stilt houses** (p. 184) in dramatic **Ba Bể National Park** (p. 182); when you wake up, take a boat ride across the calm, crystal waters of Ba Bể Lake, visit Montagnard **villages** (p. 185), and go on any number of hikes. If you go on a weekday, the park will be yours and yours alone.

LẠNG SƠN   ☎25

Over the last 2000 years, the pass at Lạng Sơn has seen many uninvited, heavily armed Chinese guests. Most recently, Chinese troops razed Lạng Sơn in 1979 as part of Deng Xiaoping's effort to "teach the Vietnamese a lesson" in response to the country's invasion of Cambodia (see **Reunification and Rebuilding**, p. 68). The lesson, however, was ultimately taught to the Chinese instead. Today, Lạng Sơn boasts neither Thái Nguyên's charm nor Cao Bằng's beauty; most travelers pass through only briefly en route to China. Those who choose to stay, however, will discover that the city's warm residents are quite enthusiastic and happy to welcome the rare visitor. The constant price-gouging and hustling of the big cities is almost nonexistent here, and travelers are treated with a level of respect unknown in the bigger tourist cities—which for some travelers compensates for the area's profound lack of memorable attractions.

◪ **TRANSPORTATION.** Buses usually drop people at the **Ngô Quyền bus station,** left off Trần Đăng Ninh and 1km north of the Lê Lợi intersection. Those that have to transfer buses en route from Hà Nội are let off at the **Lạng Sơn bus station,** off Lê Lợi

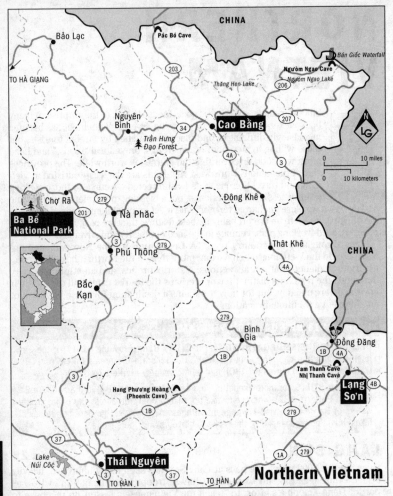

on Ngô Quyền, 2km east of the intersection with Trần Đăng Ninh. **Buses** run from Ngô Quyền bus station to Đồng Đăng (20-30min.; 30,000Đ); Cao Bằng (5hr.; 5, 8am, 5:30pm; 50,000Đ); Thái Nguyên (every 30min.; 40,000Đ); Tiên Yên (4hr.; 11:30am; 40,000Đ). Buses from Lạng Sơn bus station leave for Hà Nội (3½-4½hr.; depart when full 6am-1pm; 45,000Đ). **Minibuses** run to Hà Nội (4hr.; 50,000-80,000Đ) and the border (20min.; up to 50,000Đ). **Trains** from **Lạng Sơn Station** (☎ 873 452), at the end of Lê Lợi, leave for Hà Nội (5-6hr.; 2, 6am; hard seat 35,000Đ, soft seat 42,000Đ).

■■ **ORIENTATION AND PRACTICAL INFORMATION.** Lạng Sơn is 130km north of Hà Nội on Rte. 1. The town's main drag, **Trần Đăng Ninh,** heads north to Đồng Đăng. In the southern part of town, **Đường Lê Lợi** branches east from Trần Đăng Ninh, passing the **post office** (international telephone and ATM; open daily 6am-10pm) and ending at the train station. Three **Internet** cafes, all with good connections, cluster near the intersection of Trần Đăng Ninh and Lê Lợi. (All 3000Đ per hr.) One hundred meters south of the intersection, Trần Đăng Ninh crosses the **Ky Cung River** and continues to **Đầu Tư Bank,** 2 Hoàng Văn Thụ, which exchanges currency but not traveler's checks. (☎870 033. Open daily 7am-11:30pm.) For merchandise and delicious fruit (locally grown pears, plums, peaches, and persimmons), try the sprawling market on **Bắc Sơn,** which runs north from Lê Lợi near the major intersection. Ethnic minority groups (especially the Nung) from nearby towns also sell their goods throughout the market. Turn left off Bắc Sơn when the stalls thin out, and straight ahead will be **Trần Đăng Ninh,** with another marketplace selling wares imported from China. There's a **pharmacy,** 79 Tam Thanh, on the road that branches left off Trần Đăng Ninh, 20m north of the Lê Lợi intersection. A personable doctor has an office in the back. (☎812 524. Open daily 5:30am-11:30pm.) **Tam Thanh** continues west through a six-way intersection to the **hospital.**

⬛ ACCOMMODATIONS. Searching for lodgings in Lạng Sơn can rapidly give travelers a case of déjà vu. Hotels provide virtually indistinguishable setups and ranges of amenities (TV, A/C, fans, and hot water). Nonetheless, rooms vary in quality—ask to see several rooms in each establishment before you decide, as rooms with views over the lake will go for the same price as those with views of construction sites. While bargaining can be difficult, inspecting rooms with visible disappointment will generally result in lower costs. Most hotels are scattered along Trần Đăng Ninh near the center of town. **Hotel Khách Sạn Mâu Sơn ❷,** 125 Trần Đăng Ninh, has bathtubs and bright rooms, many of which overlook Phai Loan Lake. (☎876 818. Doubles US$9; triples US$11.) Next door is **Hoà Bình Hotel ❹,** 127 Trần Đăng Ninh, with small, well-kept suites and comparable views. The hike to the top floor is worth the sweat, offering great views at a good price. (☎870 807. Rooms 130,000Đ.) A 10min. walk north of the major intersection, **Khách Sạn Hoàng Vũ ❷,** 240 Trần Đăng Ninh, has airy rooms with a small sitting area and amicable service. (☎873 738. Doubles 130,000Đ; triples 160,000Đ.) **Hoàng Sơn Hải Hotel ❹,** 57 Tam Thanh, might just be worth the steeper price. Turn onto Tam Thanh, just north of the intersection of Lê Lợi and Trần Đăng Ninh, and walk 100m. The entrance is up a set of marble stairs, past fish tanks and a colorful mural. A two-star rating is displayed proudly on the door. Rooms are very well kept, with spectacular views overlooking Lạng Sơn's red-roofed houses. (☎870 199. Doubles US$20; triples US$25.)

THE LOCAL STORY

SLOPPY SECONDS

A bus ride in Vietnam can be a sloppy experience. The fact that the majority of Vietnamese travel by motorcycle is telling—switchbacks and bumpy roads don't sit well with phở. Here are some ways to avoid vomit flowing in your direction.

1. Avoid sitting near anyone with his head down, or (worse) looking despairingly out the window. There is no movement yet, but he is anticipating sickness. That person is definitely the first to pop.
2. Also avoid people who ask for orange plastic bags from the money collector. They know they won't make it. You, too, can identify them. They are the ▮ewers.
3. In a crowded bu▮ a mother may place a cute child's head on your lap. Do not allow it. More often than not, that cute kid's not-so-cute sickness will end up in your lap.
4. After the break for lunch, do not sit near a window seat. Remember, those same people that were throwing up before lunch are definitely vomiting after lunch—only this time there's a lot more rice and meat in it. And those orange plastic bags get thrown out the window.
5. Carry minty-smelling nasal spray in your pocket.
6. Enjoy the experience. A chuckle to yourself at the antics of basic transportation ▮ Vietnam can make you mostl▮ get the half-digested rice on your pants not seem all that bad. Mostly.

Hotel Hoàng Nguyễn ❸, 84 Trần Đăng Ninh, has rooms with terraces overlooking a construction site, but the bubbly owners and romantic canopied beds make up for its less attractive features. (☎874 575. Rooms US$10-12.)

📭 **FOOD.** There are a few overpriced restaurants in Lạng Sơn, but your best meals will be from sidewalk vendors and market stalls. Eating your way through the market is a fun experience; regional specialties include suckling pig, roast duck, and *bánh bao* (steamed dumpling stuffed with vermicelli noodles, diced meat, and an egg). Wash it all down with the local rice wine and bar snacks like cucumber and green mango dipped in salt. Trần Đăng Ninh and Lê Lợi host the usual phở shops (10,000-20,000Đ). Walking south on Trần Đăng Ninh and turning left by the bridge onto Nguyễn Tri Phương leads to a **market.** Toward the back of the first aisle a woman sells particularly tender chicken-feet sandwiches (4000Đ)—which is to say, as tender as chicken feet get. Another good street kitchen can be found on Bắc Sơn, which intersects with the northern side of Lê Lợi near the main intersection. Under a blue tent across from the neon Bào Việt sign, boys and girls cook up hefty portions of fried rice—just point at the ingredients you want included (10,000Đ). Cheaper options line the side streets where you can usually get cơm with tofu, vegetables, and cooked meats for 6000Đ.

Minh Quang Restaurant ❷, 44 Ngô Quyền, offers a peaceful refuge from Lạng Sơn's noisy streets. Walk east on Lê Lợi and bear right when the road splits. Walk through the alley and turn into the dining room. The grilled beef is topped with sesame seeds served over a bed of pineapple. Also available are snake head, sparrow, and the regional specialty of roasted duck. Most plates are small and cheap, so you can try a little bit of everything. The service is excellent. Most entrees are 15,000-25,000Đ; be sure to check prices before you order. (☎870 417. Open daily 8am-8pm.) **Nhà Hàng New Century ❶** also provides an English menu. In a large building set off of Trần Đăng Ninh on the lake, New Century restaurant has decent food but great karaoke. The crab and chicken soups (6000Đ) are small but come out steaming hot. Sauteed pumpkin buns with garlic (12,000Đ) are another treat. Also available are various meats, including pig stomach (25,000Đ), camel (chewier and tastier than chicken; 35,000Đ), frog, and carp. (☎898 000. Open daily 6am-10pm.) For your daily dose of fruit, stop by **Ởi Xanh ❶**, before the bridge on Trần Đăng Ninh. Watch the goldfish in the bowl on your table bump into the glass while slurping a fruit cocktail (10,000Đ) made with *máng câu* (mangosteen), *xoài* (mango), and many other tropical fruits. Even the durian shake (12,000Đ) makes the noxious fruit seem quite appealing. (☎278 188. Open daily 7am-11pm.)

🄂 **SIGHTS.** A motorcycle taxi (10,000Đ) can take travelers to **Tam Thanh Cave** and **Nhị Thanh Cave,** located in the mountains 3km west of town. For a nice walking tour, start in Nhị Thanh Cave's main entrance and walk along the path, which opens into an enormous, stalagmite-filled chamber. Continue to the opposite entrance of the cave. From there, a 10min. walk straight ahead will bring you to Tam Thanh Cave, home to Buddhist altars and their faithful companions, bats. An opening at the cave's rear offers a great panoramic view of the surrounding countryside. A slightly different view is accessible via the staircase to the side of the cave's entrance. Be careful, as some of the stone steps carved out of the cave can get quite slippery. (Both caves open daily 7am-6pm. 5000Đ each.)

In town, walking around **Phai Loan Lake** takes about 30min. and provides some nice views of Lạng Sơn. Another pleasant option is in the southern part of town where there is an attractive temple, set by the bridge on Trần Đăng Ninh, that overlooks the Ky Cung River. The bridge lets out onto a wide avenue full of government buildings and a few plazas in recognition of fallen soldiers. Next to the first plaza is a market; beyond the usual fruit vendors is a row of barbers, for those whose five o'clock shadow has turned into a two-week jungle.

⚓ BORDER CROSSING: ĐỒNG ĐĂNG. Just north of Lạng Sơn, at the northern terminus of Route 1, lies the tiny border town of Đồng Đăng, one of three legal places in Vietnam to enter China (see **Border Crossings,** p. 37). While Đồng Đăng has little for tourists, the customs procedures there are low-key, quick, and easy. There is an impressive, multi-tiered **temple** with brightly painted ◪dragons on Khu Lô Rèn, the town's main drag. The surrounding countryside, too, is breathtaking, and worth some exploration on a *xe ôm.*

Minibuses run frequently between Đồng Đăng and Lạng Sơn (30,000Đ). On the ride over, large rocks jut out from rice paddies and steep streets twist along rolling hills. **Motorcycle taxis** wait at the intersection of the main highway and the entrance to Đồng Đăng. They can take you to the border (7000Đ), which is past two check-points, 3km beyond Đồng Đăng at the **Hữu Nghị (Friendship) Crossing.** To enter China here, your visa must have a Đồng Đăng exit stamp. Tourist cafes in Hà Nội can procure Chinese visas (US$34, plus US$20 extra for American, Canadian, German, and Japanese citizens) and can change the exit stamp on Vietnamese visas (US$35). **Trains** to Beijing, China leave from Đồng Đăng train station, just south of town. Tickets should be booked in Hà Nội. There is also a daily train from Đồng Đăng to Hà Nội (7hr.; 1:20pm; 40,000Đ). Over the border at **Pingxiang,** in Guangxi Province, there are rail and bus connections to Nanning, China.

CAO BẰNG

☎ 26

Cao Bằng is magical. Financially poor but culturally rich, the region remains the archetypal undiscovered gem for travelers, with genuinely kind inhabitants, decent food, and scenery so spectacular that it seems unreal. Cao Bằng town, the capital of the province, acts as an ideal base from which to venture out into the picturesque countryside. A cave of epic size, the largest waterfall in Vietnam, and markets galore have yet to appear on the tourist radar—frequently making foreign travelers the main attraction wherever they may venture. Along the Bằng Giang River, boys fish with bamboo poles or herd water buffalo while talkative women sell lychee fruit, work in the fields, or wash clothes in the river. Though the nine different ethnic minorities who live in the province differ in many ways, they all share an unusual enthusiastic energy that makes the region feel homey and vaguely familiar. In heavy rain you might be handed an umbrella, and at an impassable road, you'll undoubtedly be offered a cigarette. Hard to reach but even harder to leave, this idyllic corner of Vietnam is not to be missed.

▐ TRANSPORTATION

The **bus station** is across the river, 50m north of the bridge. **Buses** go to Hà Nội (8 hr.; 6:30am, 7pm; direct 80,000Đ, via Thài Nguyên 60,000Đ) and Lạng Sơn (5:30am; 50,000Đ). It is also possible to get to Ba Bể National Park by taking the Hà Nội bus to Nà Phăc (2½hr.; 50,000-60,000Đ) and then taking a motorcycle taxi the rest of the way (1½hr.; 85,000Đ). **Minibuses** and provincial buses leave from Cao Bằng's bus station sporadically throughout the day, including afternoon trips to Hà Nội. The schedule changes frequently, so it's best to check beforehand to confirm times. **Motorcycle taxis** will take you anywhere in Cao Bằng for 3000-6000Đ.

✹ ORIENTATION

Like most raging urban volcanoes, Cao Bằng town extends into the surrounding area, pushing up against hills and hopping over streams. The major north-south artery is **Kim Đồng**, which runs on the western side of the **Băng Giang River.** Most of the action is centered in the northwestern side of town, around the intersection of Kim Đồng and the **Băng Giang Bridge,** where the food market is located. The river provides the best directions in town—standing at the foot of the bridge, with your back to the river, north is to the right and south to the left.

▊ PRACTICAL INFORMATION

Like every other town in Vietnam, Cao Bằng features a **goods market** in addition to standard local services. This one is housed in the enormous white building one block south of the bridge on Kim Đồng (open daily 6am-6pm). Don't miss those glamorous "Dior" and "Chanel" sunglasses you've been craving.

Tourist Office: In one of the offices through the yellow gate on Sô Nhà, accessible either from Nguyễn Du or from the southern side of the goods market. Very little English spoken—just like the rest of town.

Currency Exchange: One block north of the bridge, turn left for the **Bank for Foreign Investment and Development,** 49 Xuân Trương (☎852 163). ATM inside. Open daily 7am-4:30pm.

Police: Behind the goods market. Walk west on Đàm Quang Trưng 1 block and turn left onto Hoàng Như. The station will be on the right side of the street.

Emergency: ☎115. **Police:** ☎113.

Pharmacies: Scattered all throughout the city; 2 are located on Nguyễn Du, south of the market off Kim Đồng (☎855 069 and 852 338). Open daily 5am-7pm.

Hospital: 3km south of town on Hwy. 4A.

International Telephone: Available at the post office for 13,000Đ per min. or at the small calling center, 39 Chợ Xanh (☎841 147), just north of the bridge by the entrance to the food market.

Internet Access: Located all over town for 3000Đ per hr. Look for signs with "Internet," "chat," or "yahoo" written on them. One reliable place is **Cao Bằng Network Club,** 378 Hoàng Văn Thụ (☎858 044). Walking north of the bridge, take your first left onto Xuân Trương and then your first right. Fast connection. Open daily 7am-10:30pm.

Post Office: On Hoàng Đình Giong, which intersects Kim Đồng just south of the bridge. The post office is 2 blocks down the street, diagonally across from the Hồ Chí Minh statue. Open daily 7am-5pm.

▟ ACCOMMODATIONS

Generally, hotels in Cao Bằng are both attractive and expensive. Bargaining takes some effort, but is nonetheless a worthwhile endeavor given the high asking prices. The longer you're staying, the more bargaining leverage you have. But animal lovers beware: the theme of choice in most hotel lobbies seem to be "wilderness"—or something else that includes many, many stuffed deer and birds.

Hoàng Anh Hotel, 131 Kim Đồng (☎858 969). The best deal in town; get more Bằng for your buck. Sleepy lobby with nice owners and pleasant rooms, and a view of either the street or the neighbor's brick wall—one is only slightly better than the other. Doubles 130,000Đ, although bargaining can work wonders here. ❷

Thàn Loan Hotel, 131 Vươn Cam (☎857 026), 100m north of the bridge. A step above the rest, with spacious rooms, high ceilings, and burgundy wooden furniture. The 4th

Around Cao Bằng

and 5th floors get great light. Simple breakfast included. Enthusiastic and professional staff. All rooms US$15; prices go down slightly for extended stays. ❸

Băng Giang Hotel (☎853 431), right in the center of town on Kim Đông. A big and impersonal establishment run by the state, with large rooms and leather couches. It's hard to bargain, but it can be fun singing karaoke or getting a massage with government officials. Breakfast included. Rooms US$15. ❸

Hoáng Long Hotel, 42 Phô Thâu (☎852 477), next to the wares market along the riverbank. All rooms are similarly sized, regardless of the number of beds crammed in them. Several of the rooms have huge windows directly over the river and include all the normal goodies (A/C, TV, etc.). Perhaps not the best deal for doubles, but a bargain for larger groups. Doubles, triples, and quads 160,000-200,000Đ. ❸

Bâc Lâm Hotel, 25 Phô Hoàng Như (☎852 697). Walk 2 blocks west off Kim Đông on Nguyễn Du, which is just south of the goods market. Pass 2 pharmacies and take a left. Clean, bright rooms with canopied beds, which also serve to keep out mosquitoes from the river. Massage offered downstairs. Doubles 170,000Đ. ❸

Hotel Hương Thơ'm, 91 Kim Đông (☎856 128). A lively atmosphere, consisting of Cao Bằng's citizens munching on mangosteens in the lobby. The receptionist speaks some basic English. Immaculate (if overpriced) rooms 200,000Đ. ❸

Nguyêt Nga Hotel, 43 Kim Đông (☎856 455), directly across the river from the Băng Giang Hotel. Clean but crowded. Rooms with A/C, fridge, and a "satellite" TV that only

ON THE MENU

TOAST THIS!

Alcohol has always been intimately related to traditional aspects of Vietnamese life, even finding its way into religious rites and ancestral altars. Over the past 20 years, with the increase in wealth throughout the country, alcohol consumption has become even more central. Friendships are forged and businesses are sold to the clinking of glasses in a *chúc* (toast). *Bia hơi* (beer) flows from every tap in every town, cheaper and colder than water. Also common is *rượu* (hard liquor, pronounced *ziò* in the north), of which there are a variety of forms: *rượu nếp* (sticky rice wine), *rượu gạo* (harvested rice plant wine), and *rượu ngô* (corn wine).

Complicated etiquette accompanies the art of drinking in groups. No party is complete without everyone toasting everyone, ensuring that all present will drink themselves into oblivion. Novelties that they are, foreigners are commonly invited by locals to sit and drink *rượu*—it's a perfect opportunity to get hammered, if that's what you're after. To sit is to make an unspoken commitment to drink like crazy. However, if you're toasted more than once, you can always defer the drink to a friend. If you want to kick a few back and still walk after lunch, it's best to remain standing and *chúc* everyone at once before gulping down your glass, thereby minimizing your separate commitment to each drinker in the group.

gets 3 channels. You won't be watching it anyway, with all the time you'll be spending on daytrips. All rooms 170,000Đ. ❸

Thanh Trung Hotel, 116 Phô Cū (☎857 797), all the way down Nguyễn Du street where it terminates at Phô Cū. Elegant exterior, simple interior. Rooms have A/C, private bath, bed, and little else. A short and pleasant walk from the center of town, Thanh Trung is for those who crave a calmer, more suburban environment. Doubles 160,000Đ. ❸

🍴 FOOD

Restaurants in Cao Bằng—though limited in number—offer reasonably good food. Those on a tight budget might choose to capitalize on the endless phở and *cháo* (rice porridge) options throughout the city, or frequent the food stands that set up every evening in front of the food market and on Kim Đông (open daily 5am-6pm). Whatever you choose, be sure to eat early; most of Cao Bằng heads home around 8pm. The town is also the place to get snacks for daytrips. The fruit options are endless—awesome-looking dragon fruit, plums, lychee, and rambutan are all juicy and sweet snacks. Loaves of bread and meat are also packable picnic items.

Viêt Béo, 7 Lý Tư Trọng (☎850 087). A 10min. walk north of the bridge, past the Thàn Loan Hotel. Follow the perimeter of the stadium's gate and the restaurant is on your left. Not the place for animal-rights activists. In the first room is a large metal tank; net your sea animal of choice and bring it to the back room to be prepared. Prices are high, but the fish is cooked to perfection and comes on a hot plate with various garnishes. Most fish around 120,000Đ per kg. Shrimp 250,000Đ per kg. Sea turtle 460,000Đ per kg. For the less adventurous, steak and chicken are available for around 40,000Đ. Open daily 6am-11pm. ❹

Phô Núi, 3-10 Nà Cạn (☎850 878), across the river, a 10min. walk south of the bridge. Lengthy menu includes crab (95,000Đ per kg) and beef (25,000Đ). The tiki-torch atmosphere, with fruit hanging from the ceiling, somehow manages to make this place even more charming. Open daily 9am-8pm. ❷

Hợp Trường Restaurant, 8 Băng Giang (☎854 788), a 5min. walk north of the bridge along the riverbank. This place specializes in those meats you've been dying to try, including cat (40,000Đ) and snake (95,000Đ per kg; must be bought whole). For those who like to know what they're eating, Hợp Trường also has veggie fried rice and beef (15,000Đ each) that are superior to most places in town—any dish, it seems, is better with garlic and ginger. Open daily 9am-10pm. ❸

Băng Giang Restaurant (☎853 431), located (of all places) in the Băng Giang Hotel. Reminiscent of your high school cafeteria, except with superior food. The *bò bít têt* (beef; 40,000Đ) is particularly tender. Has an English menu. Open daily 5am-7pm. ❸

Hương Sen Restaurant (☎852 338), south of the bridge, just off Kim Đông opposite Nguyễn Du. A table by the kitchen is stacked with various meats, veggies, fish, and shrimp. If you haven't tried *bò lá lốt* (beef wrapped in betel leaves and grilled) this is just the place. Just point and pay—a full meal should cost around 20,000Đ. The food is hit-or-miss—look around to see what everyone else is having. Open daily 11am-8pm. ❷

🔘 SIGHTS

Cao Bằng is known for the attractions spread throughout the province, but if time allows, there are a few places around town worthy of exploration. There are two picturesque **Chinese temples** nearby. At the southern end of Kim Đông, the road branches; take Đông Khê and walk 10min. Just beyond an Internet cafe, there is a set of mossy stone steps leading to a small, secluded temple. Closer to the city's center, on Nguyễn Du by the Thanh Trung Hotel, there is a larger and more active temple, with the smell of incense wafting through the air at all hours.

Want to walk off the phở you ate for lunch? Head across the river, take your first right down Pác Bó and walk several hundred meters until the first phone booth. Turn left into the alley and up to the **war memorial.** The entrance to this subtly phallic marble monument is closed indefinitely, but the views from the hill are worth the trip. If you want to walk off breakfast as well, head back to Pác Bó and continue one block to the river, where there is a lovely path heading south out of Cao Bằng. Along the route sits a bastion built by the French in 1940.

🔳 DAYTRIPS FROM CAO BẰNG

Pulsing waterfalls, breathtaking caves, soothing lakes, and lively villages provide much more than a day's worth of sight-seeing, and the condition of some roads after a rainstorm might extend your visit longer than you expect. Sights are most easily accessible by *xe ôm*, which generally run 225,000-300,000Đ for a full day. Wherever you choose to go, water, sunscreen, snacks, and a camera are essential.

🔳 THĂNG HEN LAKE

Thăng Hen Lake is a 1hr. ride from Cao Bằng. Most of the road is paved, but nearing the end it narrows and fades out somewhat. The trip costs 125,000Đ round-trip by motorbike and an exorbitant 400,000Đ by SUV. It is also possible to make the trip using minibuses headed for Trá Lính—just jump off when you see a sign pointing left in the direction of the lake. Sometimes motorbike taxis wait inside a small pool hall at the junction and can take you the rest of the way for 20,000Đ. If not, the walk is just over an hour. It is possible to sleep in the large wooden house closest to the lake for 30,000Đ per night. You'd be in good company—Hồ Chí Minh himself once slept there.

Past the Băng Giang Bridge, the creekside road to Thăng Hen Lake goes over beautiful Mã Phục Pass. Above the pass, a small road with a bamboo gate branches off the main highway. Thăng Hen is a 15min. drive down this road.

The lake is calm—no artificial sounds, no unsightly telephone poles, and no pushy vendors. While there are more impressive sights in the province, no other tourist spot so fluently captures the sacred quiet of Cao Bằng's countryside. A small animal path snakes along the left side of the lake and then continues up into a pass between two mountains. Climbing towards the clouds for another 5km leads to a seven-family H'mông village. Their isolated location receives few visitors, and they are usually overjoyed to see a new face.

While you're at the lake, test out your balance on the lake's rafts. The fisherman who hang out around Thăng Hen charge 15,000Đ to use the larger bamboo rafts, and nothing at all for the older rafts, which are on their last log—they consist of four bamboo trunks tied loosely together and are usually halfway submerged in the water. Also, check out the market at Trà Lình on your way to or from the lake.

■ BÁN GIỐC WATERFALL AND NGƯỜM NGAO CAVE

A motorbike costs roughly 250,000Đ for the full-day trip. SUVs can be hired from most hotels for around 600,000Đ. Making the trip by public transportation is challenging but more affordable. Minibuses leave from the center of Cao Bằng for Trúng Khán (one-way 50,000Đ). From there it's possible to hire a motorbike to make the round-trip journey 25km farther to the falls (round-trip 70,000Đ).

Bán Giốc Waterfall and its faithful companion, **Ngườm Ngao Cave,** are a 3hr. drive northwest of Cao Bằng. The road, most of which is paved, climbs past Montagnard towns and villages—mostly Nũng and Tày—before opening into even more vast and beautiful territory. The landscape is something out of a storybook—green mountains and sheer cliffs jut straight out of grasslands, casting shadows over scarecrows wearing conical hats and rivers with shoulder-deep water buffalo. Twenty-five kilometers past the markets of Trùng Khánh, the road splits; a sign directs you right toward the cave, failing to mention that the waterfall is to the left.

Bán Giốc, which is fed by the Quay Xuan river, is the largest waterfall in Vietnam and acts as an implicit boundary with China. The approach from the parking lot is gorgeous—the road weaves through rice paddies and crosses floating bamboo bridges (which charge a frustrating 2000Đ) before arriving at the base of the trembling falls. The curtain of mist coming from the falls dampens your skin from afar, providing a pleasant cool-down to picnickers on the shore. For 20,000Đ, you can get a closer look by taking a boat up to the imaginary boundary in the middle of the Quay Xuan; check out the intense Chinese tourist infrastructure on the other bank.

An even better view entails a steep and sometimes slippery walk to the left of the main waterfall. Arriving at a small cave filled with incense, veer right toward the rickety bamboo bridge just above the rushing falls. The bridge connects to dry land, level with the waterfall. The noise created by the sheer force of the waterfall —let alone the views of the river below—is breathtaking.

The nearby **Ngườm Ngao Cave** is a castle amongst caves. The 5000Đ fee is almost laughable when compared with this sight's overwhelming beauty. A 10min. walk through corn fields, avoiding the water buffalo that block the marked path, leads to a small opening in a rock face. Inside, the cave is an elaborate and dizzying system of tunnels—to get through, one must pass under arches, climb slopes, and dodge columns. The tight squeezes open up into enormous rooms with naturally sparkling stalactites, resembling everything from giant chicken's feet to cacti and waterfalls. The sound of rushing water—its origin a mystery—is all around. The tourist-free 2414 square meters of cave makes this perhaps the best sight in the region. Tour guides can be nice, but interior lighting makes them unnecessary.

The route back to Cao Bằng passes through the town of **Phúc Sen.** There, in a field just beyond town, men forge *dao* (knives) and *liêm* (small, wing-tipped machetes). Each knife is the product of several men's efforts. Standing together with mallets in hand, they pound out frightfully sharp and attractive blades. The huts are easy to miss, so listen for the rhythm of metal beating on metal. At the end of the day, it may be worthwhile to stop back by Ngườm Ngao Lake for a quick dip. It's a short jog to the left off Highway 206.

PÁC BÓ CAVE

Pác Bó is a 2hr. drive north of Cao Bằng. There is currently no public transportation to the site; a motorcycle taxi costs around 200,000Đ and an SUV will make the 154km round-

trip journey for 400,000Đ. The trip to the cave is incredible—stilt houses dot the valleys, and bright yellow corn is laid out along the roadside to roast in the midday sun.

On February 8th, 1941, Hồ Chí Minh returned to his beloved country after decades abroad and began living in **Pác Bó Cave,** a hideout beside the Chinese border. From there, he planned the Vietnamese resistance against the French and began training his troops while allegedly living a life of extreme austerity, using a wooden board as a bed and subsisting on vegetables and bamboo. The wooden bed still sits in the cave, and people climb the small rope deterrents to absorb some of the leader-turned-hero's energy. Below the cave is a roped-off piece of stone where the leader is said to have done his best thinking. Between strategizing and writing poetry, he named a nearby creek after Lenin and a mountain after Marx. If you want to find out more, the museum in Pác Bó provides visitors with pictures and paintings of the beloved Uncle Ho as well as articles of his clothing. Regardless of your take on the man and his story, you can't help but admire his taste in hideout spots—the landscape is beautiful.

Heading back to Cao Bằng, stop at the attractive **Kim Đồng Memorial;** it's only a brief walk from the main road. Kim Đồng was a courier in the war against the French; he is said to have died when he was 14 in a successful attempt to distract French troops while his Vietnamese compatriots escaped. The sight is now used for award ceremonies honoring teenagers.

MONTAGNARD MARKETS

The confluence of ethnic minorities in the Cao Bằng province makes markets a special treat. At daybreak, everyone heads to the marketplace. Some arrive on motorbikes with baskets of animals strapped to their sides; others make the journey by bus or buffalo; most arrive on foot. Markets are not only a chance to buy and sell goods, but also to exchange information and socialize. Below is a list of some of the best markets in the area; be advised that market days run according to the **lunar calendar** (p. 448). Doing a whirlwind tour of the markets is a nice way to spend the morning (6am to noon), but the better option is to visit one town or another en route to a sight. Buy a duck, a traditional indigo shirt, or black sticky rice stuffed with mung beans. Better yet, do what many of the older local women do—take a seat and just watch the action. **Trà Lình,** near Thăng Hen Lake (see above), has the highest concentration of ethnic minorities, and overall, it's the most fun. Check it out on your way to the lake for one heck of a good day.

ETHNIC MINORITY VILLAGES	DAYS OF THE LUNAR CALENDAR
Quảng Hòa, Thạch An, Thông Nông, Nà Giang	1st, 6th, 11th, 16th, 21st, 26th
Nguyên Bình, Nước Hai, Phục Hòa	3rd, 8th, 13th, 18th, 23rd, 28th
Trà Lình, Na Nhũng, Nà Rì	4th, 8th, 14th, 19th, 24th, 29th
Bảo Lạc, Cao Bình, Nà Giàng, Tỉnh Túc, Trung Khánh, Ban Giới	5th, 10th, 15th, 20th, 25th, 30th

TRẦN HƯNG ĐẠO FOREST

Trần Hưng Đạo Forest is 1hr. from Nguyên Bình on an isolated road. There is no public transportation there; a motorcycle taxi will make the trip from Cao Bằng for 160,000Đ, including a stop in Nguyên Bình. The forest is a Vietnamese historical sight and photography is not permitted. Minibuses also run from the center of Cao Bằng to Nguyên Bình. They leave as early as 5am and charge 30,000Đ each way. The journey is 5hr. round-trip.

Trần Hưng Đạo Forest is located in the Nguyên Bình province and offers a refreshing escape from the summer's sauna-like weather—and little else. The Vietnamese Liberation Propaganda Unit originated in this isolated spot in 1944. The trail in the forest is well-maintained but short; 10min. from the parking lot is an attractive monument enclosed in a well-kept garden. The path leads to a more scenic memorial, up 500 slippery steps to an exposed summit. The view from the top is great.

Given the numerous sights in Cao Bằng province, sacrificing a full day for Trần Hưng Đạo Forest is hardly worthwhile. The only real way to justify the trip is to combine it with a stop at Nguyên Bình market, which is on the 3rd, 8th, 13th, 18th, 23rd, and 28th of every lunar month. From 6am to noon on market days, the local Montagnard women, dressed in ornate traditional garb, congregate in town to sell and trade various goods. While in Nguyên Bình, visit the tiny cemetery perched atop the hill. To get there, take the street branching left through town, pass the government building and turn right up the second dirt path (beyond the small ladder). Once on the path, a right and then a left will bring you to a tiny set of switchbacks leading to the cemetery, which has awesome views of Nguyên Bình valley.

BA BỂ NATIONAL PARK   ☎ 281

Located in the Bắc Kạn province, Ba Bể National Park was established in 1992 to preserve some of Vietnam's most thrilling natural beauty and diverse wildlife. Covering over 200 sq. km of water, limestone crags, and lowland evergreen forest, the park is home to 40 species of reptiles and amphibians, 45 types of mammals (27 of which are bats), 87 varieties of fish, 350 genera of butterfly, and 200 types of bird. Communities composed of Tày, Dao, H'mông, Nùng, and Kinh people share the natural wealth of the area. The park's major attraction is Ba Bể ("Three Basin") Lake, which is composed of three smaller, interconnected bodies of water.

Ba Bể's highlights will be determined by your approach. It is possible to do a professionally operated tour that scans the natural and cultural wonders within the park. Others might choose to have a *xe ôm* drop them at the boat landing or someplace remote and rely on intuition and the kindness of strangers to get them through. Track down the endangered Tonkin Snub-Nosed Monkey or kick back and drink iced beers by the boat landing, but don't miss the pristine Ba Bể Lake.

BA BỂ AT A GLANCE	
AREA: 233 sq. km.	**GATEWAYS:** Chợ Rã, from which buses run to Thái Nguyên and Hà Nội.
CLIMATE: Vietnam's lovable tropical monsoon climate; especially chilly in the winter.	**CAMPING:** Must be part of a trek accompanied by a guide (US$20 per day); visitors can also stay in a park-owned room or in a ▨ **stilt-house** by the lake.
ELEVATION: 145m at highest point.	
HIGHLIGHTS: Ba Bể Lake; Tày, Nùng, Kinh, Dao, and H'mông villages; caves, waterfalls, and thrilling views and landscapes.	**FEES AND RESERVATIONS:** 15,000Đ entrance fee and its trusty sidekick, the mandatory 1000Đ insurance fee.

◪ **TRANSPORTATION.** Heading into Ba Bể is relatively simple—just be sure to arrive with cash (the hotel inside the park will grudgingly change small sums of money). The park has a 15,000Đ entrance fee and a mandatory 1000Đ insurance fee, both payable at the park entrance just past Chợ Rã, a small town 15km from park headquarters.

Getting anywhere from Ba Bể using public transport takes faith, effort, and time. You can get to Bắc Kạn via occasional **buses** from the park entrance (2hr.; 6:30am; 30,000Đ), but the schedule is irregular, so inquire at the park headquarters. Frequent **minibuses** will also get you to Bắc Kạn (2hr.; 18,000Đ), where you can transfer to Thái Nguyên or Hà Nội. Buses also depart from Chợ Rã heading to **Thái Nguyên** (4hr.; 5, 6, 9am, 1pm; 35,000-40,000Đ) and **Hà Nội** (7hr.; 5am; 50,000Đ) from

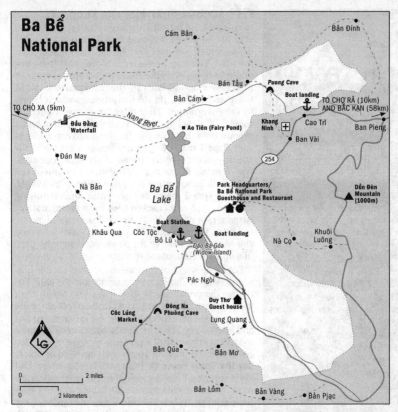

Ba Bể
National Park

the three-way intersection. You'll have to take a *xe ôm* from Ba Bể to get to Chợ Rã; the ride should take 30min. and cost 20,000Đ, but hard bargaining is necessary. Have the hotel call up to an hour ahead of time for the motorcycle.

No buses leave from Chợ Rã to **Cao Bằng**, so it's best to take a *xe ôm* to **Nà Phắc** (1½hr.; 60,000Đ) and then hop one of the buses heading north on Rte. 3 toward Cao Bằng. If you're on a tight budget, you can take a minibus from Chợ Rã bound for one of the southern destinations and have it drop you on the highway; from there, you can try to pick up a northbound bus to Cao Bằng..

WHEN TO GO. Ba Bể is cooler and drier than Vietnam's southern national parks, with a pleasant average annual temperature of 22°C. Nevertheless, visit during the dry season (Nov.-Mar.) to avoid rainouts; as always, trails and roads are more difficult to follow after a heavy rainfall.

🗺 **PRACTICAL INFORMATION. Khang Ninh Hospital** (☎894 077), just 4km from park headquarters (toward Chợ Rã), handles medical emergencies. **Internet** may be available by 2007. As a student or a scientist, it is possible to obtain a permit for the **Biodiversity Research Station** in Ba Bể National Park. Visitors will receive a homestay, office and equipment. For more information, contact Nông Thế Diên, Vice Director of Ba Bể National Park (☎894 027; thedien@hn.vnn.vn).

NORTHERN VIETNAM

LOCAL LEGEND

THE BARBELL OF BA BỂ

An unassuming rocky outcrop in the middle of Ba Bể lake is known as Đảo Bà Góa, Widow's Island. According to local lore, an old beggar went around the Tày village of Nam Mẫu asking for food and a place to stay. Every villager refused her request, except for a poor, lonely widow who offered her some food and a bed for the night.

That evening, the beggar warned the widow of a large storm that would bring devastating floods. The beggar advised the woman to throw a few grains of rice onto the ground once the rains began. Later that evening, the widow looked into the beggar's room, but the beggar was nowhere to be seen. Instead, she saw a dragon—surely this beggar was a god in disguise. The widow kept this a secret, as she was too afraid to tell anyone. (How she kept the dragon from ruining the decor is another story.)

The following night, a large typhoon threatened to flood the villagers' homes. The widow heeded the beggar's advice, and each grain of rice turned into a boat. The widow then rescued her fellow villagers from drowning. It was just in time—the deluge would eventually flood the village and connect the two lakes at the ends of the village into one—forming Ba Bể (Three Inlet) Lake's barbell shape. The bit of the village that remained above the water was the widow's house—hence the name, Widow's Island.

ACCOMMODATIONS AND FOOD. When tackling Ba Bể by public transportation, it's best to stay at the **Ba Bể National Park Guesthouse** (☎ 894 026), located just past park headquarters, 2km from the lake. You may be fooled into thinking there are multiple options by the different reception areas in the cluster of buildings by the headquarters. All of these are, in fact, Ba Bể Guesthouse, which is run by the government. They offer three types of double rooms. While all include TV, air-conditioning, and a private bath, they vary in levels of upkeep and privacy. **Type 1 rooms ❹** cost a ridiculous 280,000Đ, for which you get a room in one of six small cottages. **Type 2 rooms ❸** are across the street in one of the hotel buildings, cutting the price down to 250,000Đ. And the **Type 3 rooms ❸** have bathrooms featuring chipped paint and cracked tiles for a (comparative) bargain rate of 200,000Đ. Prices listed are high-season rates. On weekdays the place is a ghost town, but call ahead and reserve for weekends since the park fills up with Vietnamese tourists.

For those who have private transportation, it is possible to stay in Chợ Rã and commute into the park, but the accommodations in Chợ Rã are no better than those in the park. Instead, try a **homestay ❶** along the lake, where the experience can be much more fun and interesting. The park headquarters arrange these overnight stays, but it's possible to drive in and discover a guesthouse on your own. One solid option is **Duy Thọ Guest House ❶.** Pass park headquarters, and after 1km you'll see a paved turn-off (the only other road before reaching the lake); take a left and continue until you reach a bridge. Cross the bridge—Duy Thọ is the first building on the other side. (☎ 894 133. Rooms 46,000-70,000Đ; meals 30,000Đ.)

There is a **restaurant ❷** on the park premises, which is also run by the government and conveniently located beside one of the hotel buildings. The food is pricey and of limited variety—a fish entree will cost you a minimum of 50,000Đ per person. For breakfast, there are noodles with beef or a fried egg (20,000Đ) and at lunchtime, phở (15,000Đ) and dinner-type edibles are available. Alternatively, the small food stand by the hotel offers *bánh cuon* (rice crepes with dried meat) for only 1000Đ each. It is also possible to purchase drinks and snacks at the hotel or the boat landing, but prices are again inflated; it's a good idea to stock up on fruit and water before entering the park.

OUTDOORS Food and hotel accommodations in Ba Bể may be limited, but sights abound. Visitors usually come to Ba Bể for one or two days, but there is a week's worth of park to see. Whether or not you intend to take a guided tour, the park headquarters can be instrumental in planning your stay. Make sure you wear good footwear and bring lots of water wherever you go.

Guides are available for half-day (200,000Đ) and full-day (US$20) **tours;** boat rentals cost an additional 400,000Đ. Prices are the same for groups of 1-5 people, so it's best to get a group of park visitors together. While it is also possible to go without a guide, communicating with locals and following trails can prove tricky because of the lack of adequate maps (unless you speak Vietnamese). Then again, the guides don't speak English very well, either. Be sure to confirm ahead of time exactly what sites the tour will be covering and whether or not all transportation and food is covered in the original cost of the trip.

In addition to leading your way, a guide may be able to offer the local perspective on the silent war that exists between the local minority groups and the government-operated parks department. The government has offered financial compensation, drinking water, and electricity to local communities in exchange for relocating; they plan to build an electricity-generating dam at the villages' present locations. But villagers are unwilling to sacrifice their fertile land and sense of home, instead requesting better facilities where their homes now stand.

The most popular full-day trip takes 7-8hr. and briefly visits all of the park's major attractions. Beginning at the Nang River boat landing, 7km northeast of headquarters, tourists climb aboard one of the boats in the motorized fleet and head down the river, entering a gorge squeezed between impressive limestone cliffs. The Nang snakes into **Puong Cave,** an enormous tunnel that echoes and smells of bats, 11 species of which live on the high ceilings. The boat drops you off at a muddy landing and a path leads into the cave with excellent views of the river. Check out the stalagmite that (sort of) resembles the Buddha.

Upon exiting the cave, the landscape becomes welcoming and the boats stop at a trail leading 1km along the river to the Tày village of **Bản Cám.** Sitting in a modest home drinking tea, it's tempting to feel as if you're Bản Cám's first Western guest.

Leaving Bản Cám from a different landing, the trip continues down the Nang, passing dug-out canoes and local ferries before entering a small inlet on Ba Bể Lake. A short hike away is the startlingly silent **Ao Tiên (Fairy Pond).** The pond's serenity is occasionally disrupted by locals with bottles of rice wine, but it's worth a look nonetheless. From Ao Tiên, the boat heads across Ba Bể Lake. At this point in the trip, you can decide how to finish the day. Those who are short on time can truncate the tour and be dropped off at the lake boat landing (making the journey 5hr. long), but to make full use of the boat and guide, you can choose to also visit **Cốc Tộc** and **Bó Lù** villages (Tày), which resemble Bản Cám village. Another option is to head to **Đầu Đẳng Waterfall,** which has drops of 45m over an 800m span.

Other tour options abound, but require effort to set up. There is an 8hr. day hike up **Đồn Đèn Mountain** (1000m), which has impressive views overlooking Ba Bể. The way home passes Cao Trĩ Village, home to both Nũng and Tày. A strenuous two-day trip visits Puong Cave before turning up a channel to Bản Tầu and Bản Cám (Dao Trến, H'mông). The trail continues steeply to Đầu Đẳng Waterfall and an overnight in Đầu Đẳng Village (US$5). The next morning, trekkers visit Đán May Village (H'mông), Khâu Qua Village (H'mông), and Cốc Tộc Village (Tày) before circling back to Ba Bể Lake for the major attractions.

If you're averse to the guided tours, take a boat across the lake (6am-6:30pm; 10,000Đ each way) and head out from there. If you hope to visit certain minority groups, check the map by tourist headquarters with information on each village. As a general rule of thumb, **Tày, Nũng,** and **Kinh** live by rivers and do not dress in traditional garb. The **Dao** live in middle mountain regions, and the **H'mông** villages are the most remote, located in the upper mountains.

THÁI NGUYÊN
☎ 280

The people in Thái Nguyên constantly poke fun at their own city, ironically calling their markets "large" and their sights "famous...for Thái Nguyên." The source of this inferiority complex is the lack of any alluring natural wonder in the city or its surrounding countryside—something of a rarity for northern Vietnam. But from an outsider's perspective, Thái Nguyên fuses together some of Vietnam's most attractive characteristics with unparalleled grace. Sweeping colonnades from the time of the French turn into smaller, more livable avenues, then end in sprawling fields. Farmers dry corn and peanuts on the road as luxury cars drive by. On Sunday, every beer garden in the city is full of people chatting and trying to avoid the sun.

During the American War, Thái Nguyên was a target for American attacks. Supposedly, cables were strung across the streets and draped with camouflage to protect soldiers. The city today is a work in progress, suspended between the steel town that it once was and the thriving provincial capital that it hopes to become.

▐ TRANSPORTATION

Buses: The bus station (☎ 759 759), is west of the city center on Lương Ngọc Quyển (Hwy. 3), which connects Hà Nội to Cao Bằng via Bắc Kạn. Avoid the aggressive sellers by going inside to purchase tickets. Check the board for prices. Taxis wait outside of the bus station. **Buses** run to: **Bắc Kạn** (2 hr.; frequently all day; 24,000Đ); **Cao Bằng** (6hr.; 5am-12:20pm; 55,000Đ); **Chợ Rã** (4hr.; 5:30, 6:30, 10, 10:50am, 12:30, 1:30, 2pm; 35,000Đ); **Hà Nội** (2hr.; frequently all day; 20,000Đ); **Hà Giang** (6hr.; 5:20, 7, 8:15, 9:30, 11am; 50,000Đ); **Lạng Sơn** (4hr.; 4:30am-3:35pm; 20,000Đ).

Trains: The **train station** is 1km northwest of town; ask a *xe ôm* to take you there. There is 1 train per day to **Hà Nội** (7am; 11,000Đ).

▐ ORIENTATION

It's best to visualize the city as being built around a straight street composed of a western segment **(Hoàng Văn Thụ)** and an eastern segment **(Đội Cấn)**. Dividing the two segments is the central **rotary** (marked by a clocktower). Running north from the clocktower is **Đương Bắc Kạn** (also known as **Thư Minh**). The **Gia Bảy Bridge** is 400m north of the clocktower on the east side of this road. Running south from the clocktower is **Cách Mang Tháng.** One kilometer west of the clocktower, Hoàng Văn Thụ intersects with **Lương Ngọc Quyển;** the **bus station** is 100m north of this intersection. One kilometer east of the clocktower, **Đội Cấn** intersects with **Bến Tượng.**

▐ PRACTICAL INFORMATION

Tourist Office: 4 Càch Mang Tháng. Open M-Sa 7am-5pm. Very little English spoken.

Bank: Several options in town, but **The Industrial and Commercial Bank of Vietnam,** 62 Hoàng Văn Thụ (☎852 258), tends to have the best exchange rates. Open M-F 7:30am-4:30pm.

Police: (☎855 219.) On Hoàng Văn Thụ, opposite the Thái Nguyên Hotel at the rotary.

Pharmacy: Absolutely everywhere in town. Most open 7am-10pm.

Hospital: 479 Lương Ngọc Quyển (emergencies ☎934 0555), just south of Hoàng Văn Thụ. Thái Nguyên's proximity to Hà Nội makes it possible to call the International SOS clinic (p. 108), which provides much better care.

NORTHERN VIETNAM

Internet Access: Lots of options; the cybercafe at 128 Hoàng Văn Thụ (☎858 444) has an excellent connection. 3000Đ per hr. Open daily 8am-6pm. Other outlets along Lương Ngọc Quyến offer Internet for 2000Đ per hr.

Post Office: (☎858 377). 100m south of the tourist office on Cách Mạng Tháng. Open 24hr.

ACCOMMODATIONS

Hotels in town offer decent prices, and almost all rooms include TV, air-conditioning, and private bath. Because most hotels are a long walk from the bus and train stations, it's best to take a *xe ôm* (5000Đ) to the central rotary, and go from there.

Dong Sông Xanh Hotel, on Gia Bảy (☎651 732), just across the Gia Bảy bridge. Set back from the street on the banks of the Cầu River, the hotel offers a quieter retreat than most of the other hotels in town but is not too far away from the city center. Perhaps the best deal in town. Singles 120,000Đ; doubles 150,000Đ. ❷

Queenli Hotel, 648 Bắc Kạn (☎855 807), just north of the clocktower on Thư Minh. There are marble sinks and tasseled Victorian curtains in your rooms, but you may be sharing it with a critter or two. Ideal location and friendly staff. Singles 150,000Đ; doubles 180,000Đ; triples 250,000Đ. ❷

Cao Bắc Hotel, 70 Hoàng Văn Thụ (☎855 372), immediately beside the bank. Most of the sleek rooms are set on a peaceful courtyard off the street, but those that overlook the main street are a bit noisier. Doubles 160,000Đ; triples 200,000Đ. ❸

Sơn Hải Hotel, 31 Phương Trưng Vương (☎855 438). Head down Đội Cấn to the end, bear right on Bến Tượng and then left at the first intersection. Everything is very new, and it's relatively close to all the action. A good option if you can ignore the color scheme: sky blue, lime green, and pink. Doubles 160,000Đ. ❸

Đông Á Hotel, 142 Hoàng Văn Thụ (☎758 288), 200m west of the central rotary. Central location in the city's flagship hotel and office complex. Carpeted VIP suites include adjoining sitting area. Doubles 180,000Đ; VIP doubles 300,000Đ. ❸

Sông Cầu Hotel, 351 Thư Minh (☎856 410), 100m north of the Queenli Hotel, just south of the Gia Bảy Bridge. The rooms are spacious, with small terraces, but there are better deals in town. Doubles and triples 160,000-250,000Đ. ❸

Khách Sạn Hoa Hồng, 644 Lương Ngọc Quyến (☎759 337), 1km south of Hoàng Văn Thụ, gives you the whole 9 yards—doubles with fluffy beds, bathtubs, and solid wooden furniture for 200,000Đ. For 150,000Đ you lose the bathtub, but the rooms are a good deal, though they are on a busy street farther from the city center. ❷

FOOD

The people in Thái Nguyên enjoy their food and beer. A lot. **Phở shops** can be found everywhere; those found in the cluster at the intersection of Bến Túợng and Nha Trang are particularly good. Superb bread and pastries can be found at **Hương Tram,** 2 Hoàng Văn Thụ, 100m west of the second intersection. There are two **markets** in town: a small one next to the bus station and the much larger central market, which begins at Đội Cấn as it intersects with Bến Túợng. There are no tourist prices (making the rest of Vietnam seem expensive), but watch your wallet here anyway as pickpocketing is common.

Nhà Hàng Liêm Nga, 526 Lương Ngọc Quyến. From the 3rd intersection, take a left and walk several hundred meters. This place is packed with people right until closing time, and for good reason. Meat entrees around 12,000Đ. Open daily until 10pm. ❶

NORTHERN VIETNAM

Biển Xanh Restaurant, 30 to 12 Phương Quang Trưng (☎ 758 918), outside of the city center in a residential neighborhood. From the bus station, take a left onto Lương Ngọc Quyến for 800m. Look for a sign on the left side of the road above Ngõ (lane) 140. The restaurant is 100m down this lane. Very popular with the Vietnamese elite, this seafood restaurant has the best food in town. The *nem hai san* (seafood spring roll; 3000Đ), shrimp fried with lemongrass and chili (32,000Đ per kg), and the *miên xào cua* (crab fried noodles; 20,000Đ) are all delightful. 2 open-air dining rooms and private air-conditioned rooms on the 1st floor. Open daily 7:30am-10pm. ❷

Hữu Nghị Restaurant, 332 Thư Minh (☎ 854 045), a 5min. walk past the Gia Bảy Bridge. The beer-guzzling buddhas at the entrance get the message across. Ceiling fans, cold beer, and delicious food. The menu is huge and includes chicken, beef, fish, duck, goat, rabbit, and frog. Most portions run around 10,000Đ. Open daily early until late. ❶

Hiền Hương Phở Shop, located just north of Gia Bảy Bridge on Thư Minh. No-frills place with a local clientele, local food, and local prices. Full meal—vegetables, soup, rice, and meat—runs about 12,000Đ. The sweet-and-sour ribs (*sườn são chua ngọt*) is the most popular dish. Open daily until late. ❶

Thực Đơn Restaurant (☎ 855 372), located in the Cao Bắc Hotel. A very good place for *mực* (crab; 90,000Đ per kg). Fish and other seafood dishes are also available for similar prices. Open daily 7am-9pm. ❸

Nhà Hàng Hưng Restaurant, 611 Lương Ngọc Quyến. Only worth knowing about if you plan on staying in the Khách Sạn Hoa Hồng hotel. Sanitary place with limited menu of Vietnamese standards. Meat and fish are 25,000Đ, and the portions are generous. Open daily 9:30am-9:30pm. ❷

Hương Trà Restaurant, 5 Càch Mang Tháng (☎ 854 033), just off of the central rotary, across the street from the tourist office. The arsenal of fans and wind-blown curtains keeps things cool at this bread-and-butter establishment. Long menu with beef, chicken, ox, calf, and much more. Meals run around 35,000Đ. Open daily 7am-8pm. ❸

👁 📷 SIGHTS AND NIGHTLIFE

The **Bảo Tàng Văn Hóa Các Dân Tộc Việt Nam (Museum of the Cultures of Vietnam's Ethnic Groups),** located in a stately building just off the central rotary, has all you wanted to know (and more) about Vietnam's 54 ethnic groups. The museum includes ancestral altars, fishing equipment, musical instruments, life-size model homes, costumes, and plenty of photos. Captions are in English as well as Vietnamese. The place is definitely worth an hour or two, even if you don't plan on staying in Thái Nguyên. (Open Apr.-Oct. Tu-Su 7-11:30am and 1:30-5pm; Nov.-Mar. 7:30-noon and 1:30-5pm. 10,000Đ.)

Thái Nguyên province also has many **memorials** hidden on side-streets and dirt roads, but the grandest of them is directly across from the museum at the central rotary. The towering, gray marble spire commemorates Thái Nguyên's war heroes. It was constructed in 2000 for a whopping US$1 million.

For an inimitable museum-going experience, head east from the rotary on Hoàng Văn Thụ to visit the **Bảo Tàng Quân Kha 1 (Museum of Military Region 1).** It is located just outside of town on the road toward Núi Côc. The entrance is through a large green metal gate, but be sure to ask to see the museum before entering, as there are no established visiting hours. You may or may not have to pay the 10,000Đ admission fee, and you will be guided by one of the on-site officers. This place is not built for tourists, but rather for Vietnamese to stay in touch with their history. The first floor of the museum documents the French war, and the second floor—which is scheduled for construction—will document the American war. It is helpful to have a Vietnamese speaker with you to navigate the museum.

There are two nice **walks** in town. Return to the rotary and then continue west. At the end of Đội Cấn by the central market, take Oánh heading out of town. Turn left up an unmarked street (by building 182), and you'll begin passing houses and walking out toward the Sông Cầu River. Soon the road dies out and a small dirt path leads past farmers perched under umbrellas tending their plots. Đe Bao Sông Cầu is a shorter and more established walking path that begins by the gas station beside the Gia Bảy Bridge and follows several hundred meters along the river before turning back onto Đội Cấn. The path is popular with young couples looking for solitude, so your typically shocking presence might actually be ignored.

In terms of nightlife, **beer gardens** and **pool halls** fill up in the evenings and tend to stay open until 11pm. The hottest place in town is **Mêhyco,** near the central rotary across from Hương Tram bread shop. The venue is newly opened and remains packed every evening. Amateur hour is from 8pm until closing (usually midnight), with a big stage and some pretty decent performances (beer 10,000Đ).

▶ DAYTRIPS FROM THÁI NGUYÊN

HANG PHƯƠNG HOÀNG (PHOENIX CAVE). Forty-five kilometers northeast of Gia Bảy Bridge is Hang Phương Hoàng, a large cave that was once used as a meeting spot for revolutionary leaders. A short way down the path at the caves, the road splits. To the left is an incredibly steep and rugged trail that climbs a nearby mountain. While the views are a great reward, make sure to bring enough water, and a companion, as navigating the route can prove difficult (about 2hr. round-trip). The right-hand path ascends 300m before leading to Phương Hoàng Cave. The sign announcing a 100m approach is neither gross underestimation nor typographical error ("Did they mean 1000 meters?")—there is a cave entrance 2min. from the first junction, but be sure to find the others too. The inside of this first cave is illuminated, and families gather to hop from stone to stone or swim in the refreshing waters. *(Hang Phương Hoàng is a 1hr. drive from Thái Nguyên, and a xe ôm will cost 70,000-80,000Đ round-trip. It is also possible to take a metered taxi from Thái Nguyên, but prepare to dish out big bucks. There is a 25,000Đ entrance fee collected on the highway.)*

LAKE NÚI CÔC. Núi Côc (Lake in the Mountains) is an artificial reservoir amid rolling hills. The 26-square-kilometer lake is just gorgeous. However, it's more than just a lake—in the 1980s, a theme park was constructed here that might just be the most ridiculous spot in Vietnam. A labyrinth of plastic trees and concrete paths lead to a zoo (3000Đ), fake cave (10,000Đ), plastic underworld (10,000Đ), pool with a waterslide (20,000Đ), and several other money wasters. Vendors are persistent in selling their phở or *kem* (ice cream). From the port, it's possible to organize an overpriced boat ride on the lake (1hr.; 180,000Đ for 4 people), which circles a small island before heading back to shore.

Of course, no tourist lake would be complete without a man-made origin myth. As the story goes, two young lovers, Côc and Công, wanted to marry each other, but Công's father disapproved because Côc was poor and without land. The two lovers fled, but the father found them and killed Côc. Công was pretty broken up over the whole affair—so much that she broke into (a lot of) tears, which formed the river leading into the lake. Other, more boring legends whisper that the lake was created by some very intelligent engineers. Regardless of how it came to be, this DisneyWorld gone terribly wrong is worth a peek. *(Núi Côc is 20km from Thái Nguyên. There is no public transportation to the lake; a xe ôm costs 20,000Đ and takes 45min. It is also possible to circle the lake instead of being dropped off at the park entrance, but prices should be negotiated before leaving Thái Nguyên, as this is an uncommon request. Entrance to the park is 10,000Đ and most of the actual attractions are open daily until 4pm. It's best to arrive in the afternoon, when the heat is more bearable and the crowd has died down.)*

NORTHERN VIETNAM

THE NORTHWEST HIGHLANDS

Sitting over a plate of pancakes, travelers are apt to discuss the development of the tourism industry in the northwestern region of Vietnam. Throngs of adventure-seekers trek through gorgeous valleys and visit dazzling Montagnard markets. Travelers with limited time can get a taste of the region with a trip to highly touristed Sa Pa or Mai Châu. More time allows detours off the standard track, leading to worlds that are remote in a way no map can define. Beyond the city of Sa Pa, the Hoàng Liên Sơn Mountains present some of the most desolate territory and challenging travel opportunities in Vietnam. Every additional kilometer that you venture is more rewarding than the last. The roads wind through a magnificent array of highland populations, free from the chemically dyed kitsch and the tourist-chasers that are now part of the package in more touristed destinations.

The northwest affords a look at the Vietnam that has yet to reap the benefits of modernization. Many of the region's people struggle to survive on less than a dollar a day. It is a landscape of tattered homes, limp phở and cơm signs, and pyramids of luscious fruit set along the roadside, all of it simmering with a flavor distinctly different from anywhere else in the country. Local Montagnards coax water buffalo through soft, lush hills and over unforgiving mountain tops. Grandmothers sit hunched over intricate embroidery in meditative concentration while grandfathers sit and puff away on bamboo water pipes. In general, life in the highlands runs differently than anywhere else in the country—we recommend that you go, but we promise not to be upset if you never return.

HIGHLIGHTS OF THE NORTHWEST HIGHLANDS

RIDE INTO THE SUNSET on the mountain road from **Sa Pa** to **Mường Lay** (Hwys. 4D and 12; p. 208). The rugged, unearthly peaks and valleys captivate the imagination.

RIDE BACK OUT OF THE SUNSET and into one of the more remote reaches of the world on **Route 6** from Mường Lay to Tuần Giáo (p. 215), a slim ribbon of mountain road winding among isolated Montagnard villages, river valleys, and towering karsts.

MAKE A POINT OF NOT GOING TO SA PA by going to **Bắc Hà** (p. 202), the sort-of alternative to the northwest's most popular destination. Tours from Hà Nội flood the area on weekends, but during the week, the nearby markets are yours.

BE ADOPTED by a White Thái family in **Mai Châu** (p. 226). Travelers spend the night in stilt-houses; days are spent (how else?) wandering the spectacular countryside.

LÀO CAI
☎ 20

Lào Cai is one of two border crossings into Yunnan Province, China, and is the chief point of access to Sa Pa, the northernmost stop on most open-tour routes, and Bắc Hà, Sa Pa's nearly untouched neighbor to the east. Despite the booming trade between China and Vietnam, there isn't a great deal to do here; most travelers hardly pause before speeding across the border, south to Hà Nội, or directly into the mountains. While Lào Cai's main attraction may be its location, the city is a fine place to spend the afternoon before saddling up for somewhere new.

NORTHWEST HIGHLANDS

The Northwest Highlands

🖪 **TRANSPORTATION.** The **train station** lies 2km south of the Chinese border (open daily 7:30am-5pm), and travelers report that the crossing is quick and easy. There is a 3000Đ charge to cross the border on foot. Most travelers arrive in Lào Cai by train from Hà Nội or China. Ticket stubs are collected at the gate on arrival. **Trains** run to Hà Nội (10hr.; 10:30am, 7, 8:30, 9:15pm; hard seat 75,000Đ, soft seat 126,000Đ, soft sleeper 223,000Đ). Plenty of transfer options to Sa Pa await at the Lào Cai train station. Some guesthouses have **minibuses** (35,000Đ) that will take you from Lào Cai directly to their hotel in Sa Pa; you are not obliged to stay at the assigned address, only to look. If you purchase tickets directly from the drivers outside instead of at the counter, you'll pay about 25,000Đ. **Tickets cheaper than 25,000Đ are likely to be fraudulent.** Other modes of Sa Pa-bound transport include **motorcycle taxis** (1hr.; 50,000Đ), **taxis** (150,000Đ or less), or **minibuses** from the station. The central **bus station** sits between the train station and customs, immedi-

NORTHWEST
HIGHLANDS

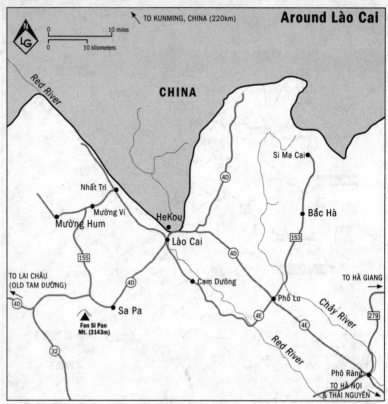

Around Lào Cai

TO KUNMING, CHINA (220km)

CHINA

Red River

Si Ma Cai

Nhất Tri

Mường Vi

Mường Hum

HeKou

Bắc Hà

Lào Cai

155

TO LAI CHÂU
(OLD TAM ĐƯỜNG)

Cam Đường

TO HÀ GIANG

Sa Pa

Fan Si Pan
Mt. (3143m)

Phố Lu

Chảy River

4E

4E

279

Red River

32

Phô Ràng

TO HÀ NỘI
& THÁI NGUYÊN

ately over the Côc Lên Bridge on the opposite side of the river. **Buses** run to: Bắc Hà (2-3hr.; 5:30am; 35,000Đ); Hà Nội (10-12hr.; 3:30am; 70,000Đ); Mường Lay (8hr.; 7am; 45,000Đ); Sa Pa (2hr.; frequently 6am-4pm; 25,000Đ).

> **ZOOM ZOOM.** There are various modes of transport for those who want to brave the northern loop. Bicycling is masochistic; jeeps are comfortable, quick, and expensive. The public bus can be onerous, but you'll share the burden with locals. Traveling by **motorbike** is the most exciting way to go, but be sure to master the relevant Vietnamese. "Landslide" *(nổ đất)*, "flat tire" *(buc sam)*, and "flood" *(lụt)* are necessary terms for those who decide to explore the breathtaking region. Whatever the mode of transportation, the crumbling road behind you will only push you onward into a mercilessly difficult and startlingly beautiful world.

There is another **bus station** located 150m down the street in front of the train station. Prices are usually fixed, and there are fewer hawkers than in town. Buses leave for: Bắc Hà (6:30am, 1pm; 28,000Đ); Diện Biên Phủ (9hr.; 7am; 95,000Đ); Hà Nội (4:30, 5am; 85,000Đ); Mường Lay (6, 6:30, 8, 9am, 3:30pm; 38,000Đ); Yên Bái (5 hr.; 4:30am, noon; 45,000Đ). The train service into China has been temporarily discontinued, but there are buses available just over the border to Kunming (9-11hr.; 7, 9am, 12:30, 7pm). Keep in mind that China is an hour ahead of Vietnam.

Motorcycle taxis will go anywhere in town for 5000Đ. **Taxis** are also available.

⚡🛈 ORIENTATION AND PRACTICAL INFORMATION. Lào Cai straddles the **Red River** (Sông Hông). Most places of interest are along the eastern bank on **Nguyễn Huệ**, which runs parallel to the river. Both the train station and the **bank** on Nguyễn Huệ offer **currency exchange** between dollars, đồng, and yuan. (☎830 013. Open daily 7-11:30am and 1:30-5pm.) The **hospital** (☎842 396) is located on the other side of the river, 2km south of the bridge on Hoàng Liên. There is a **post office** stand on the street across from the border, and behind it there is an international calling center with **Internet** (3000Đ per hr.; open daily 7am-9:30pm).

🛈🛏 ACCOMMODATIONS AND FOOD. Most hotels are clustered around the customs building and across the Côc Lên Bridge; those by customs tend to be cheaper and more conveniently located. While bargaining, keep in mind that none of the prices in town are set, and hotels don't fill up. Check the room beforehand, as most hotels rent some rooms without windows.

Just south of the border is **Hoa Lan ❷**, 82 Nguyễn Huệ. Upstairs, past the large fish tank, are fresh rooms—everything in them is new. Ask for Room 203—it has an excellent view of the Red River. (☎830 126. Doubles 150,000Đ.) **Hoàng Hiệp ❷**, 35 Nguyễn Huệ, offers spotless rooms with phone, air-conditioning, and flat-screen TV. (☎830 758. Doubles 100,000Đ; triples 120,000Đ.) **Hoa Hông Hotel ❷**, 40 Nguyễn Huệ, is just across the street from Bình Ming Restaurant. The rooms have similar amenities, but they're also a bit dark, with windows looking out at a brick wall. (☎830 495. Doubles 120,000Đ.) Nearby **Hông Phươ'ng Hotel ❷**, 17 Nguyễn Huệ, has cramped rooms with all the amenities, including a fridge. If you bargain hard, it can be a good deal. (☎830 419. Doubles 120,000Đ.) The **Sông Hông Guest House ❷** is 10m down Phan Bội Châu, which jogs east when Nguyễn Huệ terminates by the Chinese border. It has big, bright rooms with everything included, but some amenities may not work. Of all the accommodations in Lào Cai, it has the most character, even if it's the kind of character that only comes with age. Some have terraces on the Nam Thi River, overlooking China. (☎830 004. Rooms 120,000Đ.) By the train station, **Xuân Hồng Hotel ❷**, 3 Hồ Tùng Mậu, offers quiet rooms off Nguyễn Huệ. Exiting the train station, walk to the right side of the square and continue straight down the street; it's on your left. (☎832 670. Doubles 150,000Đ, prices negotiable.)

For food, try **Bình Ming Restaurant ❷**, directly off Nguyễn Huệ, around the corner from the tourist office. It has a large dining room and an extensive English menu with breakfast, lunch, and dinner options (banana pancake 10,000Đ; fried eggs 10,000Đ; lunch and dinner entrees 25,000-30,000Đ). Try the sweet and sour fried pork (30,000Đ). (☎835 577. Open daily 5:30am-9pm.) Two doors over is **Chong Long ❶**, a simple eatery that lacks a menu, but it's as good as Bình Ming, and cheaper, too. (☎830 769. Veggies 3000-5000Đ; main courses 15,000Đ. Open daily 6am-9pm.) There are several small food joints as well as **Việt Hoa ❷**, located in the hotel across the square from the train station. This place is bit of a tourist trap—it has a long menu in English with listed but steep prices. (☎830 082. Soup 10,000Đ; fried rice 20,000Đ; fish and chicken 35,000Đ. Open daily 6am-9pm.)

◎ SIGHTS. Lào Cai is starved for sights—three small temples are its main attractions. The first, **Đên Mẫu** (Mother Temple), is next to the border on Nguyễn Huệ. The temple was originally built during the Lê Dynasty, but the Chinese have destroyed it twice since. Perhaps Đên Mẫu's most interesting characteristic is its proximity to China—the temple's back gate is flush with the border. Continue down the street and bear right, passing the Sông Hông Guest House to **Bao Sỏn Pagoda**. Through a gate and a garden, this humble temple hosts three small altars.

The best of the three, **Đên Thưo'ng** (2000Đ) has been declared a Vietnamese historical heritage sight and overlooks pleasant surroundings from atop a hill. The walk from Bao Sòn Pagoda to Đên Thương is only 50m down a quiet street. To the left is the Nam Thi River, with China's rolling hills on the opposite bank. The path passes a remarkable **banyan tree** whose shade engulfs the area. Just beyond the tree—perhaps the most impressive sight in town—is Đên Thương, and beyond it, a small memorial. The complex is quite peaceful, making for a relaxing siesta.

◪ **DAYTRIP FROM LÀO CAI.** To escape from the tourist photo-ops at Sa Pa and Bắc Hà, make a trip to **Mường Hum Sunday market.** The market attracts Black H'mông, Giáy, Hà Nhì, Phù Lá, and Red Dao people. The journey alone, through Giáy villages and rugged mountains, is worth it. *(From Lào Cai, take the northwest road 19km to Bát Xát/Nhất Trí market, 6km past Bát Xát village. Take a left 25km later onto the road toward Mường Vi and then to Mường Hum. This road is in poor condition; drivers should use caution. A 2hr. xe ôm from Lào Cai costs 200,000Đ each way.)*

SA PA
☎ 20

The common sentiment among visitors seems to be: "This place is beautiful—it had better not lose its charm." Once a remote colonial hill station, Sa Pa is now the premier spot for weekend package tours. In the center of town is the spectacle of Sa Pa's famed market, which has become a fixture on standard Southeast Asian tourist itineraries. Local H'mông girls approach travelers with high fives and questions in English; suspicious travelers assume this to be the lead-in to a sales pitch, which it often is. To escape the capitalistic frenzy of the rest of the country, more and more visitors choose to come mid-week to see Sa Pa's true idyllic beauty. Treks through the surrounding mountainside are an opportunity to visit picturesque villages, most notably those of the H'mông and Red Dao people. With the recent inundation of tourism, many of these villages have transformed into glorified shops where locals sell traditional garments and mass-produced aluminum jewelry from China. Strangely, leaving Sa Pa—through the Tram Ton Pass—might just be the best part of your visit, as the Sa Pa Valley's magnificent mountains beckon dramatically westward to the untamed splendor of the provinces beyond.

⌐ TRANSPORTATION

Because the construction of a hydroelectric dam in Old Lai Châu will render the town almost uninhabitable (see **"The Fate of Mường Lay,"** p. 212), that city and several near it have changed their names. This makes traveling in the region confusing, as road signs, bus tickets, and transportation schedules all use conflicting names. The original **Lai Châu** is now also called **Mường Lay**, while old **Tam Đường** has become the new **Lai Châu (Tỉnh Lai Châu)**, once known as **Phong Thổ. Bình Lu**, between Sa Pa and new Lai Châu, is now called **Tam Đường**. Good luck.

Buses: Tourist minibuses to **Lào Cai** leave from the large square in front of the church (1½hr.; every hr. from 6am; 25,000Đ). Buy tickets at the post office or in any of the tourist cafes 1 day in advance. **Public buses** (2hr.; 7:30am, 3:30pm; 30,000Đ), as well as **jeeps, sedans,** and **minibuses** (2hr.; depart when full; up to 30,000Đ) also leave for Lào Cai from the church. Other transportation can be secured through your hotel. The public bus to **Mường Lay (Old Lai Châu;** 8hr.; 45,000Đ for Vietnamese, more for foreigners) must be flagged down at the gas station on the road toward Lào Cai. Facing the main post office, walk left down the road out of town 1km and wait at the traffic triangle. The bus usually comes between 8 and 9am, but may come as early as 7:30am or as late as 11am. **Demand a ticket with Mường Lay written on it.** Buses also run to new **Lai Châu (Old Tam Đường;** 2-4hr.; every hr. 6am-2pm; 25,000Đ), where buses can be caught to Mường Lay.

Local Transportation: Motorbikes can take you anywhere in town, but it's best to walk.

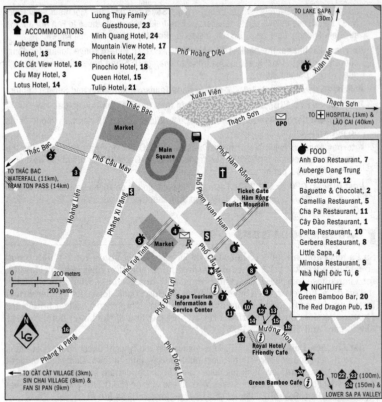

Sa Pa

🏠 ACCOMMODATIONS

Auberge Dang Trung
Hotel, **13**
Cát Cát View Hotel, **16**
Cầu Mây Hotel, **3**
Lotus Hotel, **14**
Luong Thuy Family
Guesthouse, **23**
Minh Quang Hotel, **24**
Mountain View Hotel, **17**
Phoenix Hotel, **22**
Pinochio Hotel, **18**
Queen Hotel, **15**
Tulip Hotel, **21**

🍴 FOOD

Anh Đạo Restaurant, **7**
Auberge Dang Trung
Restaurant, **12**
Baguette & Chocolat, **2**
Camellia Restaurant, **5**
Cha Pa Restaurant, **11**
Cây Đào Restaurant, **1**
Delta Restaurant, **10**
Gerbera Restaurant, **8**
Little Sapa, **4**
Mimosa Restaurant, **9**
Nhà Nghỉ Đức Tú, **6**

⭐ NIGHTLIFE

Green Bamboo Bar, **20**
The Red Dragon Pub, **19**

Rentals: Many hotels rent **Minsks** (old Russian motorcycles) and smaller **motorscooters** (US$1 per hr., US$5-8 per day). Check that the price of the bike includes gasoline and a helmet. **Jeeps** with drivers are also available (from US$30 per day).

✴ 🔢 ORIENTATION AND PRACTICAL INFORMATION

The **Sa Pa Church** faces a grass field at the town's center. From the church, it takes 10min. on foot to reach anywhere in town. One block north of the church up Thạch Sơn is the **GPO**; the **lake** is one block farther north up **Xuân Viên**. A stairway 100m southeast of the church leads down to the **market** and **Cầu Mây**, the main street, which runs northeast-southwest. Tourist services cluster here before the road heads out of town. **Phăng Xi Păng** winds southwest down the valley toward Cát Cát Village and runs perpendicular to the main street; it originates at the fruit and vegetable end of the market, where it is called **Tuệ Tĩnh**.

Tourist Office: Sapa Tourism Information and Service Center (☎ 871 975), just up the main street, offers tours and an impressive display of information on local minority groups. Maps of the Sa Pa area 15,000Đ. Open M-Sa 8-11:30am and 1:30-5:30pm. The best way to ensure a good daytrip is to ask other travelers for guide recommendations. Most companies offer competitively priced treks to minority villages or up Fan Si Pan Mountain (US$40-100). Most daytrips run US$10-15, depending on the group size, and

NORTHWEST HIGHLANDS

are all-inclusive. Overnight trips are generally US$15 per day. The Mountain View Hotel (☎871 914; see below) serves travelers well on treks, especially those to Fan Si Pan. The adjacent Friendly Cafe (☎871 313), inside the Royal Hotel, is also well known.

Currency Exchange: The bank, 1 Cầu May (☎871 107), will exchange dollars for đồng, but at poor rates. Most guesthouses will also change US$ and traveler's checks at high rates (5-7% commission).

Police: 26 Cầu May (☎871 463), next to Sapa Tourism Information and Service Center.

Hospital: (☎871 116.) 1km down Thạch Sơn from the GPO toward Lào Cai.

Telephones: Cash calls available at both post offices. US$2.35 per min. Phone cards do not work.

Internet Access: Available at most cafes for 4000Đ per hr. The post office has the cheapest connection for 2500Đ per hr., but Cát Cát Guest House offers the best connection for US$1 per hr.

Post Offices: GPO (☎871 292). Facing the church, go left on Thạch Sơn leading back to Lào Cai. *Poste Restante.* Open daily 7am-9pm. Another branch (☎871 247) is on Phố Cầu May below the market.

ACCOMMODATIONS

Sa Pa has enough rooms to house all of Vietnam. Most hotels run on both a seasonal and a weekly price schedule. During the weekend in high season (May-Jul. for Vietnamese tourists, Jul.-Oct. for foreigners), hotels charge what they want. On the off days, however, it's a buyer's market, so don't back down. As a general rule, lower prices mean lower floors and worse views. The town's budget hotels are clustered mainly on Mướng Hoa, off Cầu May. Several of the larger hotels accept Mastercard and Visa, with a 4-6% fee.

Càt Càt View Hotel (☎871 946). After taking over the Twilight Guest House, Cát Cát is now a local superpower with the best price-for-view ratio in town. Communal terraces and large windows overlook the valley, and fresh flowers are brought to your room. Great tourist info. Restaurant serves Vietnamese cuisine (30,000Đ) and the best burgers in Sa Pa (30,000Đ). Internet US$1 per hr. Rooms US$4-30. ❶

Mountain View Hotel (☎871 914), on the right side of the main street as you walk from the market toward the Auberge (see below). The name doesn't lie—but then again, it's the same view you'll get everywhere else. It's the bustling, upbeat atmosphere and the helpful English-speaking staff that set this place apart. The big communal deck can spice up a lonely evening. Good guide service and restaurant. Internet access. Humbler rooms buried in the hotel cost US$6, but still boast some fine views and small private terraces. Top floors cost US$10-20. MC/V. ❶

Minh Quang Hotel (HI; ☎871 449), south of the town center on Mướng Hoa. The 1st draw: its distance from tourist fanfare (for now). The 2nd draw: the cheapest dorm beds in town. Some rooms have small private balconies, but trees obstruct the view. Breakfast 10,000Đ, but it can be bargained into the room price. Doubles US$5-10, depending on the view and the day of the week. Dorms US$2.50, US$2 with an HI card. ❷

Auberge Dang Trung Hotel (☎871 243). From the market, head south on Cầu May and take a left onto Mướng Hoa. An old-time favorite in a stylish French villa. Relax by the bonsai garden, carefully tended by the hotel owner. French- and English-speaking staff. Internet access. A stairway leads up to the rooms, with prices increasing each step of the way. Singles and doubles at the base of the stairs US$8, US$35 at the top. ❷

Luong Thuy Family Guesthouse (☎872 310), between the Phoenix and the Minh Quang. Only a few rooms, but most have excellent views at a good value. A bit of a retreat from the tourist hubbub. Doubles $US5-6. ❶

Pinochio Hotel (☎871 876), also on Mướng Hoa. Clean rooms at a reasonable price. Communal balconies with that same great view. Doubles US $4-6. ❶

Phoenix Hotel (☎871 515). Rooms are clean and spacious. Ask for one by the roof patio, with a view of Fan Si Pan. Doubles M-Th and Su US$7-12, F-Sa US$12-15. ❷

Lotus Hotel (☎871 308), by the Auberge. Viewless rooms starting at US$5. For a dollar or two more you move out onto the avenue, and for another few bucks you head to a higher terrace. Many rooms have a TV and fireplace. Rooms Su-Th US$5, F-Sa US$8. ❶

Queen Hotel (☎871 301), on the main road below the market. Ask for rooms 403 or 503. Rooms with hot water US$4-15; you pay more for a good view. ❶

Tulip Hotel (☎871 914), on the main road just past the Queen Hotel. The Tulip is living the minimalist dream—rooms are impeccably clean and simple. Plenty of light and communal balconies. Summer rooms US$9-10; winter US$5-6. ❷

Cầu May Hotel (☎871 293). From the market, head north up Cầu May until it hits a set of stairs; then turn left down Hoàng Liên. Removed from the usual tourist hangouts, but the views are blocked by trees and buildings. The rooms are sparsely furnished, but the hot water is guaranteed to work. Doubles US$5-8. ❶

☕ FOOD

There are many culinary options in Sa Pa, varying widely in quality and price. If you head to a sit-down restaurant, be sure to check your bill carefully for mistakes. The **phở stalls** in the market and around town are always affordable.

▧ **Baguette & Chocolat,** on Thác Bac, up the stairs past the turn-off for the Cầu Mây Hotel. Run by a vocational school for disadvantaged youth. Take off your shoes and sit at one of the cushioned benches. Wonderful pastries as well as sandwiches (32,000-40,000Đ), quiche (22,000Đ), pasta (36,000-42,000Đ), and more. The pork escalope (55,000Đ) is recommended. Top off your meal with a divine ▧**chocolate mousse** (18,000Đ). Meals aren't enormous, but they're satisfying. Open daily 7am-9pm. ❷

Anh Đao Restaurant, on the main road south of the police station. Cheap, decent food. The fried potato with vegetable, onion, mushroom, and tomato (10,000Đ) is excellent, as is the fried noodle with vegetable (8000Đ). Steer clear of the fish dishes and sit in the back dining room for a more civil dining experience. Open daily 6am-10pm. ❶

Mimosa Restaurant, off Cầu May, 2 blocks from the market; a sign points up a stairway to the restaurant. This relaxed, family-owned establishment is a favorite tourist spot away from the noise. The beef kebab in BBQ sauce (40,000Đ) is tasty, as are the frog's legs with bamboo shoots (35,000Đ). Open daily 7am-11pm. ❷

Auberge Dang Trung Restaurant, in the Auberge Hotel. Terrace seating with fine views. Slightly pricey, but worth it. Pork with potatoes and mushrooms 35,000Đ. Vegetarian plates 25,000Đ. Banana or papaya shake 10,000Đ. Open daily 6:30am-10:30pm. ❸

Little Sapa, 18 Cầu May, just beyond the stairs down to the market. Exceedingly friendly staff compensates for the lack of atmosphere. While some dishes are assaulted by garlic, the food is generally quite good. Try the grilled Sa Pa chicken on a hot plate (35,000Đ) or the batter-fried pork (25,000Đ). Open daily 6:30am-11pm. ❷

Gerbera Restaurant, on the same path off the main street as the Mimosa Restaurant. Worth visiting for local specialties. Try the wild pork on a hot plate (35,000Đ), venison (35,000Đ), or red pumpkin soup with toast (17,000Đ). Open daily 7am-11pm. ❷

Camellia Restaurant, across from the vegetable section of the market, on the right before Càt Càt Guest House. Camellia breakfast (31,000Đ) comes with fried veggies and potato soup. Roast beef with ginger and butter 35,000Đ. Steamed rice with coconut milk 32,000Đ. Open daily 6:30am-11pm. ❷

Cây Đào Restaurant, on Xuân Viên, across the park from the GPO, at the turn-off for the lake. There is a menu, but just walk into the kitchen and they'll point out what they have. A half-chicken will cost 50,000Đ and a plate of fish goes for 30,000Đ. Spit-roasted pig 50,000Đ. Open daily 7am-10pm. ❷

Nhà Nghỉ Đức Tú, past the stairs to the market, on Phạm Xuan Huan. They have an English menu, but it's more likely they'll open up the fridge to see what's available. Entrees about 20,000Đ. Open daily 6am-11pm. ❶

Cha Pa Restaurant, on the main drag 50m before the Auberge. Typical backpacker staples include juices (10,000Đ) and cereal with yogurt (20,000Đ). Set breakfasts 25,000Đ. Dinner entrees 30,000-55,000Đ. Open daily 6am-10pm. ❷

Delta Restaurant, across from Cha Pa Restaurant. An elegant interior with tablecloths and wine racks along the wall. High-quality Italian food—and correspondingly high prices. Pastas US$5.50 and up. Lasagna US$7.50-8.50. Pizzas from US$5. They also offer big breakfasts for US$4.50. Open daily 7am-11pm. ❹

▣ NIGHTLIFE

At night, hotel patios fill up with travelers in search of conversation and a card game. Bars tend to remain quiet; locals congregate at the church. Mellow much of the time, this meeting place can become raucous on Saturday nights, when rice wine, musical instruments, and crowds tend to converge.

The Red Dragon Pub, on the main street across from the Green Bamboo Hotel. Serves pub food in a pub atmosphere—welcome relief from standard Vietnamese and "Western" fare. Shepherd's pie or sausage and mash 65,000Đ. Excellent drink list with the most extensive beer selection in town (6000-20,000Đ). Open daily 7am-11pm.

Green Bamboo Bar, in the Green Bamboo Hotel, down the main street past the Auberge. Tourists crowd in F-Sa 7-10pm to watch traditional music performances. No cover. Beer 10,000-25,000Đ.

◉ SIGHTS

▣**Hàm Rồng (Dragon's Jaws) Tourist Mountain** has an entrance around the corner from the church. Despite the steep entrance fee (20,000Đ), the views are some of the best and most accessible in Sa Pa. A network of paved stone paths meander through a peach garden, a "European" garden, and a stone forest, then head past a caged ostrich for some scenic lookouts. The mountain also houses a "Cultural Village of Ethnic Minorities"—it's only a few shops, but the name and gate are perhaps the most flagrant example of Sa Pa's disconcerting human-zoo element.

The best reason to visit Hàm Rồng, however, is to climb the peak hidden behind the tourist paraphernalia. Walk to the back of the cactus garden and you'll see a small dirt path leading through the brush. The zig-zagging trail branches into several smaller routes up the mountain. The most worn of these trails jogs around the left side of the peak, and a 30min. hike leads to a small ganja patch. From here, you can access one of the large boulders with views of the Sa Pa Valley. If you lose the "trail," most of the smaller paths also make their way up toward the summit.

▦ MARKETS

Sa Pa's main attraction is its market. On Saturday afternoons and Sunday mornings, minority villagers (primarily H'mông) come to sell their goods, including colorful shirts, musical instruments, and jewelry. The Dao instituted the market as a "Love Market," where friends from villages near and far came to meet, sing, impress, and entertain each other. Unfortunately, with tourists filming the villagers' every move, the event ceased. Now the market is geared toward tourists, who come by the busload and leave wearing silver bracelets and packing H'mông embroidery. For weekday visitors, there are still plenty of trinket sellers—so many that it is now difficult to distinguish which day is the official "market day." The second floor of **Chợ Sa Pa** (Sa Pa Market) is the gathering spot all week.

DAYTRIPS FROM SA PA

Hikes to ethnic villages, past waterfalls, and through green rice fields offer magnificent views and an escape from Sa Pa's commercialism. All the routes listed below charge entrance fees. Having realized that tourists enjoy being guided by H'mông girls, many tourist companies have weeded out Vietnamese guides. Most visitors opt for a H'mông guide and later report that they are the best insight into the customs and life of local minority groups. Some routes can be navigated alone; if you're going solo, don't be afraid to ask the way, as most villagers will be pleased to point you in the right direction. Use caution when taking overnight treks. You need a permit, which should be organized through a hotel; most will get one from the police for you. Some of the remote areas around Sa Pa are not open to visitors. Check before you head off into the unknown, as fines are steep.

HIKES TO MÁ CHA AND TẢ PHÌN VILLAGES

While this circuit route is described from the Sa Pa-Lào Cai road trailhead to Má Cha and then Tả Phìn, finding the way from the main highway to Má Cha Village can be difficult; we recommend hiring a guide, especially on days with low visibility. From Sa Pa, travel 5km north toward Lào Cai on Hwy. 4D to the major trail leading into the valley (between km markers 3 and 4). 150m down from the road, cut right onto a narrow path into a H'mông village, and then follow the detailed directions to Má Cha below.

You could also do the circuit in reverse by starting from Tả Phìn—probably the best way to do the route alone. The Tả Phìn entrance gate (15,000Đ), is located about 8km down a paved road off Hwy. 4D. The turn-off for the paved road is between km markers 4 and 5, before the 1st bridge heading out of Sa Pa. From the Tả Phìn entrance gate, walk past the school into the H'mông part of town. The large trail leading toward Má Cha Village is easy to pick out. There are also a series of navigable routes up the surrounding hills, all of which provide awesome views of the valley. A motorcycle taxi to Tả Phìn from Sa Pa costs 50,000Đ round-trip. Some travelers report that by starting in Má Cha and taking a xe ôm back to Sa Pa, they were able to speed through the Tả Phìn entrance gate and bypass the entrance fee.

This village circuit showcases the verdant rice fields and cultural splendor of the Sa Pa area; what it lacks are vans full of tourists and clusters of trinket dealers. Once you enter the village off the road, you'll pass small H'mông homes and large vats of water full of indigo, which are used to dye cloth. A 20min. walk down into the valley will bring you to a small bridge; just above it is a rice wheel. This ingenious invention is set up like a see-saw: one side of the plank lifts up as the other, dug-out side fills with water. The water then dumps out and catapults the elevated plank into a vat of rice, thereby husking it.

Climb above rice fields and hop over bamboo irrigation pipes to continue along the path. In the valley, the trail becomes a complex web; you'll shuffle along terrace walls deeper into the hollow. Just past a hemp patch, there is a looming limestone outcrop from where **Má Cha Village** is visible. Near the outcrop is a lone tree on the horizon. If you ever get lost on your way to Má Cha, aim for this tree (or follow the powerlines that point to it). Má Cha is a small collection of tin-roofed H'mông homes with a modern school and a few water buffalo. Follow the wide trail to the left of the school as it continues through town and into the valley.

An hour beyond Má Cha is the H'mông side of **Tả Phìn** village. Bails of hemp lie in the front yards of well-maintained homes. On the other side of the rice paddies, there are larger buildings where Tả Phìn's Red Dao people live. The Red Dao are easily identifiable by the large red headdresses worn by many of the women. Babies wear small red-and-blue beanies with metal beads. Their pants are resplendent with intricate geometrical embroidery atop dyed cloth.

From the H'mông side of Tả Phìn, walk past the school to the main road and turn left. Follow the paved path straight through the Red Dao side of town to **Hang Tả Phìn** (Tả Phìn Cave). The Dao children out front will rent you a torch (2000Đ), which is made by stuffing a piece of gasoline-soaked cloth in one end of a bamboo stick. The cave is damp, dark, and somewhat treacherous, but following the path makes for a good, Indiana Jones-like time. Back outside, take a look at the makeshift pool table dug in the dirt; with improvised cues and miniature balls, local children will beat you with embarrassing speed. Smile politely and defer to their terrifying superiority. The balls, which resemble a small squash, are called *chõ*, and their seeds are mixed into a hot drink to fight particularly nasty colds.

From Tả Phìn, most visitors choose to drive the 30min. back to Sa Pa. Off the road near the admission gate, there is an old French monastery, which deserves more than a glance from the road. The three-story shell remains fully intact. Orange lichen adorns the structure and fireplaces float on the wall, the floors below them long gone. Be careful when visiting the church—watch for barbed wire, thorny plants, and treacherous footing.

THÁC BAC (SILVER WATERFALL) AND TRAM TON PASS

The waterfall and pass are both northwest of Sa Pa on the road to Lai Châu. To visit Thác Bac Waterfall, take Đường Thăc Bac out of town, passing Baguette & Chocolat on the way. The trek will take you half a day on foot or 30min. on a motorbike. At a few points the road gets difficult to drive on—most notably during the 6th km—use caution driving after rain. After reaching the falls, it's best to buy an overpriced pork skewer from one of the stands near the entrance so that the salesperson will look after your bike. It's not unheard of for visitors to return from the falls only to encounter a motorbike "malfunction." Tram Ton Pass is 3km beyond the falls on the same road.

Thác Bac Waterfall is located 11km from Sa Pa on the road to Lai Châu. The 100m tumbling falls are impressive and peaceful, if you can ignore the photo-hungry hordes. Climbing the staircase halfway up the falls costs 5000Đ. At the top, a bridge connects both banks, and it is possible to continue down the other side. We recommend against climbing up onto the falls for photos, though you'll see many people doing it; it's worth taking note of one of Vietnam's few warning signs, which urges travelers to stay on the established route.

Three kilometers farther toward Lai Châu is **Tram Ton Pass,** where the views are spectacular, weather permitting. Often the Sa Pa side of the pass has low visibility, but heading down into Lai Châu, the surroundings are usually visible. The journey beyond the pass into Lai Châu province is highly recommended.

On the way back into Sa Pa, you will pass a small sign pointing 50m to **Đèn Thương.** The temple is unspectacular but makes a fine stop on the return journey.

CÀT CÀT AND SIN CHAI VILLAGES

Guided tours of Càt Càt and Sin Chai (US$10-12) last half a day. Most tourists choose to make the trip on their own; the road (5000Đ entrance fee) is paved and easily navigable. Walking round-trip to both villages takes 4-5hr.

Approach Sa Pa's most accessible village circuit from Phăng Xi Păng, which runs downhill past the appropriately named Càt Càt Hotel. Follow the path northwest along the valley and you'll see a French villa built in the 1930s, which is now a center for wildlife protection. About 15min. later, a set of steps splits off to the left.

This path leads down to the small H'mông village of **Càt Càt**. While it's comforting to leave Sa Pa's concrete jungle behind, Càt Càt has adapted a little too eagerly to the tourist trade. Many homes, particularly those along the well-maintained path, now sell goods and beverages. Continuing deeper into the valley, the stairs lead to an old hydroelectric power station and the small but attractive **Càt Càt Waterfall.**

After snapping a photo, most tourists opt to retrace their steps back to the road. From there you can hike back to Sa Pa or take one of the *xe ôm*s, which are strategically placed for exhausted tourists. From the bottom of the gorge, however, the path continues over the river and up onto the other side of the valley, providing even more impressive views of both the waterfall and the surrounding countryside. This short addition to the trek circles back to the main road over a suspension bridge, which revisits the original turn-off to Càt Càt village after 1km. It's likely that a motorcycle driver will spot you coming off this amended route, come meet you, and try to bring you back to Sa Pa. If you're enjoying yourself, refuse the ride and walk 100m up the paved road to a smaller paved road on the left. This turn-off travels 4km to the H'mông village of **Sin Chai**. After 45min., Sa Pa is out of sight, the pavement ends, and you enter town. Sin Chai sees its share of tourists, mostly on their descent from Fan Si Pan; nonetheless, it remains beautiful and remote. Young boys chase their dogs and locals wave calmly before continuing about their business. Water buffalo stand in pools of muggy water, their heads tilted proudly upward for air. The town is peaceful and generally free of visitors.

From Sin Chai, you must retrace your steps in order to return to Sa Pa (4km). It is possible a local will come out of the woodwork and offer to shuttle you back to Sa Pa on his motorcycle (15,000Đ), but don't count on it. If not, you'll have to walk the 5km back to the original turn-off to Càt Càt village.

THE LOWER SA PA VALLEY

The most popular trips in Sa Pa are accessed from Mướng Hoa, which heads southeast out of town, past the Auberge Hotel. This road (15,000Đ entrance fee) is so treacherous that tourists on motorbikes often turn around, and xe ôms should but don't. Before making the trek, be sure to ask at your hotel about the condition of the road. If it's being widened, head down on foot or by jeep.

If you choose to start the trek on your own, it's possible to hire a H'mông girl en route to be your guide. Many speak English. It will be less expensive than a tour company, and she may bring you to meet and visit with her family. Motorcycle taxis are also available from the turn-off to Lảo Chai for 15,000Đ.

About 7km down into the valley, a bridge appears far below and a trail leads downhill toward the river and across a footbridge to **Lảo Chai**. There is also a scenic and less-traveled route to Lảo Chai: from the entrance gate, walk downhill for 40min. to the first convenience store. Nearby, there is a trail into the valley that slowly makes its way toward Lảo Chai. This "route" is actually a series of small local trails that slowly weave down toward and then along the river. Five minutes past the convenience store, just 30m beyond the first small hut you come to, there is another clay path that meets the bridge to Lảo Chai. It's a beautiful walk through rice paddies and farmers' fields down into the valley.

The Black H'mông village of Lảo Chai experiences about as much traffic as Times Square, so it can be hard to enjoy the surroundings while being constantly bombarded by hawkers. By the bridge there are some wonderful spots where people swim. From Lảo Chai, the river leads 4km to the Giáy village of **Tả Van**. For a light day, backtrack across the bridge from Tả Van and return to the main road. It's about 2hr. back to town. Otherwise, you can stay on the far side of the river and continue through rice paddies and bamboo forests to **Giàng Tả Chải**. The trail between these two villages take 1½hr. and is steep at points. While at times the route can be difficult to follow, the steady stream of tourists and guides are not. Giàng Tả Chải is home to several minority groups, most notably the Red Dao and H'mông. There is a very nice waterfall on the path through the village. Two trails leave town: one small path along the river and a more established route clinging onto the mountainside. After 15min. they converge at a bridge onto the main road. Near a sharp bend on the western side of the main road are fascinating stones inscribed with pictures of stilt homes, people, and symbols.

An hour and a half farther down the main (dirt) road is the H'mông town of **Sử Pan**. The small shops along the road attract nearby Red Dao traders. There is a small, beautiful, and rarely used path that leads to Sử Pan from Giàng Tả Chải, but you will need a guide. To ensure that you have enough time for this trail, start in Tã Van as opposed to Sa Pa. Sử Pan is the launching point for many multi-day treks into the region; it's also a good place to turn around for Sa Pa. Motorcycle taxis will take you to Sa Pa for 40,000-50,000Đ.

FAN SI PAN MOUNTAIN (3143M)

Provisions and a competent guide are necessary for the 2- to 4-day trip to the summit and back. Rain often renders the route impassable. Though weather is impossible to predict at any time of the year, Nov. and Dec. are the best months to attempt the summit. Headlamp, bug spray, and snacks are all worth bringing. All guesthouses can arrange tours complete with sleeping bags, tents, rain gear, guide, porter, and 3 meals per day. Most guides, however, do not bring medical kits. Prices depend on the number of people in the group and the number of days, but generally run US$50-100 per person.

Fan Si Pan Mountain, across the valley from Sa Pa, is Vietnam's highest peak and a popular expedition for those willing to brave its deceptively steep slopes. The trail starts at the pink building just 1km before Tram Ton Pass. From that permit checkpoint, it's a 3-4hr. hike up to base camp (2200m). Everyone sleeps in the small hut at base camp, and you will be provided with a sleeping bag, but you might want to bring your own sleeping bag or at least a liner. The base camp has a makeshift bar and a river, where you can take a cold bath. Typically, trekkers reach the summit and return to base camp on the second day. The steep, muddy trail travels through jungle and bamboo forest, and ropes have been set up on the larger rock faces. The round-trip from base camp to the summit takes roughly 8hr., and there are great vantage points along the way. On top, you can take a picture holding the Vietnamese flag or a photograph of Hồ Chí Minh. On the third day, hikers generally leave base camp on a different route, heading down to Sin Chai, where a jeep or motorbike will pick you up and bring you back to Sa Pa.

BẮC HÀ ☎ 20

Tourism is to Bắc Hà what God is to weekend worshippers—praised on market days and forgotten the rest of the week. One hundred kilometers northeast of Sa Pa, Bắc Hà (elevation 700m) recently came into the crosshairs of Hà Nội's tourist cafes, which tout it as an "alternative to Sa Pa." Once a mountain hamlet of hill-tribe traders and old wooden homes, the village is now adapting to its post as a tourist destination. And unlike its more popular neighbor, Bắc Hà remains free of road tolls and hustling H'mông. Accommodations are overpriced, and many of the restaurants have printed English menus. Since few travelers attempt to visit on their own, from Monday to Saturday Bắc Hà really does become an alternative for those who wish to encounter northern Vietnam's ethnic minorities and mountain scenery without having to fend off busloads of tourists. Mid-week, you're likely to be alone among the Tày and their livestock, roaming the streets or nearby hills.

⌐ TRANSPORTATION. The **bus station** (☎ 880 510) is on the right fork of the town's main road. Only buses that originate in Bắc Hà stop at the station; all other buses stop along Highway 153. **Buses** run to Lào Cai (2-4hr.; 6am, noon, 2:30, 4pm; 25,000-50,000Đ) and Phố Lu (1½hr.; 7, 9, 10:45, 11:30am; 15,000-20,000Đ). Buses to Lào Cai are often full. The earliest bus to Phô Lu is rarely punctual, coming either very early or very late; the 10:45am bus is not recommended. **Buses** or **trains** can be caught from here to Hà Nội (the 9:15pm train from Lào Cai does not stop in Phô Lu). Be suspicious of buses with signs saying "Bắc Hà-Phô Lu-Lào Cai"; they've been known to charge full price and then terminate in Phô Lu, where you'll have to pay for another bus to Lào Cai. The easiest way to leave Bắc Hà is by **xe ôm** to Lào Cai (2hr.; 130,000Đ); Phô Lu (1hr.; 100,000Đ); or Sa Pa (3hr.; 200,000Đ).

Around Bắc Hà

[Map showing: Si Ma Cai, CHINA, 153, SI MA CAI, Cán Cấu, Lũng Phìn, 154, Lầu Thí Ngài, Bản Phố, Tà Chải, Thải Giàng Phố, Na Hối, Bắc Hà, BẮC HÀ, Cốc Ly, TO LÀO CAI, Bảo Nhai, 4D, Chày R., Nậm Lức, N LG, 4E, 70, TO HÀ NỘI, 0 — 5 miles, 0 — 5 kilometers]

■ **ORIENTATION AND PRACTICAL INFORMATION.** Bắc Hà has one main road that splits into three near the north side of town. The **right fork,** as you head northeast away from Lào Cai, leads to the bus station. The **central fork** and the town's main road is **Highway 153.** Heading into Bắc Hà from the south, the **post office** is on the right side of the main road, 150m before the three-way fork. You can make **international calls** from inside, but phone cards don't work. (☎880 262. Open daily 7:30am-9pm.) There is a **pharmacy** 60m uphill from the post office on the right. (☎880 365. Open daily 8am-noon and 1:30-5pm.) On the main drag are several **Internet** parlors. Expect to pay 4000-6000Đ per hr. for a mediocre connection. At the first triangular park, a road cuts right just past the post office and leads past the **bus station** to the rear entrance of the **market.** The middle fork heads out of town, first toward nearby minority villages and then on to Cán Cấu. A 5min. walk down this road brings you to the **police** (☎880 204) and then the **bank,** which exchanges currency. (☎880 226. Open 7:30-11:30am and 1:30-5pm.) The left fork runs past the Sao Mai Hotel to the **hospital** (☎880 263), 50m beyond the hotel.

ACCOMMODATIONS. Prices are high on the weekends, but during the week you're likely to be asked how much you can pay. All accommodations listed come with TV, hot water, and a fan. **Toàn Thắng ❷,** on the left branch of the forked road, is overshadowed by the Sao Mai Hotel, directly across the street. Simple rooms are housed in an attractive wooden building out back. (☎880 444. Doubles 100,000-120,000Đ.) The **Sao Mai Hotel ❸** is 150m down the left branch of the road described above. The rooms are spacious, but the prices are still higher than they should be. Some rooms have great views of the surrounding peaks. There's also a **restaurant ❷** (entrees 30,000-50,000Đ) and bar that stays open as long as there are customers. (☎880 288. Weekday doubles US$10-30; weekends US$40-45.) **Tuấn Anh ❶,** between Hoàng Vũ and Nga Nan, has clean and basic rooms. (☎880 377. Singles 80,000Đ; doubles 100,000Đ-120,000Đ.) **Hoàng Vũ ❷,** at the main intersection, has a dark lobby and basic rooms. Those in the back are quieter and overlook nearby peaks. (☎880 264. Doubles 100,000Đ; triples 150,000Đ.) **Nga Nan ❷,** also at the main intersection, has rooms with office desks, TVs, and balconies overlooking the street. (☎880 251. Doubles 100,000Đ.)

PHỞ'D OUT?

While spring rolls and phở are known as the signature staples of Vietnamese cuisine, the Montagnards of the north have their own specialties. Any trip to their festival markets would not be complete without trying some of these dishes:

Cơ'm lam, dried sticky rice with bamboo shoots. Keeps for several weeks, so it's great for the minorities' long treks to markets and journeys to the forest to hunt and collect supplies.

Thắng cố, a meat soup with every imaginable part of the cow and goat ▇ ▇mmered with maize, chili, tsáoko, and herbs. Often, coagulated blood, made by boiling a mixture of blood, water, and salt, is added into this heartwarming mix.

Lau long heo, a H'mông soup made from pig innards.

Au tau soup, made with pigs' feet and the *au tau* bulb, which is said to have medicinal properties.

Thịt lợ'n muối xông khói, a slab of bacon mixed with herbs and dried over a fire place. Often preserved for years.

Mèn mén, steamed Mông maize cakes.

Ru'ợu cần (stem spirits), part of any Montagnard festive meal. Made from sticky rice, herbs, and spices, this concoction is boiled and then poured into terra cotta jars. After being buried in rice husks for a month, the jars are unearthed and the liquid ambrosia is sipped through bamboo straws from a communal vessel.

The **Đăng Khoa Hotel ❷,** on the main road 75m up from the post office, has terraces overlooking the street. Ask to be on the top floors. (☎ 880 290. Doubles 150,000Đ; triples 200,000Đ; prices negotiable.)

◖ FOOD. Bắc Hà is renowned for its small plum-like fruit *(mân tam hoa)*, a must-try. Locals dip them in salt and eat them when they are still green and sour. For breakfast, be sure to try *bánh quân* (see **"Phở'd Out?"** p. 204), made from a rice batter and available all over town. A spoonful is spread thinly over a boiling pot of water until it solidifies. This pseudo-crepe is topped with grilled onion. Across from Đăng Khoa hotel is a small joint serving Vietnamese standards. The portions of meat are small but tasty and come with rice. (10,000Đ. Open daily 6am-8pm.)

The food at Sa Pa's restaurants is cheap, fresh, and tasty. **Công Fú ❷,** just off the main intersection on the street veering right toward the bus station. They'll hand you a pen and an oversized menu so that you can mark what you want. Công Fú has obviously seen its share of tourists, but it's still a good option, with food that's greasy but fresh. (☎ 880 254. Fried rice 15,000Đ; spring rolls 20,000-25,000Đ; beef with Sa Pa mushrooms 25,000Đ. Open daily 6am-10pm.) **Thanh So'n Restaurant ❷** is across the street from the bus station, 30m from the main intersection. A friendly family will hand over the English menu, which includes tofu stuffed with ground pork and tomato (20,000Đ), omelettes with veggies and mushrooms (10,000Đ), and pork with onions and bean sprouts (25,000Đ). For a smaller meal, the yogurt with pureed mixed fruit costs 10,000Đ. (☎ 880 407. Open daily 6am-10pm.) **Hoa Ngân Restaurant ❷,** at the main intersection, has a decent English menu, though you might have trouble getting food during the week. Along the back wall, some of the tables have lovely views out into the valley. (☎ 880 736. Rice soups 5000Đ; beef with green peppers 25,000Đ. Open daily 6am-11pm.) **Xuân Về ❶,** opposite the Sao Mai Hotel and beside the Toàn Thắng Hotel, has standard dishes for low prices. The noodle soups (6000-8000Đ) are cooked with packaged noodles, but lots of spices and veggies are thrown in to compensate. English menu includes braised pork with onions (30,000Đ), tofu and tomatoes (15,000Đ), and omelettes (7000Đ) that are as good for dinner as for breakfast. (☎ 880 352. Open daily 6am-11pm.) At the hotel restaurants in town, you generally pay more and get less.

◧ ◪ SIGHTS AND ENTERTAINMENT. There is very little to see in Bắc Hà proper. If you have an hour to kill, turn right at the corner by the post office and walk until the paved road ends. Continue over a suspension bridge to another road. To the right it leads away from town, and to the left it circles around to the opposite side of Bắc Hà. The road isn't particularly scenic, but it's a fine way to see town from a distance and escape the mass of humanity that converges on market days. When you re-enter town (over a different bridge), you'll see a dilapidated but grandiose building, the **Hoàng A Túông Palace ("Old King's House of H'mông")**. Most of the building is off-limits to visitors, but it's worth walking up the steps into the main courtyard. If nothing more, the peeling paint and boarded windows are an interesting representation of the time that has passed since French colonization.

Most people in town relax by playing games in a cybercafe, drinking beer on the street, or watching TV at home. On Saturday nights, you can see traditional dancing at the Sao Mai Hotel, but only if there is a package tour staying the night.

🔲 **HIKING.** Many visitors choose to visit the nearby florid markets over lacing up and heading off for a trek. If you have the time, you may look into staying overnight with any of the ethnic groups around Bắc Hà. There are endless options for multi-day treks. If you take a guided trip, plan on 5-6hr. of light hiking each day. More strenuous trips are available if you make it clear that's what you want. There are also routes in the area that can be done unguided—be sure to obtain a **permit** (US$10) beforehand and prepare for an adventure.

The quickest and most accessible trek from Bắc Hà is a circular route (2½hr.; 7km) that passes the H'mông village of **Bản Phố.** The town has been exposed to its fair share of visitors, but that has not disrupted the kindness of the locals or the pristine landscape. It's possible to stop in one of the Flower H'mông homes, which are made from a mixture of mud and rice plants. Inside, large cauldrons of corn are cooked to make the local **corn liquor.** If you're offered a shot, it most likely means you'll be given several more. This stuff isn't weak—if you drop a match on top of the cup, the liquor will ignite. (To get on the trail to Bản Phố, take a left after the main intersection and turn left by the hospital. A new road now allows you to access the village by motorcycle or car. Guides are available but not necessary.)

One nearby circuit visits **Thải Giàng Phố** before looping back to Bắc Hà via **Na Hối.** The 16km loop, which takes 6hr., is not strenuous. On the way, you'll pass Flower H'mông, Tày, Nùng, and Phù Lá homes. Another popular trek visits **Tà Chải** (Tày) and continues upward to **Lầu Thí Ngài** (Flower H'mông) before circling down to Bản Phố and back into town. This route is 15km and takes 6hr.; it distinguishes itself from the rest with some impressive mountain views. Some tourists choose to combine the popular **Cốc Ly** market with a trek (6hr.; 18km on trail) and a boat trip down the Chảy River (1½hr.). On the boat, you'll be able to see Cốc Ly's **waterfall** (Thác Cốc Ly) and a large **suspension bridge** (Cầu Treo Cốc Ly) built over the river by local hill tribes. This route is done with a guide, who can arrange transportation from the boat landing straight to Lào Cai train station.

🔲 **DAYTRIPS FROM BẮC HÀ: MINORITY VILLAGES.** English-speaking guides lead one- and multi-day treks through nearby minority villages, markets, and mountains. They are often fluent in some of the hill tribe languages and can be hired at the Hoàng Vũ Hotel or the Sao Mai Hotel. (US$5-15 for day treks and US$20-25 per day for all-inclusive, longer treks with village overnights. Prices quoted are per person in a four-person group. For more information, contact Nguyễn Nghệ (☎880 264; hoangvutours@hotmail.com.) Daytrips tend to be hassle-free, but overnight stays require a **permit** (US$10) that can be purchased at the police office (no English spoken) or through a tourist office. It's possible to take unguided trips; ask in town first for relevant information before you set out.

The hills surrounding Bắc Hà are home to the Flower H'mông, Red Dao, Black Dao, Tày, Nùng, La Chí, and Phù Lá people. The town's ethnic diversity is impressive, as is the sheer number of markets in the area. Each has its own distinct flavor, but most visitors opt to visit Bắc Hà for its own **Sunday market** (open 6am-3pm). While the town is adapting to an influx of tour buses, the market remains genuine: Flower H'mông come from all around to buy and sell animals, clothes, and accessories. The market is also known for its cheap food stalls. At 8am, things begin to get crowded, and the tour buses from Sa Pa arrive; coming early allows you to watch as locals stream in from the surrounding hillside with dogs, pigs, and other goods to sell. Come during the week and you'll have the place to yourself. If you're eager for more, head 12km north to **Lũng Phin.** This small market is predominantly attended by the Phù Lá minority of the Tibetan-Burman language group. They dress colorfully and often wear coins, metals, beads, and bits of animal fur.

There are several other markets scattered throughout the area. These countryside markets tend to have a gentler atmosphere, with fewer tourists and Kinh. The **Bảo Nhai** market, held on Thursdays, draws Flower H'mông, Black Dao, and Red Dao people. It's smaller and less touristed than some of the other markets around Bắc Hà. Your presence will also be met with appreciative surprise in **Nâm Lúc,** home of a Saturday market with little tourism. This market attracts Flower H'mông, Black Dao, Phù Lá, and Nũng minority groups. In Nâm Lúc, things get going before 8am and start slowing down at 10am, so be sure to start the 2hr. drive early. **Cốc Ly** hosts a Tuesday livestock market attended by Flower H'mông, Tày, Red Dao, Black Dao, and Nũng people. This market has become a popular tourist destination and trips are now offered from Sa Pa (car or minibus from Bắc Hà takes 2hr.; 48km). There's another market on Saturday in **Cán Cấu** (open 7am-2pm; best visited at 9:30am), frequented by the Flower H'mông. Cán Cấu is 20km from Bắc Hà; the drive is on a mountainous road and takes 1¼hr.

HÀ GIANG ☎ 19

The capital of one of Vietnam's poorest provinces, Hà Giang bears witness to material poverty that lies in stark contrast with its wealth of natural beauty. Though situated on the banks of the Lô River and framed by limestone peaks, Hà Giang's scenery is not its only attraction: the town also serves as the gateway to the rugged Đồng Văn-Mèo Vac road, one of the country's most breathtaking journeys. Transportation to and around this city is painfully inconsistent, but you'll hardly notice the delays once you hit the stunning highway. In addition to those amazing mountain views, Hà Giang itself has begun working to become a major border crossing into southern China.

▐ TRANSPORTATION. The **bus station** (☎866 075) is located 2km south of town on Nguyễn Trãi. A new bus station is under construction 500m north of this one on the same road. **Buses** run to: Hà Giang (6-8hr.; 4, 4:15, 4:30, 5am; 55,000Đ) via Tuyên Quang (2-3hr.; frequently 4am-3:30pm; 25,000Đ); Mèo Vac (6hr.; 5 am, noon, 12:30pm; 38,000Đ) via Đồng Văn (5hr.; 37,000Đ); and Thái Nguyên (6hr.; 5, 7, 9am; 40,000Đ). Those heading to the northwest and Lào Cai must backtrack to Doan Hung, located at the junction of Hwy. 2 and Hwy. 70, 28km south of Tuyên Quang. Buses to Lào Cai run through this junction until early afternoon. Otherwise, catch a **minibus** from Tuyên Quang to Yên Bái, which is on the Hà Nội-Lào Cai rail line. **Taxis** are available for hire in Hà Giang (☎860 860).

▓▐ ORIENTATION AND PRACTICAL INFORMATION. The **Lô River** splits Hà Giang in two. Parallel to the river on the western half of town is **Nguyễn Trãi** (Highway 2). On the other side is **Nguyễn Thái Học,** east of which is **Trần Phú,** which becomes **Anh Phú** after crossing **Minh Khan** to the south. Two bridges connect the two sides of town: **Yên Biên I** (Dương Trần Hưng Đạo) to the north and **Yên Biên II** (Dương Minh Khan) 1km to the south. The eastern half of town is home to the **market** on Nguyễn Thái Học, north of Trần Húng Đạo, the **police station** (☎869 163) at

ROAD RULES. Traffic accidents are the leading cause of death and serious injury in Vietnam—every day, 31 people are killed on the road, a statistic particularly frightening for those traveling on the Northwest Highlands' mountainous and unkept roads. Though travelers sometimes have no choice in their method of transport, some of these tips can maximize your road safety.

1. **Stay off the roads during and after heavy rains.** After bad weather, the hills may be soaked with water and prone to landslides, particularly on Hwy. 12 between Lai Châu and Mường Lay.

2. **Hire an older xe ôm driver.** The older the driver, the more experience, and usually the more cautious the driving. Young drivers, thrilled by the speed of the road and the chase for the next commission, tend to be more reckless.

3. **Ride in newer-looking vehicles.** The vehicle's upkeep may reflect the driver's overall character and attitude toward driving. Cleaner is safer, dirtier is riskier.

4. **Sit in the middle section of the vehicle.** While the front may provide the best view, it's the least safe in the event of a crash. If you can withstand the amplified bumps, the back of the bus may be even better.

5. **Always be aware of the nearest safety exits.** These could be windows, the air vent in the back, or holes in the bottom of the bus. Be sure you will fit through these exits, or find an alternative.

28 Anh Phú, and the **hospital** (☎ 866 411) at 11 Minh Khan. The western half of town is where most of the provincial government buildings are located. There are two **post office** branches in town. The southern branch is 500m south of the Yên Biên II bridge at 13 Nguyễn Trãi, where international phone calls, **Internet** (3000Đ per hr.), and Hà Giang's best air-conditioning are available. (☎ 863 915. Open daily 7am-8:30pm.) Two **banks** are on Nguyễn Trãi; both exchange currency. **Pharmacies** are found throughout town; one is at 344 Nguyễn Trãi (open daily 7-11am and 1-5pm).

ACCOMMODATIONS. Despite Hà Giang's small size and seclusion, the town offers a generous selection of hotels. Most cater to Chinese entrepreneurs and offer business-class amenities like elevators, air-conditioning, fans, TV, and hot water. The **Thủy Tiên Hotel** ❷, 19 Nguyễn Thái Học, just north of the Yên Biên II bridge, has clean rooms with large bathrooms. The back rooms have views of the river. (☎ 875 156. Singles 120,000Đ; doubles 130,000Đ.) The **Khách Sạn Duc Giang** ❷, 14 Nguyễn Trãi, north of the bus station, has some of the best-kept rooms in town. (☎ 875 648. Singles 110,000Đ; doubles 130,000Đ.) Closer to the bus station is the slightly older **Sao Mai Hotel** ❷, 9 Nguyễn Trãi, where each room comes with an office desk. (☎ 863 019. Singles and doubles with bath 150,000Đ.) The **Hà Dương Hotel** ❷, 300m north of the bus station, is a good value; the large rooms in front have bay windows and balconies. (☎ 862 555. Singles 100,000Đ; doubles 120,000Đ.)

FOOD. While Hà Giang is famous for its **goat salad** (shredded goat wrapped in a dry pancake with citronella, peppers, green banana, starfruit, and herbs), there are only a limited number of eating establishments where it can be found. **Quán Hái Yến** ❶, just north of the Thủy Tiên Hotel at 51 Nguyễn Thái Học, serves local dishes with local prices. The *cha cha lot* (minced pork wrapped in leaves; 6000Đ) and pork cooked with coconut (8000Đ) are recommended. There's no menu; simply select your own dishes behind the glass case. The largest restaurant in town is **Hoàng Đại Gia** ❷, 6 Nguyễn Trãi (☎ 875 658), located just south of the Yên Biên II bridge in the western half of town. Beef dishes (35,000-45,000Đ) and vegetarian dishes (30,000-45,000Đ) both come with sticky rice. **Tửu Lầu Trung Quốc** ❸, 19 Trần Hưng Đạo, just west of the Yên Biên I bridge, has a small English menu, but the portions are equally as small. The Vietnamese menu, which includes dog, is much more extensive. Try the beef in wine sauce for 60,000Đ. (☎860 316. Open daily 7am-10pm.) **Beer gardens** line the promenade on the western bank of the Lô River.

◙ **SIGHTS.** Besides its scenic location, the only attraction in town is the **Hà Giang Provincial Museum,** located at the corner of Trần Húng Đạo and Nguyễn Trãi. While it takes a creative eye to discern the building's metaphorical form—a "big lotus opening up its petals"—this red-and-white citadel houses the obligatory shrine and photos of Hồ Chí Minh on the ground floor. One floor up, you'll find mannequins dressed in minority costumes and local archaeological finds. Highlights of the small exhibit include the bronze drum collection and a topographical diorama of the province—which may whet your appetite for the Đồng Văn-Mèo Vac road. While nothing remarkable, the museum does kill at least half an hour. *(Open daily 8-11am and 2-4pm; M, W, F-Su, 7:30-9:30pm as well. Free.)*

▶ **DAYTRIP FROM HÀ GIANG: ĐỒNG VĂN AND MÈO VAC.** Though it takes several days to complete, the ◙**Đồng Văn-Mèo Vac driving loop** is best accessed from the town of Hà Giang; in fact, it's the main reason even to go there, as it boasts some of Vietnam's most spectacular mountain scenery. Bordering China, the region is home to many ethnic minorities and is a politically sensitive area. **Beyond Hà Giang, all foreigners must bear a special permit and travel with a guide.**

When the road going northeast out of town forks, take a right to head northeast. At a second fork about 40km away, turn left toward Đồng Văn. The first major site on the loop is **Quan Ba (Heaven's Gate) Pass** (elevation 1000m), 45km northeast of Hà Giang. The pass offers tantalizing views of the voluptuously named Thạch Nhũ Đôi (literally "Double Stalagmites," but known also as "Two Stone Breasts") in the valley below. Another 70km from Hà Giang, the minority village near Lang Si Pass is home to White H'mông who hold a market every six days.

Just 12km before Đồng Văn in the White H'mông village of Sa Phin is the **Vương mansion.** Designed according to Chinese geomantic principles and built by the French in 1903, the building signified the colonial government's recognition of Vương Chi Đuc as king of the H'mông. Sanctioned by Nguyễn kings and the French to suppress rebellions by the ethnic minorities, the Vương dynasty remained loyal to the French until 1945, when Chi Đuc's son pledged his loyalty to Hồ Chí Minh.

After another 16km you'll arrive at **Đồng Văn,** a market town of little interest besides a government **guesthouse** (☎856 265) where you can spend the night. Alternatively, you can push on to nearby **Mèo Vac** and stay at the guesthouse there (☎871 176). While both villages are situated amidst limestone backdrops, the road connecting the two takes center stage. The height of the trip is at the **Ma Phi Leng Pass,** which overlooks the Nhô Quê River nearly 1500m below.

Tours organized from Hà Giang to Đồng Văn and Mèo Vac are expensive. As this region is still a politically sensitive area, travelers are required to purchase a **permit** (technically 150,000Đ per 1- to 5-person group, though it can only be obtained through the travel company, which charges much more) and travel with an even more expensive guide. **Foreigners are not allowed to wander on their own in the hills or villages outside of Mèo Vac and Đồng Văn.**

The sole tour operator in town charges astronomical prices for the necessities: 800,000Đ for the permit, 200,000Đ per day for the guide, and 600,000Đ per day for private transport. You must also pay for food and accommodations for the guide and driver. A five-day tour of Mèo Vac, Đồng Văn, and Bắc Hà with a hired jeep and guide runs US$230-350 at more established travel companies in Sa Pa.

SA PA TO ĐIỆN BIÊN PHỦ

The landscape between Sa Pa and Điện Biên Phủ—a succession of majestic mountains, ethnic villages, and gorgeous rice fields—is simply superb, bordering on sur-

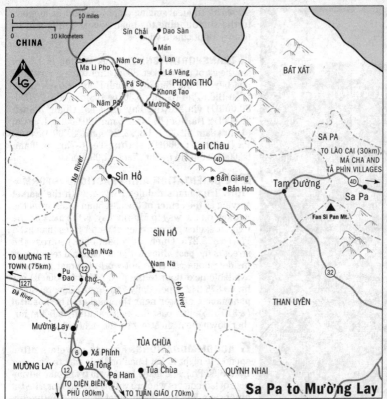

Sa Pa to Mường Lay

real. Small detours and brief treks allow for an authentic look at life in the region. Even if you don't plan on stopping anywhere along the 300km stretch, be sure to grab a window seat. Along the road you will see a wonderful array of headwear—hats of horse hair and straw, aluminum headdresses, conical hats, and thick turbans. Travelers generally stop in one of two towns for the night: Lai Châu (old Tam Đường) or Mường Lay (old Lai Châu). The mountains and villages surrounding both of them are their biggest draw. The relatively unscathed Rte. 6 that bypasses Điện Biên Phủ—instead connecting Mường Lay directly to Tuần Giáo—is by far the most unbelievable stretch of road in the country, passing through some of the most untouched villages in all of Vietnam. Connecting Sa Pa and Điện Biên Phủ, Highways 4 and 12 manage to communicate the diversity and splendor of Vietnam's various ethnic groups in a way that H'mông-heavy Sa Pa can not.

LAI CHÂU (OLD TAM ĐƯỜNG)   ☎23

In the past decade, Lai Châu has suffered from some serious identity crises. Just two years ago, this concrete strip was known as Tam Đường, and before that, Phong Thổ. Today, signs and maps with all three names still pop up, but most road signs say Lai Châu. It's a lot of confusion for what is essentially nothing more than a convenient stopover, 90km west of Sa Pa and 103km northeast of Mường Lay (Old Lai Châu). Though the town itself offers little or nothing to travelers, Lai Châu

POPULAR MECHANICS

In Vietnam, motorbikes have redefined the term "all-terrain." Drivers navigate the roads with alarming speed, rounding turns better-suited to sports cars and traversing floods that would look impassable even in a Jeep commercial.

Secretly I had wondered how these machines would respond to damage in a remote locale. Afraid that vocalizing my concern might render it a reality, I let it linger. But when a rock caught our bike's tire a day's hike from the closest repair shop or phone, my silent question was answered.

The driver and I rolled the bike to a small collection of Thài stilt homes. Everyone quickly emerged to see what was happening. A teenage boy magically produced a bicycle patch and glue. The village watched as we looked for a leak in the tube. Finally, we found the break and fixed it. The town laughed and smiled.

But we weren't home free. We filled the tire with air and...it popped. No patch could fix it. While the driver went to hitch a ride to a repair shop, I settled in for lunch. The local children showed me how to mount a water buffalo, and I sipped tea with the crafty boy's family, engaging in a dialogue of different tongues. While I may not have processed a word, I finally knew what can happen when you get a flat. By never making it to where I needed to go, I ended up where I wanted to be.

—J Zac Stein

serves as an ideal staging point for short excursions to the surrounding tea-bush-covered hills and to nearby Montagnard villages.

TRANSPORTATION. The **bus station** is 1.5km southeast of the market, 800m after the left fork, and just beyond the Phương Thanh Hotel. Buses run to Điện Biên Phủ (5-7hr.; 5:30, 6, 10am, noon; 70,000-80,000Đ) via Mường Lay (Old Lai Châu; 3-4hr.; 38,000Đ); Hà Nội (12-14hr.; 5am; 120,000Đ); Lào Cai (4-6hr.; 9am, 12:30, 1, 1:30, 2, 2:30pm; 38,000Đ) via Sa Pa (2-4hr.; 26,000Đ); Mường Tè (6-7hr.; 6:30am; 68,000Đ); Sìn Hồ (4-6hr.; 7am; 41,000Đ).

ORIENTATION AND PRACTICAL INFORMATION. Lai Châu straddles Hwy. 4, with the **market** serving as the center of town. A 5min. walk from the market, on the way to Mường Lay, is the **bank** on the right. It exchanges currency at better rates than in Sa Pa. (☎875 275. Open M-Sa 6am-6pm.) Across the street is the **post office** with international telephones inside; phone cards do not work. **Internet access** is available next door to the post office for 3000Đ per hr. (☎875 242. Open daily 7am-9pm.) Several small **pharmacies** cluster near the market. The **hospital** (☎875 185), just past the **police** station, is 500m farther down the main street on the right side.

ACCOMMODATIONS. Foreign travelers often spend the night in Lai Châu on their way to Sa Pa or Điện Biên Phủ, and many hotels will try to take advantage of latecomers who are willing to settle for a bed at any price. **Phương Thanh Hotel** ❸ is currently constructing two new buildings past the market toward Sa Pa. Rooms in the back of the main building have gorgeous views of the valley. (☎875 235. Doubles US$10.) **Tây Bắc Hotel** ❸, down the main street toward Mường Lay, has cramped but cozy rooms. A newer addition in the back has standard hotel-chain-quality rooms for US$15. (☎875 879. Doubles US$10; triples US$18.) **Tam Đường Hotel** ❷, on the main street across from the market, has uninspiring, musty rooms. (☎875 288. Singles 120,000Đ, doubles 150,000Đ.)

FOOD. **Tuấn Anh Restaurant** ❷, on the right 100m from the market toward Sa Pa, has an impressive menu in English and French. The food is good but relatively pricey. They also do standard Western breakfasts. (Spring rolls 18,000Đ; beef with vegetables or pineapple 25,000Đ; fish soup 25,000Đ. Open daily 6:30am-10pm.) **Bình Dân** ❶, on the right side of the alley leading to the market, is a simple room with a stove. A pleasant staff serves phở (5000Đ) and other dishes; a heaping plate of delicious tofu costs only 5000Đ. (Open daily 4am-8pm.) **Nhà Hàng Đức Mạnh ❷,** on the right side of the street when walking toward Mường Lay, is popular with locals. There is no menu, but they'll show you what they're cooking in the back. Meals cost about 20,000Đ. **Lanh Anh Restaurant ❷,** on the left side of the road southeast of the market, has oily Vietnamese standards and an English menu. (Phở 5000-6000Đ; fried rice or noodles 20,000-25,000Đ; meat entrees 20,000-55,000Đ. Open daily 7am-8pm.) **Bình Lai Restaurant ❷,** in the back of the Phương Thanh Hotel, has a long English menu (though not all of it will be available) and mess hall-style seating. (Soup 8000-10,000Đ; eel 30,000-40,000Đ. Open daily 7am-8pm.)

◪ SIGHTS. There isn't much to see in Lai Châu besides a pair of markets. In the morning, local Montagnard women buying food and goods fill the **Chợ Tam Đường Nhúa** (Tam Đường Plastic Market). Lai Châu also hosts **Chợ Tam Đường Đất** (Tam Đường Stone Market), which is held on Sundays 7km down Hwy. 4 toward Sa Pa. This market tends to be a frenzy of colors, with White H'mông, Flower H'mông, Nhắng, and Pu Nà peoples all in attendance.

A few hours in Lai Châu is enough time for a brief stroll into the **countryside.** Walking toward Mường Lay, pass the post office and take a left; this road quickly turns to dirt as it leaves town. Herd paths branch off from the main one and run to nearby peaks. Below these hills, planners have laid out a new residential area, and the concrete of the main strip may soon engulf this area, too.

Those with a free day or afternoon can, through the Phương Thanh Hotel, arrange for a local guide to take them on a 4hr. trek to visit nearby **minority villages.** Most villages around Lai Châu are accessible by jeep, motorbike (weather permitting), or foot, though it is difficult to hike without a guide, because the buffalo herd trails are tough to follow. One possibility is to head southeast, passing H'mông and Red Dao homes before arriving at villages of the Lư minority. The Lư, who still live in stilt houses, departed China during the 9th century and made their way to this region by the 12th century. Traditional Lư dress is black; women have horizontal and vertical embroidery along the bottom of their clothing. Traditionally, couples of this group who wish to marry out of love must go to a fortune teller to ensure they are compatible. One of the Lư women's most noticeable characteristics is their black teeth. They rub lemon inside their mouths and then apply *phèn đen*, a darkener made from charcoal. **Bản Giăng,** which is 15km from Lai Châu, is the closest Lư village. **Bản Nà Bỏ** and **Bản Hon** villages are farther out along the same road. To access any of these villages, head to Tam Đường Đất, 7km from Lai Châu on Hwy. 4 to Sa Pa. A track leads south to Duy Phong, from which Nà Bỏ is 7km. From Nà Bỏ, a fork in the road leads to Giăng, 1.5km down the right fork, and to Hon, 5km down the left fork. Day treks can be arranged through the Phương Thanh Hotel for 30,000Đ. Local guides cost 100,000Đ per day. Lunch and dinner can be obtained en route, but if you want breakfast you'll have to pack it.

VILLAGES BETWEEN LAI CHÂU AND MƯỜNG LAY

A 103km stretch of road connects the stopover points of Lai Châu and Mường Lay for travelers en route to Sa Pa or Điện Biên Phủ. Weaving across peaks and along the Na river valley by any mode of transportation is magnificent. For those traveling by *xe ôm* or jeep, however, there are several worthwhile detours, including **Phiêng Ban,** a Black Dao and White H'mông village 21km west of Lai Châu.

Nearby, a road off of Hwy. 12—on the right from Sa Pa or on the left from Điện Biên Phủ—stretches for 33km of village bliss before terminating at Dao Sàn, near the Chinese border. Use caution: the road is in poor condition. Early-morning public buses depart from Lai Châu to many of these villages, but it may be difficult to find transportation back to town in the afternoon.

THE FATE OF MƯỜNG LAY

The construction of Vietnam's largest hydro-powered dam, on the Đà River by Mường Lay, began in 2006. When completed in 2012, the USụ2.5 billion dam is expected to produce between 7.5 and 9.2 billion kilowatts annually—enough electricity to meet the national demand.

One point of contention, though, is the "safe" height of the dam. Two earthquakes rocked Old Lai Châu in 2001, and despite government reassurances, critics fear that another could break the 115m high walls.

Additionally, the dam will create a reservoir that will flood low-lying areas of Mường Lay permanently. Officials report that the dam will leave existing settlements on higher ground untouched. Since 2002, hundreds of families have been given food, land, and money from the government and resettled out of the valley. New homes for displaced Thài families have been built to "preserve ethnic cultural identities."

Despite government reports that people are happy, the change has been difficult, and it affects even those who will be allowed to remain. The town's name, though, refuses to drown. In 2004, Old Lai Châu was renamed Mường Lay, taking over the name of a settlement 50km southwest. Tam Đường, 100km to the northeast, is now called Lai Châu.

Three kilometers past the turn-off, a path on the right travels 500m to Phuong Thổ market, commonly called **Mu'o'ng So**. The market is held every Monday from 8am to noon, and its primary participants are the Nhắng minority. The Nhắng—whose name is Vietnamese slang for what is officially the Giáy minority—belong to the Tày-Thài language group. Nhắng women wear either blue or pink shirts with black, silky trousers, and often wrap their hair in plaid cloth. Buses to Mường So depart from Lai Châu at 9am, noon, and 2 pm (10,000Đ).

Farther down the road lie the Thài villages of **Lá Vàng** and **Lan**. On Sunday, Lan hosts a colorful market, amassing H'mông, Thài, Nhắng, and Black Dao people. Roughly 7km farther down the road is the Red Dao village of **Mán**. Past Mán, a small road branches left 1.5km to the H'mông village of **Sín Chải**. At the end of the road is **Dao Sàn commune**. On Sunday, it holds an alluring market, especially large on the 1st and 15th of each lunar month. High-elevation minority groups gather there to buy and sell goods. Perhaps the most striking of these groups is the Hà Nhì—Lai Châu's Hà Nhì women have incredibly colorful garb—beads, tassels, and stripes abound. Buses to Dao Sàn from Lai Châu depart at 5am (20,000Đ).

It is possible to head back to the main road from here, but if you have time, retrace your steps to Khong Tao, 5km before Hwy. 4 (28km away from Dao Sàn). Turn right; for 16km this road passes homes of the Black Dao, Thài, Giáy, and Dau Quần Chẹt, who wear white stockings and beret-like hats attached under their chin. This road then meets another at Nam Cay. You can turn right and continue for another 12km to visit more Dao homes before reaching the border at the village of **Ma Li Pho (Ma Li Thang)**. Buses to Ma Li Thang depart Lai Châu at 5am (18,000Đ). Your other option is to turn left at Nam Cay and travel 7km back to Hwy. 12, which empties out in the center of the Thài village of **Pá So**. Pá So has a small and uninspiring Sunday market attended by H'mông, Black Dao, and Thài. From the junction, it is less than 1km toward Sa Pa to the **Lan Anh Hotel II ❷**. This newer version of Mường Lay's Lan Anh Hotel has 60 rooms with all-wood interiors. Set along the river, it boasts a **restaurant,** will provide a local map, and rents motorbikes (US$6) for the day—enough time to do the aforementioned circuit. (☎896 337.) Singles and doubles US$7-35.) Three kilometers southeast of the Lan Anh Hotel are the **hot springs** (free). An unmarked path leads 200m in from the highway to the pools; use your odometer or ask around for the *suối nước nóng*.

SÌN HỒ

The road to **Sìn Hồ** (elevation 1700m) from Hwy. 12 begins at Nam May, 4km south of Pá So, and three-quarters of the way from Lai Châu to Mường Lay, a distance of 100km. This 38km detour takes almost 2hr. to drive and is only paved for 10km, although it improves gradually as you climb. As difficult as the road may be, the views are excellent. The H'mông village of **Lăng Mô** is halfway up the mountain. The other noticeable collection of homes is the H'mông **Bản Mông** village, 11km before Sìn Hồ. While most of the homes belong to the Black H'mông, it is also possible to see Red H'mông along the road. The women are identifiable by their incredibly long hair, which is twisted and then wrapped around their heads. Traditionally, Red H'mông women collect the hair that falls from combing and weave it into their existing hair. Younger women now tend to collect their old hair for wigs. The road terminates in the drab town of Sìn Hồ, perched on a prairie 1km above sea level. Staying there is a chore, but it isn't easy to leave. Two **buses** depart daily from opposite the market and head to Mường Lay (4-6hr.; 6am; 30,000Đ) and Lai Châu (3-4hr.; 6am; 38,000Đ). Expect to pay 100,000-150,000Đ for a *xe ôm* to Mường Lay and 150,000-200,000Đ to get to Lai Châu. It is also possible to get dropped off on Hwy. 12 and flag down a bus bound for Lai Châu or Điện Biên Phủ. If you want to visit Sìn Hồ as a daytrip from Mường Lay, you can rent a motorbike and make an adventurous circuit. If you're not arriving on market day, your presence will likely be met with suspicion by local authorities. Visit the **police** station (☎ 870 251), beyond the market up the paved road on the left, to register yourself. This formality is also necessary if you plan on traveling to Sìn Hồ's nearby villages.

MƯỜNG LAY (OLD LAI CHÂU)   ☎ 23

Nestled in a pastoral river valley, Mường Lay (elevation 600m) sits in a subdued state, awaiting its watery doom. By 2012, a reservoir formed by a colossal hydro-electric dam will flood low lying parts of the region, including most of the town (see **"The Fate of Mường Lay,"** p. 212). Already, the town seems to have given in to its poignant, predetermined fate. Business has slowed and visitors rarely stop for more than a meal and a night's sleep. Once a power base for White Thài chieftains, Mường Lay used to be a French administrative center during the colonial period. Today, the town has its own sleepy charm, serving as a restful base for exploring the surrounding valley, which is home to some of the best trips in the northwest.

TRANSPORTATION. Buses leave from a lot labeled "Bến Xe Thị Xã Mường Lay," 2km south of Mường Lay proper. They head to: Hà Nội (18-30hr.; 6am; 125,000Đ) via Điện Biên Phủ (3hr.; 5, 6, 7, 8, 9:15, 10:30am; 35,000Đ); Lào Cai (10-14hr.; 6am; 55,000Đ) via Lai Châu (Old Tam Đường; 3-4hr.; 5, 10:30, 11am; 38,000Đ) and Sa Pa (7hr.; 45,000Đ); Mường Tè (5hr.; 6am; 35,000Đ); Sìn Hồ (3hr.; 7am; 30,000Đ). It's also possible to flag down buses to Điện Biên Phủ and Lai Châu along the road throughout the day.

ORIENTATION AND PRACTICAL INFORMATION. The Lan Anh Hotel has a solid but incredibly expensive **Internet** connection (20,000Đ per hr.); it also happens to be the only place in town for currency exchange, and the rate is fair. The Lai Châu **GPO**, at the far end of town toward Sa Pa, has *Poste Restante*, **Internet** (3000Đ per hr.), and international phones. (☎ 852 301. Open daily 7am-9pm.) Six hundred meters toward Điện Biên Phủ, a street turns off to the right and continues straight 200m to the **Na River.** On the left side of the street, halfway to the river, is the local **market,** in front of which is a **pharmacy.** (Open daily 8am-8:30pm.) A suspension bridge leads over the river 100m farther down. The **hospital** (☎ 852 492) is 4km down the road to the right on the other side of the bridge. The **police** (☎ 852 486) are closer to town on the same road.

📷📱 ACCOMMODATIONS AND FOOD. The most popular lodging is town is the **Lan Anh Hotel ❷,** where independent travelers and package-tour junkies collide. The hotel is just off of the main street, immediately before the bridge. Free bananas, rooms with all-wood interiors, and fans are all part of the deal. Shop the hotel rooms to avoid getting thrown in claustrophobic quarters. The manager has lots of information on nearby treks and activities. (☎852 370. Motorbike rental US$6 per day. Singles and doubles US$7-35.) The dull **Song Da Hotel ❷,** a short walk down the highway from the main intersection toward Điện Biên Phủ, has rooms with air-conditioning, TV, and private bath. Don't expect charm or natural light. (☎852 527. Doubles 100,000Đ; triples 120,000Đ.)

Lan Anh Hotel boasts the only **restaurant ❸** in town. It serves a set menu (40,000-80,000Đ) with large and greasy portions, including spring rolls, pork, fried noodles, vegetables, rice, and fruit. Main dishes are also available (30,000-40,000Đ). Simple breakfasts cost 10,000Đ. There are also plenty of cheap phở shops in town.

🔳 DAYTRIPS FROM MƯỜNG LAY

The mountains are not as vast as those in Sa Pa, the hotels and restaurants aren't as bountiful, and the conversations tend to be held in Vietnamese. With so little to do in town, Mường Lay offers visitors no choice but to venture out into the pristine surroundings. Since most people stop in Mường Lay only long enough to eat and perhaps sleep, the surrounding villages and treks remain breathtakingly unspoiled and merit a stay in Mường Lay.

DỐ AND NÂM CẢN VILLAGES. The closest and easiest trip from Mường Lay follows the He river valley upstream. After walking over the first suspension bridge on the main street, turn left to reach **Dố Village,** home to White Thài villagers. While there are plenty of locals wearing Western clothes and driving motorbikes, the stilt houses with firewood stacked below the floors are lovely. Many homes have old looms, and some women continue to dress in traditional garb.

Past Dố, the path goes by two more suspension bridges before turning inward to hug the mountainside. Trekking between the second and third bridges takes about an hour, and the road is generally flat. Roughly 300m before the third bridge, a small path leads up to the high reaches of **Nậm Cản** (about 4km from the first bridge), which is inhabited by the White H'mông. Chickens and children play while Thài men and women wave from their doorstep or smile while working in the fields. Visiting the H'mông takes almost 4hr. round-trip; unlike the riverside path, this route is uphill and difficult to follow. Going solo? Prepare to say "H'mông" to many, many Thài people, in hope that they'll point the way. If getting lost isn't your thing, cross the third bridge to Hwy. 12; from here, it's an easy 4km back to Lai Châu. Despite the drab pavement, hiking back is fairly interesting, and small detours prove rewarding. It is also possible, though not always easy, to take a *xe ôm* back to town or catch a bus coming from Điện Biên Phủ. Another option is to continue upriver along the far riverbank to (surprise, surprise) the next suspension bridge. This extension takes about 1½hr.

PU ĐAO AND CHỞ VILLAGES, LÊ LỢI STONE, AND CHĂN NƯA. From Mường Lay, cross over the first suspension bridge and bear right 3km until you reach the boat landing. There, you can take a brief ferry ride across the river (5000-10,000Đ). Turn upstream along the Đà River toward Mường Tè. A short trek up the road brings you to the ruined **house of Dèo Văn Long,** the last of the White Thài kings. When this French-backed autocrat fled Vietnam in 1953, it is said that he poisoned all of his servants so that they could not tell the incoming Vietnamese army of his

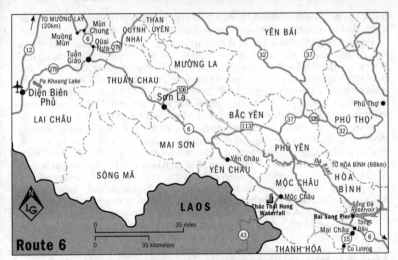

whereabouts. Needless to say, he is not thought highly of by the locals, and the sight is closed permanently. Immediately beyond the house is an 18km trail that leads to **Pu Đao.** The route is navigable, but much of it is uphill and the trip takes 3-4hr. Both White and Blue H'mông reside in the village.

Without a guide, the most viable option is to retrace your steps back to the ferry landing. If you do so, bear right when you reach the road to Mường Tè, turn right, and hike past Thài homes to see **Emperor Lê Lợi's poem,** which he inscribed into a rock overlooking the Đà. The small plaque on the roadside that leads the way is easy to miss. The poem was written in Chinese, but a nearby marble stone bears English and Vietnamese translations. Lê Lợi is nationally beloved for expelling the Chinese from the region in the 15th century, and the poem recounts the importance of ethnic minority chiefs' loyalties to the security and peace of the country.

There are two alternative routes back down from Pu Đao. A 2hr. trek down a hazy trail brings you to **Chơ' village,** of the White Thài minority—this hike requires a guide. From here it's a 1½hr. trek back out to the suspension bridge, which is close to where the ferry dropped you off. To catch a ferry back, turn right up the road to Mường Tè. Going left over the wood-planked bridge will lead you quickly out to Hwy. 12. Be ready for a lengthy trip; the road back is long and circuitous.

To return to Mường Lay, a third trail from Pu Đao, which is also difficult to navigate, takes you down to **Chăn Nưa.** It is possible to get a bus into town, assuming you time things correctly: the trail from Pu Đao takes a mere 1½hr., and while it's necessary to have a guide, this is the best option for travelers who are in a hurry. Be sure to verify departure times from Chăn Nưa in advance.

If you'd like to visit these sights with a guide, the Lan Anh Hotel in Mường Lay will set you up with a local guide (US$10) and a boat trip (US$10) to do so.

ROUTE 6 FROM MƯỜNG LAY TO TUẦN GIÁO

Directly across the street from the Mường Lay post office, a Montagnard path pretending to be a road called ⧨Route 6 eases up into the mountains. This road is an empty, scenic alternative to the highway, and its beauty rivals any found in Vietnam. Except for the last 26km before Tuần Giáo, no public buses venture through this route, and with good reason: its 96km connecting Mường Lay with Tuần Giáo are in various—and sometimes extreme—states of disrepair. Though there is little traffic, narrow sections, sheer drops, and abrupt changes in the quality of the road merit slow and cautious driving and sometimes quick maneuvering.

Route 6 quickly climbs out of the He river valley, revealing fantastic views as rice paddies shrink into nothingness. A quick trek or motorbike ride 5km up this road is worthwhile for the panoramas alone. Ten kilometers from Mường Lay, the road levels off by a small collection of buildings. Sandwiched between two convenience stores, a well-maintained trail branches left to **Xá Tổng**. Another 2km down this path is the White H'mông village of **Phi Hay**, a collection of 50 houses that provides an opportunity for several hours of undisturbed wandering and exploration.

Route 6 continues southeast, only to become even more magnificent. Corn and rice fields become tangled jungles and high mountains, hiding just a sliver of road. Jutting peaks surround Montagnards with machetes strapped loosely about their hips walking their livestock along the road. Baskets and babies are latched to locals with intricately embroidered baby-carriers. The road is dotted primarily with H'mông women, who sport colorful stripes on their arms and wraps on their heads. Other women are clothed in vivid pinks, oranges, and greens. The men typically wear black suit-like tops and matching pants, often with a thin floral trim.

The best part of the trip, however, is the 20km descent into a valley beyond Xá Tổng, where the hidden village of **Pa Ham** is nestled. This Thài village is not to be confused with the more modern and well-maintained one 3km before it. Pa Ham is a large collection of stilt homes with bamboo roofs. At the far side of town, the river and road become one as the water flushes out the trail. If it has just rained, the children will undoubtedly be playing out in the river—some naked, others more modestly clothed but soaked nonetheless. The village continues past the flushed-out trail. Your presence, which is likely to cause quite a stir, will be met with smiles, waves, and general hilarity. The women in Pa Ham wear cloth headwraps along with typical Western attire. It is possible to take a *xe ôm* round-trip (roughly 3hr.) from Mường Lay to Pa Ham for 70,000-80,000Đ.

The road gradually climbs out of the valley to cling midway along a ridge paralleling the Múc River. While the coy river often plays peek-a-boo behind the trees and hills below, views of the river eventually open up to a wide panorama. Farther along, limestone karsts rise out of the rolling green hills before the road drops to the level of the river and then crosses it. Route 6 then follows a smaller tributary until 37km before Tuần Giáo, where it climbs up to a pass. Looking back from there, you can trace your journey to the farthest peak.

From Mùn Chung, the final 26km before Tuần Giáo is a victory lap. For those who have braved the bumps, mud, and sheer drops of the rest of the road, this final segment of smooth pavement is well-deserved. The landscape continues to introduce new vistas, and the sides of the road are increasingly peopled by Black Thài women. Their piled-up buns of hair hold up elaborately embroidered head scarves. The 4hr. *xe ôm* ride from Mường Lay to Tuần Giáo should cost 150,000-200,000Đ.

For those driving the road in reverse from Tuần Giáo to Mường Lay, the route is no more difficult to follow. At Minh Thắng, 91km before Mường Lay, bear left at the fork in the road. When the smooth pavement ends at Mùn Chung, 72km from Mường Lay, be careful not to follow the pavement to the right of the bridge. This is Highway 129, which leads to Tửa. Route 6, unsurprisingly, goes straight up a rocky path—and stays on it for the rest of the way.

ĐIỆN BIÊN PHỦ   ☎ 23

Điện Biên Phủ (ĐBP) is a destination for history buffs and a stopover for everyone else. Though set in a beautiful valley, this unattractive but historically significant town is easy for foreign tourists to miss. As the site of the French defeat in 1954 at the hands of Hồ Chí Minh's Việt Minh, Điện Biên Phủ remains one of the best-known symbols of

European colonialism's collapse in Vietnam. Today, the town is adjusting to its relatively new role as the capital of Điện Biên Phủ Province. Only time will tell whether or not authorities will allow a second wave of Western invaders by opening the border to Laos, which lies 34km west of town. In the meantime, the tanks and bunkers scattered throughout the Điện Biên Phủ Valley remain interesting to some Westerners, positively exciting to a select few, and a source of pride and reflection to the Vietnamese.

TRANSPORTATION. The **airstrip** runs parallel to Hwy. 12 and the **terminal** is on the left, 1km north of the bus station on the road to Mường Lay. **Flights** to Hà Nội leave daily at 12:30 and 3:30pm (465,000Đ). You must connect in Hà Nội to get to: Đà Nẵng (1,120,000Đ plus 25,000Đ airport tax); Hải Phòng (1,120,000Đ); HCMC (1,990,000Đ); Huế (1,120,000Đ plus 20,000Đ airport tax). You can buy tickets at the **Vietnam Airlines** office in the Airport Hotel on Trần Đăng Ninh. (☎824 692. Open daily 7-11am and 1:30-4:30pm.) **Buses** leave from the station beside Hwy. 12 and run to: Hà Nội (20-30hr.; 4:30, 8:30, 10:30am; 130,000-155,000Đ); Lai Châu (5-6hr.; 5, 7, 10am, 12:30pm; 70,000Đ); Lào Cai (8-10hr.; 6, 7:30am; 84,000-115,000Đ) via Sa Pa (75,000Đ); Mường Lay (3hr.; 8, 9, 11am, 1:30pm; 33,000Đ); Mường Tè (8hr.; 5:30am; 67,000Đ); Sìn Hồ (6hr.; 5:30am; 55,000Đ); Sơn La (6-7hr.; 4:30am, noon; 55,000Đ); Tuần Giáo (2hr.; 6:30, 11am, 3:30pm; 27,000Đ). Buy tickets from the booth before boarding. (☎825 776. Open daily 3:30am-7pm.)

ORIENTATION AND PRACTICAL INFORMATION. Over 450km northwest of Hà Nội and 34km from the Lao border, Điện Biên Phủ is in the Mường Thành Valley. The bus station is west of town on **Highway 12**, which continues northeast to Mường Lay. From Hwy. 12, **Trần Đăng Ninh** heads east from the bus station into town, bridging the Rốm River and passing the **police** station (☎827 240). After 300m, it intersects **Đường Mường Thành**, the town's main drag. From this main intersection, a right leads south toward the rest of town, where Đường Mường Thành is known as **Đường 7-5**. Đường 7-5 heads into Laos (34km) after passing the post office, the Điện Biên Phủ Museum, and the majority of the military sites, including **A-1 Hill**. The **Bank for Investment and Development of Vietnam**, 3 Đường 7-5, halfway to the post office, exchanges foreign cash. (☎825 774. Open M-F 7-11am and 1:30-5pm.) The **GPO** is just past the bank on the right. It has *Poste Restante* and an international telephone office. (☎825 833. Open daily 7am-9:15pm.) A **hospital** (☎825 463) is on Hoàng Văn Thái, left off of the main street between A-1 Hill and the Vietnamese cemetery. Back at the main

ON THE MENU

THE TRUTH ABOUT CATS AND DOGS

Ever been bothered by your pets scrounging under the table for scraps of food? Rest assured that in Northern Vietnam, pets wouldn't want to—they could be eating their childhood playmates. In Vietnam, dogs are multi-purpose animals, serving as both man's best friend and his best meat—making for some surprisingly tasty entrees. The smell and taste of dog meat is fairly powerful and well complemented by alcohol. Fido is generally fried up and served with a raw green called *lámơ*. You can order *thịt chó*, which is a stir-fried dog meat, but the most supple part of a dog is *loñg chó*, the stomach.

Given the recent rat problem, eating cats has actually been outlawed in Hà Nội. But think again if you imagine that cute little kitties get off the hook. Farther north, you can feast on *con mèo* in local establishments. The meat from these introspective animals is fatty and can be difficult to chew, but when stir-fried with some veggies, it's actually a real treat.

Even travelers who consider themselves oblivious to animal rights may be a bit unnerved to witness dogs experiencing the same treatment as chickens or cattle. If the house pets up north seem a bit timid, just consider the psychological stress they're suffering. Friend and food have never been so close.

intersection, a left leads north into the **market.** Several hundred meters farther is a cluster of **Internet** cafes, of which **Trung Tâm Tin Học Trẻ** has the best connection. (4000Đ per hr. Open daily 7am-8pm.) While there are plenty of **pharmacies** in town, **Công Ty TNHH Dược Phẩm Hoa Ban,** located several hundred meters farther up the street, is definitely the best option. (☎824 445. Open daily 7am-10pm.)

⌐ ACCOMMODATIONS. Hotels in Điện Biên Phủ are similar to the sights gracing its valley: numerous and unexciting. Some pleasant establishments have sprung up in response to the growing number of jeep tours passing through town, but they are farther removed from the action. **Khách Sạn Him Lam ❹** is the best hotel in town. Look for the sign on the right outside of town on the road to Tuần Giáo; the turn-off is 4km from the central rotary in town. The beautiful rooms have lakeside views, air-conditioning, TV, bathtub, fridge, phone, and terraces. The hotel grounds include a well-maintained swimming pool, tennis courts, pool tables, steam baths, and swan paddleboats. (☎811 999. Doubles US$20; triples US$25.) **Bình Long Hotel ❷,** 761 Mường Thành, is a small, family-run establishment with clean rooms, air-conditioning, and some English-speaking staff. Walk up the main street from the market toward Sơn La; it's on the right. (☎824 345. Doubles 120,000Đ; triples 150,000Đ.) **Lottery Hotel (Khách Sạn Xo So) ❷** has pleasant rooms with bathtub, TV, and fan. It is close to the town center but still manage to remain quiet. Walking from the main intersection toward A-1 Hill, bear right on the street before the post office. (☎825 789. Doubles 110,000Đ; triples 165,000Đ.) **Khách Sạn Điện Biên Phủ-Hà Nội ❸,** 279A Đường 7-5, between the post office and A-1 Hill, has overpriced rooms but luxurious suites for just a few dollars more. Modern suites have a living room, air-conditioning, TV, and bathtub. (☎825 103. Singles US$10; doubles US$13; triples US$16; one-person suites US$13; two-person suites US$20.) **Khách Sạn Công Ty Bia (Beer Factory Hotel) ❶** is a bit out of the way, but a good deal. Between A-1 Hill and the Vietnamese soldiers cemetery, turn up Hoàng Văn Thái. Pass Liên Tươi restaurant and turn onto the second street that angles right. Through the alley beside the hotel is a *bia hơi* factory. (☎824 635. Singles 60,000Đ; doubles 120,000Đ; triples 180,000Đ.)

🗀 FOOD. There is good food in ĐBP. Phở and cơm are best in the market, but can also be bought along Mường Thành. Stalls past the GPO offer a wider selection of eats, and Trần Đăng Ninh has little restaurants serving dog meat (*chó;* see **"The Truth About Cats and Dogs,"** p. 217). **Ngọc Mai Restaurant ❷,** on Hoàng Văn No, serves the best ethnic minority dishes around. It's famed for local dishes like sticky rice with maize (10,000-20,000Đ) and dried beef (*thịt say;* 40,000Đ). It's across a retention pond from the GPO. (☎825 932. Open daily 8am-9pm.) **Liên Tươi Restaurant ❷,** 300m down Hoàng Văn Thái (the street between A-1 and the cemetery) has good food at fair prices. The spring rolls (40,000Đ) are excellent, but the Vietnamese menu offers more adventurous, seasonal meats, such as iguana, *kỳ đà.* (☎824 919. Open daily 6am-11pm.) **Mường Thành Restaurant ❷,** in the Mường Thành Hotel, offers set breakfasts (15,000-20,000Đ), pasta (35,000-40,000Đ), fried tofu with veggies (25,000Đ), and a range of meats including frog and chicken. (☎810 043. Open daily 5am-10pm.) **Nhà Hàng Van Tuế ❷** is just off the main drag on Đường Trường Chinh, on the way toward the Mường Thành Hotel and Sơn La. The beer (4000Đ) is fresh and the food is good but spicy, as the owners know that nothing washes down hot peppers like beer. Check on the prices of non-listed foods to ensure there are no surprises. (☎829 652. Open 24hr.) **Romantic Coffee-Snack Bar ❶,** 68 Nguyễn Chí Thàng, is a nice break from the streets of ĐBP. Coffee (5000-14,000Đ), tea (4000Đ), and mixed drinks (15,000Đ) are available. Printed masterpieces such as *Guernica* adorn the walls. Despite its name, there are no snacks in sight. (☎830 650. Open daily 7am-midnight.)

🗀 SIGHTS. Điện Biên Phủ's main appeal is its history. Travelers who arrive by bus can easily imagine why the French reckoned the valley too remote to be threatened by the Việt Minh. In 1953, the French air-dropped 9000 troops into the region, securing eight hills surrounding Điện Biên Phủ, and constructed an airbase under the command of Colonel Christian de Castries. Less than a year later, General Võ Nguyễn Giáp, commander of the Việt Minh, began to drag artillery to the ridges around Điện Biên Phủ Valley. On March 13th, 1954, the Việt Minh unloaded roughly 9000 shells on the 9000 French troops. For 56 days a battle ensued; the French desperately tried to fly in supplies and reinforcements, but the Việt Minh successfully hindered their efforts. Rough estimates suggest that 2500 French and 8000 Vietnamese died during the battle. Nevertheless, on May 6, 1954, the French lowered the *tricouleur* and hoisted the white flag of surrender. A day later, negotiations began in Geneva, ultimately leading to the division of Vietnam along the 17th parallel. National elections were supposed to take place in 1956 and allow for the reunification of Vietnam, but these elections never occurred, and a decade later General Giáp was again called to duty, this time against the Americans.

ĐIỆN BIÊN PHỦ MUSEUM. In the white-and-yellow building across from the cemetery, on Đường 7-5 heading toward the Lao border, lies the city's museum chronicling the battle of Điện Biên Phủ. This collection of pictures, models, and artifacts is well displayed with descriptive labels in English, French, and Vietnamese. The museum is small, and it looks like they had a difficult time choosing what to include, given the rope (used to pull heavy artillery) and the bathtub (salvaged from the captured Colonel De Castries's bunker) that are both prominently displayed. Nonetheless, the museum is worth a look. French and Vietnamese weapons and equipment are on display outside. *(Open daily 7-11am and 1:30-5pm. 5000Đ.)*

A-1/ELIANE 2 HILL. Opposite the museum, 60m toward Hwy. 12, is A-1 Hill, known to the French as Elaine 2—purportedly, the French named all of the city's strategic hills after De Castries's mistresses (others include Anne-Marie, Beatrice, and Gabrielle). Some of the fiercest fighting of the campaign took place on this saucy (ha!) hill, and today it stands as a scarred reminder of the war. A-1 is a large network of paths, bunkers, and tangled barbed wire. Plaques dish out information in Vietnamese along the way. At the top of the hill (accessible via the second small path branching left) is a tank, memorial, and bunker you can enter. A-1 also provides good views of the ĐBP Valley. *(Open daily 7-11am and 1:30-5pm. 5000Đ.)*

COLONEL CHRISTIAN DE CASTRIES'S COMMAND BUNKER AND FRENCH SOLDIERS' MEMORIAL. From A-1 Hill, head back toward town and turn left onto Bế Văn Đàn. This leads past the unkempt bunker where Commander Pirot killed himself. Allegedly, the French artillery commander committed suicide because the Việt Minh were too well camouflaged for him to counter their advances. Over the wooden-planked Mường Thành Bridge is a tank on your right. Turn left to visit a re-creation of Colonel Christian de Castries's Command Bunker, rebuilt in 1994. *(Open M-Sa 7-11am and 2-5pm. 3000Đ.)* Turn the corner from the bunker and walk 300m, passing a tank, to the French Soldiers' Memorial. Through the cast-iron gate is a small garden with a white obelisk. *(Open M-Sa 7-11am and 2-5pm. Free.)*

NGHĨA TRANG LIỆT SẠ ĐIỆN BIÊN PHỦ (ĐBP CEMETERY). Directly opposite the museum, this cemetery was constructed in honor of fallen Vietnamese soldiers. Inside the entrance is a long wall of names which, ironically, resembles the Vietnam War Memorial in Washington, D.C. The grounds are filled with nameless gravestones, many of which are lit with incense to honor the dead. The landing up a flight of steps near the entrance has a good view over the grounds. The entire complex is beautifully designed, and along the outside wall is a gold-painted, socialist-realist frieze depicting the war. *(Open daily 7-11am and 1:30-5pm. Free.)*

TUONG ĐÀI CHIEN THANG ĐIỆN BIÊN PHỦ (ĐBP VICTORY MONUMENT).
Perched on top of D-1 Hill, the Vietnamese monument is in sparkling contrast to its diminutive French counterpart in the valley below. Weighing 200 metric tons, it's the largest bronze-cast statue in the country. *(Take the first left off of Đường 7-5.)*

HOÀNG CỘNG CHẤT TEMPLE AND THE CITADEL OF THIRTY THOUSAND. Built in honor of the 18th-century peasant leader Hoàng Cộng Chất, this temple houses a few archaeological remains of Chất's citadel. Leading a coalition of ethnic minority chieftains, Chất expelled the armies of southern China who had invaded the region during the early 18th century. The event represented just a piece in the recurring narrative of ethnic minorities uniting against foreign invaders. The temple offers a quiet retreat from the traffic of ĐBP. Nearby, 15th-century Lù lords built the Citadel of Thirty Thousand, said to have housed—surprise surprise—30,000 people. The remains of the outer wall are still visible in the nearby village of Xam Mứm. *(To get to the temple, head toward the Lao border on Highway 279. After 4.5km, you'll pass by the Long Nhai Memorial (Đài Kỷ Niệm Long Nhai), built to commemorate the ethnic minority POWs held by the French in 1954. At Bản Phủ market, 10km from ĐBP, bear right. 1km down the road, the temple is on the left. Another 1km down this road will take you the remains of the Citadel of the Thirty Thousand, located just beyond the right fork in Xam Mứm village.)*

■ DAYTRIP FROM ĐIỆN BIÊN PHỦ

PA KHOANG LAKE (HỒ PA KHOANG)
Driving northeast out of ĐBP on Hwy. 279, turn right after 17km. After another 5.5km, you will see a road branching down to the lake. 20m up from the hotel is a boat launch, where tours (200,000Đ) of the lake, the Thài and Sa villages, and General Giáp's bunker depart.

Pa Khoang Lake is pretty, but it doesn't quite compare to some of Vietnam's other, more beautiful lakes. Trees guard the banks and the wooded swamp on the outskirts of this exceptionally quiet and tourist-free spot.

If the boat tour threatens to break your bank, continue along Hwy. 279 to Mường Phăng. After a 25min. drive through forested marshlands, the road reaches town and opens onto beautiful rice paddies and Thài stilt houses. **General Giáp's Bunker** (5000Đ) is five minutes down the road. Born to a Mandarin family in 1912, Giáp became the commander, under Hồ Chí Minh, of the armed propaganda forces, which later became the People's Liberation Army. He was declared Defense Minister in 1946 and proceeded to defeat the French at ĐBP in 1954. The bunker is one of the more interesting historical sites in the ĐBP area. A 10min. hike from the entrance brings you to a hut containing model Vietnamese soldiers. The path continues through a string of bunkers and huts before arriving at a tunnel and Giáp's own command post. Though not overly exciting, it's worth visiting in conjunction with a trip to the lake. On the way out, veer off the established path and follow the trickling river through rice paddies back out on to the road. The round-trip from ĐBP to Pa Khoang Lake should take about half a day (3-4hr.). On the return trip, consider stopping at the Him Lam Hotel for a drink by the lake.

On your left on the road to the lake is the decaying **Pa Khoang Lake Hotel ❶**, where you can find a double bed for 80,000Đ. The damp, decaying rooms include fan and private bath. The top floor has nice views of the lake and proper beds; bottom-floor rooms have mattresses slung on platforms. A **restaurant** is attached to the hotel, but the tables are rarely set up; don't expect a menu or quick service.

TUẦN GIÁO   ☎ 23

Eighty kilometers from Điện Biên Phủ, 75km from Sơn La, and 98km from Mường Lay, the small town of Tuần Giáo is a centrally located and necessary stop on any tour of the Northwest Highlands. Residents here are a mix of Kinh and Thài, all of whom seem contented to go about their business as travelers roll through to someplace else. For those who wish to skip Điện Biên Phủ, the stretch of ⊠Route 6 connecting Tuần Giáo and Mường Lay is magnificent (p. 215). If you haven't gotten enough of the Montagnard scene, continue on Rte. 6 another 5km toward Mường Lay to the Thài village of **Qũai Nư'a**. Bear right and continue for 5km more to visit **Pú Nhung**, a H'mông village. The scenery is spectacular. For another pleasant walk, head toward Sơn La and, 100m from the main intersection, cut down the path right of the bridge. You'll pass small houses and bamboo on the river's edge; luscious rice paddies cover the opposite bank.

The best rooms in town can be found at the impressively named **Nhà Khách Huyện Tuần Giáo Tỉnh Điện Biên Phủ Hotel ❶**. To reach it from the center of town, turn up the small street beside the post office and walk on the left side of the grass field. For 120,000Đ you can sleep in style in one of the fresh, attractive rooms with air-conditioning, TV, fan, and a clean bathroom in the new wing. For 80,000Đ you get a TV, fan, and a private bathroom. For 60,000Đ the room is the same—but you have to brave dirtier facilities. Rooms have two to four beds. Across the street from the post office lies **Khách Sạn Tuần Giáo ❷**, which has a very friendly staff. The rooms are clean and come with ceiling fan and TV—make sure that they operate. Price quotes start at 100,000Đ for a single and 150,000Đ for a double, but be sure to bargain it down to about half of that. (☎862 613.)

The three restaurants in town are about 300m down the road from the pharmacy. Housed in the large building on the left side of the street is **Nhà Hàng Thanh Thủy ❷**. They have a short menu in Vietnamese and English—ask about prices before ordering. Specialties include sweet-and-sour pork (20,000Đ), fried chicken (40,000Đ), and spring rolls (20,000Đ). In the back there are tables where you can look out at the hillside through a chicken-wire fence. (☎862 408. Open daily 5am-8pm.) Across the street, **Thư'c Do'n Hoàng Quát ❷** has clearly seen its fair share of tourists. The walls are plastered with tour companies' stickers and business cards. The short English menu lists appetizing dishes such as beer-steamed fish (20,000-30,000Đ) and grilled pork (20,000-40,000Đ) at reasonable prices. (☎862 482. Open daily 6:30am-8pm.) **Huyền Trang ❶**, in a baby-blue building just north of the post office, doesn't have a menu, but they'll make up some tasty dishes and you're guaranteed to leave full. (Entrees 20,000Đ. Open daily 6am-8pm.)

Tuần Giáo lies on three roads leading from the three towns it connects—Hwy. 279 southwest to Điện Biên Phủ and Rte. 6 northwest to Mường Lay and southeast to Sơn La. The **bus station** is just up the street on your left as you walk toward Mường Lay. **Buses** run daily to: Điện Biên Phủ (2-3hr.; 6:30, 7, 8:30, 11:30am, noon; 27,000Đ); Hà Nội (5:30, 7, 9, 11:30am; 105,000Đ); Sơn La (3hr.; 5:30, 6:30am; 30,000Đ); Thái Bình (6:30, 7am; 135,000Đ). The ticket booth is rarely functional; be sure to set a price before you depart. The **bank** (☎862 294) is 150m up on the left, and beside it is the **post office**, which has international calling booths and **Internet** for 3000Đ per hr. (☎862 386. Open daily 7am-9pm.) One hundred meters farther up the street toward Mường Lay is a small and lively **market** filled with Thài women selling fruit, veggies, clothes, and watches. There is a **pharmacy** just off the three-way intersection toward Điện Biên Phủ. (☎862 876. Open daily 6:30am-9:30pm.) Farther down the road toward Điện Biên Phủ is the **hospital** (☎862 342). The **police** station (☎862 348) is by the main intersection in town.

SƠN LA   ☎22

Nestled among limestone karsts and rice paddies, Sơn La (elevation 676m) is an attractive town used as an intermediate point between Hà Nội and Điện Biên Phủ. Political prisoners were held there by the French, and even now the town has a self-contained air, hemmed in by the surrounding hills. Their astounding natural beauty—

where Black Thài and H'mông were wise enough to set-tle—offers an escape from the construction and rattling *xe ôm*s that remain caged up in town.

ROUTE SICKS

Having heard endless, wildly con-flicting accounts of the treacher-ous road conditions between So'n La and Mai Châu, I wasn't sure which tale was the most reliable. Who was I supposed to trust?

The bus scheduled to go from So'n La to Moc Châu chose, endearingly, to show up at the station over an hour late. The 120km stretch of road that fol-owed then took six hours to traverse, not counting a roadblock while en route. There were three severe episodes of motion sick-ness—know that the phrase "severe episodes of motion sick-ness" has a more dire meaning in Vietnam than in the rest of the world—and one woman cracked her head on a rough handrail so hard that she began bleeding.

This casualty rate didn't seem to surprise anyone—just another day on the battlefield. General Giáp once explained to the Ameri-cans, "You can kill 10 of my men for every one of yours... Even at those odds I will win and you will lose." This stretch of road seemed to confirm that unflinching, stony Vietnamese mentality. So if every-one was basically wrong, what did I learn? In whom should I have placed my confidence? The real lesson is that it's worth steering clear of construction, which is likely to include dynamite and large, falling rocks. Most of us can't stomach ten-to-one odds.

—J Zac Stein

■ TRANSPORTATION

Most buses going through S'on La drop passengers off at the town's main intersection. The **bus station** is 7km outside of town on Rte. 6 toward Hà Nội. A *xe ôm* from the station to town should cost 10,000Đ. From the bus station, **buses** and **minibuses** leave for: Điện Biên Phủ (6-7hr.; every hr. 5am-noon; 42,000Đ), Hà Nội (8-10hr.; every hr. 4am-noon; 78,000Đ), and Mộc Châu (2hr.; 5, 7, 9am, 1:30pm; 32,000Đ). Occasional buses driving the Hà Nội-Điện Biên Phủ route can be hailed as they cross the bridge. To get to Mường Lay, take the bus to Điện Biên Phủ and transfer in Tuần Giáo (30,000Đ), taking a *xe ôm* to Mường Lay (4hr.; 150,000-200,000Đ).

■ ORIENTATION AND PRACTICAL INFORMATION

Sơn La is 320km west of Hà Nội and two-thirds of the way from there to Điện Biên Phủ on **Route 6**. The inter-section of Rte. 6 with a smaller street forms the main intersection and the center of Sơn La. Entering town from the west, Rte. 6 is known as **Đường Điện Biên**. After the main intersection, Điện Biên becomes **Nguyễn Lương Bằng**. Entering town from the southeast, Rte. 6 is known as **Trường Chinh** and becomes **Chu Văn Thinh** after the main intersection. A left off of Trường Chinh onto Điện Biên will lead across a small bridge. Directly after the bridge, turning right from Điện Biên on **Tô Hiệu** leads past the **GPO**. After passing the park, Tô Hiệu curves to the east, hitting the end of Chu Văn Thinh at a rotary, before continuing northward out of town as Rte. 106. After the bridge, Điện Biên curves northward as it goes uphill to parallel Tô Hiệu. Sandwiched between Điện Biên and Tô Hiệu is the **Đồi Thanh Niên (Youth Hill)**, crowned by the prison and radio tower.

On the right side of the street, 100m down Chu Văn Thinh from the main intersection, is the brown, four-story **Bank for Agriculture and Rural Development,** where you can exchange currency. (☎852 409. Open M-Sa 7:30-11:30am and 1:30-4:30pm.) A large **market** (Chợ Trung Tam) sits 1km down Chu Văn Thinh from the main intersection and sells fresh fruit, meat, and vegetables along with clothes. The largest **pharmacy** in town is **Nhà Thuốc Trấn Minh Sáu**, 37Đ Điện Biên, just across the bridge. (☎852 905. Open daily 6:30am-10pm.) The **hospital** (☎852 325) is 2.5km down Tô Hiệu on the right. (Open daily 6am-6pm.) The **police station,** 53 Tô Hiệu (☎852 289), is nearby. The **GPO**, 200m down Tô Hiệu, has an international telephone office and **Internet** for 3000Đ per hr. (☎852 421. Open daily 6:30am-9pm.)

ACCOMMODATIONS

There are dozens of hotels in Sơn La, ranging from dingy dens of prostitution to snazzy accommodations offering all the amenities. Competition to fill rooms makes good deals even better, so bargain hard.

Nhà Nghỉ Thanh Bình, 7 Chu Văn Thinh (☎852 969), located 100m down from the main intersection across from the bank. Simple but pleasant rooms are some of the cleanest. Doubles with fan 100,000Đ, with A/C 120,000Đ; triples 140,000Đ. ❷

Nhà Nghỉ Hoa Ngọc, 6 Ngoi So 3 (☎350 133). Walk past the post office on Tô Hiệu and bear right at the first street. The guesthouse is 20m down on the right. The rooms are brand-new and very attractive, and all include A/C, TV, and fans; if you ask, they'll give you a room with a sparkling bathroom. Doubles 120,000Đ. ❷

Nhà Nghỉ Phương Bắc, 260 Tô Hiệu (☎857 589), between the post office and the park. Cramped lobby, but pleasant rooms with new amenities and access to a rooftop terrace. Be sure to bargain. Doubles with fan 120,000Đ, with A/C 140,000Đ. ❷

Hoa Hồng Hotel, 39 Đường 3-2 (☎854 301), 800m down Nguyễn Lương Bằng from the main intersection. Take a left after the second intersection. The bulky-looking (and slightly dilapidated) building has surprisingly clean and well-maintained rooms. A bit removed from the sights. Singles, doubles, and triples with bath and A/C 130,000Đ. ❷

Nhà Nghỉ Thu Hà, 282 Tô Hiệu (☎852 997), across from the park. The business advertises "Rest Room for rent," but it is possible to get a bed, too. Rooms are anything but special; all have fans. Singles 60,000Đ; doubles 80,000Đ; triples 90,000Đ. ❶

FOOD

The local brew, "Bia Sơn Dương," is on tap all over town. Though less tasty than "Bia Hà Nội," it has some kick to it, making up for the town's utter lack of nightlife.

Hải Phi Thịt Dê, 189 Điện Biên. For a local gastronomic specialty, head 800m up Điện Biên from the bridge; as the road curves past the War Memorial Park, look for the sign on the left. The name means "goat meat," which the cook will roast, stir-fry, or grill for 40,000-50,000Đ. We recommend it grilled. Open daily 11am-9pm. ❷

Nhân Đặt Cơm (☎854 444), on Tô Hiệu across from the park. A good local joint where you can eat a large Vietnamese meal for 10,000-15,000Đ. They're happy to fry up your favorite meat-and-veggie combo or, better yet, their delicious stew of thịt heo với dưa (pork with bamboo shoots) for a measly 10,000Đ. Open daily 6am-noon and 5-8pm. ❶

Hoàng Chương, 13 Trương Chinh (☎854 718), beside the main intersection, has a large buffet of local dishes for fair prices. Most dishes cost 5000-10,000Đ; the beef skewers and tofu are both safe bets. You can ask them to heat your food or cook something fresh. Open daily 6am-10pm. ❶

Nhà Háng Thanh Lanh, 96 Tô Hiệu, on the way to the post office. Fine Vietnamese standards in a bright, clean setting. Though the servings are small, the thịt bê (veal; 20,000Đ) is quite good. Open daily 10am-10pm. ❷

Nhà Háng Hop Dự, 452 Tô Hiệu (☎855 959), 1km up from the post office. Run by a smiling family that uses the food section of a phrasebook to take your order. Bean curd soup 5000Đ. Sweet-and-sour pork 20,000Đ. Open daily 7am-9pm. ❶

SIGHTS

NHÀ TÙ CŨ CỦA PHÁP (OLD FRENCH PRISON). The French first constructed a small local prison here in 1908. By the 1930s and 1940s, it was used to hold thousands of Vietnamese patriots; it now stands as a reminder of the French oppression of the Việt Minh. The complex was bombed in 1952 and most of the grounds have been left to stand in ruin. The left wing, however, has been reconstructed and now hosts an exhibit containing blueprints, artifacts, and photographs explaining the prison's history. A poem by Xuân Thủy stands above a diorama of the prison and its surroundings, setting the mood for your visit: "The four faces of the mountain sadden immense wild forests oppress by night the cold wind blows gently, but the days are covered with gloomy dew." (Something might be lost in translation, but you get the idea.) You can venture downstairs into the small, cramped cells where leg irons remain. The main yellow building, which once housed the prison guards, now hosts a small museum. The interior rooms contain some artifacts of local ethnic minorities, a photo history of the prison, and, naturally, several walls dedicated to the beloved Uncle Ho. *(To get there, head northwest on Điện Biên for 400m. Take the first right uphill onto Khẩu Cả and follow it to the top. The entrance to the prison is down a path to the right. Prison and museum open daily 7-11am and 1:30-5pm. 5000Đ for both.)*

LOOKOUT TOWER. For the best views of the town and its surroundings, there is a lookout tower on top of the hill behind the Công Đoàn Hotel. Take the paved path on the far side of the hotel for 100m. When it splits, go right and cut quickly onto the stone path. Try to ignore the intimidating dogs, who will not be pleased to see you. The round-trip hike takes 40min., and the steep climb is not for the weak, although a camera is definitely worth the extra weight. *(Free.)*

█ HIKING

Bản Bó is the closest Black Thài village to Sơn La, and makes for a pleasant trek. Head down Tô Hiệu straight past the post office and toward the town limits, where it becomes Lò Văn Giá. Roughly 3km down you will see a sign on the left side of the road with an arrow pointing to "Di Tích Hang Thẩm Tat Toòng," 450m farther. Follow the path, passing a swimming pool on your right. On the left, you will see a small shack in the rice paddies and a path beside it. This trail leads to **Tat Toòng Caves**, which, at the time of publication, had been placed off-limits. Ask at your hotel if they are again open for exploration. Back on the small paved road, turn left and continue toward Bản Bó. Stilt houses begin springing up soon after the path to the caves, and the road terminates after 3km. The area is beautiful and the village of Bản Bó is a charming and quiet place to visit.

For another hike, start down Tô Hiệu in the direction of Bản Bó and turn left in front of the guesthouse Khách Sạn Hoa Ban ❷ (at the intersection of Tô Hiệu and Chu Văn Thinh). Take the first right and walk for nearly 1km until you come to a small path on your left, marked by two small signs. One says "Gữ Xe" and the other reads "Có Bán Hương Vàng." This dirt road leads up to **Lê Thái Tông King's Temple**, whose Chinese architecture, complete with wooden doors and a wing-tipped roof, is remarkably beautiful. *(Officially open 7:30-11:30am and 1:30-5:30pm, but the gate often stays shut.)* **Stela Cave**, 200m to the right, contains a small altar near the entrance, but the path ends not far into the cave. While you can explore the smaller crevices of the cave, there are some enormous drops. If you're reckless enough to venture in, bring a very good flashlight and an even more reliable companion. *(Free.)*

MỘC CHÂU ☎ 22

Mộc Châu boasts some of Vietnam's best dairy and tea products, but little else. On Rte. 6 between Sơn La and Mai Châu, its location and elevation (1500m) makes for cool temperatures around 20°C in the summer. It's a pleasant stop and a fine place to spend the night. Every street in town leads into the beautiful countryside.

█ TRANSPORTATION. Buses often drop passengers off at the main intersection before pulling into the small station, 300m down Rte. 6 toward Hà Nội. There is a small office beside the lot, but it is difficult to buy a ticket there. Be persistent and

NORTHWEST HIGHLANDS

set a price before leaving. There is one bus daily to Hà Nội; it generally leaves between 5 and 7am, most often at 6am. Buses coming from Điện Biên Phủ on the way to Hà Nội also pick up passengers along Hwy. 6 until 1pm (50,000Đ). There are also departures to Sơn La (7, 9am, 1pm; 32,000Đ). To get to Mai Châu, take a Hà Nội-bound bus to Tòng Đạo (35,000Đ) and hire a *xe ôm* (6000-10,000Đ).

■ ♂ ORIENTATION AND PRACTICAL INFORMATION. Mộc Châu is 120km from Sơn La and 70km from Mai Châu. While there are patches of town scattered over several kilometers, most of the action is concentrated along Rte. 6 near the post office. **Đường Uỷ Ban Huyện** runs perpendicularly from Rte. 6 beside the GPO, creating a T that marks the center of town. The **GPO** has an international telephone and **Internet** for 3000Đ per hr. (☎860 160. Open daily 6:30am-9pm.) Across the street is the central **market,** which primarily sells tea, although other goods are up for grabs. (Open daily 7am-6pm.) The **police** station is down Đường Uỷ Ban Huyện (☎866 113), and a **hospital** (Bệnh Viện Nông Nghiệp) is roughly 5km up Rte. 6 toward Hà Nội (☎869 204). There is a **pharmacy** 100m down Đường Uỷ Ban Huyện across from the hotel. (☎866 518. Open daily 7am-10pm.) Of the three banks in town, none exchange currency.

♂ ♦ ACCOMMODATIONS AND FOOD. The few hotels in Mộc Châu are all close enough together that you can shop around easily, using one set of prices to bring down another. Prices typically tend to reflect quality. **Khách Sạn Hương Sen ❷,** across from the post office, offers the best and quietest rooms in town. (☎866 174. Doubles 120,000Đ.) **Nhà Nghỉ Bình Nguyễn ❷** is across the bus station on Rte. 6. Though the location is convenient, the newest rooms may also be noisy at night. (☎866 398. Doubles 120,000Đ.) **Nhà Nghỉ Đức Dũng ❷,** 100m down from the post office on Đường Uỷ Ban Huyện, has basic rooms. Feel free to bargain. (☎866 181. Doubles 120,000Đ; triples 150,000Đ.)

Spending any amount of time in Mộc Châu will likely influence you to become a dairy fanatic. The ▧**sữa chua**—something like yogurt—is sweet and incredibly fresh. For a delicious dessert, ask for *sữa lạnh*, an icy, creamy, blissful cup of frozen sugar. Both local specialties cost a modest 1500-3000Đ and can be purchased at the shops along Rte. 6. **Bánh Ngọt Hồng Nhương ❶,** 300m on the left as you head toward Hà Nội from the GPO, also sells *bánh sữa* (milk cake; 2000Đ), another local specialty. Perhaps more appropriately called butter cake, it consists of a piece of fluffy bread doused in butter. (Open daily 6am-8pm.) In town itself, good meals are elusive. A friendly family runs **Các Món Ăn ❷,** 280m toward Hà Nội. For a rapturous 20,000Đ, you may enjoy a hefty serving of soup with veggies thrown in, a steaming bowl of rice, and a large meat dish—the beef is quite good. If you don't like pepper, make that very clear. As always, phở is also available for 6000Đ. (Open daily 6am-9pm.) **Quang Thắng Phở Bò ❶,** across from Nhà Nghỉ Đức Dũng and next to the pharmacy on Đường Uỷ Ban Huyện, serves decent Vietnamese standards in a clean setting. Most dishes cost 10,000-15,000Đ. Act like you know what you're doing to avoid being ripped off. (☎866 551. Open daily 6am-9pm.)

◙ SIGHTS. Hang Dơi Cave is 400m past the center of Mộc Châu, on the right as you head toward Sơn La. It's perched atop 240 stairs, which are marked by a sign on Rte. 6, and flaunts some excellent views. A guard sits by the door from 8am-6pm; bargain the entrance fee from 5000Đ down to 3000Đ. The cave has several skylights that allow enough sun in to highlight the first of the stalagmite-filled chambers. To go farther into the cave, you'll need to bring along a flashlight. There is also a nice waterfall near Mộc Châu known as **Thác Thái Hưng;** the easiest way to get there might be to draw a picture of a *xe ôm* driver and write "H₂0" beside it. To visit Thác Thái Hưng on your own, head out of town on Rte. 6 toward Sơn La. You will see a sign pointing 600m to Bệnh Viện Mộc Châu (Mộc Châu Hospital). Turn left on this road and follow it past the hospital to its end, before bearing left. Follow this beautiful stretch of paved road roughly 6km out of town. The falls run below the road; despite their size, you need to keep a keen eye out to spot them. A small dirt path leads from the road down to the base of the falls. Take the footpath over the small bridge and cut left through the corn fields. If the path is steep and treacherous, you're going the correct way. The slope of loose rocks leads down until you're practically beneath the falls. Thác Thái Hung is dwarfed by Thác Bac in Sa Pa and Thác Bán Giốc near Cao Bằng, but it is impressive nonetheless and remains entirely undeveloped. A *xe ôm* round-trip from the post office to the falls costs 20,000Đ. If you have time, continue along the road for a while as it becomes even more isolated and beautiful farther out from Mộc Châu.

MAI CHÂU   ☎ 18

Surrounded by steep mountains and stunning rice paddies, tiny Mai Châu is a refreshing change of pace in a region packed with challenging travel opportunities. Just outside of town, the White Thài villages of Bản Làc and Pom Coọng allow visitors to step into Thài life by spending nights in stilt houses, eating home-cooked meals, and observing rural Thài and Vietnamese culture. Whether sipping tea under palm-leafed roofs with a host family or venturing out to nearby hills and villages, you'll find Mai Châu an accessible gateway into the slow and peaceful White Thài lifestyle. Those looking to escape into the silence of the countryside, however, will leave disappointed—you'll wake to the hum of motorbikes and chatter of TV soap operas. These are, after all, the sounds of modern Vietnam.

⊑ TRANSPORTATION. Buses depart from the station for Hòa Bình (2-3hr.; 6, 6:30, 7, 10am, 12:30pm; 25,000Đ). From there, you can catch frequent buses to Hà Nội. You can also take a **motorcycle taxi** from Mai Châu to Tòng Đậu (6000-10,000Đ) and catch a bus from there to Hà Nội (40,000-50,000Đ) or Sơn La (3hr.; 40,000Đ) via Mộc Châu. Locals can tell you when to expect buses (as early as 6am).

⛏🛈 ORIENTATION AND PRACTICAL INFORMATION. Mai Châu is 140km west of Hà Nội and 6km from Tòng Đậu, which is at the junction of Rte. 6 and Rte. 15. The entire town stretches along 1.5km of **Route 15,** from the post office at the northern end to the Mai Châu Guest House at the opposite end. About halfway between the two, at kilometer zero, is the **market,** across from the bus station.

The **bank** is two blocks before the GPO from the market. (☎867-258. Currency exchange. Open 7:30-11:30am and 1:30-5pm.) The largest **pharmacy** is on the main road 100m south of the market. (☎867 129. Open daily 6am-7pm.) Another 200m in the same direction is **Bệnh Viện Mai Châu hospital.** (☎867 244. Open daily summer 7-11am and 1:30-5:30pm, winter 7:30-11:30am and 1-5pm.) There are three **Internet** cafes in town: one charges foreigners US$1 per hr., another 7000Đ per hr., and the last 4000Đ per hr. This last option is near the hospital on the way to the market. (Open daily 8-11:30am and 1:30-11pm.) The **post office** is 500m north of the market, with international telephone and fax services but no calling card access. It also has Internet for 3000Đ per hr. (☎867 209. Open daily 7am-9pm.)

🏠🍴 ACCOMMODATIONS AND FOOD. Mai Châu's unique accommodations are its primary attraction. **Pom Coọng** and **Bản Lác** are the most popular White Thài villages that provide lodging to tourists. The villages are next to each other off Rte. 15 on a semicircular detour. Pom Coọng is the closer and quieter of the two, located a few hundred meters into the rice paddies on the road that branches to the right beside the Mai Châu Guest House. A majority of the traditional stilt houses now serve as **guest-houses ❶,** and for 40,000-50,000Đ visitors can sleep on a floor mat in the main room. Mosquito nets are provided. One particularly nice house lies near the entrance of Pom Coọng village. To get there, walk down the road from Rte. 15, take a right at the small junction, and turn left into the first small street that you come to. At the end of the row, at **Number 28 ❶** (☎ 867 318), you'll find Ms. Chung, who speaks a bit of English. The food is good, the family is welcoming, and the toilet is Western. In Bản Lác, the nicest views are available from the **guesthouse ❶** at the entrance of the village. For an extra 30,000-40,000Đ, Bản Lác families also serve a filling Vietnamese dinner. The meals are generally quite good, especially compared to the lack of culinary delights in Mai Châu proper. In addition to these homestays, there are two standard accommodations in town. The **Mai Châu Guest House ❶** is by the lake at the end of town farthest from Tòng Đậu. A modern exterior and a haunted-house-like interior await. The large rooms have balconies with views of the surrounding rice paddies. (☎ 867 262. Singles and doubles 70,000-100,000Đ.) **Nhà Nghỉ Ngọc Bách ❸**, on the west side of Rte. 15, is the only place in town with good air-conditioning. Its pleasant terraces lack good views. (☎ 867 340. Overpriced doubles US$15; highly negotiable.)

Culinary choices in Mai Châu proper are few. The **market** sells fruit, vegetables, and deep-fried pastries. Full meals can be purchased at phở shops. **Hoàng Anh Cóm Phở ❷**, just after the bridge on the right heading toward the post office, offers generous portions of standard Vietnamese fare. The *bo sáo* (beef and green bean stir-fry) comes with soup and rice for 25,000Đ. (☎ 867 752. Open daily 7am-11pm.) If you've been in rural Vietnam and are used to local prices, prepare to be frustrated in Mai Châu—even after intense bargaining, the cost of goods remains inflated.

◙ SIGHTS. There are a couple of neat caves and plenty of ethnic villages in the hills surrounding Mai Châu. Across Rte. 15 from the hospital, a paved side-street is marked with a sign pointing to **Hang Chiều**, an impressive cave hidden by thick brush and a twisting bonsai tree. This street soon meets a massive stairway ascending a mountain slope. Over 1000 steps later, you will arrive at a tiny landing that marks the entrance to the cave. The stairmaster never burned as bad as this climb does, but it also never rewarded you with such spectacular views. Catch your breath and head into the cave, where stalactites abound. The path drops steeply to the chamber floor, from which point you can explore freely. While the first compartment is well lit, venturing farther into the cave requires a flashlight.

Nearby **Hang Mỏ Luông cave** is a must-see for cave enthusiasts, and it has some areas where flashlights are not required. Stalagmites sparkle, bats flutter around you, and after it rains, you'll be ducking through tunnels in knee-deep water. The entrance to the cave (10,000Đ) is up a flight of stairs opposite the Mai Châu Guesthouse. The cave stays locked; come in the morning and be ready to wait while someone fetches a key from the hotel—or you can make an appointment the day before at the drink stand out front. While the paved floor and graffiti in the first chamber detract from the spirit of the space, all is forgotten once you climb the ladder into the tunnels. Lights have been strung up roughly 400m into the cave; you can go farther, but you will have to bring your own flashlight.

Another option is to spend an afternoon or overnight at the well-manicured village of **Bản Văn**, 1km from Mai Châu. The village offers homestays with fewer tourists than Pom Coọng and Bắc Làc. The road to Bản Văn is well marked, beginning on the right side of Rte. 15 just north of the market. At the far end of the village the road turns to gravel and does a short loop before coming back to the village's paved entrance. While not adventuresome, the trip is undoubtedly pretty.

▶ DAYTRIPS FROM MAI CHÂU. The town of Mai Châu is an excellent hub from which to explore the surrounding hills and valleys, which are densely populated with White Thài villagers. Some roads are paved, while others are no more than narrow muddy lanes or rough mountain trails. All villages can be reached by foot and many are accessible by bicycle, which some guesthouses rent for 20,000-25,000Đ per day. Get psyched to push your rusty wreck to its limits, and be sure to check the brakes before heading out. Guesthouse Number 28 in Pom Coọng has the newest—and priciest—bikes for rent (60,000Đ per day). Even if your vehicle disappoints, rest assured that Mai Châu is one of Vietnam's few locales where getting lost doesn't automatically equate with getting stranded—everyone will happily point the way. If you're still not convinced, get a local **guide** in either Pom Coọng or Bản Lác to show you around. Guides are necessary on more remote routes and multi-day treks in the Mai Châu area (100,000Đ per day), such as the popular **Bản Lác-Bản Xa Linh** trek. This two-day, 18km trek climbs 600m in altitude and ends at the H'mông village of Xa Linh, near Rte. 6. Another option is to plan your trip with the Hòa Bình Hotel I (p. 230).

HIKES THROUGH CHIỀNG SAI, XÒM CHA, BẢ CHA LONG, XĂM PÀ, NÀ CʺT, AND BẢ NA TÀNG VILLAGES. All of the villages on these trails have seen their fair share of visitors. Nonetheless, you're more likely to hear a "hello" in English than the all-too-familiar call of "money, money" that echoes along the more frequented circuits. From Mai Châu, take the street across Rte. 15 to Bản Văn, which runs directly into **Chiềng Sại** village. There, you can work in a rice paddy for the day. Continue straight over the bridge to a fork. The road to the left ends along the mountainside; the right path is an access route to more rice paddies used by local farmers. Stretching for nearly 2km, this muddy route offers the ideal opportunity to get down and dirty in the paddies that have been feeding you, in addition to providing you with choice photo ops. Heading out into the knee-deep slosh, you'll likely receive brief instructions and a wide smile before being set to work. The path eventually reaches **Xòm Cha,** where you'll be confronted by three roads. The paved road to the right leads back to Rte. 15, 2km from the Mai Châu market, but the path to the left, which cuts deeper into the mountains, soon reaches **Bả Cha Long.** Here, the path narrows, skirting corn fields, before arriving at a small drainage in the brush, with a rusty blue sign secured overhead. This drainage is used by locals as a bridge; crossing it and heading farther up leads to **Xăm Pà,** where there is another small herd path cutting through brush. The trail curves left and climbs to **Nà Cụt.** Unless you hike to Nà Cụt and circle back down to Mai Châu on the other side of the mountains to a paved road, you'll have to retrace your steps to Bả Cha Long and back to the three paths at Xòm Cha. The third, central path acts almost as an extension of the trail from Mai Châu to Bả Cha Long, running perpendicular to Rte. 15 through rice paddies. Crossing a decrepit, wooden bridge onto the knife-edge path, you'll soon come to **Bả Na Tàng,** leading out to Rte. 15.

HIKES THROUGH NÀ PHÒN, BẢN NHÓT, PIỀNG PHUNG, BẢN NẢ MÉO, AND NẢ CʺT VILLAGES. From the Rte. 15 turn-off to Bản Lác, turn onto the road branching left, circumventing the village. Cross over Cầu Lác and continue straight until the dirt path begins to curve back toward Rte. 15, at which time you should cross the small river (or riverbed, depending on the season). Follow this trail to **Nà Phòn.** For a small and worthy detour, hike a few hundred meters and cut right along the drainage to the opposite side of the rice paddies. From there, you can follow a path up to the top of the mountain for views over the valley. Back on the "main" trail, you'll soon be in Nà Phòn, which has seen plenty of visitors but has yet to lose its earthy charm. When the trail splits in town, take a sharp right; this trail connects to a sidewalk. Continue out to the paved road, where you'll find yourself in the heart of **Bản Nhót** village. Five hundred meters farther down this road leads to **Piềng Phung** on the left, where the slope steepens for a kilometer and ends at an intersection along a gushing river. Following the road left brings you to **Bản Nả Méo.** Better yet, turn right up the sidewalk into **Nả Cụt** village. High, peaceful, and pavement-free, Nả Cụt is one of the better villages in the Mai Châu valley. Trails branch in all directions, and everyone, it seems, will be happy to point you the way to Xăm Pà or the remote path down to Rte. 15 through Xòm Cha. It's also possible to retrace your steps down the paved road; instead of turning off at Bản Nhót, continue down to Mai Châu and Rte. 15. For those who battled through the tour on a bike (which is possible despite the warnings), the long downhill from Nả Cụt is quite a reward. The only exercise you'll be getting is with your brake hand.

ROUTE 15 TO CO LƯƠNG AND TURN-OFFS. The quiet village of **Co Lương** is set beside a river with a sheer wall of rock towering behind it. Local Thài have adopted Western clothing and there is little to see in town. Beyond Co Lương, Rte. 15 follows the Mã River with beautiful panoramas of limestone karsts in the background. The 15km stretch connecting Mai Châu and Co Lương is paved and perfect for a bicycle or motorbike. Along the way are a succession of Thài villages, bamboo groves, and roads branching into the rice paddies. The first turn-off is 2km from Mai Châu proper, just before the "Van Mai 9km" road marker. Once over a bridge, the trail turns to dirt. Continue straight through a football pitch onto the small, rough path. The trail loops for roughly 1.5km, spilling out onto the pavement near Cầu Lác, beside Bản Lác village. The second turn-off goes to **Mai Hạ.** The road is rough but passable on a motorbike. Just on the other side of the rice paddies is the small town of **Tiên Phong;** the leftward path then continues a few more kilometers to Mai Hạ (about 5km from Mai Châu). This is an unspectacular route, save for the fact that it sees virtually no visitors. The third turn-off is marked "Khoè 9km," pointing the way to **Xăm Khoè,** a village advertised as a trekking destination by Hà Nội travel agencies. It is home to both Thài and Mường residents, who now live in similar stilt houses. It is difficult for most Westerners to distinguish between the two groups. You'll need a **guide** trek the 14km to Khoè on local paths. **Homestays ❶** in the village are permitted. (50,000Đ for a mat on the floor.)

HÒA BÌNH ☎ 18

For many travelers, Hòa Bình functions as the gateway either to or from the Northwest Highlands. Having absorbed more of the raucous charm of Hà Nội than the silent beauty of the northwest, the streets remain noisy and active. Mountains tease the outskirts of town toward Sơn La; the sights found within them are an underwhelming primer for Mai Châu and other remote regional destinations. The nearby Sông Đà Reservoir is the area's most impressive feature.

▐ TRANSPORTATION

The **bus station** (☎853 378) is on Trần Hưng Đạo, directly across from the post office. There are daily **buses** to: Hải Phòng (6am; 26,000Đ); Hà Nội (1½hr.; 10-15min. after the hour 5:15am-6pm; 18,000Đ); HCMC (2pm; 265,000Đ); Kim Bôi (7 per day 5:30am-noon; 12,000Đ); Mai Châu (1hr.; 5:45, 10am, noon, 2pm; 20,000Đ); Thái Nguyên (7:15am, 1:50pm; 30,000Đ). Note that the Hà Nội bus terminates at Hà Đông province, 13km from the city center.

✳ ORIENTATION

Hòa Bình is located 74km southwest of Hà Nội. Rte. 6 follows the **Đà River** and becomes **Đường Cù Chính Lan** in town, Hòa Bình's main drag. As this road heads southwest toward Mai Châu, it turns sharply to the left and becomes **An Đường Vương.** At this turn, **Đường Đà Giang** bears right, and 5km later becomes **Bích Hạ Port** on the reservoir. Running parallel to Đường Cù Chính Lan through most of the town center, **Đường Trần Hưng Đạo** hits An Đường Vương roughly 1km toward Sơn La. Back in the town center, a huge bridge, **Cầu Hòa Bình,** turns off Đường Cù Chính Lan to cross the Đà River.

NORTHWEST HIGHLANDS

▨ PRACTICAL INFORMATION

The **Khách Sạn Hòa Bình I (Hòa Bình Hotel I)**, 2km down Rte. 6 after it turns toward Mai Châu, doubles as a **tourist office**, organizing tours of Mai Châu and the surrounding area. (☎858 796 or 858 910. US$20-30 per person per day for groups under 10 people.) For currency exchange, head up Rte. 6 from the police station and the **bank** will be on your left just before the sharp turn. (☎852 769. Open daily 7-11:30am and 1:30-5pm.) The **Bank for Foreign Investment and Development of Vietnam** will also change currency; they are located on Trần Hưng Đạo near the intersection with Rte. 6. (☎854 359. Open daily 7-11:30am and 1:30-5pm.) Đường Nguyễn Trung Trực serves as a **market** for fruit and wares—to get there, turn left off Rte. 6 roughly 200m southwest of the bridge. The **hospital** (☎857 644) is 2km down Rte. 6 from the bridge, in the direction of Hà Nội. Across the street is the largest **pharmacy** (with the longest name) in town, **Trung Tâm Dược Phẩm Mỹ Phẩm Hòa Bình**. (☎852 373. Open daily 7am-9pm.) The **police** (☎852 723) are on the left side of Rte. 6 as you continue toward Sơn La. There are **Internet** cafes clustered across from the bridge on Đường Chi Lăng. All charge 3000Đ per hr. and have temperamental connections. The connection at **25 Đường Chi Lăng** is the best. Across from the bus station, roughly 800m farther down Trần Hưng Đạo, is the **GPO** with international calling booths. (☎853 805. Open daily 7-11:30am and 1-5pm.)

▨ ACCOMMODATIONS

Most hotels are clustered on and around Rte. 6 near the bridge.

Nhà Nghỉ Hiệu Nhung (☎853 029). Walk from the bridge toward Sơn La, pass the market, and bear left onto Chi Hội 8. Cozy and attractive rooms with A/C, TV, private bath, and small balconies. Doubles with fan 100,000Đ, with A/C 120,000Đ. ❷

Khách Sạn Tháp Vàng, 213 Đường Cù Chính Lan (☎852 864), just up Rte. 6 from the bridge. A classy establishment set off of the main street. Rooms have wooden furniture, A/C, TV, and ceiling fans. Singles 150,000Đ; doubles 230,000Đ; triples 250,000Đ. ❷

Hà Giang Hotel, 18/6 Đường Cù Chính Lan (☎852 337), before the Đường Đà Giang turn-off. A double staircase, a terrace with city views, and an iguana tank in the lobby distinguish this hotel from others. Its location on the main drag, with traffic outside and karaoke inside, doesn't. Air-conditioned doubles 120,000Đ; triples 180,000Đ. ❷

Khách Sạn Hoàng Gia, 12/25 Đường Chi Lăng (☎853 634), on Rte. 6 across from the bridge. Slightly worn rooms with A/C and TV. Doubles 150,000Đ. ❸

Nhà Nghỉ Bình Dân (☎894 012), 500m down Trần Hưng Đạo from the bus station toward Mai Châu. This bare-bones establishment has rooms with TVs, fans, and uncomfortable beds. Singles with fan 60,000Đ; doubles with fan 100,000Đ; singles and doubles with A/C and private bath 120,000Đ. ❶

▨ FOOD

Quality food options are more difficult to find than good hotels in Hòa Bình. Then again, it's hard to go wrong with phở.

Nhà Sản Tối Thanh (☎853 951), on the left side of Rte. 6, just 5min. from the bridge toward Hà Nội. A lengthy English menu that is geared toward more adventurous eaters. Standard dishes include potato and carrot soup (6000Đ), deer (40,000Đ), and wild boar (40,000Đ), but iguana, snake, and, everyone's favorite, *tiết dúi* (mole blood) also grace the menu. Adventurous meats are in stock randomly. Open daily 7am-11pm. ❷

Nhà Sạn Hiền Lương (☎857 238), beside Nhà Sạn Tới Thanh. No menu and little variety. Nonetheless, the food remains a step above other local hangouts. They're big on deer (30,000Đ). Fried tofu 5000Đ. Open daily 7am-10pm. ❷

Phở Bò Gia Truyền Nam Định (☎683 256), 80m before Rte. 6 turns sharply toward Mai Châu. No frills and nothing special, but it does serve one of the better bowls of phở in Hòa Bình (7000Đ). Open daily 5am-10pm. ❶

Cơm Rang, Mỳ Tôm (☎856 664), on Ngô Quyền beside Nhà Nghỉ Hiệu Nhung. The lady behind the counter has her hands full frying, boiling, and chopping to prepare meals for hungry locals. The table of meats, phở, and veggies serves as the menu. Entrees around 20,000Đ. Open mid-day until late; breakfast is next door at its identical counterpart. ❶

🄶 SIGHTS

Hòa Bình is known more as a gateway to Mai Châu than for its own sights. While the surroundings are not home to the same captivating scenery found elsewhere in the northwest, it's worth poking around before moving on.

■SỐNG ĐÀ RESERVOIR. Located 5km up Đường Đà Giang, which cuts off from Rte. 6 in Hòa Bình proper, this splendid reservoir stretches for 200km. Formed during the construction of the Hòa Bình hydroelectric dam, the power station is one of Vietnam's largest. The 200m walk up Đường Đà Giang to see the impressive dam wall is probably the best activity in Hòa Bình. Directly across the Đà River, a large orange-and-red-roofed memorial stands to honor the 161 workers who perished during the dam's construction. You can pay your respects to a colossal statue of Hồ Chí Minh by climbing the stairs to the top of the dam and following the road up a hill to the left. This point also offers a beautiful panorama of the city below. *(It is possible to travel over the dam wall out to Bích Ha port and take a public or private boat out onto the reservoir. You can also rent a private boat from Khách Sạn Hòa Bình I (p. 230), which will take you to visit the Mường village of Vấy Nưa and the Dao village of Dương. 4hr.; US$30 for a boat with 1- to 15-person capacity.)*

KIM BÔI "HOT" SPRINGS. Kim Bôi Hot Springs, located 32km west of Hòa Bình, is, strangely enough, rumored to be the best place in Vietnam to buy inner tubes. The spring water is suitable to drink and allegedly has medicinal properties. Water is pumped into two large indoor swimming pools filled with gossiping Vietnamese. Kim Bôi is disappointingly tepid during the summer months, but the water reaches 36°C during the winter. Phở shops and guesthouses now surround the complex, preying on its popularity with Vietnamese tourists. *(11km west of Hòa Bình, a sign indicates the 25km road to Kim Bôi. This stretch of paved road is arguably the highlight of the trip, as it meanders through gorgeous hills and rice paddies. 4km before Kim Bôi, an inauspicious blue sign reads "Điểm Du Lịch Tắm Nước Khoáng Nong Kim Bôi." Take a sharp left here and travel 500m to the entrance gate. Open daily 6am-6pm. 10,000Đ.)*

BẢ TANG HÒA BÌNH (HÒA BÌNH MUSEUM). This small museum, located on Rte. 6 as it turns to the northwest, has an enthusiastic staff and two rooms that contain excavations and artifacts dating back to 10,000 BC. There are bronze drums dating back to the 14th century, ceramics from the 12th century, and a Mường stilt house with a loom. *(☎852 177. Open M-F 8-10:30am and 2-4:30pm. Free.)*

XÓM MÔN VILLAGE. This small Mường village is worth visiting en route to Kim Bôi or as an alternative to Mai Châu. Locals no longer wear traditional attire, but they produce plenty to sell to tourists. The village has been officially approved by the government for tourist visits. At the end of the village, the paved sidewalk turns to dirt and climbs into the unexciting hills nearby. *(To visit Xóm Môn, head 5km out of Hòa Bình on Rte. 6 toward Mộc Châu. Bear right at the sign to Cảng Thương Lư; it is 6km down this road to the village entrance.)*

NORTHERN CENTRAL VIETNAM

Rushing from Hà Nội or Hội An, most visitors opt to skip over the treasures of Northern Central Vietnam. Removed from the traditional backpacker beat and deprived of the safe comforts of catered travel packages, a zigzag through the region offers foreign visitors a truer taste of Vietnamese life. Vietnamese visitors are mesmerized by Kênh Gà and Tam Cốc's golden rice paddies topped with limestone mountains, the majestic grottoes of Phong Nha adorned with rocky formations that fire the imagination, and the mountainous coastlines that cruise over turbulent waters near the Ngang Pass. Those who take their time in the north find that the locals there are the friendliest in the country. Farther south, the countryside turns to jungles that sprawl across the Lao border. Rejuvenated by time, abandoned battlefields, bomb shelter tunnels, and cemeteries become more numerous as the roads approach the old divide between North and South, now known as the Demilitarized Zone. The city of Huế is the jewel of central Vietnam—as the ancient imperial capital, it is surrounded by grand tombs of intricate architecture and spotted with peaceful lotus ponds. Its historical ambience provides a tantalizing taste of the concentrated old-town beauty found in nearby Hội An, while its streets are spiced with culture and some of the country's—and the world's—best food.

HIGHLIGHTS OF NORTHERN CENTRAL VIETNAM

RELIVE THE IMPERIAL DAYS in mellow **Huế** (p. 270), where the citadel and royal tombs recall ancient glory. The city's remarkable cuisine is also insanely good.

TAKE MANY, MANY PHOTOS of the magnificent landscape at **Kênh Gà** (p. 238) and **Tam Cốc** (p. 237); rafts take travelers among towers of sheer limestone rising up from the rice paddies. Ninh Bình province has one of the most amazing natural landscapes in the country, as well as a famous **cathedral** (p. 239).

ESCAPE ALL TOURISTS AND INFRASTRUCTURE in **Hà Tĩnh Province** (p. 252). Pristine beaches and lonely hilltop pagodas accentuate the undisturbed natural beauty.

LET THE HOURS SLIP INTO THE OCEAN atop the rocky cliffs of **Sầm Sơn Beach** (p. 245) as you sip milk straight from a coconut.

SAVOR THE RAINFOREST of eminently accessible **Bạch Mã National Park** (p. 290), featuring hikes past waterfalls and to summits with spectacular views.

VISIT ABANDONED BATTLEFIELDS in the **DMZ** (p. 264), either solo or by tour from Huế or Đông Hà. The weathered relics of the bitter, tragic struggle are deeply moving.

NINH BÌNH ☎ 30

One day, travelers will wise up and notice that Ninh Bình is more than just a rest-stop on the way to Hà Nội or Huế. Until then, one of the most beautiful parts of

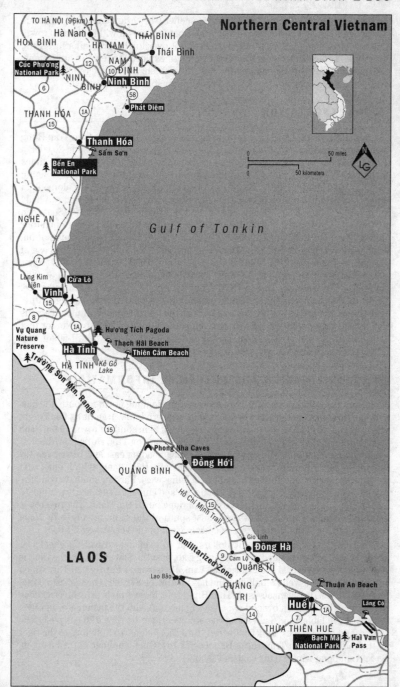

TO HÀ NỘI (96km)

Hà Nam

HÒA BÌNH

HÀ NAM

THÁI BÌNH

Thái Bình

Northern Central Vietnam

Cúc Phương
National Park

NINH

BÌNH

NAM
ĐỊNH

Ninh Bình

Phát Diệm

6

12

10

58

1A

THANH HÓA

15

Thanh Hóa

Sầm Sơn

Bến En
National Park

0   50 miles

0   50 kilometers

NGHÊ AN

Gulf of Tonkin

7

Làng Kim
Liên

Cửa Lò

Vinh

15

8

Vụ Quang
Nature
Preserve

1A

Hương Tích Pagoda

Thạch Hải Beach

Hà Tĩnh

Thiên Cầm Beach

HÀ TĨNH

Kẻ Gỗ
Lake

Trường Sơn Mtn. Range

15

Phong Nha Caves

QUẢNG BÌNH

Đồng Hới

Hồ Chí Minh Trail

15

LAOS

Demilitarized Zone

Gio Linh

Đông Hà

Cam Lộ

Quảng Trị

9

Lao Bảo

QUẢNG
TRỊ

Thuận An Beach

Huế

Lăng Cô

14

7

1A

THỪA THIÊN HUẾ

Bạch Mã
National Park

Hải Vân
Pass

Vietnam is yours for the taking. Dramatic scenery, historical intrigues, religious pilgrimage sites, and an endangered animal sanctuary are all within 50km of town. A slowly blossoming city, Ninh Bình itself is not overflowing with alluring sights, but instead serves as an ideal base from which to explore the region's attractions. Accommodations here are among the best in Vietnam; an intense (and hilarious) rivalry among lodging choices keeps prices reasonable and quality high.

TRANSPORTATION

The **bus station** is on Lê Đại Hành opposite the bridge that connects to Trần Hùng Đạo. **Buses** leave for: Hải Phòng (6hr.; 5:45, 6:30, 7:15am, noon, 1, 2pm; 20,000Đ); Hà Nội (1½-2hr.; every 15min. 5am-5pm; 25,000Đ); HCMC (42hr.; 6am, 3-5 times per week; 211,000Đ); and Phát Diệm/Kim Sơn (50min.; every hr. 7am-5:30pm; 7000Đ). Additional buses to Hà Nội can be flagged down anywhere along Trần Hùng Đạo. Another option is to catch one of the many **tourist buses** that run daily to Hà Nội (1½-2hr.; 5:30, 7:30am; US$3-4) and Huế (11hr.; 9pm; US$8-9). Seats can be booked at any hotel, but the best seats are usually taken as part of open-tour tickets. The **train station** lies at the end of Hoàng Hoa Thám. From the bus station, walk north two blocks on Lê Đại Hành and turn right; the road ends at the base of the station. **Trains** go to: Hà Nội (2-3½hr.; 5 per day; 26,000-60,000Đ); HCMC (40hr.; 404,000-920,000Đ); Huế (12½-15hr.; 134,000-282,000Đ); Vinh (3-5hr.; 30,000-130,000Đ). If traveling to Huế or HCMC, buy your ticket at least a day in advance. To get to Vinh, arrive no later than 15min. before the train's scheduled departure. Train times and prices are posted on a bulletin outside the main entrance. There is also a local **taxi** service. (☎876 876; www.universe.fpt.vn. 14,000Đ per km for first 2km, 7000Đ per km next 3-20km, 5000Đ per km for the following 21-50km, and 2000Đ per km or negotiable for longer journeys.)

ORIENTATION AND PRACTICAL INFORMATION

Ninh Bình lies 96km south of Hà Nội on Hwy. 1A. Running north to south, the narrow **Van River** bisects the town center. On its western bank, **Trần Hưng Đạo** (Highway 1A) runs parallel to the river before crossing it 2km south of town. **Lê Đại Hành** runs parallel to the river's eastern bank. Heading south on Trần Hưng Đạo, the first major intersection in town is with **Lê Hồng Phong** heading east and **Lương Văn Tuý** heading west. The next major intersection is with **Vân Giang,** which goes east toward the market, and **Trương Hang Sieu,** heading west. Farther south, beyond the radio tower, Trần Hưng Đạo goes over a bridge and curves to run nearly parallel to Lê Đại Hành. The bus station is across this bridge on Lê Đại Hành. The two roads eventually merge 3km south of town. Just south of the radio tower, **Lý Tự Trọng** heads west from Trần Hưng Đạo and ends in front of the **hospital** (☎871 030).

Hotels will exchange đồng for dollars, but to exchange traveler's checks or obtain a cash advance, head up Trần Hưng Đạo, past the Star Hotel. On the right is the brand new **Industrial and Commercial Bank of Vietnam**, 1 Lương Văn Tuý, which is housed in a large yellow building and has an **ATM.** (☎872 675. Open M-Sa 7-11am and 1-4:30pm.) The **pharmacy** is on Trần Hưng Đạo. Many hotels provide easy **Internet** access, though it's slow and expensive compared with the cybercafes in town. Access is available at 58 Trần Hưng Đạo for 5000Đ per hr. The **GPO** has post, telephone, and fax services; look for the red "Bưu Điện" sign two buildings to the right of the radio tower on Trần Hưng Đạo. (☎871 104. Open summer M-F 6am-10pm, Sa-Su 7am-9pm; winter daily 6:30am-9:30pm.)

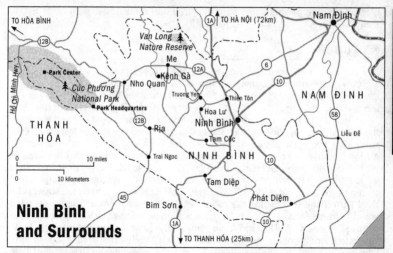

Ninh Bình
and Surrounds

ACCOMMODATIONS

In anticipation of the town's increasing popularity, new hotels pop up almost daily. All accommodations offer restaurants, bike rentals for US$1 per day, motorbike rentals for US$4-5 per day, tourist information, and tours of the surroundings. Guests are not obliged to rent only the services of their hotel, as those right next store may be much cheaper. **Queen Mini Hotel ❶**, 21 Hoàng Hoa Thám, 150m from the train station, has some of the best deals in town and a helpful and smiling staff. It's home to the excellent English-speaking guide, Luong, who organizes tours throughout Vietnam. (☎871 874; luongvn2001@yahoo.com. Tiny single with fan and no bath US$4; comfortable rooms with bath and A/C US$5-15.) The English- and German-speaking owners of **Thanh Thuy's Guest House ❶**, 128 Lê Hồng Phong, just off of Trần Hưng Đạo, have added a new wing with sparkling bathrooms and powder-white walls to join their older (but still clean) rooms. (☎871 811; fax 880 441. Sturdy Japanese mountain bikes 15,000Đ per day, Chinese models 8000Đ. Internet 3000Đ per hr. Private massage 50,000Đ per hr. Laundry 10,000-15,000Đ per kg. Tiny attic single with fan US$2; old doubles with fan and bathtub US$5-6; new, spacious doubles with private bath and fan US$8, with A/C US$10-20.) **New Guest House ❶**, right next door to the train station, is a family operation offering small but clean rooms. (☎872 137; fax 874 252. Doubles with bath, TV, and fan 70,000-80,000Đ, with A/C 100,000Đ.) **Kinh Đô ❷**, 99 Phan Đình Phùng, located one block north of Vân Giang off of Trần Hưng Đạo, has some older rooms as well as newer luxurious ones, the latter of which bask in a twist of imperial culture with carved wooden furniture. (☎871 352; kinhdohotel-nb@hn.vnn.vn. Older rooms with fan 120,000Đ; newer rooms with A/C 150,000Đ.) One of the quietest options in town is the **Nhà Nghỉ Quốc Bình ❷**, located in a residential district away from the train station and noisy streets. From Trần Hưng Đạo, turn west onto Trương Hang Sieu and walk for 150m. Turn right onto An Thành; watch for the "Nhà Nghỉ" sign. (☎881 605. Doubles with fan 120,000Đ, with A/C 150,0000Đ; triples with A/C 180,000Đ.) **Thuy Anh Hotel ❷**, 55 Trương Han Sieu, in the center of town, has luxurious rooms at hefty prices. The English-speaking staff can arrange full-day tours (US$18-22) and motorbike rentals (US$6 per day). Internet is available for 500Đ per min. (☎871 602; fax 876 934. Free transport to and from train and bus stations.

Overpriced, tiny rooms with fan and shared bathroom US$7, with A/C US $10. Doubles with A/C and bath US$15-35. MC/V.)

FOOD

For the local breakfast specialty *miện lươn* (eel in vermicelli noodle soup; 10,000Đ), or Vietnamese standards like *canh cua* (crab soup; 10,000Đ) with *cà ghém muố* (a local pickled vegetable delight), stop by **Cơm Bình Dân ❶**, at the intersection of Trần Hưng Đạo and Vân Giang, diagonally across from the Thuy Anh. Grab the purple paper on the table to wipe off your chopsticks and bowl like the local guests do. The most famous restaurant in town is **Hường Mai ❷**, 12 Trần Hưng Đạo, just north of the intersection with Lương Văn Tuý. Patrons can sample a Ninh Bình delicacy: *cơm cháy* (deep-fried rice cakes doused in a hot soup of pork or cow kidneys and hearts; 35,000Đ). They're also famous for their free-range *dê tái* (30,000Đ), boiled goat served with citronella, lemon leaf, ginger, and wrapped with rice paper. (☎871 351 Open daily 8am-9pm.) Across the street is its rival **Trừo Giang ❷**, offering the same fare for the same price. The tree-shaded street in front of Queen Hotel to the train station has numerous local phở and cơm shops. The one at 22 Đường 7 Trần Phú, with its kitchen-turned-cafeteria look, caters to friendly young twentysomethings. (Open daily 11am-8pm. Plates of tofu, veggies, or various meats 1000-4000Đ.) Numerous **cafes** line the streets off of Trần Hưng Đạo. For a cool mid-afternoon or late-evening snack, the clean and friendly **Sinh Tố ❶**, 49 Phúc Lộc Phúe Thánh, scoops out *sinh tố bo* (guava ice cream; 7000Đ) and blends mango or orange juice (3000Đ). You might be served a slew of friendly questions along with your drink. (☎880 709. Open daily 7am-11pm.)

NIGHTLIFE

Like many Vietnamese businesses, Ninh Bình's nightlife operates for the most part out of private homes, with lawn furniture arranged inside open homes and spilling onto the sidewalks. The stretch of garage pubs and lawn furniture arranged along Vô Thị Sán, on the May Xay Lake, is especially popular. Locals enjoy cheap beer and pleasant company in the twilight. It is easiest to reach Vô Thị Sán by motorbike; women traveling alone might feel more comfortable bringing along a companion to prevent inquisitive stares from a largely male following. To get there, turn right out of the bus station onto Lê Đại Hành and continue until the intersection and small roundabout of Lê Hồng Phong. Hook the next right to reach the local pub scene. (Most open 11am-11pm, later on weekends. Beer 5000Đ per liter; soda 2500Đ.) Though more expensive, **Bia Hơi Hà Nội**, 31 Đường Trần, bops with hungry locals late into the night. A young and friendly staff (some English-speaking and eager to practice) is ready to serve *xúp gà* (chicken soup; 5000Đ), *xúp luon* (pea soup; 5000Đ) for vegetarians, and *tran* (buffalo; 20,000-25,000Đ) for those daring enough to try. (☎884 598. Open daily 11am-midnight.)

DAYTRIPS FROM NINH BÌNH

The best way to reach any of the local sights is to hop on a *xe ôm*. If you book a guide, ask to take the longer route that passes villages and majestic limestone mountains. The government is building a scenic road (to be completed in 2008) that will bring busloads of tourists to the Trang An grottoes, located in the cliff-covered landscape between Hoa Lư and Tam Cốc. Until they finish, exploring the relatively quiet ▨**backroads** on your own is highly recommended for those who don't mind getting a little lost. Be extremely careful traveling alone on Hwy. 1A, as the condition of the road makes it quite dangerous.

TAM CỐC (THREE GROTTOES)

From Ninh Bình, head south on Highway 1A for 3km. Take a right at the huge Tam Cốc bill-board. The boat basin is 3km farther down this road. To take a boat trip through the three caves, buy a ticket at the booth 300m before the boat basin. The 2hr. ride costs 50,000Đ and includes admission to the nearby temple and pagoda (open daily 7am-5pm). Arrive early to beat the crowds, sun, and boat vendors. Local merchants have umbrellas ready for rent (5000Đ), while camera-toting locals paddle boats alongside tourists (2000Đ).

Ninh Bình's premier tourist attraction is an otherworldy landscape, appropriately nicknamed "Hạ Long Bay without the sea." Bamboo skiffs float to and through the caves, past towering limestone cliffs, working fishermen, and occasionally hordes of tourists. Midway through the trip, the boat stops at a small shrine. The break is often used for the female rowers to present their embroidery for purchase. Float-ing alongside tourists, boat vendors approach these tours and try to cajole visitors into buying drinks or food for themselves or their rower; but many times the row-ers simply sell the drinks back to vendors at a lower price. Tipping the guide might be a more direct option for those wanting to thank him or her—they'll probably ask for one anyway.

Before the first bridge, visitors can either return back to the boat basin or be let off at a landing to the right. From the landing, they can walk 500m to the **Thaí Vi temple**. Erected in 1273, the temple was dedicated to Emperor Trần Thaí Tông and his three royal descendants. Inside, locals come to pray and leave gifts at the altar. The temple can also be explored after being dropped off at the boat basin. With your back toward the basin, take the first dirt road on the left. Continue past the hotel, crossing the small bridge as boats pass under you. The road terminates at the temple. Temple admission is included in the Tam Cốc Tour.

The tour also includes admission to the **Bích Động (Blue Grotto) Pagodas.** These pagodas date back to 1428, when two Buddhists, Chí Klên and Chí Hề, joined forces to search for a place where they could continue their religious studies. When they found the breathtaking sights of Ngũ Nhạc Sơn, or "fire mountain," they built the first and highest of the three Bích Động Pagodas, which perch at varying heights on the mountainside. A stairway leads past these beautiful temples and through a grotto, yielding fantastic views of the cliffs and surrounding farm-lands. They are especially beautiful during the harvest season in June, when the fields resemble a yellow sea. It's possible to enter the pagodas from the rear, via a torchlight boat trip through the low-hanging cave, followed by a short climb over the front side of the mountain. To reach the pagodas, take the road on your left when facing the boat basin. This road curves around town, passing a memorial to veterans of the French and American Wars. Continue past Tam Cốc until the road ends in a small square in front of the pagodas (about 3km from the boat basin). For the back entrance, backtrack 50m and take a right on the narrow path. Follow this for another 100m around the mountain, until you see the boats and cave entrance.

TIÊN (FAIRY) CAVE

To reach the cave, follow the path leading to the back door entrance to the Bích Động Pagodas. Take the first left on a very narrow path. This path will circle around a limestone outcrop before ending at a temple. A set of stairs to the right of the temple leads to the cave entrance. Suggested group donation 10,000Đ.

Largely undiscovered by foreign tourists, this stalagmite-filled cavern pierces through a limestone outcropping. Locals come to the cave to pray for a good har-vest and for luck in front of formations called the "money plant" and "rice plant." While it may be hard to see the likenesses, the incense that locals burn inside adds to the mystical atmosphere. The journey through the cave is fully lit, but visitors will have to practice their Vietnamese or think of creative hand gestures to get the temple attendant to unlock the gate and turn on the lights.

KÊNH GÀ

From the Ninh Bình post office, head north up Trần Hưng Đạo (Hwy. 1A) 11km out of town. Turn left 400m after passing a bridge, following the sign to Cúc Phương National Park. Continue straight for another 10km. In the center of Me town look for the telecommunications tower and main post office. Turn left onto the road at the corner with the post office. After 2km, you'll come to a cafe with a thatched roof. The ticket office is in the cafe parking lot. ☎868 560. 2½-3hr. trips available daily 6am-6pm. Sightseeing ticket 15,000Đ. Boat ride 30,000Đ per person (min. 2 people); 75,000Đ for singles.

The best time to catch Kênh Gà's natural beauty is in July, the first of three months when the river floods, swallowing many village homes and leaving locals to roam the river on houseboats until the water level recedes. Still largely undiscovered, though gaining popularity with adventurous backpackers, Kênh Gà remains mostly tourist-free. Though its name means "chicken canal," chickens are nowhere to be seen. Rather, the inhabitants of this small village subsist off surrounding rice fields as well as the snails, crabs, and fish that get tangled in their nets. Though the boat tour is named after the floating village, the excursion follows the Hoàng Long (◀King Dragon) River, surrounded by limestone mountains that jut out from the rice fields. Passing through the village, visitors are charmed by smiling children and the occasional mother holding a baby while paddling along with her feet, all against a breathtaking mountainous backdrop. After passing the village, boats dock to allow visitors to embark on a 2km walk to the **Vân Trình Cave** entrance. The cave can be explored at leisure, without crowds or guards. As in all caves, visitors should refrain from touching the precious stalactites; human contact can do a great deal of harm by rubbing away thousands of years of mineral and rock formations. If you're taking the route without a guide, just follow the bamboo poles that run along the embankment from the boat landing. At the entrance to the cave, a person at the small refreshment stand on the left will ask for your sightseeing ticket. A light switch rests to the right of the entrance, though visitors are best advised to bring their own flashlight; the lighting is poor and the stairs can sometimes be wet and slippery. Bring your own lunch or wait to return to the mainland, where you can snack at slightly inflated prices or try your bargaining skills at the local food stands sprinkled throughout the town.

HOA LƯ

From Ninh Bình, head north on Hwy. 1A for 6km to Thiên Tôn, then take a left toward Truong Yen. After another 5km, take a left at the "Welcome to Hoa Lư ancient capital" sign and continue to the ticket booth and parking lot. From there, continue straight and hook a right over the bridge. The entrance to the first temple is about 30m farther. The second temple is 300m to the right. Hoa Lư can also be accessed through the beautiful backroads from Tam Cốc or Kênh Gà; ask your hotel owner to draw a detailed map. Open daily 7am-6pm. Access to both temples and the mountain stairway 10,000Đ, children 12 and under 3000Đ. To catch a ferry, wave to the villagers on the opposite side of the bridge and ask for a ride. 30,000Đ per person.

Hoa Lư, the capital of Đại Cồ Việt, the first independent Vietnamese state following a millennium of Chinese rule, lies 12km north of Ninh Bình in a valley ringed by limestone peaks. It was chosen for its location, which made it virtually impregnable to the invading Chinese, and served as the capital from AD 968 until Lý Công Uẩn of the Lý Dynasty, moved it to Thăng Long (modern-day Hà Nội) in AD 1011.

While little survives of the original city, two 17th-century replicas of 11th-century **temples** remain. The first, on the way from the ticket booth, commemorates Đinh Bộ Lĩnh (Đinh Tiên Hoàng), the first Vietnamese king to declare himself emperor. It is said that he had a tiger and an urn placed in the palace courtyard and declared that anyone who violated the law would be boiled and eaten. Gilt statues of Đinh Tiên Hoàng and his sons are housed in the second inner sanctuary.

On each side of the temple stand two smaller structures. The one on the right is an imperial exhibit (in Vietnamese) with great views of the surrounding countryside; the other is a simple display of nearby fauna that includes 577 various species of plants. While modest on the outside, the interior of the temple is carved from dark wood and decorated with golden signs and numerous dragons. The second temple, **Đến Lê Đại Hành,** is dedicated to Đinh Tiên Hoàng's successor. After Đinh Tiên Hoàng was assassinated, Lê Hoàn, the commander of Đinh Tiên Hoàng's army, seized power and declared himself king. He took control not only of the deceased king's throne, but of his wife as well, who was purportedly his lover well before the king's death. Her statue is housed in the rear of the temple.

To visit Đinh Tiên Hoàng's tomb, take the road to the left of the entrance to the temple gardens and quickly veer left to find over 300 steps that lead to the top of Saddle Mountain (Núi Man Yên). Though the tomb itself is simple, the climb reveals a panorama of the countryside. Continue past the tomb and up 2m of jagged stairs to see the view of the other side. Remember which way you climbed up—this path is unmarked. Three hundred meters past the gate of the first temple lies the garden and place of worship of Lê Hoàn. The site is still used for occasional village and religious festivities.

Though Tam Cốc (p. 237) is the more picturesque and popular spot for a ride on the river and through nearby caves, Hoa Lư offers its own aquatic excursion. Before crossing the small bridge, a blue sign tells visitors of the chance to take a 2hr. ferry ride around the mountain and through its nearby caves, where national treasures were kept and prisoners punished.

On the way to Hoa Lư from Ninh Bình, 700m after turning off Hwy. 1A, is the **Vestige Pagoda** and **Cave of Thiên Ton** (Heaven King), just before the road makes a sharp turn to the left. Behind the main structure is the outer cave, dedicated to Buddha. An 18th-century Nguyễn Dynasty stone altar, carved with supernatural creatures, lies next to a bronze bell dating back to Lê Hiến Tông's reign (1497-1504). In the inner cave, the altar holds a bronze statue of the king standing on the back of a tortoise. The entrance to the cave is usually locked. Ask the temple attendant to let you in; a 10,000Đ donation is suggested.

HANG MÚA

From Tam Cốc, head back toward Hwy. 1. After 1.5km, pass a 2-story yellow building, and turn left before the small lake. Then take your first right and the first left onto a poorly paved road leading through a village. Continue straight down the road for 1.5km, and after you cross a small footbridge, you should see a big sign pointing you to the left. 20,000Đ.

Hang Múa, the area's newest attraction, lies on the way to Hoa Lư from Tam Cốc. Five hundred steps ascend past billowing red, yellow, and blue flags and painted concrete animals to a breathtaking vista 200m above the rice paddies at the mountain's summit. At the base is a peaceful garden with big concrete sculptures and a small man-made island; there is also a cave at the base of the stairs, which requires a flashlight. The poor condition of the access road prohibits tour buses from getting there, for now. While the view at the top is fantastic and the gardens are quite tranquil, this mountain's well-kept landscape feels a little out of place in its surroundings, lacking the beaten-down charm of the region. Don't forget your camera, water, and sunblock. Shoes, rather than sandals, are a good idea.

PHÁT DIỆM

The streets of Phát Diệm (Kim Sơn) are worth exploring for their numerous sewing shops *(cắt may)*, a plentiful but untouristed market, and the majestic Catholic Cathedral, which illuminates the surrounding streets and canals. The center of Vietnamese Catholicism is the **Phát Diệm Cathedral,** one of the 30 or so churches in this area built by French Jesuits. Built between 1875 and 1899 by Vietnamese

Father Sáu, it was nearly destroyed in 1972 by American bombs, but was quickly repaired afterward. The stone-and-wood edifice is an amalgamation of pagoda towers, Buddhist lotuses, and crosses laid out in a cathedral plan. Wander into the monastery grounds and ask for an English- or French-speaking guide to give you a tour of the small museum of Vietnamese Catholicism behind the cathedral, as well as a glimpse of the cathedral's interior, where you'll find a two-ton bell that resounds across a 10km radius. Even if you forgo the detailed tour of the one-room museum (housing clothes, pictures, and maps of the region), you can still sneak a peek at the wooden interior and the ornate golden altar through the windows next to the main entrance. A map located near the entrances at either side of the cathedral orients English- and French-speaking visitors, while plaques nearby relate the history of Phát Diệm. *(From the bus station, head right over a bridge, and pass two more bridges. About 1km later, look for a sign reading "Nhà Thờ Phát Diệm" on the left. The cathedral is 300m down the road to your right. Mass is held daily at 5am and 5:30pm, though curious onlookers are requested to come during visiting hours only. ☎862 058. Open daily 7:30-11:30am and 2:30-5pm. Free tour, although it's customary to give a 10,000Đ donation.)*

The selection of accommodations in Phát Diệm is meager. However, those wanting to stop here on their way south can spend the night at **Thu Hương Hotel ❶**, 53 Phát Diệm Tây, on the main street to the cathedral. Eager to help, the Vietnamese-speaking staff offers clean doubles with air-conditioning, dark wood furniture, and clean sheets. Some rooms have private baths. (☎862 336. Singles 80,000-100,000Đ; doubles 150,000Đ.) While phở and cơm shops proclaim their presence with brand-new red-and-blue signs, little else is available in the way of food save home groceries and food stands. You can pick something up at the town **market** on your way from the bus stop, or walk up the main road past the turn to Phát Diệm until you reach the corner of Lưu Phương and the small fruit and veggie stands.

You can reach the town and the Catholic Cathedral with an organized tour from any hotel in Ninh Bình, or simply by renting a motorbike and a guide for the day (US$4-5; with guide US$6-9). The town is 28km southeast of Ninh Bình. From Trần Hưng Đạo (Hwy. 1A), head east over the river, pass the bus station, and cross over the railroad tracks. Head straight into Phát Diệm (Kim Sơn), then continue 1km and veer right at a blue sign with an arrow to the Phát Diệm Cathedral. Public buses to Kim Sơn run frequently, though the trip will take longer, and the "hourly" buses leave only when full. Those wishing to daytrip from Hà Nội or simply to bypass Ninh Bình on their way south can do so. The **bus station** is on the north end of town on the main road, Đường Pho. **Buses** run to Ninh Bình (45-90min.; about every hr. 6am-3pm; 7000Đ) and Hà Nội (3-4 hr.; 20,000Đ). To reach the **Ngân Hàng Nông Nghiep Va Bank** (Bank for Agriculture and Rural Development), head south from the bus station, pass the bridge, and veer left to pass over one street. Then make the first right before you hit the town market, and continue 100m. Though there's no ATM, you can change cash inside. For cheap **Internet** access, look for **Đào Tạo Tin Học**, 140 Phát Diệm Đông, slightly to the right of the left-side entrance to the Cathedral. (☎862 219. 2000Đ per hr.) Next door to the bus stop is the **post office**, 16 Trí Chính. (☎862 101. Open daily 6am-10pm.)

CÚC PHƯƠNG NATIONAL PARK

Home to endangered species like the cloud leopard, the Asiatic black bear, and the red-bellied squirrel, Vietnam's first national park was dedicated by Hồ Chí Minh in 1963 to preserve the dense forest and wildlife of the area. While visitors would be lucky to see any of the park's rare wildlife, nature lovers are drawn here for its 307 species of birds and 1000-year-old trees. Located 45km northwest of Ninh Bình, most people see the park in a day, but two- to three-day stays allow for longer treks deeper into the park and a more thorough visit of Cúc Phương's attractions.

With Cellular Abroad, talk is not only cheap, *it's free.*

Unlimited FREE incoming calls and no bills or contracts for overseas use!

1-800-287-5072
www.cellularabroad.com

Otel.com

Are you aiming for a budget vacation **?**

US & CANADA
1-800-820-4171 OR 1-212-594-8045
EUROPE
00-800-468-35482 OR 44-207-099-2035

CÚC PHƯƠNG AT A GLANCE

AREA: 222 sq. km.

CLIMATE: Very humid from Apr.-Sept.; dry and more pleasant Dec.-Mar. Average year-round temperature is 23°C.

GATEWAYS: 45km north of Ninh Bình via Nho Quan.

HIGHLIGHTS: Bird watching; hikes; overnight stays at Mường Village.

FEATURES: Limestone caves, dense forest, and 1000-year-old trees.

ACCOMMODATIONS: Camping and bungalows within the park. Homestays in Mường Village.

FEES AND RESERVATIONS: Entrance fee 40,000Đ (children 20,000Đ). Guides required for some hikes.

■ ORIENTATION

Once inside, it is easy to maneuver around the park. The main road splits the park in two, with trails branching off in either direction. The **Visitor Information Center** resides in a white building on the right at the park headquarters. The ticket booth and entrance gate are 500m down the road from the information center. The park center and the starting point of six of its trails lies 20km from the entrance gate. The closest trail open to visitors without a park guide begins after a 10min. ride into the heart of the forest from the entrance gate.

■ TRANSPORTATION

The best way to reach the park is on **motorbike.** To get there, follow the directions from Ninh Bình to Kênh Gà (p. 238), but pass over the left turn at the post office and continue straight for another 20km. If you can't drive yourself, a round-trip *xe ôm* from Ninh Bình will cost 100,000Đ to park headquarters and 150,000Đ to the park center; it may be wiser to hop on an organized tour from Ninh Bình. (Motorbike US$10-18; 2-day trip by car US$45-70 at the Thuy Anh Hotel.) A bus from the park center back to Ninh Bình can be chartered for US$20-35. Alternatively, **buses** from Hà Nội's Giap Bat bus station head to Nho Quan (2½ hr.; 8, 9am, noon, 1, 3, 4pm; 27,000Đ). A *xe ôm* from Nho Quan to park headquarters will cost 30,000Đ.

■ PRACTICAL INFORMATION

WHEN TO GO. If you want to admire the caves at their best, hit the park during the dry season (Oct.-Apr.). The park peaks just over 400m above sea level; temperatures remain consistent with those of the surrounding central coast region, although they are slightly cooler due to the dense, luscious forests. The average temperature is 23°C, and humidity hovers around an impressive 85% for most of the year, although it is a bit cooler in the winter and in the north of the park. The ample rainfall (2200-2500mm per yr.) keeps the Botanical Gardens blooming, but you should still bring lots of water for drinking. Be sure to bring a flashlight and batteries if you plan to explore any caves.

The **National Park Information Centers** can be reached at ☎ 30 848 0006 or www.cuc-phuongtourism.com. Local hotels offer one- or two-day **tours** of the park, the latter including a night at the Mường Village. However, only tours led by a guide and arranged through the park authorities have full access to both marked and unmarked trails. These can last from one to six days and are meant for those wishing to fully exhaust the park's possibilities. (One-day hikes US$10-15 for groups of 1-5 people. Groups and full-day guide US$20 per day.) Entrance to the park costs 40,000Đ for adults and 20,000Đ for children under 15.

INIQUITOUS DELICACIES

Vietnam is renowned for rare culinary delicacies, including monkeys' brains. Most accounts of the dish fail to mention, however, that the practice is neither legal nor common. Poachers capture the animals and sell them to Chinese tradesmen and Vietnamese restaurants. The former use the brains and blood for medication, while the latter prepare them as gourmet meals for the wealthy.

The process is far from pleasant: the scalp and brain are removed from the stunned animal. This practice has caused several species to dwindle in numbers; some are even endangered. Their survival lies in the hands of educators, rescue centers, and those willing to sacrifice an adventurous appetite.

Other "exotic" delicacies are also problematic. *Rượu den*, snake-blood vodka, is a famed Vietnamese alcoholic rite of passage. The two available types are yellow and white snakes: yellow ones taste like chicken and need no special preparation. Their poisonous white counterparts must be neutralized before being dropped in vodka. More than just a delicacy, vodka mixed with snake blood is believed to have healing properties against health problems like rheumatism. Unfortunately, locals and travelers fail to realize that endangered species get mixed up in the lot. The message, as always, is: think before you drink.

ACCOMMODATIONS AND FOOD

There are four ways to spend the night in the park. The government accommodations range from **luxury bungalows** ❸ with air-conditioning and TV (singles US$15, doubles US$20 at headquarters; US$17/25 at the park center) to **rooms** ❸ with a simple fan and private bath (US$15/20 at headquarters and park center; US$15 at Mac Lake area, 2km from headquarters) to shabby **dorm beds** ❶ with a shared bath at headquarters (dorms US$5, rooms US$10 at headquarters; US$6/12 at the park center). All accommodations include mosquito nets. A full listing of accommodations is available at the ticket booth. Those wishing to **camp** ❶ with their own tent may do so in designated areas for US$2 per night. An overnight on cots in the **Mường Village,** following the park tour, costs US$5 per person. An alternative to sleeping right in the park is the privately owned **Nhà Nghỉ Guest House** ❸, Thôn Ngāba Xā Cúc Phương. Only 1km from the park gate, the hotel provides pleasant and colorful singles with fan and private bath. (☎848 033; fax 030 848. Rooms US$10.)

Though refreshment stands greet visitors both at the head of the trail to the Cave of Prehistoric Man and at the park center, they have little to offer but water, soda, and snacks. Those staying in park accommodations can order a **meal delivery** ahead of time (30,000Đ min., or US$7-12 for three meals), or eat in the Mường Village for similarly inflated prices.

SIGHTS

Hidden behind a metal fence, the **Endangered Primate Rescue Center** lies across from the Visitor Center. Inside are 15 of Vietnam's 25 species and subspecies of primates, which are brought to the center for rehabilitation before being released into the wild. Some of the residents have been confiscated from hunters, who sell the monkeys to restaurants where they are consumed illegally (see **"Iniquitous Delicacies,"** p. 242), or to China, where the primates are killed and used to make medicine. Opened in 1993, the center, once strictly a research facility, now allows animal lovers to visit its current residents. (Open daily 9-11am and 1:30-4pm. Short tours every 30min. Buy tickets at entrance gate 400m past the Rescue Center. English tour 10,000Đ.) On the way back to the entrance stop by the Visitor Center to sneak a peek at small **ecological exhibits** as well. (Open daily 8am-4:30pm. Free.) Across from the ticket booth is the **Botanical Garden** (5000Đ).

🏔 HIKING

You can pick up a free brochure with a map of the park's routes at the ticket booth. The trails open to self-guided visitors are limited to the Cave of Prehistoric Man, the Ancient Tree, the Thousand-Year-Old Tree, and the Palace Cave. The **Cave of Prehistoric Man** (Don Người Xưa) is a 30min. climb up the mountain. Once inside, crawl through small passages to reach the innermost enclosure where the tap of stalactite-like formations somehow fills the cave with sounds of drums. Don't forget to bring a flashlight. When making your way back, take heed of the ladder to the right of the exit—those daring enough to climb arrive at a cave above, from which the ladder (or a steep climb and a somewhat difficult first drop) leads back to the cave entrance in about an hour.

Another local favorite is a walk in the forest that leads from the Park Center (to the right of the pillar house) to the monumental **Thousand-Year-Old Tree.** Rest along the way on tree-stump stools. After 3km along the path you can take the 10-15min. climb up the mountain to the smaller **Palace Cave,** then backtrack to the original trail. When you reach the tree, continue along the trail on the other side for two to three hours. With a park guide you can step off the Thousand-Year-Old Tree trail to mount the park's highest peak, **Silver Cloudy Top Mountain** (650m; 4-5hr.; US$10).

Other hikes that require a guide include a difficult 450m climb to the **King's Son-in-law Cave** (6-9hr.) and a spectacular view of the park. You can also take an overnight camping trip to the **Ancient Tree** (US$20). One popular guided walk is the 3hr. nightspotting tour, where visitors might get glimpses of civets, Samba deer, Indian Flying Squirrels, and tree frogs. You're at least guaranteed to see lots of insects, so bring repellent. (US$15 per group, max. 5 people.) Other speciality tours, including bamboo rafting along the Buoi river or biking, can be arranged at park headquarters or by email prior to your visit.

The major road from Cúc Phương to Ninh Bình passes by **Van Long,** Northern Central Vietnam's largest wetland reserve. The main attraction for visitors is the 1½hr. ride on board bamboo rafts. You'll be able to spot a lot of waterfowl if you bring your binoculars, and, if you're lucky, one of the reserve's 40 Delacour langurs—of only 300 alive worldwide. (*From Ninh Bình, take Hwy. 1A 11km north. Turn left, heading towards Kênh Gà and Cúc Phương for 5km. A turn-off to the right will take you to the entrance, 2km down this road. Open daily 7am-4pm. 20,000Đ.*)

THANH HÓA ☎ 37

A large, sprawling, and primarily commercial city, Thanh Hóa at first appears to have little to offer to tourists in search of historical or spectacular sights. However, its proximity to Sầm Sơn's spectacular beach and Bến En's amazing natural sights, as well as streets filled with delightful cafes, outdoor markets offering delicious treats, and quality, affordable hotels, merit a stop. Though the city lacks a well-established infrastructure for foreign tourists, those who have the patience and time will find a visit worthwhile.

🚆 TRANSPORTATION. The **train station,** Thanh Hóa, lies at the western edge of town, at the end of Phan Chu Trinh. **Trains** to northern destinations leave five times daily; southbound trains leave four times daily. Trains depart for: Hà Nội (3-5hr.; 43,000-190,000Đ); HCMC (33-40hr.; 396,000-830,000Đ); Huế (9-11hr.; 133,000-275,000Đ); Nha Trang (33-37hr.; 294,000-610,000); Ninh Bình (1-2hr.; 15,000-30,000Đ); Vinh (2-3hr.; 36,000-73,000Đ). If you're going to HCMC or Huế, get tickets a day in advance (☎851 527). There is no central bus station. **Buses** leave from different stops near the edge of town, depending on their destination. A **minibus**

JUL. 17

FROM THE ROAD

MORE MONEY MORE PROBLEMS

One of the things I enjoy most about traveling is getting to know the locals. My experiences with them in Vietnam, though, has been a surprisingly mixed bag.

In Huế, a stranger on a motorcycle offered to take me around the city to practice his English—"Please come. No money." I jumped at the opportunity, and it started out great—he showed me around the royal tombs while I peppered him with questions. At the end of the day, though, he asked for money for his family. When I gave him some, he asked for more. The exchange of money soured it all; I started to wonder whether everything had been an act to get into my wallet.

Only one week later, in Đông Hà, I met Sy, a 23-year-old student. His family invited me for a modest dinner four nights in a row. The father filled my bowl with rice and veggies, demanding that I eat more and more. They appreciated the fruit I brought them as a gift, but when I asked what they wanted as a going-away present, they requested only my friendship and my attendance someday at Sy's wedding.

There is no real formula to avoid being used; as with many things while you're traveling, you just have to trust your instincts. But despite the scams, it's important to remember to take some risks—you might just be fortunate.

—Ross Arbes

station—locals, for some reason, call it a "car" station—is located at the intersection of Nguyễn Trãi and Đình Nghệ, 1km south of Trần Phú, and goes to all the major cities. Minibuses to Hà Nội leave every 15 to 30min. during the day (40,000Đ). You can also flag one down along Trần Phú. There are also frequent minibuses to Vinh (20,000-30,000Đ).

ORIENTATION AND PRACTICAL INFORMATION. Though maps of Thanh Hóa are hard to come by, the city's grid layout makes it easy to reach your destination, as long as you remember your position in relation to the city's two main streets, **Lê Lợi** and **Trần Phú**. Much of the city is concentrated on and near Trần Phú (Hwy. 1), which pulses through the city from north to south. Lê Lợi, named after the 14th-century hero who was born in this city, bisects the city from east to west. The two streets intersect at **Lê Lợi Square,** which has a large statue of the hero and marks the center of town.

While **tourist offices** in the city are few and far between, one can be found in a small booth at 34 Lê Lợi. The lady inside speaks decent English, sells maps, and can arrange tours within the province. (☎860 384. Open daily 7-11:30am and 2-5pm.) Another tourist office, **Trekking Travel, Inc.,** 25A Quang Trưng, is next to Hotel Thanh Hóa, two and a half kilometers south of the city center. (☎758 812. Open daily 7-11am and 1-5pm. Sells open-tour bus tickets from Thanh Hóa to all major cities.) To reach a **bank,** head from the city center 500m north to the roundabout and take a left on Phan Chu Trinh. Immediately on your left and right, you'll pass a slew of banks. To exchange money or traveler's checks, or to get cash advances, stop into a branch of the **Incombank,** 17 Phan Chu Trinh. (☎852 318; www.icb.com.vn. Open 7am-5pm.) A **24hr. ATM** stands outside. The **post office** (Bưu Điện), 33 Trần Phú, stands at the intersection of Lê Lợi and Trần Phú, near Lê Lợi Square. Telephones are inside. (☎752 700. Open daily 6am-10pm.) There is a **pharmacy** next to Hotel Thàn Công at 27 Triệu Quốc Đạt. (☎836 720. Open daily 7am-11am and 1-9pm.) For **Internet** access, head west down Lê Lợi, taking your first right onto Hàng Đồng; a small Internet shop can be found right on the corner of the intersection at 132 Hàng Đồng. (☎853 020. 2000Đ per hour. Open 7-10:30pm.) There are **markets** scattered all over the city; the largest is **Chợ Quảng Cao,** in a huge stadium on Lê Lợi, where everything imaginable is sold. There is also a fish market on Phan Chu Trinh, right across from the Incombank. The most enjoyable market, though, is one along Lê Duy Doán that sells fish, fruit, veggies, and local specialties. All markets are open from dawn to dusk.

▟▙ ACCOMMODATIONS AND FOOD. In Thanh Hóa, there is a variety of lodging options scattered around the city. There is a surprisingly large number of four-star hotels set up for the businessmen and international investors that pass through the city. Though less visible, budget options are around, too. The best value can be found at the sparkling new, family-run **Hotel Miền Tây Xanh ❷,** 212 Đình Nghệ, located at the western end of Nguyễn Trãi, right near the minibus station. The rooms are clean and spacious with crisp white sheets, fluffy pillows, TV, and private bath. The family that runs it is extremely kind, helpful, and generous. (☎851 718. Doubles with fan 120,000Đ, with A/C 150,000Đ.) Another inexpensive option is **Nha Kach Thanh Bình ❷,** 2 Nguyễn Du, located at the city center. The rooms are dark and small, but have air-conditioning, TV, and private bath. Going north up Trần Phú, take your first left after the post office, and it's 50m down the road on your left. (☎752 543. Doubles 120,000Đ.) For good quality at a higher price, head to **Hotel Thàn Công ❹,** 29 Triệu Quốc Đạt, where the rooms are comfortable, spacious, and spotless, and come with air-conditioning, TV, refrigerator, and tubless baths. The staff is helpful and some speak English. From the post office, head north along Trần Phú for 600m, taking a left onto Triệu Quốc Đạt just slightly before Phan Chu Trinh. The hotel is about 50m down, on the left side. (☎710 224; fax 710 656. 1 double bed 170,00-210,000Đ; 2 double beds 230,000-250,000Đ. Prices vary depending on room size.) There is a **restaurant ❷** downstairs. (Soup 15,000-20,000Đ; crab 35,000Đ; juice 5000-7000Đ; beer 10,000-15,000Đ. Open daily 7am-7pm.) The city's specialties mostly involve shrimp, shellfish, and fish. Stalls selling shrimp chowder (*chau tôm;* 10,000Đ) can be found all over the city, especially near Lê Hoàn. There are a few vendors in the outdoor market on Lê Duy Doán that cook egg pancakes with scallions and shrimp (6000Đ), but the most famous of the city's culinary specialties is *nem chua,* pig meat and skin cooked in a banana leaf. It can be found in nearly any restaurant or market for 4000Đ. Wash it down with *nược dau má,* a sweet and bitter drink with supposed medicinal powers. One of the city's few good restaurants is **Sộng Dá ❷,** 13 Cao Thằng, a street that runs parallel and 50km east of Trần Phú. Their specialties are *cá bóng supa* (fish soup; 30,000Đ) and spring rolls (4000Đ). There's good service, too. (☎853 864. Entrees 30,000-90,000Đ. Open 7am-10:30pm.)

◪▟ SIGHTS AND NIGHTLIFE. There are no sights of real interest for travelers in Thanh Hóa, save a pleasant park and a gray Catholic church. To reach the **park,** head west on Phan Chu Trinh toward the train station. The park is across from the now-abandoned movie theater; it's a beautiful spot for a lazy afternoon walk. To get to the **church,** go 100m north of Phan Chu Trinh on Trần Phú and take a right onto Nguyễn Trương Tỗ when you see the church's gray steeple looming on your right. In the evening, the city's residents sit in cafes drinking coffee or sugarcane juice and enjoying *kem* (ice cream). To mingle with the local night crowd, head to Lê Lợi Square. There are stands all around the square filled with teens and adults eating ice cream and socializing. This laid-back crowd stays until 10:30pm and then heads home. Outside of the square, there is—you guessed it—karaoke.

◪ DAYTRIPS FROM THANH HÓA

SẤM SƠN

Public transportation to Sấm Sơn is scarce, so most tourists arrive by car or motorbike. However, minibuses make the trip from Thanh Hóa to Sấm Sơn about 4 or 5 times per day and can be flagged down at the intersection of Lê Lợi and Trần Phú. To get there on your own, head east out of the city along Lê Duy Toàn. Cross a bridge and continue 16km to the beach.

The most developed beach resort of the north, Sầm Sơn, which lies 16km east of Thanh Hóa, offers two very different types of beaches. While Sầm Sơn's **northern beach,** where tourists swim and relax on umbrella-covered beach chairs (typically you must buy a drink to claim a chair; sodas 8000Đ), is the more popular, the rocky **southern beach** is the real jewel. Visitors sit in bamboo shacks built upon the cliffs drinking milk straight out of a coconut (10,000Đ) and watching small fishing boats float around in the ocean. Beautiful and serene though it is, Sầm Sơn's waters are not as clear as other beaches, and its views aren't as stunning—but the cliffside huts along the northern coast make this beach unique.

To reach the rocks, head south along the coast until you see several staircases. As you reach the top of the cliff, you will come across the small and simple **Chùa Dền Dòc Cuốc pagoda,** where locals come to pray. Past the pagoda are 20 to 25 bamboo shacks offering coconut milk (10,000Đ), beer (10,000Đ), soda (8000Đ), or a chair with a view of the waves and the small fishing skiffs below (5000Đ per hr. without a drink). Nestled in the boulders is what looks like a museum and park dedicated to the town's hero, Than Đoc Choc, which details his adventures with a ride and moving displays. Geared towards Vietnamese children, the short tour has little English and can be boring for those who know nothing about the hero. (Open daily 6:30-11am and 1:30-10:30pm. Tour 19,000Đ.)

Those wanting to spend a night at the beach will have no problem finding a hotel—the northern part of the beach is a jungle of hotels and restaurants. It is nearly impossible to distinguish between the sea of hotels, both private and government-run. Finding a specific hotel can be even harder, as the numbers on streets are not very well marked. Hotels with up-front views of the beach are generally priced higher; cheaper rooms can be found in the numerous hotels farther from the shores. Some of the best deals in town can be found near the southern tip of Sầm Sơn. There, you will find a cluster of 200,000Đ options along Trung Tâm Bãi Tắm. **Hoa Hồng I ❸,** almost directly behind the rocky shore, has bare, clean rooms with air-conditioning, fan, TV, private bath, and views of the ocean. (☎821 459. Bargain doubles to 200,000Đ.) Another group of relatively inexpensive hotels can be found one and a half kilometers north along Bà Triệu, the main drag running alongside the coast, perpendicular to Hồ Xuân Hương. **Thế Anh ❸,** on Nguyễn Văn Cừ, offers small, simple rooms with air-conditioning, TV, wooden furniture, and small private baths. (☎821 459. Doubles 200,000Đ.) To get there from Lê Lai, take a left onto Hồ Xuân Hương when you arrive at the ocean. Continue straight for one kilometer; turn left onto Bà Triệu and left again onto Nguyễn Văn Cừ. The hotel will be 20m up on your left. Just north of Thế Anh, at the intersection of Bà Triệu and Nguyễn Văn Cừ, is **Hotel Tùng Lâm ❸,** 4 Bà Triệu. Though beginning to reveal its age, clean and colorful doubles with air-conditioning, fan, private bath, and a balcony with a pleasant view make this a pretty good choice. (☎821 479. 200,000Đ per person; doubles 250,000Đ.) The **restaurant ❸** downstairs serves set menu meals of fish, beef, and chicken with very generous portions to the tune of 50,000Đ per person. (Open daily 6am-11pm.) There is a grouping of clean and friendly seafood restaurants along Bà Triệu on the walk from Hotel Tùng Lâm to the beach. (Shrimp chowder 8000-10,000Đ; rice with fish 30,000-40,000Đ; beer 8000-10,000Đ.) You can buy snake wine about anywhere for 150,000Đ per kg or dried octopi for 30,000Đ per bunch.

If you visit this beach during the summer, expect to share the it with a lot of Vietnamese tourists, especially on weekends. However, as the beach is large, you should be able to find a quiet spot for yourself on the northern or southern edge of the beach, even at the height of the season. Be prepared for intense heat as well.

ctpnh@hn.vnn.vn. Doubles US$20; 2 double beds US$22; deluxe suites with bar and living room US$35.) Don't miss the hotel's rooftop **restaurant ❷**; no meal could be complete without stewed eel and banana (35,000Đ) or fried frog with butter. (Open daily 5am-10pm.) Across the highway and 150m north, **Hồng Ngọc 2 ❸**, 24 Lê Lợi, is really only a good deal for those in search of quads. The walls in this dark, cabin-like arrangement are old and the TVs and toilets are equally worn and undependable (sometimes refusing to turn on or flush). The staff, however, is friendly and always willing to help fix any problems. Rooms come with air-conditioning, TV, fan, fridge, and likely some ants. (☎841 314. Doubles 120,000Đ; quads 180,000Đ.) The accompanying **restaurant ❷** offers well-spiced but expensive Vietnamese dishes (35,000Đ for spicy fried beef), good french fries (20,000Đ) for those craving a taste of home, and cheap beer on tap (4000Đ per pint).

During lunchtime, locals head to one of the many **com shops ❶** offering nearly identical dishes along Phan Chu Trinh, near its intersection with Quang Trung. The shops, such as the one at 225 Phan Chu Trinh, serves filling and delicious servings at affordable prices (5000-15,000Đ). For a vegetarian soup that you can mix with veggies and rice, ask for *nước lay muống cochans*, and then specify "các món ăn chay." (☎841 1369. Open daily 6am-10pm.) If you plan on a picnic, crave a midday snack, or are simply looking for products with set prices, head to the **supermarket** located on the ground floor of the newly erected **Maximark**, 166 Nguyễn Thai Hoc. Though the prices will be far higher than those of the market, there's a good selection of imported foods. From the bus station, walk 50m south on Hwy. 1. (☎561 322. Open daily 8am-9:30pm.)

👁 SIGHTS

Though most of the regional attractions lie in the towns surrounding Vinh, visitors should absolutely not miss **Hồ Chí Minh Square,** with a gigantic statue of the hero standing tall in the center. In the crisp morning hours, locals stroll in the park, some on the way to work and others simply out to enjoy the cool and peaceful morning. At night, the square and park light up with life. Motorcycles line the parking lot as teens and adults alike walk, eat ice cream, and dance under the stars. For directions to the square, see **Nightlife,** below. The family altar of laureate **Nguyễn Du,** author of the *Tale of Kieu,* is 13km south of town. To reach it, head out of town south on Hwy. 1, pass the Bến Tuy bridge and follow the signs for 10km.

🎭 NIGHTLIFE

Visitors might be surprised to learn that the streets of Vinh burst with life in the late evening hours, with the largest volume of partiers emerging from their homes at 7 or 8pm and returning at 10 or 10:30pm. A drive down Nguyễn Văn Cừ from its intersection with Nguyễn Sỹ Sách reveals popular cafes decorated with colorful Christmas lights sitting alongside garage pool halls and packed Internet and game rooms. The drive ends at the crowded Hồ Chí Minh Square, where a shockingly white statue of the socialist leader looms over groups of laughing locals. The park's surroundings are a fun mix of bars and ice cream shops. A small carnival is set up for children, and colorful Communist-symbol light fixtures light the way.

For some Vinh-style singing and dancing, visit the star-lit **Cafe Karaoke,** 51 Hồ Tùng Mậu, which rests on the northeastern corner of the park about three blocks north of the statue, directly across from the post office. (☎835 026. Beer 8000Đ; soda 6000Đ. Music daily 7-10:15pm.) For good people-watching, head to the two-story **Tuấn Euro,** at the intersection of Hồ Tùng Mậu and Nguyễn Văn Cừ, and grab a seat on the balcony of the second floor. As the crowd is almost all male, women might want to come here with a friend rather than venturing in alone. (☎562 384.

Beer 8000Đ; coffee 6000Đ.) To escape motorbike traffic and the packed park, seek out the romantic mood lighting and peaceful atmosphere of the **cafe** situated in the southeast corner of the park, on Thúc Mẫu off of Hồ Tùng Mậu, one block south of Nguyễn Văn Cừ. To reach the cafe, pass the booming karaoke bars and hook a left on Thúc Mẫu, which will reveal a round structure. Patrons are an eclectic but mellow crowd drinking coffee and fruit shakes in the abundant seating on the third floor. (Open daily until 10:30pm. Coffee 6000-12,000Đ; fruit shakes 10,000-12,000Đ; mixed drinks 20,000-25,000Đ.) To take part in a small **carnival** filled with a ring toss, gambling games, and—of course—karaoke, head 100m north on Hồ Tùng Mậu from the main statue and turn right into the often-crowded parking lot. Prizes for these child-oriented carnival include chips, gum, and cans of soda.

◪ DAYTRIP FROM VINH

LÀNG KIM LIÊN

To reach Làng Kim Liên, 14km from Vinh, you can hop on a bus from the station to Nam Đàm, although it will likely be easier and quicker to flag one down right outside of the market at the intersection of Đinh Phùng and Quang Trưng, about 3km south of the bus station (30min.; 6-8 trips daily; 5000-10,000Đ). Hop off when you see a huge blue billboard welcoming you to Làng Kim Liên. The first sight is about 1km down the road that winds past the post office and fishing fields. Make the journey on foot, or hire a local to drop you off and pick you up at each place. Negotiate a price in advance (5000-15,000Đ). Alternatively, you can hire motorbikes (30,000-40,000Đ round-trip). Both sights open daily 6am-8pm. Free.

Communist party members flock from across the country to pay homage to Hồ Chí Minh at his birthplace in the village of **Hoăng Thi** and at the thatched house to which his family returned for his formative years (ages 5-10) in nearby **Làng Sen** or **Làng Kim Liên** (Lotus Village). Don't expect much in the way of tourist information for English speakers, except for a few signs. However, the absence of English will not at all take away from the experience—the real attraction for non-Vietnamese is the carnival-like crowds taking pictures, buying souvenirs, and burning incense around these houses. The first sight is Hồ Chí Minh's place of birth, two kilometer on the unnamed road past the post office; swing a left immediately after passing a small lake on your left. Among the bustling souvenir stands are the three hatched huts that form Hồ's proper birth house in **Hoăng Thi**. While two are furnished exactly as the socialist leader knew them during the first years of his life—showing his truly modest roots—the third contains a shrine where visitors are requested to place the first of three bouquets of flowers. To get to the second sight, continue down the road from the post office for one kilometer until you reach a roundabout, at which point you should follow the sign to Bai Xé Que Noi for 200m. This is **Làng Kim Liên;** Hồ Chí Minh's family settled here in 1901 after returning from Huế, where Hồ's father had traveled to study. Here you'll find three more thatched houses, one of which is another shrine awaiting your second bouquet. Farther down the path is a museum, which is closed for construction until 2010. However, the most interesting and telling part of the two sights is in the building next to the museum, where there's a giant white bust of Vietnam's socialist hero. Flowers, food, and burning incense lie at his feet, just as in the temples of ancient kings; large families gather round to take pictures to show their friends.

Snack and souvenir shops selling socialist books, Hồ Chí Minh photos, shirts with pictures of the thatched houses on them (15,000Đ), and even busts (90,000Đ) crowd both sights. To purchase flowers, head to the museum office located across from the entrance to the leader's birth house in Hoăng Thi. (10,000Đ per bouquet. Open daily 6am-8pm.)

CỬA LÒ
☎ 38

A short distance northwest of Vinh, Cửa Lò is a beautiful resort-filled beach town. Nearly all of the restaurants and hotels lie on one main road, Bình Minh, just steps away from the shoreline covered in bamboo-hut cafes and the warm, wavy ocean. Though the water lacks the crystal-clear quality of some of Vietnam's other beaches, the tranquil ocean sounds and the view of the nearby islands make for a pleasant getaway. Come during the weekends to see the beach dotted with locals; during the weekdays, you can have the beach to yourself. Prices of accommodations and food are considerably higher than those of Vinh; it might be more affordable to make a daytrip to this beach town.

TRANSPORTATION. Only 20km from Vinh, the new beach resort is easily accessible by motorbike. From the bus station, take a left onto Lê Lợi and continue for two kilometers until it spills into Nguyễn Trãi. Continue north on this road for another two more kilometers until you see a big blue sign directing you to take a right on Hwy. 46. After 16km, you will be staring at the ocean as the road comes to a stop at Cửa Lò's main drag, Bình Minh. A one-way trip to or from Vinh on by **motorbike** costs 25,000-35,000Đ. To take the **bus** to Cửa Lò, just stand along Nguyễn Trãi or Lê Lợi, north of the bus station, and flag one down as it heads northwest to Cửa Lò. The bus to the beach runs about every hour 7am-5pm (6000Đ). Be advised that the bus returns less frequently, with the last bus passing through Bình Minh at 6pm. An abundance of motorbike drivers, though, guarantees you won't be stranded.

ORIENTATION AND PRACTICAL INFORMATION. Simple in structure, most of the town of Cửa Lò lies along the main street **Bình Minh,** which flows parallel to the beach. The town's twin islands lie to the north, while a small palm forest stretches to the south. The town **bank,** 66 Bình Minh, lies near the post office across the street from the shore. Exchange your money here or take advantage of the ATM in front. (Bank and ATM open 6:30-11am and 1-5pm.) For **Internet** access, continue north on the road to 26 Bình Minh, just across the street from the post office. (☎951 224. Open daily 7am-10pm. 5000Đ per hr.) Next door, at 32 Bình Minh, there are fewer computers, but the connection is cheaper. (☎949 854. 3000Đ per hr. Open 7am-10pm.) The **post office,** 1 Bình Minh, lies on the beach side of Bình Minh. (☎824 106. Open daily 7am-9pm.)

ACCOMMODATIONS AND FOOD. Peace, beauty, and inflated prices are a package deal in Cửa Lò. While lodging below 200,000Đ is difficult to find—especially in the hot summer months—the comfortable rooms in Vinh rarely rise in price, so you might be better off daytripping to the beach. Those who would rather avoid the commute can find a good value at the **Lộc Anh Hotel ❸,** 26 Bình Minh, across from the post office, with extremely clean, green-and-white tiled floors in breezy rooms with nice views. (☎038 824. Doubles 200,000Đ.) The best prices on the beach can be found at **Hotel Hồng Tấn ❸,** 46 Bình Minh, 100m south of the post office, which offers small, clean, and mostly viewless rooms. (☎824 387. Doubles with air-A/C, TV, and baths 180,000Đ for 1 person and 200,000Đ for 2.) If the owner gives a higher price, bargain until it comes down. Smack in the middle of the hotel-packed Bình Minh is the family-friendly **Hotel Việt Đức ❸,** with tiny but well-groomed double beds and small balconies. To reach the hotel, make a left onto Bình Minh when coming in from Vinh, then hook a left into the small alley filled with food shops around 90 Bình Minh. The Việt Đức is 50m down and to the right. (☎824 557. A/C, TV, and private baths. Doubles 200,000Đ.) Phở and cơm shops are scattered every 20m on Bình Minh. A large cluster of these restaurants can be

THE LOCAL STORY

WHEN THE SMOKE CLEARS

While having lunch in Hà Tĩnh with a family I had met at the bus station, I noticed a tattoo on the father's arm. The tattoo was of a a peace sign with two dates around it. Curious, as this was the first tattoo I had witnessed on a local, I had to get to the bottom of it.

LG: What do the dates on your tattoo stand for?
A: The one above the peace sign is my birthday. The one below is the day an American bomb dropped 20 feet away from me when I was fighting for the country's unification during the war. I was badly injured and had to undergo surgery, and my back to this day is still very weak.
LG: Did many people you know die in the war?
A: Many. I had many friends who died, one brother, and several cousins.
LG: How do you feel now about Americans? Is it strange that you just had an American for lunch in your house?
A: Not at all. I tattooed this peace sign on my arm because I bear no grudge. All I want is peace now. I do not want to remember the war. The memories are no good. I think Americans are Number 1. Some of my family has moved to America, and I hope, though I think I will never have the money, to visit your country. Now eat up. Your fish is getting cold.

found on the alley near 90 Bình Minh on the way to Hotel Việt Đức. (Phở 10,000Đ; rice and beef 30,000Đ; beer 9000Đ. Open 7am-11pm). For a more tropical atmosphere, settle down at the phở and cơm shop of **Lộc Anh Hotel ❷,** 26 Bình Minh, where you can eat sitting underneath a palm tree in the semi-outdoor lobby. (☎824 788. Open daily 5am-11pm. Entrees 12000-35,000Đ.) Food, refreshment, and snack stands dot both Bình Minh and the beach pathway. A chair on the beach, rented from one of the bamboo refreshment huts, costs 10,000Đ. The cafe also has a water well where you can rinse yourself off before leaving the beach (5000Đ).

HÀ TĨNH ☎39

Despite the fantastic array of beaches and sights nearby, Hà Tĩnh has not yet caught the attention of the tourist industry. As a result, there are few English-speakers and no English menus in town. Though Hà Tĩnh is not incredibly tourist-oriented, travelers should not shy away from the challenges of this enjoyable coastal city. Amazing undeveloped beaches, a peaceful mountaintop pagoda, and an enormous lake nestled in the forest are attractions that are by far worth the hassle. More importantly, the amiable and receptive people of the city want nothing more than totake travelers to dinner and karaoke. Hà Tĩnh is a great town—it won't be long before tourists realize it.

Ｅ TRANSPORTATION. Hà Tĩnh is only accessible by bus. The **bus station** is across from the post office on Trần Phú. **Buses** leave irregularly every 15-45 minutes 6am-7pm for: Đồng Hà (4-5hr.; 40,000-60,000Đ); Đồng Hới (3hr.; 20,000-40,000Đ); Hà Nội (7hr.; 60,000-80,000Đ); Hồng Lĩnh (40min.; 10,000-15,000Đ); Huế (6hr.; 50,000-70,000Đ); Vụ Quang (2hr.; 20,000Đ). These buses, as well as those going to smaller provincial cities, can be flagged down anywhere along Hwy. 1. **Open-tour buses** to Hà Nội (40,000-60,000Đ) can be booked at the Hà Tĩnh tourist office on Trần Phú and at many hotels. To get a **taxi,** call **Taxi Hà Tĩnh** (☎896 896).

🖪🔃 ORIENTATION AND PRACTICAL INFORMATION. While most of Hà Tĩnh is centered on **Highway 1** (called **Trần Phú** in town), the town also branches east toward the ocean along **Phan Đình Phùng** and a few smaller, parallel roads. The Hà Tĩnh **tourist office,** 9 Trần Phú, lies to the left of Bình Minh Hotel. The friendly, English-speaking staff provides brochures and information on the various sights of the province, as well as the available modes of transportation. (☎853 610; vkchi2008@yahoo.com. Open M-F

7-11am and 2-5pm.) To change currency and get AmEx/MC/V cash advances, head to **Vietcombank,** 11 Phan Đình Phùng, 50m down the street from Trần Phú. (☎821 202 or 857 002. Open daily summer 7-11:30am and 2-5:30pm, winter 7-11:30am and 1:30-5pm.) A **24hr. ATM** hides behind the bank. For pharmaceutical needs, you can go to **Nhá Thuôc So Lu,** 97 Phan Đình Phùng, where no one speaks English, but there is a good selection. (☎856 559. Open daily 6am-8pm.) Or head to the town **market,** where vendors are ready to heal your aches and pains. The bus station and the **post office,** 4 Trần Phú (☎855 312; open daily summer 6am-10pm, winter 6:30am-9:30pm), face each other along the highway.

⊓⌐ ACCOMMODATIONS AND FOOD. So far there are only a handful of hotels (all specializing in hosting conventions) in all of Hà Tĩnh. The helpful, English-speaking owner at **Hotel Bình Minh ❶,** 9 Trần Phú, 50m from the post office is the town's budget steal, providing affordable, comfortable, and fully equipped rooms with air-conditioning, TV, fridge, and private bath. (☎857 890; fax 857 857. Breakfast included. Singles with two twin-beds 80,000Đ; twin-bed doubles 155,000Đ; double-bed doubles 300,000Đ. Reserve well in advance.) Budget travelers can try to negotiate a discount at **Tân Giang ❷,** 25 Nguyễn Công Trứ, which has comfortable rooms and a friendly staff. Relatively bare singles, doubles, and triples (140,000-160,000Đ) have air-conditioning and TVs. (☎857 063 or 855 583.) Next door is the **Thành Sen ❸,** 23 Nguyễn Công Trứ, offering similar lodging at slightly higher prices. The walls are somewhat marked up but the doubles are spacious and the singles comfortable and clean. (☎855 706. Singles and doubles 150,000Đ.)

Though overflowing with refreshment stands and some delicious phở and cơm shops, there isn't much in the way of culinary choice in Hà Tĩnh. Decent food can be ordered at the restaurant on the ground floor of **Hotel Bình Minh ❷.** (Entrees 10,000-30,000Đ. Open daily 6am-9pm.) A sweet snack called *cư do,* made of peanuts, honey, and rice paper—vaguely reminiscent of Cracker Jacks—is a specialty of Hà Tĩnh. The tasty snack can be bought all along Hwy. 1 and in the market. Popular shops and refreshment stalls that remain busy into the night line the left stretch of Phan Đình Phùng, near its intersection with Trần Phú.

⌐⊓ SHOPPING AND ENTERTAINMENT. The **Chợ Hà Tĩnh** on Nguyễn Chì Thanh is a shabbily erected and sprawling warehouse that sells food, clothing, accessories, and even medicine. (Open daily from dawn until dusk.) You can reach the market by making a right from Phan Đình Phùng onto Nguyễn Chì Thanh about 1.5km south of Trần Phú. Locals teenagers frequent the **karaoke** shops along Nguyễn Biệu from 8-11pm every night. If you meet any young adults, you will likely end up in a karaoke shop, where you pay by the hour. Most karaoke shops offer a small booklet of English songs if you ask the manager, so tune up those vocal chords and get ready to sing like a Vietnamese popstar.

⊠ DAYTRIPS FROM HÀ TĨNH. If you're looking to escape into relatively undisturbed natural beauty, you need not travel far from Hà Tĩnh. Several white-sand beaches, a surreal mountaintop pagoda, and a nature reserve are all within a day's travel. Though most are best done as daytrips, some offer overnight accommodations for those who wish to lengthen their peaceful retreat.

⊠ THẠCH HÂI BEACH. Lying 12km east of Hà Tĩnh, Thạch Hâi is the perfect getaway for a day or just for a quick swim. Though not as popularly acclaimed as Thiên Cầm beach (p. 255), Thạch Hâi, with its crystal-clear waters, is certainly just as beautiful. Not (yet) a resort, the white shore stretches along a green forest, with merely a few beach volleyball courts, scattered refreshment stands (coconut milk 6000Đ), and seafood restaurants serving fresh clams (20,000-30,000Đ) and crabs (about

KARA! OK!

The first time I did karaoke was in Hà Tĩnh. Although I had become increasingly aware throughout my stay of just how many neon "karaoke" signs littered the city, I didn't realize that Hà Tĩnh was the country's unofficial capital of karaoke. As for me—well, I never really considered myself the type to sing outside of the shower, and the idea of karaoke never quite sat well with me. One night, though, while eating coconut with a group of Vietnamese twenty-somethings, the uneasy thought abruptly became a reality. Within 20 minutes of meeting these strangers, one asked whether I could sing. Naively (for it seems that the coconut milk has affected my reasoning abilities), I responded in the affirmative. Immediately, my questioner yelled "KARA!" and his companions yelled back "OK!" Within seconds I was on the back of a motorcycle heading for one of the many neon-lit alleys.

The karaoke I would take part in that night (and the next) was completely unlike what I had imagined. I had envisioned a large room with a single stage and a crowd, listening eagerly as singers performed their favorite tunes. I've since learned that, though such karaoke places exist especially in Vinh), the majority of karaoke shops in the country consist of small rooms. Inside each room is a couch, a table

Cont'd on next page...]

100,000Đ per kg). These stands and restaurants are concentrated at the mouth of the road leading to the undeveloped beach. Come in the late afternoon to see a spectacular sunset and watch locals (who avoid the sun during the day) enjoy the beach at night. You can rent bathing suits (5000Đ) and lockers (8000Đ) at any of the main restaurants along the beach. The drive there is pretty fantastic; watch as the landscape changes from city to rice fields to forest to lakes to sandy beach. *(The beach is 30min. from Hà Tĩnh and costs 20,000-25,000Đ each way by motorbike. To reach the beach on your own, turn south down Phan Đình Phùng and continue down the road 1.5km until a blue billboard on your right invites you to head right on Nguyễn Chí Thanh for 12km.)*

■ **HƯƠNG TÍCH PAGODA.** Situated in Thien Loc village, 15km northwest of Hà Tĩnh, Hương Tích Pagoda ("Pagoda of Fragrant Traces") lies atop Ngàn Hồng mountain. Not merely a tourist attraction, the pagoda remains a site of pilgrimage for local Buddhists, whose signs of worship—freshly burned incense and gifts of food—are impossible to miss. The oldest shrine rests at the peak of the mountain trail, where it is carved into the stone itself; a newer pagoda has been erected at the foot of the steps that lead to the original place of worship. This one is more ornate in design, decorated with intricate golden carvings and Chinese letters—an echo of the time when Vietnam lacked its own written language. Though worthwhile in and of itself, the pagoda is only a part of this impressive site. Once you reach the launch point of the visit, the journey begins with a short boat trip on the lake (20,000Đ per person one-way) that brings you to the base of the mountain path. The owner of the boat may try to overcharge you, but make it clear when bargaining that you can forgo the boat trip by heading to the steps that lie to the right of the launch point, traversing the side of the mountain on foot (1km). However, the boat trip through the placid Ho Nhá Đương Lake is a fitting beginning for the journey to the tranquil and remote pagoda. After the boat ride, climb past picturesque rivers and dense forest to a statue of a Buddhist monk atop a dragon emerging from a small pool of water. As the climb continues, the steps become progressively steeper, and the views of the lake and surrounding forest become progressively more spectacular. This hike, however, is not for the faint of heart. Just the ascent to the top can take anywhere from 1½-3hr., and the final 250m is incredibly steep. Visitors are advised to bring sunscreen, tennis shoes, and water; try to avoid a midday climb, when the blazing sun burns the rocky steps. While the pagoda itself is very beautiful, the hike is the highlight of the daytrip. Those hardy souls undaunted by the trek should continue past the old altar along a slippery dirt path to the peak of the mountain. *(Boats run daily 7am-5pm. To reach the launch point of the boat, head north out of Hà Tĩnh on Hwy. 1 for about 12km until you spot a blue sign on the right urging you to take a right and follow the small, poorly paved road for 5km to Hương Tích. Two more turns along the way are both very well marked with blue signs. A motorbike with driver will cost around 30,000Đ one-way. Arrange pickup in advance.)*

KẺ GỖ LAKE. Just 13km south of Hà Tĩnh lies the beautiful and undeveloped natural reserve of Kẻ Gỗ Lake. Spanning 350m and at points 50m deep, the gorgeous, freshwater lake is surrounded by forest-topped mountains. Developers are planning to make some of the area surrounding the lake into a tourist health resort, but for now, a walk along the perimeter of the lake leads you out of earshot far away from the minimal construction and landscaping that has taken place. Sandy shores and rocky walls provide relaxing and strangely romantic hideaways, and easy hikes through the forest feel peaceful and secluded. Though there are no lifeguards at the abandoned resort, both swimming and water sports are allowed in its clear, sea-green waters. Visitors should make sure to bring an umbrella and sunblock; there is no place, save the forest, where you can escape the punishing sun. If you plan on staying a while, bring plenty of food and water, as there are no vendors and most often no tourists disturbing the solitude of Kẻ Gỗ Lake. *(No public transport goes down the narrow paved path that leads to this lake. To reach Kẻ Gỗ by motorbike, head south on Hwy. 1 for about 1km until you reach a sign for the reserve. Take a right, and continue on the path for 12km until you come to a small bridge. Just before the bridge, head right and up the very small incline until you see the enormous, breathtaking lake. A motorbike with driver costs about 30,000Đ one-way. Arrange a pickup in advance.)*

THIÊN CẨM BEACH

Proclaimed by locals to be the most beautiful beach in Hà Tĩnh province, Thiên Cẩm is a popular beach resort in the initial stages of development. Cut off from the eastern coast by mountains to the north and the south, Thiên Cẩm's golden shores entertain weekend vacationers looking to escape the hassle of city life and provide unprepared short-term visitors with every necessity to enjoy both the sand and the water. Sitting atop a mountain at the northern tip of the beach is the **Cẩm Sơn Pagoda,** built in AD 600 on the Thiên Cẩm mountain. Though the pagoda itself is a simple structure, the view of the beach below is worth the climb to the top, especially at sunset. At

for your glass of beer or energy drink, and, inevitably, ominously, a microphone.

My new friends poured out beers, yelled "Yo!" (cheers) and programmed the first song. The first singer was a natural, who had to stand up and at times close his eyes to properly convey his passion. The next singer belted out a painfully insistent Vietpop tune. Finally, it was my turn. The majority of the songs in the programming book were Vietnamese, or English songs I had never heard of. I settled on Toni Braxton's "Unbreak My Heart," which for some reason is almost as well known in Vietnam as their national anthem; everyone sang along with me. Over the course of the night I also sang Boyz II Men's "I'll Make Love to You," the lyrics of which my friends did not understand, as well as Sam Cooke's "Twisting the Night Away."

And I had a great night. What I enjoyed most about it all was the kind of playful innocence surrounding the process. None of my fellow singers were at all self-conscious, and they weren't singing to impress anyone. They were singing because they loved to sing. And it's a national passion, alive in the countryside as much as the city. As you explore Vietnam, be ready to sing—it's a fun time and a great way to make friends, whether around a TV prompter or an old farmhouse guitar.

—*Ross Arbes*

the beach itself, you can rent a bathing suit (5000Đ) and leave your things to be watched with the attendant next to the showers (5000Đ). When you're done, a shower and mini-shampoo will cost 3000Đ and a small towel 10,000Đ. To take a 30min. boat ride to a small island that rests amid the crashing waves, stop by the reception at the Thiên Ý Hotel (250,000Đ for 25-55 people). On the island, you can wine and dine or simply splash around.

Still in its first stages of becoming a major resort, Thiên Cầm's secluded atmosphere and relatively undisturbed shores come with a price: a lack of affordable or diverse housing options. Air-conditioned triples (250,000Đ) with private baths but no hot water can be found in **guesthouses ❸** hidden in the woods along the beach. To the right of the post office stands the bright green **Thanh Lịch Hotel ❸.** Bare but brightly lit, rooms with a twin and queen bed, air-conditioning, TV, private baths, and pleasant service cost 250,000-290,000Đ for one person and 300,000Đ for two (☎862 520). For higher-quality rooms and significantly higher prices, stop by the **Thiên Ý Hotel ❹.** The staff speaks English, and the rooms have air-conditioning, TV, and phone. (☎862 345; thienyhotel@yahoo.com. Breakfast included. Check-out noon. Deluxe singles and doubles with brand-new shower and bath 360,000Đ; comfortable triples 410,000Đ.) For deluxe meals and big portions of cooked eel (38,000Đ), stewed chicken (8000Đ), or simple but delicious boiled spinach (6000Đ), grab a seat at the **beachfront restaurant ❷** of the Thiên Ý Hotel. (Open daily 6am-11pm.) A few phở and cơm shops line the beach walk, while others can be found near the steps that ascend to the pagoda and in the village which lies about 500m southwest of the beach resort.

Though accessible by paved roads, the beach lies 9km away from the closest bus stop on Hwy. 1, and as such, must be reached by **motorbike** (one-way from Hà Tĩnh 35,000Đ). To reach the beach on your own, turn right out of the bus station and head south along Hwy. 1. Continue for about 20km until you reach the center of a town and a sign that signals a left turn to Thiên Cầm. A 9km drive leads to another sign marking a left and a 1.4km drive that lands you at the beach. The road that runs along the sandy bank hosts guesthouses, cafes, and phở and cơm shops. There is no bank or ATM, but you can exchange money at the Thiên Ý Hotel, across the street from the post office, at a decent rate. While there is no pharmacy or Internet access, a **post office** stands across from Thiên Ý Hotel on the road that leads to the beach. (☎862 205. Open daily 7am-9:30pm.)

ĐỒNG HỚI ☎52

While the Quảng Bình province boasts historical importance as a focal point of the American War, Đồng Hới provides peace for those looking to escape the noise and tumult of most of Vietnam's other major cities. Though its sleepy streets have little to offer, local beaches to the northeast and the town's friendly, laid-back atmosphere lure visitors to lounge on nearby shores and relax in local coffee shops. It's an ideal rest stop before the requisite trip to Vietnam's famed Phong Nha Caves or to the head of the Hồ Chí Minh Trail—the path that kept provisions flowing to hidden armies in the mountains and caves of the Kẻ Bàng National Park.

▛ TRANSPORTATION

The easiest way to head north or south is to flag down one of the **buses** on Hwy. 1 heading north to Hà Nội (60,000-80,000Đ), south to Huế (40,000-50,000Đ), or to one of the many smaller cities in between. The rarely used and out-of-the-way Đồng Hới **bus station** (☎825 254) lies 1km west of the center of town, at the corner of Trần Hưng Đạo and Nguyễn Hữu Cảnh. **Buses** leave irregularly every 15-45 minutes daily for: Đà Nẵng (7½hr.; 50,000-60,0000Đ); Hà Nội (12hr.; 60,000-80,000Đ); HCMC

NORTHERN
CENTRAL VIETNAM

(15hr.; 120,000Đ); Huế (4½hr.; 40,000-50,000Đ). **Open-tour bus** tickets are available at the few tourist offices in town, and go to: Đà Lạt (260,000Đ); Hà Nội (100,000Đ); Hội An (110,000Đ); Huế (75,000Đ); Mũi Né (280,000Đ); Nha Trang (210,000Đ); Savannakhet, Laos (220,000Đ). The **train station** lies 3km west of town, 1km past the market. (☎836 789. Open daily 7:30am-5pm.) Continue 2km past the bus station on Trần Hưng Đạo and take the first right after the bridge onto Hoàng Diệu, turning right again 700m later into the path that leads to the station's steps. Five northbound trains leave daily very early in the morning; five southbound trains leave in the afternoon. To: Hà Nội (9-13hr.; 122,000-177,000Đ); HCMC (23-30hr.; 280,000-408,000Đ); Huế (3-4hr.; 40,000-57,000Đ); Vinh (4hr.; 48,000-70,000Đ). To hail a **taxi**, try **Quảng Bình Taxi** (☎828 282) or **Taxi Đồng Hới** (☎841 841).

✈ ? ORIENTATION AND PRACTICAL INFORMATION

Though it is a relatively small town, Đồng Hới is spread out along Hwy. 1, which enters from the north as **Lý Thường Kiệt** and turns into **Quang Trưng** at its intersection with **Trần Hưng Đạo,** which in turn heads west toward the bus and train stations and east toward the Nhật Lệ river. There are very few English-speaking **tourist offices** in Đồng Hới, as the city does not presently receive many foreign tourists. Small offices selling open-tour bus tickets to Hà Nội line Lý Thường Kiệt. Most large hotels can set up private cars with a driver for a daytrip to Phong Nha (350,000-400,000Đ).

Your best bet if you want to find information about the province and its sights, or if you want to book an open-tour bus ticket, is **Nhà Nghỉ Du Lịch** tourist office, 102 Lý Thường Kiệt. Though a 1km hike north of the post office, the tour agent speaks decent English and is very helpful. (☎828 228. Open daily 7am-4pm.) Exchange dollars for đồng at one of the best rates in town at **Vietinde Bank,** 3 Nguyễn Trãi. (Open M-F summer 7:30-11:30am and 1:30-4:30pm, winter 7-11:30am and 1-4pm.) To reach the bank, turn left onto Nguyễn Trãi, a small road intersecting Quang Trưng 800m south of the post office. You can purchase medication or first-aid needs at **pharmacy** stalls found inside Chợ Ga, the major town market on the western outskirts of town. The town **hospital** (☎822 443) lies just off Hữu Nghi on Trần Quang Khải, about 2km northwest of the post office. From the bus station, head west on Trần Hưng Đạo and keep right as the road splits off and becomes Hữu Nghi. Continue down this road for 1km and take a left on Trần Quang Khải. Check out the new-ish computers at the **Internet** cafe at 1 Lê Trực, on a small road off Quang Trưng, one block south of Nguyễn Trãi. (☎824 694. Open daily 7am-11pm. 3000Đ per hr.) Alternatively, pop into one of the Internet shops along Đinh Tiên Hoàng, a small alley on your left 100m north of the post office. (Open 7am-10:30pm.) The **post office**, 1 Trần Hưng Đạo, marks the center of town, standing at the intersection where Lý Thường Kiệt transforms into Quang Trưng. (☎822 579. Open daily 6:30am-10pm.) There's a Vietcombank **ATM** inside.

⌂ ACCOMMODATIONS

There are numerous hotels scattered all over town, most of which offer comfortable doubles at affordable prices. For the most part, the hotels with the best value in the city are the smaller, family-owned establishments, offering good rooms for slightly lower prices than the larger hotels.

Kim Liên Hotel ❷, 2 Lê Văn Hưu (☎822 154), behind the Quảng Bình Gate. Spacious and clean rooms with comfortable beds, a friendly staff, and all the regular amenities—A/C, TV, toilet, and fridge—offered at some of the lowest prices in town. Singles 100,000Đ; doubles 120,000Đ.

Thanh Long Hotel ❷, 56 Nguyễn Du (☎822 462), is another great family-run lodging. Head east from the post office until you get to Quách Xuân Kỳ; take a right, and the hotel will be on your left about 1.5km. Situated conveniently between the city center and the beaches, the Thanh Long Hotel boasts spacious, comfortable, and cheap rooms with balconies overlooking the ocean. Singles 100,000Đ; doubles 120,000Đ.

Hotel Hoàng Nhật Anh ❷, 28 Quang Trưng (☎822 409; fax 840 269). Though slightly pricier than some of the other options, this hotel has refurbished and roomy singles and doubles, with gorgeous wooden furniture, marble floors, and radiant baths. Standard doubles 140,000Đ; deluxe rooms with king-size bed 300,000Đ.

Đồng Hới Hotel ❷, 50 Quang Trưng (☎822 289; fax 828 117), has standard two-bed doubles with A/C, TV, and fridge in its old wing. Some of the rooms overlook a small, peaceful lake. Doubles 150,000Đ.

Hotel Tân Bình ❷, 4 Lê Vân Hưu (☎822 181), right next to the Kim Liên. Popular with Vietnamese tourists. The rooms are old but clean and are fully equipped with A/C, TV, fridge, office desks, and private baths. Prices are somewhat negotiable. Singles 150,000Đ; doubles and triples 200,000Đ.

Mỹ Ngọc Travel Hotel ❸, 5 Lý Thường Kiệt (☎822 074), opposite the post office. Rooms are small and somewhat overpriced, but they're in a prime location and are clean, with A/C, TV, and bath. Doubles 200,000Đ but highly negotiable.

Nhà Nghi Điện Ảnh ❶, 1 Lê Trực (☎821 839), is the tight-budget option. Next to an Internet shop, about 850m south of the post office, this hotel has old, small triples with few windows. These dark rooms with A/C are some of the cheapest chambers in town. Triples with fans 50,000Đ, with A/C 80,000Đ.

🍴 FOOD

For an inexpensive, delicious bite to eat, explore the popular shops and cafes that crowd the market area on Mẹ Suốt near the river, 300m east of the Quảng Bình Gate on Quang Trưng. For delicious fruit smoothies (*sinh tò*), settle down at one of the street cafes across from the province's prized gate. There is one stall across from 2 Mẹ Suốt that serves a fantastic blend of fresh mango and banana with ice (8000Đ). Just say "*sinh tò*" and point to your fruits of choice.

Phở Saigon ❶, 32 Quang Trưng (☎828 402). Near the Quảng Bình Gate, next to the Hotel Hoàng Nhật Anh. This small phở shop serves what might be the most perfectly seasoned bowl of phở (8000Đ) on Vietnam's central coast. Open 7am-9pm.

Tiến Thành bakery ❶, 104 Trần Hưng Đạo, 300m west of the post office. Run by one of the friendliest families around. Try the delicious slices of fluffy cake (4000Đ), cupcakes (2000Đ), or pork and beef sandwhiches made with freshly baked baguettes (7000Đ).

Đồng Hới Hotel ❸ has a restaurant that serves guests a variety of traditional and international set-menu meals at somewhat inflated prices. Dinner entrees 50,000Đ.

Hotel Tân Bình ❷ has a restaurant downstairs from the hotel serving typical Vietnamese fare at decent prices. This is also a reasonably popular bar; Vietnamese men drink beer here late into the night. Rice and beef 20,000Đ.

🏛 SIGHTS

The only real sight of interest in Đồng Hới town is the **Quảng Bình Quan**, a gate which stands in the southern part of town on Quang Trưng, 1km south of the post office. The tower-like structure was once part of a larger wall that marked the territory of the province; now it stands as a lonely reminder of Vietnam's royal history. **Quách Xuân Kỳ**, which runs parallel to Hwy. 1 alongside the river, makes for a

It's morning in Vietnam. Your thoughts turn to breakfast. Out on the street, though, coffeeshops and corner bakeries are conspicuously absent. The Western traveler, bereft of so much as a croissant, begins to panic. Americans, wide- and bleary-eyed, scan the streets for evidence of doughnuts; British tourists, already unhappily resigned to a dearth of ham and cheese, realize with a horrible jolt the paucity of toast as well; Australians twitch and shiver as residual traces of Vegemite leave their bodies. What, you might ask in desperation, hunger-induced hallucinations of Muesli and orange juice dancing before your eyes, am *I* supposed to eat?

The good news is that the traditional Vietnamese breakfast is one of the country's great national dishes, and perhaps one of the greatest breakfasts the world has ever known. The bad news is that it's not also the automatic default choice for lunch and dinner. The breakfast of choice in Vietnam is a piping hot bowl of fragrant beef broth and rice noodles called phở (pronounced "fuh"—think "funk" without the "nk"). Incredibly inexpensive on its home turf, it will fill you up nicely for a pittance. Though many phở shops have opened across the Western world in the last 15 years or so, particularly in the United States, they are not what most consider breakfast spots unless they happen to be in a large community of transplanted Vietnamese. Why hot rice noodle soup for breakfast? It may have something to do with Vietnam's steamy climate; it may also be the soup's absurdly high health quotient. Whatever the reason, phở's deliciousness gives it an insistence that is not to be ignored, so the only question is when to have it. Early, in whatever cool the morning has to offer, is probably the best answer, but many phở stalls stay open into the afternoon for the sake of late risers and breakfast-for-lunch types.

Although phở is one of the traditional dishes of Vietnam, the tradition itself doesn't date back as far as one might expect. Chef and author Mai Pham writes that the use of beef broth in Vietnam, canonical in the preparation of phở, began only during the late 1800s during the French colonial period. Cows were rarely considered a food animal in Vietnam until the French and their appetite for beef and beef stocks arrived. Vietnamese cooks made that stock their own by adding ginger, star anise, a few other herbs and spices, and their ubiquitous seasoning ingredient—fish sauce.

It's true that the pungent saltiness of fish sauce on its own tends to have non-Vietnamese travelers running for the doors. However, the employ-ment of fish sauce in phở stands as a synecdoche for Vietnamese cuisine in general—a powerful, frankly offensive-smelling agent subordinated through culinary alchemy to the greater good of the dish, creating a gastronomic masterpiece of extreme subtlety and wealth of taste. When properly combined with beef stock, fish sauce creates an incredibly balanced and rich flavor unequaled by any other broth; the fishy taste is subsumed in the greatness of the whole.

The streets of urban Vietnam are awash in the tantalizing aroma of phở; look for shops with people slurping happily as they hunch over bowls, or just simple street stands, again with people clustered around bowls of soup. Be aware that phở comes in a range of sizes, starting with large and ending with enormous. It's probably best for novices to stick to large. Order phở bò (with beef) and a large bowl will be filled with rice noodles; perhaps a bit of finely chopped herbs, and some paper-thin layers of raw lean beef are draped on top. (A bit of chewier cooked beef may be added, and there are many other variations: tripe, little meatballs, tendons, and so forth.) Finally that wonderful broth—the essence of phở—is ladled in, instantly cooking the beef to the perfect degree. Eat as is or—better yet—squeeze in some lime wedges, stir in fresh chili slices (or some chili sauce), and shred leaves of basil and *rau ram* (another herb) to sprinkle over the bowl. Your breakfast can be soothing, fresh-tasting, and zippy simultaneously.

Although final assembly takes only a minute, proper preparation of the stock takes hours. Consequently, few in Vietnam make phở at home; most get their fix out on the street. Going out for a phở breakfast may seem like a great way to meet locals, but there's an etiquette to keep in mind; most connoisseurs of phở (which is to say, most people you will meet) like to eat their soup quickly, while the rice noodles are at just the right ratio of softness to chewiness. You should do the same, and then strike up a conversation after the soup is gone and that profound sense of well-being sets in.

Finally, to really jump-start your day, try a Vietnamese coffee, alias *cá phê*. A metal filter is placed over a glass with a layer of sweetened condensed milk in the bottom and hot water is poured over the dark, espresso-like coffee in the filter. Very strong coffee slowly drips into the milk. When finished, the two are stirred together and often poured over ice to drink. It's the perfect accompaniment to your phở breakfast, and together they'll leave you prepared to face anything the day brings. More likely than not, your day will bring more phở. Welcome to Vietnam.

*Noodle soup enthusiast **Jeff Fortescue** is a reference librarian who regrets he can't get phở for breakfast in Pittsburgh.*

peaceful stroll, with a fantastic view of the nearby Xã Bảo Ninh Island. Another 2km brings you to the simple and ever-popular **Nhật Lệ beach,** full of small stalls offering fresh fruit, soda, beer, and coconut milk (4000-8000Đ). Another 3.5km past the beach, Quách Xuân Kỳ turns into a small red dirt road and leads to enormous **sand dunes.** The major town **market** (Chợ Ga) lies on the western outskirts of town, about 400m before the train station. Inside this market (also known as Chợ Nam Ly), you'll find stalls filled with clothing, shoes, books, bags, pharmaceuticals, and food. Outside, more vendors crowd the market to sell fruits, vegetables, seafood, and slabs of meat. To reach the market, turn onto Trần Hưng Đạo at the post office and head west for about 2.5km. The second, slightly smaller market, **Chợ Cá,** lies near the river bank at the end of Mẹ Suốt, facing the Quảng Bình Gate.

▶ DAYTRIPS FROM ĐỒNG HỚI

PHUONG NHA CAVES

There is no public transportation to the caves. You can join an organized tour (400,000Đ car rental for up to 4 people from the Nhà Nghỉ Du Lịch tourist office), take a taxi (300,000Đ one-way), or hire a xe ôm (125,000-175,000Đ round-trip). To reach the caves by motorbike, head north along Hwy. 15 until you reach one of the many highways (10, 12, 16, 18, or 20) that leads to the Hồ Chí Minh Trail. Turn right on the trail and continue north until it ends at Kẻ Bàng National Park. Follow the signs for less than 1km to the parking (1000Đ). The tourist reception office to the left of the ticket counter offers 3½-5½hr. tours of the caves that include the boat trip to the entrance. (☎ 675 001; phongnhanp@dng.vnn.vn. Open 6:30am-4:30pm. One-person tours 50,000Đ; cheaper for larger groups. Huế tourist agencies also offer combined tours of the caves and DMZ.

The caves in Kẻ Bàng National Park are some of Central Vietnam's most interesting natural land formations. The park has 62 caves, of which only two are open to tourists. The first stop on the tour is the 1000m long **Đồng Tiên Sơn Cave,** which was discovered by a local villager in 1935 but wasn't opened to visitors until 1999. A 30min. boat trip brings you to the base of a small mountain. From there, it is a steep 45min. climb up stairs flooded with Vietnamese tourists and ice-cream vendors all the way to the mouth of the cave. Inside, colorful lights illuminate various stalactites and stalagmites to create an amazing scene filled with colors, shapes, and echoes. One of the more popular attractions of this spectacular rock formation is the **Lovers' Cave,** a small nook with what looks like two stools, illuminated by green lights. Tourists tend to pose here for pictures.

To see the three chambers of the second and more famous **Phong Nha Cave,** visitors must head down the mountain and back along the river. As you enter the mouth of the cave in your boat, look up to see marks left by US bombs, whose impact enlarged the cave entrance. The 700m-long cave is bathed in natural light reflected by the water and the white stone walls. The center chamber has the most spectacular views: a tiny bridge carved in the rock leads to the **Chamber of Fairytales,** where one can marvel at what appears to be a fairy's flowing hair, the bed of a sleeping king, and a solid waterfall flowing down majestic stairs.

Natural beauty aside, the caves are an important historical site for Vietnamese visitors. The abandoned houses along the river leading to the cave and the small, difficult-to-spot bomb marks all over the area remind visitors and inhabitants alike of the conflict waged a generation and a half ago. Many of these caves served as military bases, hospitals, and even banks during the country's wars.

There are English-speaking officials at the **Phong Nha Tourist Center,** at the base of the mountain leading up to the first cave, providing visitors with information about the caves and the surrounding historical and natural sights. Snack and drink vendors crowd the cave entrances, and they are joined by restaurants and cơm shops around the parking lot and information and ticket booths.

HỒ CHÍ MINH TRAIL

(To travel down the trail, head from Đồng Hới onto road 15, turning west onto road 10, 12, 16, 18, or 20, all of which are branches the trail.)

This historically important road begins at Quảng Bình's most popular tourist destination, the Phong Nha Caves, and runs south. During the war with the US—known to some here as "the war to fend off American imperialists"—the trail served as the main route of transportation for the NLF as well as the main supply line for the rebel Việt Cộng in the south. As one of the primary ways to reach the caves, where provisions were stored, the road provides a view of the mountainous and forested inland that three decades ago was entrenched in war. Bomb pits, sometimes filled with water, are scattered along the road in the midst of forests or rice fields.

ĐÔNG HÀ ☎ 53

Đông Hà is a gateway city. Largely unimpressive in its own right, but located in the center of the DMZ, the city sees an amazing number of tourists passing through on historically oriented tours each day. Most of them, however, don't stay longer than the time it takes to eat a meal. Though it was the seat of a major US base three decades ago, the city today is entirely lacking in historical relics, and instead serves only as a stopover for visitors wanting to get a glimpse of the past in the hills surrounding it. Don't overlook this place entirely, though—the locals there are some of the kindest, most inviting people in all of the country.

█ TRANSPORTATION. Located at the intersection of Lê Van Hữu and Lê Duẩn, the **southbound bus station** runs buses every 15-30min. between 5am and 7pm. Buses leave when they are full, and tourists should expect high but bargainable prices from the drivers. **Buses** run to Đà Nẵng (4½hr.; 50,000-60,000Đ), Huế (1½hr.; 25,000Đ), and Lao Bảo (1½hr.; 25,000-30,000Đ). To catch a bus to any northern city, get a motorbike to drop you off along Hwy. 1 about 800m north of the Đông Hà Bridge for 5000Đ. From there, you will have to flag down a passing **northbound bus** to Đồng Hới (1½hr.; 30,000-40,000Đ) or Hà Nội (12-15hr.; 74,000-100,000Đ). The **train station** is 700m farther south on Trấn Phú; to get there from the bus station, head west along Lê Van Hữu and take your first left on Trấn Phú. Continue on this road until it ends. Five trains daily leave to: Đồng Hới (1½-3hr.; 28,000-100,000Đ); Hà Nội (9½-10hr.; 185,000-622,000Đ); HCMC (23-28hr.; 300,000-1,100,000Đ); Huế (1-1½hr.; 18,000-66,000Đ); Vinh (6-8hr.; 82,000-303,000Đ). Trains going south leave in the morning; trains going north leave in the afternoon. Sinh Cafe and the Quảng Trị Tourist Company sell **open-tour bus** tickets to Hà Nội (US$7); HCMC (US$14); Huế (30,000Đ); Laos (US$11-12); Ninh Bình (US$7).

█ ORIENTATION AND PRACTICAL INFORMATION. Pulsing from north to south, **Highway 1** (known as **Lê Duẩn** in Đông Hà) is the city's main thoroughfare. Heading in from Hà Nội, Lê Duẩn flows over a bridge, passes the main market and the park, and draws close to a mix of housing options. Twenty meters south of the bus station is **Quảng Trị Tourist Company**, 66 Lê Duẩn, which operates from the Mekong Hotel. Quảng Trị has excellent English-speaking tour guides and organizes tours of the DMZ (1-day tours US$10; 2-day single and small-group tours with guide and car US$45-50). An English-speaking guide with motorbike costs US$15-20 per day. Special remembrance tours, tailored for veterans of the American War, are also offered. (☎852 927; dmzqtri@dng.vnn.vn. Open M-Sa 7-11am and 2-5pm.) North up Hwy. 1, 800m past the market, is **Dong Que Restaurant and Tourist Information Center.** If you are interested in a personal tour of the DMZ by motorcycle, ask at the front desk of the restaurant for Hoan Chiến. He speaks fantastic English, is incredibly knowledgeable about the sites, and does not rush through them as

GIVING BACK

WHAT'S YOURS IS MINE

MAG, Mines Advisory Group, was started in 1992 to demine Afghanistan after the war there with Russia. Today, it has spread even as far as Vietnam. MAG has two main goals—the removal of mines and, unexpectedly, the promotion of the local economy. MAG teams are composed almost exclusively of locals who are trained and paid for their work in the field. Even the present head of Đồng Hới's team, brought in from England for the planning and project management stages, will soon be phased out as locals are trained to do his job.

Though its mission is fairly straightforward, MAG is constantly faced with difficult decisions. The office received one request from a hotel developer to clear out an area for a new hotel. But would the project really be helping the community? Locals would probably never see the profits of the hotel; then again, they'd be the ones building it, and they would pay the price for finding an unexploded object.

Some choices are easy. A year ago, 160 items were removed for an area that afterwards housed a school. Recently, a large area was cleared to create housing for poor locals previously living in areas with high rates of flooding.

Some unpaid volunteer opportunities may be available. Check out their office in Đồng Hới at 15 Lê Thành Đồng. ☎842 852; www.magclearsmines.com.

some other guides do (US$15-18 per day). Dong Que also offers open-tour bus tickets and DMZ tours by bus (US$10) and by car (US$45-50) for a maximum of 4 people. (☎852 303; dongqueqt@dng.vnn.vn. Open daily 7am-11pm.) Just south of the bus stop, facing the bridge, is **Trung Tâm Quán**, 201 Lê Duẩn, where you can book DMZ tours and open-tour bus tickets. (☎852 972; ttquan@dng.vnn.vn. English tours daily 8am-4pm; US$10. Open daily 6am-11pm.) To change money or get MC/V cash advances (with 3% commission), hook a right immediately after the town park. The **Vietnam Bank for Agriculture,** 1 Lê Quý Đôn, is right on the corner. (☎852 100. Open daily 7-11am and 1-5pm.) There are a couple of **ATMs** scattered along Lê Duẩn, including ones at 183 Lê Duẩn, in front of the Hiệu Giáng Hotel, and 189 Lê Duẩn, behind the gas station. The **Thuốc Tây pharmacy,** 10 Lê Duẩn, is on the way from the market to the bus station. (☎851 919. Open daily 7-11:30am and 1-9pm.) To check email and avoid a hotel's exorbitant prices, head to **Dich Vu Internet,** 177 Lê Duẩn, across from Mêkông Hotel. The computers there are good and the owner is friendly. (☎857 177. Fast connection 3000Đ per hr. Open daily 7am-11pm.) From the Vietnam Bank for Agriculture, continue straight for 1km until you reach an intersection with train tracks on the left. The huge glass tower in the center of the intersecting streets is the main **post office,** 20 Trần Hưng Đạo. (☎852 206. Open daily 6am-9pm; phone service available 6am-10pm.) A smaller post office, at 291 Lê Duẩn (☎846 001; open 7am-9:30pm) offers Internet for 3000Đ per hr.

⌐⌐ ACCOMMODATIONS AND FOOD. There is a surprisingly wide variety of overnight options in Đông Hà. Backpackers will likely feel most comfortable at the original **Phụng Hoàng ❶,** 295 Lê Duẩn, 300m south of the bus station. The singles (80,000Đ), equipped with air-conditioning, TV, private bath, and a comfortable bed, are the best value in the city. Doubles (120,000Đ) have nearly the same amenities in slightly bigger rooms. (☎853 359; phunghoanghotel2001@yahoo.com.) **Đông Hà Hotel ❷,** 16 Trần Hưng Đạo, stands opposite the Buddhist temple, slightly west of the town market. It has colorful, spacious rooms with air-conditioning, TV, fridge, and private bath. (☎551 670; fax 554 200. Singles 100,000Đ; doubles 150,000Đ; triples 200,000Đ.) To live in luxury, stay a night at the **Phụng Hoàng II ❸,** 146 Lê Duẩn, where king-sized rooms with beds to match, fridge, living room, and whirlpool tubs cost US$25 per night. Less upscale, though still spacious rooms have twin beds, fridge, and a sparkling private bath. Even smaller, but still comfortable doubles have clean baths. (☎854 567; phunghoang2001@yahoo.com. All rooms have air-conditioning and TV. Internet 20,000Đ per hr. Twin beds US$20; small doubles US$15. Prices may be slightly negotiable.) One kilometer south of the bus station, **Nhà Khách 261 ❷**, 260 Lê Duẩn, has clean, affordable, and generic rooms with air-conditioning, TV, and private bath. (☎854 425. Singles and doubles 120,000Đ; triples 160,000Đ. Deluxe suites with an additional room 300,000Đ.) **Mekong Hotel ❷**, 66 Lê Duẩn, located conveniently in the center of town, offers clean, fresh rooms with air-conditioning, TV, private bath, and a helpful staff. Rooms are a little more expensive than other hotels in the city, but offer equal quality. (☎852 292. Singles 150,000Đ; doubles 200,000Đ). **Nhà Nghỉ Ga Đông Hà ❷**, 2 Lê Thánh Tong, located right next to the bus station, is a good place to sleep if you get in late or are catching an early morning train. The sheets leave something to be desired and the paint is peeling a bit, but the rooms have air-conditioning, TV, and private bath with toilet. (☎857 756. Singles and doubles 130,000Đ.)

The choice of restaurants in town is not spectacular, as most locals eat at streetside cafes—follow their lead and try out some of the phở and cơm shops along Lê Duẩn and in the market. As usual, these shops serve great food and are extremely cheap. For those craving the comfort of an English menu, there are a few restaurants in the city, especially along Lê Duẩn heading south from the bus station. On the corner across from the station is **Tân Ngọc Sang ❶**, 72 Lê Duẩn, where the Vietnamese food—mostly glorified street food—is decent, but no better than the food stalls. (☎853 366. Cooked beef and rice 25,000Đ. Open daily 5am-10pm.) Many DMZ tour and open-tour buses make a rest stop at the **Mekong Hotel restaurant ❷**, where decent meals come at slightly inflated prices. (☎852 292. Breakfast 8000-12,000Đ; lunch and dinner 15,000-25,000Đ. Open daily 6am-11pm.) **Trung Tâm Quán ❶**, 201 Lê Duẩn, doubles as a phở and cơm shop with a friendly staff. (☎852 972. Vegetable soup 7000Đ; phở 10,000Đ; rice or noodles with meat 13,000Đ.) Some other hotels, like the Phụng Hoàng II **restaurant ❷**, 146 Lê Duẩn (open daily 6-8am and noon-midnight), and the Đông Hà Hotel **restaurant ❷**, 16 Trần Hưng Đạo (open daily 6am-8pm), offer Western food options. Both offer lunch and dinner options ranging from sautéed chicken to American steak (25,000-40,000Đ).

🖸 **SIGHTS.** Though the city was once a military base, the remnants of US occupation that survived the NLF were destroyed by inhabitants who returned to reclaim their ruined homes. Now the only war-related sight within the city limits is a trio of **US tanks** abandoned in 1972. After the war, the tanks were retrieved from the DMZ and brought to the city center, and they now sit opposite the main post office. The other sight of interest is an old **Buddhist temple,** whose vibrant colors and walls engraved with ancient tales seem out of place among the gray, weathered buildings and simple modern structures of the city. To reach the temple from the post office, head down Trần Hưng Đạo towards the market. Alternatively, head down the curving road that starts at Lê Duẩn to the left of the market. The temple is about halfway between the post office and the market. Though it is not a tourist attraction, the curious can peek respectfully through the temple door window to get a glimpse of the inside. The friendly monks are usually happy to show visitors around despite their limited English. The town **market** sits about 1km north of the bus station at the fork where Lê Duẩn splits into Hwy. 1 and Trần Hưng Đạo. The city's central location between Huế and Hà Nội makes for an interesting market, surprisingly large and filled with goods from all over the country, including electronics, clothing, and the requisite packaged and fresh food.

🔀 **BORDER CROSSING: LAO BẢO.** No more than a village, Lao Bảo is a small post to the west of the DMZ attractions. Though not a destination in itself, the city receives a sizable number of visitors passing through the border to Laos. Most of them choose not to step out of their vehicles in this small, unmemorable village.

About four or five hotels offer housing, primarily for those who get stranded in Lao Bảo waiting for the bus or want to rest before heading on. The best value is **Hoá Bình Hotel ❷**, on Hwy. 9 near the market, which offers clean, spacious rooms with tall ceilings, air-conditioning, TV, minifridge, and private bath. (☎777 348. One person 130,000Đ; two people 140,000Đ.) A small family-run hotel, **Thiên Nga ❷**, has comfortable rooms with air-conditioning, TV, and private bath. Veer right as Hwy. 9 splits into two branches; the hotel will be on your left about 100m up the hill. (☎877 282. One person 150,000Đ; two people 180,000Đ.) The **Bảo Sơn ❸**, visible from Hwy. 9 and across from the bank, is 700m from the border. The staff speaks little English, and the rooms are standard, clean, and comfortable, with air-conditioning, TV, private bath, and faded paint on the walls. (☎877 848. Check-out noon. Singles and doubles 160,000Đ.) Both Bảo Sơn and Hoá Bình hotels have attached **restaurants ❸** serving Vietnamese and Western fare. (25,000-60,000Đ. Open daily 7am-11pm.) For cheaper and often better food, visit the town **market**, where phở and cơm shops and a few vegetable and fruit stands are interspersed among standard goods. This huge market is really the town's only sight of interest. Inside, alcohol, fake designer shirts, electronic goods, and perfumes, all rumored to be smuggled from Thailand and Laos, attract hordes of Vietnamese shoppers.

To reach Lao Bảo, head west on Hwy. 9, which runs perpendicular to Hwy. 1 from Đông Hà into Laos. Buses leave for Lao Bảo from the Đông Hà bus station irregularly every 15 minutes (1½hr.; 20,000-30,000Đ). Tourist companies in Đông Hà and Huế run buses between the two countries for US$11-13 with no more than a rest stop in Lao Bảo. Most of the town itself lies on Hwy. 9. The **bus station** (☎877 503; open daily 5am-7pm) lies in the center of town near the market, off Hwy. 9. Daily **buses** go to Đông Hà (1½hr.; sporadically every 15 min. 5am-7pm; 20,000-30,000Đ). Turning left off Hwy. 9 before the bus station and market leads to the **Agribank,** where you can exchange dollars and kip, Laos's adorably named currency, or receive a Western Union transfer. (☎877 246. Open M-Sa 7-11am and 2-4pm.) The **border crossing** lies at the end of Hwy. 9, about 1.5km (a 15min. walk or a 5000Đ motorbike ride) from the town market. You can cross into Laos daily from 7am-9pm. If you don't have a visa, it will cost you a half an hour's wait and US$21 to get one. (Visa office open daily 7am-5pm.) Coming from Đông Hà, there is a large blue-and-white **post office** on the right off Hwy. 9, a block before you reach the market. Inside you can send mail, make calls, or exchange US dollars for đồng. Though the rate is not as favorable as in banks or at ATMs, the difference is usually less than 200Đ per dollar. (☎877 601. Open daily 7am-8pm.)

THE DEMILITARIZED ZONE (DMZ)   ☎53

With military sights scattered along and around Highway 9, the Demilitarized Zone covers a radius of about 25km south and west of Đông Hà. A complete visit to the tourist-approved sites takes time, energy, and a fair amount of money if you're planning to go with a guide. Touring solo and still seeing everything is nearly impossible, and Let's Go recommends that independent explorers take at least two days in the area. A good motorcycle, an excellent map, and patience are also useful—it can be tricky to spot sights whose importance now remains merely in national, and sometimes personal, memory.

HISTORY

After the French were defeated by the Việt Minh in 1954, a conference was set up in Geneva to decide the future of Vietnam. Virtually without its consent, the coun-

STAY ON THE BEATEN TRACK. As per the guidelines of the Geneva Accords of 1954, Vietnam was divided at the 17th parallel, which runs through the DMZ, until 1975. During the war, the Americans placed mines in this area to keep North Vietnamese soldiers out of the South. After the war, locals attempted to clear the area by hand or with sticks. Since then, 5000 Vietnamese lives have been claimed by mine explosions. Foreign powers such as the UK's Mine Advising Group, Germany's SOEI, and the US military have come to Vietnam's aid in the effort to de-mine the former DMZ. However, **live mines and undetonated shells still litter the area.** Be careful and stick to well-established paths.

try was split into two, divided by the Bến Hải River at the **17th parallel.** For 55 days, people could move between the two nations. Then the borders closed—and the national election, scheduled to take place two years later and reunite the country, never occurred. During this time, **Hồ Chí Minh** was given control of the Communist northern state, powered by the **Việt Minh,** while power-hungry **Ngô Đình Diệm** ruled over the supposedly democratic South Vietnam. US troops, afraid that the spread of Communism to the southern state would have a domino effect in Southeast Asia, came to central Vietnam in 1965 to "aid" the **Army of the Republic of Vietnam (ARVN;** the southern army) by building a string of bases in the DMZ. Though it was the French who first created Hwy. 9, it was American troops who paved the road. Việt Cộng ambushes, however, soon made the road dangerous. To prevent attacks and improve visibility along the highway, US troops sprayed nearly 20 million gallons of **Agent Orange,** the now-infamous toxic chemical, throughout the area to kill the jungle vegetation that crowded the road. The troops also used Agent White to kill the bamboo that often hid rebels from view. A third chemical, Agent Blue, targeted rice fields. When American troops retreated from the DMZ, they heavily bombed their own bases to ensure that the Vietnamese would not be able to use them. By 1972, the Americans, realizing that they could not win the war, decided to leave. A new demarcation line between the North and South was established at the Quảng Trị River. This shaky peace did not last long—the **National Liberation Front (NLF)** conquered the South by 1975, reunifying the country at last.

Memories of the war are rekindled as visitors traverse landscapes familiar to them through first-hand experience or second-hand knowledge. The mark left by the war and the occupation remains alive within the memories of the area's inhabitants. Some Vietnamese recall the lingering US soldiers as their first English teachers. Others simply remember those days as a time when many men were forced to fight, often without a choice. In recent years, Agent Orange's adverse effects on both Vietnamese and US citizens has become the subject of many lawsuits. During his November 2000 visit to the country, US President Bill Clinton promised to aid the Vietnamese government in its efforts to ameliorate the caustic effects of the chemical. Also in 2000, the US donated US$3 million of mine-clearing equipment to the country and began to research the locations of mines, though many remain, making the countryside dangerous to wanderers.

▐ TRANSPORTATION

You can book tours or English-speaking guides at tourist agencies in **Đông Hà** (p. 261), in order to avoid the 2hr. commute from **Huế.** Đông Hà serves as the best base from which to explore the DMZ. Most tourists, though, opt for an easy, pre-arranged daytrip from Huế. Tourist offices and many hotels offer full-day trips with transport and air-conditioning (US$8-12). Some tours also include breakfast. Two-day trips to the DMZ run US$20-30. Shop around before signing up, as smaller agencies often offer tours of equivalent quality for lower prices; keep in mind, however, that sketchy, disreputable outfits abound. The **Phú Xuân Tourist Office,** 21 Trần Cao Vân (☎848 686), offers full-day tours with breakfast, guide, and air-conditioned transport for US$10, while Mr. Do at the **Stop and Go Cafe,** 4 Bến Nghé, arranges motorbike trips for US$15 per person. Tours leave at 6am and return around 7pm, with drop-off at your hotel. Visitors who want to visit the **Quảng Trị Citadel** can catch one of the frequent buses heading south on their way to Huế (30min.; 15,000Đ). The short distance (13km) makes Quảng Trị easily accessible by motorbike (20,000Đ one-way; 40,000-50,000Đ round-trip, including wait).

■✦ ❓ ORIENTATION AND PRACTICAL INFORMATION

Many former military bases and other sights of the DMZ lie west of Đông Hà on **Highway 9,** itself a historical landmark. Paved by the US military in 1966, it was designed to facilitate the transport of ammunition and supplies from the east to the bases that stretched toward the mountains of Laos. Tours of the DMZ usually begin on this road, but require backtracking to Đông Hà more than once. **Cam Lộ** lies 13km west from Đông Hà down Hwy. 9, while another 5km reveals a dirt road which leads to the spot where **Camp Carroll** once stood. Head 15km west from Cam Lộ to get a glimpse of the **Rockpile.** Thirty kilometers from the Rockpile after the **Đa Krông Bridge** is the former **Khe Sanh** combat base and the memorial museum that stands in its place. About 20km farther, the remains of the **Làng Vây Special Force Camp** rest on a ridge 9km before the Lao border. To visit the sights north of Đông Hà, head back on Hwy. 9 past Camp Carroll, and about 15km before Đông Hà town, turn left onto Hwy. 15. Built by the French before the war, this road is now known throughout Vietnam as the **Hồ Chí Minh Trail.** Fourteen kilometers north is a short dirt path that leads to the bunker at **Cồn Tiên.** Continuing 8km north on Hwy. 15 leads to the **Trường Sơn National Cemetery.** From here, head back down to Hwy. 9, taking a left onto Hwy. 75, which connects Hwy. 15 to Hwy. 1. Heading north on Hwy. 1 will take you to **Gio Linh,** a town where the former Doc Miếu military base was located. The DMZ tour continues north with a stop after 4km at the **Bến Hải River** and the **Hiến Lương Bridge.** Two kilometers after the bridge, turn right onto **Cai Lai.** A 15km drive east will take you to the **Vĩnh Mốc Tunnels.** To get to **Quảng Trị Citadel** and **La Vang Church,** head back south to Hwy. 1 and, after passing Đông Hà, continue for 13km past the remnants of the American military airport at **Ai Tự.** Alternatively, flag down a bus heading south and make sure to exit when you hit the city of **Quảng Trị** (15,000Đ).

◉ SIGHTS

Though the actual Demilitarized Zone spans 5km north and 5km south of the Bến Hải River, the sights in the area today known as the DMZ reach as far as 60km west, 15km south, and over 25km north of Đông Hà. About 17 American military bases were set up in the area; today, some of these bases have museums or monuments, while others have been entirely erased from the landscape.

CAM LỘ. Fifteen kilometers west of Đông Hà lies the town of Cam Lộ. Though it was once a small US military base, today no remnants of war can be found. When the US troops abandoned the area in 1972, the NLF took over the town. After the war, its citizens destroyed any remaining battle scars and slowly rebuilt their town, placing markets on the foundations of bases.

CAMP CARROLL. Five kilometers west of Cam Lộ, an unpaved road turns left off Hwy. 9 to the old US base at Camp Carroll. Four kilometers farther from the paved road lies a bunker foundation and a pile of rocks that marks the spot of the former military base, whose function was to supply the Rockpile and Khe Sanh with artil-

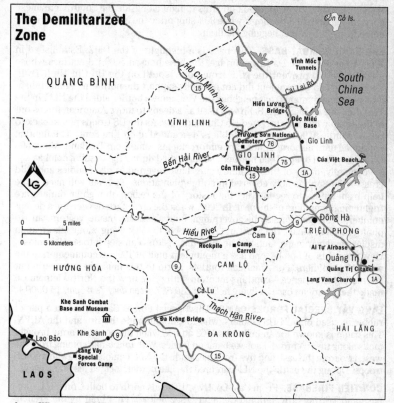

The Demilitarized Zone

QUẢNG BÌNH

VĨNH LINH

Hồ Chí Minh Trail

South China Sea

Cồn Cỏ Is.

Vĩnh Mốc Tunnels

Cai Lai Rd.

Hiền Lương Bridge

Dốc Miếu Base

Trường Sơn National Cemetery

Gio Linh

GIO LINH

Cửa Việt Beach

Cồn Tiên Firebase

Bến Hải River

Đông Hà

TRIỆU PHONG

Hiếu River

Cam Lộ

Rockpile

Camp Carroll

CAM LỘ

Ái Tử Airbase

Quảng Trị

Quảng Trị Citadel

Lang Vang Church

HƯỚNG HÓA

Cà Lu

Thạch Hãn River

Khe Sanh Combat Base and Museum

ĐA KRÔNG

Đa Krông Bridge

HẢI LĂNG

Lao Bảo

Khe Sanh

Làng Vây Special Forces Camp

LAOS

0 5 miles

0 5 kilometers

N LG

lery. When the DMZ was attacked in 1972 by the NLF troops arriving from Laos, Camp Carroll was where ARVN Colonel Phạm Văn Đính surrendered to the North. Ironically, after the surrender he became an officer in the NLF—part of a propaganda effort to assure southerners that surrender would not be fatal.

THE ROCKPILE. Twenty-eight kilometers from Đông Hà and 7km from Camp Carroll lies a 288m tall, unassuming green mountain—alias the Rockpile. The valley in between it and its neighboring mountain, Razor Back, harbored the Dậu Mậu military base. US Marines thought the base to be a safe helicopter landing pad until 1967, when it was assailed by Việt Minh commandos. Now nothing remains of the old base except for the mountains that harbored it. Some guides have pictures of the mountains and the surrounding region during the war, and they invite visitors to compare the empty stretch of land—cleared by Agent Orange—to the coffee fields which presently fill the countryside. Like some of the other sights, the Rockpile should be no more than a short stop on the way to Khe Sanh.

ĐA KRÔNG BRIDGE. Built in 1999, this bridge connects the Hồ Chí Minh Trail to the Phong Nha Caves (p. 260)—during the war, troops traversed the waters by ferry. From the bridge, it's about 1000km to the former southern stronghold.

BRU MINORITY VILLAGE. Though it wasn't a site of battle itself, the village of the Bru minority has become a stop on some tours of the DMZ. During the American

War, 10% of the Bru people took up arms to fight alongside the South Vietnamese government and the US troops, while 90% supported the North. Today, there is not much to see other than begging children.

KHE SANH COMBAT BASE. This base is a highlight of the DMZ. Established in 1966, 10km from the Đa Krông bridge, the base housed 5000 US marines whose mission was to prevent the NLF from going south on the Hồ Chí Minh Trail. Though the Lao government did not officially support the northern regime, inhabitants of the mountains that neighbor the Vietnamese border aided the NLF. In the Tết Offensive of 1968, Khe Sanh was used as a decoy to move American forces out of the south while they targeted Hồ Chí Minh City. As the US troops pulled back to return south, 40,000 more NLF soldiers descended upon Khe Sanh. The fighting continued until airborne American reinforcements came from Thailand. About 500 US soldiers and over 10,000 northern soldiers died during the ensuing combat.

Poignantly, many of these military sites have reverted to rice paddies and wild grass—Khe Sanh is now covered in coffee plantations. Tourists will need some help from guides to reconstruct the history of the region, though landmines are frightening reminders of the past. In 2002, when the area started receiving a decent number of foreign tourists, the government built a **museum.** Inside, visitors can see photographs of locals, the NLF, and members of the Việt Cộng, alongside weapon displays and war maps. Outside the museum, visitors can step into small bunkers, view remnants of bombs, and see a monument built in 1999 to commemorate the war's NLF soldiers. For American tourists, a trip to this museum is an eerie but interesting experience—captions mention with pride how the North Vietnamese made the American base "a living hell." (☎ 780 587. Open daily 7am-5pm. 15,000Đ.)

LÀNG VÂY SPECIAL FORCES CAMP. This Special Forces Camp, not just a pile of rubble, housed only 24 US soldiers, who fought alongside the Bru and the ARVN. This camp is known for an infamous 1968 attack, when the northern army brought tanks along the river from Laos via bamboo ferries. With four tanks coming from the west, two from the east, and five from the south, the NLF completely bewildered US troops. During the battle the NLF captured the Lao border, located just 7km away.

CỒN TIÊN FIREBASE. From Cam Lộ, Hwy. 15 heads north to both Cồn Tiên Firebase and Trường Sơn National Cemetery (see below). First built by the French, Cồn Tiên was taken over by American troops when they arrived in Vietnam. In 1967, the base was attacked and taken by the NLF. About 14km west on Hwy. 15, there is a 2km dirt path, accessible by motorbike or foot, that leads to the site of the former base. At the top of the path is a concrete bunker used by American troops. If you look closely at the wall to your left upon entering the bunker, you can see, in addition to many bullet holes, the word "CALIFORNIA" inscribed by a homesick soldier. So much crossfire took place between NLF and US forces that new battalions had to be sent constantly to sustain the firebase.

TRƯỜNG SƠN NATIONAL CEMETERY. Eight kilometers farther north on Hwy. 15 are signs that point visitors to the gate of Trường Sơn, one of the three national cemeteries in Vietnam. Created in 1975, the cemetery holds over 10,000 graves. During the war, when a soldier or fighter fell, he was buried on the spot of his death. However, since neither of the Vietnamese armies wore identification tags, friends of the fallen would write down the deceased soldier's name and the name of his village. In 1975, when the war was over, the government began to exhume corpses of northern army soldiers and supporters of the northern government. Thanks to the efforts of their comrades, many of the soldiers' remains were retrieved, allowing families to identify their loved ones and engage in proper ancestor worship. Many grievers who were unable to find their family members' burial sites turned to fortune tellers. You might therefore see pictures and fake tombstones placed on the unmarked graves that psychics pick out. Most graves are marked by tombstones with the words "Liệt Sĩ," meaning "martyr," followed by the name of the deceased, his home village, the year that he entered the army, and the year of his death. The tombstones' inscriptions relay that some of the dead NLF soldiers (those with the middle name "Thi") were women and others were boys as young as 12. However, only those who fought with the north were afforded a place in the national cemetery. When the corpses of ARVN soldiers were retrieved, they were buried in civil cemeteries, denying their claim to a place in military memory. In the center of the cemetery is a large monument of NLF soldiers and Việt Cộng guerrillas with the inscription "Lest we forget."

GIO LINH. North of Đông Hà on Hwy. 1 is a small town that was once Doc Miều military base for US troops. A US Army M41 tank and two reconstructed bunkers mark the landscape; littering the sides of the path are bombshells and impact craters. The area around the base is bare; its trees were chopped down by the American army for a better view of the surroundings. Farther down Hwy. 1 is a memorial commemorating NLF soldiers, with a sculpture of three soldiers standing victoriously atop stone stairs. The large central character is a woman, representing the many females who volunteered to fight with the NLF.

BẾN HẢI RIVER AND HIẾN LƯƠNG BRIDGE. Dividing North and South Vietnam, the small gray bridge that connects the two banks was destroyed in 1967. During the time of separation, the two sides are said to have placed speakers on either side of the river to communicate with one other. To send a letter from the southern bank of the river to the northern bank took two months, as it was sent first to HCMC, then to Laos, then to Bangkok, then to Moscow, and then to North Vietnam. Rebuilt in 1975 to commemorate the Demilitarized Zone, the Hiến Lương Bridge stands as a monument, while a newer and larger bridge serves as the means of transportation. Both foreigners and Vietnamese visit the historical junction, whose yellow gate and red signs reclaim the once-imperial colors of the king for the new socialist government with a sign that reads "Hồ Chủ Tịch Muôn Nâm"—"Hồ Chí Minh alive forever."

VĨNH MỐC TUNNELS. Located on the northern side of the Hiến Lương Bridge, these tunnels were built by locals in an effort to shield themselves from the US forces. While the American Army never crossed the northern border on land, the area was constantly under aerial attack. Aware that many soldiers of the NLF and their armed supporters resided in the area, the US incessantly bombed the villages that stretched along the northern border. The network of tunnels you can visit today is only one of the 11 built in the area, but it's the only one that survived. While the underground village took only 18 months to construct, its inhabitants remained in the dark corridors for four years during the war. Over those years, 300 people occupied the 2km long tunnels of Vĩnh Mốc. Children attended school and adults had town meetings in a main "meeting chamber." Aware that similar structures had collapsed under the force of US bombs, the inhabitants of Vĩnh Mốc built a bomb shelter as part of the tunnels that descended 23m into the ground. Throughout the tunnels, visitors can see the small rooms that served as cramped living quarters for families of four to five people, the fresh-water wells, and the tiny corridors that marked the village walls. There are 13 entrances to the tunnels. Villagers would leave the tunnels in between bombings to get food from the woods above and the sea below. Before entering the tunnels, visitors can peruse pictures of inhabitants and other images of the war on the walls of the small pink museum. Behind the tunnels is a beautiful stretch of beaches, where tourist buses often make a stop and allow visitors to rest and sunbathe. Twenty-eight kilometers north of the tunnels is **Cồn Cỏ Island,** which was used by the NLF to prevent US and southern Vietnamese soldiers from moving north. (☎823 238. Open daily 6am-6pm. Informational booklets in Vietnamese and English 10,000Đ; collections of war pictures 30,000Đ. 15,000Đ.)

QUẢNG TRỊ CITADEL. On the 13km journey to the Citadel, you will cross over the Quảng Trị river, the newer demarcation line between North and South (as of 1972), where prisoners of war were swapped. Two kilometers down the road are the remains of Ai Tự military airport, a huge cement area where US planes brought supplies to the south. About 3km farther down Hwy. 1, take a left on Trần Hưng Đạo. The remains of Trương Bồ Dệ, a school riddled with bombs and gunfire during the war, is preserved by the Vietnamese government as evidence of American destruction. About 500m down the road, take a right at Lý Thái Tô to the Citadel. Constructed in 1820 by King Minh Mạng, it was occupied by the ARVN during the American War. In May of 1972, the Citadel was attacked by northern forces, who took hold of the southern camp. In July of the same year, the southern army attempted to reclaim the Citadel: intense warfare lasted 81 days, at the end of which 328,000 metric tons of American bombs claimed the lives of the northern attackers, along with the Citadel walls. Though the structure was totally devastated by the war, a war memorial commemorating those who fought and perished has been built in its place. Check out the affecting before-and-after pictures of the Citadel. (Open daily 7am-5:30pm. 15,000Đ.)

LA VANG CHURCH. Along Hwy. 1, about 12km north of Đông Hà and 1km south of the Citadel, is the road to La Vang Church. The road is new and has no name, but a large sign marks the site. The church was originally constructed in 1889 by the French to mark the spot where the Virgin Mary was sighted in 1798. While much of the area was destroyed by American bombs during the war, the bombs that landed immediately next to the memorial miraculously never exploded. In early August, many locals gather to praise Mary, and every third year there is a much larger pilgrimage attended by Catholics from around the world.

HUẾ ☎ 54

Huế is delightful. It is Vietnam's spiritual, artistic, and culinary center. History buffs will be fascinated by Huế's Citadel, originally constructed in the 19th century under the rule of the Nguyễn Dynasty, as well as historical relics of both the French and American wars. Art aficionados can admire the unforgettable architectural wonders of the Imperial City. Meanwhile, just a small trip outside of Huế leads to the grandiose and ornate tombs of the various Nguyễn emperors, softened by picturesque lotus ponds and majestic mountains. These sights transplant visitors into another world—ancient, imperial, magnificent Vietnam. Though many foreign visitors rush through the city after visiting only its historic Citadel, Huế's tantalizing flavor permeates the calmer days of those who take their time. The city's parks are adorned with modern and traditional representations of Vietnamese art, and its streets are graced with tiny galleries of original art. The city's markets are large and bustling. But it's the food—the insanely good, superbly subtle, masterfully prepared food of Huế—that sets the city above all others. Huế's culinary specialties and Buddhist restaurants are the best in Vietnam. Do not miss them.

◪ INTERCITY TRANSPORTATION

FLIGHTS

Phú Bài Airport, 15km south of the city off of Hwy. 1. **Vietnam Airlines,** 7 Nguyễn Tri Phương (☎824 709), in Thuận Hóa Hotel. Open M-Sa 7-11am and 1:30-4:30pm, Su 7:30-11am and 2-4:30pm. **Vietnam and Pacific Airlines,** 48 Hùng Vương (☎829

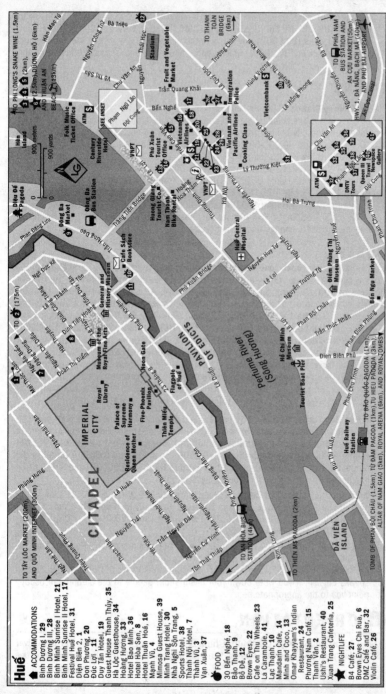

Huế

▲ ACCOMMODATIONS
Bình Dương I, **29**
Bình Dương III, **28**
Bình Minh Sunrise I Hotel, **21**
Bình Minh Sunrise II Hotel, **17**
Festival Huế Hotel, **31**
Diễn Biên 2, **1**
Don Phương, **20**
Đức Lợi, **11**
Duy Tân Hotel, **19**
Guest House Thanh Thủy, **35**
Hà Lộc Guesthouse, **34**
Hoàng Hương, **33**
Hotel Bao Minh, **36**
Hotel Hòa Sen, **8**
Hotel Thuận Hoà, **16**
Mạnh Vũ, **4**
Mimosa Guest House, **39**
Minh Trang Hotel, **30**
Nhà Nghi Sơn Trang, **5**
Sports Hotel, **38**
Thành Nội Hotel, **7**
Thành Vũ, **3**
Van Xuân, **37**

● FOOD
30 Bến Nghé, **18**
Bảo Thanh, **9**
Bồ Đề, **12**
Brown Eyes, **22**
Cafe on Thu Wheels, **23**
La Carambole, **41**
Lạc Thành, **10**
Mandarin Cafe, **14**
Minh and Coco, **13**
Omar Khayyam's Indian
  Restaurant, **24**
Phương Nam Café, **15**
Thanh Van, **2**
Ushi's Restaurant, **40**
Xuan Trang Cafeteria, **25**

★ NIGHTLIFE
B4 Café, **27**
Brown Eyes Chi Rua, **6**
DMZ Café and Bar, **32**
Violin Café, **26**

829; fax 823 336). Open daily 7am-7pm. AmEx/DC/MC/V. Three planes per day go to **Đà Nẵng** (USụ25), **Hà Nội** (USụ53), and **HCMC** (US$53). **Taxis** (50,000-55,000Đ) and **motorbike taxis** (80,000Đ) run between the airport and city center. Vietnam Airlines runs airport **buses** (30,000Đ), which can be booked at hotels, tourist offices, and the Vietnam Airlines booking office.

TRAINS

Huế Railway Station, 2 Bùi Thi Xuân (☎822 175 or 822 686), at the southwest end of Lê Lợi and over the small bridge that spans the canal. Motorbike taxis (20,000Đ) head there from the city center. Trains go to: **Đà Nẵng** (3-4½hr.; 1:05, 2:50, 4:25, 8:10, 10:30, 11:25am; 40,000-60,000Đ); **Đồng Hà** (1½-3hr.; 11:30am, 12:30, 7:55pm; 20,000Đ); **Đồng Hới** (3-5hr.; 9:15, 11:30am, 12:30, 3:30, 4:55, 7:55pm; 45,000-98,000Đ); **Hà Nội** (12-15hr.; same time as Đồng Hới; US$18-32); **HCMC** (21-24hr.; same times as Đà Nẵng; US$20-44) via **Nha Trang** (14-18hr.; US$12-26); **Lăng Cô Beach** (1½hr.; 1:05, 4:25, 11:25am; 20,000-30,000Đ); **Ninh Bình** (12-13hr.; 9:15, 11:30am, 12:30, 7:55pm; 120,000-150,000Đ); **Vinh** (7-9hr.; 9:15, 11:30am, 12:30, 3:30, 4:55, 7:55pm; US$6-8). Prices vary based on comfort and speed of train. Times may be subject to change. Purchase tickets early.

BUSES

For most tourists, **open-tour buses** are the best way to get to Huế. Travel agencies are everywhere in the city—about three per block, and even more in the tourist centers of Hùng Vương, Lê Lợi, and Bến Nghé. All sell open-tour bus tickets. Nearly every restaurant and hotel will also sell you these tickets for roughly the same price. To: **Đà Lạt** (18hr.; 8am, 2pm; 120,000Đ); **Đà Nẵng** (3hr.; 8am, 2pm; 35,000Đ); **Hà Nội** (14hr.; 8am, 2pm; 100,000Đ); **HCMC** (22hr., 8am, 2pm; 210,000Đ); **Hội An** (3½hr.; 8am, 2pm; 35,000Đ); **Nha Trang** (12hr.; 8am, 2pm; 120,000Đ); **Ninh Bình** (10hr.; 8am, 6pm; 120,000Đ); **Savannakhet, Laos** (8hr.; 8am; 190,000Đ).

Huế has three **public bus** stations. These buses do not cater to tourists; there is no English or air-conditioning, and foreigners are charged much more than locals. Buses come and go to most destinations every 30 minutes while the station is open. Prices are subject to severe inflation, and bargaining yields little.

An Hòa Bus Station (☎822 716), on Lê Duẩn, outside the Citadel at the northwest corner of town. Motorbike taxis (5km; 30,000Đ) run to the station from the city center. All buses departing from this station go north to: **Đồng Hới** (5hr.; 25,000Đ); **Hà Nội** (24hr.; 80,000Đ); **Khe Sanh** (5½hr.; 40,000Đ); **Vinh** (11hr.; 70,000Đ). To get to the border crossing at Lao Bảo, catch a bus to **Đông Hà** (3hr.; 15,000Đ) and transfer to a bus bound for the Lao border. Open daily 5am-5pm.

Phía Nam Bus Station (An Cựu), 97 Hùng Vương (☎810 954 or 825 070). 2km southeast of the Perfume River on Hwy. 1. Buses go south to: **Buôn Ma Thuột** (18hr.; 78,000Đ); **Đà Lạt** (20hr.; 100,000Đ); **Đà Nẵng** (3hr.; 20,000Đ); **HCMC** (30hr.; 120,000Đ). Open daily 4:30am-5pm.

Đông Ba Bus Station (☎823 055), right next to Đông Ba market on Trần Hưng Đạo, on the Citadel side of the Perfume River. Buses to: **Đồng Hà** (2hr.; 20,000Đ) and **Thuận An Beach** (35min.; M-F about every hr., Sa-Su every 30min.; 5500Đ). Though no one speaks English, if you write down your destination, people in the station can usually point you to the appropriate bus.

✈ ORIENTATION

About 15km inland from the South China Sea, Huế is bisected by the **Perfume River (Sông Hương).** The northern bank, the cultural center of the city, is home to the

Old City, hidden within the Citadel's walls. The **Flagpole of Huế**, which marks the front gate of the Royal Palace and the Imperial City, is inside the Citadel. Farther north of the Palace and stretching along its sides are surprisingly less touristed streets, inhabited by locals and permeated by a more traditional Vietnamese flavor. One of the busier streets in this section of the city is **Đinh Tiên Hoàng**, filled with food, clothes, and Internet shops. On the Citadel side, **Lê Duẩn** runs parallel to the river, becoming **Trần Hưng Đạo** after passing **Phú Xuân Bridge** from the west, and eventually leading to Đông Ba market, between the river and the Citadel wall. Across the river, on the southeast side, stands the commercial capital known as **New Huế**, which is overrun with hotels, restaurants, and Westernized services. On the southeast bank of the Perfume River, **Lê Lợi**, the main tourist strip, runs parallel to the water. **Bến Nghé** is known for pricey shops, tourist restaurants, and other services geared toward foreigners; it runs its course from the intersection of **Trần Cao Vân** and **Đội Cung**, near the eastern tip of Lê Lợi, and continues until it merges with **Hùng Vương**, the other major tourist drag. Starting at the **Tràng Tiền Bridge**, Hùng Vương crosses Lê Lợi and heads southeast to **Highway 1**. Farther upstream (southwest) on the Perfume River, the Phú Xuân Bridge spans the river between Lê Duẩn and Lê Lợi. Heading north toward **Thuận An Beach**, Lê Lợi becomes **Nguyễn Sinh Cung**, which pulses through the city's northeast.

◪ LOCAL TRANSPORTATION

Cyclos swarm around the city. 10,000Đ per ride. Bargain like it's going out of style.

Motorbikes are often cheaper than cyclos. 3000-7000Đ per ride; around the city 10,000-15,000Đ per hr. For longer distances, approximately 1000-1500Đ per km.

Taxis: Mai Linh (☎898 989). Metered and unmetered rides to almost anywhere. For unmetered rides, agree on a price beforehand. **Gili Taxi** (☎828 282) is all over town.

Boats: Half-day boat trips to visit the Royal Tombs are booked at nearly every restaurant, hotel, and tour office (with English-speaking guide US$5-6). A cheaper option is to ask for a 1hr. dragon boat ride (20,000Đ) from one of the boat owners along the boardwalk on Lê Lợi, north of the Tràng Tiền Bridge. Though many of these guides don't speak English, the sights speak for themselves.

Tourist Boat Pier, 7 Lê Lợi, right next to the HCMC Museum. 1-day tours (8am-4pm; 200,000Đ) up the Perfume River to Thiên Mụ Pagoda and the Royal Tombs, or to Thuận An Beach, on 10- to 15-person boats. Lunch included. Those traveling solo or in pairs can buy individual tickets at the pier or at tourist agencies, hotels, and the Mandarin and Stop and Go Cafes (US$1.50 per person). The acclaimed **Folk Songs of Huế** (see **Entertainment**, p. 285) boat tour leaves every night (1½hr.; 7, 8:30pm; 80,000Đ, 350,000Đ for groups of 10-15 people). The booking booth at 51 Lê Lợi (☎828 945) is at the northernmost end of the street. Open daily 6am-10pm.

Huong Giang Tourist Company, 17 Lê Lợi (☎832 220; www.charmingvietnam.com), arranges nightly folk song excursions (1½hr.; 7, 8:30pm; 50,000Đ, 350,000Đ for groups of 5-10 people). Also arranges tours of tombs and the Citadel and books Vietnam and Pacific Airline tickets. Open daily 6:30am-9pm.

Rentals: Most guesthouses, hotels, and outfits on Hùng Vương rent motorbikes for US$3 per day. Some also rent them with hired drivers. **Minh & Coco Mini Restaurant,** 1 Hùng Vương (☎821 822), provides motorbikes with drivers for US$6.50 per day. However, probably the easiest and most enjoyable way to get around Huế is to pedal around on a **bicycle**. There are several bicycle rental shops along Lê Lợi: **Nam Thanh,** 48 Lê Lợi, has a large selection of bikes. The shop inside Hoàng Hương Hotel, at 46/2 Lê Lợi, has very friendly service. Both are open 6:30am-10pm and rent bikes for 10,000-15,000Đ per day. Don't forget to bargain. Hotels and cafes, such as the **Mandarin**

Cafe, 3 Hùng Vương (☎821 281; mandarin@dng.vnn.vn), **Stop and Go Cafe,** 4 Bến Nghé (☎889 106), **Phương Nam Cafe,** 38 Trần Cạo Vân (☎849 317), and **Minh & Coco's** provide bikes with locks for the same price. **Phú Xuân Tourist** (see below) rents cars with drivers for US$25 per day.

🛈 PRACTICAL INFORMATION

TOURIST AND FINANCIAL SERVICES

Tourist agencies: Nearly all tour agencies, restaurants, and hotels offer identical services at nearly identical prices. Most sell one-day motorbike tours of the royal tombs and the Citadel (US$5-6); half-day Perfume River tours (20,000-25,000Đ); One-(US$10) and two-day (US$20) DMZ tours with meals included; one-day Bạch Mã tours (US$20-30); and open-tour bus tickets.

Phú Xuân Tourist, 21 Trần Cạo Vân (☎848 686), a small office that offers DMZ tours (11hr.; departs 6am; US$10; breakfast included) and boat trips on the river (8am-3pm; 25,000Đ). Open-tour tickets to Hà Nội (100,000Đ) and HCMC (220,000Đ).

Mandarin Cafe, 3 Hùng Vương (☎845 022 or 848 626). Sells Sinh Cafe open-tour tickets to Hà Nội (US$7) and HCMC (US$16) and arranges full-day DMZ tours (US$10) and dragon boat excursions (55,000Đ).

DNTN Tours, 1 Phạm Ngũ Lão (☎824 010; cell 0914 007 316), offers low prices on dragon boat trips (20,000Đ), full-day DMZ tours (US$10, 70,000Đ for private car), and city tours (US$6). Open daily 8am-9pm.

Banks: Most banks, exchange desks, and ATMs are scattered throughout the southern bank, around the tourist and commercial districts to the southeast of Lê Lợi. Some ATMs around the city close at 9pm; those on Hùng Vương tend to stay open 24 hr. **Vietcombank,** 78 Hùng Vương (☎846 055; fax 824 631). 3% charge on MC/V cash advances. Cashes traveler's checks (US$2.20 per check if cashed to US$; no fee if cashed for VNĐ). Open M-Sa 7-11am and 1:30-4:30pm. **24hr. ATM** outside. ATMs abound on Hùng Vương, Lê Lợi, and Bến Nghé. They simply aren't hard to find in Huế. The vast majority serve foreign credit cards.

Beyond Tourism:

Từ Đàm Pagoda doubles as a religious school where monks pass on their knowledge of languages to the local children; English and French classes are popular parts of the lesson plan. Foreigners interested in joining these monks as teachers would be warmly welcomed. For details, contact Thuh Phap Tri, 1 Lieu Quan (cell ☎0914 190 109; dha_wisdom@yahoo.com).

Global Volunteer Network (www.volunteer.org.nz/vietnam/orphanage) accepts volunteers ages 18-65 interested in teaching English in an orphanage. See **Beyond Tourism,** p. 92.

Volunteers in Asia (www.viaprograms.org) has a program for undergraduate and graduate students to teach English at the city university during the summer. See **Beyond Tourism,** p. 93.

Cooking Class: For those interested in the culinary specialties of Huế (and come on, who isn't?), try the **Thánh Hôi Phu Nứ Women's Group,** 11 Ly Thượng Kiệt (☎823 231). Teaches nightly classes M-F to men and women in English.

Bookstore: Cafe Sách, 131 Trần Hưng Đạo (☎847 745), at the intersection of the Tràng Tiền Bridge and Trần Hưng Đạo, on the northern side of the Perfume River. Sells maps of Vietnam and English books about the food, culture, and history of the country.

EMERGENCY AND COMMUNICATIONS

Police Station: 52 Hùng Vương (☎822 160).

Immigration Police: 45a Bến Nghé (☎825 819). Visa extensions US$20. Open M, W, F summer 7-11:30am and 1:30-5pm; winter 7-11:30am and 1-4:30pm.

Pharmacies: The pharmacy at 9 Hoàng Hoa Thám (☎821 319), close to the main post office, offers a good selection, but don't expect much English. Open daily 7am-9pm. **Thanh Xuân,** 6 Chu Văn An (☎830 675). Open daily 7am-9pm. There are also several pharmacies scattered along Hùng Vương, Trần Hưng Đạo, and Đinh Tiên Hoàng.

Medical Services: Huế Central Hospital, 16 Lê Lợi (☎822 325, ext. 2247). General check-ups and services open M-F 7-11am and 1:30-4:30pm. Emergency entrance on Nguyễn Huy Tự open 24hr. Small **dental offices** line Phan Đăng Lưu, just outside the eastern wall of the Citadel, as well as Lê Thán Tôn in the eastern corner inside the Citadel walls. Look for the large smiles with white teeth.

Internet Access: Many hotels offer a computer in the lobby for guests to check their email. With the arrival of DSL, numerous cheap Internet cafes have sprung up all over Huế, though prices near hotels and popular tourist areas are often inflated. A somewhat pricey but friendly shop is **Jerry.net,** 66/1 Lê Lợi, in an alley filled with cheap hotels. Offers 30 computers with fast connections for 5000Đ per hr. and Internet phone for around 5000Đ per min. Open 7am-11pm. To check email in the comfort of A/C, head to the main post office (VNPT; see below). 2000Đ per hr. Open daily 7am-9pm. The Internet cafe at 51 Bến Nghé charges 80Đ per min., with a 1000Đ minimum, and has Internet phone for 3000Đ per min. Open daily 7am-10pm.

Post Office: Mini post offices abound. **VNPT,** 8 Hoàng Hoa Thám (☎825 825; bdt-thue@dng.vnn.vn), 1 block southwest of Hùng Vương, on the southern bank. Offers a strangely diverse selection of calling cards, money order services, and flower delivery services. Open daily 7am-9pm. International parcels and *Poste Restante* are dealt with at window #1 (open daily 7-11:30am and 1:30-5pm). Near the Citadel is a post office on **91 Trần Hưng Đạo** (☎531 927), which sells calling cards and offers Internet downstairs for 2000Đ per hr. Open daily 6:30am-9:30pm. To ship large pieces of **luggage** and **oversized items,** go to the luggage office at Huế Railway Station, 10m from the main waiting room entrance. A 50kg parcel to Hà Nội costs 40,000Đ; to HCMC 50,000Đ; to Nha Trang 25,000Đ. Open 7-11:30am and 1-5pm.

⚐ ACCOMMODATIONS

Popular with backpackers, the alley at 46 Lê Lợi has a dense cluster of inexpensive and quality accommodations—some of the best for the budget traveler. Venture elsewhere for more luxurious quarters and to forgo the area's foreign traffic. In guesthouses and less-established hotels, bargain until the quality matches the price. Most establishments arrange tours. Every other year, for a few weeks in June, the **Huế Festival** (p. 285) takes over the city and makes accommodations prices soar. To find out the dates for the 2008 festivities, check online at www.huefestival.com/index.htm.

SOUTHERN BANK

EAST OF HÙNG VƯƠNG

The largest selection of budget accommodations are concentrated on and just northeast of Hùng Vương, especially between the main drag and Phạm Ngũ Lão, a few blocks up. Amenities range from the bare minimum to everything imaginable, but a little bargaining may be necessary to get a fair price.

🏨 **Sports Hotel,** 15 Phạm Ngũ Lão (☎828 096; sportshotel15@yahoo.com), is a 2-star hotel at a 1-star price. Located on one of the main tourist drags, this hotel has rooms that are simple but elegant. The floors are marble; the pillows and beds are comfortable; the rooms are quiet, clean, air-conditioned, and delightfully bug-free. Private baths with tubs. Motorbike rentals 60,000Đ per day. DVD player and movie rentals. Singles US$10; doubles US$12-20. ❸

Hà Lộc Guest House (Halo Guest House), 66/7 Lê Lợi (☎828 403). Family-friendly, with pleasant, bright rooms and sparkling baths. Top-floor balcony has a swing. Breakfast US$1. Has laundry service. Singles and doubles with fan US$6, with A/C US$8, with balcony US$10-15; quads with 2 double beds and private balcony US$15. ❷

Guest House Thanh Thủy, 64/4 Lê Lợi (☎824 585; thanhthuy66@dng.vnn.vn). Nice, clean, air-conditioned rooms. Breakfast US$1. Laundry service 13,000Đ per kg. Rooms have either 1 double bed with public bathroom (US$4-6) or 2 twin beds and private bathroom (US$5-7). Front rooms (US$10-12) have quiet balconies overlooking the alley. Discounts for long stays. ❶

Mimosa Guest House, 64/6 Lê Lợi (☎828 068), down a small alley just off of the eastern tip of Lê Lợi. Friendly owner and nice, quiet rooms—a great option for the true budget traveler. Breakfast on the terrace US$1. Tiny singles with fan US$3. Doubles US$5, with A/C US$7-8. Prices fluctuate seasonally. ❶

Hotel Bao Minh, 66/8 Lê Lợi (☎829 953; baominh2673@dng.vnn.vn), next to Mimosa. Standard doubles with A/C, TV, refrigerators, and lovely private bathrooms, complete with tubs. Breakfast included. Rooms US$10, with balcony US$22. ❸

Hoàng Hương, 64/2 Lê Lợi (☎828 509). Cheap and friendly. Rents motorbikes (US$4 per day) and bicycles (10,000-15,000Đ per day). Boat trips US$1-2. Small single with fan and private bathroom US$3; doubles with fan US$6, with A/C US$8. ❶

Vạn Xuân, 10 Phạm Ngũ Lão (☎826 567). Run by a friendly old couple, this small hotel has a social communal balcony, where people have breakfast, relax, and chat. Rooms are cheap and comfortable, with cramped but clean private baths. A great deal, despite the mosquitoes. Breakfast on the balcony (eggs and bread) 5000Đ. Coffee 3000Đ. Singles US$5, with A/C US$6; doubles and triples US$6, with A/C US$7. ❶

Don Phương, 60 Nguyễn Tri Phương (☎825 333; fax 825 480). Newly renovated and in a great central location. All rooms come with A/C, satellite TV, and clean baths. Rooms US$8-12 depending on shower, bath, and size of room. ❷

Binh Minh Sunrise II Hotel, 45 Bến Nghé (☎849 007; www.binhminhhue.com). Reception keeps a collection of English and French novels left by former guests. Comfortable quarters with bathtub, window, and A/C. Free Internet in the lobby. Breakfast included. Rooms US$18, with balcony US$20. Prices vary slightly with season. MC/V. ❹

Hotel Thuận Hoá, 7 Nguyễn Tri Phương (☎822 553; www.thuanhoatravel.com), near the intersection where Hùng Vương meets Bến Nghé. Plain hallways hide large and extravagant rooms with A/C, satellite TV, beautiful baths, fancy drapes, and plants. Outdoor swimming pool for guest use. Rooms USụ25-35. MC/V. ❹

SOUTHWEST OF HÙNG VƯƠNG

Less crowded and more spacious streets give visitors space to breathe and relax. Slightly removed from the tourist center, these hotels have less to do right outside their doors, but they're only a short walk from the action. The streets southwest of Hùng Vương house some inexpensive old hotels that are well past their glory days, as well as some newer and more luxurious options for city living.

Minh Trang Hotel, 27 Nguyễn Thị Minh Khai (☎828 148; khoithanh@dng.vnn.vn). Dark but comfortable rooms hidden on a street near the western tip of Hùng Vương, just past its intersection with Đống Đà. All rooms have A/C, and most have refrigerator and tub. Smaller rooms with double beds or 2 twins 120,000Đ; spacious rooms with 1 queen bed, 1 twin bed, and tub 140,000Đ. ❷

Festival Huế Hotel (Đống Đà Hotel), 15 Lý Thường Kiệt (☎826 177; www.festivalhue-hotel.com), at the intersection of Lý Thường Kiệt and Đống Đà near the radio tower. Clean, comfortable, resort-like rooms with A/C, satellite TV, minibar, and a swimming pool outside (free for guests, US$3 for non-guests; open 7am-10pm). Breakfast included. Check-out noon. Singles and doubles US$35; deluxe rooms US$45; luxury suites with hot tub US$105. Prices fluctuate seasonally. MC/V. ❺

Hoàn Mỹ, 44 Đống Đà (☎821 560; fax 821 561). Do not expect much English here. 1st-floor rooms have high walls and small windows. Smaller upstairs rooms are sunny and pleasant but may lack a tub. All rooms have private bath, A/C, TV, and fridge. Rooms with double bed 200,000Đ; 2 twin beds 230,000Đ; 1 double and 1 twin 300,000Đ. ❸

Bình Dương I, 4/34 Nguyễn Tri Phương (☎828 058; binhduong1@dng.vnn.vn), next to Omar's (see **Food**, p. 279), off of Hùng Vương. The older of the two Bình Dương buildings has affordable rooms with TV, refrigerator, and private bath. Breakfast included with rooms US$10 or more. Computers in the lobby have free Internet. Singles with fan US$5-7; doubles with fan US$5-15. Rooms with A/C and balconies more expensive. ❶

Bình Dương III Hotel, 17/34 Nguyễn Tri Phương (☎833 298; binhduong3@dng.vnn.vn). The newer Bình Dương has luxurious rooms for good prices. Spacious, light-filled rooms with A/C, TV, refrigerator, and sparkling bathrooms with tubs. Check-out noon. Currency exchange offered in the lobby at good rates. Rooms US$12-25; prices vary according to floor, season, room size, and view. ❸

Bình Minh Sunrise I Hotel, 36/12 Nguyễn Tri Phương (☎825 526; www.binhminh-hue.com). Big, beautiful rooms with A/C and satellite TV. Downstairs, the hotel library has an extensive collection of English, French, and German books. Free Internet for guests located at the Bình Minh Sunrise II Hotel, just down the street. Breakfast included. Doubles US$12, with bathtub US$15, with private balcony US$25-30. ❸

Lê Lợi Huế, 02 Lê Lợi (☎824 668; www.hotels-in-vietnam.com/hotels/hue/leloihotel.html), near the train station. Each building has different kinds of rooms, varying in age, ambience, and price. Fortunately, prices tend to match the quality of the rooms. In a remote location, but it might be worthwhile if you come in on a late train. All rooms have A/C and satellite TV. Old singles and doubles US$10; newer, somewhat cramped rooms US$14-15; doubles with modern furnishings US$20. ❸

Duy Tân Hotel, 12 Hùng Vương (☎825 001; www.duytanhotel.com.vn). A monster building compound near the city's commercial center. Newly redone with comfortable, sunny rooms and soft beds. Rooms have A/C, satellite TV, refrigerators, and clean bathrooms; some have balconies. Standard doubles US$25-40. Ornate larger rooms US$40-80. ❹

THE FAR NORTHEAST

As Lê Lợi heads north, it becomes the slower-paced and less developed Nguyễn Sinh Cung, where Vietnamese tourists tend to stay. Though a little farther from the center of things, there are affordable and quality accommodations surrounded by local phở and cơm shops, without the constant harassment of motorbikes and cyclos demanding your business.

Thành Vũ, 53 Nguyễn Sinh Cung (☎823 934). Stay where the Vietnamese tourists stay. One of the best values in the city, with a friendly staff that speaks very little English. Rooms are surprisingly large and cozy, although there might be an occasional bug. Singles and doubles US$8. ❷

Nhà Nghi Sộn Trang, 29 Nguyễn Sinh Cung (☎849 846). The rooms are reasonably spacious with A/C, TV, and refrigerator. Like most rooms, though, they aren't mosquito-proof. Singles and doubles USụ10. ❸

Mạnh Vũ, 46 Nguyễn Sinh Cung (☎845 745). No English is spoken at this friendly, family-run affair. Small rooms are simple but nice. Rooms with double bed 150,000Đ. ❷

NORTHERN BANK

Inhabited by locals rather than short-term visitors, few guesthouses and hotels stand within the walls of the Old City, Huế's historical and cultural center. However, those who choose to sleep here get to experience a slower, less Westernized pace of life. While the majority of tourists come only to see the Imperial City, those who choose to further explore the Citadel will find tailor shops, clothing stores, and local restaurants with non-English menus serving impressive traditional cuisine. Purchasing rooms, meals, and most anything else here is done in true Vietnamese bargaining style, at prices lower than on the southern bank.

Điện Biên 2, 164 Mai Thúc Loan (☎527 456 or 531 246; www.viethotel.com/thanhnoihotel). Near the northeast corner of the Palace walls, with a huge African tree outside. Large, spacious rooms with A/C, TV, and old private baths. Bargain like it's your job. Big singles US$10, even bigger doubles and triples US$12-22. ❸

Thành Nội Hotel, 57 Đặng Dung (☎522 478; www.vietnamtourism.com/thanhnoihotel), next to the Forbidden City in the old town. A worthy upscale choice with ornate Chinese furniture and comfortably spacious rooms. Small outdoor swimming pool is heaven on a hot day (free for guests; 15,000Đ for non-guests). Rooms with A/C, satellite TV, and refrigerator. Check-in 2pm. Check-out noon. Singles US$18-25; doubles US$18-45. ❹

Đúc Lợi, 3 Đinh Tiên Hoàng (☎524 920), accessible from the Citadel's easternmost gate. Some of the cheapest rooms in the city, but they're not for the claustrophobic. Singles (US$6) feature a double bed in cramped and worn-down quarters with A/C, TV, and just enough room to breathe. Doubles (US$8) are a little more spacious, with queen and twin beds and an attached balcony. ❶

Hotel Hoa Sen (Lotus Hotel), 51 Đinh Công Tráng (☎525 997; hotelhoasen@dng.vnn.vn), sits on a quiet street a block from the Museum of Royal Fine Arts, east of the Palace walls. The old and worn cabin-like rooms have A/C, TV, refrigerator, and private bath. The rooms are small, but the location is good, and the staff is very helpful. Rooms with double bed US$12; with double and twin US$13. ❸

🗋 FOOD

Huế is the culinary heart of Vietnam. It has the most region-specific dishes and the most impressive and varied flavors. According to researcher Trưởng Đinh Giàn, Vietnamese cuisine has 1700 different indigenous specialties, of which 1400 originated in Huế. Try *bánh chứng nhât lệ* (Huế's specialty sticky rice pancakes, made on Nhât Lệ street in the Citadel), *bánh nam* (shrimp and pork with sticky rice in a banana leaf), *cợm hến* (cold rice and mussels), *bánh bột lọc* (clear dumplings with shrimp and pork), *nem lụi* (grilled pork and greens in rice paper with peanut sauce), *bánh khoái* (fried rice pancakes stuffed with bean sprouts, shrimp, and beef, usually called the "Huế pancake" on menus), and *mè xửng* (sesame candy). Vegetarians should be delighted to hear that not only do most restaurants cater to their needs with at least a few enticing options, but that the relatively large concentration of pagodas, monks, and Buddhist vegetarians has ensured the survival of strictly vegetarian restaurants *(quán chay)*. Vegetarian or carnivore, Huế is an food-lovers' dream. Just try the *chè*—though it's served elsewhere, this dessert treat (made from ice, coconut milk, beans, lychee fruit, and nuts) is a specialty of Huế, and it's heaven. Today, *chè* (2000-4000Đ) stands can be found all over the city, especially along Trần Hưng Đạo, south of the Đông Ba market. Keep an eye out for the **Nước Mia** 1 stands, where vendors squeeze out sugar from sugarcanes and mix it with sour fruit and ice, creating refreshing cocktails (1500-3000Đ).

SOUTHERN BANK

Scores of eateries on Hùng Vương and Lê Lợi entice patrons with greasy but delicious dishes. Some cater specifically to tourists, with English menus and welcoming signs. For more authentic victuals and a variety of tastes, venture farther into the streets less frequented by tourists.

Phương Nam Cafe, 38 Trần Cao Vân (☎849 317). Like other tourist cafes—except better and cheaper. Serves typical Vietnamese and Western fare, with English and French menus. The best banana pancake in the city (5000Đ). Huế pancake 5000Đ; fish hot pot 25,000Đ; wine 8000Đ per glass; smoothies 5000Đ. Open daily 7am-11pm. ❶

Bồ Đề, 35/1 Bà Triệu (☎832 594). Easy to miss, the restaurant hides in a small alley between 49 and 51 Bà Triệu, with a black sign showing the way. Don't be put off by the plastic decor. Delicious dishes prepared by a hospitable Buddhist family. A menu is on the wall, but just point at what looks most appealing—it's difficult to go wrong. Entrees 4000-5000Đ. Open daily 7am-10pm. ❶

Xuan Trang Cafeteria, 16 Hùng Vương (☎832 480). Decent meals at decent prices. This is one of the few restaurants in the city where local and tourist tastes agree. Omelette with bread 7000Đ; delicious country-style tofu 10,000Đ; authentic Huế specialties such as fish hot pot 30,000Đ. Open daily 7:30am-10pm. ❶

La Carambole, 19 Phạm Ngũ Lão (☎810 491; fax 826 234). Decent French and Vietnamese fare, but hands down the best sherbet and sorbet (18,000Đ) in the city. Bamboo decor, velvet-covered menus, and Frank Sinatra playing in the background. Entrees 20,000-70,000Đ. Open daily 7am-11pm. ❸

30 Bến Nghé (☎848 532), across from Binh Minh II Hotel. Head here for a break from the grease. Delicious and filling freshly squeezed juices and desserts, enjoyed by locals and tourists alike (2500-6000Đ). Open daily 11am-8pm. ❶

Omar Khayyam's Indian Restaurant, 10 Nguyễn Tri Phương (☎821 616), right in the center of the touristy New City. Huế's best Indian cuisine, prepared by the Indian owner and his family. Delicious dishes and a classy atmosphere. Potato masala 22,000Đ. Vegetable samosa 6000Đ. Entrees 12,000-43,000Đ. Open daily 10am-10:30pm. ❷

Ushi's Restaurant, 42 Phạm Ngũ Lão (☎821 143), across from La Carambole. This is the place to go for dessert if you are pining for home. Very large Coke and orange soda floats taste better than any you've had before (20,000Đ). Also splurge for delightful apple pie covered in vanilla ice cream (20,000Đ). The owner, Ushi, is very friendly, speaks fantastic English, and loves to chat with customers. Open daily 8am-11pm. ❷

ON THE MENU

THE WONDERS OF CHÈ

Originating in Huế, the Vietnamese delicacy known as *chè* is the nation's snack of choice. Both sweet and refreshing, it's the perfect midday treat or evening dessert. Though the craze originated in the ancient Vietnamese capital, the love of the healthy dessert has permeated all of Vietnam, even managing to invade remote Cát Bà and its Bái Tử Long Bay twin city, Cái Rồng.

A mixture of soft lychee meat, chunks of various fruits, juicy tapioca balls, crushed ice, and veggies, touched with a splash of coconut milk and sugar, one cup of *chè* has an immense variety of sweet flavors along with a wide array of strange and delicious textures. Almost no two cups of *chè* are identical; the variety of ingredients is as boundless as the cook's imagination and resources. Simple, fresh fruit mixes are a cheap alternative to Western cravings for fruit salad, while red or white beans mixed with coconut milk and sugar are a heavenly delight that can turn into a nightly addiction.

As *chè* comes with home-made ice, those wary of the local water supply should request a cup "*không đá.*" Costing only 2000Đ in markets, or 3000Đ in slightly cleaner street-corner stalls, the delicious temptation has charmed all of Vietnam. Don't be put off by its chunky appearance and generally gooey texture; give it a try. You won't regret it.

Mandarin Cafe, 3 Hùng Vương (☎821 281; mandarin@dng.vnn.vn). A veritable Huế institution for backpackers. Owner Mr. Cu is an excellent amateur photographer, and his photographs of Vietnam cover the walls. Books Sinh Cafe tours. Greasy, affordable entrees 15,000-30,000Đ. Banana pancakes 7000Đ. Open daily 6am-10pm. ❷

Tịnh Tâm, 54 Chu Văn An (☎832 674). All of the dishes are made of tofu and are intended to taste like real meat. Great for vegetarians, or for those curious about the phenomenon that is faux meat. Try the "deer" (25,000Đ). Entrees 10,000-25,000Đ. ❶

Brown Eyes, 10/1 Nguyễn Tri Phương (☎832 512; baong137@yahoo.com). A clone of neighboring Cafe on Thu Wheels. A decent eatery serving Western dishes from mushroom pizza (27,000Đ) to hamburgers (18,000Đ), along with traditional Vietnamese dishes such as tofu in tomato sauce (7000Đ). Popular with tourists; books tours at cheap prices (city tour US$5, dragon boat US$1). Open daily 6am-midnight. ❷

Cafe on Thu Wheels, 10/2 Nguyễn Tri Phương (☎832 241). Hidden away in the alley next to Omar's. Serves Vietnamese dishes and greasy American fare, to the dulcet tones of the Red Hot Chili Peppers. At night, it's filled with lively tourists in search of a late dinner or friendly drink. Fried eggs 8000Đ. Vietnamese steak 25,000Đ. Tuna mayonnaise sandwich and french fries 35,000Đ. Open daily 5am-1am. ❷

Minh & Coco, 1 Hùng Vương (☎821 822). A small, dark, but friendly mini-restaurant with generous portions of typical, greasy tourist fare at low prices. Lively in the evenings, as the bubbly owners entice visitors to join the crowd, but not the cleanest joint in town. Rice with meat and vegetables 20,000Đ. Eggs with bread 15,000Đ. Books tours and open-tour tickets and rents bicycles. Open daily 6am-midnight. ❶

NORTHERN BANK

While locals eat in phở and cơm shops scattered around the Imperial Palace, foreign tourists often eat at the first centrally-located restaurant they see. But a peek into the alleyways and streets slightly removed from the sights of the Old City reveals delectable cuisine, for now enjoyed only by locals and expats in the know.

Lạc Thạnh, 6A Đinh Tiên Hoàng, by the river outside the Citadel's easternmost gate. A backpacker institution famous for its extremely friendly, deaf and mute owner who skillfully takes orders by hand signal. Serves Huế specialties at good prices (5000-25,000Đ). There's a friendly but intense rivalry between Lạc Thạnh and next door Lạc Thien, a restaurant with a nearly identical menu and a similarly deaf staff. The portions at Lạc Thạnh are bigger, but the interior at Lạc Thien is cleaner. Sizable serving of *nem lụi* 12,000Đ. Open daily 7am-11pm. ❶

Thanh Vân, 137 Lê Thánh Tôn (☎511 776). Popular with locals and expats and frequented by foreign chefs. No English menu or English-speaking waiters, but nearly anything you choose will be good. During peak meal times, arrive early at this hidden hotspot. Grilled shrimp 30,000Đ. Steamed fish 50,000Đ. Open daily 11am-10pm. ❸

Bảo Thanh, 149 Trần Hưng Đạo, across from the Đông Ba market. This small bakery sells delectable desserts (2000-25,000Đ) and has a nice selection of imported chocolates. Rolls filled with custard (2500Đ) are cheap and heavenly. Very little English spoken; just point at whatever looks appealing. Open daily 7am-9pm. ❶

◉ SIGHTS

The ancient Citadel, Imperial City, and Royal Tombs (see **Daytrips from Huế,** p. 287) dominate the tourist landscape of Huế. Most attractions are pricey; only some are worth it. A few less-visited spots are free and really worthwhile. Pay admission in đồng to avoid higher rates.

THE CITADEL

Emperor Gia Long, founder of the Nguyễn Dynasty, began building the Citadel in 1805. Today, the massive square fortress has a 10km perimeter. Its enormous walls are surrounded by majestic moats and covered in lotuses, which blossom in the summer. There are four gates along the Perfume River side, and two more on each of the other three sides. Within the Citadel lie the remnants of the **Imperial City,** the spectacular and picturesque royal palace of the Nguyễn Dynasty. *(Just off Hwy. 1 on Lê Duẩn. The flagpole, pavilion, and cannons are free open-air monuments.)*

FLAGPOLE OF HUẾ. The 47m high **flagpole** stands just inside the Citadel and can be seen all over the city. The pole is placed atop three large concrete bases, representing either the heavens, people, and ground or, to some, the gods, the emperor, and the citizens. Today, the tops of the Citadel walls and the flagpole are closed to visitors, who instead marvel at their grandeur from below.

PAVILION OF EDICTS. The large square opposite the flagpole and outside the Citadel was built in 1810. The square was used by Emperor Gia Long to announce successful national exam candidates and declare important decrees. In 1929, the function of the pavilion was extended to host spectator sports when Emperor Minh Mạng used it for fights between elephants and tigers.

NINE CANNONS OF THE DYNASTY. Immediately inside the front gates of the Citadel are nine cannons constructed by Emperor Gia Long after his victory against the rebellious Tây Sơn brothers. The emperor ordered his enemies' possessions melted down and the bronze used to construct these cannons, which were meant to symbolize the dynasty's perpetual power. The five cannons to the west of the square represent the five elements—earth, fire, wood, water and metal—while the four to the east stand for the four seasons.

IMPERIAL CITY. The saffron-colored **Noon Gate** (Ngọ Môn), the grand entrance to the Imperial City, is opposite the flagpole. The city was modeled after China's much larger Forbidden City in Beijing, and the Chinese influences are obvious in this grandiose entrance. This is where the last emperor, Bảo Đại, handed power over to Hồ Chí Minh and the new government on August 30th, 1945. Constructed in 1833, the **Five-Phoenix Pavilion,** which sits atop the main entrance gate to the Imperial City, served as a platform from which the emperor could observe ceremonies. There are five gates below it: the center one was used only by the king; those to the left and right were for the mandarins (the court's intellectual elite who advised the king); the one farthest to the right was for animals and food; and the one farthest to the left was for citizens coming for festivals. Behind the entrance, past a pair of lakes on the left and right, the **Palace of Supreme Harmony** once housed the emperor's throne. Nine dragons decorate the roof, symbolizing the perfect power of the emperor. Behind the throne room, check out the small replica of the Imperial City to get a sense of the vastness and complexity of the original royal residence. Today, only about one third of the original 150 buildings are intact. Elaborate inscriptions explain what once stood in place of the piles of rubble, which serve as unpleasant reminders of the American War. The **Forbidden Purple City,** the formerly walled-in residence of the royal family, is directly behind the palace. Between the Forbidden Purple City and the Palace of Supreme Harmony are a small museum and a building where tourists can dress up as the emperor, sit in a throne, and get a picture taken for 20,000Đ. The **Royal Library,** in a lush garden on the northeastern side of the Citadel, is one of the few structures that has remained almost fully intact. In the southern corner of the Imperial City is **Thiên Miếu Temple,** dedicated to Gia Long and eight of his successors (those who died within a year of taking the throne, and the one who abdicated to the French, are not remembered). Take a look at the **Nine Dynastic Urns,** located right outside the temple, each of which is decorated with the landscape and animals found in Vietnam. All of the structures inside the Imperial City will be soon undergoing extensive restoration with funds from UNESCO, which has declared Huế a World Heritage Site. *(Open daily 6:30am-5:30pm. 45min. English-language tour 50,000Đ, but tour guides aren't really necessary. 55,000Đ.)*

MUSEUM OF THE ROYAL FINE ARTS. A beautiful example of Vietnamese architecture, the Long An Palace was built in 1845 under Triệu Trị, third Emperor of the Nguyễn Dynasty. In 1923, the Palace became the showroom of the museum, where visitors can peruse 300 objects, among which are gold-, silver-, ivory-, and pearl-decorated porcelains, bronze weapons, majestically crafted furniture, and original garments worn by the royalty of the Nguyễn Dynasty. The museum courtyard displays cannons, statues, bronze cauldrons, and bells. *(3 Lê Trực, directly north of the Imperial Museum, on a small street off of Đoàn Thị Điểm. ☎524 429. English-speaking guide inside the museum available for questions 7-11am and 2-5pm. Open daily 7am-5pm. 22,000Đ.)*

GENERAL AND HISTORY MUSEUM. Also called the Imperial Museum, this yellow complex consists of a courtyard exhibit and three small buildings, once a school for princes and the sons of nobility. The building opposite the main entrance houses a small exhibit of Vietnamese decorative sculpture and ceramics. To the right is a small structure with a more interesting exhibit on the US invasion and Vietnamese counter-attack. The building on the left houses an exhibit about the war with France. The exhibits have English captions and are worth a short visit. Both museums are good but far from exhaustive. The imperial theme spills out onto the courtyard in front of the historical buildings, where visitors can wander among US tanks and artillery. *(1 23 Tháng 8 Street. ☎522 397. History museum and yard display open Tu-Su 7:30-11am and 1:30-5pm. 10,000Đ for all three exhibits and the courtyard.)*

OTHER SIGHTS

THIÊN MỤ PAGODA. On a hill overlooking the Perfume River, this pagoda is dedicated to a legendary woman who predicted great prosperity if a Buddhist pagoda were to be built on the site. Lord Nguyễn Hoàng heard her decree and constructed the pagoda in 1601. In the front of the complex is a seven-story tower with a fantastic view of the Perfume River. Though the main entrance is under construction, a dirt road to the right of the pagoda leads to a side entrance to the active monastery. The grounds of this pagoda are nice, but the perfectly manicured lawn gives it an almost resort-like feel. The highlight is a small exhibit in the southeastern corner of the pagoda about Thic Quảng Đức, the first monk to immolate himself publicly in protest of Diệm's discrimination against Buddhists and violation of religious freedoms. While his act of martyrdom inspired others to follow his example, it elicited a different response from the president's wife, who infamously proclaimed that her husband's opponents would do well to burn themselves to death. The monk's car is on display in a small exhibit that is always open to visitors. *(3km southwest of the Citadel. An easy and enjoyable riverside bike ride. Head west on Lê Duẩn and continue across the train tracks on Kim Long for 3km.)*

THE ROYAL ARENA. Before the construction of the arena, death matches between elephants and tigers took place on Da Vien, a small island near the Perfume River, or at the Pavilion of Edicts. Both, though, were dangerous to the spectators, so Emperor Minh Mạng constructed this arena in 1830 as a safer environment for the fights. The elephant, symbolizing the power of the emperor, was the favorite of the people. If the tiger was winning, the crowds would cry; conversely, if the elephant

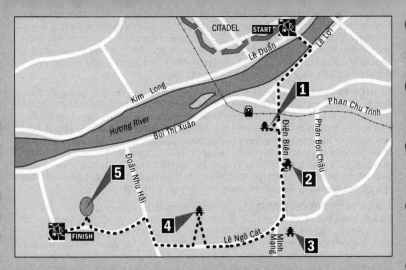

The architecture in Huế is unbeatable. Pagodas, gardens, and ruins maintain a calm imperial majesty. Biking through the countryside provides a chance to admire it all—try this route.

1 BẢO QUỐC PAGODA (P. 284). Serenity, thy name is Bảo Quốc. Monks tend luscious fruit and vegetable gardens, while local students spread out over the small but characteristic tree-covered green and bask in the peace. From the city center, head south down Lê Lợi toward the train station; 150m before getting to the parking lot, veer left and take the next right onto Điện Biên Phủ. After crossing the train tracks, turn right.

2 TỪ ĐÀM PAGODA (P. 285). The architecture may not be Huế's most breathtaking, but this pagoda was the center of Buddhist associations against oppressive and imperialist regimes. To make a stop at Từ Đàm Pagoda, head back onto Điện Biên Phủ from Bảo Quốc Pagoda, continuing down the street and up a steep hill. At the top of the hill, turn left onto Sư Liễu Quán, and the entrance to the pagoda will be 20m later on your right.

3 ALTAR OF NAM GIAO (P. 284). Get back onto Điện Biên Phủ and follow it away from the city center until it ends at a park and the Altar of Nam Giao. The alter is an Eastern representation of the cosmos in which the three levels represent humanity, earth, and sky, respectively. The trees around the altar were planted by Minh Mạng and his subjects. Those that were tended by the king bear a plaque commemorating their royal treatment.

4 TU HIEU PAGODA (P. 284). Facing the altar, veer right onto Lê Ngô Cát and continue straight for about 1km until an imposing gate leading to a forest appears on the right. Follow the road to the grounds of the Tu Hieu Pagoda. Monks and visitors mingle in the forest and lotus ponds, a picture of serenity. The grounds harbor a temple as well as school for young monks-to-be. If you're lucky, you might catch the monks playing soccer.

5 ROYAL ARENA (P. 282). Pedal through the streets along Huế's periphery and soak in the bucolic bliss. The Royal Arena, itself hidden amid homes and shops and secluded from Huế's other attractions, is a mini-coliseum where elephants and tigers were once forced to fight for the emperor's viewing pleasure. To reach the arena, continue straight past the Tu Hieu Pagoda, turning right at the road's end. About 1km down this road (Đoàn Như Hải) before it flows into Bùi Thị Xuân, a small path leads through the bustle of local houses that surround the arena. If you reach Bùi Thị Xuân without finding the path, just ask a local to point you in the right direction.

stomped the tiger to a bloody, mangled pulp, they would cheer. Today, the mini-colosseum is tucked behind houses and trees, hidden from the surrounding town. *(The Royal Arena is difficult to spot. From Lê Lợi, head west toward the train station. Across the small bridge, turn right on Bùi Thị Xuân and continue for 3km. After you pass Huyền Tân Công Chúa, start asking locals for directions to Hô Quyền. They'll point you to a small alley off the left side of Bùi Thị Xuân. Head down the alley for about 100m.)*

TU HIEU PAGODA. Located 5km southwest of the city, on the way to the Tự Đức Tomb, Tu Hieu should not be missed. Hidden beneath tall trees, its serenely beautiful garden is sprinkled with quaint wooden bridges and ponds full of pink lotus flowers. It's a great escape from the busy city architecture. In 1848, it was expanded to include a cemetery for castrated mandarins of the Nguyễn Dynasty. It's especially interesting to come during prayers at 4pm or the occasional post-prayer soccer match at 4:30pm. *(To reach the pagoda, travel west toward the Altar of Nam Giao. When Điện Biên Phủ ends, veer right. About 1km down the road is a gate on the right. Pass through, into the woods, and take the second marked path to the pagoda grounds.)*

THANH TOÀN COVERED BRIDGE. Six kilometers from Huế is a prized covered bridge, built out of wood in 1776. The bridge overlooks a small river covered in pink, green, and white blossoms. In the distance, picturesque rice fields fade into purple mountains. The bridge makes for a popular date destination for local couples and a relaxing bike ride through Huế's surrounding villages and countryside. *(Follow Hùng Vương south and turn left onto Bà Triệu. Head east and hook a right onto Trường Chin. A sign marks 6km to Thanh Toàn. Follow the road through villages and country-side. When it splits, turn left into the heart of the small village until you reach the bridge.)*

BẢO QUỐC PAGODA. Built in 1670, this pagoda looks out on a beautiful red-clay courtyard. Its altar is flanked by classrooms, where monks have taught for 50 years. Behind the pagoda, monks tend their own fruit and vegetable gardens, while the peaceful garden on the side is used by students looking for a quiet spot to study or relax. *(From the city center, head south down Lê Lợi, take a left on Điện Biên Phủ, and then take a right just after the train tracks. The large staircase leads to the pagoda.)*

ĐIỀM PHÙNG THI MUSEUM. This one-room museum displays the work of Điềm Phùng Thi, one of Vietnam's prized modern artists. Born in 1920, Điềm Phùng Thi grew up in Huế, but spent many years studying abroad in France. With Eastern calligraphy, older Asian and Vietnamese traditions, and European modernism among her influences, she developed her own harmonious and unique blend of styles. You'll invariably tumble upon the domineering sculpture "Earth" ("La Terre"), but make sure to take a peek at the more hidden "The Acrobats" ("Les Acrobates"), a fantastic sculpture that subtly captures motion and excitement despite its blocky style. Though a bit out of the way, this unique museum is worth a short perusal. *(1 Phan Bội Châu. ☎ 823 257. Open daily 7:30-11am and 2-5pm. Free.)*

ALTAR OF NAM GIAO. Sitting in the corner of a quiet park on the southwestern fringes of Huế's southern bank is the Altar of Nam Giao, a giant open-air monument. This now abandoned and desolate-looking structure, whose name means "Plane of Worshipping Heaven," was once the site where the emperors of the Nguyễn Dynasty would worship their fathers and perform Confucian rituals. It was also where the king would go if there was a flood or a sickness in the city. Legend has it that he would stand naked in the center of the top platform, surrounded by his family and mandarins, fasting and performing rituals to appease the gods. The three platforms represent heaven, earth, and man. The surrounding trees were planted by Emperor Minh Mạng and his subjects, and those planted by the Emperor himself proudly bear a bronze mark. The park and altar remain open to visitors looking for a quiet spot to read, picnic, or soak up the mid-morning sun. *(To reach the park, head southwest on Lê Lợi, then left on Điện Biên Phủ. Following it all the way down leads you straight to the park gates. Open daily 7am-5pm. Free.)*

TỪ ĐÀM PAGODA. Less architecturally impressive than its neighbors, this pagoda holds an important position in Vietnamese and Buddhist history. First founded in 1695 under the name An Tôn, the pagoda was renamed Từ Đàm in 1842 by Emperor Thiệu Trị. In 1945, Từ Đàm became the center of Buddhist anti-colonial activism, and from 1960 to 1963 it harbored the Buddhist movement against the regime of Ngô Đinh Diệm. Today, monks here study and impart their knowledge—especially of languages—to others. Inside the pagoda grounds is a small park. Near the main gate stands a large tree donated by the Buddhist Association of France in 1936. The pagoda remains an active place of worship, as yet unmarred by flocks of visitors. It is currently being renovated and expanded in order to properly capture its historical importance, but construction should be completed by 2007. *(1 Sư Liễu Quán. Head west on Lê Lợi, turning left onto Điện Biên Phủ just before the train station. Continue straight. About 1km up the hilly road, veer right onto Sư Liễu Quán.)*

PHI LONG. Not a restaurant and by no means a museum, this small house makes for a rather unusual visit. The owner, Phước Lộc, sells big jars of fermented snake wine, which he makes in the back room of his house and claims has medicinal value. Two of the biggest glass jars hold huge king cobras. Stop by and take pictures. Phước will probably offer you a taste of the bitter snake wine and will show you the scar on his foot from when he was bitten by a king cobra. *(8/23 Nguyễn Sinh Cung. ☎822 986; nhuha75@hotmail.com. Open daily 2pm-7pm. If the front gate is locked, knock on the gate and see if Phước appears to show you around.)*

HỒ CHÍ MINH MUSEUM. A one-floor display dedicated to Vietnam's political hero and the country's strife. This museum is much like every other Hồ Chí Minh museum in the country, filled with pictures and replicas. The only truly unique part of the museum is a small bit about the hero's time as a child in Huế; a few old photographs show a glimpse of Vietnamese life in the old city. *(7 Lê Lợi, on the second floor. ☎822 152. Open Tu-Su 7-11am and 1:30-4:30pm. Free. Short informational pamphlets 10,000Đ, but they're unnecessary.)*

THE TOMB OF PHAN BỘI CHÂU. Near these two small tombs you'll find a giant bust of the famous Vietnamese philosopher's head. The bust is an amazing piece of artwork; notice the faces and hands of Vietnamese people subtly carved into the philosopher's cheeks. Unfortunately, there is not much more here to see. *(119 Phan Bội Châu. The tomb is just across the street from the Từ Đàm Pagoda. Open Tu, Th, and Sa-Su 7:30-11am and 1:30-4:30pm. Free.)*

ENTERTAINMENT AND FESTIVALS

The largest festival in the country, the famous **Huế Festival** takes place every two years and is jam-packed with music, dance, art, and entertainment. Visual, culinary, and musical performers travel from all over the world to put on shows throughout the city, ranging from medieval plays in the Citadel to giant food festivals. Each evening of the week-long festival, visitors can enjoy **traditional folk songs and music** by musicians and singers in costume. Boats filled with visitors leave daily from the southern side of the Perfume River and float amid city lights as songs of glory and love are performed on the banks of the river. Mid-performance, a break allows visitors to send candles floating on the river, following an Imperial tradition in which the king would make a wish and send paper boats carrying candles into the Perfume River. In the afternoons or evenings during the festival, take a stroll along the southeastern shore of the river; artists often bring their art to the streets or simply decorate the walkways themselves. The festival typically takes place in early to mid-June. To find out the dates for the 2008 festivities, check online at www.huefestival.com/index.htm. During this time of the summer, Huế tourism peaks, and visitors are advised to make housing plans well in advance.

Other than the biennial festival, there isn't much in the way of organized entertainment. Luckily, all is not lost. Visitors can look inside the many **art galleries** on the streets that shoot off of Lê Lợi, or else listen and watch from a dragon boat on the Perfume River as musicians play traditional folk music and traditional dances are performed. (Tickets sold at 51 Lê Lợi. 1½hr.; 80,000Đ.)

MARKETS

The locals' source of fruits, veggies, meat, cheap shoes, and clothes, the markets are packed with people and goods. The vastness of the markets makes shopping fun but overwhelming for some visitors. To avoid higher prices, never accept the price offered by the seller—always offer a price at least one third lower than what originally offered. To get even better deals, venture farther from the center and away from tourist-heavy markets. **Đông Ba Market,** Huế's largest, sprawls on the Citadel side of the Perfume River at the far northeast end of Trần Hưng Đạo. This is the true Vietnamese market experience. (Open daily 6am-6:30pm.) The **Tây Lác Market** is across from 184 Nguyễn Trãi, about 3km from the Citadel's westernmost gate along the Perfume River. This market is about an eighth of the size of Đông Ba and is rarely visited by tourists, but it has a pretty good selection of food, clothes, toys, and shoes, often at better prices than the bigger market. (Open daily 7am-6pm.) On the southern bank is the slightly smaller **An Cựu Market,** near the southern end of Hùng Vương, 2.5km from Lê Lợi and before the small bridge. Shoppers are enticed by fresh fruit, meat, and veggies, as well as electronics, gadgets, and all sorts of accessories. (Open daily 7am-6:30pm.) The **Bến Ngự Market** is near the southwest edge of the Citadel. Heading down on Lê Lợi, veer left at the Hồ Chí Minh museum onto Trần Thúc Nhẫn. The market sits at the road's end and is mostly filled with fish. (Open daily 7am-6pm.)

SHOPPING

Huế's streets overflow not only with galleries selling local art, but also with stores and stalls pitching clothing, music, and other goodies to tourists and locals alike. On the southern side of the river, galleries and stores that double as art displays are concentrated on the eastern tip of Lê Lợi, on Phạm Ngũ Lão, and on Chu Văn An. Farther south, restaurants, clothing and electronics stores, and Internet cafes clutter the touristed Hùng Vương and Bến Nghé. A walk across the river and into the heart of the Citadel reveals stores and shops where locals stock up on clothes. In true Vietnamese style, the tags lack prices and everything is up for bargaining. Prices are 30-50% lower than on the southern bank. Art galleries cluster near the entrances to the Citadel; those to the south tend to be cheaper, while those to the north are even more expensive than galleries across the river. The eastern side of the Citadel, too, has a good concentration of extremely inexpensive shopping, from clothes to electronics. Peruse the stores on Mai Thúc Loan, or venture into the nearby alleys to strike good deals.

NIGHTLIFE

Night owls take warning: Huế is known for its lack of a late-night scene. While locals and Vietnamese tourists crowd street cafes near the Citadel, the city's streets quiet down by 10 or 11pm, leaving late-night, thrill-seeking tourists thirsting for entertainment. Most people simply wander the streets and congregate at the few decent late-night bars on the southern bank of the Perfume River.

BARS AND CAFES

The nightlife scene is heavily segregated between locals and foreigners. Tourists, especially the younger backpacker types, head to bars around the northeastern end of Lê Lợi. Many locals, on the other hand, venture into the Old City and gather near the flagpole and Citadel where street vendors provide refreshments.

DMZ Cafe and Bar, 44 Lê Lợi. Popular with backpackers, tourists, and locals refusing to give in to Hué's sleepy streets. An unpretentious hangout with Italian food, free pool, plenty of beer, and a lively crowd of repeat customers. The staff is very friendly, and makes an effort to befriend its clientele. Beer 9000-17,000Đ. Open daily 2:30pm-2am.

Violon Cafe, 65 Bến Nghé (☎826 009; www.violoncafe.com). A local cafe popular with the more sophisticated (read: "well-off") crowd. A pleasant, classy environment, and a singer with piano accompaniment (daily 8-10pm). Vietnamese coffee 6000Đ, after 8pm 22,000Đ. Tea 12,000Đ, after 8pm 21,000-23,000Đ. Open Tu-Su 7am-midnight.

B4 Cafe, 75 Bến Nghé (☎0914 065 618; www.geocities.com/b4hue). A relatively new establishment, this is one of the few places in Vietnam where you'll find Belgian beer, served by the English- and French-speaking owner. Happy hour daily 4-7pm (beer 6000Đ; mixed drinks 15,000Đ). Prices double after happy hour. Free pool. Open daily 3pm-late.

CLUBS

While a few bars struggle to inject Hué with a nightlife, there is only one genuine dance club in town, where tourists and locals come to unwind.

Brown Eyes Chi Rua, 55 Nguyễn Sinh Cung (☎827 494; browneyes@pmail.vnn.vn). Several blocks away from the tourist quarters, Brown Eyes is quiet on weekdays. On the weekend, though, this club livens up when the rest of the city goes to sleep. Locals and wandering tourists mingle, dance, drink, and (if you arrive during football season) cheer for the cup all night. Expensive drinks come with the nightclub territory. Corona 50,000Đ. Coke 15,000Đ. Liquor 30,000-45,000Đ. Try the flaming B52 (45,000Đ). A wide selection of loud music and free pool tables in the back.

▶ DAYTRIPS FROM HUÉ

A trip to Hué is not complete without a short excursion to the history-infused, ruin-strewn countryside. The highlights, of course, are the Royal Tombs, the grandiose burial sites of Vietnam's former emperors.

THUẬN AN. Heading northeast from Hué leads to the wave-lined shore of Thuận An. Only 13km from the city center, this pristine beach is abandoned during weekday mornings and early afternoons, but visitors flock here in the evenings and on weekends. The golden, burning sand stretches south alongside warm, green-blue waters. Colorful covered lawnchairs provide protection from the beating sun and can be rented at the beach (M-F about 10,000Đ, Sa-Su 20,000-30,000Đ). Try renting a large inner tube (10,000Đ) from one of the tents; few things are more enjoyable than rocking back and forth on the wavy sea. As you venture farther east along the beach, the number of visitors, vendors, and seaside eateries you'll see decreases. Stalls and showers (2000Đ) are behind the food and drink shops. Cafes and restaurants line the beach, and fresh seafood is available for 30,000-60,000Đ. *(Buses leave from Đông Ba Market every hr. 5:30am-3pm for 5500Đ. Only one bus makes the journey back into the city. To catch it, walk back from the beach onto the main road and flag down the bus as it rumbles back at 3 or 4pm. Motorbikes are 30,000Đ each way; taxis are 90,000Đ each way. To reach the water by yourself, follow Lê Lợi as it makes its way east and turns into Nguyễn Sinh Cung. Continue on the winding road for 6km until the Huda factory. Take a right and continue for about 7km. Look for signs to the beach.)*

ROYAL TOMBS

Hué is home to the spectacular, awe-inspiring tombs of seven emperors of the Nguyễn Dynasty, each of whom spent a large chunk of his lifetime planning his final resting place. Each tomb expressively represents the spirit of the emperor as well as the architecture of the time, blending Vietnamese and French styles to create structures in harmony with their natural setting. The tombs are a few kilometers southwest of the city center, quite accessible by motorcycle or bike. Most visitors, however, opt for a 25,000Đ dragon-boat trip, which, though charming,

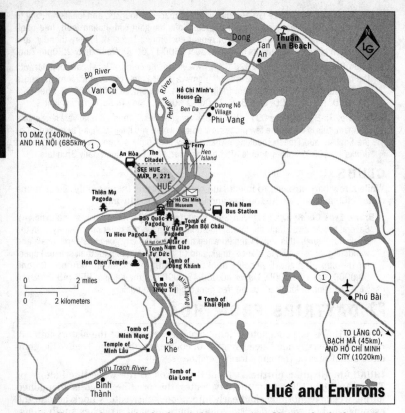

Huế and Environs

throws all sorts of overpriced sales pitches at tourists. If you take the boat trip, you'll still need an additional motorbike ride to reach the tombs from the drop-off point, which may cost upwards of 50,000Đ. On the other hand, poorly marked roads connect most of the sights, making it tough to navigate between tombs. Locals are usually helpful in pointing confused tourists in the right direction. After visiting a few tombs, you'll begin to see patterns in their architecture: a triple gate leads to a courtyard and a temple (and often a Stele house), surrounded by a pond filled with beautiful lotus flowers, while a spectacular pavilion and garden are final run-ups to the tomb itself. After noticing these similarities, it becomes possible for visitors to pick up on the more subtle differences, each of which reveal how the emperor wanted to be remembered. The tombs are listed in geographical order, but if you're short on time, be sure not to miss those of Tự Đức, Minh Mạng, and Khải Định. *(All tombs open daily 7am-5pm. English-speaking guides inside can answer questions, provide some information, or give guided tours. Requested tour donation 50,000Đ.)*

TOMB OF TỰ ĐỨC. The tomb of **Tự Đức,** whose indecisive rule was one of the factors in the Nguyễns' quick capitulation to the French, is one of the most striking. Tự Đức was the 4th Nguyễn emperor, ruled for over 35 years, and was well versed in philosophy, history, and poetry, leaving behind 4000 original poems. He ordered the construction of his tomb when he began suffering from a heart condition; unable to produce a child and aware of impending Western military advances, the emperor used what would later be his tomb as a secluded retreat. The tomb itself is an impressive spread, with gorgeous, winding lakes leading to sprawling gardens. Its attractions include a temple dedicated to his wives and predecessors, ruins of the houses that held the Emperor's over 100 (probably bored) concubines, and the Minh Kiêm Theatre, where the concubines once performed and where visitors can now dress up to take their own royal photos. Notice how the height of the mandarins standing before his Stele house—Tự Đức was a man of short stature, and he made sure that they were constructed shorter than he was. Finally, his tomb (supposedly) stands behind a small lake bed, left dry because he never had a child; no one knows for sure, though, where he was buried, as all 100 generals involved in the burial of the emperor were afterwards poisoned to ensure against grave robbers. This may or may not have been a tad excessive. *(From the city center, travel west toward the Altar of Nam Giao. When Điện Biên Phủ comes to its end, veer right onto Lê Ngo Cat. When the road ends, take a left for 1.5km. The tomb will be on your left. 55,000Đ.)*

TOMBS OF ĐỒNG KHÁNH AND THIỆU TRỊ. It was during the short one-year reign of Hàm Nghi, Đồng Khánh's older brother, that the French took control of Vietnam. When Hàm Nghi fled from the capital to organize a resistance, the French placed **Đồng Khánh** on the throne. At the age of 25, after only three years of royal control, the Emperor died. His son decided that at a time when the country was suffering so greatly, he could not construct a grand tomb for his father. Instead, Thành Thái chose an old palace for the worship of his father, and a hill 30m to the west as his resting place. Though less visited than many of the other tombs, the temple inside this tomb is considered one of the best, with a beautifully lacquered red interior. *(200m south from the tomb of Tự Đức. 22,000Đ.)* Continuing away from Tự Đức's tomb, the well-paved road turns into a gravel track. One and a half kilometers down the track is the tomb of **Thiệu Trị**, the oldest son of Emperor Minh Mạng. At age 34, Thiệu Trị came to power; as he died just seven years after claiming power, he did not build his own tomb. However, in his dying breath, he told his son how he wanted his tomb built. This son, Tự Đức, found land at the foot of a mountain 8km from the city suitable for his father's burial place. Rather than placing his father's remains among mountain peaks, as his ancestors had done, Tự Đức located them in a valley of calm, meandering streams. The entire compound focuses on natural rather than the man-made wonders. Though the ransacked tomb stands in ruins, and the temple suffers from lack of renovation and interest, the grounds of Thiệu Trị's resting place remain peaceful and picturesque. Renovations are soon to come; until then, the tomb is only worth a visit if you have extra time. *(From the tomb of Đồng Khánh, continue to the road's end, and then take a left onto the main road. Soon after, a sign points to the tomb of Thiệu Trị. 22,000Đ.)*

TOMB OF MINH MẠNG AND TEMPLE OF MINH LẦU. Minh Mạng reigned from 1820 to 1840 at the height of the Nguyễn dynasty. Built between 1840 and 1843, Minh Mạng's tomb has more architectural balance and poise than any other. At the center of the compound, three sets of stairs lead to a Stele house that bears Minh Mạng's eulogy. Though Minh Mạng began planning for the tomb in 1826, he did not settle on the spot until 1840. Soon after the tomb's construction began, the Emperor fell ill and died; construction continued under the reign of his son. Three large courtyards sit at the bottom of the pavilion. Over a stone bridge is the tomb proper; look for a dirt mound encircled by a wall. *(From Thiệu Trị, take a left on the paved road and continue for 2km. Go over the bridge and head back down toward the river bank. Take a right onto the dirt path and cross under the bridge. Minh Mạng is 1km farther on your left. Temple of Minh Lầu 55,000Đ.)*

TOMB OF GIA LONG. The tomb of **Gia Long** was built between 1814 and 1820. Twenty kilometers from the city, this rarely visited mausoleum has a courtyard surrounded by a lotus pond and a chain of mountains. The buried emperor was an unflinching soldier who unified the country; this strength is reflected in his tomb, which is surrounded by bold mountains and tall obelisks. To peek inside the tomb, ask the keeper to open the gate. Below the steps to the tomb is a courtyard filled with figures of soldiers, elephants, and horses, mimicking the style of the king's court. Though the temple and tomb are less spectacular than the more visited tombs, the location of Gia Long's resting place has a majestic natural beauty that surpasses those of his successors. *(Several km from the tomb of Minh Mạng. Follow the access road southeast through Minh Mạng Village to a tributary of the Perfume River. Construction is underway on a bridge connecting the banks; until its completion, cross on a ferry for 20,000Đ per person round-trip. At other bank, turn left and follow the path, turning right into the fields directly after a small temple, and left again to reach a small road parallel to the first. Continue straight toward the temple and tomb. The best way to visit the tomb is to hire a motorbike for 100,000Đ round-trip from the city center. Open daily 7am-5pm.)*

▨**TOMB OF KHẢI ĐỊNH.** Though smaller and lacking the luscious green appeal of his predecessors' tombs, the tomb of **Khải Định,** built into the side of a mountain, is the most unusual, ornate, and unforgettable of all of the tombs. After 11 years of construction—longer than his nine-year reign—the tomb of the 12th Emperor of the Dynasty was finally completed in 1931. Only four years after he came to power, the French colonized the country, leaving the Emperor as no more than a ceremonial figurehead. With little power, but anxious to ensure a luxurious afterlife, Khải Định raised the country's taxes by 30% so as to collect the funds necessary to complete his final resting place. The last of the tombs to be built, it shows a distinctly European architectural influence with cement and tile floors rather than wood, iron gates rather than cement, and materials gathered from all over the world. At the top, the inside of the tomb is ornately decorated with gorgeous mosaics and houses an altar with a gilded statue of Khải Định, making it the only tomb with a visual representation of the emperor. *(From the tombs of Gia Long, head toward the ferry dock and backtrack across the Perfume River. Turn right at the top of the bluff and left after 200m. Khải Định looms atop a hill, 1km down the road on the right. 55,000Đ. From Thiệu Trị's tombs, head south along the main paved road for 2km until the road dead-ends at the tomb.)*

BẠCH MÃ NATIONAL PARK   ☎ 54

Travelers speeding along Hwy. 1 in the Huế-Hội An corridor rarely notice the turn-off leading to Bạch Mã National Park. It's their loss—Bạch Mã offers sights exceeding anything in Vietnam's cities and towns. Although the park is small relative to other national parks, its diverse climate and habitat support thousands of species of plants and animals, including gibbons and langurs. The park's 220 sq. km are home to 50% of the country's animal species. And you may actually spot some of them, as its ecotourism infrastructure is relatively well-developed and visitor numbers remain low. Ruins of a 1930s French resort and a 1960s American helicopter base are ripe for exploration, as is the outstanding road connecting the summit to Highway 1. Along this road, the park service has established several well-maintained trails and villas, a post office, and a water purification plant; it has also worked to allow for responsible ecotourism opportunities. No matter what, the magnificent clouds drifting among the valleys of Vietnam's coastal mountains will be a welcome break from highway traffic.

BẠCH MÃ AT A GLANCE

AREA: 220 sq. km.

CLIMATE: Rainy and unpleasant September-December; otherwise moderate, with temperatures not exceeding 26°C.

FEATURES: Mountains and river valleys.

HIGHLIGHTS: The summit of Hai Vong Dai; the ruins of a French resort; breathtaking views from the Rhododendron Falls; diversity of endangered species.

GATEWAYS: Cầu Hai, 3km from the entrance to the park, which in turn is near both Đà Nẵng and Huế.

CAMPING: Permitted at designated sites only; guesthouses and villas abound.

FEES AND RESERVATIONS: Entrance fee 10,500Đ (students 5500Đ). English-speaking guides (150,000Đ) recommended but not necessary for hikes.

✈ ORIENTATION

Bạch Mâ National Park stretches from the South China Sea to the border with Laos in the lowlands of the Southern Central Coast. Composed of Bạch Mâ's mountain (1450m) and its environs, the park climbs from Cầu Hai Lagoon to the summit, taking the visitor through evergreen forest to the subtropical rainforest of the higher altitudes. The peak is one of Vietnam's wettest spots, with 8000mm of rain per year. It is best experienced by hiking some of the trails near the summit; as much time as possible should be spent on the mountain's trails, which provide the best opportunity to see the wildlife, hear the birds, and smell the flowers. The park boasts eight well-maintained trails, and most of the trailheads are along the road to the summit. Bring plenty of water along on your trip, use lots of insect and leech repellent, and be sure to check yourself for leeches after every hike.

▆ TRANSPORTATION

If you have your own car, the trip to Bạch Mâ can be both cheap and easy: simply turn off of Hwy. 1 at the sign reading "Bạch Mâ," in the center of Cầu Hai Village (40km south of Huế, 60km north of Đà Nẵng), and follow the road to the gate 3km away. But if you're taking public transportation, the trip can get expensive. Take a **bus** from Huế or Đà Nẵng and tell the driver to let you off in Cầu Hai, or simply say "Bạch Mâ" (US$1-3). Once you've been dropped off along the highway, a motorbike can take you to the base for 5000Đ or less. However, the trip up the mountain is costly—no motorbikes are allowed to drive up the steep mountain road. You can either walk it (16km; 4-5hr.) or rent a jeep at headquarters (300,000Đ round-trip). The easiest way to get up the mountain is to book a one-day tour that provides transportation, a guide, and lunch for US$20-25 per person..

WHEN TO GO. Although Bạch Mâ is located in the warmer southern region of the country, the park's altitude renders it 7°C cooler than the surrounding region. Temperatures range from 4°C during the winter to 26°C during the summer. The altitude does not, however, protect the park from high levels of humidity or an exorbitant amount of rainfall. The wet season drenches the park from September to December, while March and April are the driest months. February wins the year's beauty contest, thanks to the blossoming of exquisite rhododendrons. Beware of tourist inundation on the weekends during June, July, and August. And please, please don't forget your raincoat.

▮ PRACTICAL INFORMATION

The **entrance fee** is 10,500Đ and 5500Đ for students. Maps and trail information can be found at **headquarters** (☎871 330; www.bachma.vnn.vn). English-speaking guides are available for hire (150,000Đ per day), though they're not necessary. The best time to visit Bạch Mâ is during the dry season, from February to August. Plan your hikes for the afternoon, after the morning fog has somewhat burned off. Those interested in **ecotourism** should visit the Khe Su village, 1.2km from the National Park's front office. Residents of this poor village, which harvests casava, sugarcane, pineapple, banana, and coconut, provide tours of the gardening process (40,000Đ) and homestays (80,000Đ). Ask at headquarters for information

▐▐ ACCOMMODATIONS AND FOOD

Bạch Mâ can easily be visited in a day, but overnight trips are highly recommended for spotting the park's nocturnal wildlife and impressive starscape. **Headquarters** offers rooms (100,000-200,000Đ); most are doubles, and the cheaper ones lack air-conditioning. Expensive meals, snacks, and water are available from the canteen at the base of the mountain. It's preferable, though, to stay at one of the three summit options: **National Park Guesthouse ❷** is a collection of villas organized by room price. The cavernous rooms have good views, but the cheaper rooms share a bath and provide only cold water. Camping is also available here. Meals are made from whatever provisions have been brought up that day—usually rice or noodles. The guesthouse is 3km from the summit, and it's the first one you see coming up the road. (☎871 330. Rooms 100,000-400,000Đ, with private bathroom from 150,000Đ. Campsites 3000Đ, with tent 80,000Đ.) **Phong Lan Villa ❹**, owned by Huế Tourist Company, is the newest villa on the mountain and the second one along the road. Perched on the mountain slope 2km from the summit, Phong Lan has unrivaled views of the sunset and standard, clean rooms. Its canteen offers outdoor seating and a no-frills menu. (☎871 801; huetc@dng.vnn.vn. Rooms US$18.) **Morin-Bạch Mã Hotel ❹** is at the end of the road and offers views of the ocean. The rooms are above-average, but the eating area is dark and damp, and the buildings are beginning to show their age. The hotel does, however, boast the highest altitude and the best English-speakers. (☎871 199. Rooms US$20.) When it comes to food, it's easiest just to eat wherever you stay.

🥾 HIKING

FIVE LAKES TRAIL (2KM). This 2hr. hike is by far the most interesting trail in the park. Beginning about 100m from the guesthouses, it takes you along five small lakes and several cascades before linking up with the Rhododendron Trail. The fourth and largest lake is refreshingly cool and the best for swimming, but be careful of the slippery rocks. The shores of the lakes are crowded by ferns, bamboo, and the plants that are used to make Vietnam's conical hats. The lakes themselves host a variety of fish and amphibians, including a recently discovered horned frog *(ếch sừng)*. Bringing a guide ensures that you won't miss out on all of the trail's natural wonders. The hike itself is pretty tough, winding down wooden ladders and rocky paths, so be sure to wear sturdy shoes.

SUMMIT TRAIL (1KM). The French and Vietnamese have been building along this unique trail for almost 75 years. The remains of their shops and post office can still be seen near the beginning of the trail at the National Park Guesthouse. Some villas have been reconstructed, while others have been claimed by the forest—check out the ruins near the Morin-Bạch Mã Hotel. The steep stairs at the trailhead at the end of the summit road, about 14km from the entrance gate, lead to an eerie former US helicopter base. Razor wire still pokes out from the bushes. In the ground to your right, look for the entrances to the tunnels where Vietnamese soldiers hid. Staying on the cobblestone path, you'll reach the observation point, where on a clear day you can see Huế and the South China Sea.

RHODODENDRON TRAIL (3KM). Along this stellar trail, you have the chance to see flora and fauna not found in the lowlands, including wonderful orchids and the Samba deer. The 300m high Rhododendron Falls is the climax of the trail, with a clear view of Mt. Mang, the highest peak in the area (1713m). You can climb down 689 concrete steps to the bottom of the falls, but the path is difficult and slippery. The best time to do this trail is the spring, when the top of the falls is framed by blooming flowers. The trail begins 14km up the summit road (2km before the guesthouse) and connects with Five Lakes Trail.

PHEASANT TRAIL (3KM). This trail winds through the habitat of the Crested Argus pheasant, discovered here in 1923 by Delacour, a French naturalist. Odds are slim that you'll actually see one of these birds, but you'll probably hear their whooping calls. If you look carefully, you may see patches of dug-up soil—this is the work of a wild boar rooting for food. Pick up a pamphlet at the headquarters so you can identify some medicinal plants along your way. The trail ends with a waterfall. From the road, the trail is hard to miss; the trailhead is 5km up the road from the entrance gate. Watch out for leeches along this trail.

TRƯỢT FALLS TRAIL (3KM). This easy jaunt runs over fairly flat terrain and through second-growth forest, culminating in the multi-tiered Trượt Falls. Situated on the park's western border, this trail is one of the least-visited. The summit road does not connect to the trailhead, so a guide or ranger must direct you to the trail.

PARASHOREA FOREST TRAIL (1KM). This trail is not as well marked as the others. Other than a quick skip through some of the park's virgin rainforests, it is unremarkable. The trailhead is off the main road about 8km past the entry gate.

BẠC FALLS TRAIL (1KM). Just a short diversion from the start of the summit road, this trail boasts a commanding cascade. If you've already seen some of the park's other falls, you may want to skip this one.

THỦY DIỆN FALLS TRAIL (4.5KM). Though it is the longest in the park, there is little change in altitude over the course of this trail. The climax is Thủy Diện Falls, which are impressive, but not as good as the ones on the mountain. This trail is a good option if you intend to sleep at park headquarters. From the entrance gate, the ranger can literally point to the trailhead.

LĂNG CÔ BEACH

From the top of Hai Van Pass, Lăng Cô gleams like a slice of paradise. Most tourist buses stop at one of Lăng Cô's resorts for lunch, but few travelers choose to spend more time. While Lăng Cô boasts a beautiful beach, it suffers from a problem unique to Vietnam's coast: there simply ain't nothin' there. The village is poor and underdeveloped, and the few resorts are aging and overpriced. Then again—the beach itself is truly spectacular. Green mountains curve into crystal blue waters, separated by bursts of soft, white sand. The best time to visit is between April and August; at other times, the surf is rough and the surrounding mountains bring rain.

For lodging, **Than Tam Seaside Resort ❸** is the easiest on the wallet. The resort boasts a spacious, open-air restaurant with decent food (30,000-50,000Đ) and patio seating. Simple but adequate rooms in concrete bungalows face either the highway or the beach. Most tour buses stop here, so reserve rooms in advance. (☎874 456. Rooms US$15-30.) **Lăng Cô Beach Resort ❹** is the farthest from town and currently the poshest lodging and dining in Lăng Cô. The life is sweet—if totally removed from all things Vietnamese—in this typical resort compound. (☎873 555; langco@dng.vnn.vn. Small metallic bungalows 200m from the beach US$20-25; sparkling 4-star villas US$60-65.) On the other side of town is **Lăng Cô Hotel ❹,** located on Hwy. 1 in the direction of Đà Nẵng. Rooms are old and worn, but the communal patios overlooking the beach are great places to relax. (☎874 426; codolangco@dng.vnn.vn. Rooms US$20-22.) Several **guesthouses ❸** on the other side of Hwy. 1 offer lackluster rooms for US$15-20. The beaches, though, are mostly controlled by the resorts. All resorts have their own restaurants, but a walk or drive along the highway will reveal a multitude of cheap **food stalls,** many selling fresh local seafood. As always, follow the locals for the best food.

Any local bus (30,000Đ) or tourist bus (45,000Đ) will drop you off on the highway as it makes the trip between Đà Nẵng and Huế, and a motorbike taxi to town should only cost 60,000-70,000Đ from there. Lăng Cô is also serviced infrequently by slow, non-express trains, about one per day. Lăng Cô is 30km northwest of Đà Nẵng and 40km southeast of Huế. A thin strip of green and white hemmed in by electric-blue waters, the isthmus runs north-south, skewered by Hwy. 1. To the east, an empty beach stretches along the South China Sea to the horizon; to the west is an immense lagoon of oyster farms. At the southern end is the palm-shaded village of Lăng Cô, connected to the mainland by the Hwy. 1 bridge. Moving north, the village fades and only small roadside dwellings dot the landscape. Eventually Hwy. 1 rejoins the mainland and continues north 40km to Huế. Lăng Cô has no **ATM,** so be sure to bring enough cash for your entire stay. There are a few **Internet** shacks in town, as well as one **post office** 2km south of the resorts.

THE SOUTHERN CENTRAL COAST

The Southern Central Coast is where foreigners and nationals alike come to play. Gorgeous, secluded beaches begin around Quảng Ngãi, but many tourists head farther south for the well-groomed sands and natural wonders of Mũi Né, and very few of them choose to skip the bustling beach and party scene of Nha Trang. People have been enjoying the coastal sun for centuries: the Chàm were the first to flourish there, as evidenced by their many imposing towers. The northern towns of Đà Nẵng and Hội An boast scenic environs and countless historical sites. Sadly, this region did not escape the ravages of war—Quảng Ngãi province saw intense fighting during the American War, including the infamous Mỹ Lai Massacre.

Today, though, it seems that the tempestuous past has been forgotten, at least in part. Fishing communities have become resort towns, and battlefields have been reclaimed by rice paddies. Tourists flood the coast, gorging themselves on spectacular seafood, clean azure waters, and fine white sand. After the sun goes down, the party starts up—Nha Trang boasts some of the best nightlife in Vietnam. Most foreigners travel around on cheap and convenient open-tour buses, which herd crowds from HCMC to Mũi Né and Nha Trang and then head farther north. For the more adventurous traveler, local minibuses give a less-touristy glimpse into the region, and allow for spontaneous stops at Chàm relics, fish sauce refineries, and secluded seaside coves. The region is also home to spectacular natural wonders, including Vietnam's only desert. At every stop, affordable hotels and restaurants awaits. The Southern Central Coast is, in short, a tropical paradise made easy.

HIGHLIGHTS OF THE SOUTHERN CENTRAL COAST

SUIT YOURSELF in charming **Hội An** (p. 304), where hundreds of tailoring shops line the streets; this is the place to get high-quality custom-made clothing for pocket change. The ⬛ **food** there is also famous throughout Vietnam.

DO NOTHING FOR EXTENDED PERIODS OF TIME on the beaches of **Nha Trang** (p. 323) and **Mũi Né** (p. 341), the country's touristy tropical beach towns. Mũi Né has the more picturesque beach and surrounding areas, but Nha Trang's **nightlife** scene (p. 331) might just be unparalleled in Vietnam.

FEEL VAGUELY THREATENED by the region's many Chàm towers—massive, ornately carved, crumbling structures left by the ancient Chàm empire. Aspiring archaeologists can take daytrips from **Phan Rang** (p. 333) and **Qui Nho'n** (p. 318), but **Mỹ So'n** (p. 314), near Hội An, is the center of the Chàm craze.

ĐÀ NẴNG
☎ 511

For years both the primary French port in central Vietnam and a nerve center of the American war machine, Đà Nẵng today has shifted into a low-key role. Between Huế to the northwest and Hội An to the southeast, Vietnam's fourth-largest city is skipped over completely by most tourists. Though it's a booming seaport and commercial center with a fairly large expat population, Đà Nẵng itself offers little to captivate. The surrounding countryside, however, is a different story. The environs of Đà Nẵng include mountaintop resorts with spectacular vistas, secluded beaches with fresh seafood restaurants, and rice paddies melting into jungle. All of this centers on one of Vietnam's fastest-growing cities, which boasts the nation's best Chàm museum, a newly rebuilt waterfront, trendy restaurants, and friendly locals who speak good English. With the help of foreign investment and resort-minded tourists, major areas of Đà Nẵng are under construction as the city gets back on its feet after liberation. Budget travel also exists, though under the radar; streets are lined with food and beer stalls, and budget guest-houses are sprouting up next to pagodas. For any traveler wanting to get away from camera-toting tourists, Đà Nẵng and its surroundings are worth at least a couple of days.

▣ TRANSPORTATION

Flights: Đà Nẵng International Airport (☎827 286), 4km southwest of town, off of Nguyễn Van Linh. Buy tickets at **Vietnam Airlines,** 35 Trần Phú (☎811 111; open daily 7:30-11am and 1:30-5pm) or **Pacific Airlines,** 37 Trần Phú and 135 Lê Lợi (☎825 136; fax 810 144; open 8am-4pm). Flights to: **Bangkok, Thailand** (US$156); **Buôn Ma Thuột** (M, W, F-Sa 1 per day; 550,000Đ); **Hà Nội** (3 per day; 630,000-825,000Đ); **HCMC** (4 per day; 630,000-825,000Đ); **Nha Trang** (1 per day; 575,000Đ); **Pleiku** (M, W, Sa-Su 1 per day; 430,000Đ); **Singapore** (US$230); **Vinh** (M, W, Sa 1 per day; 530,000Đ).

Trains: Đà Nẵng Railway Station, 4 Hải Phòng (☎823 810). To: **Hà Nội** (14-18hr.; 6:45, 7:15, 8:45am, 12:50, 2:30pm; 224,000-504,000Đ); **HCMC** (14-23hr.; 5:30, 7:10, 7:30, 7:40, 11:10am, 1:05pm; 135,000-281,000Đ); **Huế** (2½-3½hr.; 6:45, 7:15, 8:45am, 12:55, 2:30pm; 207,000-489,000Đ); **Nha Trang** (8-12hr.; 5:30, 7:10, 7:30, 7:40, 11:10am, 1:05pm; 166,000-

The Southern Central Coast

351,000Đ); **Ninh Bình** (12½-16hr.; 6:45, 7:15, 8:45am; 205,000-461,000Đ); **Mũi Né** (12-16hr.; 5:30, 7:30, 7:40am, 7:10pm; 276,000-473,000Đ). Ticket office open daily 6am-5pm, but tickets can also be purchased at most hotels and all tourist agencies.

Buses: Full-size **public buses** heading to Hội An can be flagged down along Trần Phú. **Open-tour buses** with A/C can be booked at most hotels and all travel agencies to: **Đà Lạt** (22hr.; 5pm; 190,000Đ); **Hà Nội** (24hr.; 5pm; 190,000Đ); **HCMC** (24hr.; 5pm; 190,000Đ); **Hội An** (1hr.; 7, 9am, 2pm; 20,000Đ); **Huế** (3hr.; 9am, 3pm; 20,000Đ); **Mũi Né** (21hr.; 5pm; 190,000Đ); **Nha Trang** (13hr.; 5pm; 100,000Đ); **Savannakhet, Laos** (19hr.; 6pm; 220,000Đ). Reserve a seat in advance; the bus will pick you up at your hotel. There are two formal bus stations in Đà Nẵng on Nguyễn Lương Bằng. Most buses stop along Điện Biên Phủ to pick up more passengers.

Interprovince Bus Station, 33 Nguyễn Lương Bằng (☎821 265), right next to Điện Biên Phủ, 6km west of town. Minibuses to: **Đà Lạt** (19hr.; 4, 8am, 2pm; 120,000Đ); **Hà Nội** (24hr.; 5-9am; 100,000Đ); **HCMC** (24hr.; 5:30-9:30am; 120,000Đ); **Huế** (3hr.; every 30min. 6am-6pm; 50,000Đ); **Nha Trang** (13hr.; 5, 8am, 2pm; 80,000Đ); **Qui Nhơn** (9hr.; every 30 min. 4:30-9:30am; 40,000Đ); **Savannakhet, Laos** (19hr.; 6am, 8pm; 300,000Đ).

Intraprovince bus station, 29 Nguyễn Lương Bằng (☎823 715), right next to Điện Biên Phủ, next to the interprovince station. Sends tiny buses to **Hội An** (every 30min. 6am-7pm; 30,000Đ) and **Ba Na** (every hr. 6am-4pm; 25,000Đ).

Local Transportation: Motorbike and **cyclo** drivers will gladly take you to the airport (15,000Đ), the bus stations (25,000Đ), **China Beach** (30,000Đ round-trip), **Marble Mountains** (50,000Đ round-trip), and elsewhere. **Taxi** service is most easily arranged through your hotel; try **Hương Lua Taxi** (☎828 282) or **Sông Hàn Taxi** (☎655 655). Metered taxi to the airport costs 30,000Đ; to the bus stations costs 60,000Đ.

✈ ORIENTATION

Almost at the center of Vietnam, 750km south of Hà Nội and 990km north of HCMC, Đà Nẵng is bounded in the east by the **Hàn River** and in the north by **Đà Nẵng Bay.** The beautiful main boulevard, **Bạch Đằng,** runs along the river's west bank. Traffic is one-way going north above the Chàm Museum. One block inland, **Trần Phú** runs parallel to Bạch Đằng, with traffic going one-way south. Four blocks inland, **Lê Lợi,** which becomes **Phan Chu Trinh** south of its intersection with Lê Duẩn, is the major north-south artery. These three streets are intersected by **Điện Biên Phủ**—also called **Ly Thái Tổ** and **Hùng Vương** as it runs east—the east-west road that branches off Hwy. 1 and bisects the city. A few blocks north, Lê Duẩn ends in a bridge across the river. The city's southern boundary, **Nguyễn Văn Trỗi,** runs east over the Hàn River and toward the Marble Mountains, China Beach, and Hội An.

🛈 PRACTICAL INFORMATION

Tourist Offices: Most hotels offer basic tour services, and private companies also abound. To arrange international flights, try **Nguyên An,** 179 Phan Chu Trinh (☎823 446; fax 820 122; open daily 7-11am 1:30-6pm) or **Transasia Travel,** 167 Trần Phú (☎812 342; www.transasiadn.com.vn), which specializes in, fittingly, trans-Asian travel.

Danatours (www.vietnamwelcomes.com), the state-run outfit, has offices all over town. Branches at 76 Hùng Vương (☎835 653; fax 821 312) and 100 Bạch Đằng (☎834 515; fax 828 262).

Mr. Hung, 4 Trần Quốc Toản (☎843 122), specializes in reserving Đà Nẵng train, plane, and open-tour bus tickets.

Minh Travel Agency, 105 Trần Phú (☎812 661; mtjraymond@yahoo.ca), in the lobby of the Minh Travel Hotel. Offers information about tours and tickets to various locations. The owner speaks very good English and caters specifically to the budget backpacker.

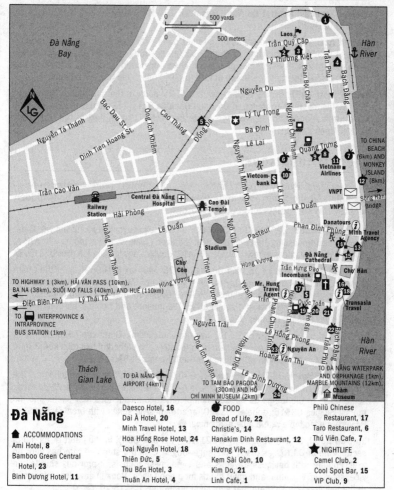

SOUTHERN CENTRAL COAST

Đà Nẵng

ACCOMMODATIONS
Ami Hotel, **8**
Bamboo Green Central
  Hotel, **23**
Bình Dương Hotel, **11**

Daesco Hotel, **16**
Dai À Hotel, **20**
Minh Travel Hotel, **13**
Hoa Hồng Rose Hotel, **24**
Toai Nguyễn Hotel, **18**
Thiên Đức, **5**
Thu Bồn Hotel, **3**
Thuận An Hotel, **4**

FOOD
Bread of Life, **22**
Christie's, **14**
Hanakim Dinh Restaurant, **12**
Hương Việt, **19**
Kem Sài Gòn, **10**
Kim Do, **21**
Linh Cafe, **1**

Philü Chinese
  Restaurant, **17**
Taro Restaurant, **6**
Thú Viên Cafe, **7**

NIGHTLIFE
Camel Club, **2**
Cool Spot Bar, **15**
VIP Club, **9**

Consulates: Laos, 16 Trần Quộ Cáp (☎821 208). Issues tourist visas to cross at Lao Bảo; 1-day processing, cheaper than in HCMC. Open M-F 8-11:30am and 2-4:30pm.

Banks: There are banks all over the city: **Vietcombank,** 140 Lê Lợi (☎823 503) cashes traveler's checks and does cash advances on credit cards. Open M-F 7:30-11am and 1-4pm. 24hr. ATM outside. There are also **ATMs** at the Orient Hotel and the Bamboo Green Riverside Hotel, as well as at **Incombank,** 36 Trần Quốc Toản (☎817 275), and on nearly every block of Trần Phú.

Beyond Tourism: Đà Nẵng Orphanage, 283 Lê Van Hiên, south of Đà Nẵng on the way to the Marble Mountains. A small but welcoming orphanage of about 30 children. Little English is spoken. Visiting hours daily 9-11am and 3-5pm.

Police: 1 Nguyễn Thị Minh Khai (☎828 371).

Pharmacies: One on every other block. Try 45 Quang Trưng or 110 Trần Phú. 2 Phan Đinh Phúng has a large selection and is located in the center of town. All open daily 7am-7pm.

Medical Services: Central Đà Nẵng Hospital, 124 Hải Phòng (☎821 118), 1 block north of Lê Duẩn.

Internet Access: Every block has an Internet parlor. The going rate is 3000Đ per hr. Options include 55 Nguyễn Chí Thanh, 30 Quang Trưng, and 61 Trần Quốc Toản. Almost all places have Internet phones for cheap international calling. Several of the hotels have free Internet; the **Bread of Life** (p. 299) offers free wireless Internet.

Post Offices: VNPT, 60 Bạch Đằng (☎821 522), north of the intersection with Hùng Vương. There's another branch at 64 Bạch Đằng (☎821 327), across the street. Both have international phones, fax, and *Poste Restante*. Located next to the Sông Hàn Bridge. Open daily 6am-10pm.

ACCOMMODATIONS

Budget travelers usually bypass Đà Nẵng, so most hotels tend to cater to businesspeople and the resort crowd; however, there are some cheap beds hidden around the city for expats and budget visitors.

▧ **Toai Nguyện Hotel,** 20 Pham Phú Thứ (☎843 098; toainguyenhotel@dng.vnn.vn). Great location next to bustling Trần Phú and near the river. Clean, spacious rooms with A/C at some of the best prices in town. Singles USụ10; doubles overlooking the river USụ15. ❸

▧ **Hoa Hống Rose Hotel,** 51 Lê Dinh Dương (☎825 740; fax 830 950), near the Chàm Museum. Buck the trend and stay in the south end of the city among the locals and trendy ice-cream and clothing shops. The Rose boasts rooftop views and endless food stalls, as well as hot water and satellite TV. Free Internet and free pickup from the airport. Singles US$12; doubles US$15. ❸

Dai À Hotel, 51 Yên Bái (☎841 511; www.daiahotel.com). Great central location and clean rooms for relatively good prices. Unfortunately, the cathedral bell tolls at 4:30am. Free Internet in the rooms, with cable provided. Rooms US$15-18. ❸

Binh Dương Hotel, 32 Trần Phú (☎821 930; binhduong32tranphu@gmail.com). The rooms are clean, delightfully quiet, and have A/C and satellite TV. Friendly staff. However, some doors to the rooms do not seal completely, and mosquitoes may sneak into the rooms. Singles US$16; doubles US$20; apartment-style suites with breakfast US$25. Prices are negotiable with a little bargaining. ❹

Thu Bốn Hotel, 8 Lý Thường Kiệt (☎821 101; fax 822 854), in the heart of the north sector. One of Đà Nẵng's many mid-range lodgings. An old standard that has kept up well. Popular with business travelers and Vietnamese tourists, it provides shuttle service, satellite TV, sauna, and quiet rooms for a good price. Book in advance; this is one of the few hotels in Vietnam that gets filled up. Rooms US$15-20. ❸

Ami Hotel, 7 Quang Trưng (☎824 494; ptscdn@dng.vnn.vn). This brand new hotel offers good quality for decent prices. Clean, quiet, and dark. Rooms US$14-25. ❸

Thuận An Hotel, 14 Bạch Đằng (☎820 527), at the north end of the street. Puts the "budget" in "budget mini-hotel." Doubles with fan US$8-12, with A/C US$10-15. ❷

Minh Travel Hotel, 105 Trần Phú (☎812 661; mtjraymond@yahoo.ca). Caters to the backpacker who is willing to rough it a little for the cheapest rooms in town. Owner speaks very good English. US$3 gets a tiny room with no A/C and a communal bathroom; US$7 gets a slightly less tiny room with A/C and private bath. A good budget deal if you don't mind the occasional cockroach. ❶

Daesco Hotel, 153-155 Trần Phú (☎892 808; www.daescohotel.com). Part of the city's 3-star business hotel fleet; this high-rise's claims to fame are its location at the heart of the city and its rooftop restaurant. Rooms 270,000-650,000Đ. ❹

Thiên Đức, 187 Đống Đa (☎825 232). Head north on Phan Chu Trinh until it turns into Lê Lợi. A few blocks up, hook a left onto Lý Tự Trọng. At the road's end, swing to the right onto Đống Đa. The guesthouse is near the corner on the right. Small, angular rooms with an old outside toilet and a cold shower. Old ceiling fans breeze over a comfy double bed. Rooms 60,000-85,000Đ. ❶

Bamboo Green Central Hotel, 158 Phan Chu Trinh (☎822 996; bamboogreen@dng.vnn.vn; www.vitours.com.vn). Bamboo Green's flagship hotel. This highrise offers great city views and spacious, bright rooms popular with business travelers. Located in the southern end of town, a 5-10min. walk from the city center. One of the cleaner, more comfortable hotels in the city. In-room laptop connections. US$50-60. ❺

🍴 FOOD

Though the food in Đà Nẵng lacks the luster of nearby Hội An and Huế, the city is by no means a culinary wasteland. Dining options vary from the ever-present food stalls selling rice, soup, and grilled meat, to a crowd of Chinese restaurants, a smattering of Western offerings, and a growing number of expensive Japanese restaurants catering to Japanese businessmen. Fun ice-cream and bubble tea shops litter the streets. There are two markets in town: **Chợ Hàn,** on the river by the intersection of Hùng Vương and Trần Phú, sells fruits, vegetables, flowers, and various foods (open daily 6am-8pm); **Chợ Côn** is near the intersection of Hùng Vương and Ông Ích Khiêm, focusing more on cloth and clothing (open daily 6:30am-6:30pm). Hùng Vương itself is lined with Western-style goods at Vietnamese prices.

Philū Chinese Restaurant, 225 Nguyễn Chí Thanh. Everything from fried rice (30,000Đ) to braised "beef penis" with traditional Chinese medicine (no, we're not sure what it is either; 45,000Đ). Large portions of authentic Chinese at reasonable prices. Entrees 30,000-100,000Đ. ❸

Bread of Life, 215 Trần Phú (☎562 917; breadoflife@pobox.com). Western bakery and eatery staffed by hearing-impaired waiters as a project to benefit the deaf. Free wireless Internet. Great Western options, especially the Italian soda (12,000Đ) and burgers (40,000Đ), for a good cause. Open M-Sa 7am-9pm. ❸

Kem Sài Gòn, 159 Lệ Lợi (☎650 800). One of the many great ice-cream shops popping up all over the city. Delectable desserts that will satisfy anyone's sweet tooth. Freshly squeezed orange juice 10,000Đ. Small choco-vanilla swirl ice cream 10,000Đ. ❶

Taro Restaurant, 51 Quang Trưng (☎863 048). One of two authentic Japanese restaurants in the city. A little expensive, but it might be worth a one-time splurge. Most 6- to 8-piece sushi rolls US$3-6. The tuna sashimi (US$3) melts in your mouth. Open daily 11am-2pm and 5pm-10pm. ❸

Thú Viên Cafe, 46 Bạch Đằng. A large, tree-shaded cafe sprawled along the river. Serves only drinks. It's a very popular hang-out for locals to chat, people-watch, and sip tea (7500Đ), Red Bull (6000Đ), lemonade (10,000Đ), or coffee (7500Đ). Tourists should expect some confused stares from the regulars. ❶

Linh Cafe, 12 Đông Da (☎820 401). A true backpacker eatery. Very friendly staff serves pancakes and good portions of Vietnamese food. Provides tour and rental info. Far from the city center. Breakfasts 12,000Đ. Open daily 6:30am-midnight. ❶

Hương Việt Cafe, 53 Trần Quốc Toản. English, French, and German menus offer some unusual Chinese treats such as shark and pigeon. The fried chicken (30,000Đ) is excellent, but may not be filling enough for some. Entrees 30,000-120,000Đ. ❸

Hanakim Dinh Restaurant, 15 Bạch Đằng (☎830 024). Right on the water, in a white and blue ship-like building, this is one of the city's nicest restaurants. Popular with business travelers and for local weddings, it features pleasant riverside seating and an

English-speaking staff. Offers fresh seafood from snapper (120,000Đ) to fresh lobster (800,000Đ). Vietnamese dishes (40,000-100,000Đ). Vegetarian dishes are more affordable (18,000-40,000Đ). Open daily 10:30am-11pm. ❺

Christie's, 112 Trần Phú (☎824 040), inside Cool Spot Bar. The restaurant is popular with Japanese tourists; the bar, with American, Australian, and British transplants who watch movies in English on television. An extensive Western menu lures travelers. Entrees 25,000-100,000Đ. Open daily 9:30am-11pm. ❹

Kim Do, 180 Trần Phú (☎821 846). A clean, cavernous representative of the city's many kitschy Chinese places, flaunting an extensive English menu and catering to a tourist crowd. Entrees 50,000-100,000Đ. ❹

👁 SIGHTS

▨ CHÀM MUSEUM. This small but celebrated museum boasts the best exhibition of Chàm sculpture in the nation. Open-air galleries showcase sandstone sculptures from the 4th to the 16th centuries, organized by their recovery location (including Mỹ Sơn). Exquisite and well-preserved works of the Champa people have been collected from all over Vietnam and brought here. Each priceless piece of art—ranging from an "elephant-tiger" to dancing women—is labeled in Vietnamese, English, and French; tour guides and guidebooks aren't really necessary here; just enjoy the intricate and fantastical creations of the Champa. The souvenir store offers many informative books about the religion and history of the Chàm. Likewise, Mr. Louis, a kind old Vietnamese man who speaks pretty good English and French, offers thoughtful 20-minute tours around the museum for 16,000Đ. This museum is especially rewarding after visiting Mỹ Sơn, as everything missing from there is found here. Make sure to check out the Buddha and Shiva sculptures at the back of the gallery. *(1 Bạch Đằng, on the southern end of town past the merging of Trần Phú and Bạch Đằng. Open daily 7am-5pm. 30,000Đ, children 5,000Đ.)*

ĐÀ NẴNG WATERPARK. One of the largest waterparks in Vietnam, this refreshing destination boasts six big slides, a zip line, a wave pool, and a lazy river. The tallest slide is 40m high and provides a nice view of the sprawling city. Bring water shoes if you can; the bricks around the park get remarkably hot. Go on a weekday and you'll have the place to yourself. *(Lockers 3000Đ. 30,000Đ, children 15,000Đ.)*

CAO ĐÀI TEMPLE. This is the largest Cao Đài temple outside the sect's home in Tây Ninh. Many of the 50,000 believers in the region worship here daily at 5:30am, noon, 5:30pm, and midnight—all under the watchful gaze of the enormous and holy all-seeing eye, located in the orb behind the main altar. The central figures of several major world religions, as well as various ancient scientists, are represented in the temple. It's worthwhile and acceptable to come at a time when people are praying, as long as you're quiet. *(63 Hải Phòng, parallel to Lê Duẩn; just head 1 block north. Ask one of the keepers to open the temple doors.)*

TAM BẢO PAGODA. This pagoda, whose tower holds relics of the Buddha, was constructed from 1954 to 1963 and is now in the middle of renovations; locals come here to worship and occasionally to take afternoon naps. A school stands behind the pagoda. The monks who live here are incredibly friendly, and will sometimes give tours. *(323 Phan Chu Trinh. From Hùng Vương, head south down Phan Chu Trinh for about 1km, keeping the river on your left side. Open daily 7-11am and 1:30-5pm. Free.)*

HỒ CHÍ MINH MUSEUM. A more upscale version of the generic Hồ Chí Minh museum, dedicated to commemorating the life and achievements of Vietnam's most famous political leader. A small garden surrounds the entire museum. In the way back, behind a small lake, is the exhibition gallery of Uncle Ho's life. In front of the lake is a replica of the political idol's childhood home in Làng Kim Liên, Vinh province. There's also a military museum filled with wartime photographs, with planes and tanks in the surrounding garden. Though it features many of the same photos and memorabilia as other Hồ Chí Minh museums, this one at least has good English captions, is in chronological order, and is pretty extensive. Then again—it's helpful to know before going that Nguyện Tat Thánh and Nguyện Al Quoc are both names for the good Uncle. (☎ 69 775 0921. 3 Duy Tân. Open daily 7:30-10:30am and 1:30-4:30pm. 20,000Đ.)

📷 NIGHTLIFE

Đà Nẵng's nightlife options are not designed for the tourist, so if you seek a night out you'll be rubbing elbows with the locals. The traditional possibilities, karaoke and billiards, can be found everywhere. Across the southern edge of the city, and especially along Lê Dinh Dương and Bạch Đằng, there are multitudes of street-side **beer gardens** packed with young students. These open-air bars are actually just paved lots under corrugated tin ceilings; the atmosphere is created by fluorescent lights and blaring pop music. You are given a case of bottles, then you drink what you want and pay by the number of empties you have left. Even farther south on Bạch Đằng, about one kilometer past the Chàm Museum, is a group of large, brand-new hot spots; the older, more popular clubs and bars are in the north around the intersection of Hùng Vương and Trần Phú. The cheapest and most relaxing evening option in Đà Nẵng is a stroll on **Bạch Đằng**, recently reconstructed into a grand boulevard. Running along the river, this wide brick walkway is lined with palm trees and French colonial buildings. The river walk meanders from the Chàm Museum in the south to the city shipyards in the north, passing over the modern Song Hàn Bridge about half-way along the walk.

Camel Club, 18 Lý Thường Kiệt. Dance like an Egyptian in this pyramid-shaped venue. Big drink list. Draws in the young and hip, but regrettably, no camels. Open daily 8pm-2am.

VIP Club, 17 Quang Trưng, is the nightclub where young locals shake it alongside aging foreigners, often to the sound of live bands. Beer 45,000Đ. Open daily 4pm-2am.

Cool Spot Bar, 112 Trần Phú, on the first floor of Christie's Restaurant. In this expat hang-out, you'll find the chance to drink the night away under the warm glow of a satellite TV with extensive channel options, many of which are in English. Free darts. Draft beer 14,000Đ. It's also the meeting place of the Đà Nẵng Hash Harriers (see **"The Đà Nẵng Hash Harriers,"** p. 301). Open daily 9:30am-1am.

THE ĐÀ NẴNG HASH HARRIERS

If you've spent time hanging ou in cities with sizable expat popu lations, you may have heard o the Hash Harriers—an interna tional running club with a drinking problem, or a drinking club with a running problem, depending on your preference. For someone moving to a new foreign city, i offers a great way to meet fellow expats; for the passing traveler, i provides an off-beat way to ge some exercise.

In Đà Nẵng, members mee every other Saturday for morning runs with a twist: you set out a your own pace (everything from walking to sprinting) and follow a "trail" marked by pieces of pape on the ground. A circle drawn on the paper means that the route has several options; like a mouse in a labyrinth, you must selec which path to take. A piece o paper with an "X" on it is a dead end; you've gone the wrong way and need to turn back. The idea is to give the runners (who tend to find all the wrong paths) and the walkers the same time on the clock, which is usually 1-1½hr. The run ends at a local pub, which serves as the club's headquarters In Đà Nẵng's case, it's the Coo Spot Bar (see **Nightlife**, p. p 301). Look on the board next to the bar for the Hash Harriers schedule and contact information The Đà Nẵng club is a bit unique in that many locals come along fo the runs. All are welcome.

SOUTHERN
CENTRAL COAST

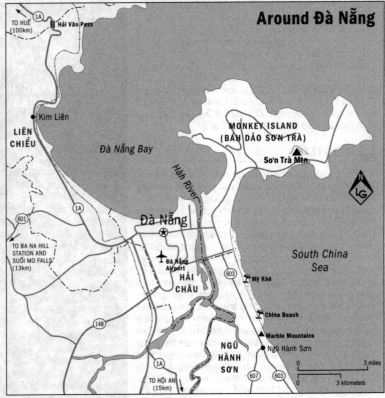

Around Đà Nẵng

TO HUẾ (100km)

1A

Hải Vân Pass

Kim Liên

LIÊN CHIỂU

Đà Nẵng Bay

601

1A

TO BA NA HILL STATION AND SUỐI MƠ FALLS (13km)

Đà Nẵng

MONKEY ISLAND (BÁN ĐẢO SƠN TRÀ)

Sơn Trà Mtn.

Hàn River

Đà Nẵng Airport

HẢI CHÂU

603

Mỹ Khê

South China Sea

N

14B

NGŨ HÀNH SƠN

1A

TO HỘI AN (15km)

607

603

China Beach

Marble Mountains

Ngũ Hành Sơn

0   3 miles

0   3 kilometers

▶ DAYTRIPS FROM ĐÀ NẴNG

The real draw of Đà Nẵng is its surroundings: within an hour's ride are a variety of noteworthy locales, including mountaintop resorts, secluded beaches, and caves.

▨ **MARBLE MOUNTAINS.** The Marble Mountains are named after the five fundamental elements: the popular Water Mountain, the thin Metal Mountain, the subtle Wood mountain, the double-peaked Fire Mountain, and the Earth Mountain. All of the mountains are close together, and most offer delightful views, pleasant pagodas, and hidden caves. The **Water Mountain** (Ngon Thủy Sơn) is the largest, with grand temples, eerie grottoes, and idols hewn from the rock, making it a tourist favorite. Most buses drop tourists off next to the limestone and marble quarries clustering around the mountain's base. From the entrance closest to the beach, stairs lead past a white Buddha to the towering **Linh Ứng Pagoda.** The Tàng Chơn Cave, hidden behind the pagoda in the back, contains a shrine flanked by three smaller chambers. In the chamber to the far left is a large standing Buddha with a large reclining Buddha behind it. Be careful not to go past the reclining Buddha, as there is a large drop. To the right of this chamber is another small chamber with a Chàm sculpture. The chamber to the far right has holes in the ceiling and, unsurprisingly, a large standing Buddha. In the main chamber there is a square stone platform, on which, according to legend, fairies and gods played checkers. (Why fairies and gods would play checkers is beyond us.)

Once back on the regular path, move on up to the "Simply Stunning Sea View," Vọng Hải Đài, which really isn't so stunning. For a grander panorama of China Beach from the mountain's highest accessible point, ascend **Động Vân Thông** (Way to Heaven), a very steep 120m climb up a dirt path, which is on your left 30m past the unmemorable **Vân Thông Cave.** Back on the path again, the **Tam Thái Pagoda** sports some beautiful bas-relief carvings and sits in front of the unimpressive **Linh Nham Cave.** To the pagoda's right, a stone representation of Quan Âm is carved in **Oa Nghiêm Cave.** The Marble Mountains' most spectacular sight lies behind it: the enormous ▨**Huyền Không Cave,** bathed in a quiet light that pierces through large holes above. Four warrior statues at the cavern's entrance, dating from Minh Mạng's time, protect it from evil spirits. Out of the cave, past the **Tam Thái Pagoda,** a path leads past two other small pagodas to Vọng Giang Đài, the perfect place to take in the five-mountain view. The Marble Mountains can provide a uniquely spiritual atmosphere if you visit when the place isn't overrun with tourists; consider visiting by motorbike in the early morning or at sunset. *(17km north of Hội An and 12km south of Đà Nẵng. Motorbikes and cyclos make the trip from Đà Nẵng for 60,000Đ round-trip. Most tourist buses stop here for an hour. Open daily 7am-6pm. 30,000Đ. A map with postcards inside costs 10,000Đ. Wear sturdy shoes.)*

▨**MONKEY ISLAND.** Fifteen kilometers from the city, Monkey Island (Bán Đảo Sơn Trà) is really a fish-shaped peninsula that juts into the ocean. Grand mountains are surrounded by gorgeous crystal-clear waters, and along the perimeter of the island, small beaches allow visitors to lounge in the hot sun. There are several beaches to choose from, all of which have resorts nearby: Tiện Sa is to the west, and Bãi But, Bãi Nam, and Bãi Bắc lie on the eastern side of the peninsula. Tiện Sa and Bãi But are some of the nicest beaches, but all are worth exploring. *(From Đà Nẵng, head past the Sông Hàn Bridge toward Hội An and China Beach, making a left when Ngô Quyền splits. Continue straight for about 10km until you reach the intersection with Lệ Van Thú street, then take a right. Continue straight until a dead end, and take a right onto Sôn Trá Đien Ngoc Street. Go another 10km until you reach your beach of choice. Ride your own motorbike or hire one for 30,000Đ each way, 60,000Đ with pickup.)*

CHINA BEACH. Along the low-lying stretch of land east of Đà Nẵng and north of the Marble Mountains are kilometers of deserted beach. The southernmost beach is China Beach, famous for being the location of a US Marine landing in 1965—however, it's unlikely that it actually was. Mỹ Khê Beach, to the north, slightly more developed but still relatively deserted, is more likely the real landing place. Along the entire waterfront are a few crumbling resorts and stalls selling outstanding fresh seafood. As of now, development has been blessedly minimal, and—though two resorts loom large—the white-sand beaches remain clean and accessible. *(20,000Đ. 7km motorbike ride from Đà Nẵng or the Marble Mountains.)* Though the beach makes for an easy daytrip, those who choose to stay overnight near the sandy shores can do so easily. Guesthouses line the thin forest near the water, and the beach's proximity to the Marble Mountains ensures a variety of tourist-oriented **restaurants ❷** that provide decent meals (soups 7000-15,000Đ; entrees 20,000-60,000Đ). There are also many local **food stalls** offering cơm dishes. **Hoa's Place ❷**, 215/14 Huyền Trân Công Chúa (☎969 978), is a 10m walk from China Beach. The rooms are small but clean and feature private baths. (Singles with fan US$6; doubles with fan US$8, with A/C US$10-15.) A friendly, English-speaking owner prepares spring rolls (20,000Đ) whose sterling reputation is confirmed by all, including visitors just passing through for a bite.

BA NA HILL STATION. West of Đà Nẵng is a world far removed from the coast: the Ba Na mountaintop resort. Founded nearly a century ago by the French, the spectacular villas here fell into disrepair in the latter half of the 20th century. Today, however, the place is being revamped and resold by the government, which hopes to draw in the weary city folk. The view is fantastic—unparalleled in the region—and the weather tends to be much cooler here than in the city. On the way up the mountain, stop at the **Tuong Phat Pagoda** and take the path up the mountain until you get to one of the largest Buddhas in the country. At the top of the mountain, there are short hiking trails, wild monkeys, the ruins of old French villas, and a rickety cable car with a spectacular view (30,000Đ round-trip). You can stay in the newer villas (around US$20) but there's no reason to stick around for more than a handful of hours after having lunch at one of the restaurants offering panoramic views. *(35km northwest of where Hwy. 1 leaves Đà Nẵng. The best way to get here is by motorbike (60,000Đ), because many roads are unmarked. At the foot of the mountain, you must pay an entry fee (10,000Đ) and wait for a special bus (35,000Đ), which leaves when full—it can be a long wait. Offering to pay 20,000Đ to other visitors with their own cars may be easier. Taxis can also bring you up (US$8-10). Once on top of the mountain, talk to the staff at a resort and they can usually set up a bus down the mountain for US$3 and back to Đà Nẵng for an additional US$2.)*

SUỐI MO FALLS. A series of small cascades around a swift river near Ba Na makes for a pleasant trek and a great way to end your day at Ba Na mountain. The spot is not heavily touristed and the hills around it are covered with forests instead of plantations or roads. *(Turn right before the Ba Na entrance gate. Follow the road for 2km and then look for the "Suối Mo" sign pointing left. It's a rocky but not overly difficult hike from here for another 10min., but the view is worth it.)*

HẢI VÂN PASS ("PASS OF THE CLOUDS"). To move north from Đà Nẵng and the South Central Coast to Huế and the North Central Coast, you must first negotiate the Hải Vân Pass, about 30km north of Đà Nẵng. A finger of the Trừờng Sởn Mountain range sticks into the South China Sea, forming a very dramatic natural barrier. In the winter, the difference in climate is quite striking: north of the pass it will be cold, wet and pouring rain, while the south side will be clear and warm. The mountain pass, at a height of 500m, is the site of spectacular cloud formations and offers a view of sprawling Đà Nẵng to the south and picture-perfect Lăng Cô Beach to the north. There are a couple of restaurants in this area catering to travelers. *(There are 2 options to get through the pass. Buses take Hwy. 1, which goes over the summit, and many tour buses stop here in the shadow of an old French fort. Alternatively, the train winds around the edge of the mountain just beyond the spray of the breaking surf.)*

HỘI AN ☎ 510

Although it traces its trading roots to the Chàm era, Hội An (known to Europeans as "Faifo") gained its reputation as a central port frequented by Chinese, Japanese, and European merchants in the 16th century. As the river began to silt up in the 1800s, the French moved the commercial center of central Vietnam to nearby Đà Nẵng. Today, Hội An does a brisk business in the tourist trade. Ancient merchants' mansions, ornate 18th-century assembly halls, delicious restaurants, local artist galleries, a nearby beach, and a general laid-back charm—and, most notably, over 100 quality, affordable tailoring shops—win over travelers' hearts. Hội An is also a UNESCO World Heritage Site, as is nearby Mỹ Son with its Champa ruins. Every day, especially during the full and new moon festivals each month, Hội An works extremely hard for the tourist dollar. Foreigners tend to stay twice as long as they'd planned, and we find it hard to blame them.

▐ TRANSPORTATION

Public buses usually drop travelers off on Hwy. 1 on the outskirts of town. Motorcycle taxis will take you the last 6km into the city (20,000Đ). The city's **public bus**

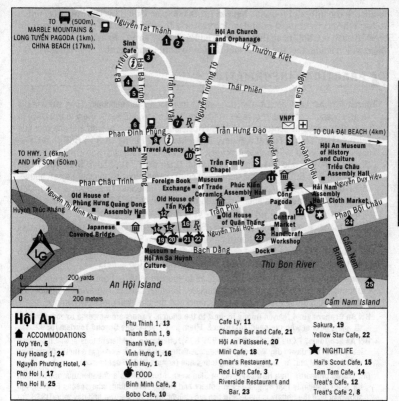

Hội An

ACCOMMODATIONS
Hợp Yên, **5**
Huy Hoang 1, **24**
Nguyễn Phương Hotel, **4**
Pho Hoi I, **17**
Pho Hoi II, **25**

Phu Thinh 1, **13**
Thanh Bình 1, **9**
Thanh Vân, **6**
Vĩnh Hưng 1, **16**
Vĩnh Huy, **1**

FOOD
Binh Minh Cafe, **2**
Bobo Cafe, **10**

Cafe Ly, **11**
Champa Bar and Cafe, **21**
Hội An Patisserie, **20**
Mini Cafe, **18**
Omar's Restaurant, **7**
Red Light Cafe, **3**
Riverside Restaurant and Bar, **23**

Sakura, **19**
Yellow Star Cafe, **22**

NIGHTLIFE
Hai's Scout Cafe, **15**
Tam Tam Cafe, **14**
Treat's Cafe, **12**
Treat's Cafe 2, **8**

station is located about 1.5km northwest of the center of town at the intersection of Nhị Trưng and Lê Hồng Phong. **Buses** leave for Đà Nẵng (1hr.; every hr. 7:30am-4:30pm; 30,000Đ), where you can transfer to a bus to Huế or other northern cities. To travel south to Nha Trang and Quảng Ngãi, flag down a bus from Hwy. 1. **Open-tour buses** are available at any hotel and head to: Đà Nẵng (1hr.; 8am; US$3); Hà Nội (14hr.; 6am, 8pm; US$12); Huế (3hr.; 8am; US$4); Nha Trang (10hr.; 6am, 8pm; US$7-12). All prices are subject to bargaining. Most hotels rent **cars** with drivers (from US$20 per day), **motorbikes** (US$5 per day), and **bicycles** (4000-7000Đ per day). **Taxis** and **freelance minibuses** hang out absolutely everywhere in the city, especially at the intersection of Phan Cháu Trinh and Hoàng Diệu.

■ ORIENTATION

Hội An is 25km south of Đà Nẵng and 102km north of Quảng Ngãi. **Huỳnh Thúc Kháng** connects **Highway 1** to the city. Just before town, the street breaks into three branches. **Phan Đình Phùng** marks the north edge of town, and it eventually becomes **Trần Hưng Đạo**, home to the **post office** and Hội An Hotel, and ultimately leads to the beach after 5km. The middle branch is **Phan Cháu Trinh**. The last branch, **Nguyễn Thị Minh Khai**, heads southeast toward the **Japanese Covered Bridge** and the river. After the bridge it becomes **Trần Phú**, the town's most sight-packed road. One block south, **Bạch Đằng** runs east-west and hugs the Thu Bon River. Though the town is growing to absorb the influx of tourists, **Nguyễn Tat Thánh** (also called Lý Thường Kiệt) tends to form the northernmost boundary for visitors. The major north-south streets, from west to east, are **Nhị Trưng** (also called Hai Bà Trưng), **Lê Lợi, Nguyễn Huệ,** and **Hoàng Diệu,** which leads over the Cẩm Nam Bridge to Cẩm Nam Island.

🄯 PRACTICAL INFORMATION

Tourist Offices: Every hotel in town can arrange tours locally and nationally. Every block in Hội An also boasts 2 or 3 tourist bureaus. A few are listed below, but nearly every tourist office in town offers the same services at only slightly different prices. Shop around and use your bargaining skills. **Linh's Travel Agency,** 27A Phan Đình Phùng (☎910 689; linhtravelagency@yahoo.com). Open-tour tickets, guides, local tours (Mỹ Son US$3), cooking classes, Internet, and bus and plane tickets. Open daily 7am-11pm. **Sinh Cafe,** 18B Hai Bà Trưng (☎863 948; www.sinhcafevn.com). Same services, plus money exchange. Open daily 6am-11pm. A far cheaper idea is to ask a fisherman to give you an hour-long **boat tour** of the nearby islands. It should only cost about US$2, but you'll have to get to the dock by 6am, and your guide may or may not speak English.

Banks: Incom Bank, 4 Hoàng Diệu (☎862 675). Currency exchange, traveler's checks services, Western Union wire transfers. Open M-Sa 7am-5pm. **VietABank,** 2 Phan Cháu Trinh, also offers basic banking services. The best **ATM** in town is at 37 Trần Hưng Đạo (open daily 8am-8pm), but there are hundreds that line the streets.

Beyond Tourism: Hội An offers alternatives to tourism ranging from volunteering at an orphanage to ecotourism to cooking classes. Informal classes are available, too—just ask for instruction at your favorite restaurant, and the chef will probably comply.

Hội An Orphanage, 4 Nguyễn Trường Tô, next to the church. Visitors are welcome to come by and sit, play, or chat with the children. Open 8-10am and 2-4pm. See **Beyond Tourism,** p. 92.

Hội An Eco-Tours, 7 Cua Đại Beach St. (☎927 808), offers several different trips in which one can learn about the day-to-day work of a Vietnamese fisherman or a rice worker in a rural village. Trips include a meal and an English-speaking tour guide (around US$25 per person).

Mr. Trung, of nearby Than Há village, about 3km west of town, offers a cheaper tour option. Than Há is a community that specializes in pottery and fishing. Mr. Trung, who speaks English, will show you how the pottery is made and fish are caught in his village. The half-day tour (US$8 per person) ends with a trip to his house where you eat a traditional meal cooked by his wife.

Hai's Scout Cafe, 98 Nguyễn Thái Học (☎863 210; info@visithoian.com). Offers nightly Vietnamese ▨ **cooking classes.** See **Beyond Tourism,** p. 96.

Banana Split Cafe, 53 Hoàng Diệu (☎861 136), near the Cẩm Nam bridge. The cheapest cooking classes in town. Offers 1 class per day 9am-noon for US$3. The teacher here knows less English than those at other cooking schools.

Bookstore: Foreign Book Exchange, 52 Lê Lợi. Good and cheap; buys, sells, and trades. Most books around 60,000Đ. Large French and German sections. Open daily 8am-10pm. There's also a smaller shop a bit to the north. Several book and CD exchanges are on Trần Phú.

Emergency: Police ☎115. Fire ☎114.

Police: 8 Hoàng Diệu (☎861 204).

Pharmacy: Several on Trần Phú. **Pharmacie No. 225,** 58 Nguyễn Trường Tô, is near the hospital. Open daily 7am-10pm. Another is at 96 Lê Lợi (☎862 470), close to the water.

Medical Services: Local hospital, 4 Trần Hưng Đạo (☎864 566), across the street from the VNPT Post Office.

Internet Access: New outlets are popping up by the day. Many hotels have free Internet access for their guests in the lobby. In the city, especially along Phan Đình Phùng, expect to see at least one Internet store per block. Try **Linh's Travel Agency,** 27A Phan Đình Phùng (☎910 689). Multiple computers and a fast connection (100Đ per min.). The best deal requires a bit of a walk: **VNC**, 47A Nguyễn Tat Thánh, is the fastest and the cheapest at 3000Đ per hr., but you might have to wrestle a computer away from a Vietnamese boy playing video games.

Post Office: VNPT, 6 Trần Hưng Đạo (☎861 480). The place to mail your clothes home, although it isn't cheap. The 1st kg costs around US$10, and about US$3.50 per kg above that to ship to the US. For other overseas countries, shipping costs between US$10-20 for the 1st kg, and US$1-5 for every kg afterwards. Free packaging. *Poste Restante.* Open daily 6am-10pm.

▟ ACCOMMODATIONS

Hội An will never have a room shortage. Such a large number of hotels has sprouted up in the last few years that it is inconceivable they could ever all fill up; indeed, how this many remain in business is a mystery. The list below is by no means exhaustive. The center of town offers older, more convenient, and more expensive establishments. The northwest corner of town, marked by Lê Hồng Phong and Nhị Trưng, tends to be newer, cheaper, and only a short walk from the town center. You'll find most backpackers here. All hotels offer different prices for rooms with and without air-conditioning.

▨ **Thanh Vân (HI)**, 78 Trần Hưng Đạo (☎916 916; www.hotelthanhvan.com). One of a handful of new, sparklingly clean hotels in the northwest corner of town. Quiet rooms, a large courtyard swimming pool, free Internet, and delicious breakfast included—all wrapped up in a pagoda-like palace. A better value than the surrounding hotels. Filled with backpackers. Rooms US$8-15. ❷

Họp Yện (HI), 16A Nhị Trưng (also called Hai Bá Trưng; ☎863 153). One of the most popular backpacker destinations. On a quiet street in the northwest corner, 7min. from the city center. The rooms are clean, air-conditioned, and comfortably small, and the staff is friendly. Free Internet in the lobby. Singles US$6; doubles US$8. ❷

Nguyễn Phương Hotel, 6 Bà Triệu (☎916 588). One of the best deals in Hội An. This small guesthouse in the hotel district provides comfortable rooms at the right price. Singles with hot water, A/C, and TV US$6; doubles US$8. ❷

Vĩnh Huy, 203 Lý Thường Kiệt (☎916 559). Another clean, cheap mini-hotel, popular with backpackers. The owner is your best friend, and guests practically move in. You can borrow a DVD player and DVDs for free. The walls are thin and the street is noisy, though, and it's far from the town center. Singles US₫5; doubles US₫7. ❶

Pho Hoi I, 7/2 Trần Phú (☎861 633; www.phohoiriversidehoian.com). A good deal in the city center. Rooms are cheap and a little noisy, but adequate. Staff is backpacker-friendly and speaks English. Singles with hot water, A/C, and satellite TV US$8; doubles US$10. ❷

Phu Thinh I, 144 Trần Phú (☎861 297; www.phuthinhhotels.com), across the street from Vĩnh Hưng 1, right in the center of town. Rooms have thin walls, but the price is good for being so close to the market and the river. Doubles with A/C $10. ❷

Pho Hoi II, Cẩm Nam Island (☎862 628; www.phohoiriversidehoian.com), right across the Cẩm Nam Bridge in the southeastern part of town. A medium-sized hotel affiliated with the large, resort-like hotel next to it. Guests can use the sister resort's fantastic pool and eat at the buffet free of charge. Smallish rooms with a garden view US$12-15. ❸

Huy Hoang 1, 73 Phan Bội Châu (☎861 453; fax 863 722). Clean rooms by the river. The main draw is breakfast on the balcony, with a spectacular view of the river and the market (which is just a hop, skip, and a jump away). Bridge traffic can be a bit noisy. Rooms US$12 and up; river-view rooms US$30. ❸

Vĩnh Hưng 1, 143 Trần Phú (☎861 621; www.vinhhunghotels.com). One of the nicest options amid the narrow streets of the old quarter. Excellent service and upscale rooms in an architecturally magnificent, Chinese pagoda-style building. Popular with an older crowd. Rooms US$25-50, though bargaining might get you a better deal. ❹

Thanh Bình I, 1 Lê Lợi (☎861 740; vothihong@dng.vnn.vn). An old standard, the "Serene Hotel" offers cheap rooms at the town's main intersection, though the building is beginning to show its age. Motorcycle taxis tend to drop off tourists at this hotel, but do not get swept away by its beautiful exterior. Once you get past the colonial-style architecture, there is nothing special. Singles US$8; doubles US$10. ❷

 FOOD

Hội An has both quantity and quality when it comes to food. The city's local culinary specialties are famous throughout the country and deserve your individual gastronomic attention. Hội An also offers a stunning variety of foreign cuisines to satisfy the whim of every passing visitor: Chinese, French, Indian, and Italian. The listings below are a good start, but every turn, nook, and alley in the city yields a new restaurant or cafe. The cheapest eats radiate out from the market in the center of town. A stroll along the waterfront reveals a string of slightly more expensive seafood restaurants—most have the same menu, and all claim to have the best seafood in town. Prices are lower the closer you move to the market.

Hội An has three specialties: **white rose** (tasty shrimp and frog in a crunchy flour wrapping), **fried wontons,** and, best of all, **cao lầu** (a superb thick and flat rice noodle served with sprouts, greens, and crispy fried rice paper in a light soup). Enhanced with mint, anise, and small chilis, *cao lầu* is both filling and flavorful.

Aside from standard restaurants, Hội An also offers two outstanding cafes that are great for shopping breaks or people-watching. **Cafe King ❶,** 10 Phan Châu Trinh, is located literally in the center of town (coffee 8000Đ). **Quán Dần Lang ❶** is tourist-free and stares down Hội An from the opposite side of the river. To reach it, cross Cẩm Nam Bridge, take the first right 20m down the road, and walk 150m to the end of the residential street.

🖼 **Hội An Patisserie,** 107-109 Nguyễn Thái Học, located at the western edge of town by the river. With a real French pastry chef and a wide selection of delectable treats, this is what you've been craving. Take a coffee and crème brulée (12,000Đ) to the terrace and be transported back to French Indochina, or grab a pastry for a late-night snack-and-stroll. You can also sit on the comfortable sofas in the lounge of next door Cargo Club, where you can wash down your pastry with a delicious smoothie (made with ice from filtered water; 20,000Đ). Pastries 7000-20,000Đ; gourmet sandwiches 40,000Đ. ❷

🖼 **Riverside Restaurant and Bar,** 58 Bạch Đằng. One of the best meals in town. Though it looks like every other restaurant on the river, Riverside's Vietnamese, vegetarian, and seafood dishes blow away the competition. Try the fantastic spring rolls and spicy peanut sauce. Affordable prices (30,000Đ-70,000Đ). ❸

Cafe Ly, 22 Nguyễn Huệ, conveniently located near the market. All of the food is great, but the banana pancakes are extraordinary. Excellent *cao lầu* (8000Đ), white roses (12,000Đ), and fried wontons (17,000Đ) are among the restaurant's top offerings. Open daily 8am-10pm. ❷

Bobo Cafe, 18 Lê Lợi, facing Thùy Dương Mini Hotel. Good value and good food make this a long-time favorite among backpackers. Offers vegetarian versions of local specialties and pleasant patio seating. The steamed spring rolls (8000Đ) and the accompanying light vinegar sauce are some of the best in town. ❶

Champa Bar and Cafe, 75 Nguyễn Thái Học. Like many other restaurants on Nguyễn Thái Học, but catering especially to the tourist crowd. Nightly concerts (9pm, except in summer), cheap beer, billiards, and cooking classes make this a foreigner-friendly food stop. Entrees 10,000-28,000Đ. ❶

Mini Cafe, 10/28 Bạch Đằng (☎861 105), across from Pho Hoi 1. On a small alley off of Trần Phú, this little restaurant has a very friendly waitstaff and serves cheap goodies from an extensive Western and Vietnamese menu (pancakes 7000Đ). Perfect for a quick bite near the markets. ❶

Omar's Restaurant, 14 Phan Đình Phùng. One of 2 Indian places in town—Omar's is the more expensive (entrees 30,000-90,000Đ) but claims the only Indian chef in Hội An. Limited selection, but excellent curry (45,000Đ). A great option if you need a break from Vietnamese and are looking to splurge. ❸

Yellow Star Cafe, 73 Nguyễn Thái Học (☎910 430; www.yellowstarcafe.com). This pleasant and relaxed restaurant offers a great selection of steaks and baguettes along with the typical Western and Vietnamese fare. Entrees 15,000-70,000Đ. ❸

Binh Minh Cafe, 27 Lê Hồng Phong, is the cheapest meal in the northwest corner of town. As the small book exchange in the corner suggests, this place caters to backpackers. Excellent breakfast (omelettes 7000Đ). Also look for the shorter Vietnamese menu. ❶

Red Light Cafe, 603 Hai Bà Trưng. A small streetside cafe in the northwest corner offering good, quick food at great prices. *Cao lầu* 8000Đ. Most entrees 8000-37,000Đ. ❶

Sakura, 119-121 Nguyễn Thái Học. Hội An's finest eatery seems like a relic from the French colonial era, but it's actually new. Overlooks the river and a quiet plaza. The menu features a strange but delicious mix of gourmet seafood, Japanese food, and steak (150,000Đ and up). The set menu is a better deal: fruit, noodles, rice, veggies, beef, white rose, and shrimp all go for US$6. ❺

🔘 SIGHTS

Below is a thorough list of sights in the city that have been preserved since the 16th and 17th centuries. Together, these sights give a good indication of what this ancient city looked like as far back as the Middle Ages and how it has changed with the powerful influences of its international trading partners. The city's assembly houses date back to when Chinese merchants came to Hội An and formed congregations *(bang)* according to their native region. The halls of these houses all follow similar patterns and purposes: four open chambers surround a courtyard, providing an ornate environment for meeting peers, worshipping gods, and honoring ancestors. You probably won't be able to see all of the sights listed here, but our favorites are the Japanese Covered Bridge, the Old Houses of Phùng Hưng and of Tấn Ky, Phúc Kiến Assembly Hall, the Museum of Revolutionary Fighting, and the Hội An Church and Orphanage. You can purchase a UNESCO **entry ticket** (75,000Đ) from 6am-5pm at any of Hội An's **tourist booths:** 81 Nguyễn Huệ (☎862 715); 5 Hoàng Diệu (☎861 114); 37 Trần Phú (☎862 118); 78 Lê Lợi (☎861 982); and 19 Hai Bá Trưng (☎861 984). Each ticket provides access to the Japanese Covered Bridge or the Cống Pagoda, as well as your choice of one old house, one assembly hall, one museum, and one additional sight. Government tour guides (100,000Đ per 2hr. tour; free for groups over 8) have a sweeping knowledge of local history.

UNESCO SIGHTS

JAPANESE COVERED BRIDGE. The pink Japanese Covered Bridge, Hội An's most famous symbol, is known locally as Chùa Cầu ("Pagoda Bridge"). Japanese traders built it in the early 17th century. The stone piles were meant to be driven into the heart of a monster, whose pesky tail supposedly caused earthquakes in Japan. Walking across the bridge today is free; entering its inner room requires your ticket but offers little to see.

CÔNG PAGODA (CHÙA ÔNG). This pagoda honors Quan Công, a general of the Han Dynasty during the 2nd and 3rd centuries. The 350-year-old temple, built in 1653, has the distinction of housing the largest deity statue in Hội An. (*24 Trần Phú, across the street from the market. Opens into the Museum of History and Culture. Open daily 7am-5:30pm. Dress conservatively.*)

HANDICRAFT WORKSHOP. "Workshop" is a misnomer—you'll be lucky to see anyone making handicrafts. However, there's a wide selection of goods on sale, all presumably made on the premises. In the far back you can see a working loom used for mat weaving. Every day except Monday there are traditional music shows at 10:15am and 3:50pm. If you are not planning on buying anything, use your ticket for a different, more exciting sight. (*9 Nguyễn Thái Học.*)

OLD HOUSES

OLD HOUSE OF PHÙNG HƯNG. This 180-year-old building is still home to eight people from the family's 8th generation. The spacious house stands in serene contrast to the busy street scene outside the Japanese Bridge. The two-story house used to hold merchandise, but today they exhibit a collection of arts and crafts. One of the family members may give you a personal tour of the house, pointing out the interesting vestiges of Chinese, Japanese, and Vietnamese architecture. Check out the trap door and removable windows on the second floor. (*4 Nguyễn Thị Minh Khai, just west of the bridge. Open daily 8am-6pm.*)

OLD HOUSE OF TẤN KY. The first old house in the city to be certified as a World Heritage Sight, the old house of Tấn Ky is now visited by national and international leaders. Visitors can only enter the stunning front chamber, as the 7th-generation family inhabits the back of the house and the second story. There is still plenty to see—the 200-year-old house displays an impressive fusion of Chinese, Japanese, and Vietnamese architecture. There are Chinese poems written in mother-of-pearl and portraits of each generation's matriarch and patriarch, beginning with Tấn Ky himself. A worthy selection for your ticket, as the owner speaks English and invites visitors to tea. (*101 Nguyễn Thái Học. Open daily 8am-5:30pm.*)

TRẦN FAMILY CHAPEL. Devoted to ancestor worship, the 200-year-old Trần Family Chapel incorporates Chinese, Japanese, and Vietnamese design into its woodwork and beams. The 8th generation of the Trần family, who live next door, explain their heritage and serve refreshments to guests. On the family altar rests a group of boxes, each one containing a small personal object from the patriarch and a wooden tablet listing his accomplishments. (*21 Lê Lợi, at the corner of Lê Lợi and Phan Châu Trinh. Open daily 7am-6pm.*)

OLD HOUSE OF QUÂN THẮNG. Built by a Chinese captain in the 18th century, this well-preserved house is said to be the oldest in Hội An. Quite a bit smaller and emptier than the other old houses, it is nonetheless a window into a world of almost 300 years ago. (*77 Trần Phú. Open daily 7am-8pm.*)

ASSEMBLY HOUSES

■**PHÚC KIẾN ASSEMBLY HALL.** This is one of the best choices for your ticket. Hội An's oldest, largest, most colorful, and most complex structure, this hall was first constructed in 1697 by immigrants from China's Fujian Province. Passing the pink columns of the Red Phoenix Gate, look down to see the symbol for longevity surrounded by five bats of happiness (as if there were any other kind of bat). The first courtyard contains stonework and a statue called "Carp Contemplating a Moon." Above the inner archway, five bats frame the phrase "The goddess will give her fellow man favor." This goddess is Thánh Mẫu, Holy Mother, Protectress of

Sailors, and Goddess of the Sea. Just inside the main building, a mural depicts Thánh Mẫu preparing to rescue a ship from a wipeout-caliber wave. The main altar pays tribute to the congregation's ancestors; a smaller one to the right honors the God of Prosperity. *(46 Trần Phú. Open daily 7am-6pm.)*

QUẢNG DONG ASSEMBLY HALL. This hall served the families of Cantonese merchants, who arrived during the 17th century, built the hall in the 18th century, renovated it in 1885, and added the courtyard's colorful dragon fountain 20 years ago. A large bas-relief mural at the entrance depicts a red-faced Quan Công, a deified military hero from the 3rd century. The main sanctuary houses a three-dimensional image of him with the Goddess of Mercy and the God of Prosperity on either side. To the right side of the main building, a small alley takes you to a contemplative sculpture garden, where fantastical and colorfully tiled creatures twist and turn with impressive complexity. *(176 Trần Phú. Open daily 6am-6pm.)*

TRIỀU CHÂU ASSEMBLY HALL. Intricate wood carvings lure a select handful of visitors to this 150-year-old hall. Inside the sanctuary, a first-century Han emperor sits surrounded by tiny figures carved and painted on wooden panels. Younger than some of the other houses and at the east end of town, this hall sees the fewest visitors. The quiet courtyard provides welcome relief from Hội An's bustling streets, but the interior of the house is less inspiring than that of some of the other old houses. *(362 Nguyễn Duy Hiệu, the eastern extension of Trần Phú. Open daily 6am-6pm.)*

MUSEUMS

MUSEUM OF HỘI AN SA HUỲNH CULTURE. This museum displays remnants of the Sa Huỳnh civilization that were first unearthed around Hội An in 1993. As with Oc Eco in the south and Đông Sơn in the north, much of the history of this prehistoric, pre-Champa culture remains elusive. Most of the exhibits focus more on the archaeology that unearthed the artifacts than on the culture itself. In any case, the ancient burial jars, holding ashes of the dead, are pretty interesting. Also check out the **Museum of Revolutionary Fighting**, on the second story of the museum. While very few of the displays have captions in English, it is interesting to see the old artillery and the pictures of revolutionary characters, many of whom were females. *(149 Trần Phú, opposite the Quảng Dong Assembly Hall. Open daily 6:30am-6pm. Free.)*

HỘI AN MUSEUM OF HISTORY AND CULTURE. This 300-year-old museum, which used to be a Quan Âm Pagoda, provides a decent overview of the city's history. Today, this one-room museum's secular displays trace local civilization through the early Sa Huỳnh culture, the Champa Empire, and the Đại Việt Era. The majority of displays have captions in English. The museum is worth seeing, but it will provide few real answers to your historical questions. *(7 Nguyễn Huệ, connected to the Công Pagoda. Open daily 7am-6pm. Free.)*

MUSEUM OF TRADE CERAMICS. The front room of this museum introduces visitors to the global maritime network through rather boring displays, including a map of ocean routes, a model of a trading ship, and a 17th-century Japanese painting of Hội An. More engaging exhibits on modern-day architectural preservation efforts, along with a section of Hội An's signature *yin* and *yang* roof tiles, await visitors in the back room, though it is unfortunately crowded with distracting pieces of wood and small purses for sale. *(80 Trần Phú. Open daily 7am-5:30pm. Free.)*

OTHER SIGHTS

HỘI AN CHURCH AND ORPHANAGE. The church services the area's Catholic population and supports the orphanage next door. While the church is unimpressive, a visit to the orphanage is rewarding. Visitors are more than welcome to stop by and play

HOT NEW THREADS

I first heard about Hội An a month before I arrived in Vietnam. I was talking to a previous *Let's Go: Vietnam* researcher who had really enjoyed Hội An, in part because he had had a couple of great suits made there. I didn't pay much attention; clothing, as a regional attraction, didn't strike me as all that compelling. I pulled into town with tailoring low on my list. Then everything changed for me.

Having tailored clothes made for you in a day is a rush. While the constant invitation into clothing shops may try one's patience, all is forgotten as the imagination runs wild with the prospect of creating a new outfit.

The process begins with the selection of the desired article of clothing. Almost all shops have a collection of Western catalogues to help with selection. You can either choose something exactly as shown or mix and match, creating completely unique gear. After you select the item and the fabric (from a remarkable variety), it's time to settle on the price.

I chose to have two suits and a pair of pinstripe trousers made, and I got the price down from US$145 to US$115. I gave the seamstresses two days and they were very thankful—most customers ask for it back in a day. The following day, everything was finished—I almost wished that I was returning home to a professional job, or at least a job interview.

—*Danny Koski-Karell*

with the children who live there. While some children will be excited simply to practice their English, it is worthwhile to bring a gift, such as markers or bouncy balls. *(See **Beyond Tourism**, p. 306. Church located at 4 Nguyễn Trường Tô, and orphanage at 2 Nguyễn Trường Tô. Mass services: Su 5:30am and 4pm; M, W, F 5:45pm; T, Th, Sa 4:45am. Orphanage visiting hours: daily 8-10am and 2-4pm.)*

LONG TUYỀN PAGODA. This pagoda, whose name means "dragon's stream," is the largest and youngest of Hội An's pagodas. Because it isn't over 200 years old, it's not on the tourist radar—but it definitely warrants a visit. Down a dirt path, the brightly colored pagoda towers rise above the surrounding cemetery. On the grounds, there are several unique Buddha statues and altars—the styles and stances vary wildly—as well as living quarters for the monks. At the very back of the compound is the entrance to the cemetery and a statue of a bearded white man that looks, strangely, like a traditional rendering of Jesus. *(Head 1km west on Nguyên Tat Thánh from its intersection with Hai Bà Trưng. The pagoda is down a dirt path on the left—follow the towers. About a 15min. walk from the town center.)*

TRƯỜNG FAMILY CHAPEL. A less polished house of ancestral worship, the Trường Family Chapel was first constructed in 1840 and then rebuilt in 1897. The edifice honors a family that came from Fujian, China, 10 generations ago. The central altar honors the family's first three generations; the left altar, generations four through six; and the right altar awaits those next in line. The best time to visit is after 5pm when guide Trường Tri is home. *(69/1 Phan Châu Trinh. Open 7am-7pm.)*

HẢI NAM ASSEMBLY HALL. For a glimpse of amazing woodwork, visit this hall. The congregation came from the island of Hainan near the coast of North Vietnam. In 1851, 108 of their merchant sailors were wrongfully killed by local mandarins, who in turn were executed by the emperor. The assembly hall was built in the sailors' memory. *(10 Trần Phú. Open daily 6am-5pm.)*

🛍 SHOPPING

In a region renowned for its tailors and dressmakers, Hội An tops all other cities in central Vietnam. Though lower-quality US$20 suits are not difficult to find, a good suit should cost about US$40, and a pair of silk pajamas US$10. All can be made within a day and according to the shopper's specifications. Shops are concentrated on Lê Lợi, but can be found everywhere in the city. Most have old pattern books and fashion magazines to aid the design process. The **cloth market,** which houses about 60 cloth stalls, is farther down Trần Phú toward Hoàng Diệu at 1 Trần

Phú. (Open daily 6am-5pm.) While visiting, you will be mobbed by women trying to sell you fabric and make you clothing. To avoid some of the noise, go between noon and 1:30pm when some of the vendors are napping. The cloth market is worth exploring, as the seamstresses can use any fabric in the entire warehouse, and the prices are often cheaper than those of true tailor shops. Inside the market, **Mai,** stall number 7, produces superb work, and its vendors speak excellent English. But almost every tailoring shop offers great value and quality, and nearly all can be bargained down to the same price. To ascertain quality, talk to the dressmakers (not just the shopkeepers), look at their previous work, and ask other customers' opinions. The trilingual (English, French, and Vietnamese) seamstress at unassuming **Ngọc Huệ,** 61 Phan Đình Phùng, does excellent work at reasonable prices. Another solid option is **Thu Thủy,** 60 Lê Lợi. Ask to see the exquisite hand-carved wood beams in the showroom in the back.

There is also the vast **central market,** with everything from fruit to knives to T-shirts, at the intersection of Nguyễn Huệ and Trần Phú. (Open daily 6am-7:30pm.) The southern area of the market is more geared to the locals, while the northern part is for tourists. Be ready to bargain and to turn away the numerous hawkers.

SHOP LIKE A PRO. There are a few things to keep in mind while shopping.
1. Clothes are cheap and made quickly here, but allow yourself a day or two for modifications after the clothing is made.
2. Always try your clothing on, and do not hesitate to ask for changes.
3. If you have a difficult or special order, try to make sure the tailor, and not just the shopkeeper, is present.
4. Linings might cost extra; double-stitching (which prevents fraying) should not.
5. You can take off an extra inch; you can't add one.
6. "Chinese silk," "Japanese silk," and "Vietnamese silk" are slightly different materials and mean different things to different people, but when all is said and done, real silk burns in a flame, while synthetics melt away. Ask for a sample and test the fabric yourself with a lighter.
7. Try to be creative; if you could find it at home, keep brainstorming.
8. Don't be overwhelmed by the multitude of shops: they all sell mostly the same materials from the same cloth distributors. The trick is to find a store in which you are comfortable and that understands what you're looking for.
9. Ask them to keep your sizes on file and get their email address in case you ever want more clothes made.

Though Hội An makes its name with tailors, its **artists and craftspeople** should not be overlooked. This remarkable community produces brightly colored oil paintings. Other artists specialize in sculpture and etching—the variety of art is wide, as a stroll down Nguyễn Thái Học will reveal. If you show interest in something, it is not unlikely that the artist will invite you for tea and explain the process and meaning behind his or her work. Also be sure to stop by **Reaching Out,** 103 Nguyễn Thái Học, a handicraft shop that sells work made by the town's disabled population. (☎862 460; www.tbonet.f2s.com. Open daily 8am-5pm.)

◧ NIGHTLIFE

Hội An is chock-full of tourists, but at heart it remains a quiet riverside town. Nightlife centers around bars, billiards, and cafes. For those bent on liver destruction, rice whiskey and 8000Đ glasses of draught beer flow in the several bars on the corner of Lê Lợi and Trần Phú until 4am most nights; most other bars are hopping until 2am, with Happy hour lasting from 4 until 9pm.

Tam Tam Cafe, 110 Nguyễn Thái Học, one block toward the river from Trần Phú. Early evening is quiet, as diners enjoy pricey but superb Western cuisine (Australian steak 90,000Đ). Price range varies wildly from 15,000-150,000Đ. By 10pm every Westerner in town has elbowed his way in, dressed in brand-new threads; by 1am the French owners begin coaxing out the raucous crowd.

Hai's Scout Cafe, 98 Nguyễn Thái Học (☎863 210). The quieter neighbor of Tam Tam. Equally popular with tourists, this place nevertheless promotes a more relaxed, elegant atmosphere which attracts a slightly older crowd. The cafe features darts, (slow) Internet, a book exchange, and a small shop. Inquire about Vietnamese cooking classes (see **Beyond Tourism,** p. 96).

Treat's Cafe, 158 Trần Phú, and **Treat's Cafe 2,** 31 Phan Đình Phùng. Pool, darts, huge TV, and loud Western music bring in droves of tourists. Offers the same Western and Vietnamese menu as other cafes, but at a slightly better price (burgers 25,000Đ). Happy hour 4-9pm, beer 8000Đ. Most entrees 10,000-25,000Đ.

▶ DAYTRIPS FROM HỘI AN

■ **MỸ SƠN.** Declared a UNESCO World Heritage Site in 1999, the ruins of Mỹ Sơn were once the major religious center of the ancient Champa Kingdom. These temples reveal the ancient integration of different cultures. The walls, pillars, and pyramid-like temples rising out of the jungle are a blend of Hindu and indigenous culture. The earliest artifacts date from the 4th century, though more permanent temples were not built until the 7th century. From the 7th to the 13th centuries, over 70 towers were built. Today, the ruins are organized into groups A through H. Regrettably, there is little written description of the sights. The path from the entrance leads first to the E and F groups, then to the G group. These groups do not offer much to see and are really just a warm-up for the crown jewel B-C-D group. The C1 *kalan* (main tower) is the most prominent; the broad, rectangular D1 and D2 were once *mandrapart* (meditation chambers) for the B and C temples, respectively. Unfortunately, the best sculptures have been moved to Đà Nẵng's Chàm Museum. US bombs reduced the A1 tower—once a spectacular testament to 10th-century Chàm artistry—to a sad perimeter of stone. Today, A1's best offering is a small rise which offers a picturesque view of the B-C-D group. Check out the Chàm Museum in Đà Nẵng, too—this helps to imagine the site in its full majesty. Also, try to arrive early to beat the swarms of visitors. Being alone at Mỹ Sơn will allow you to appreciate the serene grace and beauty of the site. (*Mỹ Sơn is 50km west of Hội An. Minibus tours allow 2hr. at the ruins (leave 8am, return by 2pm). You can book the minibus trip at any tourist office or hotel lobby for around US$2-3, usually including a tour guide. Motorbikes US$5-6 round-trip. Open daily 6:30am-4:30pm. To reach the ruins, visitors must take a brief bus ride from the entrance and proceed 300m on foot. 60,000Đ entry fee. English-speaking guides cost an extra 30,000Đ (up to 4 people) or 50,000Đ (5 or more); they're rarely available on the spot, so try to book them from the tourist offices in Hội An.*)

CUA ĐẠI BEACH. A picturesque beach 5km down Trần Hưng Đạo from Hội An, Cua Đại warrants at least one lazy afternoon spent with its palm-lined shores and beachfront seafood stalls. A motorcycle taxi ride to the beach should cost no more than 10,000Đ, but it's an easy and relaxing bicycle ride. If you choose to visit around the month of June, expect tons of local children celebrating the end of the school year. Restaurants on the beach rent out beach chairs with umbrellas for 10,000Đ. Though the beach today is bustling with pineapple and bracelet hawkers, Cua Đại was once the departure point for many fleeing refugee "boat people" embarking on the 10-day passage to the Philippines.

Down on Bạch Đằng, **boat tours** depart from the dock near the market between 6am and 10pm. Independent operators, mostly local fishermen, charge 30,000Đ per hour for a trip on the river as the sun rises; Hội An Tourist's Tours are more expensive (around US$8 for a 2hr. cruise) but better planned. Stops are made along the way at three handicraft villages: **Ceramics Village** (Làng Gốm), **Carpenter's Village** (Làng Mộc), and **Carpet Village** (Làng Chieu). Staying on the beach is not cheap. **Victoria Hội An ❺**, 101 Trần Hưng Đạo (☎861 740), is the most lavish option, and also one of the priciest (US$100 and up), but it offers a variety of watersports, free shuttle service to and from downtown Hội An, and a stunning US$18 buffet dinner every night. The pool is beautiful and overlooks the waves. **Vĩnh Hưng Resort ❺** offers slightly more affordable rooms, but sits on the Hoai River instead of the beach, though the beach is nearby. (☎910 577; www.vinhhunghotels.com. Head toward the beach on Trần Hưng Đạo from Hội An center. After about 3km, it should be on your right. Rooms US$50-100.)

When it comes to having fun at the beach, look for **Rainbow Divers**, 98 Lê Lợi, offering speedboat dive trips, snorkeling, and scuba diving. (☎911 123; www.divevietnam.com. $50 per dive. No experience necessary.)

QUẢNG NGÃI ☎55

Straddling National Highway 1, this unremarkable provincial capital has little to boast except for its long tradition of nationalistic resistance. The area first saw an uprising against French and Japanese troops in 1945 and later became a Việt Minh stronghold in the 1950s. Heavy fighting took place in Quảng Ngãi Province during the American War, and it was home to the tragic Mỹ Lai Massacre of 1968. Such a legendary history once drew visitors to the riverside city, which was a launching point for tours of Mỹ Lai. Today, however, most Mỹ Lai tours originate in Hội An, and tourists have forsaken Quảng Ngãi. With almost no city sights and a 12km drive to the nearest beach, the city is little more than a convenient stop for Vietnamese heading south on the highway; since few foreign tourists drop by, English is not widely spoken and hotels are a bit more expensive.

█ TRANSPORTATION. The **bus station**, 26 Nguyễn Nghiêm (☎822 895) is located in front of the market. Buses head to: Buôn Ma Thuột (13hr.; 5:30am; 62,000Đ); Đà Lạt (16hr.; 3am; 74,000Đ); HCMC (24hr.; 8am; 100,000Đ); Hội An/Đà Nẵng (3-4hr.; about every hr. 5am-8pm; 36,000Đ); Kon Tum (11hr.; 5am; 43,000Đ); Nha Trang (9hr.; 5am; 49,000Đ); Pleiku (10hr.; 5am; 37,000Đ); Qui Nhơn (4hr.; about every hr. 5am-noon; 30,000Đ). Another option is to flag down buses in front of the **Petro-Sông Trà Hotel** on the north side of town as they travel the new Hwy. 1 bypass. Buses often circle near the bypass for as long as 30min. until the bus is full before heading to their respective destinations. The **train station** (☎820 272) is 2km west of Hwy. 1, at the end of Hùng Vương (which turns into Nguyễn Chanh). Trains go to all major stops in either direction on the Reunification Express, including Hà Nội (24-35hr.; hard seat 230,000Đ; soft sleeper 460,000Đ) and HCMC (20-30hr.; hard seat 145,000Đ; soft sleeper 295,000Đ).

█ ▞ ORIENTATION AND PRACTICAL INFORMATION. Quảng Ngãi is 150km north of Qui Nhơn, 100km south of Hội An, and 120km south of Đà Nẵng. Hwy. 1 runs north-south through town, where it's called **Quang Trứng**. The town, which stretches north-south, is bordered on the north end by the **Trà Khúc River**. The main east-west road running through the center of town has two names: west of Quang Trưng it's called **Hùng Vương**, and east of Quang Trưng it's called **Lê Trung Đình**. The center of town is about 1km south of the river.

Quảng Ngãi Tourist Company, 310 Quang Trưng, is the only tourist outfit in town and is accustomed to dealing only with Vietnamese tourists. They speak pretty good English, and they have a decent selection of helpful and free pamphlets and maps. (☎825 293; fax 922 836. Open M-Sa 7-11am and 1:30-5pm.) The **Incombank,** 87 Hùng Vương, cashes traveler's checks and changes money. There's an ATM outside. (☎822 626. Open daily 7-11:30am and 1-5pm.) A few blocks away, there's also a **Vietcom Bank** inside a hotel lobby at 45 Hùng Vương. The same services are available. (Open M-Sa 7-11:30am and 1:30-4:30pm.) There is a **hospital** 2km west of Quang Trưng on Hùng Vương (☎822 598; very little English spoken) and a **pharmacy** at 316 Quang Trưng, 100m north of Hùng Vương, near the tourist company (☎515 270; open daily 7am-6pm). More pharmacies line both Hùng Vương and Quang Trưng. The indoor and outdoor **market** is at the intersection of Nguyễn Nghiêm and Ngõ Quyền. Though smaller than those in big cities, this market nevertheless has a huge selection of fresh fruit and vegetables. **P and T Internet,** 415 Quảng Trung, has decent Internet access. (☎823 717. 4000Đ per hr. Open daily 7am-10pm.) There are also several Internet kiosks in a row between 324 and 334 Hùng Vương; all cost the same. The **General Post Office,** 62 Phan Đình Phùng, at the intersection with Hùng Vương, has international phone service and is located at the center of town. (☎815 598. Very little English spoken. Open daily 6:30am-9pm.)

⚑ ACCOMMODATIONS. There are two areas with hotels in Quảng Ngãi, but rooms abound due to the stream of Vietnamese traveling along Hwy. 1. On the north end of town, hotels line the river and tend to be pricier. In the center of town, hotels cluster around the intersection of Quang Trưng and Hùng Vương. **Du Lịch Cẩm Thành ❸,** 118 Lê Trung Đình, has clean, simple rooms and a central location. The desk staff is very friendly but speaks little English. It's also near the highway and quite noisy. (☎822 606; fax 825 610. Singles US$10; doubles US$15.) **Hùng Vương Hotel ❹,** 33 Hùng Vương, is a lavish hotel in the center of town. The large and comfortable rooms have nice artwork and a pleasant atmosphere. (☎818 828. Rooms US$25-30.) **Petro-Sông Trà ❹,** 2 Quang Trưng, is the cheaper of two three-star hotels on the river. As this sprawling complex is rarely full, you're bound to get a deal. Deluxe rooms come with leather chairs, a bar, and a view; all guests get access to the pool and fitness room. Desk staff speaks better English than those at most other hotels in town, and they can organize local bus trips upon request. (☎822 665; fax 822 204; pvstc@dng.vnn.vn. Rooms US$25-45.) **Đồng Hựng ❷,** 497 Quang Trưng, has some of the cheapest rooms in town and is conveniently located near the market. However, you get what you pay for in terms of cleanliness. (☎825 322; fax 825 321. Singles US$8; doubles US$10.)

◻ FOOD. The streets of Quảng Ngãi, particularly Quang Trưng and Nguyễn Nghiêm, are choked with food stalls that offer the most convenient—and often the tastiest—meals in town. Along Nguyễn Nghiêm, **Cộ Loan ❶** (at 318) and **Ràm 72 ❶** (at 320) are exceedingly popular with the locals. Cộ Loan offers a wide array of traditional Vietnamese dishes, all cooked with chicken, for 6000-10,000Đ. At Ràm 72, you can wrap chicken or beef in rice paper with lettuce for 8000Đ. Another row of outdoor food stalls, known to locals as **Bờ Kè,** is located along the Trà Khúc River. In a little enclave by the Hai Bà Trứng road, grab a smoothie or eat a rice dish with the locals while looking out onto the dried-up river. As most locals are content with such eateries, Western-style restaurants are few and far between. **Cơm Việtnam ❷,** 21 Hùng Vương, is located in the city center and has an English menu with a large selection of typical Vietnamese dishes and Western breakfasts. Though more expensive than the food stalls, it is a popular place for the city's few tourists and locals wanting to practice their English. Good selection of vegetarian options. (Dishes 15,000-40,000Đ. Open daily 7am-11pm.) **Cafe Bich Quân ❷,** 42 Hùng Vương, is a cafe-restaurant full of local hipsters. This cafe, situated in the center of town where Hùng Vương forks, has a dark interior and sidewalk seating, encouraging a lingering visit—come for noodles, stay for coffee. (☎823 971. Dishes 10,000-30,000Đ. Open daily 8am-11pm.) **Trà Khúc ❸**, 2 Quang Trưng, is behind the Petro-Sông Trà Hotel, which owns this riverside restaurant. Serving the best (and priciest) food in town, and offering a diverse menu, it caters to Vietnamese tourists and local officials. (☎822 665. Breakfast 10,000Đ; entrees 10,000-80,000Đ. Open daily 7am-10pm.)

■ **SIGHTS.** Quảng Ngãi proper offers next to nothing to see or do. In the city center there is a French-built church. Still in use today, the church shows its age with a fading pink exterior and crumbling walls. Before you head out of town, take a look at the untouched fortification built by the US military when it occupied the town. The concrete bunker is at the southern end of the highway bridge.

▶ **DAYTRIPS FROM QUẢNG NGÃI.** At the site of the 1968 Mỹ Lai Massacre—during which an entire civilian village was wiped out in the most infamous of the US's Search and Destroy missions—the ▨**Sơn Mỹ Memorial** is one of Vietnam's most moving experiences, especially for Americans. Set amid peaceful rice fields in a landscape that has hardly changed since the war, the memorial does not fail to impress. At first, the unkept garden, simple sculptures, and typical Stalinist monument seem an awkward attempt at remembrance; continue to the small artillery shelters in the back of the grounds, though, and the atmosphere changes. Crawl inside the damp, cramped space, and you'll feel the ghosts of a terrified family praying for their lives. This space, along with bullet-ridden trees and an irrigation ditch where more than 100 villagers were executed, accurately and acutely conveys the horror of the massacre. In the way back, there is a beautiful and gripping mural depicting the event. Head to the second story of the museum to view personal items and chilling photographs. While the captions are obvious government propaganda, the photographs do not hide the gruesomeness of death; avoid them if you have a weak stomach. The museum also provides a one-sided view of the US attempt to cover up the massacre and the investigation that followed it. (Go 1km north of Hùng Vương along Quang Trưng, cross the highway bridge and take the 1st right (My Tra Hotel sits at the intersection) onto Hwy. 24B. Sơn Mỹ is 9km down the road. From the center of town, a motorbike trip should cost 40,000-50,000Đ round-trip. No buses service this route. Open daily 7am-5pm. Admission 10,000Đ.)

Once a base for American, Australian, and South Korean troops, today **Thiên An Hill** is the site of Thiên An Pagoda, a monument to Huỳnh Thúc Kháng (an important figure in the anti-colonial movement) as well as a little Buddhist monastery. The pagoda is the oldest in the province, a product of the 17th-century Nguyễn Dynasty. The monastery, nestled atop the mountain under trees and looking out on Quảng Ngãi, is incredibly peaceful and houses several valuable relics, including an aged bronze bell and a supposedly 2km deep well. The monks are extremely friendly, and if you're lucky, they may offer you a delicious meal or chat with you in broken English. (On the way to Sơn Mỹ, 7km down 24B from the city; take a left into the road with banners above it. Free.)

Located 35km southwest of Quảng Ngãi in the Minh Long province, **Thác Thrắng Waterfall** is an adventurer's dream. The waterfall, situated in the middle of the jungle, is 2km high and lined with palm trees and green bushes. Bring a picnic or buy a snack at the small shack 75m from the falls. It's difficult to get there, but the waterfall is a real gem. Watch for leeches, though. (The trip by motorcycle taxi costs about 100,000Đ round-trip from Quảng Ngãi and lasts about 2½hr. Take Hwy. 4 south of Quảng Ngãi until Hwy. 627, which will eventually become a dirt road for the last 750m. From there, hop from rock to rock for 100m until you arrive at the base of the waterfall.)

BA TO'   ☎ 55

Ba To' is the name of a small town in southern Quảng Ngãi Province, as well as of the mountainous district that surrounds it. While this area is quite beautiful, the town itself is unremarkable. The main reason to visit is the town's unique history: it's the site of the first Communist guerrilla action in Vietnam. In response to the occupying Japanese forces during World War II, the local Communist Party cell organized a small guerilla army. After months of secret meetings and battle training in Ba To' and the surrounding mountains, the motley rebels seized the town on March 11, 1945. After that, Ba To' and Quảng Ngãi became Communist strongholds. Today, the uprising is commemorated by a small **museum.** On the whole, the museum needs a lot of help, but it does house original Party literature from the 1930s and 1940s, as well as the machetes, spears, and handmade rifles used during the insurrection. Outside, visitors can purchase crafts made for tourists by the local H're people. (Open daily 7am-5pm. Free.)

Ba To' is 70km south of Quảng Ngãi. From Quảng Ngãi, go south down Hwy. 1A until you reach Hwy. 24, where you take a right. Buses are nearly impossible to find; motorbikes are your best bet, with round trips starting at 100,000Đ. The ride should last around 2½hr. round-trip.

SA HUỲNH   ☎ 55

Sa Huỳnh is a small seaside town sandwiched between the beach and Hwy. 1. The beach, dotted with groves of palm trees, is clean and easily accessible to passersby. Most people stop and eat at the seafood stalls or beachside restaurants (each with its own access to the sandy stretch), but they rarely stay much longer, as the town lacks decent accommodations or sights. Though it might not be worth the long drive, it's a quiet and relaxing place to spend a day on the beach.

Small hotel outfits line Hwy. 1 at the southern end of town. **Thế Vinh ❸** is the most prominent and has the best view of the beach, as well as a restaurant downstairs. (☎860 385. Singles US$10; doubles US$15.) Next door, **Vinh ❸** serves excellent seafood and a variety of Vietnamese dishes. It caters to tourists, so prices are a bit steep (20,000-70,000Đ). As always, **food stalls** line Hwy. 1A throughout town.

Sa Huỳnh is located on Hwy. 1A, 60km south of Quảng Ngãi and 114km north of Qui Nho'n. Local buses usually stop there. Flag one down and head to Quảng Ngãi; it should cost around 20,000Đ; to Qui Nho'n will be 30,000-40,000Đ. Round-trip motorbike rides from Quảng Ngãi run about 80,000Đ and last about three hours.

QUI NHO'N   ☎ 56

This low-key seaport town is the capital of Bình Định Province and the less-touristed alternative to the beach parties of Nha Trang. In the 18th century, the Tây So'n brothers led a great rebellion from here, ending two centuries of division between the North and South. This region, the Tây So'n district, was also home to two of Vietnam's greatest poets, Hàn Mạc Tu (1912-1940) and Xuân Diệu (1916-1985). Contemporary Qui Nho'n is a hectic seaport masquerading as a resort destination: the beautiful beach is also the site of a small fishing village and a shipping port. Still, Qui Nho'n has its highlights, such as the fleets of fishing boats that become ethereal points of light in the horizon after the sun sets and the untouched public beaches free of Western tourists.

▄ TRANSPORTATION

Any tourist bus originating in Hội An or Nha Trang will drop passengers off on Hwy. 1, 10km west of Qui Nho'n. To get to the city center, pick from the smorgasbord of motorized vehicles that hover around the junction (motorbikes and taxis 3000-15,000Đ). The **airport** is 34km out of town. **Vietnam Airlines** is the large blue building near the corner of Nguyễn Tất Thành and Nguyễn Thái Học. (☎825 313. Open daily 7-11:30am and 1:30-5pm.) Planes fly to HCMC (8:25am; also 3:30pm on M, W, Sa; 515,000Đ) and Hà Nội (M, W, Sa 12:30pm; 1,165,000Đ) via Đà Nẵng (365,000Đ). For **trains,** ignore the cargo transport station and head to **Gà Diêu Trì** (☎822 036), 10km outside the city (15,000Đ by motorbike). Tickets and schedules are available at **Gà Qui Nhơn,** on Lộ Thường Kiệt across from Quang Trưng Park. (☎833 255 for reservations; 834 706 for timetables. Open daily 7am-4:30pm.) Northbound trains depart daily at 6:50am and go to Đà Nẵng (6hr.; 87,000-129,000Đ), Hà Nội (22hr.; 246,000-484,000Đ), and Huế (8½hr.; 117,000-172,000Đ). Southbound trains depart daily at 4:45pm and go to HCMC (12½hr.; 138,000-282,000Đ) and Nha Trang (4½hr.; 69,000-101,000Đ). The **bus station,** 2km west of Quang Trưng Park on Lam Son, runs buses to Buôn Ma Thuột (9hr.; 7am; 43,000Đ); HCMC (15hr.; 6am; 78,000Đ); Huế (11hr.; 6am; 48,000Đ) via Đà Nẵng; Nha Trang (6hr.; every 2hr.; 28,000Đ); Pleiku (4hr.; 8am; 20,000Đ). Minibuses arriving in Qui Nhơn may drop passengers off along Trần Hưng Đạo on the north side of the city, rather than at the bus station. In-town taxi service is provided by **Davi Taxi** (☎812 812), **Taxi Dan** (☎818 881), and **Hương Tra Taxi** (☎847 777).

ORIENTATION

Qui Nhơn is on a triangular peninsula 220km north of Nha Trang, 180km south of Quảng Ngãi, 150km east of Pleiku, and 10km east of Hwy. 1. **Highway 19** runs east into town along its northern edge as **Trần Hưng Đạo.** It eventually skirts **Quang Trưng Park,** which marks the center of town. From here, **Phan Bội Châu** runs east past the market, **Lê Hồng Phong** runs southeast toward the beach, and **Lộ Thường Kiệt** curves southwest, connecting to the airstrip-turned-boulevard, **Nguyễn Tất Thành.** The other end of this street terminates at the beachside boulevard, called **Nguyễn Huệ** to the north and **An Dương Vương** to the south.

PRACTICAL INFORMATION

The staff at **Barbara's Backpackers** (see **Accommodations,** p. 320) provides great tourist services; owner Barbara, a Kiwi, knows the local scene in and out. **Chương Tringh Tour Agency,** adjacent to Seagull Hotel, provides free maps of the region, and arranges 3-day tours (800,000-900,000Đ) around the province. (☎747 747. Open daily 8am-8pm.) **Vietcombank,** 152 Lê Lợi, at the intersection with Trần Hưng Đạo, does currency exchange and has an **ATM.** (☎822 408. Open M-F 7-11am and 1-4pm, Sa 8am-noon.) **Agribank,** 44 Le Thành Tôn, at Phan Bội Châu, cashes traveler's checks and has a Western Union inside. (☎892 498; www.vbabinhdinh.com.vn. Open daily 7-11:30am and 1:30-4:30pm.) The **police** can be found at 247 Lê Hồng Phong. There are **pharmacies** across the street from the hospital and at 345 Lê Hồng Phong and 264 Phan Bội Châu. The central **hospital** (☎822 900) is located at 104 Nguyễn Huệ; there is a branch at 255 Trần Hưng Đạo in the city center. **Internet** access is abundant. Try **Binh Dinh,** 245 Lê Hồng Phong, in the center of town (3000Đ per hr.; open daily 7am-10pm), or 405A Nguyễn Huệ, at the south end. The **General Post Office,** 197 Phan Bội Châu, has international phone service and a Vietcombank **ATM.** (☎821 441. Open daily 6:30am-10pm.)

ACCOMMODATIONS

Qui Nhơn accommodations can be divided into two groups: large, old, and noisy hotels frequented by Vietnamese tourists in the city center, and newer, quieter, beachside accommodations that house foreign tourists. Of the latter, it is best to stay at the southern end of the beach, where the sands are cleaner.

▨ **Barbara's Backpackers,** 18 Nguyễn Huệ (☎892 921; nzbarb@yahoo.com). This old favorite continues to draw in budget travelers. The rooms are aging, but the location, across the street from the beach, is tough to beat. Pleasant eating area with Western menu on the 1st floor, as well as tourist services and a helpful staff. Same-day laundry 10,000Đ per kg. Dorms 30,000Đ; private rooms with fan US$8, with A/C US$2 extra. ❶

▨ **Hotel Anh Vy,** 8 An Dương Vương (☎847 763). With an exceedingly friendly staff, this family-run guesthouse is clean, well-kept, and attractive. All rooms have cable TV and fan. The higher-priced rooms have a private balcony with seaside view. Don't even bother with English—a smile will go further. Check-out noon. Rooms 120,000-200,000Đ. ❷

Hotel Âu Cơ, 8-24 An Dương Vương (☎747 699; hotel_auco@yahoo.com). A mirror image of the neighboring Anh Vy, Âu Cơ has slightly more to offer for a slightly higher price. All rooms have A/C, cable TV, and minibar. Friendly English-speaking manager happily offers advice on local diversions. Some rooms have funky treehouse decor. Singles 160,000Đ; doubles 200,000Đ; triples 300,000Đ. ❸

Hai Au (Seagull Hotel), 489 An Dương Vương (☎846 473; www.viehotel.com/seagull-hotel). One of Qui Nhơn's resort hotels, this renovated oldie is fully equipped with sauna, massage parlor, pool, tennis courts, and gym. The rooms are a little small, but the hotel is located on the city's attractive southwest beach. 24hr. room service. All rooms have A/C and satellite TV. Breakfast included. Rooms US$20-50. ❹

Sai Gon-Quy Nhơn Hotel, 24 Nguyễn Huệ (☎829 922; www.saigonquynhonhotel.com.vn). Qui Nhơn's newest resort hotel, this 4-star establishment lives up to its rank. Ironically, this quintessence of luxury sits across from Qui Nhơn beach's bleak Stalinist liberation statue. Money exchange at reception. Breakfast included. Check-in 2pm; check-out noon. Singles US$35-50; doubles US$45-60. AmEx/D/MC/V. ❺

◖ FOOD

Qui Nhơn brings little to the table besides fresh seafood along the beach and typical rice and soup dishes in the city center. The cheapest eats, as always, are at the **food stalls** in the beachside fishing village and across from Quang Trưng Park and at the brand-spanking-new **Qui Nhơn Trade Center.** This Western-style supermarket is one of the first in the country and deserves a visit even without a grocery list. Drive along Nguyễn Tất Thánh and you can't miss it. The city **market,** with indoor and outdoor stalls, is at 1 Tháng 4 between Phan Bội Châu and Tăng Bạt Hổ. At night, the cafes along Nguyễn Huệ bring out full drink menus and pumping music into the street, creating some semblance of a social scene.

Hồng Phat Thai Food, 261 Lê Hồng Phong, right in the main square. Better-than-average Thai food and filling portions for a decent price. Both the restaurant and the bar upstairs—Qui Nhơn's only discernible nightlife—are popular with the locals. Pad Thai 30,000Đ. Open daily 10am-late. ❷

Ngọc Nga, 324 Phan Bội Châu, on Quang Trưng Park. Popular with young hipsters for its excellent ice cream and comical flavor names, including Cream of Funny Man and Cream of Birthday. You can even steal a glance into the company's expansive factory. Ice cream 4000-8000Đ. Coffee and milkshakes 2500Đ. Open daily 8am-11pm. ❶

Kiwi Cafe, 18 Nguyễn Huệ (☎892 921), on the ground floor of Barbara's Backpackers. An English-language menu, large portions, and familiar Western food. Check the chalkboard for daily specials. Excellent smoothies (Kiwi Sunset 20,000-25,000Đ). Fresh-baked muffins 5000-8000Đ. Entrees 15,000-30,000Đ. Open daily 7am-10pm. ❷

Thanh Minh, 151 Phan Bội Châu, near the city's main pagoda. Inexpensive vegetarian food and soy products. Most entrees under 15,000Đ. Open daily 7am-8pm.

Sanh Phương, 251 Lê Hồng Phong. If you're craving typical Vietnamese dishes but avoiding food stalls, then this is your place. Pull up a stool by the satellite TV and order a *cơm gà* (15,000Đ). Open daily 7am-11pm. ❶

Phương Thảo, 423 Nguyễn Huệ. The most stylish of the seafood restaurants in the fishing village, and one you won't have to trudge through the noxious streets for. Quality seafood and other Vietnamese dishes 20,000-30,000Đ. ❷

Việt Úc Bakery, 104 Phan Bội Châu. It looks just like any other streetside joint, but the green tea muffins (5000Đ) are exceptional. Open daily 7am-10pm. ❶

👁 SIGHTS

Qui Nhơn is home to few sights besides its deserted beaches, but the museums and religious sights in town make for a relaxing break from all the sun and sand.

BEACHES. Qui Nhơn's biggest draw is its long, curved beach. With heavy fishing going on just offshore, the water isn't the cleanest along the coast, but the sands remain clean and well-loved by locals and visitors alike. The municipal beach is at the northeast end and is bordered by a wide, palm-shaded promenade, ideal for strolling. Check out the half-submerged US tank just a meter from the beach. The central portion of the shore hosts a fishing village. At the southwest end is Genh Rang Beach, the least-visited portion of sand. Though this beach is deserted during the day, it has a carnival-like atmosphere at night.

> **STAYING HYDRATED FOR POCKET CHANGE.** For those hot and humid seaside afternoons, try a **coconut** for an all-purpose fluid- and electrolyte-packed snack. You'll see them in the markets with their shells peeled off and husks cut into various white shapes. When you purchase one from a fruit seller, she'll hack off the top and hand it to you with a straw. Half a liter of sweet juice later, she'll take it back and crack it in half, yielding a core of filling white flesh. This combined meal-and-drink usually runs 3000-5000Đ.

LONG KHÁNH PAGODA. A giant white Buddha rises from the province's primary place of worship. Dating from 1715, this pagoda mirrors Qui Nhơn: generally unremarkable, but holding a few precious gems. Within its walls lies a bell dating from 1805, prayers printed on paper almost 200 years old, and a small memorial to the monk Thích Quảng Đức, who set himself on fire in 1963 in protest of the Diệm regime. *(Turn down the dirt road next to 143 Trần Cao Vân. Doors open at 5pm. Free.)*

THÁP ĐÔI CHÀM TOWERS. Although the shape of these towers is slightly unusual—they have pyramid tops instead of the more common, square-terraced ones—their real wonder comes from their location. Situated in the middle of a poor section of Qui Nhơn, the towers have become fully integrated with the surrounding shanty-town, a stark visual metaphor for the fluid, dynamic relationship between past and present that is common throughout Southeast Asia. *(Walk along Trần Hưng Đạo away from the city center. You'll see the towers rising above the rooftops one the right once you hit the 800s. Turn right onto Tháp Đôi, then right again after 50m to access the tower grounds. Open 7am-5pm, but often closed for lunch between noon and 2pm. Free.)*

QUI HOA LEPER COLONY AND QUEEN'S BEACH. Strangely, tourists can't get enough of this leper colony, taking note of its pristine medical facilities and various homages to caretakers and doctors. The seaside colony is a well-maintained village where you'll see residents farming, making crafts, receiving visitors, or just enjoying the sea air. At the center sprawls a sizable and immaculate hospital. The beach, named for the wife of Vietnam's last emperor, is shaded by palm trees and situated in a gentle cove. Along the beachfront are a series of busts of medical luminaries from Hippocrates to Pasteur. At the northernmost point of the beach is an interesting monolith, decorated with Christian figures. At the south end of the colony is a large cemetery, with Christian and Buddhist tombs. Stick to the main paved paths: trudging into the smaller alleyways will leave you feeling intrusive. *(2km from Qui Nho'n's southern edge, east of the new seaside road to Song Cau, and 300m from the tomb of Hàn Mạc Tu. Open daily 8-11:30am and 1:30-4pm. 3000Đ.)*

SHIPYARDS. Just offshore, stretching from Qui Nho'n to Nha Trang, are fleets of brightly colored fishing boats. These electric-blue vessels with red, yellow, and white trim form the core of Vietnam's fishing industry, and Qui Nho'n is the center for their production. The shipyards are on the northwest end of Đong Đa, where you can see boats at various stages of construction: some being painted, some being sealed, and some with ribs still exposed. Visitors can venture into the actual construction zone, where massive logs are turned into boats by hand under the glaring sun. Each boat takes approximately two months to build. Just past the shipyards is the official Port Authority of Qui Nho'n, full of cargo holds and huge lorries, which is closed to visitors. *(Along Đong Đa, past Phan Dinh Phu'o'ng. Free.)*

BÌNH ĐỊNH MUSEUM. A collection of Chàm sculptures, dioramas of ethnic tribal housing, maps of local ecology, and Communist Party history are just the beginning of this museum. Recently renovated, it has signs in both English and Vietnamese. Check out the well-preserved US war machines in the entrance courtyard. *(26 Nguyễn Huệ. Open M-Sa 8am-5pm. Free.)*

TOMB OF HÀN MẠC TU. Qhi Nho'n is home to the tomb and shrine of one of Vietnam's most revered poets. The commemorative house behind the tomb has a bust of the late poet, as well as relics from his past—family pictures, calligraphic scrolls, and anthologies translated into French. Exhibits are in Vietnamese. *(5km south of Qui Nho'n, at the base of Hàn Mạc Tu Mountain, where Genh Rang beach ends. 5000Đ.)*

⚡ DAYTRIPS FROM QUI NHO'N

The countryside around Qui Nho'n is dotted with huge **Chàm towers** that dwarf even the most visited Chàm site, Mỹ So'n (p. 314). Though these towers are impressive, they differ little from one another. Located down a maze of dirt roads, the towers can be visited via tours organized at the Bình Định Tourist Office, or via motorbike. Inquire at Barbara's Backpackers (see **Accommodations,** p. 319) or call the excellent, English-speaking Mr. Chu Nguyễn Văn (☎ 091 413 0992), who gives tours for around US$10 per day.

BÁNH ÍT CHÀM TOWERS. This is the best Chàm site around Qui Nho'n. Bánh Ít, built at the end of the 11th century, is a collection of four towers at the summit of a solitary hill. Interestingly, each tower has been built in a completely different style, although all four are capped with a statue of Shiva. The value for visitors is the pleasant walk up the hill and the commanding view of the coast and the surrounding countryside from the top. *(20km north of Qui Nho'n, just east of Hwy. 1. Towers are visible from the road. Open daily 7:30-11am and 1-5pm.)*

DU'O'NG LONG CHÀM TOWERS. This trip may be worthwhile only to Chàm tower enthusiasts. These towers, built in the 12th century at the height of the Chàm artistic development, are notable for their beautiful decorative carvings and large size (the largest is 24m tall). On your way to the towers, check out the cashew orchards. *(50km northeast of Qui Nho'n, down a long, unmarked dirt road. Follow the tall central tower. Open daily 7:30-11am and 1-5pm.)*

CÁNH TIÊN CHÀM TOWER (CHA BAN). The unremarkable Cánh Tiên tower stands in the center of what used to be Cha Ban, a former Chàm capital. The capital has all but disappeared beneath farmland; only a sprawling cemetery and the tower remain. *(26km north of Qui Nho'n, 5km west of Hwy. 1 down an unmarked dirt road. Open daily 7:30-11am and 1-5pm.)*

QUANG TRU'NG MUSEUM. Forty kilometers northwest of Qui Nho'n, in the middle of the arid countryside, is a museum on the grounds of the Tây Sơn Palace. The palace was home to the three brothers who led the Tây Sơn Rebellion. The museum itself honors the middle son, who crowned himself Emperor Quang Trưng in 1771. In 1789, he led his forces to defeat an invading Chinese army near Hà Nội—a remarkable battle that's still celebrated today. Unfortunately, the museum's exhibits of old clothing and weapons, as well as other artifacts from the Quang Trưng court, are uninspiring. All signs are in Vietnamese. The grounds of the museum and palace are serene, though, and you can still see the tamarind tree and the water well that are original to the palace compound. *(40km west of Qui Nho'n, about 8km north of Hwy. 19. Open daily 7am-5pm. Free.)*

BIRTHPLACE OF XUÂN DIỆU. Bình Định is the birthplace of revered poet Xuân Diệu. A museum has been set up in the village of Túng Giản at the late great's former home. *(Approximately 23km north of Qui Nho'n. Open daily 7:30-11am.)*

HÂN HO CASCADES. Extremely popular with local Vietnamese, but completely off the foreign tourists' radar, this is a relaxing place to spend an afternoon. You can amble down the river in a boat (30,000Đ), take on the rapids in a kayak (40,000Đ), or climb along the cascades and surrounding park trails. The scenery is nice and the trails are well maintained, but on the whole this place isn't too exciting. *(60km from Qui Nho'n, down several unmarked dirt roads. Open daily 7am-5pm. 5500Đ.)*

HỒ NÚI MỘT. Surrounded by hills, tranquil Hồ Núi Một (First Mountain Lake) is a peaceful and romantic spot. Boatmen will ferry a four-seat boat to a waterfall upriver. *(30km west of Qui Nho'n, off Hwy. 19; look for a small sign and head south. USụ10.)*

BẢI BAO AND BẢI XÊP PRIVATE BEACHES. Bải Bao is a brand-new beach complex. The beach itself is private, and the cleanest around Qui Nho'n; visitors can swim, sunbathe, and generally enjoy the atmosphere. The complex is complete with fountains, footbridges, and even a caged baboon. Bải Xêp has less sand and more huge stone monoliths. The boulders are fun to scale and provide great vistas of the sea. *(10-12km south of Qui Nho'n, on Hwy. 1. 5000Đ.)*

NHA TRANG ☎ 58

Nha Trang is beach party central—its sparkling turquoise water is the stuff of dreams. Once Vietnam's peaceful emerald oasis, the city has recently exploded into a full-fledged resort spot, feeding rapaciously on tourist dollars. Unchecked growth threatens to choke the city with over-development—on bad days, smog completely blocks the nearby islands from view—but good times still abound. Budget hotels and luxury resorts are packed with visitors enjoying cheap, high-quality snorkeling and scuba diving, daily jaunts to offshore islands, and nightly parties care of the city's lively club scene. Fresh seafood dominates the menus, making Nha Trang an epicurean adventure. Vietnam's great municipal beach and a laid-back, tourist-friendly population round out the closest thing the country has to a Pacific island resort atmosphere. But travelers should be careful to strike a balance in Nha Trang—don't go, and you'll regret it; stay too long, and you'll get irritated. The town's surreal beauty has created a tourist oasis, quite removed from the "real" Vietnam, to the extent that establishments (and prices) are designated either for foreigners or for locals.

▐ TRANSPORTATION

Due to its booming tourist industry, getting into Nha Trang is easy. Most of the city's sights and attractions can be visited on foot.

Flights: Nha Trang Airport (☎827 286), just south of the city center, off of Trần Phú. **Vietnam Airlines,** 91 Nguyễn Thiện Thuật (☎826 768) or 1 Trần Hưng Đạo (☎822 753). Both offices open daily 7-11:30am and 1:30-5pm. Flights to: **Đà Nẵng** (Sa-Th and Th 2pm; 555,000Đ), **Hà Nội** (10am; 1,450,000Đ), and **HCMC** (3 per day; 650,000Đ). Many upper-end hotels will pick you up at the airport.

Trains: Nha Trang Station, 17 Thái Nguyễn. Open around the clock except 12:30-1:30pm. There are 5 trains per day to: **Đà Nẵng** (9-12hr.; 113,000-222,000Đ); **Hà Nội** (25-34hr.; 326,000-632,000Đ); **HCMC** (7-10hr.; 86,000-166,000Đ); **Huế** (12-16hr.; 136,000-263,000Đ).

Buses: Northbound buses depart from the end of 2 Tháng 4, 10km north of the city center. Southbound buses leave from **Liên Tỉnh Station,** 58 23 Tháng 10 (☎822 347). Buses go to: **Buôn Ma Thuột** (4-6hr.; 4 per day; 36,000Đ); **Đà Lạt** (5hr.; frequent; 40,000Đ); **Đà Nẵng** (14hr.; daily; 40,000Đ); **HCMC** (10hr.; 7 per day 5:30am-8pm; 65,000Đ) via **Phaïn Thiết** (5hr.; 45,000Đ); **Huế** (15hr.; 5am; 68,000Đ); **Pleiku** (7hr.; daily; 54,000Đ); **Quảng Ngãi** (8hr.; daily; 43,000Đ); **Qui Nho'n** (6hr.; daily; 33,000Đ). Negotiate with the driver. Faster, private **minibuses** leave from many hotels for **Đà Lạt** (US$5), **Hội An** (US$8), and **HCMC** (US$8).

Rentals: Most hotels rent **motorbikes** (US$5-10) and **bicycles** (10,000Đ) by the day.

▐ ORIENTATION

Nha Trang lies 450km northeast of Hồ Chí Minh City and 175km northeast of Đà Lạt. Two-lane **Trần Phú** runs north-south along the length of the 6km beach; its north end offers spectacular views from the **Trần Phú Bridge. Hùng Vương,** a block inland, becomes **Trần Hưng Đạo** and then **Pasteur** on its way northward. **Lê Thánh Tôn** shoots northwest from Trần Phú's **memorial tower** on the central beach, and hits a six-way intersection by **Nha Trang Cathedral,** after which it becomes **Thái Nguyễn** and then **23 Tháng 10** past the train station and bus station. Near the northern end of Trần Phú, **Yersin** heads east toward another six-way hub; from here, **Quang Trưng** runs north and continues out of town as **2 Tháng 4. Lê Lợi** runs west from Trần Phú's northern end to the town market. **Biệt Thự** and **Trần Quang Khải** run west from Trần Phú's southern stretch until they hit **Nguyễn Thiện Thuật,** forming the main square where hostels, nightlife, and tourist activity abound.

▐ PRACTICAL INFORMATION

Tourist offices, banks and Internet cafes abound; Internet prices are highest in tourist areas. There are also **film-developing services,** with branches at both 4 Yersin (☎823 028) and 2 Biệt Thự (☎828 030) that offer 2hr. film developing (40,000Đ), digital conversion to CD (50,000Đ), and passport photos (20,000Đ).

Tourist Offices: Nha Trang is bursting with agents. Most line Biệt Thự and Trần Hưng Đạo; typically, they open between 6 and 7am and close at 10pm. Most accept MC/V.

Sinh Cafe, 10 Biệt Thự (☎521 981; www.sinhcafevn.com), handles everything under the sun.

An Phu Tour, 4 Trần Quang Khải (☎524 471; anphutour@yahoo.com), is another popular option.

SOUTHERN CENTRAL COAST

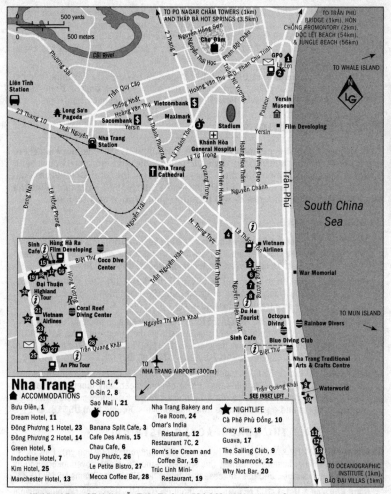

Nha Trang

ACCOMMODATIONS

Bưu Điện, 1
Dream Hotel, 11
Đông Phương 1 Hotel, 23
Đông Phương 2 Hotel, 14
Green Hotel, 5
Indochine Hotel, 7
Kim Hotel, 25
Manchester Hotel, 13

O-Sin 1, 4
O-Sin 2, 8
Sao Mai I, 21

FOOD

Banana Split Cafe, 3
Cafe Des Amis, 15
Chau Cafe, 6
Duy Phước, 26
Le Petite Bistro, 27
Mecca Coffee Bar, 28

Nha Trang Bakery and
    Tea Room, 24
Omar's India
    Resturant, 12
Restaurant 7C, 2
Rom's Ice Cream and
    Coffee Bar, 16
Trúc Linh Mini-
    Restaurant, 19

NIGHTLIFE

Cà Phê Phù Đồng, 10
Crazy Kim, 18
Guava, 17
The Sailing Club, 9
The Shamrock, 22
Why Not Bar, 20

Highland Tour, 97/1 Nguyễn Thiện Thuật (☎524 043; highlandtourvn@yahoo.com), specializes in excursions to the Central Highlands.

Du Ha Tourist, 8 Nguyễn Thị Minh Khải (☎811 160), organizes canoe tours of the river.

Banks: Vietcombank, 17 Quang Trưng (☎824 093). Currency exchange and MC/V cash advances. Open daily 7:30-11am and 1:30-4pm. Branch at 5 Hùng Vương has an **ATM.** Open daily 7am-9pm. **Sacombank,** 54 Yersin, and **Incombank,** 86 Trần Phú, both have a **24hr. ATM.** There are more along Trần Phú, about every 500m. Most hotels and tourist offices exchange cash and traveler's checks, but at punishing rates.

Emergency: ☎115.

Pharmacy: 7 Hùng Vương (☎812 857). Open daily 8am-6pm.

Medical Services: Khánh Hòa General Hospital, 94 Yersin (☎822 168), at the intersection with Quang Trưng. 24hr. emergency service. Some English and French Spoken.

Internet Access: Rates can be exploitative depending upon location. Most tourist offices charge 100Đ per min. 8C Biệt Thự, 10 Pasteur, and 2 Hùng Vương provide the best connection at this rate. For the best compromise between price (3000Đ per hr.) and speed, follow the locals to 3/10 Trần Quang Khải, down a side street. This place has cheap Internet phones and decent music. Open until 11pm.

Post Offices: General Post Office, 4 Lê Lợi (☎829 657). *Poste Restante,* Internet access, international calling, and a DHL Express office. Open daily 6:30am-10pm. Smaller branch at 110 Nguyễn Thiện Thuật. (☎811 718. Open daily 7am-10pm.)

■ ACCOMMODATIONS

Nha Trang's survival depends upon tourist visits, and its citizens know it. There are hotels and guesthouses in every style imaginable, and more are being built. There are plenty of options on almost every street, but the tourist hotels are concentrated in the square between Biệt Thự and Trần Quang Khải. Most offer the same services; the emptier ones will be more open to price negotiation.

ALONG TRẦN PHÚ

☒Đông Phương 2 Hotel, 96A₄ Trần Phú (☎522 580; fax 521 138). This hotel's popularity with the backpacker set has led it to open up a beachside wing. Good location and standard amenities; excellent value for the price. Rooms US$6-15. ❷

Manchester Hotel, 96B₁ Trần Phú (☎524 620; fax 524 630). One of the countless mini-hotels in Nha Trang, notable for its elevator. Spacious rooms have beach views, although they are inconveniently located along a busy street. Rooms US$10-15. ❸

Dream Hotel, 96A₇ Trần Phú (☎524 247; fax 524 245). An airy, neon hotel on the sea, Dream provides a comfortable night's sleep with all the amenities (A/C, satellite TV, and minibar). Go somewhere else for your Internet (12,000Đ per hr. in the lobby). Laundry 15,000Đ per kg. Rooms US$10-20. AmEx/D/MC/V. ❸

Bưu Điện, 2 Lê Lợi (☎821 252; posthotel@dng.vnn.vn), located (appropriately) next to the post office. A quality mid-range place offering clean, airy rooms with satellite TV. Provides a pleasant escape from the noisy streets. Extremely popular with Vietnamese tourists and a good escape from backpackers. Rooms from US$18. ❹

SOUTH OF BIỆT THỰ (BACKPACKER DISTRICT)

☒Kim Hotel, 124 Nguyễn Thiện Thuật (☎810 402; anhtuanns@dng.vnn.vn). Run by an English-speaking, hospitable owner, this small guesthouse is often overlooked. Rooms are clean and simple, and the staircase is empty of loud tourists. Rooms US$5-10. ❶

Đông Phương 1 Hotel, 103 Nguyễn Thiện Thuật (☎/fax 526 986). The sky-blue original Đông Phương. Rooms are clean and quiet; all are equipped with satellite TV. Laundry service 10,000Đ per kg. Rooms with fan US$6-10, with A/C US$10-20. ❷

Sao Mai ("Morning Star") I, 99 Nguyễn Thiện Thuật (☎/fax 827 412). An old favorite with backpackers, who crowd the lobby and swap stories. Rooms are basic and tidy, but have thin walls and are starting to show their age. Rooms from US$5. ❶

NORTH OF BIỆT THỰ

Green Hotel, 6 Hùng Vương (☎821 404; www.greenhotelnhatrang.com). An excellent choice for upscale living. Spacious bamboo-decor rooms with hardwood floors are clean and sunny. The views make it hard to leave. Breakfast included. Rooms US$39-89. ❺

O-Sin 1, 4 Nguyễn Thiện Thuật (☎825 064; osinhotel@hotmail.com), and **O-Sin 2,** 15 Hùng Vương (☎822 902), are old standards that have been through the wash and are looking ragged. However, they have the ultimate budget prize: the only dorm beds in Nha Trang. Dorms US$3; rooms US$5-10. ❶

Indochine Hotel, 14 Hùng Vương (☎815 333; indochinehotel@yahoo.com). This elegant and spacious hotel ensures a quiet and comfortable stay. Top floors have beach views. Rooms US$10-14. ❸

⬛ FOOD

Due to the waves of tourists who crash upon Nha Trang's shores, most restaurants offer all types of international food. Most also leave something to be desired. Head for the fresh local seafood instead—restaurants in every price range serve succulent dishes featuring the daily catch. There are two supermarkets in town: **Maximark,** at the intersection of Quang Trưng and Lê Thánh Tôn, and **Đại Thuận,** 17A Biệt Thự, provide all the necessities. The latter specializes in imported goods and seafood. Both open daily 7am-9:30pm. The town's central **market** (Chợ Đàm), best known for its dried squid, is west of the post office at the end of Hoang Hòa Tham.

RESTAURANTS

▨ **Nha Trang Bakery and Tea Room,** 99B Nguyễn Thiện Thuật (☎526 562). Offers a cheap but extensive international menu. Breakfast options include an extensive mashed and "jacket" (baked) potato menu (20,000-35,000Đ) and melt-in-your-mouth chocolate croissants (5000Đ). Other dishes 15,000-20,000Đ. Open daily 6am-midnight. ❶

Trúc Linh Mini-Restaurant, 11 Biệt Thự. One of the best values in town: tasty seafood at reasonable prices. Leaves the frills behind and focuses on the fish. Frequented by locals and visitors alike. Entrees 20,000-50,000Đ. ❷

Chau Cafe, 42 Hùng Vương (☎826 336). A small restaurant with an extensive international menu. The Indian fare here is the best in Nha Trang, and the ice cream with hot fudge (20,000Đ) is fantastic. Most dishes around 25,000Đ. ❷

Duy Phước, 99 Nguyễn Thiện Thuật (☎812 055). A great spot for authentic streetside phở (8000Đ). Open daily 6am-midnight. ❶

Restaurant 7C, 7C Lê Lợi. Run by an amiable German, this is the place to satisfy your bratwurst craving. 7C enjoys a patronage beyond Teutonophiles, though, as it's one of the few places to offer brown, multi-grain bread. An airy beer garden is open daily 9-11pm. Entrees 15,000-30,000Đ. ❷

Cafe Des Amis, 2D Biệt Thự (☎521 009). Good food in a relaxed atmosphere—this place is never empty. The owner, Mr. Trương Hoa Đôn, is a skilled painter whose works, along with those of other local artists, are featured on the cafe's walls. Full vegetarian menu. Entrees 10,000-20,000Đ. Open daily 7am-10pm. ❶

Le Petit Bistro, 26D Trần Quang Khải (☎527 201). This bistro offers French cuisine in a cozy atmosphere. Try the gratinated onion soup (30,000Đ). Cold meats 30,000-60,000Đ. Specialty stews 85,000Đ. Open daily 11am-11pm. AmEx/D/MC/V. ❸

Omar's Indian Restaurant, 96A₈ Trần Phú (☎814 489). Part of a nationwide chain, Omar's has quality Indian food at slightly inflated prices. Entrees 30,000-40,000Đ. 5-course meals US$7 (US$6 for the vegetarian version). ❸

CAFES

▨ **Rom's Ice Cream and Coffee Bar,** 1C Biệt Thự (☎527 677; rommeley@web.de). German-owned and French-managed, these guys know their ice cream. Sizeable fruit-and-ice-cream sundaes. Ice cream concoctions with liqueurs 60,000-80,000Đ. 1-5 scoops 20,000-80,000Đ. Takeout available (12,000Đ). Open daily 9:30am-late. ❸

Banana Split Cafe, 60 Quang Tru'ng. A Nha Trang institution whose fame is well-earned. Excellent ice cream and desserts are worth the trip. Also organizes highly regarded tours. Desserts 5000-20,000Đ. ❶

Mecca Coffee Bar, 18 Trần Quang Khải (☎524 455; mecca_coffee@hotmail.com). This L-shaped coffee bar has a menu that sets it apart. Choose from fruit juices (12,000Đ) or "special" fruit juices (15,000Đ) like the Golden Dream, which combines orange, grenadine, and lime with egg yolk. Try the rum-spiked Suzette pancakes (20,000Đ) or the mango crepe with chocolate sauce (20,000Đ). ❷

🔍 SIGHTS

A tour of the following sights takes 2-3hr. You can hire a motobike driver to take you around for 100,000-150,000Đ, and tour companies in town offer more formal, more expensive city tours, with English-speaking guides.

 YES, SIR. If you want a proper English-speaking guide, whether as a full guide or a motorbike driver, don't just take their language skills at their word. Be sure to have a full conversation with the fellow first, and ask multi-part questions: many guides have perfected the art of knowing just enough English to snag your business, but will only give you "Yes, sir"s thereafter.

■ NHA TRANG TRADITIONAL ARTS & CRAFTS CENTRE. Enter the Craftwomen's Poetry Garden to sip tea and watch threads of raw silk being spun into elaborate tapestries. Every step of the process, from needle and thread to pattern and seamstress, is on display. The end products are absolutely stunning (from US$40). Staff speaks English and will show you around this privately-owned gallery. *(64 Trần Phú.* ☎*826 879; xqhandembroidery.com. Open daily 7:30am-9:30pm. Free.)*

LONG SO'N PAGODA. Built at the base of a hill, far enough from the beach to discourage tourists, is Nha's Trang's largest pagoda—and one of Vietnam's most interesting. Home to a community of monks and orphans (who serve as guides), the pagoda is teeming with life. The main hall has been rebuilt several times and has a modern feel; it's dedicated to the Buddhists who gave their lives protesting the US-backed Diệm regime in the 1960s (see **The Long Haul Toward Independence,** p. 65). The real treat of the pagoda is the 24m tall Buddha on the hilltop. A narrow pathway to the statue begins to the left behind the main hall, and goes up the hill to the Buddha. From this point, the entire city and the sea are visible. The statue holds a shrine inside. To the right of the Buddha are rows of over 5000 urns, which hold the ashes of the community's deceased. *(At the west end of Yersin, 2km from Trần Phú; look for the hilltop Buddha. Free.)*

PO NAGAR CHÀM TOWERS. Some of the finest Chàm towers on the country's coast. This site is wonderfully preserved and still serves as a place of worship; Buddhists place offerings at altars in each tower. It's a fascinating example of the appropriation of one faith's deity (the Hindu goddess Po Nagar) by another faith's followers (Mahayana Buddhists). From the entrance, a brief ascent to the left leads from the former *mandapa* (meditation hall; now a series of sturdy pillars) to the hilltop towers, where there's a great view of the Cái River. The most impressive tower is the northernmost one; over its entrance is a sculpture of Shiva, and the door posts are covered with inscriptions. Remove your shoes before entering. *(At the north end of 2 Tháng 4, just over Xóm Bóm Bridge. Open daily 6am-6pm. 4500Đ.)*

NHA TRANG CATHEDRAL. An excellent example of French Gothic architecture, this stone-and-cement cathedral, set on a hilltop, appears deceptively simple but conceals an elaborate interior. A spiral staircase in the back leads to the balcony, a good vantage from which to view the colorful stained glass windows. A portrait to the left of the main alter shows Jesus presiding over a congregation of Vietnam's priests. A beautiful relic of the colonial era, the cathedral still inspires Nha Trang's Catholic community. Along the road up the hill, urns hold the ashes from a disinterred cemetery. (*At the west end of Lê Thánh Tôn, 1km from Trần Phú. Su mass 5, 7am, 5, 9:30pm; M-F mass 4:45am and 5pm. Free.*)

OCEANOGRAPHIC INSTITUTE. This institute has thrown open its French-colonial doors to invite tourists to learn about local marine biology. A tour of the institute begins with tanks of colorful tropical fish, deadly tiger fish, and a variety of sharks and other sea life. But most spectacular is the ■warehouse of preserved specimens, farther inside the compound, where hundreds of species representing the region's biodiversity sit in jars of formaldehyde. Other exhibits inside the building include traditional and modern seafaring equipment and an old French nautical map with certain regions marked *"dangeureuse inexploée."* Exhibits are explained in English and French. (*At the south end of Trần Phú, near the docks. Open daily 7:30am-noon and 1-4:30pm. 15,000Đ.*)

YERSIN MUSEUM. Housed in the Pasteur Institute of Nha Trang, this clinic and research facility was founded by doctor/bacteriologist/farmer/explorer Alexandre Yersin (1863-1943) in 1895. To the left of the main building, the collection features Yersin's laboratory equipment and his library. Even more interesting are the original maps of his expeditions in the Central Highlands and an old globe from the French colonial era. Also noteworthy is the exhibit on the history of the bubonic plague and of the development of an anti-plague serum in Nha Trang. Documents are in French with some Vietnamese and English translations. (*10 Trần Phú. Open M-Sa 7:30-11am and 2-4:30pm. 26,000Đ.*)

HÒN CHỒNG PROMONTORY. Tourists (mostly Vietnamese) climb over the rocks here to reach a large granite boulder with an disproportionately large handprint on it. Scale the rocks your own way or follow the steps cut into the stone on the left. Legend explains that the handprint was made by a giant while he spied on a beautiful fairy bathing on nearby Fairy Beach. After a failed romance, the fairy lay down in grief to form the Fairy Mountains, just to the north. From right to left, the three peaks are her profile, her breasts, and her knees. From this point, Nha Trang is fully visible. (*Located at the northern end of Trần Phú. Open daily 6am-6pm. 3500Đ.*)

BẢO ĐẠI VILLAS. Emperor Bảo Đại's former villas are now open to the public, both as a tourist attraction and for accommodations. The five villas themselves are unimpressive, and the small beach is largely overshadowed by the neighboring port, but it's secluded and offers a fantastic view. Most visitors are tourists from HCMC or local teens looking for a quiet, romantic spot. (*Just behind the Oceanographic Institute, off the south end of Trần Phú. Open daily 7am-5pm. 5000Đ.*)

☑ BEACHES AND WATER-RELATED ACTIVITIES

The city's splendid beach, its serene waters, and the life that lies underneath are Nha Trang's *raison d'être*. Its soft sands and turquoise waters are open to anyone; a few private restaurants and resorts rent out beach chairs and umbrellas along the length of the beach. Some parts are deserted while others are mobbed, but one constant is the roving vendor traffic, offering everything from fresh mangoes to oil massages. The beach becomes less crowded the farther north you go, culminating in an empty patch north of the Hòn Chồng Promontory. Hotel managers warn their guests against walking along unlit parts of the beach late at night—there have been rumors of muggings, though none have been officially reported.

THE BIG SPLURGE

UNDER PRESSURE

Diving is an excellent way to experience Vietnam. Ten minutes of swimming through Vietnam's coastal waters will show you a greater quantity and diversity of organisms than ten hours of trekking in one national park. This is partly because the ocean world is so multifarious in its own right, and also because, unlike jungle creatures, animals under the sea are often less intimidated by human presence.

In the long run, getting basic certification means having an entire world open to you. Professional Association of Diving Instructors (PADI) and Scuba Schools International (SSI) certifications are governed by international standards and, accordingly, accepted worldwide. This means that any time you are next to an ocean or lake and you want to take a guided "fun dive," you are entirely qualified to do so. Fun dives are less expensive than "try dives" and allow more flexibility under the water and freedom to explore. So splurge—these dives are a great way to see a part of Vietnam inaccessible to the average tourist, and they're a great way to spend an afternoon.

*Open-water courses last 3 days and are offered at a standard rate of US$220 in Nha Trang (see **Scuba Diving**, p. 330). The price is notably lower than the US$600-700 required for the same instruction in Australia, New Zealand, or the US.*

SCUBA DIVING

Although it's not one of the world's premier diving locations, Nha Trang definitely has the best scuba diving in Vietnam. Diving here is cheap and easy, as is certification (see **"Under Pressure,"** p. 330). The city has plenty of dive companies offering a range of services at international standards. A first-time diver can choose between a "try dive," a shallow (6m) hand-holding experience (US$30), and a "discovery dive," which also serves as a first step toward certification (US$55). "Fun dives" (for the certified) run US$28-35; basic certification takes three days and costs about US$220; rescue-diver certification is around US$280. Most establishments also offer nitrox (enriched air) diving, which extends your bottom time, for an extra US$10-12. Book at least one day in advance.

▧ **Coral Reef Dive Center,** 6 Hùng Vương (☎524 993; fax 524 996). Highly-skilled, fun crew, with English- and French-speaking instructors. Manager Fred is an excellent instructor for first-timers. Also offers a full-day, 3-island trip in Nha Trang, weather-permitting (US$60 to Mun, Diamond, and Pyramid Islands). Open daily 7am-10pm.

Rainbow Divers, 55 Trần Phú and at other locations all over town (☎829 946; www.divevietnam.com). The most reputable company in Nha Trang. Extensive services and top-notch experience. Open daily 6:30am-10pm.

Blue Diving Club, 66 Trần Phú (☎825 390; www.vietnam-diving.com). Another of Nha Trang's gold-standard dive operations. Open daily 6:30am-10pm.

Coco Dive Center, 2E Biệt Thự (☎522 900; www.cocodivecenter.com). International crew boasting the first and only Vietnamese PADI Master and Instructor, Miss Xuan. Managed by former French Navy diver Jean Pierre. Offers both SSI and PADI courses. Private and speed boats available. Open daily 7am-10pm.

Octopus Diving (Sailing Club Divers), 62 and 72 Trần Phú (☎810 629; www.octopusdiving.com). A newer company with plenty of young, hip, Western and Vietnamese instructors. Open daily 7am-10pm.

BOAT TOURS

Boat tours (approx. US$6) are big business in Nha Trang. Back when the city was a tourist frontier, the tours were raucous, lawless affairs specializing in sun-soaked hedonism. Today they have become much tamer package deals, but they still provide an opportunity to cruise the South China Sea, snorkel among tropical fish, eat excellent seafood, and meet other travelers. After you buy a ticket, a minibus picks you up wherever you're staying between 8 and 9am. You're then shuttled to the hectic dock and packed onto a wooden boat. The cruise takes you and

30-40 others to **Mun Island** (Black Island, p. 332) for an hour of snorkeling and then anchors at **Mot Island**, where a fantastic lunch is served. Next comes Nha Trang's signature "floating bar," which essentially translates into free-flowing complimentary Vietnamese wine. Then it's off to **Tam Island** (5000Đ) with its zoo-like beach, overpriced drinks, and jet skiing and parasailing opportunities. A refreshing fruit buffet helps you absorb the alcohol on the way to the traditional fishing village on **Meiu Island**, where a ride in a colossal bamboo basket boat costs 5000-10,000Đ. Some boat tours also stop at Trí Nguyễn Aquarium. You should be back to your temporary abode no later than 5pm. (Tickets can be booked at nearly every hotel and tourist office, or you can go directly to the operators: **Mama Hanh**, 44 Lê Thánh Tôn; **Mỹ A**, 10 Hùng Vương; or **Mama Linh**, 2A Hùng Vương.)

More sophisticated travelers and families often opt for a calm, **glass-bottom boat tour.** The journey begins with an early hotel pickup and a visit to the **Oceanographic Institute.** Then you're whisked away to Mun Island in a glass-bottom boat. Lunch is at a secluded "floating village" which also offers a variety of activities, including kayaking, swimming, and jet skiing. Next up is a trip to the **Trí Nguyễn Aquarium.** You'll be back in the city by 3pm. (Inquire at VN Seaworld Offices, 110A/14 Trần Phú (☎828 242; www.vnseaworld.com. 145,000Đ, children 85,000Đ).

OTHER WET VENUES

Simply referred to as the "mud baths," **Tháp Bà Hot Spring Center** lies just north of the city. It's quite possibly one of the most relaxing spots in all of Vietnam. Visitors have the luxury of swimming in hot mineral spring water, soaking in tubs of soothing warm mud, and receiving massages. Prices range from 25,000Đ to 250,000Đ, depending on the level of pampering you desire. (☎835 335; www.thapba-hotspring.com.vn. Follow the signs along 2 Tháng 4, 2.5km north of the Po Nagar Chàm Towers, onto Son Thuy. Most hotels can arrange a shuttle for 20,000Đ.)

Waterworld, an outdoor waterpark, is fun for locals and visitors alike. There's a variety of clean, well-maintained pools and waterslides for all ages. (Between the beach and Trần Phú. Lockers 5000Đ. Open daily 7am-5pm. 20,000Đ.)

◙ NIGHTLIFE

People come to Nha Trang to party, and there is no shortage of options. Local expats know what the tourists want, and the result is a bustling nightlife scene dominated by Western-style bars and clubs. Most are found at the southern end of town, along Trần Quang Khải and Biệt Thự. A typical night starts at **Crazy Kim** or **Guava,** which have the most extensive food menus, and then moves on to **The Sailing Club** after midnight and **Why Not Bar** until the sun comes up. Beware that Nha Trang's nightlife scene is rife with illegal activity—namely drugs and prostitution—especially at the larger venues.

Crazy Kim, 19 Biệt Thự. A large, hip bar with a huge MTV-style lounge complete with a dance floor and pool table. The crowd here tends to be more laid-back but no less inebriated than at other bars in town. Also has outdoor seating and free wireless Internet. Happy hour 6-10pm. Open daily 8am-1am.

Guava, 17 Biệt Thự. An equally hip but more English-friendly bar run by 3 youthful Canadians. Caters to young partyers. Quality pub food, great music, pool table, and lounge chairs. Happy hour for mixed drinks 5-10pm; for beer, 5-9pm. Open daily 11am-late.

The Sailing Club, beachside Trần Phú, across from Trần Quang Khải. An unassuming Italian and Indian restaurant during the day; the ultimate bar at night. Everyone's evening somehow ends here. Spacious dance floor, pumping beats, and a big seating area. A young crowd happily partakes in the general bacchanalia of sweaty bodies and endless shots. Comes alive at midnight. Open daily until very late.

HE ANTI OPEN-TOUR

Sylvio Lamarche, originally from Canada, has been living in Vietnam with his wife and children for 0 years and runs the not-quite-resort of Jungle Beach, about 50km north of Nha Trang. As a soil conservation scientist, Mr. Lamarche is turning Jungle Beach and its environs into an eco-friendly destination for travelers. He also wants it to become an escape from the city rush—a place to experience Vietnam at a slower pace.

When I came here in 1994, there was nothing here; I saw two foreigners in Hà Nội. My first day here I was close to going back to Thailand because it was so much easier there; here, no one spoke English, it was very different. There was no road to Hải Phòng Bay—there was no Hải Phòng City. It was difficult, but it was fun because it was difficult.

Nowadays people go on this tour bus and they don't really see anything—they miss everything. Back then it was all local bus, nothing was ready for tourists. You could go anyway, and stop anywhere because the buses only went 50km before you had to change. I finally got to Nha Trang...and there was a beach, and it was quiet and warm, and they had great food.

I had a market garden in Canada and everything I had grows here, plus tropical fruit. The goal is to grow all that on Jungle *Cont'd on next page...]*

The Shamrock (Hoa May Mần), 56A Nguyễn Thiện Thuật (☎527 548). No party town would be complete without the token Irish pub. Behold The Shamrock: large, green, lively. Get your Guinness (10,000Đ) and old classics like beef stew and mash (50,000Đ) and fish and chips (60,000Đ). Open daily 5pm-late.

Dream Bar, 96A₇ Trần Phú, (☎524 247), on the 8th fl. of the Dream Hotel. Offers high-priced drinks and one of Nha Trang's only high-rise views. Happy hour 6-8pm. Open daily 6-10am and 6pm-midnight.

Why Not Bar, 93 Nguyễn Thiện Thuật (☎522 625). A small but hopping bar with good music. TV and pool table. Incredible deals on drinks: Happy hour 5-10pm, but free mixed drinks pop up throughout the night. Open daily 9am-4am.

Cà Phê Phù Đồng, on Trần Phú, on the beach next to Water-world. Open-air seating, Vietnamese pop, and a view of the waves. More low-key than the Western-run establishments, this tropical bar offers standard mixed drinks (15,000-50,000Đ) and ice cream sundaes (10,000-22,000Đ) without the constant noise. Open daily 5-11pm.

■ DAYTRIPS FROM NHA TRANG

A few of the beaches and sights near Nha Trang offer some peace from the noise of the city. When you tire of partying or if you want something to do during the day, head north and east of town to see what the surrounds have to offer.

■ **MUN ISLAND.** Mun Island is Vietnam's place for underwater adventure and exploration. The island itself is uninhabited except for Army guards, but its surrounding waters are teeming with colorful coral and schools of fish. The ocean floor terrain has shallow shelves suitable for beginner divers as well as 18-20m depths for the more advanced. Mun Island is shaped in the form of a spoon, with the handle jutting out to the east. On the south side, at the junction between the handle and ladle, is **Fisherman's Bay,** marked by shallow sands and colorful corals. Snorkelers and divers alike should easily be able to spot schools of fish there, including tiger fish and clownfish. Sailing east around the handle, in the channel between it and Rom Island, are the illustrious ■**Madonna Rocks.** Three separate swim trails at 8-10m make this a thrilling dive. Across from Madonna Rocks is **Padi Beach,** the shallow area where many dive instructors practice basic skills with their pupils. Farther around the island, at its westernmost tip, is **Moray Beach,** inhabited by the native Moray eels. The unaggressive eels are easily teased out of their coral refuges. Finally, at the southwestern edge of the island are the **Coral Gardens.** *(Mun Island is a 45min. boat ride* *from Nha Trang. Tours are best arranged through dive shops in Nha Trang (p. 330), which offer snorkeling and a range of scuba dives. Private boats for unguided excursions may be rented from most dive shops.)*

JUNGLE BEACH. Sandwiched between an isolated white-sand beach and the jungle-covered Hòn Hèo Mountain (813m), the underdeveloped Jungle Beach isn't exactly a resort, but it isn't exactly anything else, either (see **"The Anti-Open Tour,"** p. 332). Guests stay in basic rooms and eat around a communal table, enjoying the exquisite food prepared by the *madame* of the home. A relaxed atmosphere permeates everything—a result of the hammocks down by the beach, the outdoor four-post beds (covered with mosquito netting) and the treks through untouched forests to nearby waterfalls. There is no other place like this in Vietnam, and it's only going to get better. Although it's a bit hard to reach, Jungle Beach has a stellar reputation that's made it quite popular, so reservations are recommended. *(☎ 622 384; syl@dng.vnn.vn. Take a motorbike from Nha Trang up Hwy. 1 heading north about 36km and turn off at the huge Hyundai-Vinashin sign. You can also have tour buses drop you off here. Follow the road to its terminus, about 20km down. Overnight stays, including meals US$15.)*

WHALE ISLAND. An exclusive, remote resort for those who really want to get away from it all. It's 2hr. by boat from Nha Trang; except for a small fishing village, the island is unpopulated. Guests stay in rustic yet pleasant bamboo bungalows. During the day, scuba diving (Feb.-Nov.), windsurfing, canoeing, and catamaran sailing are all options. A nature walk around the island offers superb bird-watching opportunities, and a small communal canteen is the favorite evening hangout. Whale Island is a true escape, although it can get a little too quiet during the winter months. *(For more information, visit the Whale Island office in Nha Trang, 11B Nguyễn Thiện Thuật. ☎ 811 607; www.whaleislandresort.com. Bungalows US$75-140. Includes meals and transport from Nha Trang. Discounts for children.)*

PHAN RANG ☎ 68

Phan Rang, the capital of Ninh Thuận province, is slowly growing into a respectable metropolis, leaving its immediate neighbor, Tháp Chàm, behind. Though they're set in the sandy and arid southern central coast, Phan Rang and Tháp Chàm are known for their grape production; stalls selling every possible grape product line the roads. The surrounding landscape is unlike any other in Vietnam, supporting only vineyards, salt beds, and the occasional corn field. But like its environment, Phan Rang does not offer much, and Tháp Chàm offers even less. But there are a few noteworthy sights in the

Beach, so people can come to my house and say "Oh, this is a coffee tree; I've never seen a coffee tree before." When a little kid reaches up and picks a papaya off a tree and then cuts it up and eats it, he will never forget it... Jungle Beach is a place to get away from the rat race.

I think people who come here do not realize how big a country this is, north to south. People come here wanting to see it all, but the only way is to rush through; people go to a lot of places but they don't really see Vietnam. They hang out with each other—they don't hang out with the families. I had a buddy who stayed with me for a month and went to some nearby villages. He learned all about Vietnam: he drank with them, he went to a wedding, he went to a funeral. Most tourists just come here and hang out at the bar; they miss out on a whole lot. It's always, "I got to get to Sa Pa, I got to get to Hà Nội." They don't see the country—it's beautiful out there.

*See **Jungle Beach**, p. 333. ☎ 622 384; syl@dng.vnn.vn. Take a motorbike from Nha Trang up Hwy. 1 heading north about 36km and turn off at the huge Hyundai-Vinashin sign. You can also have tour buses drop you off here. Then follow the road to its terminus, about 20km down. Overnight stays including meals US$15.*

area, including one of the finest Chàm towers in Vietnam. There's also a sizable Chàm population and even a small Muslim one in and around Phan Rang.

▣ TRANSPORTATION. The **bus station** is between 228 and 231 Thống Nhất. Buses leave when full for: Buôn Ma Thuột (60,000-90,000Đ); Đà Lạt (20,000-30,000Đ); HCMC (50,000-70,000Đ); Phan Thiết (24,000-30,000Đ). **Minibuses** sometimes stop at the gas station, near the market in the center of town. **Tourist buses** stop at the nearby Poklongarai Chàm tower but bypass the city. The **train station** is 6km west of Hwy. 1 and is serviced only by non-express trains.

⬥ ORIENTATION. Phan Rang is 120km south of Nha Trang, 147km north of Phan Thiết, and 110km east of Đà Lạt. The town is skewered by **Highway 1** and **Thống Nhất**, which run north-south through the town. At the north end are the post office and bus station; at the south end, a bridge leads out of town. Several east-west streets intersect Hwy. 1 perpendicularly; the intersection with **16 Tháng 4**, a main street, forms the heart of town. At the south end, **Ngô Gia Tư** runs east, then curves up to the northeast, forming the eastern perimeter of town. Tháp Chàm is Phan Rang's sister city, with **21 Tháng 8** serving as its main road.

▨ PRACTICAL INFORMATION. The **Agriculture Bank**, 540-544 Thống Nhất, handles basic banking needs, including currency exchange. (☎824 619; fax 822 716. Open M-Sa 7:30-11am and 2-4:30pm.) **Markets** are spread along Thống Nhất south of Trần Hưng Đạo. A Western-style **supermarket** sells everything under the sun (except food) at 251A Thống Nhất. Several **pharmacies** line Thống Nhất and offer the same selection. The large Ninh Thuận provincial **hospital** is at the intersection of Lê Hồng Phong and 16 Tháng 4, 50m west of Thống Nhất. Several **Internet** parlors also line Thống Nhất; most charge 3000Đ per hr. The **General Post Office** is at 217A Thống Nhất and offers all basic services, including international calling. (☎824 430. Open daily 6:30am-9:30pm.)

▨▣ ACCOMMODATIONS AND FOOD. The few accommodations in Phan Rang cater primarily to Vietnamese tourists, but backpackers shouldn't have trouble finding a decent place to rest. **Ninh Tuan Hotel ❹**, 1 21 Tháng 8, is just west of the intersection of Thống Nhất and Quang Trưng. Phan Rang's premier hotel is ever-mindful of its road-weary clientele, offering a 24hr. check-in. (☎827 100; fax 822 142. Decent rooms all have A/C and satellite TV. Best English in town. Rooms US$25-35.) **Thống Nhất Hotel ❸**, 343 Thống Nhất, another quality hotel, is situated right on Hwy. 1. It provides clean, comfortable rooms but lacks the extras. (☎825 406; thongnhotel_pr@hcm.vnn.vn. Rooms US$12-18.) **Trang Hà ❷**, 562-564 Thống Nhất, is Phan Rang's budget option for a reason—it's along a noisy stretch of the highway and the rooms are slowly crumbling away. Nevertheless, it's very popular with Vietnamese tourists. (☎822 606. Rooms from US$8.)

When in Phan Rang, you have little choice but to do what the locals do. Almost everyone eats at the festive **market stalls** or at the small eateries lining Thống Nhất that dish out traditional Vietnamese food. For the few who feel the need for a table and service, there are two restaurants near the market offering similar fare. Mostly, though, what you'll find in Phan Rang are cafes serving highlands coffee. Small cafes line the highway; larger, newer ones are along Ngô Gia Tư to the east. **Cafe 407 ❶**, 407 Thống Nhất, is small and simple, serving golden brew from the highlands. It is also one of the few cafes that sells the coffee in bulk (under 10,000Đ). **Cafe Uyên Trinh ❶**, 1 Lê Lợi, is one of the two restaurant-type cafes in town. You may savor the pleasant seating more than the typical Vietnamese food and local specialties. (Entrees 15,000-20,000Đ.) **Cafe Hoàng Gin ❶**, near the market on a sidestreetacross from the gas station, offers local specialties and shade from the glaring sun. (Entrees around 15,000Đ.)

▨ DAYTRIPS FROM PHAN RANG. The sights in Phan Rang are not in the city itself, but on the outskirts. To reach most of them, you'll need your own transportation—most likely a motorbike (2-3hr.; 50,000Đ). Tour buses do, however, stop at the most striking sight, the Poklongarai Chàm Towers.

The **Poklongarai Chàm Towers** are possibly the most spectacular Chàm site in all of Vietnam. Set upon a hilltop amidst otherwise-drab country roads, the four towers of Poklongarai have been well-preserved for eight centuries and are an awe-inspiring sight. The most spectacular view in the complex is the entrance to the central tower: the doorposts are covered in ancient inscriptions, and above the entrance is a bas-relief sculpture of a dancing Shiva. Just inside the entrance is a statue of the bull Nandi, the overseer of local agriculture and Shiva's celestial vehicle. The inside shrine honors King Poklongarai (AD 1151-1205), the Champa ruler credited with constructing the local irrigation system. Remove your shoes before entering. Outside, spend a few moments appreciating the skill needed to construct the elaborate tower caps. The ornate multi-tiered towers rival anything else in Southeast Asia. Several of the groundskeepers, who can be found at the booking office, are themselves Chàm descendants; they will happily speak of their ancestry and write for you in the Chàm script. For a more personal account of this experience, see **"Heritage Hunting,"** p. 336. (Poklongarai is on Trau Hill 7km northwest of Phan Rang, north of Hwy. 20. Most tour buses from Đà Lạt to Nha Trang or Nha Trang to Mũi Né stop there. Pay at the booking office at the end of the compound. 5000Đ.)

> **TIP**
>
> **GOOD MORNING, FASCISM.** Western travelers in Vietnam may at first be appalled by the prevalence of **swastikas** throughout the country's religious sites, recognizing them only as the symbol of Nazi Germany. But Vietnam is not a country of fascists: the swastika was a holy and auspicious symbol in Hinduism long before it was reappropriated by the Nazis. Buddhism, founded by a Hindu prince, inherited the swastika, and it is at countless pagoda entrances, on statues of the Buddha, and marking Buddhist headstones.

The solitary **Pô Rô Mê** Chàm Tower is off the tourist radar. Situated on a long hilltop near a mud-and-brick Chàm village, Pô Rô Mê is the center of Chàm New Year celebrations. The tower is beautiful in its peaceful surroundings—a windswept hill alone in a shrub desert—but unremarkable in itself, except for the curious bas-relief sculpture of a mustached man that adorns the tower's terraces. The inner sanctum remains locked shut, awaiting the New Year. The most interesting part of the tower, however, is getting there. A lone road twists and turns through the arid landscape, past fields of cacti and small Chàm villages, with road signs written in both Chàm and Vietnamese scripts. A single sugarcane juice (1000Đ) stand is on the access road, and it's a traveler's best bet for refreshments out here. (To reach Pô Rô Mê, head 15km south of Phan Rang on Hwy. 1. After Ninh Phước village, take the last right immediately before the bridge, a few meters short of mile 1567 on Hwy. 1. Take the next immediate right, then the first left. After a few kilometers you'll see a school on the right and a blue sign on the left. Take the first left after the sign. Continue on this cement road past a Chàm village until the Pô Rô Mê sign. From here, turn onto the dirt road on the right. Take a left where the dirt road forks; you will see the tower 500m ahead, a total of 7km from the highway.)

Thuấn Tú Hamlet is a village living in grinding poverty and struggling to survive. The only thing that distinguishes this from Vietnam's countless other such villages is that the residents are Muslim—an extreme rarity in this country. In fact, with the hamlet set among sand dunes and shrubs, and the residents wearing headscarves and herding sheep, Thuấn Tú seems to belong thousands of kilometers away on the shores of the Mediterranean. There is not much to see except a small, plain mosque—any visitor, to the people living here, is the real sight. A more elaborate mosque sits on Hwy. 1, 1km south of Ninh Phước village. (To reach Thuấn Tú, take the first left off Hwy. 1, just before the bridge leading out of Phan Rang. This same dirt road will continue through a few villages until a gate announces your arrival at Thuấn Tú, 8km from Hwy. 1.)

The lonely **Thàp Chàm Towers** have been abandoned to the elements. Overgrown and decaying, they are nonetheless worth a visit because of their massive size. Indeed,

HERITAGE HUNTING

When my father used to tell me that my family descended from great Indian kings who once conquered lands throughout Southeast Asia, I was sure it was all just exaggeration and lore. But the stunning Chàm Towers around Phan Rang—tall, imposing remnants of a long-gone empire—substantiate his claim, and a tour of the towers began, for me, to feel like a personal exercise in heritage hunting.

The similarities between these religious sights and those so familiar to me confronted me immediately. Presiding over most towers is a depiction of God that I grew up with—dancing Shiva. His eight arms flail with power, holding in their hands familiar symbols like the trident, the drum, and the eternal flame. The Chàm script, prolifically spread across the archway stone, appears eerily Dravidian: watching the ethnically Chàm tower guard pen my name reminds me of my grandmother first teaching me to write Telugu, my family's native tongue.

Perhaps the most profound and gratifying moment, however, comes when visiting the inner shrines themselves. It is clear that Hindu rituals are still followed here, and my literacy in those rituals enables me to participate, not just spectate, in honoring the living legend of that archaic empire. To receive blessings in one's own faith in a far

[Cont'd on next page...]

their empty bellies are cavernous. The south tower is decayed almost beyond recognition, but the north one still displays beautiful, intricate carvings on its brick walls. (Right on Hwy. 1, 15km north of Phan Rang.)

CÀ NÁ ☎ 68

Cà Ná is fish sauce country. More than a dozen ■**refineries** of the traditional Vietnamese condiment *nước mắm* line the 1km stretch of Hwy. 1 that cuts through the town. Otherwise, the small fishing port is unremarkable. Just west of the village along Hwy. 1 are a few resorts squished between the highway and the South China Sea, which provide great access to the beach, despite the large boulders scattering the shore. Unfortunately, this beach is never more than 50m from the highway, and it's battered by high winds from October through March, so most travelers bypass Cà Ná for Mũi Né or Nha Trang, unless they're staying at the scuba resort, specially designed for diving enthusiasts.

■■ **TRANSPORTATION AND ORIENTATION.** Cà Ná is 32km south of Phan Rang and 115km north of Phan Thiết. The resorts and seafood stalls begin just west of the turn-off to the port and continue in that direction along **Highway 1.** Local **buses** typically pass here; just ask to be let off. **Open-tour buses** sometimes stop in Cà Ná as a rest stop. Otherwise, hire a **motorbike** from Phan Rang (40min.; 70,000Đ). Hwy. 1 is the main drag through this town, and almost everything in town is on one side or the other of this highway.

■■ **ACCOMMODATIONS AND FOOD.** Three large resorts, complete with restaurants and tennis courts, can be found around Cà Ná. **Cà Ná Hotel ❷,** close to the village and next to the Hòn Cò Cà Ná Motel (see below), has the cheapest bungalows along this stretch of pavement. They're a bit past their prime, but are still clean and comfortable. The nearby section of beach is not the nicest, but the staff is friendly and helpful, and they can arrange for motorcycle tours of the surrounding areas or schedule bus pickups. The cheapest rooms have fans; all others have air-conditioning and TV. (☎ 760 616; fax 761 320. Bungalows 120,000-180,000Đ; more spacious villas 200,000Đ.) **Vietnam Scuba Resort ❸,** 3km west of the village, is a plush resort catered to divers. Secluded bungalows face the beach, and a small army of dive instructors await your beck and call. (☎ 062 853 919; www.vietnamscuba.com. Room and 3 meals US$75; diving and 1 meal US$80; diving, room, and 3 meals US$130.) **Hòn Cò Cà Ná Motel ❹** is the closest to the village. Although it calls itself a motel, it's actually a full-fledged resort, outfitted with a minimart, bar, restaurant, massage parlor, Internet

access (12,000Đ per hr.), and private beach. Bungalows are spacious and clean, and there's parking outside. (☎ 760 998; honcocana@hcm.vnn.vn.
Bungalows US$25. MC/V.)

Biển Vinh Hảo Seafood Restaurant ❷, east of the
scuba resort, serves excellent seafood and has an
English menu. This roadside restaurant, with
thatched roof and bamboo decor, faces the sea.
(Entrees from 25,000Đ.) **Phương Thảo Restaurant ❶**,
across from Cà Ná Hotel, offers basic Vietnamese
dishes—bland but filling—in a spacious room. (Soup
8000Đ; rice dishes 20,000Đ.)

◪ SIGHTS. Fish sauce is what really sets Cà Ná
apart from any other highway town, and fish sauce is
the reason this city is worth a stop for any coastal
traveler. The locals here create *nước mắm* from
scratch, and observers can see every step in the nine-
month-long refining process by visiting the town's
◪nước mắm stalls. Anchovies are netted from the
nearby sea, set upon wire racks, doused and layered
with rock salt, and plunged into huge wooden barrels. The liquid that seeps from the barrels is then filtered and siphoned in several stages, until the final
product is packaged in a fine plastic bottle. Whatever
culinary genius happened upon this convoluted and
counterintuitive process deserves a high-five. The
barrels can be seen from the highway, and any of the
refineries can show you around; some will even
insist that you have a taste of their freshly fermented
sauce, using rice paper for dipping. Tài Sang (☎ 861
311) has an easy-to-follow layout and a particularly
friendly staff. You can take home the finished product by the liter (15,000Đ).

PHAN THIẾT ☎ 62

This provincial capital, one of Hồ Chí Minh's childhood homes, has grown from a fishing port to a small
but bustling city and a major production center for
nước mắm, Vietnam's staple fish sauce. Though it
features the scenic Cà Ty River, Phan Thiết struggles
to capture the tourist crowds. It offers relatively
cheap accommodations, friendly people, and an
excellent beach, but most visitors opt for nearby
resort paradise Mũi Né (p. 341). Phan Thiết serves as
a great daytrip from Mũi Né for anyone looking to see
one of the less touristed parts of Vietnam.

▣ TRANSPORTATION

Trains: Phan Thiết station, 1 Hoàng Hoa Thám, near
the intersection of Lê Hồng Phong and Cao Thắng, 1km
north of town. Non-express train for HCMC leaves daily
at 7:30am (4hr.; 60,000Đ).

and foreign land is to feel
one's ancestry at the deepest level.

Experiencing these archaeological relics in real time has been a
more personal experience than I
expected. But I imagine that it is
not necessarily an exclusive experience. Vietnam is a land of mixture—many empires have entered
here, with many cultures and
many faiths imposing themselves
upon the local terrain. Though the
Vietnamese have consistently
thrown off the administrative yoke
of foreign oppressors, their culture
has carefully absorbed the positive
traditions of those foreign influences—from those tasty French
baguettes to the (less tasty, but
still important) Chinese legal system.

Thus, in a seemingly paradoxi-
cal way, while Vietnam is homoge-
neously nationalistic, its culture
and way of life reflects many heter-
ogeneities. The scattered and
adopted traditions of other cultures are the thousand spices
which make the Vietnamese way
of life so incredibly unique. A
Christian will see cemeteries bearing crosses scattering the countryside. A Muslim will see crescents
and green minarets. If he or she
looks closely, a Western traveler,
or any traveler, is bound to find
echoes of their own heritage
within the mix.

-Saritha Komatireddy

Buses: Buses leave from the station 2km north of where Từ Văn Tư intersects with Trần Hưng Đạo. Buses to nearby cities like **Long Hai** and **Ben Trễ** leave frequently throughout the day on their own schedules. Buses go only as far south as HCMC and as far north as Đà Lạt. Service to **Đà Lạt** (6hr.; 4, 4:30, 5pm; 50,000Đ), **HCMC** (4hr.; every 30min. 2:30-6pm; 38,000Đ), and **Phan Rang** (3hr.; every 15min. 4:45am-6pm; 30,000Đ).

Tâm Hanh Travel Company (☎833 277). Open-tour buses leave daily at noon for **Hà Nội, HCMC,** and **Nha Trang.** They'll stop at your destination if it's close to their route. Catch the bus (US$9-12) next to the Phú Gia Hotel on Tôn Dức Thắng.

Motorcycle Taxi: You can rent a taxi for about 100,000Đ per day plus the cost of gas.

ORIENTATION

Phan Thiết is 200km northeast of HCMC and 100km south of Đà Lạt. It lies just off Hwy. 1, where the **Cà Ty River** spills into the South China Sea. The city straddles the river, with the more condensed old quarter and the fishing port on the south shore and the sprawling, chaotic new quarter on the north shore. **Trần Hưng Đạo** runs south into town from Hwy. 1 and crosses the river between quarters. Stretching to the north and then east from Trần Hưng Đạo is **Thủ Khoa Huân,** which heads toward Mũi Né (19km). To the southeast is **Nguyễn Tất Thành,** which leads to the beachside **Lê Lợi** (also called **Võ Thị Sáu**). In the old quarter, **Trần Phú** and **Nguyễn Huệ** are the two largest arteries, meeting at the market in the center of town.

PRACTICAL INFORMATION

Tourist Office: Bình Thuận Travel Service Agency, 82 Trưng Trắc (☎816 821; www.binhthuantourist.com). The state-run provincial agency; you can arrange package tours here and get limited walk-in help. The friendly staff can book Vietnam Airlines and Pacific Airlines tickets. City map $1. Open daily 7:30-11:30am and 1:30-4:30pm.

Banks: Agriculture Bank, 2-4 Trưng Trắc, near the center of town. Offers currency exchange and MC/V cash advances. Open M-Sa 7-11am and 1:30-5pm. **Industrial and Commercial Bank,** at the intersection of Nguyễn Tất Thành and Trần Hưng Đạo, offers the same services. ATM outside. Open M-Sa 7-11am and 1:30-4pm.

Pharmacy: 29 Thủ Khoa Huân, at the north end of town. Several others are near the market and along Trần Hưng Đạo.

Hospital: (☎822 733), across from 133 Hải Thượng Lãn Ông. A large UNICEF-certified, "baby-friendly" hospital. Also look for a newer, shinier version to the north, off of Hwy. 1.

Internet: 20A Thủ Khoa Huân, at the north end of town. Offers Internet phone. A 2nd cafe at 121 Trần Phú, near the post office, has a more convenient location but no Internet phone. Both charge 5000Đ per hr. More shops along Trần Hưng Đạo have same rate.

Post Offices: Government Post Office (GPO), at the intersection of Nguyễn Huệ and Trần Phú, in the heart of the old quarter. International phone service. Open daily 6:30am-9:30pm. **Provincial Post Office,** a bigger building at the intersection of Nguyễn Tất Thành and Tôn Dức Thắng, near the beach.

ACCOMMODATIONS

The accommodations in Phan Thiết are segregated geographically: cheap hotels, mostly used by Vietnamese tourists, are in the crowded city center and to the north, near the train and bus stations. Posh resorts catering to foreign tourists are along the beach. There's also a string of nearly identical budget guesthouses along Trần Hưng Đạo, between Thủ Khoa Huân and Nguyễn Tất Thành.

Nhật Linh, 337 Lê Lợi (☎831 141; fax 823 473; nhatlinhhotel@pmail.vnn.vn). A clean, spacious hotel lacking in character. It makes up for its average interior, though, with a prime location: only 1 block from the beach, it's the closest non-resort accommodation to the sand. Singles 200,000Đ; doubles 300,000Đ. ❸

Phan Thiết Hotel, 364 Trần Hưng Đạo (☎819 907; fax 815 930). With its tropical court-yard, cavernous conference rooms, and attached restaurant, this attractive hotel is a popular Vietnamese wedding spot. The rooms are cheap, and it's one of the few hotels located near the city center. Singles 150,000Đ; doubles 210,000Đ. ❷

Hotel 19/4, 1 Từ Văn Tư (☎821 794; 19-4hotel@hcm.vnn.vn), next to the bus station. The largest hotel in the city that isn't on the beach. With its long halls and spacious rooms, it's the closest thing in the city to a Western inn. Staff is friendly and helpful. Rooms have A/C, fridge, TV, and small lounge area. Free luggage storage during the day. Perfect if you pull into the city on a late bus. Singles 200,000Đ; doubles 250,000Đ. ❸

Tây Hồ, 401 Trần Hưng Đạo (☎821 710). A short walk from the city center. One of the least expensive accommodations along the strip of budget hotels. Staff is friendly, and there is an array of tropical trees growing in the lobby. Rooms are small and quiet, but may have slightly musty smell. Doubles 140,000Đ. ❷

Phương Hưng, 166 Trần Hưng Đạo (☎825 619; fax 825 300), near the bus station and easily accessible from Hwy. 1. This modern hotel offers standard rooms bathed in fluorescent glory, along with a discotheque, massage services, a sauna, and rental cars. Helpful staff. Clean but plain rooms, many with balcony, though the hotel is situated on a noisy road. Singles 170,000Đ; doubles 250,000Đ; triples 350,000Đ. ❸

Hải Văn Hotel, 102 Thủ Khoa Huân (☎823 783; fax 832 028). Large, comfortable, non-descript rooms and a friendly owner (fluent in German). Rooms have A/C, TVs, and small fridge. Spacious garage is convenient for drivers. On the road to Mũi Né, but not too close to the beach or the city center. Doubles 200,000Đ. ❸

Đổi Dương Hotel, 403 Lê Lợi (☎821 579; ksdoiduong@vnn.vn), right across from the beach. Great rooms, great views, and great sunbathing. Beautiful swimming pool and tennis court. Stellar English-speaking staff. A towering, upscale hotel with all the expected amenities—a good value in Phan Thiết, but you can do better in Mũi Né. Rooms US$26-48. Breakfast buffet included; expensive but tasty restaurant attached to hotel. ❹

🍴 FOOD

Although Phan Thiết has been a successful fishing town for years, it has yet to dis-cover seafood restaurants. Most of the day's catch is bought and sold at the port and goes directly to private homes or roadside vendors. You can check out the numerous stalls along Ngư Ông, or those on Trần Hưng Đạo between Thủ Khoa Huân and Nguyễn Tất Thành. Many of the city's restaurants are attached to hotels; beyond that, *bún* and *phở* shops can be found on every other block. For even cheaper food, the indoor and outdoor **market** is along Nguyễn Huệ at its intersec-tion with Trần Phú, where inexpensive fruits and vegetables can be found.

🦴 OShin Cafe, on the beach at the end of Nguyễn Tất Thành. The largest and most popular of a string of open-air, beachside ice cream and drink shops. The perfect place to let the hours slip into the sea. Drinks from the extensive menu 6000-14,000Đ. ❶

Kim Sơn Lâu, 34 Nguyễn Thị Minh Khai. Located near the city center. One of only a hand-ful of sit-down restaurants in Phan Thiết. Serves a variety of dishes including seafood. Friendly atmosphere. Beautiful view from the second fl. Extensive English menu with a great selection of vegetarian options. Dishes 20,000-80,000Đ. ❸

Nam Thanh Lâu, 50 Nguyễn Thị Minh Khai. Two doors down from Kim Sơn Lâu is another full-fledged restaurant serving excellent seafood and good Vietnamese and Chinese cui-sine. Extensive English menu and fast service. Dishes 12,000-50,000Đ. ❷

🌅 SIGHTS

Phan Thiết offers only a few things to see or do, but its sights are a nice alternative to the beach. Two of the city's most interesting sights are free: the century-old watertower, built in a distinctive Chinese pagoda style, stands on the north shore of the Cà Ty River, and the river itself teems in spring and summer with an armada of primary-colored wooden fishing boats.

■ **ĐÚC THẮNG TEMPLE.** Hidden inside this seemingly ordinary temple is Southeast Asia's largest preserved fin whale. The enormous 20m long whale skeleton has been held intact for 200 years. The adjoining building houses the typical array of Buddha sculptures and incense, but tucked behind these statues are tons of enormous whale bones. In the mornings, local fishermen pray to the "sea genie" for good luck. The temple is well worth the visit while you are in the old quarter of the city. *(54 Nguyễn Du. Open daily 7-11:30am and 1:30-5pm. 3000Đ.)*

HỒ CHÍ MINH MUSEUM. Yet another monument to Uncle Ho, who lived in Phan Thiết for a short time back when he was called Nguyễn Tất Thàn. The exhibits in this two-story museum have aged and are not entirely tourist-friendly—the few English captions don't adequately explain why preserved octopi belong underneath pictures of Hồ Chí Minh. The museum's gems include the original handwritten statutes of the Vietnamese Communist Party and old photos of Hồ Chí Minh's early life. Across the street is a well-preserved schoolhouse where Hồ Chí Minh taught in 1910. *(At the end of Trưng Nhi, on the river. Open Su, Tu-Sa 7:30-11:30am and 1:30-4:30pm. 5000Đ; 3000Đ for groups.)*

ÔNG PAGODA. Located on Trần Phú three blocks north of the market, this colorful and elaborate pagoda is the city's finest. Four distinct chambers—particularly the middle two—are filled to the brim with ornamentation and have altars in every corner. Watch locals' worship and be sure to examine the craftsmanship of the large ■**dragon head** inside. *(Open daily 5am-5pm.)*

♫ ENTERTAINMENT

Phan Thiết's biggest tourist draw is its top-notch golf course. The **Ocean Dunes Golf Resort** is attached to the Coralia Ocean Dunes Resort, 1 Tôn Đức Thắng, but it's open to walk-in guests. This 18-hole course is set along the beach and almost doubles the size of the city. (Weekday 9-hole US$35, 18-hole US$65; weekend US$50/US$85; driving range US$5-15; lessons US$30 per hr.; caddie or cart US$15; equipment rental US$5-25.)

▶ DAYTRIPS FROM PHAN THIẾT

TÀ CÚ MOUNTAIN. This mountain, 28km southwest of Phan Thiết, is one of many extinct volcanoes that dot the landscape of Bình Thuận Province. The pagoda built into its side, dating from 1861, holds Vietnam's **largest Buddha statue.** At 49m long, the sleeping Buddha is truly awesome. Unfortunately, huge crowds of Vietnamese and foreign tourists have created an amusement-park atmosphere, especially on weekends, making this distant daytrip more suitable as a stop on the way into or out of Phan Thiết. A shuttle brings visitors from the entrance gate to a cable car that heads up the mountain. You can choose to hike up instead: bear left at the only fork in the road leading to the cable cars. The rocky and steep 2500m trail is a neat hike overlooking a beautiful green, brown, and blue patchwork landscape, but the garbage along the trail is distracting. *(Tà Cú is 3km south of Hwy. 1; turn off the highway at the large billboard. A round-trip motorcycle taxi ride to the mountain from Phan Thiết takes about 45min. each way and costs 60,000-80,000Đ. 5000Đ.)*

PÔSHANU CHÀM TOWERS. Some 12km down Thủ Khoa Huân (the road to Mũi Né) are two Chàm towers set on a seaside hill. They're easily visible from the road, and the walk to get closer is probably not worth it. They've fallen into disrepair, and much of the sculpture and ornamentation have eroded away. Nonetheless, the area around the towers is appealing, offering spectacular views of the coastline and Phan Thiết itself. But many more spectacular Chàm towers await in the north. *(A round-trip motorcycle taxi ride takes about 30min. each way and should cost you 40,000-60,000Đ. 2000Đ to hike up to the towers.)*

MŨI NÉ ☎ 62

Mũi Né offers a glimpse into Vietnam's most surprising terrain—its desert. The canyons of red clay and the dunes of orange and white sand that are so insanely, hilariously unique in this country flooded with rainforests, mountains, and aqua-blue water make Mũi Né a must-see. But the gorgeous beach is what really draws the tourists in. Located on a peninsula 19km east of Phan Thiết, this small fishing village is, simply, gorgeous. The subject of a thousand postcards, Mũi Né is a tropical paradise. Sparkling and playful waves crash along fine white-sand beaches, all under the gentle shade of swaying coconut palms. Over the past few years, numerous developers have realized this obvious fact and have saturated the area with resorts. The advantage is that almost every accommodation offers private access to the superb and often uncrowded beach. The disadvantage is that Mũi Né lacks a social fabric; the resorts are spread out and closed off from one another, so travelers may find it hard to meet people.

⌐ TRANSPORTATION

Tour buses shuttle visitors in from HCMC, Đà Lạt, and Nha Trang. The nearest local **bus station** is in Phan Thiết, which is accessible by motorbike taxi (20,000-30,000Đ). Most hotels rent out **motorbikes** (US$5 per day) and **bicycles** (US$2 per day) for travel along the peninsula, but you can walk almost everywhere in town.

✳ ORIENTATION

One lone street, **Highway 707** (also called **Nguyễn Đình Chiểu** and **Huỳnh Thúc Kháng,** west and east respectively of the **Fairy Stream Bridge**), runs parallel to the crescent-shaped beach and connects Phan Thiết and Hwy. 1 to Mũi Né village. The north side of the road is lined primarily with restaurants; the south (beach) side has the resorts. Establishments often give their addresses by kilometer number along the highway. The beach on the western side is the nicest one while the one in the center of town tends to be the most battered by winds and surf; it's also quite narrow and steep on account of erosion. The beach on the eastern side is also pleasant, but sometimes the wind carries the ever-pleasant odor of fish and fish sauce here. Budget accommodations and restaurants are concentrated on this end.

⁇ PRACTICAL INFORMATION

Mũi Né is visited by the major nationwide **tour agencies.** Most places can book you tickets from Mũi Né to the surrounding tourist destinations (Đà Lạt, HCMC, and Nha Trang). They also rent out jeeps, motorbikes, and bicycles. **Sinh Cafe,** 144 Nguyễn Đình Chiểu (☎847 542; www.sinhcafevn.com), is located inside the Sinh Cafe Mũi Né Resort. **An Phu Tourist,** 45B Huỳnh Thúc Kháng (☎847 543; www.anphutouristhoian.com) is another popular company. **Hanh Cafe,** Km 14 (☎847 347), has a good restaurant and arranges local exploration. **Vietcombank** has a **24hr. ATM** adjacent to the Saigon Mũi Né Resort (AmEx/MC/V). For currency exchange and MC/V cash advances, try **Incombank,** which has branches at Swiss Village Resort, 44B Nguyễn Đình Chiểu, and Tropico Resort, 73 Nguyễn Đình Chiểu. (Both branches open M-F 7:30am-noon and 1-4:30pm.) Many resorts ask guests not to handwash laundry in their bungalow bathrooms and instead use the **laundry services** that line the town's main street and charge about 15,000Đ per kg. A local **pharmacy** is at 85A Huỳnh Thúc Kháng, across from Canary Resort. There is a small strip mall at 75 Nguyễn Đình Chiểu, across from the Vinh Sương Seaside Resort, with groceries, souvenirs, necessities, a liquor store, laundry service, and film developers. **Internet** access is easy but expensive in Mũi Né; you can pay 5000Đ per hr. at streetside cafes or as much as 12,000Đ per hr. inside resorts. A branch of Phan Thiết's **post office** is at Swiss Village Resort, where stamps, postcards, phone cards, and international calling are available. (☎741 015; fax 741 017. Open daily 8am-8pm.)

ACCOMMODATIONS

Mũi Né is all accommodations. The entire beach is lined with resorts of every shape, size, and smell. No resort ever wants their guests to leave the grounds, so most are outfitted with restaurants, entertainment venues, and sometimes Internet access. Constant construction means the number of rooms is growing rapidly. Budget accommodations are almost as plentiful, and the summer months (June-Sept.) yield discounts of 10 to 30 percent. Don't bother trying to lower the price of your room; few hotel owners in Mũi Né bend to hagglers.

EASTERN BEACH

Hải Gia, 72A Huỳnh Thúc Kháng (☎847 555; haiga_muine@yahoo.com). A cozy resort kept immaculately clean. Spacious rooms, all with attached bath, set into long concrete units with thatched roofs. Opens onto a small, narrow beach. Rooms US$6-10. ❷

Thai Hòa, 56 Huỳnh Thúc Kháng (☎847 320; www.vngold.com/mn/thaihoa). Popular with the youthful backpacker set. Individual bungalows face a large open space, creating a communal atmosphere—a rarity in Mũi Né. Owner speaks superb English. Bungalows with outdoor shower US$5, with private indoor shower US$12. ❶

Canary Resort (☎847 258; www.canaryresort.com), at Km 18. An attractive place with bamboo bungalows, grassy lawn, a friendly owner, and a large open-air restaurant. A great deal, despite the occasional whiff of fish. Bungalows US$15. ❸

CENTRAL BEACH

The Sanctuary Resort (☎847 232; www.asiatravel.com/vietnam), at Km 4. Living up to its name, this isolated resort is set far back from the road and boasts exquisite rooms, set in a large coconut grove facing the sea. Everything is calm and peaceful, including the horses grazing on the grounds. Rooms US$20. ❹

Hồng Di, 70 Nguyễn Đình Chiểu (☎847 014; hdhongdi@yahoo.com). A series of bungalows stretched along the sand. Laid-back vibe, quiet beach, and fast Internet. Bungalows with bath US$10. ❸

Hồng Hà (☎847 327), at Km 16. A small resort with brick bungalows and a family atmosphere. Completely off the tourist map; an ideal escape from other travelers and crowds in general. Bungalows US$5. ❶

Pin Pon, 233 Nguyễn Đình Chiểu (☎847 076), across the street from the beach. Caters to Vietnamese tourists—perfect if you want to escape the backpacker crowds. Spectacular seafood and large, cheap rooms. Rooms with bath US$5-8. ❶

WESTERN BEACH

Keng, 72 Nguyễn Đình Chiểu (☎847 015; songhaisgon@yahoo.com). Friendly, English-speaking owner and helpful staff. Private back patio and accompanying beach are free from heavy tourist traffic. Breakfast included. Bungalows US$8-12. ❷

Small Garden, 48 Nguyễn Đình Chiểu (☎847 012; smallgarden@hcm.vnn.vn). One of the best and cleanest budget resorts, with a perfect beachfront. Isolated bungalows discourage socialization among guests. Rooms US$7; bungalows US$12. ❷

Blue Ocean Resort, 54 Nguyễn Đinh Chiểu (☎847 322; www.blueoceanresort.com). As good as it gets. Gorgeous, expansive grounds and a wide, flat beach. A manufactured tropical paradise. Rooms US$65-110. ❺

◐ FOOD

All the resorts provide their own private restaurants. Outside food options in Mũi Né are scarce, and not necessarily better than what the resorts offer. Along the road near the village, there are many small seafood shacks frequented by locals.

▨ **The Sand Dollar,** 79A Nguyễn Đinh Chiểu (☎847 409; thesanddollar@yahoo.com.vn). This self-proclaimed "Abba-, Kenny G-, Gypsy King-Free Zone" has an attitude all of its own, and a menu to match. Internationally styled and simply delicious main dishes (35,000-55,000Đ) and classic Vietnamese appetizers (20,000-45,000Đ). A pool table helps pass the waiting time; if you lack company or competition, try challenging the ever-eager Hanh. Open daily 9am-late. ❸

▨ **Luna D'Autonno,** 51A Nguyễn Đinh Chiểu. Some of the best Italian food in Vietnam. Italian chef serves superb pizza, pasta, and seafood. Quality jazz played in the background. Sa is salsa night. Dishes 70,000-150,000Đ. Open daily 10am-10pm. MC/V. ❹

Keng, 72 Nguyễn Đinh Chiểu. The roadside restaurant at this resort serves tasty Vietnamese dishes for unusually reasonable prices. The crepes (20,000Đ) are particularly good. Entrees 15,000-30,000Đ. Open daily 7am-11pm. ❷

Xuân Phát, on the beach, next to Mũi Né village, 1km east of the resorts. Carries the freshest, most authentic seafood in town. You will likely be the only tourist there, but the food is worth the stares. Entrees 12,000-40,000Đ. Open daily 7am-10pm. ❷

Trung Duong, on the village end of Coco Beach Resort. Special Vietnamese-style barbecue, which includes fresh meats, veggies, lemon, salt, and a table-top grill. Barbecue 25,000-50,000Đ. Open daily 10am-11pm. ❷

Sàigòn Cafe, Km 18. A backpacker haunt on account of its cheap meat and beer. Low-key atmosphere, plus plenty of pancakes and barbecue. Happy hour daily 6-9pm. Dishes 15,000-50,000Đ. Open daily 7am-midnight. ❷

Xua & Nay (Before & Now), opposite Coco Beach Resort. The offerings at this tiny pizzeria are not too different from the rest, but this place delivers to your door (regular 40,000-70,000Đ; large 62,000-97,000Đ). Open daily noon-midnight. ❷

◉ SIGHTS

The sights around Mũi Né are a testament to what nature can come up with when wind, sand, and sea collide. These phenomena are unparalleled in the rest of Vietnam and are well worth the two to three hours it takes to see all of them. The drive along the Pacific highway is a sight in itself. Most local tour companies offer half-day tours (US$10-15), or you can hire a motorbike to do them on your own (90,000Đ with driver; full-day rental US$5).

▨ **FAIRY SPRING.** A warm, clear stream has created a narrow gorge where the dunes and clay meet jungle palms and brush, exposing a fantastical geological display of reds, pinks, oranges, and whites. Hollywood could not have created a better alien world. Local tour agencies arrange "expeditions" to the spring and the surrounding waterfalls. (*To get there on your own, follow the stream from where it flows underneath the highway. Go along the right bank, past fences and shrubs, and then drop down into the stream itself and walk another kilometer to the source. The water never gets more than a foot deep, but wear sandals or quick-drying shoes. You can usually hire a guide right on the spot.*)

SAND DUNES. The area east of Phan Thiết has a fascinating climate. Besides strong heat and winds, it receives only a fraction of the rainfall that surrounding provinces and the city itself do, creating a unique landscape famous throughout

Vietnam. Just a few kilometers northeast of Mũi Né village are large orange sand dunes, which lie just off the main road. Visitors can climb over the dunes and slide down them on sheets of plastic. They don't cover a very large area, but there's something inspiring about standing atop one and looking out at the ocean. There are bigger, more impressive "white" dunes another 35km down the road, with a mini-oasis and water lily-filled lake in the center. *(To reach the first dunes, head east on Hwy. 1 toward the village. After entering the outskirts of town, take a left at the market immediately after the blue-and-yellow "Chợ" sign. The dunes will be on the left about 5km down the road.)*

HÔNG RUM (RED CANYON). Flowing water and dry red clay come together to form this small but impressive canyon, a sight unlike any other in Vietnam. Visitors can walk through the dried streambed, as the red peaks rise up on both sides. Two paths lead to and through the gorge. To the left, the trail passes a water pump station and proceeds through a briar patch into the center. The path on the right leads higher into the gorge and gives a better view of its topography. *(The canyon is about 3km down the road from the first set of sand dunes. A break in the fence marks the entrance.)*

🎵 ENTERTAINMENT

Entertainment in Mũi Né centers around the water. Several establishments offer a range of water sports, from bodyboarding to windsurfing. While the waves here are not particularly suited to normal surfing, the winds make Mũi Né Vietnam's kitesurfing capital. ◪**Windchimes,** based at Saigon Mũi Né Resort, is highly professional and has skilled, multi-lingual kite surfing instructors. (www.windchimes-vietnam.com. Open daily 8am-6pm.) **Jibe's Beach Club,** 90 Nguyễn Đinh Chiểu, was the first in Mũi Né and is still a reputable place to get your adrenaline rush. (Open daily 8am-7pm.) The staff at **Airwaves,** with branches at the Sea Horse Resort, Sailing Club Resort, and Bon Bien Resort, is a fun and informal bunch. (☎903 308 313; www.airwaveskitesurfing.com. Open daily 8am-6pm.) All offer equipment rental, lessons with experienced instructors, and, of course, a bar. All of these places offer similar services at roughly equivalent prices: windsurf equipment US$12 per hour or US$45 per day; kitesurf equipment US$20/75; surfboard or boogie board US$3/10; kite surfing lessons with equipment US$85.

🎹 NIGHTLIFE

Since most vacationers stay in their resorts, nightlife in Mũi Né is nowhere near as happening as in Nha Trang, Vietnam's other premier beach destination. But that doesn't stop the few local bars from pumping music and flashing lights all night long. If you go out, be aware that in the wee hours you'll be at the mercy of only a few motorbike drivers to get home, and gross overcharging is not unusual.

Hot Rock, across from Small Garden. An Aussie-themed bar that's a rollicking good time. Funky interior is a welcome change from the resorts. Pool table, meaty menu (20,000-50,000Đ), free-flowing taps (beer 30,000Đ), and great music. Open daily 4pm-late.

Jibe's Beach Club, 90 Nguyễn Đinh Chiểu. Relaxed, youthful crowd enjoys the comfy atmosphere, quality music, and seaside views. Come in off the beach, dry off, and have a drink (30,000-50,000Đ). Open daily 10am-late.

Dany's Pub, at Coco Beach Resort. This air-conditioned refuge gives Westerners a welcome break from the heat. With a pool table, dartboards, and widescreen TV, the atmosphere gives ample reason to stay. Beer 25,000-35,000Đ. Hard liquor 35,000-50,000Đ. Guinness 125,000Đ. Open daily 2:30pm-2am.

Gecko Bar & Lounge, 55 Nguyễn Đinh Chiểu. This hotspot keeps things alive with jazz and Latin music. Beer 20,000-30,000Đ. Happy hour 9-10pm. Open daily noon-late.

THE CENTRAL HIGHLANDS

Most foreigners, if they're familiar with the Central Highlands at all, heard about them 35 years ago, when the region saw some of the bloodiest combat in the American War. Today, some veterans return here on remembrance tours, but the region's natural beauty and native cultures—not its battle grounds—are its real attractions. The agricultural production of the region is tremendous, moving well beyond the traditional rice paddies into vast fields of strawberries, artichokes, and flowers. Thanks to the Central Highlands, Vietnam is the world's second largest coffee producer. Many of Vietnam's 54 ethnic minorities make their homes in the Central Highlands: the Banhar, Jarai, and Sodang live around Kon Tum, the Ếdē and M'nong live around Buôn Ma Thuột, and the K'Long dwell outside Đà Lạt. Unfortunately, most (if not all) minority villages are living under a destructive policy of "Vietnamization," which is erasing their unique cultures and keeping them in miserable poverty. Violent uprisings in the region have moved officials to close some villages to tourists for security reasons.

The Central Highlands is one of Vietnam's most fascinating and adventurous regions, and it's at its best in the fields and mountains outside the provincial capitals. As such, cities in the highlands should be used primarily as jumping-off points: Đà Lạt for mountain treks and hilltop pagodas, Buôn Ma Thuột for surging waterfalls and ethnic minority villages, and Kon Tum for ruined war sites. Most other cities in the region are all but devoid of foreigners—tourist buses don't venture past Đà Lạt—so in its fields and small villages, the Central Highlands offers an unobstructed view into the reality of Vietnam: an industrious nation struggling to recover from the past and determined to create a better future.

HIGHLIGHTS OF THE CENTRAL HIGHLANDS

BIKE THROUGH THE HILLS of **Đà Lạt** (p. 345), home to monk artists, Vietnamese cowboys, and an **✦enormous concrete chicken** (p. 357). Yes, this confuses us as much as it does you.

BEFRIEND AN ORNITHOLOGIST in peaceful, luscious **Cát Tiên National Park** (p. 358), one of Vietnam's youngest national parks and a birdwatcher's paradise.

DRIFT UP THE DAKBLA from **Konkoitu** village (p. 372) in a Banhar dugout canoe; from nearby **Kon Tum** (p. 369), daytrips to American War sites like Đắk Tô and Charlie Hill emphasize the region's violent history.

ĐÀ LẠT   ☎ 63

Forget everything you know about Vietnam—Đà Lạt is different. The mountainous city's flourishing artistic community, easygoing atmosphere, and frankly bizarre "Đà Lạt Eiffel" have led to the affectionate nickname "Le Petit Paris." French doctor/adventurer Alexandre Yersin became smitten with the alpine climate and pine forests during an 1892 expedition. Following his suggestion that they build a city, the French displaced ethnic Vietnamese and K'ho people to establish the resort city of Đà Lạt (elevation 1500m) in 1910. Today, the hills are alive with the sounds of tour-

CENTRAL HIGHLANDS

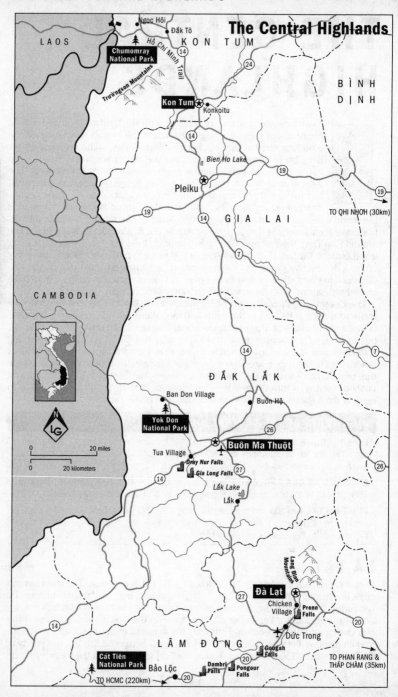

The Central Highlands

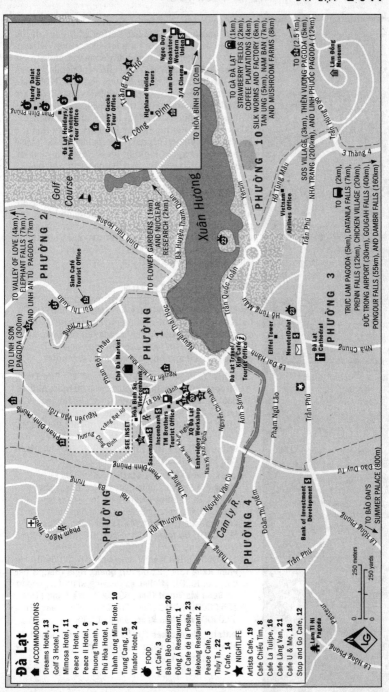

CENTRAL
HIGHLANDS

EASY RIDER EXTRAORDINAIRE

The hills of Đà Lạt are the turf of a loosely knit band of motorcycle guides who call themselves the "Easy Riders." Most of these jovial, well-weathered bikers have left behind typical jobs to persue the lucrative guide business, especially now that they have become a tourist attraction in their own right. Easy Riders are easily identifiable by their Soviet-era Minsk motorbikes and characteristic baseball caps. They'll find you, however, and offer their guide expertise, motorbike, and excellent command of English for the day, charging about US$10. Recently, the most senior member, Chau Thiệt, talked about the birth of this phenomenon at the group's de facto clubhouse, the **Peace Cafe** *(p. 351).*

On the Name: The group is more than 15 years old, having come together in 1991-92, but the name is very new. It was given to us by a travel-writer in 2003. He said "Easy Rider" was the name of an American film about hippies and that it was a good name. Before then, we were just called "Group of Moto-tour."

On the Origin: Before 1992 we were not allowed to take tourists anywhere on motorbikes, but after that changed, some of us started taking them from the local bus station to hotels, just like taxis. Most of us only did this at *[Cont'd on next page...]*

ism. Known as "The City of Flowers" for its abundant flower markets, Đà Lạt has perfected the art of the vacation destination, for both foreigners and Vietnamese. Every other March, the city's market and streets are flooded with colorful collections of petals to celebrate the biannual Đà Lạt Flower Festival. Elaborate potted arrangements, floral sculptures, and floats are crafted in preparation for the festival, and the sounds of music and poetry readings fill the streets. Romantic lakes and a booming flower industry make this the kitschy honeymoon capital of Vietnam; it's also a base for escapist expats looking for a European haven. Travelers looking for the real Vietnam can use the city as a base from which to explore the fascinating agricultural and anthropological sites in the surrounding hills. Đà Lạt has also become the epicenter of adventure- and eco-tourism in southern Vietnam, luring the brave into ravines and onto mountaintops. No matter what you fancy—a taste of Paris, a moutainside hike, or a giant concrete chicken (p. 357)—Đà Lạt and its surroundings have something for you.

◤ TRANSPORTATION

Đà Lạt's local bus industry has been hit hard by the tourist influx and the accompanying private tour bus operations. With only a few roads out of town, most locals and tourists just take the tour buses. Tickets can be booked and buses boarded at any hotel.

Flights: You can reach Đà Lạt by flying into **Đức Trong Airport,** 30km south of the city. The **Vietnam Airlines** booking office is in Hotel Hàng Khôi, 2 Hồ Tùng Mâu (☎833 499; fax 531 720). Though there's some fluctuation in departure times, daily flights via **HCMC** (40min.; 430,000Đ) go to **Đa Nẵng** (90min.; 950,000Đ), **Hà Nội** (3hr; 2,250,000Đ), and **Huế** (2hr.; 1,400,000Đ).

Buses: The public **bus station** (☎822 077) is on 3 Thàng 4, southeast of the city center. Buses start running at 7am; arrive before 8am for longer trips. The best option is to haggle directly with departing drivers. Local buses to: **Buôn Ma Thuột** (5hr.; 3 per day; 60,000Đ); **Đà Nẵng** (15hr.; daily; 105,000Đ); **HCMC** (6hr.; every 2hr.; 50,000Đ); **Huế** (26hr.; daily; 120,000Đ); **Nha Trang** (7hr.; 3 per day; 32,000Đ) via **Phan Rang** (3hr.; 21,000Đ); **Quảng Ngãi** (8hr.; 3 per day; 86,000Đ). **Minibuses,** leaving when full, depart for **Buôn Ma Thuột** (5hr.; 60,000Đ); **Đà Nẵng** (15hr.; 105,000Đ); **HCMC** (6hr.; 50,000Đ); **Nha Trang** (7hr.; 32,000Đ) via **Phan Rang** (3hr.; 21,000Đ).

Rentals: Motorbikes (US$5 per day) and **mountain bicycles** (70,000Đ per day) are easy to rent at any tourist office or hotel.

Train: A train runs from **Ga Đà Lạt Train Station** to **Trai Mát** (30min.; 7:30, 9am, 2, 3:30pm; 70,000Đ), the site of Linh Phước Pagoda (p. 355).

Taxi: Several taxi services are available, including **Anh Dao Taxi** (☎570 570), **Mai Linh Taxi** (☎511 111), and **Thang Loi Taxi** (☎835 583).

✺ ORIENTATION

The capital of Lâm Đồng Province, Đà Lạt is 300km north of HCMC on Hwy. 20. Built on several adjoining mountaintops, the streets twist, turn, rise, and fall, making initial ventures disorienting. The slope rising north out of the west end of Xuân Hương Lake supports the city's center and the central market. To the left of the market, steps lead up to Hoà Bính Sq., dominated by the 3/4 Cinema. **Trương Công Định** heads north from the cinema and turns into **Phan Đình Phùng**, which also runs roughly north-south. Most of Đà Lạt's backpackers stay in this area. Below the square, **Nguyễn Chí Thành** and **Lê Đại Hành** run southward to the lake. The slope facing it from the southeast, marked by the "Đà Lạt Eiffel" and the cathedral, is the location of the post office and high-end accommodations. In this neighborhood, **Trần Phú** runs east-west, from which **3 Thàng 4** runs southeast out of the city.

🛈 PRACTICAL INFORMATION

Tourist Offices: There are 2 kinds of tourist offices in Đà Lạt: those that organize bus tickets and package tours around the city itself, and those that manage more specialized adventure tours and ecotourism (see **Outdoors**, p. 357).

Đà Lạt/Kim Travel, 9 Lê Đại Hành (☎822 479; dltoseco@hcm.vnn.vn), is a government-run agency on the south side of town, with slightly cheaper prices than its main competitor, Sinh Cafe.

Easy Riders (see **"Easy Rider Extraordinaire,"** p. 348) offers exclusive motorcycle tours. Their headquarters are at the Peace Cafe.

Sinh Cafe, 49 Bùi Thị Xuân (☎822 663; sinhcafe2dl@hcm.vnn.vn) offers all typical services.

TM Brothers, 2 Nguyễn Chi Thanh (☎828 383; dalat.tmbrother@yahoo.com), is another HCMC outfit expanding its territory.

Currency Exchange: Incombank, 46 Hoà Bính Sq. (☎824 495; fax 822 827). Traveler's checks cashed, MC/V advances, and an ATM. Open M-Sa 7-11:30am and 1-4:30pm. **Vietcombank,** 6 Nguyễn Thị Minh Khai (☎510 479), up the stairs from the market. 24hr. ATM accepting AmEx/D/MC/V. Open 7:30-11am, 1:30-4:30pm. Other ATMs include: **NovotelDalat,** 12 Trần

night. I used to be a farmer during the day, then drive tourists sometimes until 1am. When the tourists met us they would be very excited because we spoke some English. For some tourists, it was the first English they had heard in weeks, so they wanted us to show them around all day.

On learning English: I learned all of my English in high school in '69-'72. The VAA (Vietnamese-American Association) would come to school and teach us. Some others learned English while in the Army; half of the first group served in the South Vietnamese Army during the War.

On Đà Lạt's Tourism: Đà Lạt has changed so much in the last ten years. Before 1992, people were starving. There wasn't enough food—and there were only 10 government-owned hotels. Then, when the country opened up and life got better, things changed. People don't care about food anymore—they grow flowers! Today, one in 10 of Đà Lạt's farms grows flowers! And the hotels: when Vietnamese had enough food, they started traveling and there wasn't enough room for them here. Many slept in parked buses. And then when foreigners started coming, the government agreed to allow private guesthouses to be built. Now Đà Lạt has over 400 hotels!

Phú (☎825 444); **Bank of Investment and Development,** 30 Trần Phú (☎821 171); **Bank of Commerce and Trade,** 46-48 Khu Hoà Bính (☎833 263). A **Western Union,** 28 Khu Hòa Bính (☎822 308), offers currency exchange and AmEx/MC/V cash advances.

Beyond Tourism: SOS Village, 67 Hùng Vương. Volunteer, mentor, and teach English at a branch of the international SOS orphanage network. The village originally housed the orphaned children of American soldiers and Vietnamese women. When US soldiers left after the American war, many Vietnamese women were left with children, some of whom ended up in the SOS Village. The village is located in a villa-style complex on the south side of the lake, hidden among pines. Volunteers should dress conservatively and arrange for their own food and accommodations. Open daily 7am-5pm.

Emergency: ☎ 115. **Police:** 19 Trần Phú (☎113). **Fire:** ☎114.

Hospital: Provincial General Hospital, 4 Phạm Ngọc Thạch (☎834 158).

Pharmacy: On the square at 34 Khu Hoà Bính (☎822 570). Open daily 7am-10pm.

Internet Access: Small Internet parlors dot the town, offering service at a standard rate of 3000Đ per hr. The fastest option is in the second story of the **Lam Dong Bookstore** at 18-20 Khu Hoà Bính. It features mainly Vietnamese works, but includes some dual-language dictionaries, a complete stationary section, and an all-purpose 2nd fl. with everything from toothbrushes to puzzles to Tupperware. Open daily 7:30am-10:30pm. After the bookstore closes, enter through the propped-open side door. **Việt Hưng,** 7 Nguyễn Chi Thanh, is a true Internet cafe, offering 10min. free if you order drinks and 30min. free if you order food.

Post Office: 16 Trần Phú, under the Đà Lạt Eiffel (☎822 571). Offers fax, Internet, Internet phone, international phone calls, and *Poste Restante.* Open daily 7am-9pm.

ACCOMMODATIONS

Like Vietnam's other tourist meccas, Đà Lạt has plentiful rooms varying widely in price. Almost all accommodations provide mosquito nets and hot water. Some prices vary by season: February, June, and July are high season in Đà Lạt. The following list is not exhaustive; if you aren't satisfied, there are tons of hotels and hostels lining every street. Trương Công Định and Phan Đình Phùng, north of Hoà Bình Sq., form Đà Lạt's backpacker quarter. The area south of the city center—under the shadow of the "Eiffel"—has more upscale offerings.

PHƯỜNG 1

Peace II Hotel (Hoà Bình II), 67 Trương Công Định (☎822 982; peace12@hcm.vnn.vn). A more homey offshoot of its larger, older sibling (see below). Rooms are large, bright, and provide just what you need. Popular with backpackers. High-season rooms US$8-15. Low-season US$5-10. ❷

Dreams Hotel, 151 Phan Đình Phùng (☎833 798; dreams@hcm.vnn.vn). Clean, modern rooms at a low-end price. Its great reputation among travelers keeps the place full. Exceedingly friendly staff and convenient Internet access. Breakfast included. Check-out noon. Reserve in advance. Rooms US$8-15. ❷

Phuong Thanh, 65 Trương Công Định (☎825 097), consistently offers some of the cheapest rooms in town. Central location. Rooms are aged and a little dark, but there's hot water and clean sheets. Basement rooms are slightly cheaper. The lobby offers a full-service local tourist bureau. Friendly family management. Rooms US$4-6. ❶

Thành Long Mini-Hotel, 23 Trương Công Định (☎823 932; lanchidl@yahoo.com). This guesthouse lives up to its inspired motto of "polite, quiet, clean." It's situated near the backpacker quarter but manages to maintain a calm atmosphere. Popular with Vietnamese tourists. Friendly staff. Rooms US$7-13. ❷

Phú Hòa Hotel, 16 Trăng Bat Hổ (☎822 194; fax 007 293). Run by the experienced staff of the Peace Hotels, this large, apartment-style hotel is popular with vacationing Vietnamese. The open-air interior isn't pretty, and the hotel gets a bit noisy, but it suits the budget traveler. Basic amenities available in the lobby. Rooms US$4-10. ❶

Peace I Hotel (Hoà Bình I), 64 Trương Công Định (☎822 982; peace12@hcm.vnn.vn). The venerable granddaddy of Đà Lạt's backpacker accommodation family, this large, central hotel keeps up. The hallways are dark and impersonal and the rooms are unexceptional, but budget travelers still flock here. Cable TV and phones in all rooms. More expensive front rooms have balcony. Same-day laundry US$1 per kg. Check-out noon. High-season rooms US$8-15. Low season US$5-10. ❷

Golf 3 Hotel, 4 Nguyễn Thị Minh Khai (☎826 042; golf3hot@hcm.hdm.vnn.vn). Location, location, location. The most central of Đà Lạt's own Golf Hotel chain, and by far the most popular. Right on the market, Golf 3 trades the seclusion and views of its peers for a ring-side seat in front of the city's action. Standard, plain rooms, but shinier and newer than most other options. Rooms US$30-80. ❺

ELSEWHERE IN ĐÀ LẠT

Mimosa Hotel, 170 Phan Đình Phùng (☎822 656; fax 832 275). Cell-like rooms are truly budget, and they're a bit of a walk from the city center, but they offer satellite TV. Rooms US$5-15. ❶

Vinafor Hotel, 16 Hùng Vương (☎822 417; vinaforhotel@hcm.vnn.vn). For those looking to "get away from it all." Lose yourself in Vietnam naturale. Hidden in a pine forest a few hilltops from the city center, Vinafor's large, wood-paneled rooms and quiet surroundings tempt those weary of Vietnam's urban life. Rooms US$10-16. ❸

Trung Cang, 4A Bùi Thị Xuân (☎822 663; trungcangdl@sinhcafevn.com). One of the newest outposts of Sinh Cafe's empire, Trung Cang is a great combination of quality and price. The staff speaks excellent English, and the rooms are clean and comfortable, with satellite TVs. Internet and tourist office in the lobby. Rooms US$12-20. ❸

🗋 FOOD

As befits a holiday destination, Đà Lạt's restaurants tend to be either pricey, Western-style restaurants or crowded rice-and-phở eateries. Though there is little in between, there are many on either extreme; take a cue from pedestrian traffic as to which are worth a visit. The fruits, vegetables, and fried meats served up on the streets are often more tasty than what you can get in the restaurants. Đà Lạt's most renowned culinary contributions, however, are strawberries and strawberry jam. They are sold throughout the city, but if you have wheels, head to the specialty shops along Phù Đổng Thiên Vương, which heads north from the golf club, to pick up a jar of unrivaled strawberry preserves.

The cheapest eats, as always, are at the food stalls around the market. After dark, the market is lit with vendors selling home-cooked meals and local specialties. A food stall along Trương Công Định, near the bookstore, sells superb pastries for 1000Đ. The main market, ▨ **Chê Đà Lạt,** in the town center, is down the steps from Hoà Bính Sq. Vendors offer hordes of fruits, vegetables, and flowers, all grown in the surrounding hills. (Open daily 4am-1am.) **Ngọc Duy** supermarket, 6 Trăng Bat Hố, next to Phú Hòa Hotel, is a good stop before heading out for daytrips and hikes. (☎822 293. Open daily 7am-10pm.)

▨ **Peace Cafe,** 66 Trương Công Định (☎822 787), next to the Peace I Hotel. The center of Đà Lạt's backpacker scene. It doubles as the Easy Rider clubhouse. Travelers rest their feet, swap stories, and mingle with their motorbike drivers, all to the joy of the exuberant manager and cook, Tú Anh. Front half of the menu features Vietnamese, Western, and vegetarian entrees (10,000-40,000Đ); back half is filled with travel stories in multiple languages. Breakfast 8000-12,000Đ. Cigarettes 8000-17,000Đ. Try the tofu mushroom cheeseburger (20,000Đ). Open daily 6am-10pm. ❶

Bành Bèo, 20A Nguyễn Chi Thành. Past the bank from the Hoà Bính cinema. One of the tastier local eateries, it's named after its specialty: rice cakes with pork rinds, sprinkled with shrimp powder (3000Đ). Always packed. Open daily 6am-6pm. ❶

Le Cafe de la Poste, 12 Trần Phú (☎825 444). Located in the colonial district, this European-style restaurant is one of the best around. Excellent interior decoration and a pleasant patio area do justice to the nearby Đà Lạt Eiffel. Exclusively Western fare. 3-course meal including wild boar and amazing chocolate mousse US$8; bottles of French wine from US$10. Open daily 6am-10pm. ❹

Đông Á Restaurant, 82 Phan Đình Phùng. Foreign and Vietnamese tourists rub elbows at this simple restaurant with quality Vietnamese fare. A selection of wild beasts fills the menu: the more exotic, the higher the price. Chicken 35,000Đ; frog 50,000Đ. Or opt for the rice dishes (10,000-15,000Đ). Open daily 7am-10pm. ❷

Mekong Restaurant, 70A Phan Đình Phùng. Serves "Western and Asian" dishes. This family restaurant offers basic fare but leaves everyone satisfied. Remarkably similar to neighboring Đông Á. Entrees 15,000-50,000Đ. Open daily 7am-10pm. ❷

V Cafe, 1/1 Bùi Thị Xuân (☎837 576). A favorite of Westerners, this casual restaurant has Western food figured out. A friendly staff and detailed English language menu make this a safe and tasty choice. Dishes 25,000-60,000Đ. Open daily 7:30am-11pm. ❷

Thủy Ta, 1 Yersin. Literally on the lake. This bar-restaurant's blue-accented, futuristic design has made it a Đà Lạt landmark; its location has made it a tourist favorite. The food, though, isn't nearly as remarkable as the view. Breakfast 15,000Đ; entrees 25,000-50,000Đ; drinks 20,000-40,000Đ. Open daily 10am-11pm. ❷

Art Cafe, 70 Trương Công Định (☎510 089), right next to Peace Cafe. Exclusively for Westerners, with A/C and corny background music. Immaculate white tablecloths and the patrons' hushed whispers almost make you feel bad about your cargo pants. French soups, sides, and salads (15,000-30,000Đ); Vietnamese entrees (32,000-40,000Đ). Try the steamed fish with coconut sauce (35,000Đ). Open daily 10am-10pm. ❷

⬛ NIGHTLIFE

Due to the grip that French culture still has on the city, Đà Lạt has an abundance of true cafes, as relaxing as any found in Paris. And with a booming coffee industry in the Central Highlands, an evening in a cafe is a must while in the City of Flowers. The stretch of Nguyễn Chí Thành, south of Khu Hoà Bính and before the road turns sharply westward, is lined with cafes. Come nightfall, the cafes turn into spirited bars, with live music and karaoke emanating into the street.

▨ Stop and Go Cafe, 2 Lý Tự Trong. Be welcomed to coffee (6000Đ) and cake (4000Đ) by aging Vietnamese poet and calligrapher Duy Việt. Scrolls of poetry (US$2) and self-portraits line the rooms, books of verse (US$1) in English, French, and Vietnamese are scattered among the tables, and a few guitars lean upon the walls. Add poems of your own to the well-worn guestbook (now in its 4th volume), and leave with a full stomach and a freshly plucked flower in hand. See **Artist Community,** p. 356.

Artista Cafe, 9 Nguyễn Chí Thành (☎821 749). Another cafe around Hòa Bình Square with nice decor and a great view of the market. Popular place for locals to meet up with friends. Menu includes mint and lotus teas (8000Đ), toasted sandwiches (12,000-15,000Đ), and spiked coffee drinks (14,000-25,000Đ). Try the special apple cake a la mode (18,000Đ). Open daily 7am-11pm.

Cafe U & Me, 14 Nguyễn Chí Thành (☎831 876). Swanky cafe and bar with a menu to match. Full separate drink menu with milkshakes (13,000Đ), beer (12,000-42,000Đ), mixed drinks (30,000-45,000Đ) and Đà Lạt red wine (70,000Đ). Also features specialty pizzas (29,000-32,000Đ). Open daily 7am-11pm. V.

Cafe Chiều Tím, 18 Trăng Bat Hồ (☎821 776). This is where the locals go for their coffee. The faux-leather couches lining the walls are constantly filled with local motorbike types. Coffee (3000Đ); hot chocolate (5000Đ); artichoke tea (2500Đ). Best iced milk coffee in town (3500Đ). Open daily 7am-11pm.

Cafe La Tulipe (☎831 876), at the intersection of Nguyễn Chí Thành and Khu Hòa Bình. Busy with locals and tourists alike, this centrally located cafe sports a peaceful morning atmosphere with outdoor seating and roof-top seating that overlooks the marketplace. Try their dark roast coffee, excellent but overpriced at 10,000Đ. Also serves lunch and dinner, with an exhaustive meat menu that includes rabbit (35,000-40,000Đ), pigeon (25,000Đ), and eel (45,000Đ). Open daily 7am-11pm.

Cafe Làng Van, 40 Nguyễn Chí Thành (☎511 021). Plush red-and-white chairs huddled around dark wooden tables make this a comfortable cafe. Inset sculptures and paintings on the walls provide sufficient eye candy to pass the time with imported French wines (35,000Đ) or sweet ice cream with rum (18,000Đ). Open daily 6am-midnight.

◴ SIGHTS

Đà Lạt's attractions have gained notoriety around the nation and abroad, fueling the city's reputation as the premier resort in Vietnam. Đà Lạt's more interesting sights are scattered around the surrounding hills, and are most conveniently accessed by motorbike, though some more rugged souls choose a mountain bike.

Near the city center are traditional, unexciting sights popular with Vietnamese tourists. Farther into the hills are waterfalls and secluded pagodas. Some backpackers venture even farther with an adventure tourism outfit. Incongruously located among it all is a unique artist community. No matter what you choose to do, Đà Lạt has enough to keep you occupied for at least a few days.

All of the rural and agricultural sights are free of charge, and tourable at the pleasure of the owners and farmers. Pagodas are similarly open to all. Select museums and tourist sites charge entrance fees. Steer clear of the heavily guarded nuclear research center.

ON THE MENU

OF HEARTS AND RINDS

Đà Lạt is widely known for its flowers and strawberries, but the town is quietly growing a new and wilder crop to liven up its menus: *Cynara scolymus*, the all-powerful artichoke. First cultivated in the Central Highlands by the French at the turn of the 20th century, the vegetable is known to have a variety of uses, from simple table vegetable to working medicinal charm, treating everything from liver inflammation to insomnia.

Artichoke stems, leaves, roots, and flowers are each valuable in their own right: the roots are chopped into small pieces, dried, and made into a sweet-tasting drink for the hot summer months, while the bitter leaves are used to treat fevers. The plants produce optimum yield at 10-20°C, and are thus well complemented by Đà Lạt's year-round, temperate alpine climate.

The new vegetable is taking the town by storm. Visitors can spot artichoke fields in the highlands surrounding Đà Lạt by the large violet-colored flowers that appear at the ends of the 1m high plants. Many cafes and restaurants in the city serve various concoctions using the vegetable, including tea, ice cream, and even pancakes. A local specialty is the elaborately prepared artichoke hearts with stewed pig's leg.

Đà Lạt, City of Flowers...and Artichokes.

IN ĐÀ LẠT

XUÂN HƯƠNG LAKE. This man-made lake is the first thing you see in Đà Lạt. The city is built on the slopes rising from its shores, which curve eastward from the city center. Around it are swan-shaped paddle boats, opportunities to ride a horse with the famous and wonderfully kitschy "Đà Lạt Cowboys," and a couple of bar-restaurants on the lake shore. Though the waters are calm, the traffic around the lake isn't. Still, the 7km sealed path around it makes for a pleasant stroll.

FLOWER GARDENS. "The City of Flowers" takes its nickname seriously, and these gardens are the proof. The gardens should be accompanied by visits to the flower groves in the surrounding hills to get a true sense of the region's diversity. The orchid house at the back of the grounds is the highlight; make sure to look up, as the most exquisite specimens are hanging from the roof. These gardens are definitely worth a quick stroll. *(Located at the intersection of Bà Huyện Thành Quan and Phù Đổng Thiên Vương, at the eastern end of the lake. Open daily 7am-6pm. 4000Đ.)*

XQ ĐÀ LẠT EMBROIDERY WORKSHOP (DIỂM THAM QUAN). Part craftshop and part art gallery, the XQ Workshop is, in a word, awesome. At first glance, the framed artwork spilling from the walls rivals anything else in Vietnam—and its impact only increases when you realize that it's all embroidery. The staff of the shop will be happy to provide a free tour, showing you ready-to-buy pieces (US$50-200) on the first and third floors. The second floor houses the actual workshop. XQ employs 250 women but only 20 work at a time. The chosen few must go through a selection process and then a six-year training course before they put needle to silk. The second floor also has a small exhibit showing how the intricate patterns are made. An excellent site for both the art-lover and the shopper. *(56-58 Hoà Bính. ☎ 830 042; www.xqhandembroidery.com. Open daily 7am-5pm.)*

ĐÀ LẠT CATHEDRAL (NHÀ THỜ CHÍNH TÒA ĐÀ LẠT). On Trần Phú near the Eiffel, Đà Lạt Cathedral holds its own against its European cousins. The French Romanesque style and salmon color give the cathedral a unique appearance. A giant cross is carved into the front tower, and inside, an intricate series of stained-glass windows will entrance even non-believers. A refreshing departure from the usual squat concrete churches of contemporary Vietnam. *(M-Sa mass at 5:15am and 5:15pm; Su mass 5:15, 7, 8:30am, 4, 6pm.)*

BẢO ĐẠI'S SUMMER PALACE. Built in 1933, the palace was the Emperor Bảo Đại's midsummer retreat. It's been well-maintained and looks much like it did in the 1930s, resplendent in art deco magnificence. However, it's sparsely furnished, and a grand golden bust of the emperor and a glass map of Vietnam are the only artifacts of note. *(Up Lê Hồng Phong. Open daily 7-11am and 1:30-4pm. 7000Đ.)*

NEAR ĐÀ LẠT

◼ **SILK WORMS AND FACTORY.** It takes a village to make a silk pajama shirt. Actually, three villages. First, near the coffee plantations are fields of large green mobary leaves, the primary feed of silk worms. The worms are kept in huts alongside the fields and can be observed by visitors. After a one-month period of feeding, the worms are sent to Nam Ban ("bamboo village") to lie on bamboo racks assembled by the villagers. The worms' cocoons are then sent to the local silk factory, the **Cường Hoan Traditional Silk Centre** (☎ 852 338), 6km northeast of Đà Lạt on Hwy. 9. The factory is a truly bewildering and amazing place, where visitors can watch silk thread being extracted from the cocoons, dried, spooled, and then woven into florally patterned cloth. One silk worm's cocoon turns into 500m of silk thread. Not surprisingly, the Vietnamese consider the remaining silk worm larvae a culinary specialty.

PAGODAS. ▨**Linh Phưởc Pagoda** is a bustling, colorful building in the nearby village of Trai Mát. Newly renovated, the ancient pagoda is the site of nationwide pilgrimages, and the intricate beauty of the building only begins to explain why. Inside the main building sits a giant gold Buddha under a massive molded bodhi tree. Visitors can climb the tower of the main building for a stunning view or climb the tower of the smaller building to see the 8400kg bell. Between the two buildings lies a sculpture garden exhibiting a phantasmagorical ▨**dragon** made of more than 20,000 bottles of beer. The pagoda can be reached by train from Đà Lạt. *(Train station: 1 Nguyễn Trãi, east of the lake. 30min.; 7:30, 9am, 2, 3:30pm; 70,000Đ. Or drive the 8km east to 120 Tư Phưởc Pagoda. Open daily 6am-7pm.)* The hills around Đà Lạt are sown with beautiful and peaceful pagodas, but after a while, they all begin to blend together. There are a few truly remarkable ones, including **Trưc Lam Pagoda,** one of Đà Lạt's newer pagodas. Locals boast of this recently built pagoda as the most beautiful in south Vietnam, but by "beautiful" they mean new, clean, and large. Trưc Lam lacks character, but it remains noteworthy as a renowned Zen meditation center. How the monks can meditate with the noisy influx of tourists remains a mystery. *(5km south of Đà Lạt, down 3 Thàng 4.)* Down the hill sits **Tuyền Lam Lake** and small hamlets selling crafts, drinks, and boat rides. *(2km from Hwy. 20, 5km south of town. Follow the signs. Also accessible by cable car from the bus station nearly 2km away; 30,000Đ one-way, 50,000Đ round-trip.)* **Thiên Vưởng Pagoda** (Chinese Pagoda), built by Đà Lạt's Chinese community in 1958, sits on a lonely pine-covered hilltop. The main pagoda holds three large, gold-painted wooden statues brought from China and thought to date from the 16th century, representing power, infinite light, and mercy. Behind the pagoda is a large statue of Buddha. *(5km southeast of town on Khe Sanh.)* **Linh Sơn Pagoda** is Đà Lạt's oldest and most centrally located pagoda. Built nearly a century ago, the pagoda served as a hiding place for Việt Cộng guerrillas during the American War. Inside the central sanctum is a uniquely human Tích Ca (Gautama Buddha). The gardens and grounds feature sculptures and depictions from Buddha's life. Vien Nhu, an elder monk at the pagoda, speaks good English and is happy to explain Mahayana Buddhism's basic tenets. *(On Nguyễn Văn Trỗi, 1km north of the city center.)* **Linh An Tư,** Đà Lạt's newest pagoda, sits next to Elephant Falls, northeast of the city. Built in 2002, the pagoda bears marks of both Hindu symbolism (the swastika) and Chinese symbolism (dragons), emphasizing Vietnam's mixed influences.

WATERFALLS. The mountainous terrain of Đà Lạt provides quality waterfall exploration, even though the majority of them have been fenced off and turned into pseudo-amusement parks. The closest to town is the **Datanla Falls.** At the bottom of a steep climb through lush forest, the falls spray mist over anyone in the proximity. Although not very high, they are the strongest in the region. After the steady climb back out, stop at the restaurant (drinks 10,000Đ, rice dishes 25,000Đ) to re-energize over a drink and a spectacular view. *(5km south of town off Hwy. 20; look for the sign. Open daily 7am-5pm. 5000Đ.)* **Prenn Falls** is beloved by Vietnamese tourists. Above the falls are a gaggle of mock thatched-roof huts selling a variety of drinks, but the real action is below the falls. You can descend by stairs or mini-cable car and, once below the falls, paddle around the lagoon or visit the crocodile pond. The falls themselves are quite a sight as they tumble over a large outcrop—it's even possible to walk underneath them. The really worthwhile attraction here, though, is a walk to the top of the hill for a view of the surrounding countryside. *(10km south of town off Hwy. 20. Open daily 7am-5pm. 8000Đ.)* The area south of Đà Lạt also has many spectacular waterfalls, formed as the highlands flatten into the Mekong Delta. These are easily accessible from Hwy. 20, yet are refreshingly free of visitors. In the dry season, their full force is not apparent. **Gougah Falls,** 40km south, can be seen from the highway; **Pongour Falls,** 55km south, are massive and amenable to peripheral trekking; and **Dambri Falls,** the best and highest, are about 20km north of Bảo Lộc. North of town, off of Hwy. 9, are the **Elephant Falls.** Though the former elephant inhabitants migrated north after military disturbances in 1971, the waterfall is still enjoyable, especially with the metal footbridges and slippery rock steps that lead visitors delightfully close to the waterfall's base.

STRAWBERRY FIELDS. Northeast of the city, between Phù Đổng Tiên Vương and Phan Chu Trinh, are vast expanses of terraced fields. The rich soil of these fields produce a multitude of vegetables—carrots, onions, cauliflower, potatoes, and others—famous across the country, as well as Đà Lạt's gastronomic specialty, strawberries. Strawberries here are harvested four to five times a year, so with some luck you might see them in full bloom. Vast fields of flowers, protected from the wind by outdoor greenhouses, checker the vegetable fields. The big Danish flower-farm is closed to the public, but smaller, privately managed Vietnamese farms are usually hospitable and will offer a tour if they're not busy.

COFFEE PLANTATIONS. Past the fruit fields along Hwy. 9 are the coffee plantations of Tan Ung. The coffee plants reach heights of five to six feet tall, and feature small haphazard flops of white flowers. During maturation, clusters of small berry-like globes appear, hanging off the limbs of the bush, and ripen from green to deep crimson. At this point, the bean is hand-plucked and sent to factories nearby.

ARTIST COMMUNITY. The Đà Lạt Artist Community is as famous as it is expansive, awash in relaxed, enlightened attitude and crisp invigorating mountain air. The scene here is dominated by three very different—and very eccentric—titans. Fortunately, all are welcoming to tourists, but all too have been swamped by visitors, gradually making the experience of meeting them less personal. **Stop and Go Cafe** (p. 352), hidden down a windy street, is a must-see on the artist circuit. Squirreled away among flowers, greenhouses, and pine trees, and located in the living room of local poet, painter, and ex-mayor Duy Việt, this is one of the rare urban hideaways in the country. Speaking English or French, and sporting his signature beret, Duy Việt will show you his work while serving up excellent home-made cakes; you are also free to explore his greenhouse. Duy Việt has hosted a multitude of visitors, including John F. Kennedy, Jr., and he remains sincere and welcoming. Once you get settled in, it's hard to leave. *(Follow the unmarked Lý Tự Trong from the intersection of Bùi Thị Xuân and Phan Bội Châu to the end. The cafe is on the right at 2 Lý Tự Trong.)* **Lam Ti Ni Pagoda** is an old, incomplete building where the famous "crazy monk" Viên Thức is holed up. Exceedingly friendly and enjoyable, the prolific painter, poet, and musician has turned this pagoda into his studio, gallery, and home, situated among shanties and dirt roads. Show yourself through the gate and unkept garden to the sealed doors. A knock will bring Viên Thức to the door. He will happily show (and sell for US$10-50) his work, and he'll talk about himself in fluent English, French, or Thai. Unfortunately, waves of visitors have turned this more into an attraction than an authentic experience, but it still remains unlike anything else in the country. *(2 Thiện My.)* **Hang Nga Guesthouse,** called the "The Crazy House" by locals and tourists alike, is comprised of a squat building and two towers molded to form a giant treehouse. Each of the 10 rooms is designed with an animal motif—the Ant Room rivals all. Imagine Gaudí gone wild. The artist who gave birth to this craziness is Dang Việt Nga, an architect trained in Moscow who also happens to be the daughter of Vietnam's second president (Trương Chinh, successor to Hồ Chí Minh). A small art gallery near the exit sells bamboo paintings for US$40-60. *(3 Huỳnh Trúc Kháng. Open daily 7am-5pm. 7000Đ.)*

CHICKEN VILLAGE. This K'ho village outside of Đà Lạt is widely known by its nickname, which comes (predictably) from the **two-story concrete chicken** in the center of the village. The legend—or at least a variation of it—begins with a young couple in love who wanted to marry. The boy's family did not approve of his fiancée, so, in an effort to derail the marriage, they demanded that the girl present a chicken with nine spurs on the back of its legs. The girl searched throughout the village unsuccessfully and, just as she was going to lose all hope, she heard a rumor that such a chicken lived on the nearby mountain. She left for the mountain and never returned. Stricken with grief, the villagers built the monument in her memory. Why it's a chicken, and not a woman, baffles us to this day. The K'ho village is a rarity among the ethnic minority villages of the Central Highlands—they do not live in crushing poverty, keep a clean village, and are quite comfortable with visitors. The center of the village is dominated by cloth shops, but for a more low-key view of the village lifestyle, walk through the quieter south side. *(Located 18km south of Đà Lạt off Hwy. 20, in the shadow of Elephant Mountain.)*

MUSHROOM FARMS. Nam Ban is also home to several mushroom farms. Mushroom harvesting, surprisingly enough, makes for a fascinating sight—unwieldy white fungus sprouts from plastic bags packed with sawdust, dirt, and tapioca. The result is moist, dark warehouses filled with rows upon rows of mushroom columns hanging from the ceiling. It's a fun stop when coupled with the Silk Factory.

◪ OUTDOORS

Đà Lạt's rugged environs make it the adventure tourism and ecotourism capital of Vietnam. Fueled by backpacker dollars—and an increasing number of young Vietnamese—the industry is quickly dominating the city. There are a number of companies to choose from, but they offer the same basic services and tours for nearly the same price. Common activities include rock climbing, trekking, overnight camping, and mountain biking. The best area to hike or mountain bike is **Lang Bien Mountain** (2169m). Going with a guide keeps things interesting, as there is much flora and local lore to discover; just make sure you aren't talked into being driven to the summit. Below are some of the specialty outdoors tourist offices, but all bureaus can handle excursions, so shop around:

Groovy Gecko Tour, 65 Trương Công Định (☎836 521; ggtour@yahoo.com). This small operation offers all the

THE LOCAL STORY

WHERE THE ART IS

Poet and calligrapher Duy Việt's unassuming demeanor carefully conceals the international recognition his art has received. Featured in international journals and travel magazines, Việt and his multilingual work (in English, French, and Vietnamese) evoke simple messages of love, dynamism, and optimism. At the age of 65, the former city deputy spends his days tending to his backyard and welcoming guests into his home, the artistic haven that is **Stop & Go Cafe** *(p. 352).*

LG: How did you start doing art?
A: When I was a young man, I brought a small poem to woo my girlfriend. She said, "Very good!" and so I continued. If you are in love, this is what happens.
LG: How did you come about opening this cafe?
A: Before, I was a journalist in the [American] war—a captain in the South Vietnamese army. After the war, I started planting some orchids and selling some flowers, and eventually it grew into this cafe.
LG: Why do you like self-portraits so much?
A: Because life is not permanent. We change a lot. We change day by day. Sometimes our hair is short, sometimes it's long. The world changes a lot, but through it all, the heart never changes.

usual services, including multi-day trips into the highlands and local city tours. Daytrips US$13-16; longer trekking tours US$40 per day; biking tours US$60 per day. Open daily 7:30am-8:30pm.

Đà Lạt Holidays/Phat Tire Ventures, 73 Trương Công Định (☎829 422; www.phat-tireventures.com). American company Phat Tire teamed up with local Đà Lạt Holidays in 1996 to establish the most reputable operation in the area. For the hard-core, they also offer canyoning trips (US$22-28). Trekking daytrips US$16-42; rockclimbing daytrips US$28; 1-2 day mountainbiking trips US$30-135. Open daily 7:30am-8:30pm.

Hardy Dalat, 22B Nguyễn An Ninh (☎836 840; www.hardyadventuretours.com). Another experienced institution in Đà Lạt, Hardy Dalat also offers long excursions into the Central Highlands by army jeep and down to Mũi Né by bike. Most daytrips are under US$20. Open daily 7:30am-8pm.

Highland Holiday Tours, 47 Trương Công Định (☎832 221; hhtours@yahoo.com). New to the business, this tour service is humble and accommodating, offering 2-5 day treks, mountain biking, and elephant-riding excursions. Standard rate $35 per person per day, not including food and accommodations. Open daily 7:30am-8:30pm.

CÁT TIÊN NATIONAL PARK ☎ 61

Easily reachable from HCMC or Dà Lạt, Cát Tiên National Park *(Vườn Quốc Gia Cát Tiên)* offers the traveler a haven from the noisy, overtouristed coast. It also provides a glance into Vietnam's young national park system and its growing efforts at environmental conservation. Cát Tiên boasts a stunning array of flora and fauna, but the average visitor will need patience and persistence to see this side of the park. Songbirds and park rangers keep each other company during the day while geckos and tropical constellations lull you to sleep at night. Though you probably won't see a the extremely endangered Javan rhinoceros, biologists—lured by the endangered animal—abound. Nightlife consists of passing the evening hours at the riverside canteen, listening to the stories of international biologists—a fate sometimes more enjoyable than partying at a big-city disco.

In 2001, UNESCO designated the park for inclusion in the World Network of Biosphere Reserves. The low-latitude tropical rainforests and jungle contain over 1300 species of vascular plants, 435 species of butterflies, 314 species of birds, and a slew of mammals, reptiles, amphibians, and fresh-water fish. Besides goofy-looking rhinos, the park is also home to one of the few remaining populations of Siamese crocodiles, which became extinct in the park in 1996 and were re-introduced in 2001. The park's 58 endangered species also include the orange-necked partridge, the white-winged duck, and the white-shouldered ibis.

CÁT TIÊN AT A GLANCE

AREA: 739 sq. km.

CLIMATE: Moderate to wet, with an annual temperature range of 15-35°C.

FEATURES: Jungle, steep hills, and lake plains. Endangered species abound but are generally inaccessible to casual visitors.

HIGHLIGHTS: Crocodile Swamp and Heaven Rapids; chatting with local and visiting biologists is also a treat.

GATEWAYS: Buses run from HCMC and Đà Lạt. Park offers outgoing transport for a fee.

CAMPING: Ask at the reception building for sites (15,000Đ); rooms at the park headquarters also available for rent (120,000-180,000Đ).

FEES AND RESERVATIONS: Entrance fee 50,000Đ. Accompaniment by a park ranger recommended (60,000-100,000Đ per half-day).

TRANSPORTATION. Cát Tiên is located 125km north of HCMC and 175km southwest of Đà Lạt and lies 24km off National Hwy. 20. From HCMC, take a **bus** directly to Nam Cát Tiên from Miền Đông Station (4hr.; 8am and frequently thereafter; 30,000Đ). Upon arrival, take a right out of the village bus station and walk down the road. The second building on your right is the entrance office. Two minutes more bring you to the ferry departure point.

Alternatively, take a **tourist bus** to Đà Lạt (from any tour office; 4hr.; 7:30, 8:30am; 77,000Đ). Tell the driver that you are going to Cát Tiên and ask to be let off at Ma Đu Guí Junction. If you're coming from Đà Lạt, use the same procedure in reverse; take an HCMC-bound bus (public or open-tour) and ask to be let off at the junction. From there, hire a motorbike to take you the remaining 24km (40min.; 20,000-50,000Đ) to the entrance office and ferry departure point.

The easiest, most comfortable option is to take a tourist bus directly to the park. **Sinhbalo Adventures,** 283 Phạm Ngũ Lão, HCMC (☎ 8 837 6766; www.sinhbalo.com), arranges private tours to the park; contact them early, as tours fill up quickly.

ORIENTATION AND PRACTICAL INFORMATION. Foreign visitors must purchase a park entrance ticket at the brown wooden entrance office to Cát Tiên. (50,000Đ, children under 15 admission 20,000Đ. Open daily 7am-7pm.) The ferry ride is included in the cost of the ticket. Across the Đong Nai river is **Park Headquarters,** also called "The Center for Eco-tourism and Environmental Education." (☎ 669 228; fax 669 159. Open daily 7am-10pm.) Walk up the path from the ferry landing point and take a left; it's the first large building on the left. A public **telephone** and a **pharmacy** are available; take a left out of Park Headquarters, and they will be down the path on your right, across from the Guesthouse (both open 7am-7pm). While some gear can be rented from Park Headquarters (leech socks 3000Đ per day; forest shoes 5000Đ per day; electricity generator 30,000Đ per hr.), there is no comprehensive store with amenities and hiking gear, so be sure to pack all necessities beforehand. Film (145,000Đ) and camera batteries (55,000Đ) are sold at the new canteen. A park curfew begins at 10pm.

WHEN TO GO. Located in the lowlands monsoon region of Vietnam, just north of HCMC, Cát Tiên receives a fair amount of rainfall (2300mm per year), though not nearly as much as its northern park neighbor Bạch Mã. The rainy season lasts from Apr.-May and Oct.-Nov., with the dry season falling in Nov.-Dec. and Mar.-Apr. It's best to come to the park during the dry season, as the central floodplains and the northern plains tend to flood during the wet season, due to poor drainage. Average temperatures range from 15° to 35°C, and the 80% average humidity will keep you sweating whatever time of year you choose to come. If you plan on hiking (which you should), be sure to have an extra shirt or two in addition to the raingear you'll undoubtedly need.

ACCOMMODATIONS AND FOOD. Staying in Cát Tiên is easy. The park has large but impersonal **rooms for rent ❷** with private baths and mosquito nets. (Doubles and triples with fan 120,000Đ, with A/C 140,000-180,000Đ.) There are also colorful **villas ❸**, complete with kitchen, mini-fridge, and separate dining and living rooms. (600,000Đ; single floors 200,000-300,000Đ.) Private wooden **huts ❶** are also available, though they're bare and basic. (Doubles with fan 90,000Đ.) All accomodations can be rented at Park Headquarters. Check-out is at noon. Large parties should make reservations. **Camping sites ❶** are also available (15,000Đ per day), and the truly adventurous can spend a night in the Crocodile Swamp (see below). There is a small building you can sleep in at the edge of the swamp for the same rate as the rooms above, but it requires advanced booking; call Park Headquarters (☎ 669 228).

There are two canteens at the main compound. Giant geckos join visitors at the thatched-roof **old canteen ❶,** to the right of Park Headquarters, where they serve decent breakfast and late-night beers. (Entrees 10,000-20,000Đ; beer 12,000Đ. Open 7am-late.) Lunch and dinner are served at the newer, bigger, more sterile **new canteen ❷.** Take a left out of Park Headquarters and walk down the path; it will be on your left. (Fruits and omelets 8000-12,000Đ; entrees 10,000-40,000Đ; specialty meats, such as fried eel, kidney, or squid 50,000-100,000Đ. Open daily 7am-10pm.)

 SIGHTS AND ENTERTAINMENT. The government recommends that all hiking be done with a guide (60,000-100,000Đ per half-day). If you do venture out on your own, inform the staff at Park Headquarters of your departure time, destination, and when you plan to report back. Visitors can rent pickup trucks (120,000Đ per hr.), engine boats (300,000Đ per hr.), high-speed boats (500,000Đ per hr.), or bicycles (10,000Đ per hr., 35,000Đ per half-day, 60,000Đ per day; must return by 6pm) to tour the park. Individual site visits and tours may incur additional charge; rates vary depending on time of day and length of trip. Contact park staff in advance to arrange custom tours.

Near Park Headquarters are trails that lead you among an impressive variety of flora, ranging from mango trees to trees with eight-foot-tall roots. Also nearby are the **Heaven Rapids,** a relaxing place to sunbathe, though not very striking in the dry season. But to have any chance of seeing large animals, you must either push deeper into the forest or head to the **Crocodile Swamp,** where you can rent a paddle boat (15,000-25,000Đ per hr.) with or without a driver. Taking a **nightspotting** trip (155,000Đ) through the park might improve your chances of seeing wildlife, and the drive through the jungle under the stars is well worth the price. Volcanic landforms also abound in and near the park. Cinder cones, lava rocks, and volcanic ash can be found at Ben Cu forest guard station and at the Mo Vet rapids.

> **TIP** **HOW TO RUN FROM A CROCODILE.** Crocodiles can move at surprising speeds—often quick enough to catch up to a human. Their velocity, however, is hindered by their lack of agility. The best way to outrun a crocodile is to run away in a zig-zag pattern, which the wily reptiles find difficult to match.

Be sure to apply lots of insect repellent. Also be sure to pack rain gear at all times, as storms can appear suddenly. During a storm, it is best to get shelter and head to the nearest guard station or back to Headquarters if possible.

Across from the new canteen is a small entertainment center, with table tennis, billiards, and karaoke. Farther down the path is a swimming pool and tennis, soccer, and volleyball courts. Visitors can also buy T-shirts (20,000Đ) and woven bags (15,000-30,000Đ) at the souvenir shop inside the new canteen.

ĐẮK LẮK PROVINCE

Đắk Lắk province has two things in abundance: minority villages and coffee. Vietnam is home to 54 different ethnic groups, despite the government's harsh efforts at assimilation; 46 of these groups live in Đắk Lắk province. The largest are the Êđê and the M'nong, which number in the thousands in the area surrounding Buôn Ma Thuột. Traditionally, the Êđê built their thatched-roof, longhouse-style homes from wooden planks. To see these traditional longhouses, you must visit one of the villages open to tourists. The M'nong, closely related to the Malay, traditionally live in homes on stilts. Legend explains such architecture: originally the M'nong were a seafaring people, and they build their homes to look like the boats of their ancestors. Today the M'nong are famed as elephant handlers.

To visit these ethnic groups, one can arrange a group tour through the government-owned Daklak Tourist (☎852 108) or hire out a motorbike driver who knows the villages. There are a few villages set up to host tourists 20-40km south of Buôn Ma Thuột along Hwy. 14 and some near Lắk Lake (see Daytrips, p. 365). Villagers are generally welcoming and as curious about you as you are about them. Both the Êđê and the M'nong are Christian tribes, and a drive along Hwy. 14 passes several roadside churches and Christian cemeteries.

A drive on any of the roads leaving Buôn Ma Thuột also takes you through coffee country. The landscape is blanketed by coffee bushes, grown both on large plantations and on smaller, private farmland. There are a few ways to see the early stages of the booming Vietnamese coffee industry. The most expensive way is to take an arranged guided tour. A better experience is to hire a *xe ôm* driver who personally knows coffee growers. But the cheapest and most convenient way is simply to take a ride through the country, checking out the coffee beans being sorted and dried on the road. Locally grown coffee can be bought wholesale in the Buôn Ma Thuột market or sampled at one of the city's ubiquitous cafes. Vietnam is the second largest coffee exporter in the world. Đắk Lắk is the reason why.

BUÔN MA THUỘT ☎50

The capital of the Đắk Lắk region was developed in 1899 by the French colonial *Compagnie d'Agriculture d'Asie* for the production of coffee and rubber, which grow well in the fertile red soil. On March 10, 1975, the NLF swept through the region, signaling the beginning of the end for the South Vietnamese forces. Today in Buôn Ma Thuột (BMT; elevation 1100m), rubber is still stripped, coffee is still grown, and the first tank to arrive on "Liberation Day" still sits at the town center. Around this imposing monument, Buôn Ma Thuột has grown into a bustling provincial capital, specializing in the coffee trade. The city itself is simple and welcoming, but it has little to offer tourists except fresh wholesale coffee at bargain prices. Its location, however, serves as a convenient home base for trips to nearby waterfalls, minority villages, and Yok Don National Park.

▢ TRANSPORTATION

There is a small airport in Buôn Ma Thuột that flies to two other cities in Vietnam. Flights can be very crowded, so you'll need to reserve your seat. Public buses and their cheaper alternative, minibuses, run frequently from the station a few kilometers northwest of the city center. An excellent way to tour the area surrounding BMT is to hire a motorbike driver who doubles as a guide.

Flights: **Buôn Ma Thuột Airport** (☎862 248), 13km northeast of town via Hwy. 14. **Vietnam Airlines Booking Office,** 17-19 Nơ Trang Long (☎954 442; open daily 8am-6pm), at Lý Thường Kiệt. Flights go to **Đà Nẵng** (noon; 520,000Đ) and **HCMC** (3:55pm; an additional flight at 8:10pm Tu, F, and Su; 420,000Đ). Book flights early.

Buses: **Buôn Ma Thuột Station,** 71 Nguyễn Tất Thàn (☎852 603), 3km northeast of the city center. Regular buses go to: **Đà Lạt** (5hr.; 6am; 60,000Đ); **Đà Nẵng** (19hr.; 11am, noon, 8pm; 80,000Đ); **HCMC** (9hr.; every 2hr.; 100,000Đ); **Huế** (25hr.; 6am; 70,000Đ); **Kon Tum** (7hr.; 6am; 40,000Đ); **Nha Trang** (5hr.; 6am; 30,000Đ); **Pleiku** (4hr.; 6am; 30,000Đ); **Quảng Ngãi** (16hr.; 6am; 50,000Đ); **Qui Nho'n** (11hr.; 6am; 50,000Đ). Travel time varies depending on the weather. Minibuses leave throughout the day to all of the above destinations for 10,000-20,000Đ cheaper; negotiate prices with the driver when you get on and expect a cramped ride. The roads in and out of the

CENTRAL HIGHLANDS

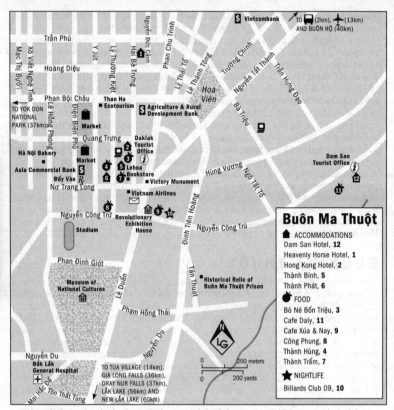

S Vietcombank TO 🚌 (2km), ✈ (13km) AND BUÔN HỘ (40km)

Trần Phú

Hoàng Diệu

Phan Bội Châu

Than Ha Ecotourism

TO YOK DON NATIONAL PARK (37km)

Market

Quang Trưng

Hà Nội Bakery

Asia Commercial Bank

Market

Đấy Vào

Nơ Trang Long

Nguyễn Công Trứ

Stadium

Phan Đình Giót

Museum of National Cultures

Phạm Hồng Thái

Nguyễn Du

Đắk Lắk General Hospital

TO TUA VILLAGE (14km), GIA LONG FALLS (36km), DRAY NUR FALLS (37km), LẮK LAKE (56km) AND NEW LẮK LAKE (60km)

Hoa Viên

Agriculture & Rural Development Bank

Daklak Tourist Office

Lehoa Bookstore

Victory Monument

Vietnam Airlines

Revolutionary Exhibition House

Historical Relic of Buôn Ma Thuột Prison

Nguyễn Công Trứ

Dam San Tourist Office

Hùng Vương

N LG

0   200 meters

0   200 yards

Buôn Ma Thuột

▲ ACCOMMODATIONS
Dam San Hotel, 12
Heavenly Horse Hotel, 1
Hong Kong Hotel, 2
Thành Bình, 5
Thành Phát, 6

🍴 FOOD
Bò Né Bốn Triệu, 3
Cafe Daly, 11
Cafe Xúa & Nay, 9
Công Phung, 8
Thành Hùng, 4
Thành Trầm, 7

★ NIGHTLIFE
Billards Club 09, 10

city wind unrelentingly through the mountains; those susceptible to motion sickness should consider taking a window seat and traveling on an empty stomach.

Motorbike guides: Buôn Ma Thuột has many English-speaking motorbike drivers who will be happy to play guide for the right price. **Tam H.** (☎091 342 1053; hwtam9999@yahoo.com) is a patient and accommodating driver, well-connected with the locals who run the sites. **Lê Trung Kiên** (☎091 404 2980) is a friendly and fair driver who can be reached on his cell phone. He also rents out motorbikes for 15,000Đ per hr.

✳ ORIENTATION

Buôn Ma Thuột is 230km south of Kon Tum, 180km northwest of Nha Trang, and 350km northeast of HCMC. National Hwy. 27 connects BMT to Đà Lạt. The big tank in the center of town is a navigational godsend, as the turret points northeast down **Nguyễn Tất Thành** (Hwy. 14) toward the bus station. The back left corner of the tank points down **Nơ Trang Long,** which runs west past the market and through the central district, where you can head for cheap rooms and eats. Off of this street **Hai Bà Trưng, Lý Thường Kiệt,** and **Y Jút** run north-south. The right side of the tank faces **Lê Duẩn,** which becomes Hwy. 14 as it heads south out of town.

▶ PRACTICAL INFORMATION

Tourist Offices: ◼ **Dam San Tourist,** 212-214 Nguyễn Công Trú (☎851 234; www.dam-san.com.vn), located in the Dam San Hotel (see **Accommodations,** p. 363), about 1km from the town center. A very helpful English-speaking staff gives out free city maps and sells regional maps (12,000Đ). They also arrange guided tours for individuals and groups. Packages range from daytrips (US$10) to the surrounding villages and water-falls to 4-day excursions (US$75) in the jungle. Prices are negotiable and depend on group size. Open daily 7am-5pm. AmEx/DC/MC/V. **Daklak Tourist,** 3 Phan Chu Trinh (☎852 108; daklaktour@dng.vnn.vn), located in the center of town next to the Thang Loi Hotel. Sells maps (10,000Đ) and books half-day to 5-day group tours of the area. Open M-Sa 7:30-11am and 1:30-11pm, Su 7:30-11am and 1:30-5pm.

Banks:

Agriculture and Rural Development Bank, 37 Phan Bội Châu (☎853 930; fax 855 546). Offers all typical banking services.

Asia Commercial Bank, 60-62 Lê Hồng Phong (☎810 198; fax 810 199), 1 block south of Quang Trưng. Cash advances on Visas. Western Union located inside. Open daily 10am-6pm.

Vietcombank, (☎855 039; fax 855 038), on Lê Thánh Tông. Cashes traveler's checks and provides cash advances. 24hr. **ATM** is at 2 Nguyễn Tất Thàn, facing the tank in the center of town.

Bookstore: Lehoa, 1 Hai Bà Trưng (☎852 971; fax 853 947). Carries English Dictionaries and stationery, in addition to a full stock of Vietnamese reads.

Pharmacy: Đẩy Vào, 86 Nơ Trang Long (☎852 009), at the corner with Lê Hồng Phong. Open daily 7am-9pm.

Hospital: Đắk Lắk General Hospital, 2 Mai Hắc Đế (☎852 662), off of Lê Duẩn heading south.

Internet Access: Internet cafes are sparse but cheap—around 3000Đ per hr. **Theheso,** 36 Lý Thường Kiệt (☎856 842), has the fastest connection. Open daily 7am-10pm.

Post Office: Central Post Office, 4 Lê Duẩn. Regular post service and international calling. Open daily 6:30am-9pm.

▶ ACCOMMODATIONS

Buôn Ma Thuột, though a provincial city, offers a range of accommodations, but no budget steals. Rooms are typically bare and soulless. Many lower-end hotels are clustered in the city center. They tend to be multi-story buildings offering concrete cells, but they're all clean and outfitted with fan or air-conditioning. The upper-end hotels are on the periphery of the city center and boast English-speaking staff, satellite TV, and hot water. Rooms are only a bit cleaner and warmer than their cheaper cousins. All prices are negotiable.

Thành Phát, 41 Lý Thường Kiệt (☎854 857; thanhphat@pmail.vnn.vn). This seems to be where the few Western backpackers congregate. Rooms are a squeeze, but the grounds are clean and well-kept. Little English is spoken. Rooms with fan and shared toilet US$6; with fan and private toilet US$8; with A/C and private hot bath US$12. ❷

Hong Kong Hotel, 35 Hai Bà Trưng (☎852 630). An older and sparser version of its neighbors, but the staff speaks English. Rooms US$6-12; pricing as above. ❷

Thành Bính, 24 Lý Thường Kiệt (☎811 511). The friendly staff speaks English well enough to keep you on your bargaining toes. Rooms are just like the others in town except all come with fridges. Some rooms come with maintenance issues, too—be sure to check thoroughly before accepting a room to make sure nothing's broken. Rooms US$6-12; pricing as above. ❷

ON THE MENU

MỘT CÀ PHÊ SỮA ĐÁ (ICED MILK COFFEE)

Ordering coffee is easy in Vietnam—cafes are everywhere—but foreigners may be a bit confused by what they get.

The Vietnamese serve coffee in individual cup-top brewers. The contraption consists of a brewer cup, an internal filter, and a saucer—all essentially pieces of aluminum with holes in them—and a thin lid covering it all. Ground coffee is placed inside the brewer cup above the filter, and hot water is poured in just before the entire thing is brought out. Thus, by the time you have enjoyed your meal, the coffee will have filtered through into the glass below.

To hurry it along, you can open the lid and press down on the watery grounds with a spoon. Once enough coffee has come through into the glass, remove the entire contraption and set it aside on the table, placing the inverted lid underneath the brewer cup to catch any extra liquid.

If you have ordered coffee with milk, a thin layer of sweetened condensed milk will have already been placed into the glass. Be sure to mix the two liquids thoroughly before drinking. Iced coffee comes with a separate tall glass full of ice, a long spoon, and a straw. Mix your coffee with the milk before pouring it over the ice. Use your spoon periodically to mix up the three separating liquids. Do this without toppling the ice, and you'll gain some serious cafe cred.

Heavenly Horse Hotel, 50 Hai Bà Trưng (☎850 379 or 853 963). Proclaims its 2-star status in neon glory. The remarkable rooms are the nicest in the city—all include hot-water private baths and satellite TV. Singles US$25; doubles US$35. ❹

Dam San Hotel, 212-214 Nguyễn Công Trú (☎851 234 or 852 505; damsantour@dng.vnn.vn). Removed from the city's center, has a helpful, English-speaking staff. The hotel also houses a tourist office. Rooms US$15-30. ❸

🍴 FOOD

Buôn Ma Thuột offers plenty of dining options, but not much variety. Cafes and street-side eats line Lý Thường Kiệt. The best value in a sit-down restaurant is the traditional *phấn* (ground pork in banana leaves, for use in spring rolls; 8000Đ). Cheaper meals can be found at road-side vendors, which usually sell phở (3000Đ) along Quang Trưng. The **market,** stocked with fresh fruits, is also located along this street. The best grocery store in town is **Hà Nội Bakery,** 123-125 Lê Hông Phong, which carries packaged meats and cheeses (20,000-40,000Đ) as well as fresh pastries (2500-3500Đ), loaves of bread (8000Đ), and pound cake. (☎853 609. Open daily 7am-7pm.) If you're itching to be served and you crave some Western-style food, head to one of the upscale hotel lobbies: all have full restaurants on the first floor for wealthier tourists and local weddings (entrees 30,000-40,000Đ).

BMT lies in the heart of coffee country, and no visit here would be complete without a trip to one of the numerous local cafes. Most cafes serve generic Trung Nguyễn coffee; a few, however, serve from a private stock. Visitors can buy packs of ground coffee from the cafes themselves (about 2500Đ for 250kg), and if you ask nicely, you may even be able to buy one of the traditional Vietnamese cup-top brewing sets in which your coffee will be served (10,000Đ). A string of cafes sit along Nguyễn Công Trú between Lê Duẩn and the Dam San Hotel.

Thành Hùng, 14 Lý Thường Kiệt (☎834 910). Popular with the locals, probably because it serves noodles with its spring and summer rolls. ❶

Bò Né Bốn Triệu, 33 Hai Bà Trưng. Meals are filling. Ask for *bò né,* the breakfast specialty: eggs, beef, scallions, and a pork ball on a sizzling cow-shaped plate (10,000Đ). Open daily 6am-10pm. ❶

Thành Trâm, 22 Lý Thường Kiệt (☎854 860). Offers a particularly delightful ensemble of custom spring rolls (20,000Đ). The owners are eager to host customers and speak English to visitors. Open daily 7am-11pm. ❶

Công Phung, 27 Nguyễn Công Trú (☎857 885). A wholesale coffee shop that offers fresh coffee beans dried and ground by hand (20,000Đ per kg). English spoken. Open daily 7am-7pm. ❷

Cafe Daly, 188 Nguyễn Công Trú (☎812 243). One of the most comfortable (and commercial) cafes in town. ❷

Cafe Xúa & Nay, 1 Lê Duẩn (☎850 143). Another similar cafe, with a large, vine-covered patio, frequented by locals. ❷

🅞 🅡 SIGHTS AND NIGHTLIFE

Any sightseeing tour of Buôn Ma Thuột begins and ends at the **Victory Monument,** located conspicuously in the center of town. Play with the local children in the fountain at the base of this towering monument and get a close-up view of an old Soviet tank. Head a bit south and you'll run into the first building of the **Đắk Lắk Province Museum,** which is composed of three separate, small museums. The **Revolutionary Exhibition House (Bảo Tàng Cách Mạng),** at 1 Lê Duẩn, houses Hồ Chí Minh paraphernalia and a presentation about the liberation of Buôn Ma Thuột, along with a comic attempt at displaying indigenous wildlife. With your back to the museum, turn right onto Nguyễn Công Trú for one block, and then right again on Đinh Tiên Hoàng to check out the **Historical Relic of BMT Prison (DTCM Nhà Đay BMT)**—the prison is always open, though tours only run during museum hours. This abandoned 19th-century French colonial prison offers its contemporary guests a reprieve from the hectic center of BMT. The final part of Đắk Lắk Province Museum is the **Museum of National Cultures (Bảo Tàng Văn Hóa Bân Tộc),** 182 Nguyễn Du, off of Lê Duẩn and a bit farther down from the Victory Monument. Housed in the former Bảo Đại Palace, it displays a variety of traditional tools, instruments, weapons, and dress. (Museum main desk ☎850 426. Open Su and W-Sa 7:30-11:30am and 2-5pm. 10,000Đ per museum.)

To hang out with the locals at night, check out the karaoke bars that line Hai Bà Trưng near the Heavenly Horse Hotel, or the **Billiards Club 09,** 29A Nguyễn Công Trú (☎816 101), next door to Cafe Xúa & Nay.

🔆 DAYTRIPS FROM BUÔN MA THUỘT

Around Buôn Ma Thuột, along Hwy. 14, are several daytrips that make the city well worth the trek from the coast. The best way to get around is by motorbike, either by yourself or with a driver. A one-hour trip should cost 30,000-50,000Đ and a full-day trip will cost 120,000-150,000Đ. If you're heading to the lakes or Buôn Hồ, consider flagging down a bus on the highway.

■**DRAY NUR FALLS.** Picturesque Dray Nur Falls—half an hour away by motorbike—is an excellent place to beat the heat for an afternoon. Follow the well-marked concrete steps down to the foot of the falls and the dramatic rock pier, and check out the red wooden bridge to the left to see a miniature tributary of the falls. In the dry season, you can jump in to take a shower in these mini-falls and feel the force of the water first-hand. **Bâng Giá,** a restaurant near the entrance, serves drinks (sodas 6000-7000Đ; beer 7000-8000Đ; local rice wine 40,000Đ). A longhouse on the premises even offers a place for midday naps for US$5 per person. *(Head 27km south on Hwy. 14. Exit south toward Ea Tling Village until the fork in the road; take a right and continue 10km to reach the falls. 5000Đ.)*

■**TUA VILLAGE.** A bit closer to BMT is Tua Village (also called Buôn Tuôr), whose 450 Êđê inhabitants are Protestant and are thought to have migrated from Indonesia and Malaysia over two centuries ago. The village is quiet and immaculately clean, and the people are welcoming. Ask after Siu Thồm, a village elder who was a first lieutenant in the ARVN. Though he spent six and a half years in prison, Thồm happily discusses politics, religion, and life in general with excellent English. He gives tours of the village, including one of the village's 80 longhouses, in which the Ếdễ live with all their extended relatives. The longhouses are made of wood and contain one window per nuclear family. The village also has a small church, which leads Sunday prayers (8-10am), a Sunday school (11am-noon), and a Sunday women's circle (1-2pm). A visit to the village is free, but small change or gifts, such as cigarettes, are always appreciated. Try to go on a Sunday—the villagers are all at rest and more amenable to conversation than during the work week. *(Tua Village is 14km south of Buôn Ma Thuột off of Hwy. 14. You must turn off at an unmarked road, so your best bet is to hire a local driver if you're on your own.)*

GIA LONG FALLS. About 30km down Hwy. 14 are the Gia Long Falls, somewhat less impressive than the Dray Nur Falls. Upon arrival, descend into a small rainforest, complete with strangler figs and hanging vines, then follow the path along the Krông Knâ river to the lower falls. The waters run through the mountains from Cambodia, which is only 40km away. The best view is from the suspension footbridge, but several cleared rock trails bring you within misting distance. The trails are unmarked but easy to follow; exploring the area provides relief from noisy BMT. Near the lower falls is a gazebo where locals and tourists are free to picnic. Near the entrance to the falls is a model longhouse in which tourists can nap for US$5 per person. *(The waterfalls are 27km south of BMT along Hwy. 14. Exit south toward Ea Tling Village until the fork in the road; take a left and continue 6km to reach the falls. 5000Đ.)*

LẮK LAKE. A M'nong community of 200 lives by this lakeside growing rice, raising livestock beneath elevated longhouses, and offering tours to visitors. Đực and Mai Bui (☎586 280 or 0905 371 633), who coordinate local activities out of their Hợp Tac Xà souvenir shop, are particularly hospitable guides to the surrounding Zun Village. Visitors can also tour the site by dugout canoe (US$10 per hr.) or by elephant (1hr.; 2 people US$30; call ahead or expect to wait). Accommodations are available in the village's sparse but spacious **longhouses ❶**, which have fans, mattresses, pillows, and an outhouse (US$5 per person). Alternatively, the **Lắk District Guesthouse ❶** in nearby Lắk village offers overnight stays for 80,000-90,000Đ. Try timing your visit to catch the description-defying sunrises and sunsets. *(Lắk Lake is 56km south on Hwy. 27—you can't miss it, as the highway runs right along the lake. You can take a motorbike there for 30,000-50,000Đ or flag down a minibus en route to Đà Lạt. Free.)*

LẮK LAKE FOR POCKET CHANGE. Lắk Lake sees many more Vietnamese than foreign tourists, and masses of incoming city-dwellers can work in your favor. Catching a ride on a dugout canoe filled with Vietnamese can mean getting your boat ride at local, not foreign, prices (about 100,000Đ cheaper).

NEW LẮK LAKE. On the other side of Lắk market from Zun Village is the New Lắk Lake—a quieter, cleaner, and more romantic site. The area consists of just the lake and a few small guesthouses, without the bustle of an accompanying village. Accommodations include wooden **longhouses ❶** with outhouses (US$5 per person) or the newly built **lakeside villas ❸** (US$10 per person). Staying in the villas requires prior arrangement with **Bào Đai Villa** (☎586 184; open daily 7am-7pm). The open-air **Lắk Lake Floating Restaurant ❶** literally rests upon the water amidst a grove of waterlilies. (Vegetable dishes 12,000Đ; fish dishes 15,000Đ; phở 5000Đ; drinks 3000-5000Đ. Open daily 7am-8pm.) Secluded and serene, the New Lắk Lake, complete with wooden swing, volleyball court, and hammocks, is perfect for a quiet highland retreat. *(New Lắk Lake is 60km south on Hwy. 27, past Lắk Village. A 1hr. motorbike ride costs 30,000-50,000Đ, or you can flag down a minibus going south on Hwy. 27.)*

BUÔN HỘ. This quaint town northeast of BMT is a fun afternoon visit. The town's attractions are all adjacent to each other along Hwy. 14 (called Hùng Vương in town). They demonstrate religious diversity in remarkable proximity: a large cathedral is followed by a white stone pagoda that features a plump "happy" Buddha, and a squat green Protestant church sits a little farther down the road. Tour the religious sites and sip the local coffee straight from the neighboring fields. *(Buôn Hộ is 40km northeast of BMT on Hwy. 14. Hire a motorbike for 30,000Đ or catch a ride on any minibus heading northeast for 20,000Đ.)*

YOK DON NATIONAL PARK

Yok Don is Vietnam's largest national park. This expansive wildlife preserve now encompasses over 1000 square kilometers, stretching from 37km northwest of Buôn Ma Thuột to the Cambodian border. The park is primarily a nature reserve and—like many of Vietnam's national parks—hosts an abundance of animals, including elephants, monkeys, buffalo, and deer. Like in other parks, though, visitors are unlikely to see any of these animals. The park is officially home to five endangered species, including the panther and a rare species of wild dog, but more are still being discovered. Yok Don borders a stretch of the regal Srepok River, which flows into Cambodia and meets up with the Mekong River before turning back into southern Vietnam and emptying into the South China Sea. Yok Don, though, is not your idyllic jungle park. Besides a thin strip of rainforest along the Srepok and the inaccessible mountains along the border, most of the landscape is grasslands and sparse hardwood forest.

YOK DON AT A GLANCE	
AREA: 1155 sq. km.	**GATEWAYS:** Buôn Ma Thuột.
CLIMATE: Hot and wet May-Sept.; somewhat less hot and wet Oct.-Apr.	**CAMPING:** Tents available at Park Headquarters and in Ban Don village. Rooms are available as well.
AVERAGE ELEVATION: 200m.	
FEATURES: Deciduous and evergreen forests, grasslands, and river valleys.	**FEES AND RESERVATIONS:** In-depth tours of the park require a guide; inquire at Park Headquarters. Pre-arranged tours (US$30-100) can be organized at tourist offices in Buôn Ma Thuột.
HIGHLIGHTS: Endangered species; Ēdē and M'nong ethnic minority villages.	

In addition to remarkable flora and fauna, several ethnic minorities, including the Ēdē and the M'nong, inhabit the area and its surrounds. The M'nong have made a name for themselves in Đắk Lắk Province as skilled elephant catchers and tamers: Vua San Voi N'thu Knul, also known as Khun Sa Nup ("elephant hunter king"; 1827-1937), is famed for having caught 244 elephants in his lifetime. Legend holds that he once captured a white elephant and gifted it to the king of Thailand, who coined the tamer's nickname. **Khun Sa Nup's tomb,** just outside of Ban Don Village, is worth a visit. It is built in a hybrid architectural style, the squat square building representing the heritage of his M'nong mother and the tall steeple representing that of his Laotian father. A few master elephant catchers still live in the area.

The M'nong people hold elephants in extremely high regard, treating them as they treat their human kin. Indeed, the elephant may be the only animal that does not appear as part of Vietnamese culinary fare. Elephant hunters take pride in capturing, not killing, the majestic beasts. Much of the respect for the animal comes from their utility and helpfulness. Elephants play an important role in M'nong agricultural life, pulling timber and carrying heavy loads. Accordingly, local goods made of ivory are crafted from fallen tusks, not from poaching.

☰ TRANSPORTATION. Visitors must arrange their own transport to Yok Don National Park. The park is best reached from Buôn Ma Thuột, where groups can arrange transportation at **Dam San Tourist** or **Daklak Tourist** (see **Practical Information, p. 363**). The cheapest and most convenient way to get there is to rent a motorbike or hire out a motorbike and driver (US$5-7). The entrance to the park cannot be missed from the road that continues west from Buôn Ma Thuột's Phan Bội Châu. The turn-off for Ban Don Village is 2km up the road on the left. The entrance is also well marked.

⚠ PRACTICAL INFORMATION. Despite the breathtaking biodiversity of Yok Don, the sightseeing options for tourists are limited—tourist infrastructure in Vietnam's national parks is new and still largely undeveloped. Arranged tours are, unfortunately, the only way you're guaranteed to see anything, and even then, guides are full of disclaimers. The heavily traveled trails in the park are completely devoid of wildlife, save a few lizards, insects, and occasionally a distant herd of buffalo. **Park Headquarters** (☎783 049; yokdon@dng.vnn.vn) offers overpriced informational treks by elephant (US$25 per hr., US$100 per day) and foot (US$20 per hr.), as well as overnight stays, but these visits do not venture beyond the Administrative and Ecorestoration Zones, which are devoid of major fauna. For longer and more in-depth excursions (from US$200), contact Headquarters in advance to arrange a two-day tour to Yok Don mountain (482m), the only tour that penetrates the Strictly Protected Zone of the park, home to most of the endangered species. Another option for prearranged touring is to inquire at **Daklak Tourist** in Buôn Ma Thuột, but they only deal with group tours.

WHEN TO GO. Yok Don's dry deciduous forest might detract from the park's botanical diversity, but a large variety of animal species still roams the grounds. Did we mention that it's *dry* deciduous forest? Over 75% of the year's rain falls between May and September, and the average annual rainfall is about 1500mm. The park is located in a tropical monsoon region, but the humidity only ranges from 60% during the rainy season to 40% around March, which is remarkably arid for Vietnam. Temperatures hover between 24° and 26°C all year long, with the highest temperatures coordinating with the wettest time of the year in May and the coolest during January.

The best bet for short, budget stays is to show up at **Ban Don village** (see p. 369), 2km past the park entrance. At Ban Don, motorbike or boat tours and trekking trips can be arranged. Also available are elephant rides (US$30 per hr.) and music demonstrations (10,000Đ). If you come in late winter, don't miss the traditional elephant competitions. Tours from Ban Don range from 3hr. to three days (half-day tours US$5). Excellent village tours are run by Mr. Vu (☎090 505 7890 or 090 783 079). You can also arrange tours in Buôn Ma Thuột at **Than Ha Ecotourism,** 45 Phan Bội Châu (☎854 903; xuanvupaulbmt@yahoo.com). If you don't feel like exploring the forest, stay in Ban Don; the locals put on a show for tourists with traditional dress, music *(cong-chieng)*, and rice wine.

🏠🍴 ACCOMMODATIONS AND FOOD. Yok Don Guesthouse ❷ (☎853 110) is located at Park Headquarters and is serviced by a small canteen. The concrete guesthouse offers limited amenities but easy access to the park's tourist services (doubles and tents 150,000Đ). **Ban Don Village ❶** offers an ethnic alternative. Guests can stay in traditional M'nong longhouses, but share relatively close quarters with other tourists (US$5). Alternatively, more private bamboo houses with private bathrooms are available in the village (US$10). If there is a large enough group, locals will put on a traditional ceremony at night. The **canteen ❶** serves typical Vietnamese food (dishes 10,000-20,000Đ).

⬛ **SIGHTS. Ban Don** is a kitschy village 2km northwest of Yok Don. Near the entrance to the village is a longhouse that doubles as a museum, featuring traditional instruments, multicolored textiles, elephant lassos made of buffalo twine, and pictorial histories of the M'nong people. Most M'nong families work the land, as their ancestors have for centuries; you'll stumble on a few fields and families if you follow the river 500m upstream from Ban Don. They are used to Westerners stopping by and will be hospitable, though most speak no Western languages and are focused on their work. **Ban Don Tourist,** 45 Phan Bội Châu (☎854 903 or 783 079; www.bandontour.com.vn), offers tours and runs the local shop.

KON TUM   ☎60

Kon Tum, the capital of Kon Tum Province, is the last city before the Central Highlands swell into the mountainous jungle to the north and west. At the foot of these mountains along the Dakbla River, Kon Tum offers the most stunning scenery of the Central Highlands. Like its southern neighbors, the city of Kon Tum is an overcrowded provincial capital and altar to Euclidean concrete. Still, the city reflects the lazy Dakbla and moves at a slower pace than Đà Lạt or Buôn Ma Thuột. Kon Tum attracts returning veterans of the American War due to its proximity to Đắk Tô and Charlie Hill (see **Daytrips from Kon Tum,** p. 371). It also offers access to nearby ethnic villages and is the start (or end) of an unrivaled drive up Hwy. 14 to the coast. Because of its seclusion, you will have many chances to practice your Vietnamese language skills. Don't speak Vietnamese? Yeah, we know.

▐ **TRANSPORTATION.** The **Interprovince bus station** is 2km north of the town center on Phan Đình Phùng. All buses, even those going to the coast, head south through Pleiku. If you want to head north along Hwy. 14, you'll have to arrange for your transportation in town. **Buses** go to: Buôn Ma Thuột (6hr.; 7am; 40,000Đ); Đà Nẵng (14hr.; 6:30am; 56,000Đ); HCMC (14hr.; 7am; 40,000Đ); Huế (17hr.; 7am; 73,000Đ); Pleiku (1hr.; frequently all day; 8000Đ); Quảng Ngãi (11hr.; 7am; 40,000Đ); Qui Nhơn (6hr.; 7am; 35,000Đ).

⬛▐ **ORIENTATION AND PRACTICAL INFORMATION.** Kon Tum fits in the nook created by Hwy. 14's crossing of the Dakbla River. **Highway 14**—called **Phan Đình Phùng** in town—forms the town's western border, while the Dakbla limits it on the south. **Nguyễn Huệ** runs along the river at the bottom of town and is parallel to **Trần Hưng Đạo,** north of which is **Phan Chu Trinh** and **Bà Triệu.** Forming a grid are **Lê Hồng Phong** and **Trần Phú,** parallel to and east of Hwy. 14.

    Kon Tum Tourist, located in the Dakbla Hotel, is a state-owned agency that handles tours, permits, and transportation. The best way to see the sights of Kon Tum is to hire a knowledgeable motorbike driver who will act as your guide. Hiring such a driver from the tourist office to get to Đắk Tô costs US$15. Guide, driver, and permit to restricted hill villages runs about US$30. (☎861 826; www.kontumtourist.com.vn. Open daily 7-11am and 1-5pm.) Mr. Nhung (☎059 822 666 or 827 563; loannhung111@yahoo.com), an excellent driver and guide, is another option. Nguyễn Do Huynh (☎905 112 037; huynhguide@yahoo.com) is a thorough guide who carefully explains all sites in English. **Investment and Development Bank,** 2 Trần Phú, lies on the river and boasts an excellent English-speaking staff. The bank can only offer credit card advances when the director is in. (Open

CENTRAL HIGHLANDS

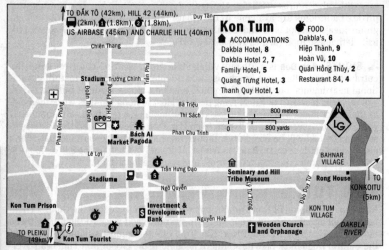

TO ĐẮK TÔ (42km), HILL 42 (44km), ▢▢ (2km), ▢ (1.8km), ▢ (1.8km), US AIRBASE (45km) AND CHARLIE HILL (40km)

Duy Tân

Chiên Thang

Kon Tum
▲ ACCOMMODATIONS
Dakbla Hotel, **8**
Dakbla Hotel 2, **7**
Family Hotel, **5**
Quang Trưng Hotel, **3**
Thanh Quy Hotel, **1**

🍎 FOOD
Dakbla's, **6**
Hiệp Thành, **9**
Hoàn Vũ, **10**
Quán Hồng Thủy, **2**
Restaurant 84, **4**

Stadium Trường Chinh
Trần Phú

GPO
Bách Ái
Market Pagoda

Bà Triệu
Thi Sách
Phan Chu Trinh

Lê Lợi

0 ⌐ 800 meters
0 ⌐ 800 yards

Trần Hưng Đạo

Stadium
Ngô Quyền

Seminary and Hill
Tribe Museum

BAHNAR
VILLAGE
Rong House TO
KONKOITU
(5km)

Kon Tum Prison

Investment &
Development
Bank

Nguyễn Huệ

KON TUM
VILLAGE

TO PLEIKU
(49km) Kon Tum Tourist

Wooden Church
and Orphanage

DAKBLA
RIVER

daily 7am-6pm.) There is no ATM in town. **Police stations** are eerily omnipresent. There's one at 90 Phan Chu Trinh. The **hospital** can be found at 71 Phan Đình Phùng (☎824 125). **Internet** access costs 3000Đ per hr. at **Vĩnh Lộc**, 99 Trần Hưng Đạo. The **General Post Office** is at 206 Lê Hồng Phong, at its intersection with Bà Triệu; look for the giant radio tower. (☎862 361. Open daily 7am-9pm.)

▐ **ACCOMMODATIONS.** All prices in Kon Tum are highly negotiable, and the hoteliers take pleasure in a good haggle, so be persistent. **Family Hotel ❷**, 55 Trần Hưng Đạo, looks and feels new. Privately owned, with bright and modern rooms, this is the best value in town. (☎862 448. Rooms US$7-15; prices negotiable.) **Dakbla Hotel ❹**, 2 Phan Đình Phùng, is Kon Tum's upper-end hotel. Situated right across the bridge into town, it's a great place for tourists, but not necessarily backpackers. (☎863 333; ktourist@dng.vnn.vn. Rooms US$25-35.) **Dakbla Hotel 2 ❷**, 163 Nguyễn Huệ, down by the river, is the smaller, more spartan sibling of Dakbla Hotel. (☎863 335.) **Thanh Quy Hotel ❷**, 215 Phan Đình Phùng, just south of the bus station, offers neat and spacious rooms at a convenient location, though there's constant traffic noise out the window. (Rooms US$8-10.) **Quang Trưng Hotel ❷**, 168 Bà Triệu, is the state-owned budget offering in Kon Tum. (☎862 249; fax 862 763. Rooms US$6-12.)

▐ **FOOD.** Most restaurants in Kon Tum open around 7am and close around 11pm, although day-to-day schedules depend upon local events, festivities, and sports matches. Expect all menus to be in Vietnamese. **Dakbla's ❷**, 168 Nguyễn Huệ, is Kon Tum's best tourist option, with reasonable prices and an extensive Vietnamese and Western menu. It's one of the few places in the Central Highlands that serves dessert. It also sells the cultural artifacts from local Bahnar villages that decorate its walls. (☎862 584. Entrees 30,000-40,000Đ.) **Restaurant 84 ❷**, on Trần Hưng Đạo across from Family Hotel, has photocopied the Vietnamese portion of Dakbla's menu and serves up the same dishes in a pared-down setting for slightly cheaper prices (20,000-30,000Đ). **Quán Hồng Thủy**, 211 Phan Đình Phùng, is a friendly local place, with an excellent table-top stir-fry and a center-stage TV for sports matches. (☎915 261. Entrees 30,000-40,000.) **Hiệp Thành ❸**, 29 Nguyễn Huệ, is a newer, nicer restaurant along the river, with an immaculate eating area and a typical menu. (☎862

470. Entrees 40,000-50,000.) **Hoàn Vũ ❸**, 81 Nguyễn Huệ, is a shiny upscale restaurant catering to Western tourists and prosperous government officials. The second-story seating area has a commanding view of the river and the surrounding countryside. (Entrees 45,000-50,000.) The cheapest eats in Kon Tom are found in the **market** (along Phan Chu Trinh) or at nearby small restaurants, such as **Phở Bò Cuoi ❷**, 70A Trần Phú, and **Restaurant 88 ❷**, 145 Trần Hưng Đạo.

◙ SIGHTS. Kon Tum does not offer many sights in town, but the ones they have are worth at least an afternoon. Near the center of town, at the intersection of Phan Chu Trihn and Trần Phú, **Bách Ai Pagoda** is a typical small-town pagoda, offering an oasis of peace in the noisy city center. Two blocks east and one block south, the **Seminary and Hill Tribe Museum**, on Trần Hưng Đạo, is another remnant of the French presence in Southeast Asia. This white-washed wooden seminary produces many of the area's priests and nuns but doesn't cater much to the tourist. Across the street is a small chapel built into volcanic rock. Walk a few minutes toward the river and you'll come across the **Wooden Church and Orphanage** at the intersection of Nguyễn Huệ and Lý Tự Trọng, Kon Tum's most-used church. The orphanage is another living relic of the French colonial era. A visit to the church and orphanage is a glimpse into a past that has been consciously erased in the Central Highlands. The church, constructed in 1913, is made completely of wood, and it combines French and Vietnamese styles beautifully. The orphanage, behind the church, is full of friendly and curious children, mostly from local Bahnar villages. The nuns who run the orphanage are more than happy to show you around. (Free, but donations greatly appreciated.) The **Rong House,** on Trần Hưng Đạo as you head east out of town, is an example of the traditional Bahnar "community center." Perched on stilts, *rong* houses stretch skyward for several stories. They're built using only wood, bamboo, bark lashing, and a thatching for the roof. It's an impressive sight, but can be unexciting unless a community festival is going on. Visitors are welcome to look inside the spacious (and empty) house; lucky visitors will arrive during a party and be invited to join in the dancing, singing, and drinking. The **Bahnar and Kon Tum Villages** are located at the eastern edge of town, just north of the *rong* house. The Kon Tum Village is the original settlement on the Dak-bla River, which eventually grew into Kon Tum. You can drive a motorbike or walk their unpaved streets to see the architecture and lifestyle of the hill tribes. Be prepared to witness grinding poverty and a dire lack of sanitation.

▶ DAYTRIPS FROM KON TUM. Forty-five kilometers north of Kon Tum are the remains of a **US Airbase** (Phượng Hoàng). The airstrip, now used to dry various tubers, is up Hwy. 14, past Đắk Tô (see below) and on the left. On the grounds near the airstrip are the remains of US bunkers; small nail-like pieces from old "beehive bombs" still litter the grounds. South of the airstrip is **Hill 42,** stretching for about a kilometer, another site where Americans were positioned during the war. Look carefully and you can still see remnants of the war, including artillery casings, old meal packets, and unexploded rockets. In the distance you can see **Rocket Ridge,** the location of a heavily used and heavily bombed helicopter base that was shared by the US and the ARVN. **Skull Hill,** the site of a clash between northern and southern Vietnamese forces in the spring of 1972, stands on the road to Đắk Tô, 17km from Kon Tum. The location of the bloody attack, where the Communists severed the land route to Kon Tum, is marked by a concrete shrine and three piles of stones where locals burn incense. **Charlie Hill,** 5km south of Đắk Tô, was the location of a southern ARVN fortification. Although the base was rather small, the fight for control of Charlie Hill became infamous. The South Vietnamese officer commanding the base refused to surrender or retreat in the

THE HIDDEN DEAL

APOCALYPSE REDUX

Like the characters in Francis Ford Coppola's movie, you can take your own boat trip through the Vietnamese jungle toward the Cambodian border. Outside of Kon Tum, young Bahnar boys of Konkoitu pass the day floating up and down the muddy, lazy Dakbla in their long dugout canoes, bringing goods up from town or sometimes just idling the day away. For 20,000-50,000Đ, they will be more than happy to take you along for the ride.

The best place to catch the canoes is on the beach of Konkoitu village, which can be reached by motorbike from Kon Tum (20,000-30,000Đ). In the village the beach is past the village center, to the left. From here you can either head downstream to Kon Tum or upstream, where the mountains close in and the road and cultivated lands fade from the shore. With a bit of imagination, you begin to feel like a modern-day Dr. Livingston.

If you take the trip alone, the looming mountains and deserted surroundings can feel a bit ominous, but it's worth it for the rare chance to explore virgin territory, free of any noise and other people. For running English commentary and a chance to hop out and inspect the surrounding flora and fauna, try a more formal tour arranged through **Kon Tum Tourist** (p. 69; US$25-35 for half-day boat and trekking trips).

face of the superior Việt Cộng force. This officer, Colonel Ngoc Minh, and his 150 soldiers endured a siege that lasted two months before the VC were finally able to overrun the hill and kill them all. The hill is unsafe to climb, as it was heavily mined during the war, but it can be viewed from Hwy. 14.

A relaxing place to spend an afternoon is Kon Tum's richer southern neighbor, **Pleiku.** Dominated by massive blocks of Soviet-style concrete architecture, this city, 48km south of Kon Tum, offers a convenient rest stop during a drive on the peerless Hwy. 14. ⚔**My Tam ❷,** 3 Quang Trưng, is a family-run Chinese restaurant that packs in the locals with its superb fried chicken (20,000Đ). Just outside of town, 7km north off Hwy. 14, **Bien Ho Lake** offers one of the best vistas in the Central Highlands, is a peaceful area to picnic or simply enjoy the scenery. The easiest way to get to Pleiku is by public bus (see **Transportation,** p. 369).

Konkoitu Village, a mere 5km to the east of Kon Tum, is the only Montagnard village in the area that you can visit without a permit. Unfortunately, there isn't much there except a few huts, a *rong* house, and poor Bahnar families. But the friendliness of the inhabitants, their willingness to show you their skills in weaving and fishing, and the stunning scenery make the short trip worthwhile. Hire a motorbike driver (20,000Đ), head east on Trần Hưng Đạo, cross over the bridge, and take a left at the fork. Follow the road to its end.

Đắk Tô, 42km north of Kon Tum on Hwy. 14, was a strategic region during the American War, valued for its proximity to the Lao and Cambodian borders. The region was a major fighting ground for American, ARVN, VC, and NVA forces. Today Đắk Tô is a booming village that nevertheless recognizes its unfortunate historical past. A Victory Monument dominates the center of the town, paying homage to the April 24, 1972 Communist takeover of the town. This Stalinist marble tower and the two Russian tanks parked beside it—the first tanks to enter Đắk Tô in 1972—are the most commanding sights in town. Next door is a pleasant *rong* house. Đắk Tô is also home to a hot spring, which bears responsibility for the town's name, which translates to "hot water."

Farther northwest on Hwy. 14, near the town of Ngoc Hơi, visitors can connect to the modern-day highway built over the **Hồ Chí Minh Trail.** The trail was used by North Vietnamese forces to infiltrate southern strongholds. The road is currently being expanded to connect into Laos, which is only 40km from Đắk Tô and 16km from Ngoc Hơi. Foreigners will be able to obtain visas at the new border crossing when it opens in December 2006.

CHUMOMRAY NATIONAL PARK

CHUMOMRAY AT A GLANCE	
AREA: 487 sq. km.	**HIGHLIGHTS:** Fairy Waterfall; endangered species; minority villages.
CLIMATE: Hot and wet May-Oct.; drier and a bit cooler Nov.-Apr.	**GATEWAYS:** Kon Tum.
HIGHEST PEAK: Chumomray Peak, 1773m.	**CAMPING:** Not yet.
FEATURES: Dense jungles, mountainous terrain, better-than-average access to flora and fauna.	**FEES AND RESERVATIONS:** In-depth tours of the park require a guide. Pre-arranged tours (US$15-30) can be organized at tourist offices in Kon Tum.

Chumomray is Vietnam's newest national park. Its borders extend to both Laos and Cambodia, where the park connects with the Vitary National Park of Cambodia and the Dong Nam Ghong National Park of Laos. What makes Chumomray different is the density of its jungle and the salty mineral water of its waterfalls. Chumomray is also particularly mountainous, as it lies along the Truongson mountain range, which reaches as high as Chumomray Peak at 1773m. The park boasts several multi-layered waterfalls, such as the 100m-tall **Fairy Waterfall** in Yaboc Valley, and is also home to several minority ethnic populations, including the Ēdē, Hlang, Leromam, Borau, Kodong, and Sedang. There are almost 1500 species of flora in the park, 131 of which are endangered. The park is also thought to contain 620 species of fauna, 114 of which are considered rare and precious, perhaps including the elusive Bossauveli, which, following a French investigation in 1920, is now considered to be extinct.

Chumomray is best visited as a daytrip, or part of an extended camping tour, from Kon Tum. Separate accommodations and food joints have not yet been set up as part of the park infrastructure. As always, bring plenty of water.

Visitors must arrange their own transport to Chumomray National Park. The park is best reached from Kon Tum, where groups can arrange transportation at **Kon Tum Tourist** (p. 369). The company also offers half-day guided trekking tours through the park (US$15). Contact park headquarters for the latest options (☎821 289; chumomray@dng.vnn.vn).

CENTRAL
HIGHLANDS

HỒ CHÍ MINH CITY (HCMC)

Hồ Chí Minh City (formerly Saigon) has long been a hotbed of activity, but it only recently became the overcrowded powerhouse that it is today. The French made it the capital of colonial *Indochine*, endowing it with wide boulevards and grand architecture. During the American War, the city served as headquarters for US forces and international journalists, many of whom were captivated by its exotic atmosphere. Today, Hồ Chí Minh City is the country's largest and most populous city, and it remains on the cusp of all things new and en vogue. Although the city was renamed after the national Communist hero, it has since come down hard with capitalist fever. With Vietnam's imminent entry into the World Trade Organization, investment is already pouring into the city. Merchants crowd every inch of sidewalk space, businesspeople broker international deals over their cell phones, and sparkling shopping centers cater to a growing number of upwardly mobile Vietnamese. The two-hour lunch is a thing of the past; people are beginning to work around the clock, without breaking on the weekends. Yet, underneath all the commercial mania is a forgotten underclass of people left behind by the progress. Hồ Chí Minh City's street people make their living selling gum or incense, and it is not clear when or if the city will pause to take stock of their desperate conditions. But Hồ Chí Minh City is nothing if not a city of contrasts. It is also home to magnificent pagodas, lush gardens, and charming cafes. For visitors, these may be a welcome respite from the city's frenetic pulse, which races at the same speed as the millions of motorbikes zipping down its streets. Given the way his namesake has turned out, Hồ Chí Minh is probably rolling over in his tomb, but the locals aren't fazed—after all, half the city still calls it Saigon.

HIGHLIGHTS OF HỒ CHÍ MINH CITY

GET LOST in Saigon's endless alleyways. You haven't seen the city properly until you've explored these hidden streets. Here is where all the normal life of the city takes place—cooking, cleaning, sleeping—and tourists are conspicuously absent. Start by diving into any alley between Phạm Ngũ Lão and Bùi Viện and see where it takes you.

BUY EVERYTHING at comically low prices in the city's sprawling, raucous markets (p. 399). Clothing, plastic fruit, and everything else that can reasonably sport a price tag can be yours. District 5 isn't called "Big Market" (Chợ Lớn) for nothing.

ESCAPE SAIGON and head for the clean air and white shores of **Vũng Tàu** (p. 404), HCMC's very own French Riviera. Stretches of waterfront abound, as do many unexplained religious statues. The ▨ **Củ Chi Tunnels** (p. 403), former Việt Cộng hideouts, also make for an ideal place to explore and awaken the claustrophobic in you.

HISTORY

HUMBLE BEGINNINGS

Compared to the rest of the country, the area around Hồ Chí Minh City is a relatively new addition to the Vietnamese nation. Set in the swampland of the Saigon River, the city that is now home to more than seven million people had its inauspi-

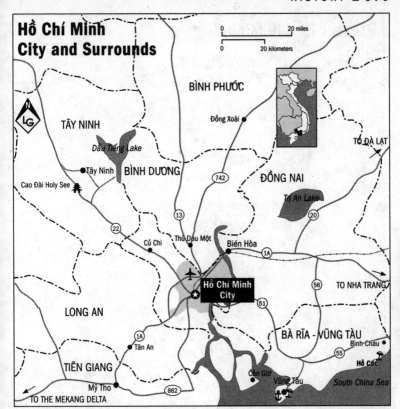

Hồ Chí Minh City and Surrounds

cious beginning as a small fishing village. It wasn't until the **Later Lê Dynasty's** expansion in the 16th century that the area's growth got seriously underway.

In the late 17th century, the northern government, realizing Saigon's ideal location as a port, began to focus its attention on the small village. In 1698, **Lord Nguyễn Phuc Chu** took steps toward development, and the swampland was filled in to facilitate overland travel and trade. The city first appeared on the European radar as a convenient locale from which to pursue economic activities during the 1700s. The atmosphere began to change, however, after the French captured the city in 1859—the first conquest in their drive toward a colonial empire in the area.

THE FRENCH KISS OF DEATH

For the next century, the French utilized Saigon as their primary trade base in *Indochine*, their Southeast Asian colonial stronghold. During that time, they provided the city with an infrastructure, building wide avenues and practical systems of transport, as well as marking their presence architecturally. With transportation and trade established in the Saigon area, rice cultivation in the Mekong Delta grew rapidly under French occupation.

During World War II, the city was briefly occupied by the Japanese. In 1945, **Hồ Chí Minh** declared the independence of the nation of Vietnam, hastening the end of French rule. But the stubborn French troops refused to leave the country and

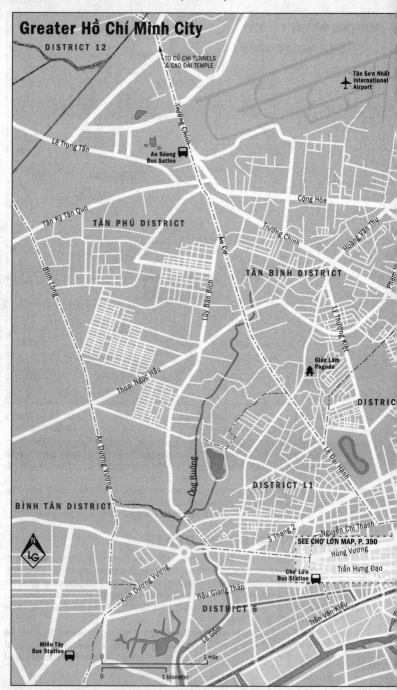

Greater Hồ Chí Minh City

DISTRICT 12

TO CỦ CHI TUNNELS
& CAO ĐÀI TEMPLE

Tân Sơn Nhất
International
Airport

Lê Trọng Tấn

Trường Chinh

An Súong
Bus Satlon

Cộng Hòa

Tân Kỳ Tân Quo

TÂN PHÚ DISTRICT

Trường Chinh

Hoàng Văn Thụ

Bình Long

Lũy Bán Bích

Âu Cơ

TÂN BÌNH DISTRICT

Pham

Thoại Ngọc Hầu

Giác Lâm
Pagoda

Lý Thường Kiệt

DISTRIC

An Dương Vương

Ông Buồng

Lê Đại Hành

BÌNH TÂN DISTRICT

DISTRICT 11

3 Thang 2

Nguyễn Chí Thanh

SEE CHỢ LỚN MAP, P. 390

Hùng Vương

Kinh Dương Vương

Chợ Lớn
Bus Station

Trần Hưng Đạo

Hậu Giang Tháp

Trần Văn Kiệu

DISTRICT 6

Lò Gốm

Miền Tây
Bus Station

0   1 mile

0   1 kilometer

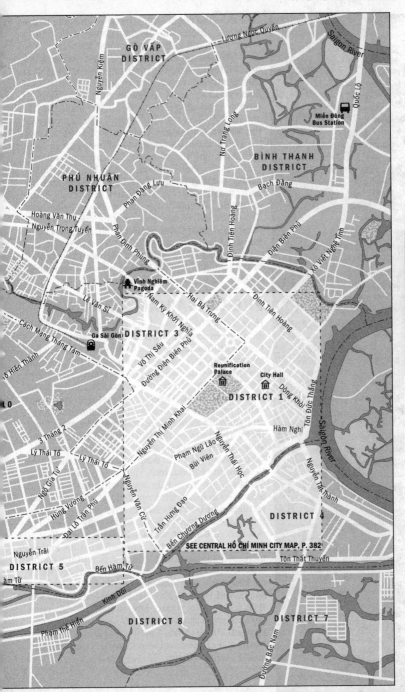

GÒ VẤP
DISTRICT

Lương Ngọc Quyến

Saigon River

Nguyễn Kiệm

Nơ Trang Long

Miền Đông
Bus Station

Quốc Lộ

BÌNH THẠNH
DISTRICT

PHÚ NHUẬN
DISTRICT

Phan Đăng Lưu

Bạch Đằng

Hoàng Văn Thụ
Nguyễn Trọng Tuyển

Phan Đình Phùng

Đinh Tiên Hoàng

Điện Biên Phủ

Xô Viết Nghệ Tĩnh

Lê Văn Sĩ

Vĩnh Nghiêm
Pagoda

Nam Kỳ Khởi Nghĩa

Hai Bà Trưng

Đinh Tiên Hoàng

Cách Mạng Tháng Tám

Ga Sài Gòn

DISTRICT 3

Võ Thị Sáu

Đường Điện Biên Phủ

Reunification
Palace

City Hall

Đồng Khởi

Võ Hiển Thạnh

DISTRICT 1

10

Nguyễn Thị Minh Khai

Hàm Nghi

Tôn Đức Thắng

Saigon River

3 Tháng 2

Lý Thái Tổ

Lý Thái Tổ

Ngô Gia Tự

Phạm Ngũ Lão
Bùi Viện

Nguyễn Thái Học

Nguyễn Tất Thành

Hưng Vương

Nguyễn Văn Cừ

Đại Lộ Trần Phú

Trần Hưng Đạo

Bến Chương Dương

DISTRICT 4

Nguyễn Trãi

DISTRICT 5

Bến Hàm Tử

SEE CENTRAL HỒ CHÍ MINH CITY MAP, P. 382

Tôn Thất Thuyến

àm Tử

Kinh Đôi

DISTRICT 8

Phạm Thế Hiển

DISTRICT 7

Đường Bắc Nam

HỒ CHÍ MINH CITY

VIETNAM'S MOMENTUM

Tam Bui is a Vietnamese-American who lives in Hồ Chí Minh City. With the support of the Fulbright Program, she is researching the role of overseas Vietnamese in the development of Vietnam's Information Technology sector. She also works as a paralegal at the international law firm of Baker & McKenzie. She spoke to us about the many changes currently taking place in Vietnam.

LG: What are some of the reasons for Vietnam's rapid development over the past several years?

A: President Clinton opened diplomatic relations between the US and Vietnam in 1996, and in 2001 the two countries signed a trade agreement. Since then, it's been a lot easier for investors to come into Vietnam, and for Vietnamese companies to export to the US. Also, Vietnam is currently trying to enter the WTO, so it's changing a lot of its regulations in order to comply with WTO standards. Furthermore, Vietnam has a very young, eager, educated labor force. A lot of investors are now looking to Vietnam as a potential outsourcing country, like India or China.

LG: Is there anything standing in the way of development?

A: There are still a number of barriers that Vietnam needs to overcome. In many industries, there is potential for growth, but problems like bureaucracy and lack of legal transparency stand in the way.

[Cont'd on next page...]

instead seized Saigon from the new Communist government, turning independence celebrations into street riots and initiating the First Indochina War between Vietnam and France. Nearly a decade later, in 1954, the French were permanently expelled from the country after their embarrassing defeat at **Điện Biên Phủ** in the north. A few months later, Western powers—including France, the Soviet Union, the UK, and the US—met with Vietnamese officials to create the **Geneva Convention.** Vietnam was divided along the 17th Parallel; the northern half became a communist state, and the southern half became a democratic state. The Vietnamese had little say in the matter, but they complied with the decision, with the understanding that two years later, in 1956, the country would be reunified and hold national elections. The northern half (the Democratic Republic of Vietnam) was handed over to Hồ Chí Minh and his Communist Vietnamese Worker's Party, while the southern half (the Republic of Vietnam) was placed in the hands of **Ngô Đình Diệm,** an anti-Communist political figure who ruled from Saigon.

PRE-LAPSARIAN SAIGON

Here's a sentence you don't see very often: things didn't go exactly as outlined at the Geneva Convention. With the help of the US, the southern contingency was able to develop an anti-Communist government with which to be reckoned. Life under Ngô Đình Diệm was far from ideal, though, for those living in the south. Determined to stay in power, he called on the US to help attack the northern army and guerrilla fighters, the **National Liberation Front (NLF),** which was established in 1960. Diệm employed violent repression as a means of rooting out opposition, passing a law that made it legal to jail suspected Communists without trial. The country's response to Diệm's oppressive rule was swift, however, and Saigon soon became a stronghold of students, intellectuals, and Buddhist monks who worked to make their dissenting voices heard. In the early 1960s, large numbers of **Buddhist monks** set themselves on fire in the streets to protest the repressive regime and its increased military and political action in the southern countryside. The US responded to the outcries by backing a coup that ended mysteriously in the assassination of Diệm in 1963, when **General Nguyễn Văn Thiệu** took over to replace him. In 1964, the American government passed the Gulf of Tonkin Resolution, guaranteeing extended military action against the North and closer involvement with (read: "control over") Thiệu in Saigon.

During the war, Saigon served as the center of US military and intelligence operations, as well as the southern capital under President Thiệu. Most of the local military action occurred in the regions north of the capital city; troops and supplies were transported along the **Hồ Chí Minh Trail,** where the NLF found plenty of wooded cover from which to operate its offensive. In 1966, the US directed its focus at the NLF in the south, who were believed to be hiding in the Củ Chi Tunnels (p. 403) north of the city; frustratingly, they failed to uncover anything. At one point, during the 1968 Tết Offensive, the NLF actually managed to penetrate the US Embassy in Saigon, prompting a speedy American counterstrike. A year later, US President Nixon met with President Thiệu to discuss the withdrawal of troops.

By 1972, more than half of the US forces had left the country. The US then began supplying bombs instead of soldiers—and plenty of bombs, at that. This offensive hindered the progression of peace talks with the North, and it wasn't until the American assault slackened that the ceasefire was signed at the **Paris Peace Accords.** By the end of 1973, the last of the US combat forces had withdrawn, leaving the South in the hands of President Thiệu. Instead of maintaining a strong base in the capital city, Thiệu spread his troops around the region, allowing the NLF to gain strength in the absence of aerial raids and tear through the south at a startling rate. South Vietnamese fled to the coast from their homes in the Central Highlands, although most were captured or killed by the northern troops en route. The confusion rapidly made its way toward Saigon, which was overrun by refugees flooding in from the quickly toppling highlands and coast. President Thiệu resigned, handing power over to **Dương Văn Minh.** The southern government was losing its grip.

THE FALL OF SAIGON

On **April 30, 1975,** hundreds of NLF tanks rolled into Saigon. The troops barreled their way through President Minh's palace and initially refused to let him surrender, proclaiming that there was nothing left to give up. Later, the president was allowed the clemency of a radio announcement.

The remaining American forces promptly evacuated the city, leaving the majority of their South Vietnamese allies to fend for themselves. A few Vietnamese managed to flee with American troops on boats and helicopters, leaving behind everything they owned. Over 2600 children had already been safely transported to the US during **"Operation Babylift,"** and others escaped during **"Operation Frequent**

This is an issue that many developing countries must address.

LG: Do you think the current growth is having any negative effects on the country?

A: One of the most notable effects of development is its impact on the environment. There is so much growth going on everywhere, and I'm not sure to what extent the government is protecting the environment or preserving historical sites. Also, most development is happening in the major cities, and people in the countryside are getting left behind. We have a situation where the rich are becoming richer and the poor are becoming poorer. The increasing disparity is definitely an issue.

LG: How are all these recent changes manifested in Hồ Chí Minh City?

A: Hồ Chí Minh City has always been the economic center of Vietnam, and I think it will continue to be in the coming years. There is so much opportunity here. My good friend Tiffany is an artist who has lived in Hồ Chí Minh City for several years, and she had her first big show in the fall. The theme of the show was "Momentum"; it was a series of installation pieces about the time she has spent here. I think that theme—"Momentum"—really captures the energy, the buzz of this city. There's always the sense of something going on, the feeling that things are moving forward.

Wind," the primary helicopter evacuation from Saigon that began only one day before the tanks rampaged the city. But for the most part, the citizens of Saigon were left in the hands of a new, Communist government and an entirely different way of life. Almost anyone who had been closely tied to the southern government, including military personnel and intellectuals, was captured and sent out of the city to re-education prison camps in the jungle. Those who avoided internment remained in rechristened **Hồ Chí Minh City,** with money that no longer had any value and no claim to their land.

PICKING UP THE PIECES

After the fall of Saigon, times were more than difficult. Southern monetary resources were scarce, and the government was relatively intolerant and corrupt (as it remains, to some extent, today). Many Southern Vietnamese continued to flee the country in order to dodge delayed reprisals for collaborating with the defeated enemy. After over a decade of communist-style economic stagnation, the government softened its stance against the market economy with the inception of **đổi mới** ("open door") liberalizing policies in 1986. The capitalism-starved Saigonese needed no second bidding.

Today, the busy Communist streets, glowing with neon signs and advertisements, look far more market-driven and American-influenced than when it was fighting Communism. Almost seven million people manage to keep up with the fast-paced lifestyle of the big city. Life is far from perfect—there's no escaping the developing world realities of high unemployment rates and widespread poverty—but reincarnation is a way of life in Saigon. It's been that way for centuries.

▣ INTERCITY TRANSPORTATION

FLIGHTS

After you land, be sure to keep your entry/exit form in a safe place, as you will need it upon your departure, along with US$14 for the departure tax. There are several means of transportation to and from Tân Sơn Nhất International Airport, including buses and (more expensive) taxis. The booth for official (though pricey) SASCO Taxis (☎842 4242; admin@sascotaxi.com; $5 flat rate to District 1) is just on the right of the airport exit, after customs.

> **Tân Sơn Nhất International Airport (SGN;** ☎842 4242; www.saigonaiport.com/ sgêothers.html), 5km northwest of the city center. ATM and currency exchange available. Tickets available locally at **Saigon Tourist Service,** 275C Phạm Ngũ Lão (☎837 7660 or 837 8961). Flights to: **Bangkok, Thailand** (1½hr.); **Hà Nội** (2hr.); **Hong Kong, China** (3½hr.); **Huế** (1½hr.); **Jakarta, Indonesia** (4½hr.); **Kuala Lumpur, Malaysia** (3hr.); **Phnom Penh, Cambodia** (50min.); **Siem Reap, Cambodia** (1½hr.); **Singapore** (3hr.); **Seoul, Korea** (6hr.); **Taipei, Taiwan** (4½hr.); **Tokyo, Japan** (6½hr.).

TRAINS

All trains depart from **Ga Sài Gòn** in District 3 and head for Hà Nội, stopping at the towns listed below. Prices are stratified according to class—the cheapest tickets will buy you a hard seat in a crowded compartment, and the most expensive will get you a bed in a sleeping car. One express train departs at 11pm every night headed north; if you take any other train you'll make many more stops than those listed and take a lot longer to reach your destination.

> **Ga Sài Gòn,** 1 Nguyễn Thông (☎843 6528). Tickets can be purchased at the station or at **Saigon Tourist Service,** 275C Phạm Ngũ Lão (☎837 7660 or 837 8961).

Express train departs daily at 11pm for **Hà Nội** (38hr.; 600,000-995,000Đ) via **Nha Trang** (6½hr.; 152,000-252,000Đ); **Diệu Trì** (10½hr.; 233,000-386,000Đ); **Đà Nẵng** (15hr.; 345,000-572,000Đ); **Huế** (17½hr.; 363,000-666,000Đ); **Đồng Hới** (19hr.; 444,000-756,000Đ); **Vinh** (24½hr.; 513,000-898,000Đ).

BUSES

There are two major bus stations in Hồ Chí Minh City. Miền Đông serves destinations north of the city and Vũng Tàu; buses going south depart from Miền Tây. Both stations are quite far from District 1; the easiest way to get there is by motorbike or taxi. The last bus of the day may leave hours before the station closes, so don't wait until 9pm to travel.

Miền Đông Station, in Bình Thạnh District on Xô Việt Nghệ Tinh (Quốc Lộ 13). Buses depart frequently every day 5am-9pm for **Vũng Tàu** (4hr.; 32,000Đ) and **north** to: **Đà Lạt** (5½hr.; 76,000Đ); **Đà Nẵng** (16hr.; 200,000Đ); **Hà Nội** (48hr.; 260,000Đ); **Hải Phòng** (50hr.; 285,000Đ); **Huế** (27hr.; 165,000Đ); **Kon Tum** (12hr.; 140,000Đ); **Mũi Né** (4hr.; 54,000Đ); **Nha Trang** (9hr., 110,000Đ); **Phan Thiết** (3½hr.; 50,000Đ); **Pleiku** (10hr.; 125,000Đ).

Miền Tây Station, in Bình Tán District on Kinh Dương Vương. In most cases, buses depart frequently every day 6am-9pm. Buses go **south** to the Mekong Delta: **Bạc Liêu** (6hr.; 115,000Đ); **Bến Tre** (2hr.; 35,000Đ); **Cà Mau** (8hr.; 47,000Đ); **Cần Thơ** (4hr.; 60,000Đ); **Châu Đốc** (6hr.; 85,000Đ); **Rạch Giá** (6hr.; 85,000Đ); **Sóc Trăng** (6hr.; 78,000Đ); **Trà Vinh** (4hr.; 55,000Đ); **Vĩnh Long** (2hr.; 47,000Đ).

Other Stations: Chợ Lớn Station, in District 5 (Chợ Lớn) on Hải Thượng Lãn Ông. Earliest buses depart at 5am and the station shuts down by 9pm. Buses go to **Mỹ Tho** (1½hr.; 21,000Đ). **An Súong Station,** in Tân Bình District on Trường Chinh. Buses go to **Tây Ninh** (1½hr.; 19,000Đ) and **Củ Chi** (1½hr.; 19,000Đ).

OPEN-TOUR BUSES

The easiest and most popular way to tour Vietnam is on open-tour buses. Operated by most of the tour companies in HCMC (p. 384), these air-conditioned buses traverse the country from HCMC to Hà Nội and stop in major cities along the way. However, they also cut out much of what's authentic about Vietnam in favor of what's easy and comfortable. Passengers can buy a ticket to Hà Nội (US$20-30) and hop on and off whenever; alternatively, they can buy tickets for individual legs of the trip. Tickets are available at any tourist office and some hotels.

FERRIES

Hydrofoils leave from the pier at the southern end of Tôn Đức Thắng. Contact Petro Express (☎821 0650) or Vina Express (☎821 4948 or 829 7892). All ferries go to **Vũng Tàu** (1½hr.; 7 per day 6am-5pm; 120,000Đ).

✈ ORIENTATION

Hồ Chí Minh City consists of 24 districts (*quận*, sometimes abbreviated Q): 12 numbered urban districts, seven named urban districts, and five named suburban districts. Most of the action takes place in **District 1;** not only is it home to the majority of tourist attractions and services, but it also contains the city's burgeoning commercial scene. On its western side, the area between **Phạm Ngũ Lão** and **Bùi Viện** is popular with budget travelers and backpackers for its cheap accommodations and food. Expatriates and luxury travelers tend to congregate near the city's five-star hotel plazas in the east, between **Đồng Khởi** and **Tôn Đức Thắng.** North of District 1, the train station and a number of other sights

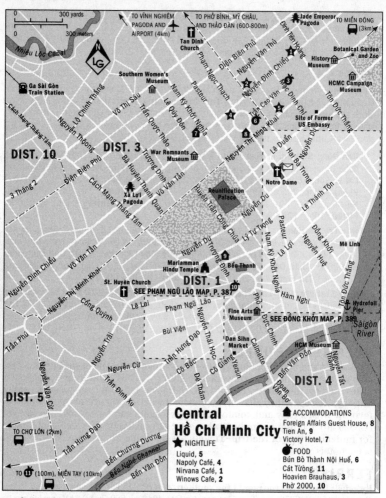

Central Hồ Chí Minh City

★ NIGHTLIFE
Liquid, **5**
Napoly Café, **4**
Nirvana Café, **1**
Winows Cafe, **2**

▲ ACCOMMODATIONS
Foreign Affairs Guest House, **8**
Tien An, **9**
Victory Hotel, **7**

● FOOD
Bún Bò Thành Nội Huế, **6**
Cát Tường, **11**
Hoavien Brauhaus, **3**
Phở 2000, **10**

are located in **District 3**. West of District 1, the ethnic Chinese population of the city is concentrated in **District 5**, also called **Chợ Lớn**.

Streets are sometimes labeled Đ for *đường* or ĐL for *đại lộ*. Alleys are often labeled *hẻm*. **Street numbering** can be quite confusing in HCMC. Street numbers on either side of a road are not necessarily close together; it is possible that 2 might be across from 303, for instance. Some numbers may appear several times in a row on the same street without any distinguishing markers. Other street numbers have a slash in them, which usually means one of two things: either the place occupies several properties (e.g., 17/13 Lê Thánh Tôn, occupying lots 17 and 13) or it is located on an alley (e.g., 40/5 Bùi Viện, located at number 5 on an alley off 40 Bùi Viện). Odds and evens are always on different sides of the street.

▣ LOCAL TRANSPORTATION

Buses: The city bus system can be confusing to foreigners. Many stops are unmarked, and route maps are hard to come by (try asking for one at ▨ **Innoviet Travel,** p. 384). Most buses are labeled with their main stops. The major depot in District 1 is **Bến Thành,** across from Bến Thành Market; **Mê Linh Square** is a smaller station on the riverfront, where Hai Bà Trưng and Tôn Đức Thắng meet. Most bus routes run between the large cities: **Miền Đông, Miền Tay, Chợ Lớn,** and **An Súong;** see **Intercity Transportation,** p. 380. Tickets are 2000-3000Đ.

Taxis: There are a number of taxi companies in HCMC, but not all are trustworthy. Check that your taxi has a meter, and make sure that the driver turns it on when you set off. Most meters start at 12,000Đ. A trip anywhere within District 1 should cost no more than 20,000Đ. Yellow Vina taxis (☎811 1111) and green-and-white ML taxis (☎925 0250) are considered reputable.

▨ **Motorbikes:** Tourists in HCMC will constantly be offered the services of motorbike drivers, who transport people on the back of their vehicles. Drivers are generally very friendly and the ride is a lot of fun, if a bit hair-raising. Motorbikes, or *xe ôms,* are not metered, so the fee involves some bargaining. A typical rate is around 2000-3000Đ per km, and a ride within District 1 should cost no more than 10,000Đ. Agree on the price before you get onto the bike. Almost nobody in HCMC wears a **helmet,** but Let's Go recommends it (see **"Promote Helmets, Prevent Death,"** p. 91).

TRAFFIC TRAUMAS. Crossing the street in Hồ Chí Minh City is a daring and dicey proposition: cars, motorbikes, and other vehicles rarely stop if they see someone waiting to cross. So how can pedestrians safely cross the street? The trick is to walk at a slow, steady pace and trust in the inscrutable god of traffic. Most drivers are accustomed to dodging pedestrians (and one another), so if they spot you in their path, they will veer out of your way. If you try to dart around them, they will only get confused, making a horrible accident more likely. Never stop dead in your tracks, or you will face a wave of oncoming drivers, all honking at you angrily. So set off confidently and trust that the mob of vehicles coming toward you will get out of your way in time. Good luck...

Cyclos: Popular with tourists, cyclos are bicycles with a seat attached to the front. Although they're slower than motorbikes, the drivers may charge more because they have to work harder to transport passengers. Consider paying 3000-4000Đ per km. Many cyclo drivers speak English and give city tours; 15,000Đ per hr. is the usual fare. Cyclos are banned on some major streets.

Car Rental: The Vietnamese government prohibits foreigners (even those with international licenses) from driving cars. You can rent a car with a driver, however, for about US$5 per hr. Inquire with a tour company (p. 384) or any large hotel.

Motorbike and Bicycle Rental: Many hotels and guesthouses rent motorbikes and bicycles to those brave enough to face the traffic. Make sure you know what you're getting yourself into. The typical rate for motorbikes is US$5-10 per day; for bicycles, around US$1 per day.

HỒ CHÍ MINH CITY

7 PRACTICAL INFORMATION

TOURIST AND FINANCIAL SERVICES

Tourist Office: There is a **SASCO** tourist booth (☎844 6666; www.saigonairport.com) at the airport, just before the baggage claim. Services include hotel reservations and tour booking. Free maps available. Open 24hr.

Tours: There are countless tour companies in HCMC, and many offer similar packages and rates. Most companies arrange city and regional tours. You can also buy **open-tour bus tickets.**

■ **Innoviet Travel,** 158 Bùi Viện (☎295 8840). Friendly service and small-group tours. English spoken.

Sinh, 246 Đề Thám (☎837 6833; www.sinhcafevn.com). Well-known and popular. Doubles as a cafe. Open daily 6:30am-10pm.

Kim, 270 Đề Thám (☎920 5552 or 920 5553; www.kimtravel.com). Nearly identical to Sinh. Open daily 6:30am-10pm.

SaigonTourist, 49 Lê Thánh Tôn (☎824 4554; www.saigontourist.net). Government-operated; sells plane, train, and bus tickets as well as tours. Open daily 7:30am-6:30pm.

Consulates: Australia, 5B Tôn Đức Thắng (☎831 7755); open M-F 8:30am-noon and 1-5pm. **Cambodia,** 45 Phùng Khắc Khoan (☎829 2751); open M-F 8:30-11:30am and 2-5pm. **Canada,** 235 Đồng Khởi (☎827 9899); open M-Th 8am-noon and 1-5pm, F 8am-1:30pm. **China,** 39 Nguyễn Thị Minh Khai (☎829 2457); open M-F 8-11am and 2-5pm. **Laos,** 93 Pasteur (☎829 7667); open M-F 8:30-11:30am and 1:30-4:30pm. **New Zealand,** 41 Nguyễn Thị Minh Khai (☎822 6907); open M-F 8:30am-5pm. **Thailand,** 77 Trần Quốc Thảo (☎932 7637); open M-F 8:30-11:30am and 1-4:30pm. **UK,** 25 Lê Duẩn (☎829 8433); open M-F 8:30-11:30am and 1-3pm. **US,** 4 Lê Duẩn (☎822 9433); open M-Th 7:30-11:30am and 1:30-5:30pm.

Visas: Most tour companies can arrange tourist visas to neighboring countries. This is usually quicker and more convenient than going to the consulate, and the price is comparable.

Banks: The banks listed below all have **24hr. ATM** service. Other ATMs are everywhere but don't always work; if your first try doesn't work, try another machine nearby.

ANZ, 11 Mê Linh (☎829 9319). Open M-F 8:30am-4pm.

HSBC, 235 Đồng Khởi (☎829 2288). Open M-Th 8:30am-4:30pm, F 8:30am-5pm.

Incombank, 211 Nguyễn Thái Học (☎837 8778). Open M-F 7:30-11:30am and 1-5pm, Sa 7:30-11:30am.

American Express: Exotissimo, Saigon Trade Center, 37 Tôn Đức Thắng (☎825 1723), a registered AmEx Travel Service office. Open M-F 8:30am-noon and 1:30-5:30pm.

Beyond Tourism:

Sozo, 176 Bùi Viện and 844 Sư Hanh (☎838 8825). Nonprofit cafes providing jobs to children who would otherwise be on the streets selling gum and postcards. See **Beyond Tourism,** p. 92.

■ **Thảo Đàn,** 451/1 Hai Bà Trưng (☎846 5410; thaodan@hcmc.netnam.vn), in the alley off 451 Hai Bà Trưng. A charity providing former street children with education in English, French, Japanese, Vietnamese, and math. See **Beyond Tourism,** p. 92.

The Network, an organization of charitable opportunities all across the city, ranging from volunteering in homeless shelters and hospitals to building schools for street children. Contact Elizabeth Copley (☎9292 0100; elizabethcopley@hotmail.com). See **Beyond Tourism,** p. 90.

Vietnamese Cookery School, 117 Diện Biên Phủ (☎823 5872; www.vietnamcookery.com). Offers day-long courses in traditional Vietnamese cooking for amateurs and professionals.

LOCAL SERVICES

Bookstores: Fahasa, 185 Đồng Khởi (☎822 4670). Huge, with a fair selection of Chinese, English, and French literature, as well as language books. Also sells stationery. Open daily 8am-10pm. **Thu Vân,** 179 Phạm Ngũ Lão (☎837 3288), behind the tourist office. Used books in Chinese, English, French, and German; also sells travel guides, language books, and popular novels. Buys and exchanges books. Open daily 8am-10pm.

Library: 69 Lý Tự Trọng. Open Tu-Su 7:30am-7pm.

Publications: *Saigon Inside Out* is an invaluable source of listings for restaurants, bars, massage places, and just about everything else. Found in hotels and big bookshops.

Laundromat: Almost all hotels and guesthouses have laundry service. Budget travelers should expect to pay 6000-10,000Đ per load.

EMERGENCY AND COMMUNICATIONS

Emergency: Ambulance ☎ 115. **Fire ☎** 114. Not all operators speak English. If you have a medical emergency, it is better to call the emergency number at one of the medical services below, or have a taxi take you directly there.

Police: ☎ 113. If you run into any problems with the law, contact your national consulate immediately.

Pharmacies: In most cases, you do not need a prescription; just ask for the medicine you need by its generic name. Hospitals recommend **Mỹ Châu,** located at 389 Hai Bà Trưng (☎822 2266; open daily 6:30am-10:30pm) for its large selection. There is a small pharmacy at 81 Bùi Viện (☎836 0050; open daily 7am-10pm).

Medical Services: The following all have 24hr. emergency service.

Columbia Asia, 8 Alexandre de Rhodes (☎823 8888; same for emergency). Open M-F 8am-6pm.

Family Medical Practice, Diamond Plaza, 34 Lê Duẩn (☎822 7848; same for emergency). Open M-F 8:30am-5pm, Sa 8:30am-12:30pm.

International SOS, 65 Nguyễn Du (☎829 8424; emergency ☎829 8520). Open M-F 7am-8pm, Sa 7am-6pm.

Telephones: General Assistance: ☎ 1080; **International Operator: ☎** 110. International direct calls are always pricey (18,000-20,000Đ per min.), but **Internet phone** calls are cheaper and usually work just as well. Many hotels and guesthouses offer this service for 5000-10,000Đ per min. You can also purchase Internet phone cards (1000-5000Đ) at most Internet cafes. International phone cards (2400Đ per min.) can be purchased only at the Central Post Office (see below).

Internet Access: Internet is everywhere in HCMC, especially around Phạm Ngũ Lão. It's harder to find in Đồng Khởi and Chợ Lớn. Expect to pay 6000-40,000Đ per hr. for a regular connection. A few places in HCMC offer wireless:

■ **Sozo,** 176 Bùi Viện (☎838 8825; www.sozocentre.com). Best connection in Phạm Ngũ Lão. Doubles as a nonprofit cafe (see **Beyond Tourism,** p. 92). Friendly staff serves Western-style muffins and cakes. Comfy couches. Free wireless for customers. Open M-Sa 7am-10:30pm.

Cafe Stay, 76 Nguyễn Thị Minh Khai (☎825 7987; cafestay@vnn.vn). All-wood decor, loud cheesy music. Free wireless for customers. Drinks 15,000-45,000Đ. Entrees 15,000-22,000Đ. Open daily 7am-midnight.

I-BOX, 135 Hai Bà Trưng (☎825 6718). Low lighting and a less reliable connection. Free wireless for customers. Snacks 35,000-95,000Đ.

Post Office: 2 Công Xã Paris (☎823 0847), opposite Notre Dame Cathedral in a huge colonial-style building. A tourist attraction in its own right. Open daily 7am-9pm. Second branch at 14 Bùi Viện (☎837 7715). Open daily 7am-9pm.

HỒ CHÍ MINH CITY

▐ ACCOMMODATIONS

Most budget accommodations in Hồ Chí Minh City have a variety of room options: with or without air-conditioning, window, bath, balcony, etc. A few dollars more will get you a larger room with better facilities. Many places do not make a distinction between singles and doubles; there is often one double bed, and the number of people you share it with is up to you. Unless otherwise indicated, the price ranges below reflect the cost of one or two people staying in a room. Check out rooms before you book them—many lack windows or are on top floors in buildings without elevators.

ACCOMMODATIONS BY PRICE

UNDER US$6/UNDER 96,000Đ (❶)		**US$10-16/160,000-255,000Đ (❸)**	
Dìn Ký (390)	CL	Canadian Hotel 281 (388)	PNL
Huong Duong (386)	PNL	Lucy (388)	PNL
Mai (388)	PNL	Madame Cúc (387)	PNL
Ngoc Guesthouse (388)	PNL	Mai Phai (388)	PNL
Phước Hưng (388)	PNL	▧ Nga Quân (389)	ĐK
		Quyền Thanh (386)	PNL
US$6-10/96,000-160,000Đ (❷)		Tien An (390)	ELSE
Cát Tường (390)	CL		
Foreign Affairs Guesthouse (390)	ELSE	**US$16-30/255,000-480,000Đ (❹)**	
Mimi (387)	PNL	▧ N. Y. Kim Phuong (389)	ĐK
Minh (389)	NPNL	Spring House (387)	PNL
▧ Miss Lợi (388)	NPNL		
Ngọc Huệ (388)	NPNL	**OVER US$30/OVER 480,000Đ (❺)**	
▧ Ngọc Minh (386)	PNL	Grand Hotel (390)	ĐK
Thanh (388)	NPNL		

> **CL** Chợ Lớn **ĐK** Đồng Khởi **ELSE** Elsewhere in HCMC **NPNL** Near Phạm Ngũ Lão
> **PNL** Phạm Ngũ Lão

PHẠM NGŨ LÃO

This area is a budget travel mecca. Every street is packed with cheap hotels; the ones listed here are just a fraction of the enormous total. Some prices may be negotiable, especially for longer stays. If you're looking for some peace and quiet, try one of the alleyways off the main streets; many have decent guesthouses. All hotels listed have air-conditioning in every room unless otherwise noted. Most places, however, have no elevator and go up over five floors; not all rooms have windows. Inquire at the front desk about specific amenities

▧ **Ngọc Minh,** 283/11 Phạm Ngũ Lão (☎837 6407; ngocminhhotel@vnn.vn), on a charming, plant-lined alley that runs off 283 Phạm Ngũ Lão and connects to Đỗ Quang Đẩu. Fresh, blue-colored rooms; lobby has pleasant cafe-style seating. Breakfast included. Free Internet. Singles USụ10; doubles USụ12. ❷

Quyền Thanh, 212 Đề Thám (☎836 8570; www.vietnamstay.com/hotel/quyenthanh), at its intersection with Bùi Viện. Located on a corner above a tourist shop, in the center of the action. Friendly staff and simple but inviting rooms with TVs. Terraces are perfect for people-watching. Rooms USụ11-12. ❸

Huong Duong, 265/3 Phạm Ngũ Lão (☎836 4442), buried in a tiny alley off Hạm Ngũ Lão between Đỗ Quang Đẩu and Đề Thám. Incredibly cheap but be prepared for basic

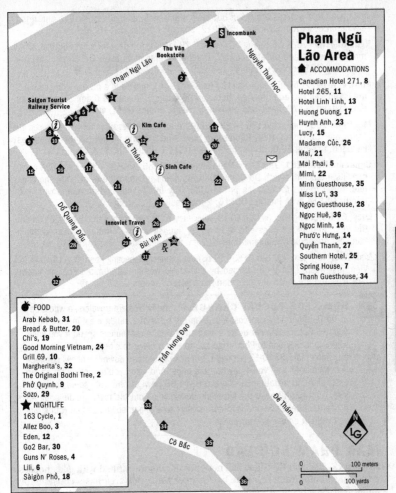

Phạm Ngũ Lão Area

🛖 ACCOMMODATIONS

Canadian Hotel 271, **8**
Hotel 265, **11**
Hotel Linh Linh, **13**
Huong Duong, **17**
Huynh Anh, **23**
Lucy, **15**
Madame Cúc, **26**
Mai, **21**
Mai Phai, **5**
Mimi, **22**
Minh Guesthouse, **35**
Miss Lo'i, **33**
Ngọc Guesthouse, **28**
Ngọc Huệ, **36**
Ngọc Minh, **16**
Phưới'c Hưng, **14**
Quyền Thanh, **27**
Southern Hotel, **25**
Spring House, **7**
Thanh Guesthouse, **34**

🍎 FOOD

Arab Kebab, **31**
Bread & Butter, **20**
Chi's, **19**
Good Morning Vietnam, **24**
Grill 69, **10**
Margherita's, **32**
The Original Bodhi Tree, **2**
Phở Quynh, **9**
Sozo, **29**

⭐ NIGHTLIFE

163 Cycle, **1**
Allez Boo, **3**
Eden, **12**
Go2 Bar, **30**
Guns N' Roses, **4**
Lili, **6**
Sàigòn Phố, **18**

HỒ CHÍ MINH CITY

living and the occasional roach. No A/C; fans in every room. Internet 10,000Đ per hr. or 300,000Đ per month for long-term visitors. Free laundry. Rooms USự1. ❶

Madame Cúc, 64 Bùi Viện (☎836 5073; madamecuc@hcm.vnn.vn), between Đề Thám and Dỗ Quang Đẩu. Comfortable rooms, friendly staff, and good value for those who capitalize on the free breakfast, dinner, bananas, coffee, and tea. One of the few hotels around with a social space: travelers can share stories over breakfast. Madame Cúc also has two cousins slightly farther from the backpacker zone, at 127 and 184 Cống Quỳnh. Rooms USự16-20. ❸

Spring House, 221 Phạm Ngũ Lão (☎837 8312; hanhhaohotel@hcm.vnn.vn), between Đề Thám and Dỗ Quang Đẩu. Bright, clean, lemon-yellow rooms with rattan furniture and a cheery atmosphere. Some have excellent views of the park. Singles US$18; doubles US$20. ❹

Mimi, 40/5 Bùi Viện (☎836 9645; mimihotel405@yahoo.fr), on the alley that runs off 40 Bùi Viện and connects to Phạm Ngũ Lão. Free, reliable Internet. Internet phone also available. Rooms are clean but have small maintenance issues. TVs and refrigerators in every room. Singles US$8-12; spacious triples US$10. ❷.

Ngoc Guesthouse, 3 Dỗ Quang Đầu (☎837 7241). A good deal for a tight budget; small rooms have TVs and private showers. Hotel also rents motorbikes (US$5 per day) and bicycles (US$1 per day). Laundry 10,000Đ per load. Rooms US$4-7. ❶

Phước Hưng, 265/1B Phạm Ngũ Lão (☎836 7040), tucked in a narrow alley connecting Phạm Ngũ Lão and Bùi Viện, between Dỗ Quang Đầu and Đề Thám. Slanting steps, fans instead of A/C; basic and obscenely cheap. Rooms US$1. ❶

Mai Phai, 209 Phạm Ngũ Lão (☎836 5868; maiphaihotel@saigonnet.vn), between Đề Thám and Dỗ Quang Đầu. Rooms are plain and bathrooms are palatial. Breakfast included. Internet 10,000Đ per hr. Singles US$13; doubles US$12. ❸

Canadian Hotel 281, 281 Phạm Ngũ Lão (☎837 8666; www.281canadianhotel.com), near its intersection with Dỗ Quang Đầu. Its name refers to the owner, not the clientele. Great rooms for average prices. Über-chic lobby and modern rooms with A/C. Rooms US$14; with Internet US$16; 2-room suite US$30. ❸

Lucy, 61 Dỗ Quang Đầu (☎836 0713; www.lucyresort.net), between Phạm Ngũ Lão and Bùi Viện. Rooms are huge and have quirky flourishes like Corinthian columns; many "singles" are actually mini-apartments. Great for longer stays. Rooms US$15. ❸

Mai, 241/41 Phạm Ngũ Lão (☎836 9176), on an alley connecting Phạm Ngũ Lão and Bùi Viện, just west of Đề Thám. Owned by a kind old woman with limited English. Rooms lack A/C and are much cheaper than most hotels. Rooms US$3.50. ❶

> **HCMC FOR POCKET CHANGE.** For many Western travelers, a whole day in Hồ Chí Minh City can cost less than the price of a single meal in their home country. But you can get by for a fraction of what most tourists spend if you know where to look. Head to Phạm Ngũ Lão to find a place to sleep—you can crash in any hostel for US$10-15 per night, but poke your head down the alleys connecting to Bùi Viện and you'll pay half the price. And when you're looking for cheap eats, skip the restaurants, where a US$1.30 bowl of phở only *seems* inexpensive, until you discover the street vendors dishing out the tasty noodle soup for 40 cents. Street-side phở is almost always safe to eat, so you can fill your stomach without emptying your wallet.

NEAR PHẠM NGŨ LÃO

Between Cô Bắc and Cô Giang is a network of alleyways filled with guesthouses. Less than a 10min. walk from the backpacker zone, this area has a considerably calmer feel. As a result, it's quite popular for longer stays; ask guesthouse owners about low monthly rates, but watch out for rooms without windows. Unless you want a workout, avoid rooms on top floors—few guesthouses have elevators.

 Miss Lợi, 178/20 Cô Giang (☎837 9589; missloi@hcm.fpt.vn), on the alley that runs off 178 Cô Giang and connects to Cô Bắc. One of the first and best in the guesthouse business. Warm staff and a great common area with inviting couches and a pool table. TVs have HBO. Breakfast included. Rooms US$8-12. ❷

Ngọc Huệ, 171/22 Cô Bắc (☎836 0089; ngochuehotel@yahoo.com), on the alley that runs off 171 Cô Bắc and connects to Cô Giang. Gorgeous rooftop garden terraces with excellent views. Long-term rooms are especially elegant; rooms for short-term stays are less impressive but still do the trick. Social atmosphere. Breakfast included. Motorbike rental around $4 per day. Visa extension service available. Rooms US$8-10. ❷

Thanh, 171/1E Cô Bắc (☎836 8469; huutri2001@hcm.vnn.vn), on the same alley that runs off 171 Cô Bắc and connects to Cô Giang. Refreshingly clean rooms. Breakfast included. Rooms US$6-8. ❷

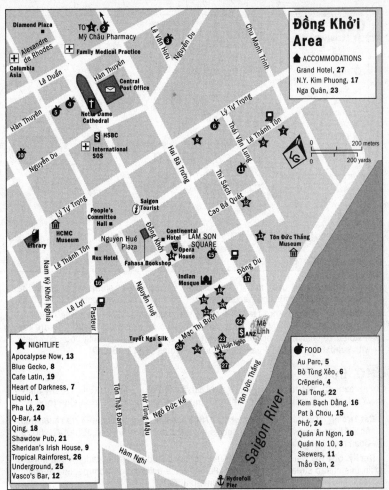

Đồng Khởi Area

⌂ ACCOMMODATIONS
Grand Hotel, **27**
N.Y. Kim Phuong, **17**
Nga Quân, **23**

0 ———— 200 meters
0 ———— 200 yards

★ NIGHTLIFE
Apocalypse Now, **13**
Blue Gecko, **8**
Cafe Latin, **19**
Heart of Darkness, **7**
Liquid, **1**
Pha Lê, **20**
Q-Bar, **14**
Qing, **18**
Shawdow Pub, **21**
Sheridan's Irish House, **9**
Tropical Rainforest, **26**
Underground, **25**
Vasco's Bar, **12**

🍎 FOOD
Au Parc, **5**
Bò Tùng Xẻo, **6**
Crêperie, **4**
Dai Tong, **22**
Kem Bạch Dằng, **16**
Pat à Chou, **15**
Phở, **24**
Quán Ăn Ngon, **10**
Quán No 10, **3**
Skewers, **11**
Thảo Đàn, **2**

HỒ CHÍ MINH CITY

Minh, 171/3 Cô Bắc (☎836 4153; minhgh@yahoo.com), on that same alley that runs off 171 Cô Bắc and connects to Cô Giang. Run by a friendly family. Cheapest rooms have fans but no A/C. Rooms US$8-12. ❷

ĐỒNG KHỞI

For those who want to be close to the city's main attractions and don't mind paying a few dollars extra, Đồng Khởi may be the place. Rooms and facilities are typically a step up from the backpacker zone, justifying the extra cost.

▨ **Nga Quân,** 10/1 Ho Huan Nghiệp (☎824 2471), on the alley that runs off 10 Ho Huan Nghiệp. Tucked away from the main drag. Rooms are spacious with lots of light. An excellent value. Rooms US$15-20. ❸

▨ **N. Y. Kim Phuong,** 22 Hai Bà Trưng (☎824 4290; www.nykimphuonghotel.com), between Đông Du and Lê Lợi. Colorful yellow and purple lobby, pleasant rooms with quirks (a

HỒ CHÍ MINH CITY

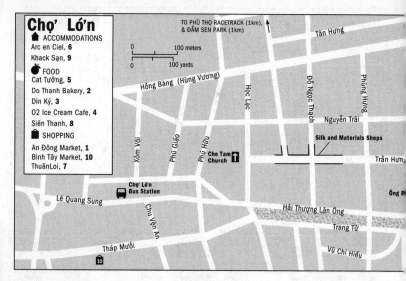

Chọ' Lố'n

ACCOMMODATIONS
Arc en Ciel, **6**
Khack Sạn, **9**

FOOD
Cat Tường, **5**
Do Thanh Bakery, **2**
Dìn Ký, **3**
O2 Ice Cream Cafe, **4**
Siên Thanh, **8**

SHOPPING
An Đông Market, **1**
Bình Tây Market, **10**
ThuânLoi, **7**

TO PHÚ THỌ RACETRACK (1km),
& ĐẦM SEN PARK (1km)

Tân Hưng
Hồng Bàng (Hùng Vương)
Hoc Lac
Đỗ Ngọc Thạch
Phùng Hưng
Nguyễn Trãi
Silk and Materials Shops
Xóm Vôi
Phú Giáo
Phú Hữu
Che Tam Church
Trần Hưn
Chọ' Lố'n Bus Station
Lê Quang Sung
Chu Vện An
Hải Thượng Lãn Ông
Ông B
Trang Tử
Tháp Mười
Vũ Chí Hiếu

small model ship in one), and a gracious staff. Fantastic views on the upper floors. The connection to New York, however, mystifies us. Internet $2 per day. Rooms US$22-30. ④

Grand Hotel, 8 Đồng Khởi (☎823 0163; www.grandsaigon.com), near the riverfront. Constructed in 1930, this luxury hotel lives up to its name. Highlights are the restored colonial elevator and the lovely tiled atrium with swimming pool, complete with sunbathing chairs. Breakfast included. Rooms US$75-180. ⑤

CHỌ' LỐ'N

Cheap eats are not hard to come by in District 5. Poke your head down any alleyway and you're bound to discover some inexpensive but tasty street-side food.

Cát Tưởng, 105 Trần Hưng Đạo (☎853 7869), near its intersection with Trần Xuân Hòa. An outdoor Chinese eatery that serves excellent dim sum. Entrees 18,000-20,000Đ. Open daily 6am-midnight. ②

Dìn Ký, 667 Nguyễn Trãi (☎867 4300). Enjoy good food alongside students and workers in this cheap streetside restaurant. Perfect for a quick break from pagoda-hopping. Meat and rice 10,000Đ. Open daily 8am-9pm. ①

ELSEWHERE IN HCMC

Tien An, 22 Trương Định (☎822 4834; www.hoteltienan.com), near the intersection with Lê Thánh Tôn, just one street from Bến Thành market. Clean rooms with warm wood accents. Rooms US$18-25. ④

Foreign Affairs Guesthouse, 1B Phạm Ngọc Thạch (☎829 7218), at the intersection with Nguyễn Thị Minh Khai—conveniently close to the Notre Dame Cathedral and the Central Post Office. This decent guesthouse is part of the International Organization for Migration; not surprisingly, the staff is welcoming to foreigners. Rooms US$15-20. ③

🍴 FOOD

Pull up a plastic chair—the true taste of Hồ Chí Min City is in the streets. Sidewalk stands and market stalls may lack the sophisticated ambience Western travelers

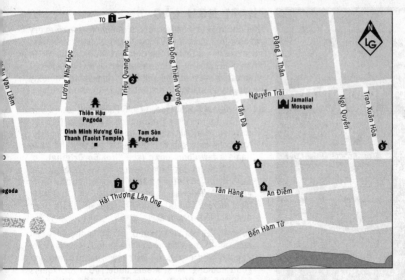

are used to, but the taste and price (most dishes under 10,000Đ) are unbeatable. There are also several Western-style **supermarkets** in the city, including Maximark (Saigon Center, 65 Lê Lợi; ☎ 821 0320; open daily 9am-9pm) and Coopmart (168 Nguyễn Đình Chiểu; ☎ 930 7384; open daily 7am-9pm).

FOOD BY TYPE

CHINESE
Cát Tường (394)	CL ❷
Dai Tong (393)	ĐK ❸
Dìn Ký (394)	CL ❶

CZECH
Hoavien Brauhaus (394)	ELSE ❸

DELI
Au Parc (393)	ĐK ❸

DESSERT/SNACKS
Crêperie and Café (393)	ĐK ❸
Kem Bạch Đằng (393)	ĐK ❷
02 (394)	CL ❸
🖼 Pat à Chou (393)	ĐK ❶

EXPAT
Chi's (392)	PNL ❷

ITALIAN
Good Morning Vietnam (392)	PNL ❸
Margherita's (392)	PNL ❷

MEDITERRANEAN
🖼 Skewers (393)	ĐK ❹

SOUTH ASIAN
Arab Kebab (392)	PNL ❷

VEGETARIAN
🖼 The Original Bodhi Tree (392)	PNL ❷

VIETNAMESE
Bò Tùng Xèo (393)	ĐK ❸
Bún Bò Thành Nội Huế (394)	ELSE ❶
Grill 69 (393)	PNL ❸
🖼 Phở 2000 (394)	ELSE ❷
Phở 24 (393)	ĐK ❷
Phở Quynh (392)	PNL ❶
Siêu Thanh (394)	CL ❷
Quán Ăn Ngon (393)	ĐK ❶
Quán No 10 (393)	ĐK ❷

WESTERN
Bread and Butter (392)	PNL ❷

CL Chợ Lớn **ĐK** Đồng Khởi **ELSE** Elsewhere in HCMC **PNL** Phạm Ngũ Lão

NOT SO ORIGINAL

Starting a restaurant in Hồ Chí Minh City's backpacker zone can be a tricky business. Restaurateurs have to manage the daily grind of cooking, serving, and soliciting customers—and in HCMC, there's the added threat of a copyright lawsuit.

The owners of "The Original Bodhi Tree" restaurant and "The Original Buddha" have been locked in a feud for years over the claim to the "Original Bodhi" name. Current "Buddha" owner, Hữu Thọ, claims that his restaurant was set up in 1995 at the current "Bodhi" address. He says that after he moved addresses, the new owner of his old plot took the name of his restaurant, bought the rights, and delivered a nasty letter to Hữu demanding that he change name.

But Phạm Thanh Há, current "Bodhi" owner, says that "Buddha" was never at the Bodhi address. Instead, she says, the current "Buddha" was set up in 2000, seven years after her "Bodhi" was allegedly in business. And Phạm says she has been the victim of a vicious publicity campaign by the duplicitous "Buddha" owner.

In an area changing as rapidly as Phạm Ngũ Lão, history can be hard to maintain. Some locals do seem to recall that the original "Bodhi" has moved, perhaps corroborating Hữu's side of the story. But whichever side is true, one thing is certain: the publicity has not been bad for business.

PHẠM NGŨ LÃO

This backpacker haven offers dishes to make every traveler feel at home. Pizzas, curries, pancakes, and tacos are just a few of the comfort foods available in Phạm Ngũ Lão. Such options are great if you just can't eat another bowl of phš; but don't dismiss too quickly the quality Vietnamese restaurants in the area, either.

The Original Bodhi Tree, 175/6 Phạm Ngũ Lão (☎836 9545), on the alley that runs off 175 Phạm Ngũ Lão (marked by a Chinese arch) and connects to Bùi Viện. Not to be confused with the restaurant with the same name a few doors down (see **"Not So Original,"** p. 392). A quality vegetarian eatery. Try the generous and delightfully crispy portion of fried spring rolls (10,000Đ) followed by banana pancakes (15,000Đ). Most entrees 10,000-15,000Đ; pizzas 40,000Đ. Open daily 7:30am-10pm. ❷

Chi's, 40/27 Bùi Viện (☎920 4874), on the alley that runs off 40 Bùi Viện and connects to Phạm Ngũ Lão. Popular with expats for its casual atmosphere and good cooking. Most meals under 40,000Đ; beers 12,000Đ-25,000Đ; drinks 25,000-40,000Đ. Free delivery. Open daily 7am-midnight. ❷

Phở Quynh, 323 Phạm Ngũ Lão (☎836 8515), at its intersection with Đỗ Quang Đẩu. A few steps away from the budget haunts, this local 24hr. favorite serves flavorful phở alongside a comically large garnish plate of fresh herbs and chilis. Phở 16,000Đ. ❶

Bread and Butter, 40/24 Bùi Viện (☎836 8452), on the alley that runs off 40 Bùi Viện and connects to Phạm Ngũ Lão; opposite Chi's. Owned by an Australian expat, this casual eatery serves simple but excellent Western food such as chicken schnitzel and fries (40,000Đ). Open daily 6am-11pm. ❷

Good Morning Vietnam, 197 Đề Thám (☎837 1894; www.goodmorningviet.com), on the alley that connects Bùi Viện and Phạm Ngũ Lão. This Italian eatery serves large but average-tasting pizzas (50,000-112,000Đ). Impressive selection of Italian liquor (30,000-60,000Đ). Open daily 9am-12:30am. ❸

Margherita's, 159 Bùi Viện (☎836 8892; mar_jewelry@yahoo.com). This combined jewelry shop and restaurant serves great Vietnamese, Italian, and Mexican food. Jewelry shop at the back; displayed paintings are all for sale as well. Most meals 20,000-40,000Đ. Open daily 7am-1pm and 3-11pm. ❷

Arab Kebab, 115 Bùi Viện (☎827 9867). Shimmering yellow-and-silver decor, waiters with good English. Decent, if rather small, kebabs (29,000-46,000Đ). Great for that late-night hunger. Open daily 11:30am-2am. ❷

Grill 69, 275H Phạm Ngũ Lão (☎836 7936; tomlyon69@hotmail.com). A wide range of dishes with a simple theme: meat. Clean and modern. Meat entrees 35,000-100,000Đ. Wine 200,000-350,000Đ. Open daily 8am-11pm. ❸

ĐỒNG KHỞI AREA

Many of the restaurants in this area cater to expatriates, middle-class Vietnamese, and luxury tourists. Prices may be a bit higher here than in the budget zone, but the quality of the food is more consistent.

▓ **Skewers,** 9A Thái Văn Lung (☎822 4798; www.skewers-restaurant.com), between Cao Bá Quát and Lê Thánh Tôn. Be treated like royalty for an evening. Impeccable service and exquisite Mediterranean cuisine make your experience well worth the higher price. Drop by during lunch for the same food at cheaper prices (60,000-90,000Đ). The ice should come from sterilized water and be safe to drink; check with your server. Entrees 70,000-250,000Đ. Open M-F 11am-2pm and 6-10:30pm, Sa-Su 6-10:30pm. ❹

▓ **Pat à Chou,** 65 Hai Bà Trưng (☎824 5873). French-style patisserie with a delicious baking smell in the air. Great for breakfast on the run. Standing room only. Pastries 7000-10,000Đ. Open daily 9:30am-6pm. ❶

Quán Ăn Ngon, 138 Nam Kỳ Khởi Nghĩa (☎825 7179; www.quananngon.com), between Hàn Thuyên and Nguyễn Du, right near the entrance to Reunification Palace. This laid-back Vietnamese restaurant serves wonderful dishes at remarkably affordable prices. Entrees 14,000-20,000Đ. Open daily 7am-11pm; kitchen closes at 10pm. ❶

Au Parc, 23 Hàn Thuyên (☎829 2772; auparc@hcm.vnn.vn), near its intersection with Pasteur. This upscale deli makes fantastic sandwiches with ingredients like baked brie and smoked salmon. Treat yourself to a meal here amid the colorful North African decor and skylights. Breakfast (served until 11am) 15,000-42,000Đ; sandwiches and salads 49,000-90,000Đ. Takeout and delivery available. Open daily 7am-6pm. ❸

Phở 24, 89 Mạc Thị Bưởi (☎825 8325; pho24@hcm.vnn.vn), between Đồng Khởi and Hai Bà Trưng. Sure, you could get cheaper phở on the sidewalk, but you'd miss out on the chic cosmopolitan atmosphere of this restaurant. Especially popular with locals for breakfast. Phở 24,000-31,000Đ. Open daily 7am-midnight. ❷

Crêperie & Café, 5 Hàn Thuyên (☎829 9117). Tucked between two larger buildings, the Creperie is marked by its pleasant, green-checkered parasols. Serves up a range of crepes and pastries. Savory crepes 50,000-70,000Đ; sweet 38,000-60,000Đ. Entrees 60,000-175,000Đ. Open daily 7am-11pm. ❸

Dai Tong, 1 Phan Văn Đạt (☎824 7025), near the Tôn Đức Thắng statue in Mê Linh Square. Delicious and beautifully prepared Chinese food, plus humorously attentive service. The whole roast suckling pig (250,000Đ) serves a large group. Most meals 30,000-90,000Đ; Chinese delicacies are pricier. Open daily 7am-11pm. ❸

Quán No 10, 10 Lê Văn Hưu (☎822 9074), between Lê Duẩn and Nguyễn Du. A great place to sample cuisine from Hà Nội. Hilarious typos on the English menu. Entrees 15,000-55,000Đ. Open daily 6am-11pm. ❷

Bò Tùng Xẻo, 31 Lý Tự Trọng (☎825 1330), between Thái Văn Lung and Hai Bà Trưng. Watch out: there are five "#31"s in a row on this road. The place to experience Vietnamese barbecue—amongst a sea of plastic chairs. The rest of the menu covers the whole animal kingdom: try the roast scorpion (60,000Đ) or just ogle the snakes in the back. Or eat them. Dishes 20,000-90,000Đ. Open daily 10am-10pm. ❸

Kem Bạch Đằng, 26-28 Lê Lợi (☎829 2707), on the corner of Pasteur and Lê Lợi. This ice-cream parlor is packed with locals in the evenings. Offers a wide variety of adventurous flavors such as durian and orange (15,000-20,000Đ). Open daily 7am-11pm. ❷

CHỢ LỚN

Cheap eats are not hard to come by in District 5. Poke your head down any alley-way and you're bound to discover some inexpensive but tasty street-side food.

Cát Tường, 105 Trần Hưng Đạo (☎853 7869), near its intersection with Trần Xuân Hòa. An outdoor Chinese eatery that serves excellent dim sum. Entrees 18,000-20,000Đ. Open daily 6am-midnight. ❷

Dìn Ký, 667 Nguyễn Trãi (☎867 4300). Enjoy good food alongside students and workers in this cheap streetside restaurant. Perfect for a quick break from pagoda-hopping. Meat and rice 10,000Đ. Open daily 8am-9pm. ❶

Siêu Thanh, 70 Hải Thượng Lãn Ông (☎857 8593), on the corner amongst several Chinese medicine shops. A simple menu: phở (30,000Đ). Relaxed and convenient. ❷

02, 27 Tân Da (☎859 4767), at the intersection with Trần Hưng Đạo. This ice-cream parlor boasts A/C and excellent scoops. A good but slightly pricey pit stop in District 5. Ice cream 22,000-38,000Đ. Open daily 7am-11pm. ❸

ELSEWHERE IN HCMC

▨ **Phở 2000,** 1-3 Phan Chu Trinh (☎822 2788; www.pho2000.com.vn), at the end of Lê Lai, right next to Bến Thành Market. With a menu described as "noodles etc.," Phở 2000 serves fantastic noodle and rice dishes (24,000-30,000Đ). Former US President Bill Clinton made a special stop here during his visit to Vietnam in 2000. Tables looking out on Bến Thành Market are great for people-watching. Open daily 6am-1am. ❷

Hoavien Brauhaus, 28 Mạc Đinh Chỉ (☎829 0585; www.hoaviener.com), near its intersection with Trần Cao Vân. Vietnam's first microbrewery serves quality Pilsner (draft 14,000-40,000Đ; bottle 20,000Đ) in a classic Czech beerhall. Enjoy Bohemian and Bavarian cuisine (entrees from 40,000Đ) or tour the brewing facilities with the manager. Call ahead to set up a tour. Open daily 7am-midnight. ❸

Bún Bò Thành Nội Huế, 47A Trần Cao Vân (☎829 9473), near its intersection with Phạm Ngọc Thạch and just outside District 1. This casual Vietnamese eatery is known for its Huế-style beef noodle soup. Despite their limited English, the staff is welcoming to foreigners. Entrees under 20,000Đ. Open daily 6am-1pm and 4-9pm. ❶

◔ SIGHTS

Most of the city's major sights lie within a short walking distance of one another in District 1. Only a few outside this area are worth visiting, but they can be reached easily by motorbike or taxi. For those who have only have a couple of days in HCMC and would like to hit the city's main attractions most efficiently, most of the tour companies (p. 384) arrange one-day sightseeing tours. Many museums and pagodas are closed over lunch, so check their hours before you head out.

MUSEUMS

▨**WAR REMNANTS MUSEUM.** This museum takes a brutal and disturbing look at the atrocities committed during the American War. Among its collection are bottled fetuses deformed by Agent Orange and gruesome photographs of the Mỹ Lai massacre. An intriguing exhibit on international opposition to the war (including the American resistance movement) provides other perspectives on the conflict. (*District 3. 28 Võ Văn Tần, between Trần Quốc Thảo and Lê Qúy Đôn.* ☎ *930 6235; warrm@cinet.vnnews.com. Open daily 7:30am-noon and 1:30-5pm. 15,000Đ.*)

MUSEUM OF VIETNAMESE HISTORY. Boasting a comprehensive collection of national artifacts dating from 500,000 years ago up through the 20th century, this museum is a must-see for the budding archaeologist. Don't miss the mummified Vietnamese woman. There are also some splendid relics from other Southeast Asian countries. A brief but charming water puppet show is performed daily. *(District 1. Nguyễn Bỉnh Kiêm at its intersection with Nguyễn Thị Minh Khai.* ☎ *825 8784. Second entrance through the Botanical Garden. Open Tu-Su 8-11am and 1-4pm. Water puppet show 9, 10, 11am and 2, 3, 4pm; also 1pm Su. 15,000Đ. Puppet show 30,000Đ.)*

FINE ARTS MUSEUM. Located in a grand French colonial building, this museum features art from the AD first century to the present day. Much of the contemporary art has a political theme, touching upon international relations, war resistance, and the benefits of Communism. *(District 1. 97 Phó Đức Chính, between Lê Thị Hồng Gấm and Nguyễn Thai Bình.* ☎ *829 4441. Open Tu-Su 9am-4:45pm. 10,000Đ.)*

HỒ CHÍ MINH CITY MUSEUM. This museum houses a collection of items related to the city, ranging from archaeological finds to photographs of recent events. The most interesting exhibit addresses the city's relationship with the Communist movement. The building's Neoclassical architecture makes it a popular spot for Vietnamese wedding photos. *(District 1. 65 Lý Tự Trọng. Entrance on the corner of Nam Kỳ Khởi Nghĩa and Lý Tự Trọng.* ☎ *829 9741; www.hcmc-museum.edu.vn. Open daily 8am-5pm. 15,000Đ.)*

HỒ CHÍ MINH MUSEUM. This museum, right on the Saigon River, takes an impartial look at everyone's favorite Vietnamese national hero and icon. Besides a lot of photographs, a number of Hồ Chí Minh's personal items and letters are on display. For an idea of how the rest of the world saw him, have a look at the international journal articles. *(District 4. 1 Nguyễn Tất Thàn, just across the river from District 1. It can be hard to find transportation back into the center of town, so it might be wise to hire a round-trip driver.* ☎ *940 2060. Open Tu-Su 7:30-11:30am and 1:30-4:30pm. 10,000Đ.)*

SOUTHERN WOMEN'S MUSEUM. This museum pays homage to the women of Southern Vietnam, from artists to athletes to revolutionaries. Photographs, artifacts, and artwork document the achievements of notable female citizens. Check out the eerie exhibit on women in prison and the huge women's history mural. *(District 3. Võ Thị Sáu, at its intersection with Lê Quý Đôn. After you pass through the main gate, enter the concrete building on the right. The museum is on the top 2 floors. Open daily 8am-1pm and 2-5pm.)*

TÔN ĐỨC THẮNG MUSEUM. For those who tire of Hồ Chí Minh, a great option is to visit this museum devoted to his successor, President Tôn Đức Thắng, who presided when Northern Vietnamese forces captured Saigon in 1975. The collection is small but well-kept and includes gifts given to the president by other communist leaders, including Fidel Castro. The exhibit about Hồ Chí Minh's time in Con Dao prison is also worth a look. *(District 1. 5 Tôn Đức Thắng, between Thái Văn Lung and Ngô Văn Năm.* ☎ *829 7542. Open Tu-Th and Sa-Su 7:30-11:30am and 1:30-5pm, F 7:30-11:30am. Free.)*

HCMC CAMPAIGN MUSEUM. Military buffs may want to check out this museum, dedicated to the communist capture of Hồ Chí Minh City in April 1975. The signs are in Vietnamese, but visitors can watch a film in English. Outside the building stand intimidating war machines, including one of the many tankers that crashed through the gates of what is now Reunification Palace. *(District 1. 2 Lê Duẩn, at its intersection with Nguyễn Bỉnh Kiêm.* ☎ *822 9387. Open Tu-Su 8-11:30am and 1:30-4:30pm. Free.)*

HOUSES OF WORSHIP

JADE EMPEROR PAGODA (CHÙA NGỌC HOÀNG). Considered by many to be the best pagoda in District 1, Jade Emperor Pagoda was built by the city's Cantonese population in 1909. Elaborately decorated in the Chinese style, the complex includes a courtyard with several shrines and a turtle pond, as well as sanctuaries where worshippers pray to Buddhist and Taoist deities. The Taoist Jade Emperor (Ngọc Hoàng), guardian of heaven, is located on the central altar just inside the main sanctuary doors. Peek upstairs (through the room on the right) for a good view of the pond and crumbling green-tiled roof. *(District 1. 73 Mai Thị Lựu, between Điện Biên Phủ and Nguyễn Văn Gia. Open daily 5am-7pm.)*

HỒ CHÍ MINH CITY

JUL 17

FROM THE ROAD

FAIR'S FAIR

With Hồ Chí Minh City's air quality in the state that it's in, I wasn't surprised to see locals sporting hats and masks—until I realized that only the women wore them. A conversation with some expats enlightened me as to the real hazard these women were protecting themselves against: the sun.

The Vietnamese do not share Westerners' penchant for glowing, bronze complexions. To them, suntanned skin is a status symbol—one that signifies the farming or street-cleaning class. Women in Vietnam will go to great lengths to preserve pale complexions, wearing full-face masks that leave only slits for eyes and smothering themselves in the Vietnamese equivalent of tan-in-a-bottle: skin-whitening cream. Celebrities sport gleaming, pale complexions.

Suddenly all the admiring stares and prods I had received throughout the city made sense. My sun-deprived pallor is actually considered beautiful here! Old women reached out to touch me as I sat by them on the bus, while younger women gestured pityingly at my few patches of sunburn.

As the economy develops to become less agricultural, the fashion might change, but it seems unlikely. After all, whatever features are most difficult and expensive to achieve in a given society will always be considered beautiful. And in Vietnam's beating sun, that makes pale the new tan.

-Juliet Samuel

CHÙA ÔNG BON. Devoted to Ông Bon, guardian of wealth and virtue, this large pagoda is one of the busiest in the district. The floor is strewn with giant sticks of incense, and every shrine has a number of worshippers. If you can see through the haze, admire the elaborate main altar and enjoy the rare sight of a temple in full use. At the back is a rock fountain and a lesser shrine. If your budget is feeling a bit tight, try burning some fake money in the furnace: it's done for good luck. *(District 5. 264 Hải Thượng Lãn Ông. Open daily 6am-6pm)*

VĨNH NGHIÊM PAGODA. The Japan-Vietnam Friendship Association helped construct this expansive pagoda complex during the 1960s, and the architecture exudes Japanese influence. The impressive main sanctuary boasts an enormous gleaming Buddha, framed by elaborate golden filigree, meditating on a lotus. Elsewhere in the complex there are several towers, a shop selling ritual items, and a school for monks. It's a bit of a hike, but well worth it for a glimpse of the sanctuary and a chance to catch the monks at their daily rituals. *(District 3. Nguyễn Văn Trỗi, near the canal. Open daily 8am-5pm.)*

NOTRE DAME CATHEDRAL. The main seat of Catholicism in Southern Vietnam, this cathedral features red bricks and stained glass imported from France during the colonial era. Inside, figures of national saints and plaques donated by parishioners provide insight into how Vietnamese Catholic practices differ from those in other regions of the world. *(District 1. In its own plaza opposite the Central Post Office, at the intersection of Lê Duẩn and Đồng Khởi. Open daily 8-10:30am and 3-4pm. Su mass in English 9:30am. Mass in Vietnamese M-Sa 5:30am and 5pm; Su throughout the day.)*

MARIAMMAN HINDU TEMPLE. This temple's elaborate and gaudy interior shocks the senses. Hindu gods and goddesses painted in neon colors adorn the walls and altars, and Mariamman sits in the center shrine amid numerous decorations and offerings. Not only Hindus worship here; the temple is also considered sacred by many Vietnamese and Chinese. The atmosphere is casual, but remove your shoes to walk in the central part of the temple. *(District 1. 45 Trương Định, between Lê Thánh Tôn and Lý Tự Trọng. Open daily 7am-10pm.)*

THIÊN HẬU PAGODA. Ethnic Chinese worship Thiên Hậu, goddess of seafarers, who occupies the main altar of this richly decorated pagoda. Also housed in the pagoda are Meh Sanh, goddess of fertility, and Long Mau, goddess of mothers and infants; both are popular with female worshippers. If you can see through the thick haze of incense, admire the intricate woodwork and huge collection of figurines along the roof. *(District 5. 710 Nguyễn Trãi, between Lương Nhữ Học and Triệu Quang Phục. Open daily 6am-6pm.)*

AN ASIDE. Except during services, most churches keep their main doors closed. This does not mean that they are closed to visitors—entry is often via an unofficial-looking sidedoor. It might seem shady, but it's perfectly acceptable to enter through these doors—you might even end up having the place to yourself.

DINH MINH HƯƠNG GIA THANH. This quiet Taoist temple—one of few in the city—is impressive for its intricate gold-and-red carvings. Also on display are the traditional shoes and hats of religious leaders and a Taoist drum (in the back left). This temple has been run by the same Chinese family for three generations—their portraits are at the back on the right. The owner speaks decent English and fluent French, and is happy to give tours. *(District 5. 380 Trần Hưng Đạo between Triêu Quang Phuc and Phù Đổng Thiên Vương. Open daily 7am-5pm.)*

CHA TAM CHURCH. This church's yellow spire is visible along a large stretch of Trần Hưng Đạo. Closer up, it is an interesting mix of traditions—look for the carved dragons where an organ would usually be located. Ngô Đình Diệm allegedly sought sanctuary here in 1963 when a coup deposed his government. The church is quiet during the day, except for the birds living in the roof. *(District 5. Facing down Trần Hưng Đạo from the western end of Chinatown. Open daily 7-9am and 5-8pm.)*

GIÁC LÂM PAGODA. Over 260 years old, Giác Lâm is one of the oldest pagodas in the city. The pagoda complex contains a modern religious tower, a gigantic Buddha, and monks' tombs. The pagoda itself, supported by dark teak pillars, is a dizzying maze of altars. The funeral hall contains photos of the deceased, while the main sanctuary houses an enormous and complicated altar to a host of Buddhist and Taoist deities. Around the pagoda are several courtyards, one of which holds a sacred Bodhi tree. *(Tan Bính District. 118 Lạc Long Quân, near its intersection with Âu Cơ'. A 25min. motorbike ride from the center of town. The pagoda is also included on many city tours. Open daily 5am-noon and 2-9pm.)*

XÁ LỢI PAGODA. The monks of this pagoda came under attack during Ngô Đình Diệm's regime, and the pagoda now commemorates their resistance. Nowadays, monks live and study Buddhism here, and are very welcoming to visitors. Murals in the impressive interior depict the story of the Buddha and are worth a look if only for the English translation of the narrative: "Queen Maya saw in a dream a six-tusk elephant enter her through the right flank. She felt very alert and became pregnant soon after that miraculous event." The courtyard houses a grafted Bodhi tree. *(District 3. 89 Su Thiện Chiêú, on a small road that connects Bà Huyện Thanh Quan and Nguyên Thông. Open daily 8-11am and 2-5pm.)*

HUYỆN SÌ CHURCH. Completed in 1847, this huge Gothic church is part of Hồ Chí Minh City's French legacy. The traditional French stained glass is a little damaged, but the overall effect remains impressive. Check out the intricate Vietnamese hanging lamps and ceiling fans. There is also an outdoor chapel in the courtyard, at the left as you enter the gates. *(District 1. 1 Tôn Thất Tùng, just northwest of Phạm Ngũ Lão. Open daily 9am-7pm. Services daily 7pm.)*

JAMALIAL MOSQUE. This small Mosque, simply colored in blue and white, provides a peaceful escape from the streets. For a house of worship it has a casual feel and is entirely devoid of tourists. Stroll the glass-enclosed terrace and have a look in at the blue ablutions pool. Visitors can listen to, but not watch, prayers, and should remove their shoes. *(District 5. 641 Nguyễn Trãi. Slightly off the road but the entrance is on the street. Open daily sunrise to sunset.)*

TAN DINH CHURCH. This church isn't afraid to make an aesthetic statement: the exterior is painted bubble gum-pink and the interior features a Jesus figure whose halo and cross both light up in glowing neon. *(District 3. Hai Bà Trưng, near its intersec-*

tion with Đinh Công Tráng. Open M-F 8am-5:30pm, Su 8am-7pm. Mass M-F 5am, 6:15am, 5:30pm; Su throughout the day.)

INDIAN MOSQUE. Unlike the city's many pagodas, this mosque is simple and unadorned. This is more a house of worship than it is a tourist attraction, but if you are going to visit, wear appropriate dress and remove your shoes upon entering. *(District 1. 66 Đông Du, between Đồng Khởi and Hai Bà Trưng. Open daily sunrise to sunset.)*

OTHER SIGHTS

■**THE NATIONAL LIBRARY.** Constructed in 1968 and home to 10 million books, the national library sits in its own mini-park opposite the Hồ Chí Minh City Museum. Most days the grounds and rooms inside are crammed full of Vietnamese students hard at work, so it's a great place to wander and observe daily life without all those pesky tourists. Take a look at the antique French globe in the room to the left of the stairs. *(District 1. 69 Lý Tự Trọng. Open Tu-Su 7am-7pm.)*

■**LÂM SỔN SQUARE.** In French colonial times, **Lâm Sổn Square** was the center of high society. The **Hotel Continental** is featured in Graham Greene's novel, *The Quiet American.* Across from the hotel on a wide plaza is the **Municipal Theater** (called the **Opera House** by locals). Constructed by the French at the turn of the 20th century, this pink Neoclassical theater was designed as an opera house, though it housed the National Assembly after the division of the country. It was restored in 1998 and now hosts dance, music, opera, and theater productions. The steps outside are a great place to people-watch at night. Inquire at the lobby for current performances. *(☎829 9976. District 1. At the intersection of Đồng Khởi and Lê Lợi.)*

NGUYỄN HUỆ PLAZA. This plaza is dominated by the **People's Committee Hall.** Once the French colonial *Hôtel de Ville*, this ornate yellow building is now ironically the meeting place for the city's Communist leadership. Visitors are not allowed inside. The park across the street features a statue of Hồ Chí Minh hugging a child. The **Rex Hotel,** famous for housing the US Information Service during the 1960s, is on Nguyễn Huệ next to the park. Its rooftop cafe (5th floor) offers a panoramic view of the city. *(District 1. At the intersection of Nguyễn Huệ and Lê Thánh Tôn.)*

REUNIFICATION PALACE. First built by the French in 1868, then reconstructed by South Vietnamese President Ngô Đình Diệm after a 1962 bombing, this palace was home to several South Vietnamese heads of state before Việt Cộng tanks crashed through its gates on April 30, 1975. When a South Vietnamese general told the Việt Cộng officers that he was prepared to transfer power to them, one officer famously replied, "You cannot give up what you do not have." Visitors to the palace today will find it frozen in its 1975 state, complete with residential rooms, subterranean war chambers, and an entertainment complex. *(☎822 1716. District 1. Entrance on Nam Kỳ Khởi Nghĩa, between Nguyễn Thị Minh Khai and Nguyễn Du. Tours available. Open daily 7:30-11am and 1-4pm. 15,000Đ.)*

PHỞ BINH. In the late 1960s, while American soldiers and officers slurped soup on the ground floor of this diner, the Việt Cộng leadership met one floor above and devised its secret plans for the Tết Offensive, including an attack on the US Embassy. Today the place is run by the son of the previous owner, a former Communist revolutionary. Be sure to look through the scrapbook and sign the guestbook. *(District 3. 7 Lộ Chính Thắng, near its intersection with Hai Bà Trưng. Open daily 7am-11pm. Phở 21,000Đ.)*

BOTANICAL GARDEN AND ZOO. The botanical garden, with a small but enjoyable collection of tropical flora, provides a pleasant escape from the grit and grime of the city. A zoo is housed in one corner of the park; unfortunately, its facilities are pretty shabby, so unless you need to entertain young children, we recommend skipping it. Just inside the park's gates on Nguyễn Bình Kiêm are the History Museum and the **Temple of King Hùng,** father of the Vietnamese nation. *(☎829 3728.*

District 1. Nguyễn Bỉnh Khiêm at its intersection with Lê Duẩn. Open daily 7am-9pm. 8000Đ, children 4000Đ; aquarium 6000Đ extra.)

SHOPPING

Hồ Chí Minh City is a shopaholic's paradise. Shops crowd every block, particularly in Districts 1 and 5—you're likely to find whatever your heart desires there. The most exciting places to shop are the city's indoor markets, which sell everything imaginable under one roof. Bargaining, as usual, is the norm here, so be sure to read up on haggling (see **"The Art of the Deal,"** p. 21). Don't be afraid to make an offer that seems too low. Most markets open between 6 and 7am and close between 6 and 7pm. It shouldn't be hard to find an entire section of a market devoted to any item you're looking for—just ask around or inquire at your lodging. The possibilities may well render your choice more difficult than you imagine.

If you're looking for slightly more upscale spending possibilities, fear not: Hồ Chí Minh City is not lacking. Over the past few years, more upscale and designer stores have been popping up, most of them concentrated along **Đồng Khởi** in western District 1. Most of the pricetags you'll find here are heftier than those at other Vietnamese markets, but still easier on the wallet than at most stores of similar value and focus in your home country.

CHỢ LỚN (DISTRICT 5)

The best budget shopping in Hồ Chí Minh City can be found at the large indoor markets on the outskirts of Chợ Lớn, where HCMC's ethnic Chinese population is concentrated. As you make your way from one market to the other, be sure to head straight through the center of Vietnam's biggest Chinatown to peruse the foreign fabric and Chinese medicine shops along the way.

MARKETS. Most markets in Hồ Chí Minh City open gradually around 8am and close between 5 and 8pm. They are meant largely for locals and usually sell goods you can buy at home—but for incredibly low prices.

The two biggest markets in the city are just outside District 5; ◪**Bình Tây** to the southeast and ◪**An Đông** to the northwest. Bình Tây, on Hậu Giang, is the most chaotic of the city's markets. If you visit one market in Hồ Chí Minh City, this should be it. The market is mostly housed in an impressive Chinese-style building with an inner courtyard, but it spills out onto many of the surrounding streets. It is unlikely that the average tourist will find much to buy here—it is mainly a place for everyday grocery shopping, wholesale vegetables, stationery, and other daily staples. But the sheer quantity of goods and the atmosphere make this market a must-see. Assume you'll be stared at and expect to get lost, but keep in mind that the vendors are not used to seeing tourists, and try just wandering aimlessly through the maze—it's the best way to see Bình Tây.

A second massive market, An Đông, is just a short walk away, between the intersections of Hùng Vương and An Dung Vương with Nguyễn Duy Dương and Sư Vạn Hanh. Enter from either Hùng Vương or An Dung Vương. Much more orderly than Bình Tây, An Đông market takes over three floors of a massive concrete block in eastern Chợ Lớn. The basement is mainly food; the first floor (called the "ground floor") has women's clothing, shoes, and jewelry, and the second floor (or the "first floor") is for clothes and souvenirs. The basement phở stalls make for a cheap meal. There is a small fruit market outside on the Hùng Vương side.

SILK AND FABRIC. Along the western end of Trần Hưng Đạo, from its intersection with Châu Văn Liêm up to Cha Tam Church, every shop on both sides of the street sells an array of materials—cotton, chiffon, silk, and velvet—making the sidewalk shine with richly patterned embroidery and glitter. The shops along

Đồng Khởi, in District 1, provide a less chaotic, though more expensive, shopping experience, with similar fabrics and less bustle.

MEDICINE SHOPS. You can't walk a block into Chợ Lớn without coming across one of the area's many Chinese medicine shops. They're worth a visit, if just to take in the sights and smells—and to learn what they call "medicine" here. The best place to explore is at the eastern end of Hải Thượng Lãn Ông where it intersects with Triệu Quang Phục. A large shop with a wide selection of products to peruse is **Thuân Lội,** 108 Hải Thượng Lãn Ông (☎865 2912; open daily 7am-6pm), but all of the shops in this area good places to investigate more exotic medicines. Even the pharmacies stock pickled snakes in this area: the Vietnamese apparently use them (along with a whole variety of products) to whiten their skin, as being pale is fashionable in Vietnam.

CDS AND DVDS. Right where the silk shops phase out, at the western end of Trần Hưng Đạo near Cha Tam Church, you will find a variety of music shops selling cheap DVDs and CDs. Most of the music is Vietnamese but the DVDs are from a range of countries. Check out the disc shop **Chuyên Kinh Doanh,** 234 Nguyễn Trãi (☎890 5563; open daily 11am-9pm), a big place with a fish tank in the entrance.

DISTRICT 1

Shops of even greater variety abound on the corners of District 1, where the markets are smaller and more tourist-friendly. We've listed a few of the highlights, but you'll have more fun just wandering through the center of town discovering places of your own.

MARKETS. You'll get fewer stares but also fewer options in the comparatively small markets of District 1. **Bến Thành,** a city landmark and popular tourist stop, is located at the big roundabout where Lê Lợi, Trần Hưng Đạo, and Hàm Nghi meet. The stalls carry mostly raw food materials, but also candy, plastic flowers, jewelry, and some clothes. In the evenings, there are lively food stalls outside. **Dan Sinh,** 104 Yersin, is the locals' hardware market, but it also contains a jumble of army gear and various unrelated items. Amongst the nails, power drills, and blenders, you'll find cheap trenchcoats, dogtags, and combat boots.

TAILORS. Hồ Chí Minh City is also a great place to have clothes made. Most rates are a great deal, considering that each product is personally tailored. Allow between one and three days to have a dress or suit made. In the Phạm Ngũ Lão area, expect to pay US$15-40 for a dress, US$60 for a suit. Pricier and higher quality versions can be found near Đồng Khởi. Though comparatively more expensive (dress US$30-50; suit US$100), shopping in this area is probably still cheaper than having clothes custom made at home. Try **Tuyết Nga Silk,** 91 Mạc Thi Bưởi (☎827 7038; open daily 8am-9pm), for both suits and dresses, or go for the slightly cheaper **Chi Chi,** 138 Pasteur (☎824 7812; open daily 8am-8:30pm).

MASSAGES. After a long day of shopping and sight-seeing, be sure to take advantage of the city's pampering services—your muscles will thank you. Finding a trustworthy massage parlor can be a bit hit-or-miss in HCMC, with many offering other "special" services to male patrons. Try to check the place out before you go, or ask around to see what's reliable. Inevitably, more established parlors will be a bit pricier. **Lady Saigon,** 242 Trần Hưng Đạo (☎837 7251), comes highly recommended by expats. (Women only. Massages 80,000Đ per hr. Open daily 8am-11pm.) Another option is **Paris Beaute,** 17A2 Lê Thánh Tôn. (☎822 4752. Massages US$11-17, half price before 2pm. Open daily 9am-7:30pm.)

♫ 🎭 ENTERTAINMENT AND NIGHTLIFE

BARS AND CLUBS

The nightlife around Phạm Ngũ Lão tends to attract mostly budget travelers, while the expatriates and young Vietnamese party in the Đồng Khởi area. Bar licensing is strict in Vietnam and most places outside the Phạm Ngũ Lão area close near midnight, though a few will stay open until 2 or 3am. To find out which bars and clubs are hottest at the moment, pick up *Saigon Inside Out* (available in may hotels and bookstores) or check out www.elephantguide.com. Many of the bars below double as restaurants during the day.

>
> **NO PHOTOS, PLEASE.** Always ask before taking photographs in bars and clubs. Many of these establishments strictly prohibit the use of cameras because of the illegal activity (drugs and prostitution, mostly) that often occurs behind their doors. So if you bring a camera, keep it out of sight.

AROUND PHẠM NGŨ LÃO

Allez Boo, 187 Phạm Ngũ Lão (☎837 2505), on the corner of Phạm Ngũ Lão and Đề Thám. Extremely popular with the backpacker crowd. Friendly staff, great music, and a popular pool table. Beers 20,000-55,000Đ; mixed drinks 55,000Đ. Happy hour 11am-4pm (2 for 1 on draft beer). Open daily 6:30am-5am.

Gossip, 76 Trần Hưng Đạo (☎821 2715), part of the Đại Nam hotel. Where all the young and hip go to party. Huge dance floor and psychedelic lights—even your shoes will vibrate with the music. Drinks around 55,000Đ. Open daily noon-midnight.

GO2, 187 Đề Thám (☎836 9575), on the corner of Đề Thám and Bùi Viện. Blaring music late into the night, this place is always packed. Colorful decor complete with Communist propaganda. Popular with travelers, but locals join the mix, too. Live music upstairs M-Sa after 10:30pm. Meals 40,000-70,000Đ. Drinks 20,000-55,000Đ. Watch out for the sneaky 20% "service charge" on all prices after 1am. Open daily 6am-4am.

163 Cyclo, 163 Phạm Ngũ Lão (☎920 1567), near its intersection with Nguyễn Thái Học. Though the bar is named for the most popular tourist-toting vehicles in town, the atmosphere is classy. Black-and-red decor; pool table upstairs. Beer 15,000-19,000Đ. Mixed drinks 50,000Đ. Open daily 9am-2am.

Eden, 296 Đề Thám (☎836 8154). Popular with travelers for its cheap beer (15,000-20,000Đ), this bar boasts both a dance floor for the energetic and street-side seating for the laid-back. Happy hour (10% discount) 6am-6pm. Open daily 6am-3:30am.

Oblivion, 180 Bùi Viện (☎836 1947). A lively but small bar with one side fully open to the street. Wander in and out or fill the place with friends. Beer 25,000Đ. Vodka 45,000Đ. Open daily 7pm-4am.

Sàigòn Phố, 266 Đề Thám (☎837 4132), between Phạm Ngũ Lão and Bùi Viện. Sidewalk tables are a relaxed place to enjoy a drink. The hostesses claim the place never closes. Beer 15,000-60,000Đ. Mixed drinks 50,000-60,000Đ. Open 24hr.

Guns N' Roses, 207 Phạm Ngũ Lão (☎836 0845), between Đề Thám and Dỗ Quang Đẩu. This biker bar plays nothing but G'n'R all night long. Free pool. Beer 15,000-20,000Đ. Mixed drinks 10,000-60,000Đ. Open daily 9pm-5am.

Lili, 219 Phạm Ngũ Lão, between Đề Thám and Dỗ Quang Đẩu. A cute but tiny bar open to the street, with a sassy staff. Bring a few friends and you'll easily fill the place. Beer 18,000-25,000Đ. Mixed drinks 35,000-40,000Đ. Open daily noon-2am.

ĐỒNG KHỞI

Underground, 69 Đồng Khởi (☎829 9079; www.underground-saigon.com), between Mạc Thị Bưởi and Ngô Đức Kế. An impressive cocktail and shooter menu (over 100 choices, 40,000-60,000Đ) draws the party crowds to this trendy, London-themed bar. Ladies' Night (free gin and vodka) W 9-10pm. Open M-F 9am-midnight; Sa-Su 8am-late.

☒ **Heart of Darkness,** 17B Lê Thánh Tôn (☎823 1080), between Thái Văn Lung and Chu Mạnh Trinh. Officially shuts down at midnight, but that's just when the wild party gets started. Different DJs every night at this well-known, dimly lit bar, which is popular with locals and foreigners. "Singles Networking and Socialize Night" daily 7-9pm (free gin and vodka). Beer 20,000-50,000Đ. Mixed drinks 30,000Đ. Open daily 5pm-3am.

Sheridan's Irish House, 17/13 Lê Thánh Tôn (☎823 0793; www.sheridansviet-nam.com), near its intersection with Thái Văn Lung. This cozy and authentic Irish pub features live music Th-Tu after 8pm; Irish tunes Sa. Happy hour 5-7pm. Two 500mL cans of Guinness 95,000Đ. Irish stout 35,000-50,000Đ. Open daily 10am-late.

Cafe Latin, 19-21 Đông Du (☎822 6363). A laid-back, sports-themed bar with walls covered in signed sports paraphernalia. A favorite amongst Aussie expats, and the weekly meeting place of the HCMC Hash Harriers (see **"The Đà Nẵng Hash Harriers,"** p. 301). Beer 15,000-50,000Đ. Shots 65,000-70,000Đ. Open daily 8am-midnight.

Vasco's (Club Camargue), 16 Cao Bá Quát (☎823 2828), near its intersection with Thi Sách. With its warm colors and red pool tables, this stylish bar is popular with young Vietnamese. Ladies' Night on W (mixed drinks US$1); free beer with pizza on Th; live music F. Beer 30,000Đ. Mixed drinks 50,000Đ. Open daily 5:30pm-late.

Q-Bar, 7 Lam Son (☎823 3479; www.qbarsaigon.com), located right under the Opera House. This small but classy venue features two bars as well as tables with a private feel. Faux classical decor and a wide selection of vodka (70,000-115,000Đ), as well as outside tables right in the middle of Lâm Sồn Square. Prime location makes it a bit pricier than average (beer 35,000-65,000Đ). Open daily 5pm-midnight.

Apocalypse Now, 2B Thi Sách (☎825 6124), near its intersection with Đông Du. An old standard in Saigonese nightlife. Draws a mixed crowd and features great music. Attractive open-air seating. Mixed drinks 30,000-40,000Đ. Open daily 7am-1am.

Liquid, 104 Hai Bà Trưng (☎822 5478), near its intersection with Nguyễn Thị Minh Khai. DJs pump out beats amid colored lasers and psychedelic video images. Packs a huge crowd (mainly Vietnamese) on the weekends. Beer 62,000-100,000Đ. Mixed drinks 70,000-80,000Đ. Tax and service not included. Open daily 7pm-midnight.

Blue Gecko, 31 Lý Tự Trọng (☎824 3483), between Hai Bà Trưng and Thái Văn Lung. Play pool, throw darts, or watch rugby at this laid-back Aussie-owned hangout. Beer 20,000Đ. Happy hour (20% off) daily 5-7:30pm. Open daily 5pm-late.

Shadow Pub, 56 Mạc Thi Buởi (☎829 0520). Play darts, chat with foreigners, or simply fill the bar with friends at this warm, red-painted pub. Happy hour (30% off) daily 4-8pm. Beer 24,000-60,000Đ. Mixed drinks 40,000Đ. Open 4pm-midnight.

Tropical Rainforest, 5-15 Ho Huan Nghiệp (☎825 7783), near its intersection with Đồng Khởi. Thumping dance music, neon strobes, sleek and modern decorations, and attractive staff make this club another hotspot for young Vietnamese urbanites. Drinks 40,000-60,000Đ. Open daily 8pm-midnight.

Qing, 31 Đông Du (☎823 2414). This wine bar is a great place to while away an evening. Locals and foreigners relax at outdoor tables by an Indian mosque. A range of wine (65,000-200,000Đ) from Chile, France, and others. Open daily 8am-midnight.

Pha Lê, 54 Mạc Thi Buởi (☎822 2481). Enjoy coffee by day and whiskey by night at this small bar. A good place to play a relaxed game of pool. Beer 30,000-60,000Đ. Whiskey 50,000-60,000Đ. Open daily 4pm-midnight.

COFFEE

A stylish coffee shop is the place to be seen in Hồ Chí Minh City, no matter what the time of day. The best cafes are full night and day, hosting trendy twenty-some-things, quiet old men, and everyone in between. A typical HCMC coffee experience can be found at many cafes around the intersection of Trần Cao Vân and Phạm Ngọc Thach in District 3. Most have outdoor seating and live music at night.

⬛ Windows Cafe, 187 Nguyễn Đinh Chiểu (☎822 2425), in District 1. A great place to people-watch. There's lots to see under the pleasant green umbrellas at this stylish cafe. Coffee 18,000-60,000Đ. Open daily 7am-11pm. ❷

Nirvana, 37 Nguyễn Đinh Chiểu (☎829 5839), in District 1. Order off roll-up leather menus while being serenaded by the garden rock fountain and Vietnam's latest hits. Coffee 8000-16,000Đ. Open daily 7am-midnight. ❶

Napoly, 7 Phạm Ngọc Thach (☎829 0583), in District 3. Relax at a pleasant outdoor table or enjoy the comfortable wicker seating inside. Live music every night after 9pm. Coffee 18,000-45,000Đ. Open daily 7am-midnight. ❷

OTHER ENTERTAINMENT

Phù Thọ Racetrack, 2 Le Dai Hanh (☎962 4319). Grab your wallet and head over to District 11 for a raucous few hours at the races. Betting is chaotic, food is cheap, and the races take place just a few feet from the spectators. Entrance tickets 5000Đ. VIP tickets (access to lounge with A/C and to horses before the race) 50,000Đ. Open M-F 8am-5pm, Sa-Su 12:30-5pm.

Diamond Superbowl, 34 Lê Duẩn (☎825 7778), on the 4th fl. of the Diamond Plaza building. Entertainment complex houses a funky bowling alley, pool tables, arcade games, and a snack bar. A favorite hangout for local teens. Bowling 20,000Đ per person; shoes 5000Đ. Open daily 9:30am-1am.

Diamond Cinema, 34 Lê Duẩn (☎822 7897; www.diamondcinemavn.com), on the 13th fl. of the Diamond Plaza building. Shows American blockbusters and other foreign films; check ahead online to see if they're subtitled or dubbed. Tickets M-F 40,000Đ; Sa-Su 50,000Đ. Open daily 10am-10pm.

Đầm Sen Park, 3 Hòa Bình (☎858 7826; www.damnsenpark.com.vn), in distant District 11. HCMC's theme park. Vietnamese families head here on weekends for the giant banana swing and various other thrills. Unless you have small children, it's not worth the trek, despite high recommendations. 18,000Đ, children 12,000Đ. Open daily 11am-5pm.

▶ DAYTRIPS FROM HỒ CHÍ MINH CITY

⬛ CỦ CHI TUNNELS

Many tour companies in the Phạm Ngũ Lão area organize guided trips to the tunnels for US$4; they are the easiest way to access them. Alternatively, take the #5 bus from Bến Thành station to Củ Chi town (1½hr.; 30,000Đ); from there, hire a motorbike or taxi to the tunnels. ☎794 6442. Open daily 7am-5pm. 70,000Đ.

Few sights capture the tenacity and ingenuity of the Vietnamese guerrillas better than the Củ Chi tunnels. The Việt Cộng developed this elaborate network of narrow passageways in order to infiltrate enemy camps while remaining almost completely hidden. At one point, the multi-level subterranean system stretched all the way from Củ Chi to the Cambodian border and included field hospitals, weapons facilities, and even kitchens. Today visitors can climb through the reconstructed 100m portion of the tunnels, although there are closer escape routes for the claustrophobic. Be aware that there is no lighting (so bring your own flashlight or lighter) and adults will have to bend double to move through the tunnels. Above ground, there are gruesome exhibitions of the booby traps used against enemy forces, some recreations of life in the tunnels, a memorial temple to Việt Cộng soldiers, and a shooting range, where visitors can fire authentic military rifles at a target (18,000Đ per bullet).

CAO ĐÀI HOLY SEE

The easiest way to see the temple is through guided tours from the Phạm Ngũ Lão area for US$4. There are no buses directly to Tây Ninh (the town nearest the temple). Instead, take the #5 bus from Bến Thành station to Củ Chi town (1½hr.; 3000Đ); transfer to another bus to Gò Dấu (30min.; 7000Đ), where you can catch a bus to Tây Ninh (30min.; 7000Đ). Once there, you'll need to hire a motorbike or taxi to the temple. Open 24hr.; ceremonies are held daily at 6am, noon, 6pm, and midnight. Free; donations accepted.

This enormous temple, constructed between 1933 and 1955, is the main seat of the Cao Đài religion in Vietnam (see **"Someone To Watch Over You,"** p. 431). While the ornate exterior is rather impressive, it is the interior that truly dazzles visitors. No color of the rainbow has been spared and no flourish neglected. The expansive main hall boasts pink columns decorated with mythical creatures, celestial ceilings sparkling with silver stars, and an immense globe upon which the divine eye observes worshippers. During the daily ceremonies, visitors look down from the balcony as the many worshippers (clad in white, red, blue, or yellow based on their level in the religious hierarchy) perform their synchronized practices, accompanied by instruments and singing.

CẦN GIỜ

Buses run from Bến Thành station to the Bình Khánh ferry crossing (50min.; 2000Đ). From there, take the ferry (10min.; 500Đ) to Cần Giờ. On the Cần Giờ side, more buses run from the ferry crossing to the town center (1hr.; 2000Đ). The Forest Park is about halfway along this route; ask the bus driver to drop you off there. Hiring a motorbike or taxi to take you around Cần Giờ is an easier but much more expensive option. Forest Park ☎ 874 3333; www.cangioresort.com. Admission M-F 7000Đ; Sa and Su 10,000Đ. Open daily 7:30am-5pm.

Cần Giờ is actually a district of Hồ Chí Minh City, but the abundant flora and fauna on this sparsely populated island will transport you light years away from the metropolis. The island's main attraction is **Forest Park** (Lâm Viên), a mangrove swamp reserve operated by SaigonTourist. The park is a playground for hundreds of monkeys, many of whom hang out along the main tourist paths. Park rangers give out free potatoes to visitors to feed to the monkeys; be aware that if you have food in your hands, the animals will stop at nothing to get it. Also, keep a handle on your belongings—the monkeys are accomplished thieves. Visitors can take a motorized canoe ride (3hr.; 250,000Đ) through winding mangrove canals to the park's **guerrilla base museum.** The canoe ride is better than the museum, which is a tiny collection of ancient archaeological finds housed in stilt huts in the middle of the forest. The park also holds a crocodile area, a small nature museum, a restaurant, and a circus stage (animal shows M-Sa at 3pm). You can stay overnight at the **Cần Giờ Resort ❹** (rooms 300,000Đ) but there is little else to do. Elsewhere on the island, the public beach (attractively named **30/4 Beach**) is whipped by strong winds, but it still draws a number of Saigonese who crave the fresh air.

VŨNG TÀU   ☎ 64

With its sun-drenched beaches, scenic vistas, and handsome promenades, Vũng Tàu is a popular weekend getaway, mostly for Saigonese. French colonists began vacationing here around the turn of the last century, and—aside from the many pagodas dotting the landscape—the peninsula still bears a resemblance to the French Riviera. Its tourist industry is still developing, however, so it remains (for now) a peaceful escape, especially midweek.

TRANSPORTATION. Buses arrive at **Vũng Tàu Station,** 192A Nam Kỳ Khởi Nghĩa (☎859 727), and go to HCMC (2½hr.; every 15min. 5am-5pm; 30,000Đ) and Mỹ Tho (4hr.; 12:30pm; 36,000Đ). **Ferries** arrive at the pier on Hạ Long (opposite Hải Âu Hotel) and go to HCMC (1¼hr.; 7 per day 6am-5pm; US$10). The best way to get around the peninsula is to rent a ▪**bicycle** (20,000-40,000Đ per day) or **motorbike**

(US$5-7 per day) from one of the many hotels or restaurants along Thùy Vân.

⚡🕐 ORIENTATION AND PRACTICAL INFORMATION. On the northwest corner of the peninsula is **Mulberry Beach** (Bãi Dâu), a quiet area with rocky cliffs and a bit of sand that doesn't see many tourists. Along the western coast lies **Front Beach** (Bãi Trước), where fishing boats dock and ferries arrive and depart. Most of the city's main activity takes place in the streets behind Front Beach. Sunbathers and swimmers flock to **Back Beach** (Bãi Sau) on the opposite coast. While less comely than Front Beach, Back Beach has more sand and is more developed than its counterpart.

For all money matters in Vũng Tàu, try **Vietcombank,** 27 Trần Hưng Đạo. (☎852 309. **ATM** and currency exchange. MC/V cash advances. Open M-F 7-11:30am and 1:30-4pm.) There are a number of **Internet cafes** in the streets near Front Beach; one of the fastest connections can be found at the main **post office,** 408 Lê Hồng Phong, which dominates the intersection with Xô Viết Nghệ Tĩnh and has a 24hr. **ATM.** (Open daily 6:30am-8:30pm; telecommunications until 10pm.)

🍴🏠 ACCOMMODATIONS AND FOOD. Since Vũng Tàu is primarily a resort city, accommodations can be expensive, and many are booked solid on weekends. Mulberry Beach is the cheapest place to stay. **Sao Mai ❸,** 80 Hoàng Hoa Thám, has well-maintained rooms and is located about halfway between Front Beach and Back Beach. (☎852 215. Rooms US$10.) The balconies at **Huy Hùng ❷,** 145 Thùy Vân, look out onto Back Beach, which is just across the street. (☎522 798. Rooms 150,000-350,000Đ.) Those on a tighter budget will appreciate **Mỹ Tho ❶,** 47 Trần Phú. Although the rooms are not exactly luxurious, there is a large common terrace built right over the water. (☎835 004. Rooms US$6; A/C 20,000Đ extra.)

Vũng Tàu is known for its seafood. Restaurants all over town serve crabs, fish, squid, and other marine cuisine. **Quân An ❷,** 7 Trần Hưng Đạo, is popular with locals for its seafood dishes and fresh fish at market prices (30,000-70,000Đ). **Good Morning Vietnam ❸,** 6 Hoàng Hoa Thám, makes decent pizzas (58,000-88,000Đ) and pasta (65,000-96,000Đ) and offers good French ice cream at 16,000Đ per scoop. (☎856 959. Open daily 9am-10pm.) **Nguyễn Vũ ❶,** 43 Thùy Vân, is a hop across the road from the beach and serves excellent rice and noodle dishes (15,000-20,000Đ).

📷🎭 SIGHTS AND NIGHTLIFE. Besides miles of beaches, Vũng Tàu also has an unusually large number of enormous religious statues. The **Madonna** and **Buddha** stand watch over Mulberry Beach, while **Jesus** faces the ocean with open arms at the tip of the

THE TẾT NOT-SO-OFFENSIVE

Foreigners are most likely to associate the word "Tết" with the 1968 Tết Offensive of the American War. The real Tết, namesake of the military operation is Tết Nguyễn Đán, the Buddhist New Year and Vietnam's most important holiday (see **Festivals,** p. 82). For three days in winter, all work ceases and the country erupts with decoration. In Hồ Chí Minh City, the square and park around Notre Dame Cathedral hosts a massive flower market with numerous traditional music performances.

Houses are festooned with *hoa mai,* a yellow flower, and *hoa dao,* peach blossoms, while families eat sweets such as coconut jam and *bánh chung,* sticky rice wrapped in banana leaves. Both children and grandparents are given small amounts of "lucky money" wrapped in red paper. The point is not the cash; red is the color of fortune in Vietnam, so the packages themselves are meant to bring good luck. During the day, the religious go to services in pagodas.

Hà Nội is probably the best place to visit during Tết, because the pace of economic change in the south means that traditions are weaker in and around HCMC. Nevertheless, the importance of Tết as a national holiday means that even the Saigonese take a break. During those few days, you're likely to find a festive mood anywhere in the country.

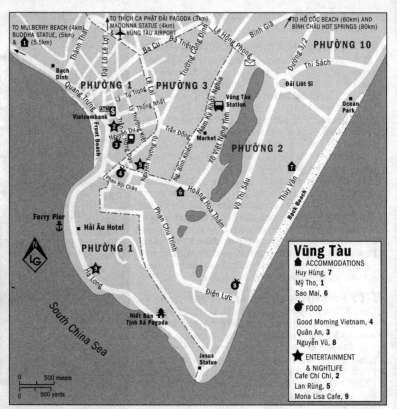

TO THÍCH CA PHẬT ĐÀI PAGODA (3km)
MADONNA STATUE (4km)
TO MULBERRY BEACH (4km) VŨNG TÀU AIRPORT
BUDDHA STATUE, (5km)
& (5.5km)

TO HỒ CỐC BEACH (60km) AND
BÌNH CHÂU HOT SPRINGS (80km)

PHƯỜNG 10

Thi Sách

Đài Liệt Sĩ

Ocean
Park

Bạch
Đinh

PHƯỜNG 1   PHƯỜNG 3

Vũng Tàu
Station

Vietcombank

Market

PHƯỜNG 2

Ferry Pier

Hải Âu Hotel

PHƯỜNG 1

Điện Lực

South China Sea

Niết Bàn
Tịnh Xá Pagoda

Jesus
Statue

0   500 meters
0   500 yards

Vũng Tàu

▲ ACCOMMODATIONS
Huy Hùng, **7**
Mỹ Thọ, **1**
Sao Mai, **6**

🍴 FOOD

Good Morning Vietnam, **4**
Quán An, **3**
Nguyễn Vũ, **8**

★ ENTERTAINMENT
 & NIGHTLIFE
Cafe Chi Chi, **2**
Lan Rừng, **5**
Mona Lisa Cafe, **9**

peninsula. At **Thích Ca Phật Đài Pagoda** on Trần Phú, the main attraction is a large Buddha meditating on a lotus leaf. **Niết Bàn Tịnh Xá Pagoda** features a massive stone Buddha reclining peacefully among jungle animals, an ancient bronze bell on the roof upon which visitors can leave written prayers (donation requested), and a mosaic-covered dragon boat containing an elaborate miniature landscape made of stone.

A more secular option, ■**Bạch Đinh (White Villa),** is situated on a hill over Trần Phú. This residence was home first to French colonial officers and later to Vietnamese royalty. Inside there are some restored rooms and a collection of antiques salvaged from shipwrecks, but the grounds of the villa are the main attraction. Winding walkways crisscross the hill among exotic trees, flowers, and butterflies, and pleasant sitting areas offer a good view of Front Beach. Go on a weekday and you'll have the place to yourself. (5000Đ. Open daily 7am-5pm.) The area around the city's main **market,** on Nam Kỳ Khởi Nghĩa one block away from the bus station, is less attractive, but the market itself offers plenty in the way of clothes, bamboo, and raw meat. **Ocean Park,** 8 Thùy Vân (☎816 319; oceanpark@hcm.vnn.vn), is a water sports complex at Back Beach that offers jet ski rental for 500,000Đ per hr. There are also two swimming pools, simple Seagull Pool (30,000Đ) and the fancier Dolphin Pool (40,000Đ) with sea-view tables and a cafe.

Nightlife in Vũng Tàu is a mix of karaoke and coffee bars sprinkled around the beach areas. To sing the night away amidst a jungle of fake fruit and animals, try **Lan Rừng,** 2 Trần Hưng Đạo. (☎530 713. Beer 14,000-45,000Đ. Karaoke 25,000Đ morning,

35,000Đ afternoon/evening. Open daily 7am-10pm.)
For a more relaxed vibe, check out **Cafe Chi Chi,** 5 Trần
Hưng Đạo, which serves coffee (5000-7000Đ) and dessert (8000-10,000Đ) in an attractive setting. (☎511 111.
Open daily 7am-10pm.) For live music and expensive
beer (12,000-15,000Đ) just across from the sea, try the
Mona Lisa Cafe, 92 Hạ Long. (Open daily 8-11pm.)

🖸 DAYTRIPS FROM VŨNG TÀU. In 1928 a French
researcher discovered **natural hot springs** around the
town of Bình Châu (see **"Blow Off Some Steam,"** p.
407). The area has since been recognized by the
World Trade Organization as a sustainable ecotourism area. Today travelers come here to relax and
unwind in the thermal waters. Aside from **thermal
bathing pools,** where the water is a blissful 37
degrees Celsius, the complex has **hot mud baths** and
foot baths. And for a mere 2000Đ, you can witness
myth in action: throw eggs (gently) into the spring
water and watch them boil. The resort also offers
typical spa services (massage and physiotherapy
80,000Đ per hr.) and sporting options (fishing
300,000Đ per hr.; tennis 50,000Đ per hr.). Bình
Châu is manageable as a daytrip from Vũng Tàu,
but you can choose to stay overnight—the **rooms ❹**
aren't cheap (300,000Đ and up; breakfast and 2
pool tickets included), but they're excellent. There
is also a good **camping area ❶** (10,000Đ per day;
water and electricity included). The resort is about
80km from Vũng Tàu. The best way to get there is to
hire a motorbike or taxi and ask the driver to take
you to Suối Nước Nòng Bình Châu. If you can get
together 12 people or more, you can book a two-day
tour from HCMC through **SaigonTourist's** website.
(☎871 131; www.saigon-tourist.com/binhchau.
580,000Đ per person.) Entrance fee (15,000Đ)
includes 1 towel and access to hot foot baths. Thermal bathing pools (50,000Đ) and hot mud baths
(120,000Đ) are open daily 5am-9pm.

Unlike the beaches of Vũng Tàu, **Hồ Cốc beach**
has seen very little development due to its remote
location. Its wide stretches of soft white sand are
interrupted only by a few bungalows. During the
week there is almost no tourism here, making it a
peaceful place to spend an afternoon. The area
around the beach is a **national forest** that is home to
a great deal of protected wildlife. Trekking through
the forest on your own is not permitted, but you
can hire a guide to take you on the trails up to the
summit of Tầm Bồ mountain and back (2hr.;
60,000Đ). Inquire at the entrance to the beach or
ask Bình Châu Eco-Resort. Hồ Cốc is just over 60km
from Vũng Tàu and can only be reached by a hired
motorbike or taxi. (Bungalows 120,000Đ and up;
includes breakfast and beach. 5000Đ.)

THE BIG SPLURGE

BLOW OFF SOME STEAM

There aren't many places in the
world where you can relax in a
natural hot-water pool the temperature of your own blood in the
middle of untouched jungle. **Bình
Châu Hot Springs** (p. 407),
though, is one of them. The resort
was founded in 2002 by Vietnam's government tourist agency,
but the hot springs themselves—
fed by 70 underground sources
and surrounded by gorgeous, government-preserved forest—have
been in use for nearly a century.

Like most natural spas, these
springs are rumored to have healing properties. The science of it
isn't clear, but don't let your skepticism deter you from diving headlong into the hot mud pools or
tearing into your spa-cooked
poached eggs. And for something
different, crocodile angling and
hiking are also available at the
springs.

Because of the resort's remote
location, it is rarely crowded. The
price might not be ideal for the
budget traveler—especially if you
choose to stay overnight—but this
relaxing haven might just be worth
the splurge. It certainly isn't going
to get any cheaper once the rest of
the world discovers it.

*The hot springs are located
80km from Vũng Tàu on Hwy. 55.
Hire a motorbike or taxi to get there.
☎871 131; www.saigon-tourist.com/binhchau. Rooms
300,000Đ. Spa entrance 15,000Đ.
Hot-water pools 50,000Đ. Hot mud
120,000Đ.*

CROSSROADS
The motorbike and modernization in Vietnam

Vietnamese drivers are among the best and worst in the world. With one million motorbikes to Hà Nội's four million people and three million bikes for Hồ Chí Minh City's six and a half million people, it comes as no surprise that the street traffic of Vietnamese cities is one of the most daunting challenges for Western travelers. But beyond the incessant momentum and almost hilarious dangers of the streets on which they drive, motorbikes have in the past decade have become vehicles of cultural change and symbols of Vietnam today.

The sounds of raucous honking and noisy motorbike engines begin before the sun comes up and continue late into the night. Streets in Vietnam's metropolises most closely resemble American highways, except without crosswalks, stoplights, or any sense of order. Yellow lines on major roads mean little, as cars and motorbikes alike use the oncoming lanes to pass, turning routine drives into harrowing games of "Chicken." Vehicles in the same lane—going in opposite directions—flash their lights and honk their horns to claim the right-of-way as they approach each other at furious speeds. Only quick last-minute maneuvering saves these drivers (and the bicyclists who dodge between them) from what seems like certain death. Even the most experienced of New York City cab drivers would be impressed at such vehicular dexterity.

For pedestrians, braving these streets presents an entirely new set of challenges. There are no "Ped X-ing" signs and no chirping "WALK" signals In Vietnam. Getting from one side of the street to the other in any Vietnamese city is not for the faint of heart and must be approached systematically. "Slow and steady pace, and whatever you do, don't panic!" were words of advice from my cab driver as he dropped me in downtown HCMC. With dozens of motorbike drivers whipping by you without giving a thought to pedestrians waiting on the side of the road, taking the first step seems like suicide. The slow and steady pace of the crossing, with constant glances to the side, is at first terrifying. You walk alone through a sea of motorbikes, which fly past you in all directions, but somehow, miraculously, each one yields to your easy, constant gait.

And after a few days, the entire process becomes almost natural. Almost.

But the break-neck pace of daily motorbike traffic and the almost monk-like equanimity of the pedestrians who pass through it are in many ways symbols of the transition to a modern Vietnam. The motorbike has provided the youth of

Vietnam with new mobility, both physical and socioeconomic. Huyen, a 24-year-old tour guide living in Hà Nội with her younger brother, is originally from a small village 2½ hours outside the city, but transitioned to urban life (like so many others her age) with the help of a motorbike. Looking at this spunky, jeans-clad, English-speaking young woman, it is hard to tell she spent the first 18 years of her life surrounded by rice paddies. "My parents wanted me to get an education so that I could help support them," she said, "so I came to Hà Nội with my brother and have been here ever since." Huyen's motorbike not only allows her to live on the outskirts of Hà Nội, where the rent is cheaper, but it also provides her with a means of traveling back to her family. And like the pedestrians who coolly and expertly traverse the chaotic streets of Vietnam's unfathomably fast-changing cities, Huyen has seamlessly adapted to the brand-new, breathtaking world surrounding her.

For others, however, this transition has been rockier. Though Vietnam—a country where rice paddies grow over old war sites and a pervasive national pride blankets personal struggles—has learned well the lessons of adaptation, the introduction of the motorbike has strained the traditional family support structure in new and difficult ways. As more young urban couples are mobile enough to work in the explosive growth sectors of Hà Nội and Saigon, the desire and ability to obtain a private residence creates tension within their families. Tradition dictates that when the eldest son marries, he and his new wife move in with his parents, where they will live and eventually inherit the house. But for young women who have grown accustomed to the independent urban life, this move can lead to a tremendous lifestyle transformation. "We'll have our own room, and his mother will watch the children while we are at work, but, ohmagod," exclaims a young woman between sips of coffee, "I can't believe I'm going to have to live with his mother and younger sister forever!"

But if the past is any indication, the country will soon pick up its new personality. Motorbike drivers already have done so, having learned (or made up) the loose rules of the road on the hectic city streets, and everyone around them has grown accustomed to the maddening roar that is Vietnamese city life today. Those in the countryside have farther to go to catch up with the modernized Vietnam, but new roads into the farmland are being built daily—it won't be long until the frantic pace of motorbike modernization reaches them, too.

Matt Norcini is high school US and World History teacher in Tampa, Florida, and a recipient of a Fulbright-Hays Fellowship to Thailand and Vietnam. He engages his students by making cutting remarks involving barnyard animals and his favorite historical character, Smedley Butler. His hobbies include traveling, writing, and challenging his intestinal fortitude by sampling open-market foods in developing nations.

THE MEKONG
DELTA

The Vietnamese call this region *Cửu Long* (Nine Dragons), in reference to the Mekong River's nine principal tributaries. As the river drains from its source in the Tibetan Himalayas, it fans out across the land in a final push to the sea, forming countless canals—the backdrop of life for Delta residents. Boat tours around the region reveal bustling river markets, natural canals lined with coconut palms, and a variety of floating homes. The flat, moist land of the delta is ideal for harvesting rice and grain, making the region one of the world's largest rice producers. The river itself is thick with traffic, from local trade in floating markets to large ships hauling precarious loads of grain to Hồ Chí Minh City. On land, fruit orchards, coconut groves, and sugarcane plantations dot the landscape. The delta's mix of elaborate pagodas signals the presence of its main ethnic minority, the Cambodian Khmer people. The Vietnamese are, in fact, relative newcomers to the region, which was dominated by the Khmer until the 18th century, when Vietnamese officials began to take control. Tensions between Cambodia and Vietnam regarding the area have persisted ever since, reaching a boiling point in the late 1970s when Vietnam invaded the tyrannical Khmer Rouge regime in Cambodia. Today, the two countries seem to be at peace, and the Delta population is a fascinating mix of Vietnamese and Khmer, along with some Chinese and Chàm influences. While the cities and towns of the Mekong Delta have the river in common, each one has something different to offer the traveler, from exotic flowers to mangrove forests to relaxing beaches. Tour companies in Hồ Chí Minh City offer trips to see the highlights of the region, but the extensive bus and boat network allows you to explore the delta on your own for as long as you like.

HIGHLIGHTS OF THE MEKONG DELTA

ABSORB THE RAYS OF THE ALMIGHTY AND VENGEFUL SUN (and the difficult-to-ignore scent of ▧**fish sauce**) in the sandy, forested paradise of **Phú Quốc Island** (p. 431), a top producer of Vietnam's favorite flavoring and an up-and-coming tourist hot spot. Get there before the rest of the world does.

GORGE YOURSELF in **Mỹ Tho** (p. 409) on sweet ▧ **coconut candy** while you lie back and drift through endless emerald canals of palms. Step off the boat to sample fruit straight off the tree in one of the Mekong's many orchards.

CHASE BUTTERFLIES with wings larger than your hands in the blissful botanical gardens of **Sa Đéc** (p. 416). After you're done chasing, head back to wander in the gorgeous market on the waterfront.

LIVE ABOVE WATER—BARELY— in the floating villages near **Châu Đốc** (p. 444), itself a sweet-tempered delta town with an attractive, well-maintained waterfront. Sobering **Tức Dụp** and **Ba Chúc** (p. 447) are two nearby sites of historical interest.

MỸ THO   ☎ 64

Just a short bus ride away from Hồ Chí Minh City, Mỹ Tho serves as the traveler's gateway to the Mekong Delta. Don't be fooled by the fact that it's a provincial cap-

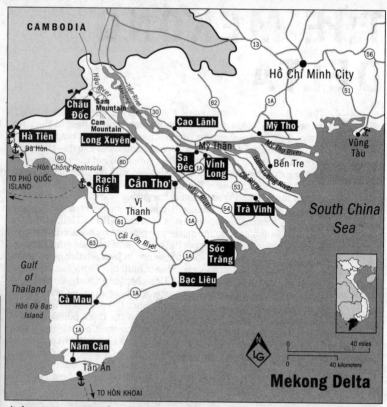

Mekong Delta

ital—you can cover the entire town by foot in about an hour. Its attractions are mostly found in and along the Tiên River, but travelers may also enjoy the peaceful riverside and busy market area.

TRANSPORTATION AND ORIENTATION. Most **buses** arrive at **Tiên Giang Station,** 42 Ấp Bắc (☎855 404), about 3km northwest of the city center. Buses go to HCMC (1½hr.; every 30min. 5am-5pm; 19,000Đ) and Mỹ Thuận (2hr.; every hr. 5-8am; 18,000Đ). The small city center is laid out in a simple grid pattern. The town is bordered to the south by the **Tiên River,** and the **Bảo Định Channel** snakes its way roughly south through the town, eventually emptying into the Tiên. **Nam Kỳ Khởi Nghĩa,** a north-south thoroughfare, intersects with **Ấp Bắc** and runs to the river. Along the main waterfront is **Đường 30/4,** which runs east-west and ends at the mouth of channel (marked by a statue). **Trưng Trắc** runs along the channel, parallel to Nam Kỳ Khởi Nghĩa. A large indoor **market** is located at the corner of **Lê Đại Hành,** which connects Nam Kỳ Khởi Nghĩa and Trưng Trắc at their centers, and **Lê Lợi,** which is two blocks inland from Trưng Trắc. In the surrounding streets, between the two bridges over Bảo Định Channel, is an outdoor market.

PRACTICAL INFORMATION. Tiên Giang Tourist Office, 8 Đường 30/4, provides free, handy maps of Mỹ Tho. (☎873 184; www.tiengiangtourist.com. Open daily

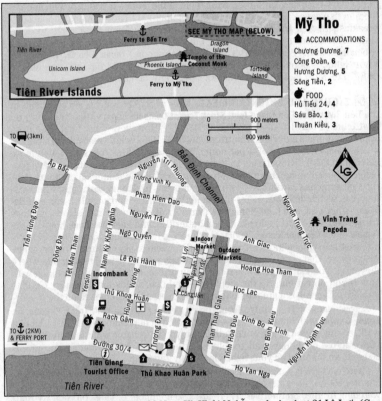

My Tho

🏠 ACCOMMODATIONS
Chương Dương, 7
Công Đoàn, 6
Hương Dương, 5
Sông Tiền, 2

🍎 FOOD
Hủ Tiếu 24, 4
Sáu Bảo, 1
Thuận Kiều, 3

MEKONG DELTA

7am-5pm.) There is an **ATM** at 33 Nam Kỳ Khởi Nghĩa and a **bank** at 31 Lê Lợi. (Currency exchange, MC/V cash advances, and Western Union. Open daily 7:15-11:15am and 1:30-4:30pm.) The **hospital** (along with a **pharmacy**) is located at 4 Thủ Koa Huân. (☎872 363. 24hr. emergency service.) **Internet** access is available at 80 Nam Kỳ Khởi Nghĩa. (☎883 993. Open daily 7am-10pm.) The main **post office**, 59 Đường 30/4, offers fax and phone services. (☎873 214. Open daily 6am-9pm.)

💈 **ACCOMMODATIONS AND FOOD.** The few tourist hotels in town are located along the Tiền River and Bảo Định Channel. At **Hương Dương ❶**, 33 Trưng Trắc, the rooms range from very basic (no A/C or hot water) to fully equipped with excellent views—all at the same price. (☎872 011. Rooms 90,000Đ.) **Sông Tiền ❸**, 101 Trưng Trắc, features neat and clean rooms, an elevator, and excellent views from the shared balconies on its upper floors. (☎872 009. Rooms 160,000Đ.) **Công Đoàn ❶**, 61 Đường 30/4, next to the post office, has spacious rooms, some with terraces overlooking the waterfront. It's a great deal when you split the cost. (☎874 324; congdoantourist@hcm.vnn.vn. Doubles 90,000-150,000Đ.) **Chương Dương ❹**, 10 Đường 30/4, is a colonial-style building set right on the waterfront, with regal furnishings and nicely manicured grounds. (☎870 875. Rooms US$25-35.)

When it comes to food, **Sáu Bảo ❶**, 1 Lý Công Uẩn, makes fantastic 🔲**bánh xèo**, a southern specialty—crispy shrimp-and-pork pancakes (13,000Đ). Don't knock 'em until you've tried 'em. Be sure to wrap them in the lettuce leaves provided and dip them in fish sauce. (☎879 835. Open daily 4-9pm.) Mỹ Tho's famous noodle soup breakfast, *hủ tiếu Mỹ Tho*, is cooked up all over town. Many restaurants and food stalls serve the dish in the mornings, but **Hủ Tiếu 24 ❶**, 24 Nam Kỳ Khởi Nghĩa, specializes in it. (Soup 4000Đ. Open daily 6am-noon.) **Thuận Kiều ❶**, 47 Nam Kỳ Khởi Nghĩa, is popular with locals and serves up fresh and flavorful rice dishes. (☎877 116. Most meals under 20,000Đ. Open daily 7am-9pm.)

◙ ▣ SIGHTS AND ENTERTAINMENT. Most of Mỹ Tho's sights are on islands in the **Tiền River**. The **Tiền Giang Joint Stock Tourist Company** has a virtual monopoly on **boat tours** (2-3hr. US$20-25; 3-4hr. US$30-35). However, many boat operators approach tourists along the waterfront and offer "unofficial" (read: illegal) tours at much cheaper rates (US$2-4 per hour). Tourists say these tours are much more catered to the individual. Due to their illegality, the boat operator may have passengers board somewhere else. Most tours cover the same sights: boats drift through gorgeous canals lined with coconut palms to ◙**candy workshops,** where visitors can watch delicious toffee-like candy being made and sample a range of flavors. Other stops include honeybee farms, fruit orchards, and islands, such as **Trưng Trắc**, rich with exotic plants and butterflies, and **Phoenix Island,** home to the **Temple of the Coconut Monk** (5000Đ). As the local hype would suggest, this island is a tourist trap of mediocre restaurants and souvenirs; skip it for the other sights. Also beware that some drivers might have deals with the island restaurants where they stop. You can bargain down the menu prices, or take your own lunch with you. If you do eat out, try the elephant-eared fish, a Mekong speciality (50,000-90,000Đ). Evening is a great time to tour the river, when fireflies flood the trees.

Across Nguyễn Trãi Bridge from the city center stands **Vĩnh Tràng Pagoda,** an active temple with impressive gates ornamented in porcelain mosaic. It's a bit of a walk, so unless you're a pagoda enthusiast, you'll probably want to skip this one. (Once across the bridge, walk to Nguyễn Trung Trực; turn left, and the entrance is 200m down the road on your right. Open daily 7am-5pm.)

There isn't really a nightlife scene in Mỹ Tho. Young people and couples tend to congregate on the waterfront in **Thủ Khoa Huân Park,** where the main activity is watching fireflies on the river. There are also a number of **cafes** on Nam Kỳ Khởi Nghĩa that pump out tunes in the evenings.

TRÀ VINH ☎ 74

The principal point of interest in Trà Vinh is its sizable **ethnic Khmer** population, which comprises 30% of the town's population. Although the Khmer people are indistinguishable from other residents in terms of appearance, they have left their mark on the city in the form of many Khmer pagodas. Today, you can admire the electric-colored garb of monks as they wander among the impressive sanctuaries.

▟ TRANSPORTATION. Buses arrive at the station on Nguyễn Đáng, near Trà Vinh's city center, and go to: Cần Thơ (3hr.; 7am; 14,000Đ); Cao Lãnh (3hr.; 7:30am; 20,000Đ); HCMC (5hr.; every hr. 1am-5pm; 26,000Đ); Sa Đéc (2hr.; 2pm; 14,000Đ); Vĩnh Long (1hr.; every 30min. 7am-4pm; 20,000Đ).

▟▐ ORIENTATION AND PRACTICAL INFORMATION. Unlike most other Mekong cities, life in Trà Vinh is not centered around its narrow river, **Long Bình,** which runs north-south on the eastern edge of town. Instead, the big **market,** at the intersection of main avenues **Phạm Thái Bưởng** (which becomes **Điện Biên Phủ**) and **Nam Kỳ Khởi Nghĩa,** is where the action takes place. The latter street runs toward

MEKONG DELTA

the river, while **Lê Lợi,** another important street, runs parallel to Pham Thái Bương, one block farther from the river.

Trà Vinh Tourist Office, 64-66 Lê Lợi, offers advice about the city and the surrounding province. (☎858 556. Open daily 7-11am and 2-5pm.) Trà Vinh has no ATMs, but there is a **bank** at 70-72 Lê Lợi with currency exchange and Western Union. (Open daily 7-11am and 1-5pm.) Surf the **Internet** at 83 Lê Lợi. (☎853 776. Open daily 6am-11pm.) The **post office** is at 70 Hùng Vương, at the intersection with Pham Thái Bương. (Phone and fax services. Open daily 6am-9:30pm.)

⌂⌂ ACCOMMODATIONS AND FOOD. Vân Trâm ❷, 6 Điện Biên Phủ, has clean, fresh rooms, helpful staff, and a prime location on the market square. The cheaper rooms lack windows. (☎858 034. Doubles 120,000-180,000Đ.) Slightly farther away, **Hoàn Mỹ ❸,** 105A Nguyễn Thị Minh Khai, has attractive, spacious rooms with wooden floors, as well as a very small but stylish bar in the lobby. (☎862 211. Rooms 160,000-340,000Đ.) **Cửu Long ❹,** 999 Nguyễn Thị Minh Khai (actually located among the early 1000s), is a modern three-star hotel with two restaurants and a karaoke bar. (☎862 615. Rooms US$17-37.)

For food, try **Túy Hường ❶,** 8 Điện Biên Phủ, which serves Chinese dishes and has a view of the market. (☎858 312. Entrees 15,000Đ.) **Tanh Bạch ❶,** 103 Trần Quốc Tuấn, makes a variety of noodle soups. (Soups 12,000Đ. Open daily 7am-10pm.)

◙ SIGHTS. In the city center, **Ông Mẹt Pagoda** (on Lê Lợi, just north of its intersection with Đường 19/5) is easily distinguished by the large Khmer inscription over its gates. Some of the buildings here are a bit run down, but they're currently being restored to their former grandeur. **Âng Pagoda,** 6km southwest of the city center off Nguyễn Thị Minh Khai, isn't particularly impressive, but it's home to some very friendly monks and is located next to **Ao Bà Om,** a square, lily pad-covered pond surrounded by the shade of trees. There is also a little collection of Khmer cultural items opposite the entrance to the pagoda. (Open daily 7:30-11am and 1:30-5pm. Free.) **▨Hang Pagoda,** about 6km south of the city center on Điện Biên Phủ, is in mint condition. The main hall boasts a brilliant multi-tiered roof. Inside, large murals depicting the life of Buddha cover the walls, and many gold statues of him adorn the altar. If you come just before dusk, especially during the rainy season, you may catch flocks of storks swooping in among the treetops. Aside from the Khmer pagodas, the only sight in Trà Vinh is the **Uncle Ho Temple (Đền Thờ Bác),** about 5km north of the city center off Lê Lợi. It's interesting how well maintained this place is when so many of the city's houses of worship are crumbling. The temple complex includes a shrine to Hồ Chí Minh, as well as a small museum displaying photos of his life and of events in Trà Vinh. There are also several US Army vehicles on display outside. Curiously, the closest translation we could find of the building's name came to "Temple of Uncle Rabbit." We don't understand it either. (Open daily 7-11am and 1-5pm. Free.)

VĨNH LONG ☎ 70

Though a bit grittier than some of its delta neighbors, Vĩnh Long attracts tourists because of its prime location on the Cổ Chiên River. A trip down this attractive waterway will take visitors through lush island canals and past floating markets, bonsai gardens, and village homes.

▣ TRANSPORTATION. Many buses do not go to directly to Vĩnh Long, instead dropping passengers off on the highway in Mỹ Thuận; from there, it's a 10km motorbike ride. There are two **bus stations** in Vĩnh Long. From the one in the city center, on the corner of Đoàn Thị Điểm and Đại Lộ 3/2, **buses** go to Cần Thơ (1hr.;

THE KINDNESS OF STRANGERS

t takes some experience to finally realize that the best way to travel s by public bus. Schedules are erratic and rides are rarely comfortable, so foreigners often opt or the smooth-riding tourist buses. But they're missing the entire point of the journey.

At Vĩnh Long station, I was overtaken by a gaggle of food hawkers, who demanded my destination and rushed me onto the correct bus. They then spent an hour hassling and questioning me while the bus was packed about 40% over capacity.

I shared a different bus ride with a basket of squawking birds and loud Vietnamese pop music as we trundled past messy haystacks, bright green paddies, and golden squares of sun-dried grain.

On Cần Giờ Island, I flagged down a tiny bus on a dusty road, only to discover that its tunes were sung in piercing children's voices. Meanwhile, a spare tire had been thrown into the aisle and the steering wheel looked in danger of rattling off its axis.

But these obstacles say more about Vietnam's people than any crumbling pagoda. Someone at the station will help the clueless foreigner get on the right bus, and someone else will see that she gets off at the right stop. Eventually, the bus will get to its destination—and some kind-hearted stranger will make sure that the foreigner gets there with it.

—Juliet Samuel

every 15min. 5am-5pm; 10,000Đ). From the other station, 4km south of the city center, buses go to Trà Vinh (1hr.; every hr. 5am-5pm; 20,000Đ).

ORIENTATION AND PRACTICAL INFORMATION. Vĩnh Long's city center is surrounded by water on all four sides: the **Cổ Chiên River** to the north, the **Long Hồ Canal** to the east, the **Cầu Lầu Canal** to the south, and the **Cái Cá Canal** to the west. Most of the action takes place on **Đường 1/5**, which runs along Long Hồ Canal, and **Phan Bội Châu**, which runs along the river. There is a large, rambling **market** behind **Đường 30/4**—one block inland from Đường 1/5—concentrated along Hùng Vương, which is another block inland from the Long Hồ Canal.

Cửu Long Tourist Office, 1 Đường 1/5, books boat tours. (☎823 616; cuulongtourist1@hcm.vnn.vn. Open daily 7am-5pm.) The main **bank**, 143 Lê Thái Tổ, is about 1km outside the city center and offers currency exchange, MC/V cash advances, **ATM**, and Western Union. (☎823 109. Open daily 7-11am and 1-5pm.) A smaller bank is in the city center, at 1B Hoàng Thái Hiếu, and does only currency exchange. (☎831 394. Open M-Sa 7-11am and 1-4pm.) The **hospital** is about 2.5km outside the city center, at 303 Trần Phú, although a new, more central one is in the works. (Entrance on Phạm Thái Bường. ☎822 653. 24hr. emergency service.) **Internet** access is available at Delta, 2G Hùng Vương. (☎822 099. Open daily 7am-11pm. 3000Đ per hr.) The main **post office**, 12C Hoàng Thái Hiếu, has fax and phone facilities and sells maps for 12,000Đ. (☎825 888. Open daily 6am-9pm.)

ACCOMMODATIONS AND FOOD. Most tourist hotels are located on or near the Cổ Chiên River. **Vân Trâm ❸**, 4 Đường 1/5, boasts fresh decor and large, sparkling rooms. All rooms have air-conditioning and some have lovely views of the nearby fruit market and river. (☎823 820. Rooms US$10.) Set back from the river, **Phượng Hoàng ❶**, 2H-2R Hùng Vương, has wonderfully sunny rooms on its upper floors and great prices. (☎825 185. Rooms 60,000-250,000Đ.) **Cửu Long Hotel ❹**, on Phan Bội Châu, is operated by the tourist office. Its carpeted rooms are quite decent and all have attached baths. Do not confuse this place with its older cousin of the same name and ownership on Đường 1/5, which is overpriced and under-kept. (☎822 494. Rooms 320,000-600,000Đ.) Another popular option for tourists is a **homestay ❸**. Cửu Long Tourist Office can arrange for visitors to stay the night on one of the islands in the home of a Vietnamese family, in an old colonial building, or in a farmhouse. Unfortunately, it's not possible to arrange one without buying a whole tour of the region's attractions, which lasts two or three nights.

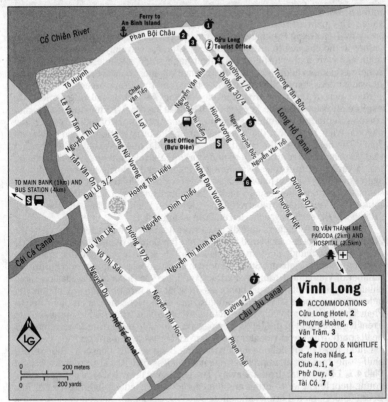

Vĩnh Long

🛏 ACCOMMODATIONS
Cửu Long Hotel, 2
Phượng Hoàng, 6
Văn Trầm, 3

🍴★ FOOD & NIGHTLIFE
Cafe Hoa Nắng, 1
Club 4.1, 4
Phở Duy, 5
Tài Có, 7

Most homestays include meals, transportation, and—most importantly—mosquito nets. (US$15-65 per night, depending on housing type.)

AVOID THE GOVERNMENT, AGAIN. Any traveler looking for a truly authentic experience will probably want to steer clear of hotels run by the government tourist office. They might have all the amenities and are generally clean and well-maintained, but they are also rather soulless. The family-run mini-hotels almost always outdo them in terms of warmth and character. -Juliet Samuel

The restaurants along the river cater mainly to the tour buses that arrive here several times each day. A cheaper and more fun way to fill up is at the **market** a block away. There are sit-down **food stalls** along Nguyễn Công Trứ and Nguyễn Văn Nhã (open during daylight hours) and on Đại Lộ 3/2 (open at night). To eat without your neighbor's elbows jabbing you in the ribs, try **Phở Duy ❶**, 106 Đường 30/4, which dishes out a variety of tasty phở options. (☎820 611. Phở 9000Đ. Open daily 5am-4pm.) On the other side of the city center, **Tài Có ❸**, 40A Đường 2/9, draws crowds for great hot pot and barbecue dishes, which patrons cook themselves. (☎824 845. Most entrees 60,000Đ. Open daily 10am-9pm.)

📷🎵 **SIGHTS AND NIGHTLIFE.** Cửu Long Tourist Office runs **boat tours** (4hr.; US$15-25) of the Cổ Chiên River. As usual, private operators offer cheaper and more personal tours (US$3-4 per hr.)—just wander along the waterfront to find them. The main attraction along the river is the **Cái Bè floating market,** an hour away in Tiên Giang Province. In the mornings, boats laden with fruit and grain gather in the channel to await customers. Although certainly interesting, it is not quite as rowdy and colorful as one might hope; trade is wholesale and the atmosphere is calm. In addition to the floating market, most boat tours include visits to bonsai gardens, handmade candy workshops, and traditional homes.

Right across the river from the city center, **An Bình Island** offers plenty to explore on your own. The key sight is **Tiên Châu Pagoda,** which features a morbid cartoon depiction of sinners suffering the many tortures of hell. To reach the pagoda, walk 10m down the stone path from the ferry station. (Open daily 6am-7pm.) The best part of the island is not the pagoda, however, but rather the fact that you can wander around here undisturbed. A stroll on its paths will take you past a variety of fruit trees, wandering chickens, and colorful homes guarded by aggressive dogs—if you pause in a gateway, they're liable to run at you, but a good shout in their direction usually makes the animals cower. During the day a commuter ferry runs nonstop between the station on Phan Bội Châu and the island. (10min.; 4000Đ each way, collected on the An Bình side.)

Though most foreigners quickly cross over it with just a glance at the view, the ◼**Mỹ Thuận Bridge** is considered the pride of Vĩnh Long Province. Opened to traffic in 2000, the strikingly modern suspension bridge is the largest one that spans the Mekong River in Vietnam. Strolling across it is a popular activity for a surprising number of Vietnamese tourists. Farther south, the **Vân Thánh Miê Pagoda** is notable chiefly because of its unusual honorees. In what is a rare practice in Vietnam, the older sanctuary pays tribute to Confucius, and the newer sanctuary is dedicated to Phan Thánh Giản, a locally born Vietnamese diplomat who tried to put an end to French domination in the 1860s. The pagoda is located on Đường 30/4; to reach it, head south from the city center about 2km and cross over a bridge.

Unlike most of its Mekong neighbors, Vĩnh Long actually boasts a proper nightclub—only one, but an impressive one nonetheless. You'll hear the dance beats of **Club 4.1,** 1 Đường 1/5, from far away. The place gets crowded on weekends when young people gather to drink and dance under psychedelic lighting. (☎826 753. Beer 30,000Đ; mixed drinks and shots 50,000Đ. Open daily noon-midnight.) For a quieter evening, **Cafe Hoa Nắng,** on the corner of Đường 1/5 and Phan Bội Châu, is a relaxed alternative. Sip drinks and watch the river flow by—but bring mosquito repellent. (Coffee 3000-4000Đ; beer 11,000-15,000Đ. Open daily 6am-10pm.)

SA ĐÉC ☎ 67

Many Mekong Delta tours make a stop in Sa Đéc to view its famous botanical nurseries. The little city is full of these gardens, whose decorative flowers and shrubs are sold all across the region. This town centers around a riverside outdoor market, and its pristine streets are lined with colorful houses. You may not want to leave this peaceful, relatively tourist-free getaway.

▐ **TRANSPORTATION. Buses** arrive at the station in the city center on Hwy. 80 and go to: Cà Mau (6hr.; 5am; 40,000Đ); Cao Lãnh (2hr.; 7:30am, 4pm; 10,000Đ); HCMC (4hr.; 6:30, 9am; 35,000Đ); Rạch Giá (4hr.; 6am; 29,000Đ); Trà Vinh (2hr.; 7am; 25,000Đ).

◼◧ **ORIENTATION AND PRACTICAL INFORMATION.** Sa Đéc's charming city center is laid out in a simple grid pattern: **Trần Phú, Phan Bội Châu, Ly Thường Kiệt,** and **Highway 80** (also called **Nguyễn Sinh Sắc**) run east-west and meet at the river. These streets are intersected by north-south thoroughfares **Hùng Vương, Trần Hưng**

Đạo, and **Nguyễn Huệ,** the last of which runs along the waterfront. There is no tourist office in Sa Đéc; the provincial office is in Cao Lãnh. However, the staff at Bông Hồng and Sa Đéc Hotels might be able to help. There is a **bank** with currency exchange and an **ATM** on the corner of Trần Hưng Đạo and Nguyễn Sinh Sắc. (Open daily 7:30am-noon and 1:30-5pm.) **Internet** access is at 124 Hùng Vương. (Open daily 10am-10pm.) The main **post office** is located at the corner of Hùng Vương and Nguyễn Sinh Sắc. (Phone and fax services. Open daily 6am-10pm.)

⌨🏠 ACCOMMODATIONS AND FOOD. The fresh, clean rooms at 🏠**Hương Thủy ❷,** 58 Lê Thán Tôn, come with excellent showers, and some have balconies looking out onto the market. (☎868 963. Rooms US$8-10.) **Nguyên Phong ❶,** A20 Trần Hưng Đạo, is a budget mini-hotel with basic but clean rooms; the highlight is the collection of posters featuring Western couples in romantic poses. (☎866 515. Rooms 60,000-100,000Đ.) **Bông Hồng ❷,** 251A Nguyễn Sinh Sắc, has some upper-floor rooms (accessible by elevator) with excellent city views. (☎868 287. Rooms US$8-20.) **Sa Đéc Hotel ❶,** 108/5A Hùng Vương, is a bit far from the center, but it is much closer than the others to the peaceful botanical nurseries in town. (☎861 430. Well-maintained rooms 80,000-150,000Đ.) **Chánh Ký ❶,** 193 Nguyễn Sinh Sắc, is a friendly place that serves Chinese noodle and rice dishes for under 15,000Đ. (Open daily 6am-6pm.) **Thủy ❷,** 439 Hùng Vương, does quality fish dishes and has a Western breakfast menu. (☎861 644. Most entrees 20,000Đ. Open daily 8am-10pm.) There are also some particularly good sit-down **food stalls** in the market area between Nguyễn Huệ and Lê Thánh Tôn. Meals should cost no more than 8000Đ.

◙ SIGHTS. Most nursery owners are accustomed to tourists taking photographs of the free 🏠**botanical gardens** that decorate the city and environs. Across the bridge from the city center, **Vương Hồng Tư Tôn** is one of the area's most popular gardens. Visitors can stroll through endless rows of colorful blooms and potted plants and relax by the fish pond under the shade of palm fronds. The nursery is open from sunrise to sunset, and is best visited during November and December, when the nurseries are in full bloom. Vương Hồng Tư Tôn is part of a village of nurseries right outside the city center. If you're walking there, cross the metal bridge at Trần Phú, turn left onto Lê Lợi (which passes under the end of the bridge) and continue along for about 2km; the village will be easy to spot on your right. On the way there you will also pass a **Cao Đài Temple** (see **"Someone To Watch Over You,"** p. 431), on your right shortly after you begin up Lê Lợi. Although the temple is not set up for visitors, the owner will gladly admit you to the colorful and elaborate interior, and he may even give you some fruit from the altar as a sign of goodwill. Sa Đéc is also notable for being the childhood home of French author **Marguerite Duras**—she set her 1998 novel *The Lover* here, and a film based on the book features footage of the city's waterfront. The city's **outdoor market** is also along the waterfront on Nguyễn Huệ. Shaded by colorful umbrellas and brimming with fruit and fish, it is one of the liveliest and most attractive in the delta. Just past the market, a small, tree-lined **canal** runs into the river and makes for a pleasant stroll around the edge of the town center. You can cover the entire town in an afternoon, and it is a viable daytrip from Cao Lãnh, but we recommend spending the night in charming Sa Đéc instead.

CAO LÃNH ☎ 67

Although this provincial capital itself offers only a few sights within the city limits, Cao Lãnh serves as a springboard for exploring the luscious forests or wild birds of Vietnam. The **Đồng Tháp Museum,** 226 Nguyễn Thái Học, off Nguyễn Huệ, houses a diverse and well-kept collection of items related to the province—unfortunately,

MEKONG DELTA

all signs are in Vietnamese. (Open daily 7-11am and 1:30-5pm. Free.) Nearby, on Nguyễn Huệ about 1km southwest of the city center, stands the ostentatious **Mausoleum of Nguyễn Sinh Sắc,** the burial place of Hồ Chí Minh's venerable father. The tomb is shaded by a giant concrete clamshell, although, and unlike his son's tomb, Nguyễn Sinh Sắc's body is not actually viewable. (Open daily 7-11am and 1:30-5pm. Free.) Farther out, **Xẻo Quít Forest,** about 25km from the city, is a national preservation site that was formerly a Việt Cộng base camp. Tall trees and tangled plants form a lush canopy over narrow waterways and a few scattered VC bunkers. You can hire a canoe to take you through the forest (5000Đ) or just walk along the path (4000Đ). Either journey takes about 30min. (From Cao Lãnh, take a motorbike or a tour from Đồng Tháp Tourist Office to the forest. Open daily 7am-6pm.) **Tam Nông Park,** 40km from Cao Lãnh, is home to thousands of red-necked cranes that migrate here between December and August—the visit is only worthwhile during these months. A 2-3hr. boat ride around the park costs 400,000Đ. (Take a motorbike or a tour to the park. Open daily 7am-5pm.)

Bình Minh ❶, 157 Hùng Vương, is the best budget hotel in town and is located just one street from the river. The owner speaks good English. (☎853 423. Rooms 50,000-100,000Đ.) **Xuân Mai ❷,** 33 Lê Quý Đôn, is on a road off Nguyễn Huệ and has comfortable rooms with attached baths. (☎853 600. Rooms 130,000-150,000Đ.) **Sông Trà ❸,** 178 Nguyễn Huệ, is run by the tourist office. The hotel has spacious rooms and offers massage and steambath services for 50,000Đ each. (☎852 504. Breakfast included. Rooms US$14-20.) In addition to the restaurants in the first two hotels, **Á Châu ❷,** 105B Ly Thường Kiệt, is a good place to fill up. They do a few Western dishes, but huge crispy meat pancakes (*bánh xèo;* 5000Đ) are their specialty, even though they're not listed on the menu. (☎852 202. Most meals 20,000-40,000Đ. Open daily 6am-10pm.) **Á Đông ❶,** 76 Nguyễn Huệ, serves big portions of great Vietnamese fare for breakfast and lunch. (Meals 15,000Đ. Open daily 5:30am-2pm.) For even cheaper eats, there are sit-down **food stalls** across from the market on Ly Thường Kiệt. (Open during the day.)

Buses arrive at the station on Ly Thường Kiệt, in the city center, and go to: HCMC (4hr.; every hr. 4am-4pm; 26,000Đ); Mỹ Tho (2hr.; 9am; 20,000Đ); Sa Đéc (2hr.; 7:30am; 9000Đ); Trà Vinh (3hr.; 8am; 19,000Đ); Vĩnh Long (2hr.; 8am; 14,000Đ). The main thoroughfare in this small town is **Nguyễn Huệ,** which runs past the main post office and bank. Intersecting Nguyễn Huệ is **Ly Thường Kiệt,** which runs past the bus station to the river. The indoor market is at the corner of Ly Thường Kiệt and **Nguyễn Du,** and towards the river is a big fish market. **Đồng Tháp Tourist Office,** 2 Đốc Binh Kiều, has informational brochures on the province and arranges boat tours. (☎855 637. Open daily 7:30-11:30am and 1:30-5pm.) The **bank** is at 87 Nguyễn Huệ. (Currency exchange, MC/V cash advances, **ATM,** and Western Union. Open daily 7-11am and 1:30-5pm.) **Internet** is in the building connected to the post office. (3000Đ per hr. Open daily 6am-10pm.) The **post office** is across from the bank, at 83 Nguyễn Huệ. (Phone and fax services. Open daily 6am-9pm.)

CẦN THƠ ☎ 71

As the unofficial capital of the Mekong Delta, Cần Thơ is the most popular tourist destination south of Hồ Chí Minh City. The wide boulevards and elegant waterfront invite leisurely strolls among some of the best restaurants in the region. Boat tours of the surrounding canals saunter past floating markets, fruit orchards, and peaceful villages. The quiet and insular demeanor of the city conveys the sensibilities of the Mekong as a whole—bustling with its unique commercial ventures, immersed in the rhythm of day-to-day business, and full of surprising peculiarities.

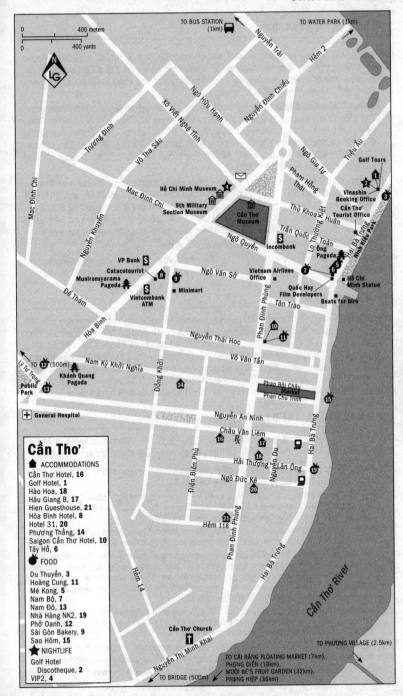

MEKONG DELTA

Cần Thơ

🏠 **ACCOMMODATIONS**

Cần Thơ Hotel, **16**
Golf Hotel, **1**
Hảo Hoa, **18**
Hậu Giang B, **17**
Hien Guesthouse, **21**
Hòa Bình Hotel, **8**
Hotel 31, **20**
Phương Thắng, **14**
Saigon Cần Thơ Hotel, **10**
Tây Hồ, **6**

🍎 **FOOD**

Du Thuyền, **3**
Hoàng Cung, **11**
Mé Kong, **5**
Nam Bộ, **7**
Nam Đô, **13**
Nhà Hàng NK2, **19**
Phở Oanh, **12**
Sài Gòn Bakery, **9**
Sao Hôm, **15**

⭐ **NIGHTLIFE**

Golf Hotel
   Discotheque, **2**
VIP2, **4**

TRANSPORTATION

Flights: Airlines are expected to start service from Cần Thơ to **HCMC** in 2007 (30min.; once daily; US$22). **Vietnam Airlines,** 25 Phan Đình Phùng (☎826 647; fax 826 650), handles domestic and international bookings for cities and other international carriers. Open M-F 7:30am-8pm, Sa-Su 7:30am-5pm.

Buses: The **bus station** is 1km northwest of the city center on Nguyễn Trãi. Buses go to: **Bạc Liêu** (3hr.; 11am; 20,000Đ); **Cà Mau** (6hr.; every hr. 6am-3pm; 43,000Đ); **Châu Đốc** (3hr.; every 15min. 3am-5pm; 29,000Đ); **HCMC** (3½hr.; every 30min. 5am-2pm; 45,000Đ); **Long Xuyên** (1½hr.; every hr. 6am-3pm; 17,000Đ); **Mỹ Tho** (2hr.; 10am; 22,000Đ); **Rạch Giá** (4hr.; every 45min. 5am-5pm; 27,000Đ); **Sóc Trăng** (1½hr.; every 30min. 5am-5pm; 17,000Đ).

Ferries: Vinashin boating company runs **high-speed boats** every Thursday to **Phnom Penh, Cambodia** (7hr.; 7am; US$45). Fare includes water, a light meal, and on-board entertainment. Contact the company Booking Office, 2 Hai Bà Trưng (☎/fax 820 527) to purchase a ticket, or contact the Head Office, 26 Lê Hong Phồng (☎888 960; www.cawaco.com.vn) to inquire about ferries scheduled on other days of the week.

Taxis: Mai Linh (☎822 266) is a reputable service in town.

Motorbikes: *Xe ôms* are a good means of exploring the city and its ever-developing surroundings. The reception desk at most hostels can arrange rentals for US$5 per day.

ORIENTATION

From the bus station, **Nguyễn Trãi** leads southeast into the city center, curving a bit to the west to become **Phan Đình Phùng,** which runs north-south through the city. **Hòa Bình,** the city's main thoroughfare, branches southwest off Phan Đình Phùng at a central rotary. The city center lies at the confluence of the **Cần Thơ** and **Hậu Rivers.** From this meeting point, **Hai Bà Trưng** runs south along the main waterfront, past a statue of Hồ Chí Minh, and into the **market** area. Hai Bà Trưng connects to **Hòa Bình** via east-west **Châu Văn Liêm,** which is called **Nguyễn An Ninh** by the river.

PRACTICAL INFORMATION

Aside from the standard tourist services, Cần Thơ offers **film developing** at Quốc Huy, 46 Hai Bà Trưng. (☎825 484. 1500Đ per picture. Open daily 8am-8pm.)

Tourist Office: Most tourist agencies offer daytrips along the river and to the surrounding sights. Half-day tours US$12-15, full-day US$20-24.

Cần Thơ Tourist Office, 20 Hai Bà Trưng (☎821 852; www.canthotourist.com.vn). Offers handy maps (10,000Đ), currency exchange, MC/V cash advance, Pacific and Vietnam Airlines booking. Also arranges trekking and cycling trips. Open daily 7am-8pm.

Golf Tours, 2 Hai Bà Trưng (☎812 210; www.vietnamgolfhotel.com), in the lobby of Golf Hotel. Rents cars, boats, and canoes. Tours are seamless and efficient. Open daily 7:30am-5:30pm.

Triết Quang Huỳnh (☎0913 618 056; triet_quang@hotmail.com) and his brother Mr. Sang (☎0913 058 794) arrange river tours, plan car or bike trips to surrounding towns, and rent motorbikes to visitors. A lower-profile guide service with small group sizes. Check to be sure your guide speaks English. The persistent Mr. Sang can be found at Hotel 31, but show the slightest bit of hesitation on his offer and he will lower his price.

Catacotourist, 5 Hòa Bình (☎829 662; fax 810 217), affiliated with Hòa Bình Hotel. Arranges daytrip river tours led by English-speaking guides. They can also help make travel arrangements for transit out of Cần Thơ. Hotel customers may be eligible for a discount.

Banks: There are a several **banks** in the city center. **Vietcombank,** 7 Hòa Bình (☎820 445), cashes traveler's checks, does currency exchange and MC/V cash advances, and has a **24hr. ATM.** Open M-F 7-11am and 1:30-4pm. **VP Bank,** 26-28 Hòa Bình (☎815 766; fax 815

770), offers similar services and includes a Western Union. Open daily 7-11:30am and 1-4pm. **Incombank,** 9 Phan Đình Phùng (☎820 858), has the same services but stays open a bit later. Open daily 7-11am and 1-5pm. There is a also Western Union inside the Vietnam Airlines office at 25 Phan Đình Phùng (see above).

Emergency: ☎115. **Police:** ☎113. **Fire:** ☎114.

Pharmacies: There is one on virtually every block in the city—the one at 29B Châu Văn Liêm is open daily 6:30am-11:30pm.

Hospital: 4 Châu Văn Liêm (☎821 288). 24hr. emergency service.

Internet: There are only a few Internet cafes in town, and access can be unreliable. **9 Châu Văn Liêm,** right by the market, charges 3000Đ per hr. Open daily 7:30am-10:30pm. **36 Hai Bà Trưng,** at the corner with Ngô Đức Kê, has A/C, a scanner, and Internet for 4000 per hr. Open daily 7:30am-10pm.

Post Office: 2 Hòa Bình. Phone and fax services. Open daily 6am-8pm. **FedEx** services can be found at 11 Phan Đình Phùng (☎825 706). Open daily 8am-4pm.

ACCOMMODATIONS

Hotels abound in Cần Thơ. Expensive options lie along the waterfront, but there are several popular budget accommodations on Ngô Đức Kê.

Tây Hồ, 42 Hai Bà Trưng (☎823 392; fax 814 239). Has sterile, white rooms in a central location. One of the few midtown lodgings. All rooms come with A/C, cable TV, and mini-fridge. Rooms US$12 per person. ❸

Hotel 31, 31 Ngô Đức Kê (☎825 287). Features spacious and airy rooms, enthusiastic staff, and a quality restaurant. Manager Mr. Sang arranges tours. Rooms US$4-10. ❶

Hòa Bình Hotel, 5 Hòa Bình (☎810 217; www.hoabinhct.com). A step up from the budget digs, this 3-star hotel boasts suites with bathtubs and minibars. Very helpful staff. Rooms US$20-45. AmEx/D/MC/V. ❹

Hien Guesthouse, 118/10 Phan Đình Phùng (☎812 718), on a narrow alley (Hẻm 118). A quirky little place with an English-speaking staff that can arrange boat tours and motorbike rentals. Rooms US$4-8. ❶

Hậu Giang B, 27 Châu Văn Liêm (☎821 950), right near the waterfront market. Comfortable rooms with full beds and lounge chairs. Rooms 80,000-150,000Đ. ❶

Hào Hoa, 6-8 Hải Thượng Lãn Ông (☎824 836), on a sleepy side street. Located in a quiet area, with decent but unimpressive rooms (60,000-180,000Đ). ❶

Phương Thẳng, 71 Nam Kỳ Khởi Nghĩa (☎811 969; fax 811 799). This mini-hotel has decent budget rooms with small balconies. Rooms 80,000-120,000Đ. ❶

Golf Hotel, 2 Hai Bà Trưng (☎812 210; www.vietnamgolfhotel.com), overlooking the river. One of the most luxurious accommodations in the city. All bathrooms are equipped with full-body-massage showers. Free glass of wine at check-in. There's a Vietcombank ATM in the lobby. Rooms from US$60. AmEx/D/MC/V. ❺

Cần Thơ Hotel, 41 Châu Văn Liêm (☎811 770). Pleasant and characterless rooms complete with A/C, TV, and clean sheets. Breakfast included. Rooms US$16-25. ❹

FOOD

Cần Thơ is blessed with a number of good restaurants, ranging from typical Vietnamese fare to exotic Mekong specialties. The main **market** is between Hai Bà Trưng and the waterfront at Phan Chu Trinh. (Open daily 7am-9pm.) To stock up on snacks or booze, try **Cầu Tre,** a minimart at 19 Đồng Khởi. (☎825 609. Open daily 6am-9pm.) There is also a **grocery store** at 27 Phan Đình Phùng, where it intersects with Tran Trào. (☎825 485. Open daily 7am-8pm.)

MEKONG DELTA

Nam Bộ, 50 Hai Bà Trưng (☎823 908), set in a restored French villa. Decadent Western and Vietnamese dishes at reasonable prices. The upper terrace is particularly elegant. Entrees 40,000-65,000Đ. Try the Mekong specialties (45,000-90,000Đ). Open daily 9am-2pm and 5-10:30pm. AmEx/D/MC/V. ❸

Sài Gòn Bakery, 15A Đồng Khởi (☎810 228). A great array of wonderful pastries (3000-5000Đ). Loaves of fresh bread 4500Đ. Open daily 5am-9:30pm. ❶

Mé Kong, 38 Hai Bà Trưng (☎821 646). A long-standing favorite for tourists. Inexpensive Western breakfasts, including pancakes and omelettes, are a big draw. Breakfast 8000-16,000Đ. Lunch and dinner entrees 20,000-35,000Đ. Open daily 7am-2am. ❷

Sao Hôm, (☎815 616), on Hai Bà Trưng behind the market complex. A dressy waterfront restaurant with gourmet Vietnamese fare. Try the French breakfast buffet that comes with a river tour (7-11am; US$13). Pre-set 6-course menus 75,000-95,000Đ. Other dishes 35,000-55,000Đ. Mixed drinks 20,000-45,000Đ. Open daily 6am-11pm. ❹

Du Thuyền. An enjoyable restaurant-boat that cruises the river nightly 8-9pm. The boat docks across from the Golf Hotel on Hai Bà Trưng. Most entrees 30,000-50,000Đ. ❸

Nam Đô, 186-188 Nguyễn An Ninh (☎820 772). Packs a crowd eager for its local dishes and friendly atmosphere. Most entrees 15,000-35,000Đ. Open daily 8am-10pm. ❷

Phở Oanh, 96-98 Lý Tự Trọng, away from the tourist scene. A street cafe offering tasty phở and cơm meals. Most entrees under 15,000Đ. Open daily 6:30am-11:30pm. ❶

Nhà Hàng NK2, 5 Hai Bà Trưng (☎811 619). A spacious riverfront restaurant, home to small local parties and karaoke at night. Offers the town's only Vietnamese buffet for 20,000Đ. Open daily 6am-10pm. ❷

Hoàng Cung, 55 Phan Đình Phùng (☎825 831) on the first level of Saigon-Cần Thơ Hotel. Order some ice cream (not on the menu) and settle in. Free wireless internet. Entrees 40,000-70,000Đ. Open daily 7am-11pm. ❸

👁 SIGHTS

Exploring the network of canals around Cần Thơ by boat is the highlight of a visit to the area. The floating markets are the city's main attraction, but they start early: the best time to visit is 6-8am. Boat operators congregate around the pier on Hai Bà Trưng, near its intersection with Ngô Quyền, eager for business—you can rent rowboats for US$2 per hr., or motorboats for US$3 per hr. Boat tours also typically pass by riverside pagodas and mangrove swamps, stopping at fruit orchards, where you can sample the bounty for a small fee (10,000-20,000Đ).

CẦN THƠ MUSEUM. As far as presentation goes, this is one of the best museums in southern Vietnam. Signs in both Vietnamese and English explain diverse and detailed exhibits, providing insight into the history and culture of the province. You can even walk through a life-size model pagoda—as if Vietnam didn't have enough real pagodas. Special exhibitions are on display periodically. *(6 Phan Đình Phùng. ☎820 955. Open Tu-Th 8-11am and 2-5pm, Sa-Su 8-11am and 6:30-9pm. Free.)*

CÁI RĂNG. The city's closest and most important floating market, Cái Răng is the most popular tourist destination in Cần Thơ. The market is dominated by farmers selling fruits and vegetables in bulk, and you'll find that the enticing smells of their goods—pineapple, jackfruit, rambutan—travel quickly to your nose. Smaller boats and canoes weave through the maze selling coffee, soda, and baguettes, just like a street market. *(7km from Cần Thơ; 2hr. by boat.)*

KHÁNH QUANG PAGODA. This pagoda features a peculiarly attractive young Buddha with a neon halo. The first floor serves as a meeting and dining room for the young monks who are schooled there; the main shrine is on the second floor.

Take the steps up at the left end of the building. *(At the corner of Hòa Bình and Nam Kỳ Khởi Nghĩa. Open daily 7am-10pm. Free.)*

CẦN THƠ CHURCH. The local Christian house of worship, built in classic French colonial style. Go in the mid-afternoon to hear the youth choir rehearse. *(On Nguyễn Thị Minh Khai, midway between Phan Đình Phùng and the bridge. Daily mass at 6:30am. Free.)*

NINTH MILITARY SECTION MUSEUM. Several Russian tanks (used by the North Vietnamese) and an enormous ground-to-air missile are the best displays in this American War museum. A damaged US fighter jet and the remains of a US helicopter are also present. The museum is worth at least a walk through. *(8 Hòa Bình. Open Su 8-11am and 7-9pm, Tu and Th-Sa 8-11am and 2-4pm. Free.)*

ÔNG PAGODA. If you're strolling along the waterfront, take a quick stop at Ông Pagoda, which stands across from the Hồ Chí Minh statue. This Chinese pagoda is notable for figurine-laden rafters, but what really sets it apart are the scores of enormous incense coils hanging from the ceiling. *(Open daily 7am-10pm. Free.)*

MUNIRANSYARAMA PAGODA. This pagoda serves the local Khmer population and stands out from its surroundings with ornate, colorful flourishes. Be careful: the monks' dormitory compound surrounds the base of the temple—don't go in through the wrong door. *(38 Hòa Bình. Open daily 7am-10pm. Free.)*

HỒ CHÍ MINH MUSEUM. Offers a look at the man and his achievements, through photos, writings, and memoirs. Just like every other Hồ Chí Minh museum in the country, but with a southern Mekong twist. *(6 Hòa Bình. Open Tu and Th-Sa 8-11am and 2-4pm, Su 8-11am and 7-9pm. Free.)*

▶ DAYTRIPS

◼ PHƯƠNG VILLAGE. Life is entirely intertwined with the waters at this serene village, built upon utter swampland with houses suspended on stilts. Every 50m or so, wooden planks form bridges over the dozens of crisscrossing canals. Take a walk or a bike ride around the village and traverse the dynamic landscape. Go in deep enough and you will reach the rice fields upon which this community thrives. *(Follow Phan Đình Phùng south, take a right at the T-junction, and cross the bridge. 2.5km outside of town, the turn-off is a dirt path with a small wooden sign marked "Phục Hồi Phuộc." Free.)*

MƯỜI BÉ'S FRUIT GARDEN. The humble and welcoming Mười will happily show you around what has

THE LOCAL STORY

WHEN IT POURS, IT REALLY POURS

For many, the summer months bring the only opportunity to trave away from home. For Vietnam they bring monsoon season. The optimistic, though, will find these tropical storms to be magnificen displays of nature's power and welcome breaks from the heat.

In the Mekong, almost ever day of the summer sees torrentia rain. The pattern begins with ar intensifying, oppressive heat after which the sky clouds ove and a warm wind sweeps in Then, with startling suddenness the skies collapse in an awe inspiring downpour. Systemati cally, motorbike traffic disappear and locals rush out of the rain to wait stoically under tents, pon chos, umbrellas, or doorways.

After about half an hour, the rain stops almost as quickly as i began. The roaring slackens to a static fuzz and the air feels mirac ulously cooler. Motorbikes reap pear, and within minutes life picks up as if there had been no interruption at all. For the Viet namese, it is all very routine.

Foreign travelers, however must take a few extra steps to sur vive the wet season. Bring ar extra pair of shoes, carry you poncho everywhere, and budge extra time to wait out the rain Most importantly, check the dates of the rainy season, as they diffe between regions (see **When To Go**, p. 2). In the meantime, don' forget to sit back and enjoy the waterworks.

become his 30-year, post-war abode. The 10,000-square-meter plot contains everything from sour cherries to hot chilis to violet orchids to the enigmatic watercoconut (a red, spiky fruit that grows on riverside palm trees). Basically, this is the place to feed your fruit curiosity. Pick whatever you like off the trees; if you ask, Mười's wife will even cook a homemade meal for you. The swinging hammocks, spotted dogs, and pet monkey Mai make it an excellent mid-day rest point. *(32km from Cần Thơ; 4-5hr. by boat. Lunch and fruit 5000-20,000.Đ)*

PHONG ĐIỀN. The market in Phong Điền is a lively scene, integrating both the streets and the river. Stalls and eateries line the banks, making it a convenient rest stop along the river. The virtually untouristed area is a pleasant escape from transit-heavy Cần Thơ. There is also a **guesthouse ❶** at 126 Ấp Thi Tu (☎850 014), to the immediate left of the bridge on the main road, which offers basic hostel-like rooms for a mere 60,000Đ per person. There's a post office, pharmacy, and Western Union along the same road. As for food, an unnatural number of sugarcane juice and sandwich stands populates the town—literally dozens line the streets half a kilometer past the bridge. For sit-down fare, **Quán Cơm ❶**, 89 Ấp Thi Tu, serves tofu-stuffed tomatoes, Mekong-spiced meats, and an unusual array of rice noodles for 5000-15,000Đ. (☎850 434. Open daily 7am-10pm.) **Cafe Trang ❶**, 155 Ấp Thi Tu, whose friendly staff leave the Discovery Channel playing in the background, serves drinks (4000-6000Đ) and some simple food. (☎850 253. Open daily 7am-8pm.) **Cafe Ngần Đuyên ❶**, 85 Ấp Thi Tu, serves simple coffee and drinks. (☎859 570. Open daily 7am-11pm.) All in all, this quiet town is worth a relaxed daytrip or overnight. *(Phong Điền is 18km from Cần Thơ; 30min. by motorbike, 2½hr. by boat.)*

PH˝NG HIỆP. Known for its trade in snakes and snake products, Phụng Hiệp's market (situated both on the water and in the street) is worth a stop. Snakes—from giant boa constrictors to small green gardeners—are sold live, and with some persistence. Vendors are highly conscious of police monitoring, as the sale of some species is prohibited, so be discreet and do not take photos. The snakes will either be crawling around in cages set on the streetside, or conspicuously empty cages will signal that the snakes are for sale deeper within the store. *(36km from Cần Thơ; 1hr. by motorbike, 4hr. by boat.)*

🎵 🎸 ENTERTAINMENT AND NIGHTLIFE

To beat the heat, you can take a dip in the **swimming pool** at the Golf Hotel; admission is US$2 for non-guests. There is also the new **Cần Thơ Water Park** on the north side of the city with plenty of slides, inner tubes, and pools. (☎763 373; www.canthowaterpark.com. Open daily 8am-7pm. 40,000Đ.) Travelers with children may consider the evening **kiddie rides** on Hòa Bình—there are some on the grounds of the Hồ Chí Minh Museum and some in the public park across from Châu Văn Liêm. The rides open up at dusk. On weekend nights, Vietnamese and foreigners alike bust out their dance moves at the **Golf Hotel Discotheque,** on the mezzanine level of the Golf Hotel. (Drinks 40,000-60,000Đ. Open daily until midnight. Happy hour 5-11:30pm. Dance music starts around 9pm.) **VIP2,** 6 Hòa Bình, serves coffee, fruit shakes, ice cream, and light mixed drinks, and is always packed with hip Vietnamese youth in the evenings. (Most drinks under 20,000Đ. Open daily 7am-11pm.)

SÓC TRĂNG ☎79

The dusty streets and muddy river of Sóc Trăng give it a bit of a down-on-its-luck appearance. But don't be surprised if you see flying bits of color in the form of monks on motorcycles—the city is known for its significant Khmer population. Several unusual temples near Sóc Trăng also set it apart from its neighbors.

 TRANSPORTATION. **Buses** arrive at the station on Nguyễn Chí Thanh and head to Cần Thơ (1½hr.; 11,000Đ) and HCMC (6hr.; 40,000Đ) throughout the day. To reach Bạc Liêu (1½hr.; 10,000Đ) or Cà Mau (3hr.; 25,000Đ), you'll need to catch a bus on the highway; ask your hotel receptionist how to do this.

 ORIENTATION AND PRACTICAL INFORMATION. From the bus station, **Nguyễn Chí Thanh** runs south and intersects with **Mậu Thân**. Heading eastward, Mậu Thân turns into **Lương Định Cúa**. In the opposite direction, Mậu Thân crosses the **Sóc Trăng River** and becomes **Hai Bà Trưng**, and then turns into **Trần Hưng Đạo** as it passes the post office. The city as a whole is quite spread out and lacks a real center, making navigation difficult. The staff at **Sóc Trăng Tourist Office,** 131 Nguyễn Chí Thanh, don't speak much English, but they'll give you a free map pointing out the municipal and provincial highlights. (☎822 292. Open daily 7-11am and 1-5pm.) **Vietcombank,** 27 Hai Bà Trưng, changes currency and handles MC/V cash advances. It also has an indoor **ATM.** (Open daily 6:30am-10:30pm.) There is a **pharmacy** at 8-10 Hai Bà Trưng. (Open daily 7am-5pm.) You can access the **Internet** at 2 Trần Hưng Đạo. (3000Đ per hr. Open daily 8am-9pm.) The **post office,** 1 Trần Hưng Đạo, has phone and fax services. (☎820 051. Open daily 6am-9pm.)

 ACCOMMODATIONS AND FOOD. The overnight options in Sóc Trăng tend to be pricey. One noteworthy exception is **Phú Quí ❷,** 41 Phan Chu Trinh, a shiny black building whose rooms feature air-conditioning, TVs, minifridges, and hot water. (☎611 911. Rooms 150,000-180,000Đ.) **Khánh Hưng ❷,** 15 Trần Hưng Đạo, has bright and spacious rooms, each with its own balcony. The staff speaks almost no English, but the budget rooms (US$8) are a pretty good deal. (☎821 026. Most rooms US$16-30.) **Phong Lan II ❷,** 133 Nguyễn Chí Thanh, is operated by the tourist office. The rooms are decent enough, but its location across from the bus station makes for a noisy stay. (☎821 757. Rooms US$8-17.) When it comes to restaurants, **Hằng Kộ ❸,** 67 Yết Kiêu, is the best place for a sit-down meal. Though it specializes in seafood, the prolific menu offers everything from simple soups to Vietnamese delicacies like porcupine and deer. (Open daily 9am-9:30pm.) Most eateries in Sóc Trăng lack menus, but the friendly waitresses at **Cẩm Húng ❶,** 1 Mậu Thân, will help you choose what to eat. (Most dishes under 15,000Đ. Open daily 6am-5pm.) The plaza next to the post office has the city's main **market.**

 SIGHTS. Sóc Trăng harbors some of the most unique **pagodas** in Vietnam. A motorbike tour to all three of them should take one hour and cost 40,000Đ. In the city center, **Chùa Khléang,** 71 Mậu Thân, is a striking Khmer pagoda with an active monk community. The rainbow-colored exterior houses an impressive sanctuary, where a golden Buddha meditates atop the enormous main altar. The lacquerwork on the columns and the detailed wood carvings on the doors and shutters are also worth a look. On Nguyễn Chí Thanh is a tiny **Khmer Museum,** housing ceremonial props, traditional costumes, and items related to Khmer culture. Signs are in Vietnamese and Khmer. (Open M-F 7:30-11:30am and 1:30-4:30pm.)

 Clay Pagoda (Chùa Phật Đất Sét, also known as Bửu Sòn Tự), 163A Lương Định Cúa, is made almost entirely of painted clay. Visitors can marvel at the clay creations here—from elaborate columns to kitschy, life-size animal statues—but should be gentle when touching, as everything is quite fragile. The pagoda also features two gigantic candles (over 2.5m and 200kg each) in memory of the original clay artist, who passed away in 1970. The pagoda is about 400m from the river.

 Four kilometers west of the city center off Lê Hong Phồng, the grounds of **Bat Pagoda** (Chùa Dơi) are home to hundreds of large fruit bats who nap upside down in the trees during the day and pillage local orchards at night. The best time to visit is at dusk, when the creatures, whose wingspans reach up to 1.5m, stir from their slumber and begin to swoop loudly around the trees. The grounds also feature a group of rare five-toed pigs. Farmers bring these swine here because it's supposedly unlucky to eat them. The pagoda itself is worth a peek inside—large, colorful ▧**murals** depicting Buddha's life adorn the walls, and the ceiling is supported by ornately carved wooden columns. The complex across from it contains more depictions of the Buddha, and the impressive murals continue on this side as well.

Several more Khmer-influenced pagodas lie on the road southward between Sóc Trăng and Bạc Liêu. The **Golden Pagoda** lies 7km from town, with a flashy golden roof and walls adorned with sculptures. **Phu Giao Pagoda** sits 32km south of town. It is a fascinating open-air pagoda with an unprotected inner shrine. Concentric red-and-gold columns surround a central sitting Buddha.

BẠC LIÊU   ☎ 781

The symbol of Bạc Liêu is the white heron—a fitting icon, as the main draw of this sleepy provincial capital is its nearby **bird sanctuary** (Vườn Nhãn), 5km outside of town. Avian enthusiasts come armed with binoculars to observe the more than 50 bird species that nest here. Rainy-season visits are recommended, as this is the best time to spot the birds. Whether you're a bird watcher or not, the ▧**view** from the sanctuary's tall observation tower takes in the vast flats around the rivers and rice that stretch between Cần Thơ and Cà Mau. (Open daily 6am-8pm. 10,000Đ.) Next to the sanctuary is a small **fruit garden,** where visitors can roam about and pick fruit straight from the trees. (Open daily 7am-8pm. 10,000-20,000Đ.) About 4km beyond the bird sanctuary is **Bạc Liêu Beach** (Bãi Biển Bạc Liêu). Leave your swim trunks at home—it's actually an enormous tidal flat. Locals come with buckets and spears to catch crabs, oysters, clams, and the many other small critters that make their home there. Roll up your pants, cast off your shoes, and wade around in the mud. Pagoda lovers might want to check out **Xiêm Cán,** about 7km southeast of the city center. This Khmer pagoda is unremarkable on the outside, but the cavernous sanctuary, decorated in carved wood and covered in murals, makes the interior worth a look.

The classiest place to stay in the city is **Công Tử Bạc Liêu ❸**, 13 Điện Biên Phủ. This "restored" French colonial villa boasts elegant rooms and a waterfront location. This may be the place to splurge—it's rare and fun to stay in an authentic French villa. (☎953 304. Rooms 220,000-500,000Đ.) In the budget range, **Kiều Hối ❷**, 28 Hòa Bình, offers cheerful rooms and a friendly staff. (☎952 185. Rooms 120,000-180,000Đ.) **Bạc Liêu Guesthouse ❶**, 8 Lý Tự Trọng, has reasonably comfortable rooms (60,000Đ-180,000Đ). For an interesting meal, head to **Hương Biển ❷** at Bạc Liêu Beach. This restaurant is built right over the tidal flat, and huge windows allow patrons to gaze out over it as it stretches toward the horizon. Not surprisingly, the specialty is shellfish. (Most entrees 25,000-55,000Đ. Open daily 7am-9pm.) Back in the city center, **Kiều Hối ❶,** on the ground floor of the guesthouse, offers tasty Vietnamese fare in a pleasant setting. (Entrees 8000-15,000Đ.)

Buses arrive at the station on Trần Phú, about 1km from the city center, and head to Cần Thơ (3hr.; 35,000Đ) and HCMC (8hr.; 68,000Đ) throughout the day. Several buses also depart in the morning for Cà Mau (1½hr.; 20,000Đ) and Sóc Trăng (1½hr.; 35,000Đ). **Trần Phú** is the city's main drag; it runs southeast from the bus station through the city center and meets the **Bạc Liêu River.** After crossing the river, it becomes **Lê Hồng Phong** and eventually **Cao Văn Láu,** which leads out to the bird sanctuary and the beach. **Điện Biên Phủ** runs along the river, past market stalls and a couple of French colonial villas. **Bạc Liêu Tourist Office,** 2 Hoàng Văn Thụ, has a helpful staff who can provide information on the region; several of them speak English. The office also does Vietnam Airlines booking. (☎824 272. Open daily 6am-10pm.) **Incombank,** 1 Hai Bà Trưng, handles currency exchange, does MC/V cash advances, and has a Western Union. (Open daily 7-11am and 1-

5pm.) There is a **24hr. ATM** at Công Tử Bạc Liêu (see above). A **pharmacy** sits at the corner of Trần Phú and Bá Triệu. (Open daily 7am-9pm.) The **post office** is located at 20 Trần Phú. (☎824 242. Phone and fax services. Open daily 6am-10pm.)

CÀ MAU ☎78

This hard-working city attracts few tourists because of its distance from Hồ Chí Minh City, but those adventurous few who make it are rewarded by the untouched mangrove-filled wilderness around the city. The major attraction is **U Minh Forest,** one of the largest mangrove swamps in the world. Honeybees feed on the mangrove blossoms; locals harvest their honey and wax. Minh Hải Tourist Office (see below) arranges boat tours of the forest, whose main point of exploration lies about 60km from the city. The normal rate is 900,000Đ per half-day in a motorboat (up to 10 people; driver and guide included)—however, solo travelers and couples may be able to bargain down to as low as 100,000Đ. Bring along insect repellent, as the mosquitoes are notoriously vicious.

Cà Mau has a large number of hotels and guesthouses, especially around Lộ Bôn and Phan Ngọc Hiển. **Kim Yến ❶,** 22A Hùng Vương (just off the roundabout), has comfortable rooms, an elevator, and a central location near the post office, bank, and markets. (☎827 308. Rooms 70,000-180,000Đ.) **Song Hùng ❷,** 28 Phan Ngọc Hiển, features clean, fragrant rooms with all the amenities. (☎822 822. Rooms 140,000-220,000Đ.) The true budget option in town is **Sao Mai ❶,** 40 Phan Ngọc Hiển. The paint in the stairwells may be chipping, but the rooms are well maintained. (☎831 035. Rooms 50,000-150,000Đ.) **Triều Phát ❶,** 26 Phan Ngọc Hiển, serves decent seafood and noodle dishes—though you might need the proprietor's son to translate the menu for you. (Most entrees under 20,000Đ. Open daily 9am-9pm.) There are also cheap, sit-down **food stalls** in the market along Phan Bội Châu. **Nam Hài ❶,** 22 Quang Trưng, is a classic streetside bakery and sandwich shop taken inside; their preparation area is immaculately clean, and their service pleasantly polite. (Open daily 7am-10pm.) **Phương Nam Hotel ❶** has a decent all-you-can-eat breakfast buffet. (Open daily 6-9am.)

Flights leave once daily for HCMC (45min.; US$26-29). **Buses** arrive at the station on Ly Thường Kiệt, about 2km southeast of the city center, and head to Cần Thơ (4-6hr.; 27,000-43,000Đ) and HCMC (8-10hr.; 57,000-86,000Đ). Both regular buses and express minibuses are available. A few buses leave each day in the morning for Bạc Liêu (1½hr.; 11,000Đ); Sóc Trăng (3hr.; 19,000Đ); Trà Vinh (6hr.; 37,000Đ); Vĩnh Long (6hr.; 27,500Đ). Heading northwest toward the city center, **Ly Thường Kiệt** curves and runs to a roundabout, which features a striking brown marble memorial. It then turns into **Ngô Quyền,** which crosses over **Gành Hào Canal** and continues northward, eventually intersecting with **Lộ Bôn,** where the tourist office and several hotels can be found. There is a second canal crossing on **Phan Ngọc Hiển,** which hits Lộ Bôn right near the tourist office. The city's main **markets** lie along **Quang Trưng,** which hugs the southern bank of the canal. **Minh Hải Tourist Office,** 1 Lộ Bôn, arranges boat tours and hands out brochures on the region. (☎831 828. Open daily 7am-noon and 1:30-5pm.) **Incombank,** 3 Ngô Quyền, changes currency and does MC/V cash advances. (Open daily 7-11am and 1-5pm.) There is a **pharmacy** (open daily 7am-9pm) at 12B Quang Trưng and a **hospital** with emergency service at 36 Lộ Thái Tốn (☎831 201), two blocks north of Lộ Bôn. Feed your **Internet** habit at 81 Phan Đình Phùng, one block north of Lộ Bôn, or at the several cafes that surround the bridge at 31 and 60A Lộ Thái Tốn. (Open daily 7am-10:30pm.) Across the street from the bank, the **post office** is just opposite the memorial. (Phone and fax services. Open daily 6am-10pm.)

MEKONG DELTA

▶ DAYTRIPS FROM CÀ MAU. Deep in this corner of the country are a few surprisingly fun islands, entirely untouched by tourism, accessible from Cà Mau.

◼ HÒN ĐÀ BẠC. These two stunning islands, set off the west coast of Vietnam, provide a glimpse into the thriving fishing villages of the Mekong and a truly authentic Vietnamese experience. A long, dainty bridge brings you across the water to the islands. Pay no attention to the first island's long red-and-blue dragon and fake plastic animals; instead, take a suspension bridge across to the second island, which holds much more intrigue. The newly built but little-known **Hotel Hòn Đà Bạc ❷** sits on the western edge of this island. It's the only lodging on the island, its **restaurant** is the only eatery, and if you stay, you'll be the only guest. Clean, tiled, and spacious rooms, decorated in beautiful soothing colors, complete the package. (☎780 897 611. Rooms 100,000-180,000Đ.) From the back courtyard of the hotel, faux-stone stairs lead into the woods. Follow the trail all the way west to a yellow-robed statue of the Buddha. Facing the setting sun, the statue sits above a small rock formation that is thought to look like the open hand of the Buddha, giving his blessings. On the opposite side of the island, facing the fishing villages of Vietnam, is a female Buddhist figure. A red liberation monument—the southernmost in Vietnam—is on top of the hill among the island's untouched foliage. If you go at sunset, the road to the islands is insanely gorgeous. *(Take the 1½hr. motorbike ride due west from Cà Mau to Vanh Thanh village for 100,000Đ round-trip, then cross the footbridge to the islands. Open daily 7:30am-5:30pm. 10,000Đ.)*

HÒN KHOAI. Part military base, part tourist attraction, Hòn Khoai is the last bit of Vietnamese property situated in the South China Sea. The island is 4km long and 15km from the mainland. One of a group of five nearby islands, Hòn Khoai is the most famous because the revolutionary teacher **Phan Ngọc Hiên** was executed there on January 8, 1941, after leading a failed insurrection in Cà Mau Province. To most, the real significance of the island is its natural beauty and isolation. Visitors can climb the 16m high **historic French lighthouse,** built in 1904, to get a better view. The granite construction guides ships around the precarious Cape of Cà Mau, into the Gulf of Thailand. *(Tours are arranged at the Minh Hải Tourist Office. Alternatively, take a 2½hr. motorbike ride down to the coast near Tân Ân and hire a boat to take you across to the islands. The availability of these ferries is unpredictable. Open daily 7:30am-5:30pm. 10,000Đ.)*

NĂM CĂN   ☎780

Năm Căn is the last real outpost in southern Vietnam before the land becomes completely claimed by mangrove swampland and merges with the sea. It is rare for the people in this fishing town to ever see tourists; you will be as much an attraction to them as their town is to you. Be sure to take along a good phrasebook, as there is no English spoken here—this is the real Vietnam, after all.

Năm Căn requires exploration. The **riverside market** is a seemingly unending stretch of vendors, with boats docking at the back side of the market, continually bringing in and taking out goods. Local boat operators will take you on a **river tour** for 20,000-30,000Đ per hr.; soon after departing town, you'll find yourself in twisting, tree-lined passageways. Back on land, a left turn off Khự Vuc 2, after the market but just before a bridge, leads to the **liberation monument,** a red sailboat with a hammer and sickle adorning the main mast. The monument faces south, and the man leading the ship has his fist thrust upward celebrating the reunification of Vietnam. Farther south along Khự Vuc 2, after crossing the bridge, the road leads through a small karaoke district to a government air base. Let's Go does not recommend trespassing on Vietnamese military property, though the gates remain open and some travelers report that looking around the area is tolerated. There is a modern-day airstrip inside, as well as a friendly, English-speaking guard.

Năm Căn has little in the way of lodging, but if you must stay, try **Khách Sạn ❷**, in the alleyway between the market and Khự Vuc 1. Its rooms are clean and reasonably comfortable. (☎877 235. Rooms 100,000-150,000Đ.) In terms of food, there are several cafes with elegant outdoor seating on the main street. Among them, **Cafe Anh Đao ❶** (☎877 226) has friendly service and tasty Vietnamese dishes (8000-12,000Đ). Farther down the road, **Pho Nui ❶** (☎247 472), across from the cell phone tower, has a funky wooden lodge-like interior and casual atmosphere for light drinks. (Coffee 4000-5000Đ; other drinks 7000-9000Đ). For the cheapest eats in town, head to the town **market,** which opens onto Khự Vuc 2.

Hire a motorbike to get to Năm Căn from Cà Mau. The ride should take 2hr. and cost 60,000Đ each way. A ferry crossing midway through the trip costs another 2500Đ. The trip south is an unrelenting show of rice fields and rivers, showing the incredible breadth of the Mekong's bread basket. The town itself has only two main roads and a few alleyways. **Khự Vuc 1** leads in from the highway and becomes the main thoroughfare. It runs into **Khự Vuc 2** (also called **Hùng Vuơng**), which runs parallel to the water. **Agribank** sits at the intersection of the two Khự's, providing foreign exchange, MC/V cash advance, and Western Union wire transfers, but no ATM. (☎877 197; fax 878 061. Open daily 7-11am and 1-5pm.) Also across the street from the post office is **Internet** access at **Cafe Tran Thanh.** (3000Đ per hr. Open daily 8am-6pm.) The **post office,** which has phone and mail services, is across from Agribank. (☎878 995; fax 878 174. Open daily 6:30am-9pm.)

RẠCH GIÁ   ☎77

Fishing, rice, and marine commerce have brought prosperity to Rạch Giá, the capital of Kiên Giang province. The seaport city's handsome waterfronts and well-lit streets are ideal for evening strolls; stately public buildings represent with due elegance what is generally considered the richest province in Vietnam. There aren't many tourist attractions here, though, so most travelers just pass through on their way to Phú Quốc Island. Still, Rạch Giá makes for an enjoyable stopover point and an enticing opportunity to savor a meal on the enchanting waterfront.

◪ TRANSPORTATION. Flights depart daily from the airport near Rạch Sởi bus station and fly to: Hà Nội (7½hr.; 9:30am; US$155); HCMC (2½hr.; 9:30am; US$47); and Phú Quốc (45min.; 9:30am; US$35). Most long-distance **buses** depart from the station in nearby Rạch Sởi, 7km outside the city center on Nguyễn Trung Trực. Buses go from here to: Cà Mau (4hr.; early morning; 60,000Đ); Cần Thơ (3hr.; every 30min. 5am-5pm; 31,000Đ); Châu Đốc (5hr.; 4 per day 5am-3pm; 35,000Đ); HCMC (6hr.; every hr. 4am-5pm; 65,000Đ); Long Xuyên (3hr.; every 30min. 5:30am-4:30pm; 21,000Đ). **Buses** to Hà Tiên (3½hr.; every hr. 6am-4pm; 24,000Đ) leave from the station on Nguyễn Bỉnh Kiêm. There are also **minibuses** that leave for Cần Thơ and HCMC from various points around the city center. The bus and minibus system is a bit confusing—ask your hotel receptionist for help. **Boats** depart for Phú Quốc Island from the pier at the end of Nguyễn Công Trứ. The tourist booking office, 6 Tự Do, runs excellent **high-speed ferries** (2½hr.; 8:30am; lower deck 130,000Đ, top deck 160,000Đ). Get tickets at least one day in advance. High-tech televisions air DVDs of the latest pop hits en route. (☎879 455. Open daily 6-11am and 1-6pm.) There are also **slow boats** (7hr.; early morning departure; 70,000Đ) that make the journey. All transportation to Phú Quốc is weather-dependent, and departures are often canceled due to storms during the rainy season.

◪◪ ORIENTATION AND PRACTICAL INFORMATION. The city center contains two branches of the **Rạch Giá River** that flow southwest into the Gulf of Thailand. **Nguyễn Trung Trực** is one main thoroughfare in the city center; coming in from the bus station, it crosses a canal and turns into **Lê Lợi,** which passes a public park

MEKONG DELTA

(featuring a statue of anti-colonialist fighter Nguyễn Trung Trực himself), crosses over a second canal, and ends when it intersects with **Trần Phú.**

Kien Giang Tourist Office, 5 Lê Lợi, is one of the better tourist offices in the Mekong Delta. The capable staff provides handy maps of Rạch Giá, Hà Tiên, and Phú Quốc Island and explains the transportation system to Phú Quốc. (☎862 018; www.kiengiangtouristmap.com. Open daily 7-11am and 1:30-5pm.) Across the bridge is **Vietcombank,** 2 Mạc Cửu, which has an **ATM,** changes currency and traveler's checks, and does MC/V cash advances. (Open daily 7-11am and 1-4pm.) There is a **hospital** with emergency service at 46 Lê Lợi and a **pharmacy** at 46 Hoàng Hoa Thám. (Open daily 7am-9pm.) **Nghĩa Thanh,** an extensive supermarket, is at 6 Le Loi. (☎640 460. Open daily 7am-10pm.) A memorable spot to access the **Internet** is inside Children's Palace on Nguyễn Công Trứ, where you'll probably catch a few karate lessons or even a quiz show in action. Once you enter the park, follow the path until you get to the opposite end; signs point to the Internet room. (Open daily 7-11am and 1:30-9pm.) Otherwise, head to 135 Nguyễn Hùng Son (open daily 8am-midnight) or 143 Nguyễn Hùng Son (open daily 7am-11pm). All Internet cafes in Rạch Giá tend to be packed with teenagers playing computer games, but at least the rate (usually 3000Đ per hr.) is reasonable. The **post office** is located at the intersection of Lê Lợi and Trần Phú. (Open daily 6:30am-10pm.)

▮▮ ACCOMMODATIONS AND FOOD. Due to the tourist traffic en route to Phú Quốc Island, Rạch Giá has a large number of lodging options. In the city center, ▮**Kim Có ❷,** 141 Nguyễn Hùng Son, boasts large, modern rooms that have an art-deco feel to them. All rooms have bathtubs. (☎879 610. Rooms with fan 120,000Đ, with A/C 160,000-200,000Đ.) **Trung Quyến ❸,** 20 Hoàng Hoa Thám, also has attractive rooms, with extra perks like make-up tables and glass-walled showers. (☎876 757. Rooms from 200,000Đ.) Shopaholics (or those looking to pick up beach towels or flip-flops) may want to stay at **Hồng Nam ❷,** B1 Lộ Thái Tố, which faces a big indoor market. As a bonus, the hotel shares its ground floor with a liquor store. (☎873 090. Rooms 100,000-250,000Đ.) The budget option is right near the Phú Quốc ferries: **Phượng Hồng ❶,** 5 Tự Do, has a friendly staff and decent rooms. (☎866 138. Rooms 90,000-140,000Đ.)

Valentine ❷, 115 Nguyễn Hùng Son, is a classy cafe by day and a karaoke bar by night, serving both Vietnamese and international food. (Drinks 10,000-12,000Đ; entrees 15,000-30,000Đ. Open daily 6am-midnight.) **Tân Hưng Phát ❶,** 118 Nguyễn Hùng Son, has a bright green neon sign, clean green tablecloths, and a menu full of green (vegetarian) Vietnamese options. (Entrees 15,000-20,000Đ; fruit 3000-5000Đ. Open daily 7am-11pm.) **Áo Dài Mới ❶,** 26 Lý Tự Trọng, is popular with locals for its hearty soups. (Most entrees under 15,000Đ. Open daily 5am-2pm.) The lovely waterfront terrace at **Hải Âu ❸,** 2 Nguyễn Trung Trực, makes it the highest-end place to eat in Rạch Giá. (Most entrees 30,000-60,000Đ. Coffee and tea 3000-7000Đ. Open daily 6am-10pm.) **Chiêu Dương ❶,** 13 Le Loi, is one of several excellent dessert and cake shops in town. (☎874 291. Large cakes 10,000-25,000Đ. Open daily 7am-10pm.) Across the street is **Thời Trang ❶,** 9 Le Loi, which also serves fresh pastries. (☎863 279. Pastries 3000-10,000Đ. Open daily 7am-10pm.)

▮▮ SIGHTS AND ENTERTAINMENT. The city's one major sight is the **Nguyễn Trung Trực Temple,** 18 Nguyễn Công Trứ. Its namesake is a local hero who led fierce resistance efforts against French invaders in the 1860s. Only when French forces took his mother hostage in 1868 did he agree to surrender, after which he was publicly executed in Rạch Giá. (What a mama's boy.) The temple features several images of the revered man, including a statue which serves as the main altar, flanked by two storks and huge (3.5m high, 360kg each) wax candles. During holidays and festivals, a large pig roast is set at the center table of the main room.

Right next door, machete-wielding women chop up plants for use in **traditional medicine.** A stunningly colorful and pungent array of dried stems and leaves—from coconut husk to marigold petals—covers every sun-exposed surface in sight. Inside **Phòng Thuốc Nam,** 14 Nguyễn Công Trứ (☎863 215), are homeopathic nurses that give consultations and prescribe the appropriate mix of natural medicine.

PHÚ QUỐC ISLAND ☎77

As one local put it, Phú Quốc has got the whole package. From fantastic beaches to wild forests to enchanting marine life, this "Emerald Island" offers treasures to every visitor. Though tourism is not yet well developed here, the island is widely known for its fish sauce, black pepper, and unique breed of dogs (identifiable by the spots of spiral hair on their back). Roughly 70% of the island is covered in jungles, and restaurants on the island cook up over 1000 different species of seafood. It's no wonder that Cambodia, Thailand, and Vietnam have all laid claim to it in the past. Not too long ago, the island was largely undeveloped, except for a few villages and some military bases. However, the tourist industry has since caught on to Phú Quốc's enormous potential, and new resorts and services are cropping up every minute. Plans are in the works to make it an international destination, and it seems only a matter of time before it loses its reputation as the best-kept secret in Vietnam—be sure to see it before it's too late.

▣ TRANSPORTATION

Phú Quốc has three entry and exit points: Dương Đông, Hàm Ninh, and An Thới.

Flights: Planes leave from the airport outside Dương Đông and go to **HCMC** (1hr.; 8:20, 11, 11:55am, 2:30pm; US$45) and **Rạch Giá** (45min.; 8:10am; US$35). The **Vietnam Airlines** booking office is in front of the Sàigòn-PhúQuốc Resort. ☎846 999. Open daily 6am-8pm.

Boats: Boats to Rạch Giá depart from **An Thới** in the south; those headed to Hà Tiên leave from **Hàm Ninh** on the island's eastern shore. Several companies run **high-speed ferries** to **Rạch Giá** (2hr.; 8, 8:30am, 1, 1:30pm; 150,000Đ) and **Hà Tiên** (1hr.; 120,000Đ), though the latter only operate for part of the year, when the water level is high enough. Booking offices line the sidewalk between 16-56 Trần Hưng Đạo in Dương Đông and next to the docks at An Thới. Slow boats go to **Rạch Giá** (7hr.; early morning; 150,000Đ) and **Bà Hòn** (4hr.; 120,000Đ), near Hà Tiên; ask for information at Hương Biển (see **Practical Information,** below) or from your hotel receptionist.

THE LOCAL STORY

SOMEONE TO WATCH OVER YOU

In 1919, on Phú Quốc Island, a huge disembodied eye floated before Ngô Văn Chiêu, a colonial bureaucrat and occult enthusiast. This sign sparked a series of heart-to-hearts between Ngô and God, who allegedly expressed frustration that all the messages he had sent to humankind had been misunderstood or ignored. His agents of the gospel had included Buddha, Lao Tse, Confucius, Mohammed, and Jesus. He was disappointed by the discord among religious groups. Inspired by this message, Ngô founded a religion incorporating elements from multiple religions, most notably Buddhism, Taoism, Confucianism, Islam, Christianity, and Hinduism. The ever-watchful eye became the symbol.

Today, the religion (called Cao Đài, meaning "High Palace") has several million followers in Vietnam, mostly in the south. The clerical structure is similar to the Catholic church; worshippers wear different robes depending upon their rank. Adherents seek to escape the cycle of reincarnation by acting lovingly toward others and avoiding sinful behavior. They believe that divine messages can be communicated during seances. Victor Hugo, William Shakespeare, and Joan of Arc were all in touch with Cao Đàists in the past. Worship ceremonies take place four times daily; the best place to see Cao Đài in action is the **Holy See** complex in **Tây Ninh** (p. 404).

Local Transportation: Many travelers rent a **motorbike** (80,000-100,000Đ per day) and explore the island themselves. Others hire a **motorbike driver** from their hotel; they tend to speak excellent English and are useful guides. The typical rate is USự10 per day.

■ ORIENTATION

Phú Quốc Island is 120km from Rạch Giá, 45km from Hà Tiên, and covers 593 sq. km in total. The island measures 48km from north to south and an average of 12km from east to west (25km at its widest point). **Dương Đông**, in the middle of the western coast of the island, is the main town, and most travelers choose to stay around here. The fishing hamlet of **An Thới** is about 28km south of Dương Đông, on the southern tip of the island. **Hàm Ninh,** another fishing town, is on the eastern side of the island, almost opposite Dương Đông. **Bai Thơm**, a small collection of fisherman's huts, is the main outpost on the northern side. Dirt and some paved roads connect smaller villages around the island.

Dương Đông itself is hardly more than a few streets. The town's two major streets are **Nguyễn Trung Trực** and **Đường 30/4**, which snake inland from the western coast. Both originate at **Bạch Đằng**, which runs along the mouth of the **Dương Đông River**. Two blocks inland, Đường 30/4 intersects **Trần Hưng Đạo** (called **Lý Tự Trọng** north of this intersection), which heads southward along the island's edge. It becomes a dirt road before passing by the resorts on Long Beach.

An Thới is composed of only two streets—**Khu Phố 3,** which runs from the entrance of the town past the market, ending at the docks, makes a T-junction with **Khu Phố 1.** There's only one street in **Hàm Ninh;** the main road threads through the town and ends as a 100m long pier jutting out into the sea.

■ PRACTICAL INFORMATION

In Dương Đông, **Hương Biển** (☎846 113), on Trần Hưng Đạo, is a hotel run by Kien-Giang Tourist Office, where the staff can provide you with free maps and general information. Tours and vehicle rentals are most easily arranged through the resorts. **Kien Long Foreign Exchange,** 41 Đường 30/4, does MC/V cash advances, cashes traveler's checks, and conducts Western Union wire transfers. (Open daily 7-11am, 1:30-5pm.) The ever-reliable **Vietcombank,** 20 Đường 30/4, offers all banking services, including currency exchange and an **ATM.** (☎981 036. Open daily 7-11am and 1-4pm.) There's also a 24hr. ATM inside the lobby of the Sàigòn-PhúQuốc Hotel. The **hospital** (☎846 074), 1km outside of town on Đường 30/4, has emergency service. There are other hospitals in An Thới, Hàm Ninh, Bãi Thơm, and Mũi Dương. There is a **pharmacy** in Dương Đông at 24 Nguyễn Trãi (☎846 369) and another at 55 Ngô Quyền. (Both open daily 7am-7pm.) Satisfy your **Internet** craving at 13 Nguyễn Trãi (4000Đ per hr.; open daily 8am-10pm). It's also free for customers at Carole (see **Food,** p. 436). The **post office,** on Đường 30/4, has international calling and fax services. (Open daily 6:30am-10pm.)

LUCKY NUMBER NINE. The people of Phú Quốc will often cite the island's 99 rolling hills, 99 pepper groves, and 99 surrounding islands. The actual count of each of these wonders is closer to a few dozen, but the fixation seems to be linked to the Vietnamese superstition that nine is a lucky number, and even luckier in succession. So the next time you're giving someone money as a gift or want to compliment them on their numerous good qualities, be sure to throw in plenty of nines.

MEKONG DELTA

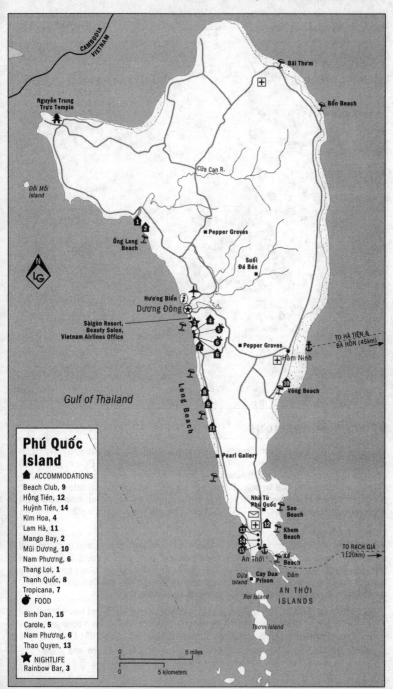

Phú Quốc Island

🏠 ACCOMMODATIONS

Beach Club, **9**
Hồng Tiến, **12**
Huỳnh Tiến, **14**
Kim Hoa, **4**
Lam Hà, **11**
Mango Bay, **2**
Mũi Dương, **10**
Nam Phương, **6**
Thang Loi, **1**
Thanh Quốc, **8**
Tropicana, **7**

🍴 FOOD

Bình Dân, **15**
Carole, **5**
Nam Phương, **6**
Thao Quyen, **13**

⭐ NIGHTLIFE
Rainbow Bar, **3**

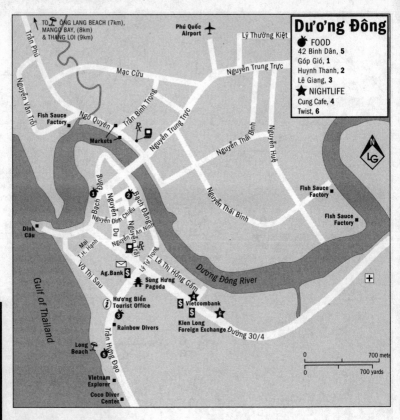

Du'o'ng Đông

🍴 **FOOD**
42 Binh Dân, **5**
Góp Gió, **1**
Huynh Thanh, **2**
Lê Giang, **3**

⭐ **NIGHTLIFE**
Cung Cafe, **4**
Twist, **6**

MEKONG DELTA

ACCOMMODATIONS

The number of accommodations on Phú Quốc Island is rapidly growing. Currently, the most popular places to stay are the resorts along Long Beach, just south of Dương Đông. The hotels in town tend to be more expensive and less convenient than those on the beach. There are also a few resorts situated on more secluded areas of the beach. Note that hot water does not come standard with accommodations in Phú Quốc, so you'll need to ask for it specifically.

LONG BEACH

Many of the resorts along Long Beach have their own restaurants and bars, as well as Internet access. In most cases, guests have the option of staying in beachside bungalows (large furnished huts, often made of bamboo) or hotel rooms. The resorts don't have numbered addresses, but they're clearly marked by signs, and most taxi and motorbike drivers are familiar with them.

Nam Phương (☎846 319). A popular budget option, with a warm and helpful staff and respectable rooms that are a short walk from the beach. There is also a book exchange, dominated by German-language books. Rooms US$6-8; bungalows US$12-15. ❷

Beach Club (☎980 998; beachclubasia@yahoo.com). A large beach and knowledgeable proprietors make this a good option. Rooms US$10; bungalows US$12-15. ❸

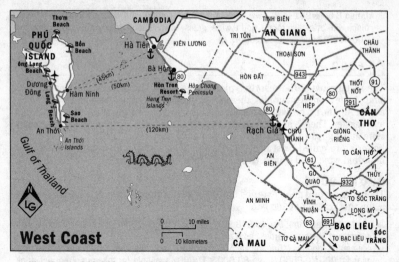

West Coast

MEKONG DELTA

Kim Hoa (☎848 969; fax 848 261). Features clean and comfortable digs, plus a nice shady piece of beach and a great pool in the back. The proprietor sells his own locally produced fish sauce. Breakfast and transportation to and from the airport are included. Rooms US$22-32; bungalows US$22-35. AmEx/MC/V. ❹

Tropicana (☎847 127). A bit pricier, but with extra perks like beach huts, an international reading rack, and a deserted beach. Rooms US$20; bungalows US$28-56. ❹

Lam Hà (☎847 369), on the south end of Long Beach. You'd never know that it's next to the beach—its grounds resemble a tropical forest. Rooms 100,000-150,000Đ. ❷

Thanh Quốc (☎980 430; www.thanhquochotel.com). The grounds resemble a suburban neighborhood, and the beach is a 5min. walk, but these bungalows-for-rent are clean, well maintained, and cheap. Bungalows US$5-8. ❶

AN THỚI

Clean beaches are far away, and the air smells persistently of fish in this southern port town. However, for those who feel the need to spend a night at the docks, or who prefer the shorter drive to Sao Beach, there are a few options.

Hồng Tiến (☎844 087; fax 844 540), on Khu Phố 3, on the left after the hospital. Clean, well-kept rooms with all the amenities. Rooms 140,000-220,000Đ. ❷

Huỳnh Phát (☎990 123), on Khu Phố 3, farther into town on the right. A smaller, cheaper mini-hotel. Friendly and attentive staff. Rooms 120,000Đ per person. ❷

ELSEWHERE IN PHÚ QUỐC

For those looking to get away from it all, the resorts along Ông Lang Beach, 10km north of Dương Đông, or Vòng Beach, 10km south of Hàm Ninh, offer a more remote setting. The resorts listed below have attached restaurants and bars.

Mũi Dương (☎849 555; fax 849 904), on Vòng Beach. Pristine, secluded, and spacious, with streams running through the grounds and bungalows set on eggshell sands. Of course, this perfection comes at a price. Rooms US$40; bungalows US$60. ❺

Thang Loi (☎0908 297 413; thangloiresort@hotmail.com), on Ông Lang Beach. Cozy bungalows where guests can celebrate the sunset with cheap drinks (most under 20,000Đ) at Happy hour, 5-7pm. Bungalows US$10-15. ❸

Mango Bay (☎981 693; www.mangobayphuquoc.com), on Ông Lang Beach. A relaxed place with attractive rooms and a wide, grassy lawn leading down to the beach. Rooms 200,000Đ; bungalows 300,000Đ. ❸

🔋 FOOD

The restaurants at the resorts typically offer both Vietnamese and Western cuisine. Aside from restaurants, there are a number of options around Dương Đông and in An Thới. The **outdoor market** on Ngô Quyền in Dương Đông has fresh fruits and veggies. There's also a **convenience store** in town at 37 Đường 30/4 and a **grocery store** at 5 Nguyễn Trãi. (☎847 367. Open daily 8am-8pm.) Additionally, a gourmet liquor store called **Twist** is at 144 Đường 30/4, carrying an impressive array of imported wines and spirits. (☎982 165. Open daily 8am-8pm.)

DƯƠNG ĐÔNG

There are several good eateries in Dương Đông, ranging from humble bakeries to a gourmet restaurant and bar.

☒ **Carole,** 88 Trần Hưng Đạo (☎848 884), at the entrance to Kim Hoa Resort. Popular with tourists of all sorts, Carole has it all: Phú Quốc squid specialties (40,000Đ), elaborate ice-cream sundaes ("Banana Hà Nội" 45,000Đ), and satisfying wood-oven pizzas (regular 50,000-70,000Đ; large 80,000-90,000Đ) available for take-out. Frequent drink promotions at the bar. Free Internet for diners. Open daily 7:30am-midnight. ❸

Lê Giang, 7 Trần Hưng Đạo (☎846 444; fax 848 383). Very popular for its delicious Vietnamese fare. Most entrees under 50,000Đ. Open daily 10am-10pm. ❸

Nam Phương (☎846 319), inside the resort. Notable for good food at low prices. Vietnamese entrees 12,000-20,000Đ, breakfasts 8000-10,000Đ. The pineapple pancakes (10,000Đ) are exceptional. Open daily 7am-8pm. ❶

Góp Gió, 145 Bạch Đằng (☎847 057), right on the harbor. Fresh local seafood cooked Vietnamese-style. Most entrees 20,000-40,000Đ. Open daily 7am-10pm. ❷

Huynh-Thanh, 88 Bạch Đằng. A small bakery tucked next to the river. Pastries (3000-5000Đ) and fresh-baked loaves of bread (10,000Đ). Open daily 7am-8pm. ❶

42 Bình Dân, 42 Trần Hưng Đạo. A clean streetside eatery with long steel tables, red plastic chairs, and Vietnamese staples. As authentic as it gets. Entrees 10,000-20,000Đ. Open daily 7am-11pm. ❶

AN THỚI

The seafood here comes right off the docks—try it. We know, it's good.

Thao Quyen (☎991 091; fax 990 479), on Khu Phố 3, on the right past the hospital. Vietnamese dishes in a pleasant atmosphere. Try the steamed tortoise. Impressive vegetarian menu. Entrees 20,000-40,000Đ. Prices seasonally. Open daily 8am-8pm. ❷

Binh Dan (☎844 126), on Khu Phố 3, next to the market. A spirited staff prepares the freshest seafood in town. Point and choose from meats, veggies, and spices behind the counter to customize your order. Entrees 10,000-20,000Đ. Open daily 7am-10pm. ❶

🌊 🏊 BEACHES AND OUTDOOR ACTIVITIES

Phú Quốc's beaches are considered some of the very best in Vietnam. The military has unfortunately claimed many of them, but ample stretches of sand still remain open. **Long Beach** (Bãi Trường) stretches from Dương Đông to An Thới. Soft yellow sand and a smooth shoreline make it the island's hot spot. Ten kilometers farther up the coast, **Ông Lang Beach** (Bãi Ông Lang) is somewhat rockier than Long Beach, making it great for marine life. But the best is ☒**Sao Beach** (Bãi Sao), on the eastern side of the island. This tranquil cove, featuring crystal-blue waters and powdery white sand, is well worth the ride down a bumpy dirt road. In the center of Phú Quốc are several **natural hot springs.** The local favorite is **Suối Đá Bán,** a series of waterfalls and bathing pools. The hilly northern part of the island is dominated by lush forests, environmentally protected but open to exploration.

The best way to explore these parts is by motorbike. Riders should be careful to heed weather conditions, as the dirt roads can become very dangerous during the rainy season. The northeastern stretch, between Hàm Ninh and Bãi Thơm, is the most beautiful, but also the most treacherous. The road follows the coastline, heading into the hills and over a number of streams, which in many cases are bridged only by precarious wooden logs. The road is being developed and paved, but for now, motorbikers should consider packing rope, a sleeping bag, and a tent, just in case they get stuck in the mud. Also, be aware of your fuel consumption: gas stations are confined to the four main cities, and huts with spare gas are few and far between, especially in the more isolated eastern side.

Beyond the southern tip of Phú Quốc are the **An Thới Islands,** an archipelago of smaller islands which offer excellent snorkeling and scuba diving. Some of the resorts rent boats (US$20-30 per day), and most can arrange transportation. Fishing trips, including the illustrious night-squid trip, run from November to June.

SCUBA DIVING

A wealth of colorful and exotic creatures dwell in the gulf around Phú Quốc. The wonderfully warm waters (15-27°C) and the trail of islands that stretches southward make the area particularly pleasant for diving. Several dive shops run organized trips, offering "try dives" for newbies (US$50), "fun dives" for the certified (US$40), and training courses at both basic (US$220) and advanced (US$180) levels. Prices include all gear and lunch.

Diving in Phú Quốc is considered second to Nha Trang in quality because of occlusion and visibility issues. However, the cities' respective diving seasons are opposite each other, due to their different rainy seasons. Most dive shops in Phú Quốc operate only from September through May, closing down in the rainy months (June to August), moving staff and instructors north to Nha Trang.

Most resorts are affiliated with one of the dive shops below, and can arrange excursions. Snorkeling equipment can also be rented or borrowed from many of the resorts, and dive shops run snorkeling trips as well (US$20). Daytrips for both diving and snorkeling depart around 7:30am and return around 2pm. Several

THE LOCAL STORY

PHÚ QUỐC GUIDELINE

So you've got your motorbike, and you're ready to explore Phú Quốc. While few travelers run into any problems on the island, keep in mind that much of the land is still undeveloped. Here are a few tips.

1. Bring at least 2 liters of water. It gets quite hot during the day, and snack stands are sometimes hard to find. Dehydration can be a serious issue, so come prepared.

2. Keep off military property. The Vietnamese government is very protective of Phú Quốc, and there are military bases (marked by signs) around the island. Although some travelers claim they've slipped through unnoticed, it is unwise to intrude upon military property. Irate officers can make your life unpleasant.

3. Take a map. Although Phú Quốc seems relatively small, its many winding paths aren't always easy to find. Bring a map with the major roads and landmarks.

4. Give yourself enough time. Poor (or practically non-existent) roads take time to navigate; it can take a whole day to explore half the island.

5. Be prepared for dust. Sunglasses are good protection unless you're already wearing a helmet with a faceshield. Wear dark clothing.

6. Bring raingear. It can turn from pretty paradise into monster monsoon in minutes. Be ready.

of the dive and snorkel sites are near the Thailand or Cambodia's maritime border, so take your passport onto the boat in case of checks by coastal police.

Vietnam Explorer, 36 Trần Hưng Đạo, Dương Đông (☎846 372; www.divingviet-nam.com). A PADI-authorized center with a friendly staff and internationally qualified Vietnamese instructors. Open year-round daily 7am-9pm.

Coco Dive Center, 58 Trần Hưng Đạo, Dương Đông (☎982 100; www.cocodive-center.com). The island's only SSI-certified dive shop. Open Sept.-May daily 7am-9pm.

◎ SIGHTS

Most travelers come to the island to explore its natural features, but there are a few quirky attractions along the way that you may want to investigate.

PHÚ QUỐC PEARL GALLERY. A series of placards and showcases explain the surprisingly complex process of creating pearls. Check out the oysters that have been made to grow heart-shaped pearls. You can also purchase jewelry here for US$50-400. *(On Long Beach, just south of Beach Club Resort. ☎980 585; www.treasuresfromthedeep.com. Open daily 8am-5:30pm. AmEx/MC/V.)*

CAY DUA PRISON. During the colonial period, the French law enforcement sent Vietnamese outcasts to this site of tropical isolation. An intimidating red fist dominates the center of the French-designed grounds. *(Open daily 7:30am-4:30pm. Free.)*

FISH SAUCE FACTORIES. Phú Quốc is widely renowned for its superb ◪**fish sauce** *(nước mắm)*, exporting six to 10 million liters each year. There are a number of fish sauce factories around Dương Đông, and many owners are willing to let visitors wander around the gigantic wooden vats. *(Open daily 8am-7pm. Free.)*

PEPPER GROVES. Another common sight (and smell) on the island are the pepper groves, easily distinguished by their neat rows of wooden posts. In 2006, Vietnam surpassed India to become the world's leading producer of black pepper. Walk through the groves to catch a glimpse of the tiny clumps of peppercorns. Again, owners generally don't mind visitors. *(Free.)*

NHÀ TÙ PHÚ QUỐC. This liberation monument has the shape of a man cut out in the middle. Look closely and you'll see that he's breaking free of his chains. The monument itself is not much, but the view of the island's hills and surrounding ocean from this point is stellar. *(On the road south, between Long Beach and An Thới. Free.)*

TEMPLES AND PAGODAS. There are several religious sites on the island. Among them, **Nguyễn Trung Trực Temple,** at the island's northwest corner near Mũi Dương, pays homage to the 19th-century anti-colonialist leader who raided the French warship *Espérance*. The **Sùng Hưng Pagoda,** in Dương Đông, is an ornate and beautiful religious complex. *(Both open daily 7am-5pm. Free.)*

DINH CÂU. While not particularly impressive, this large rock and the lighthouse on top of it provide a great view of the harbor's colorful fishing boats. *(On the end of Bạch Đằng in Dương Đông. Open daily 7am-5:30pm. Free.)*

♫ ▣ ENTERTAINMENT AND NIGHTLIFE

To be pampered and primped, try the **beauty salon** at Sàigòn-PhúQuốc Resort, which offers everything from manicures to massages. (25,000-100,000Đ; verify prices beforehand. Open daily 8am-midnight.) Alternatively, you can let the local masseuses come to you—they regularly roam Long Beach in the afternoons and evenings and will give you a one-hour rubdown for 50,000Đ.

At night, head to **Cung Cafe,** 51 Dường 30/4. It's a cafe by day, bar by night, and hip place to hang at any time. The common bookshelf includes English romance novels, free maps of the island, and guidebooks. (☎982 363; cungcafes@yahoo.com. Beer 10,000-15,000Đ; mixed drinks 30,000-50,000Đ; non-alcoholic juices and shakes 8000-12,000Đ. Open daily 7am-10pm.)

🔋 DAYTRIP FROM PHÚ QUỐC

THƠM ISLAND

Thơm Island is a 1hr. boat ride from the south end of Phú Quốc. Tours are best arranged through dive shops in Phú Quốc (p. 437) and include transportation and lunch. Dive shops typically offer snorkeling and a range of diving trips. Private boats (US$20-30) can also be arranged. Because of the island's proximity to the maritime borders of Thailand and Cambodia, foreigners should take their passports with them on the boat. The island itself is uninhabited and camping is not allowed.

Thơm Island, and the string of islands around it, offers a wonderful view into the Gulf of Thailand's underwater life. Directly south of Phú Quốc, the ocean floor here descends steeply, from three to 20 meters and deeper. Snorkelers can see a variety of corals, and deep divers have the rare chance of seeing sharks and sting rays when visibility is good (Sept.-May).

The south side of Thơm Island offers colorful **coral beds** from six to 14 meters long. Pink coral sprawls across vast portions of the ocean floor, creating tile mosaics, while green brain coral and palm-size touch-me-nots litter the landscape. Divers should be careful, as the terrain is highly variable—there are many large boulders and outcrops, so stay aware of your periphery and be careful not to hit your head. Also, be sure to avoid the thousands of black sea urchins and their long piercing tentacles. In between Thơm Island and its western neighbor, Dừa Island, you can find fan corals and sands filled with cast-away shells. More than the corals, though, the highlight of these waters are the big fish: manta rays, sting rays, barricudas, and baby sharks can be found at depths of around 15m. Shallow-water schools include striped tigerfish, bright blue parrotfish, giant purple angelfish, paired butterflyfish, and the ever-playful clownfish.

HÀ TIÊN   ☎ 77

Picturesque Hà Tiên, set on the Gulf of Thailand amid a landscape of rolling hills dotted with intricate cave temples, is a favorite Mekong stop for many travelers. Colorful houses, cheerful residents, a small-town atmosphere, and a well-kept appearance add to its appeal and render it a sweet relief—Hà Tiên is the southern hospitality you were looking for. During the American War and the subsequent transition to Communist rule, many southern Vietnamese used Hà Tiên and its offshore islands as a point of escape (by boat) to other countries. Travelers today use it as an escape from the bustling, business-minded Mekong.

🔳 TRANSPORTATION. Buses arrive at the station across the floating bridge from the town center and head to Cần Thơ (4hr.; 5:30am, 10pm; 25,000Đ); Châu Đốc (4hr.; 4 per day 6:15am-2pm; 25,000Đ); HCMC (8hr.; 8, 9pm; 50,000Đ); Long Xuyên (3hr.; 11pm; 30,000Đ); Rạch Giá (3hr.; every 30min. 6:30am-6:30pm; 15,000Đ). There are also **minibuses** to HCMC that depart in the early morning from in front of Đông Hồ Hotel. **Slow boats** to Phú Quốc (4hr.; 8:30, 9am; 120,000Đ) run from the nearby port town of Bà Hòn, 20km away; the journey often involves a short motorized canoe ride past the bridge police before boarding the larger ferry. Ask your

MEKONG DELTA

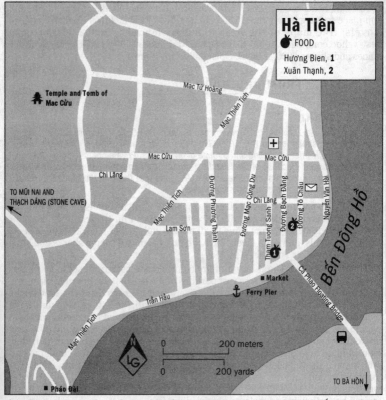

Hà Tiên

🍴 FOOD

Hương Biên, **1**
Xuân Thạnh, **2**

Temple and Tomb of
Mac Cửu

Mạc Tử Hoàng

Mạc Thiên Tích

Mạc Cửu

Mạc Cửu

Chi Lăng

TO MŨI NAI AND
THẠCH DÁNG (STONE CAVE)

Mạc Thiên Tích

Đường Phương Thành

Đường Mạc Công Du

Chi Lăng

Đường Bạch Đằng

Đường Tô Châu

Nguyễn Văn Hải

Bến Đông Hồ

Lam Sơn

Tham Tướng Sanh

Cầu Phao Floating Bridge

Trần Hầu

■ Market

⚓ Ferry Pier

N

0   200 meters

0   200 yards

TO BÀ HÒN

■ Pháo Đài

MEKONG DELTA

hotel receptionist for information about **high-speed ferries** to Phú Quốc Island, as availability depends on the season.

■ **ORIENTATION AND PRACTICAL INFORMATION.** Hà Tiên is a small town, and many tourists enjoy exploring it by bicycle. (Rentals available for 20,000Đ per day at Đông Hồ Hotel.) The main thoroughfare, **Trần Hầu,** runs along the front of the harbor, past the **floating bridge** (Cầu Phao) and the main **market,** and the **ferry station.** Just west of the town center, **Highway 80** runs north toward the nearby Cambodian border. Effective January 2007, foreigners can cross the border here (see **Border Crossing,** p. 441).

KienGiang Tourist Office runs the Đông Hồ Hotel (☎ 951 031); the staff gives out free town maps and answers general questions. **Trinh Ngoc The** rents out bicycles and motorbikes with complimentary hand-drawn maps. (☎ 0918 574 780; tinhngocthe2000@yahoo.com.) **Vietcombank,** 4 Phương Thành, has a **24hr. ATM,** changes traveler's checks, and does currency exchange and MC/V cash advances. (☎ 951 065; fax 951 067. Open M-F 7-11am and 1-4pm.) There is a **hospital** on Mạc Cửu and a **pharmacy** (open daily 7am-9pm) at 32 Trần Hầu. **Internet** is at 33 Tham Tướng Sanh (4000Đ per hr.; open daily 9am-11pm) and 21 Trần Hầu (3000Đ per hr.; open daily 7am-11pm). The **post office** is located on Tô Châu and has phone and fax services. (Open daily 6:30am-9pm.)

■ **ACCOMMODATIONS AND FOOD.** Hà Tiên offers a range of accommodation choices, from scrubby to snazzy. **Hải Vân** ❶, 55 Lam Sơn, is one of the most attractive hotels in town, and offers luggage storage and free safe deposit box in addition to quality budget rooms. The English-speaking manager Cương will happily give you a personal tour of the city and its surrounding sights. (☎852 872. Rooms 70,000-220,000Đ.) **Dú Hưng ❶**, 17A Trần Hầu, has clean rooms and a professional, English-speaking staff. All units are air-conditioned. (☎951 555; fax 852 267. Rooms 50,000Đ per person.) **Hoàng Dũ ❶**, 30 Lam Sơn, is a spiffy mini-hotel with clean and fragrant rooms. TVs are included. (☎851 463. Rooms 90,000-180,000Đ.) **Ngọc Quan ❷**, 24 Mạc Công Du, is another mini-hotel with high standards. The triples are a bargain. (☎852 652. Rooms 120,000-150,000Đ.)

In accordance with the town's congenial ambience, restaurants in Hà Tiên are usually full of chatty locals and well-served, laid-back meals. Shrimp is especially popular on menus, and the little orange critters are set out to dry all over the city streets before being put on your plate. **Giang Thanh ❷**, 36 Trần Hầu, offers a clean, white-tablecloth-covered eating terrace alongside a bustling market. Portions are quite filling, and it serves the best ice cream in town; try the milk and coconut or grilled rice milk flavors. (Ice cream 7000Đ; entrees 35,000-50,000Đ. Open daily 8am-10pm.) **Xuân Thạnh ❷**, 20 Trần Hầu, offers a great view of the market and is always bustling with locals. (Most entrees 28,000-40,000Đ. Open daily 6am-10pm.) **Hương Biển ❷**, 974 Tô Châu, is a popular place to sample local seafood dishes. (Entrees 15,000-30,000Đ. Open daily 6am-8pm.) **Cafe Hải Âu ❶**, 80 Lam Sơn, is a nice stop for the wandering pedestrian. Its second-floor terrace gives a decent view of the town. (Drinks 4000-6000Đ. Open daily 7am-10pm.)

ⓖ ♫ SIGHTS AND ENTERTAINMENT. Each of the following sights lies north of town and is a 20,000-30,000Đ motorbike ride on Hwy. 80. The most famous attraction in Hà Tiên is **Thạch Động** (Stone Cave), 4km northwest of town. This large outcrop of granite contains several Buddhist shrines and is home to a colony of small bats. Openings in the rock provide lovely views of the town, the surrounding rice fields, and the Cambodian border. There are several staircases and lookout balconies within the cave—one immediately to the left after the entrance, one to the right midway through the cave, and one at the very end of the inner walkway—so be sure to explore thoroughly. In front of the site, a fist carved in stone memorializes the massacre of 130 Vietnamese by invading Khmer Rouge forces here on March 14, 1978. (Open daily 7am-6pm. 2000Đ.) The **Mũi Nai Peninsula**, 7km west of town, offers two popular beaches: one has shallow water and a long strip of dark sand, and the other has a deeper swimming area and an attractive waterfront shaded by palm trees. Follow the local trend and rent an inner tube for 3000Đ. For the more adventurous, kayaks (10,000Đ) and jet skis (25,000Đ) are also available for rent. (Open daily 7am-11pm. Beaches 1500Đ.) The **Temple and Tomb of Mạc Cửu,** about 2km northwest of the town center, commemorates the beloved father of Hà Tiên, a Chinese governor appointed by the Khmer who shifted his allegiance to the Vietnamese Nguyễn Lords. You can climb the hill from the temple to view the decorative tombs of Mạc Cửu and his family members. Not far from here, the town's renowned **four-headed coconut tree** (Dùa Bốn Ngọn) stands in a front yard on Lâm Văn Quang. From the base of the tree, four separate trunks emerge, a biological rarity. It's near the intersection of Lâm Văn Quang and Phạm Văn Kỹ.

At night, the brightest neon signs in town come from **Cafe Nhạc Trẻ**, 1 Phương Thành, which offers karaoke, bar, steambath, and jacuzzi. (Beer 12,000-15,000Đ. Steambath and jacuzzi 60,000Đ. Open daily 6pm-midnight.)

▚ BORDER CROSSING. By 2007, travelers will be able to pass from Vietnam to Cambodia by road at the border crossing, about 10km northwest of Hà Tiên. Foreigners who do not yet have a Cambodian visa can obtain one at the border for US$22. The best way to get there is by motorbike (45min.; 50,000Đ).

MEKONG DELTA

⚡ DAYTRIPS FROM HÀ TIÊN. Nearby caves and cave temples are really what set Hà Tiên apart from other Mekong towns. Visitors in the area should not miss the chance to explore these natural formations. It is helpful to take along a flashlight. In addition, check out the beautiful beaches and archipelagos in the region. All sights are south of town, and can be reached by taking Hwy. 80 toward Bà Hòn.

▓ CHÙA HANG (PAGODA CAVE). This pagoda consists of a series of shrines built within and around a cave. Walk into the outer shrine to pay homage to several different Buddhist figures, as well as a statue of Shiva. Behind the Shiva is the entrance to the inner shrine and central cave temple. Several large Buddha statues sit in these dark and dank quarters. Follow the recessed neon lighting through to the back of the cave. On the right, you will see a spiral staircase leading up to another temple room. The back side of the cave sits alongside the beach, which is lined with a boardwalk. The beach sands are inhabited by millions of tiny crabs, and you can see the many small holes burrowed into the sand's surface. Offshore from the cave are the **Father & Son Islands,** identifiable by two large peaks; the father is on the left, and the son on the right. Legend has it that after a torrential storm, the local fishing communities all fled the coastal islands. When his son got stuck in the midst, a father allegedly swam out into the sea to save him, but neither of them returned. Their spirits are now embodied in these islands. Ferries (10,000Đ) shuttle visitors to the islands from the dock behind the cave. *(37km south of Hà Tiên. Open daily 7am-5pm. 5000Đ.)*

MOSO CAVES. This sight is composed of two white-stone ("moso" in Khmer) caves, one short and one long, which were the site of daily bombing and constant US surveillance during the American War. Inside the short cave are two giant stalactites, measuring almost 10m in height. Clumps of incense sticks also adorn the cave as altars to the deceased soldiers. The long cave stretches on for two kilometers and opens out on the other side of the mountain. A wooden-plank walkway, lit by a string of light bulbs, leads visitors through the cave. Be sure to alert the cave-keeper of your presence and pay him to keep the lights on (10,000Đ). A warning: the keeper is very old and very anti-American. It might be a better bet to pay 5000Đ at the entrance to borrow a flashlight. *(30km south of Hà Tiên. From the highway, take a left onto the paved road just before the Swiss cement factory. Open daily 7am-5pm. Free.)*

CROCODILE CAVES. Visible from the highway, these hollow caverns are marked by Swiss-cheese-like base rocks. There is usually at least half a meter of water on the ground of the cave as well. Locals insist that two large crocodiles once inhabited these caves, but when their seven crocodile children were killed by fishermen, the parents grew sullen and whiled away their lives on the inside, never again emerging. A few ladders and steps cut into the rock allow visitors a means to climb inside. Be very careful during the rainy season. *(22km south of town. Free.)*

SHRIMP FARMS. Eighteen kilometers south of Hà Tiên, travelers will notice large rectangles of water aerated by churning metal fans. These shrimp farms allow visitors to tour the farms and observe the shrimp-breeding process—a process we simply don't want to think about. *(Open daily 7am-6pm. Free.)*

HÒN CHONG PENINSULA. A fantastic beach and calm waves await visitors to Hòn Chong. With cafes aplenty and pedestrian traffic at a minimum, you could easily spend an afternoon mulling about these shores. Nearby are the Hang Tien Islands, 2km north of Hòn Chong and 4km off the main road. Inland and southeast from the peninsula is the 2km long **Dương Beach,** a great stretch of yellow sand. The star hotel of the area is **Hòn Trẹm Resort ❺,** which has large, private, balcony-laden villas radially spread out along a jutting outcrop's periphery. The resort includes a salon, sauna, karaoke, and a large restaurant, and offers tours to the nearby Ba Lua archipelago. (☎854 331; www.hontremresort.com. Rooms 400,000-450,000Đ.) Even if you're not planning to stay the night, the road toward the resort is worth a quick ride—it ascends to the top of a cliff and provides a beautiful view of the whole peninsula. *(32km southwest of town. Free.)*

LONG XUYÊN ☎76

For those travelers seeking to explore the rural attractions of An Giang Province, capital city Long Xuyên can serve as a useful jumping-off point, with the provincial tourist office located in the city. Unfortunately, the city itself doesn't have much to offer tourists, although a river tour is an enjoyable way to spend a few hours. Like so many other Vietnamese towns, the reason to come to Long Xuyên is to leave it, and there are two primary **daytrips** from town, both of which are Vietnamese historical sights. The first, situated across the river from the city center, is **Mỹ Hòa Hưng Island.** The island was the birthplace of Tôn Đức Thắng, who succeeded Hồ Chí Minh to become Vietnam's second president. A memorial area on the island features the leader's tomb, an exhibition hall with photos and remnants of his life, and the simple wooden house that served as his childhood home. Visitors can visit the island by boat or arrange a longer homestay with the tourist office. Those who stay overnight will be treated to renditions of local music and home-cooked food typical of the region. (Museum open daily 7-11am and 1-5pm. Free.) The second worthy daytrip is the more ancient **Óc Eo**, 40km from Long Xuyên. This city was once an important port at the height of the Funan Kingdom (AD first to sixth centuries), whose wealth came from controlling trade and commerce between the east and west. Its buildings were constructed on piles of stone, connected by a network of irrigation and transport canals. After the fall of the kingdom, the port went out of use, and the site lay submerged for centuries before it was rediscovered in the 1940s. Artifacts recovered from the grounds indicate that the people in this region had contact with China, Indonesia, Malaysia, Thailand, Persia, and even the Roman Empire. Among the artifacts are written accounts of the city's activities, scrawled by Chinese emissaries and travelers. (Open daily 7am-5pm. Free.)

Long Xuyên has several large luxury hotels. Its budget accommodations generally hold less appeal. **Long Xuyên Hotel ❷,** 19 Nguyễn Văn Cưng, has clean and comfortable rooms at reasonable prices and a very helpful staff. (☎841 927; fax 842 483. Breakfast included. Rooms US$9-16.) A more basic budget option with friendly staff is **Xuân Phương ❶,** 68 Nguyễn Trãi. (☎841 041. Rooms 80,000-200,000Đ.) **Đông Xuyên Hotel ❹,** 9A Lương Văn Cù, is the fanciest place in town, with services including sauna, jacuzzi, and massage. (☎942 260; dongxuyenag@hcm.vnn.vn. Breakfast included. Rooms US$20-45.) Although Long Xuyên has innumerable **cafes,** it is rather lacking in quality restaurants. **Hồng Phát ❷,** 242/4 Lương Văn Cù, is one exception—this cheerful place has a variety of delicious Vietnamese meals. (Most dishes 20,000-40,000Đ. Open daily 10am-9pm.) The restaurant atop **Đông Xuyên Hotel ❷** offers elegant ambience, excellent city views, and a surprisingly affordable menu. (Most meals under 40,000Đ. Open daily 6am-10pm.) Not far from the docking area at the end of Nguyễn Huệ is the colorful and lively **floating market,** where fruits and vegetables are piled high on boats.

Buses arrive at the Long Xuyên station about 1km outside the city center on Trần Hưng Đạo, and head to the following destinations several times each morning: Cần Thơ (1½hr.; 20,000Đ); Châu Đốc (1½hr.; 17,000Đ); HCMC (4½hr.; 68,000Đ); Rạch Giá (3hr.; 27,000Đ). **Motorboats** are available for hire (30,000Đ per hr.) at the end of Nguyễn Huệ. From the bus station, **Trần Hưng Đạo** runs along the edge of the city center and meets the **Catholic church,** whose massive spire serves as a helpful navigational landmark. Perpendicular to Trần Hưng Đạo, major thoroughfare **Nguyễn Huệ** runs from the church past a **Tôn Đức Thắng statue** and up to the **Hậu River,** whose waterfront is crowed with market stalls. **An Giang Tourimex Travel Service Center,** 17 Nguyễn Văn Cưng, is the best place to get information on the province. The office also books tours and homestays on Mỹ Hòa Hưng Island. (☎841 036; www.angiangtourimex.com. Open daily 7-11am and 1-5pm.) The main **bank,** 1 Hùng Vương, has an ATM, does currency exchange and MC/V cash advances, and cashes traveler's checks. (Open daily 7-11am and 1-5pm.) There is also a convenient Vietcombank **ATM** in the lobby of Đông Xuyên Hotel. **Internet** can be found at 312/4 Trần Hưng Đạo. (3000Đ per hr. Open daily 7:30am-10pm.) There is a **post office** on Ngô Gia Tự, near its intersection with Nguyễn Văn Cưng. (Phone and fax services. Open daily 6am-10pm.)

CHÂU ĐỐC ☎ 76

Most travelers in Châu Đốc are just passing through on their way to or from Cambodia. However, those who choose to linger here will find that the alluring and diverse city has a lot to offer, including pilgrimage sites, floating homes, and one of the most attractive waterfronts in the Mekong. Châu Đốc is an ideal escape from the inward-oriented Delta if you're craving a slightly more cosmopolitan feel, or if you simply wish to laze by the river in the well-manicured park.

▐▄ TRANSPORTATION. Buses arrive at the station 2km southeast of the city center on Lê Lợi and go to: Cần Thơ (3hr.; 5, 6, 7am; 39,000Đ); Hà Tiên (3hr.; 6, 9am; noon; 30,000Đ); HCMC (6hr.; every hr. 4-9am; 85,000Đ); Long Xuyên (1hr.; 6, 7am; 17,000Đ); Rạch Giá (4hr.; 7am; 40,000Đ); Vĩnh Long (4hr.; 6am; 40,000Đ). The **Vĩnh Xưởng border crossing** (p. 447) is 40 km west of Châu Đốc.

▐▌ ORIENTATION. The main road, **Lê Lợi** (which turns into **Trần Hưng Đạo** midway through town), runs along the **Hậu River.** The waterfront is dominated by the Victoria Hotel, a huge, yellow, colonial-style building. Beside the hotel is a lovely park with flower arrangements, vine-covered archways, and an impressive US$300,000 Bassac fish statue, symbolizing the main commerce of the city. At night, the walkways and fountains in the park light up. From the waterfront, **Nguyễn Văn Thoại** runs through the city center toward **Sam Mountain.** Market stalls crowd the streets near the riverfront between Nguyễn Văn Thoại and **Bạch Đằng,** and the **indoor market** is between Bạch Đằng and **Chi Lăng.**

▐ PRACTICAL INFORMATION. There is no tourist office in Châu Đốc, since the one in Long Xuyên serves the whole province. Various tour agencies abound with cheap and efficient multi-country trips to Vietnam's neighbors, including treks through Laos and Thailand and the ever-popular boat to Cambodia (2-3 days; US$30-40). Most boats bound for Phnom Penh, Cambodia, depart around 7am. (Fast boat 2½hr., US$15; slow boat 4hr., US$7. See **Border Crossing,** p. 447.) **Mékong Tours,** 14 Nguyễn Hữu Cảnh (☎868 222; www.mekongvietnam.com), runs everything from half-day (US$6) and full-day (US$15) trips around Châu Đốc to more extended excursions on the river (3-4 days, US$20-40). They also have a convenient sister office in Phnom Penh. Ask for the personable Đục as your guide. (Open daily 7am-9pm.) **Delta Adventure,** 53 Lê Lợi, has an energetic and friendly staff that speaks excellent English and offers the same services, plus customizable trekking tours. (☎563 810; fax 563 811. Open daily 7:30am-9pm.) The main **bank** is at 315 Lê Lợi, about 1km from the city center toward the bus station. (☎561 702. Currency exchange, MC/V cash advances, and **ATM.** Open daily 7-11am and 1:15-4:45pm.) **Hoa Sen,** 12 Nguyễn Hữu Cảnh, is a good **bookstore** that sells new and used books in English and French. (☎867 817. US$2-3 per book. Open daily 6:30am-8pm.) The **hospital** is at 5 Lê Lợi, just across from Victoria Hotel. (☎867 184. 24hr. emergency service.) The Hồng Vân **pharmacy** is at 4 Nguyễn Văn Thoại (☎866 614; open daily 8am-8pm). Connected to the post office is an **Internet** center. (3000Đ per hr. Open daily 7am-9pm.) There is also an Internet cafe at 9 Trần Hưng Đạo. (3000Đ per hr. Open daily 7am-11pm.) The main **post office** is located at 73 Lê Lợi. (Phone and fax services. Open daily 6am-10pm.)

▐ ACCOMMODATIONS. Because so many tourists pass through, Châu Đốc has a number of accommodation options. If you're unaffiliated with a tour company, go early: accommodations can be tough to find after 6pm when the masses of tour buses

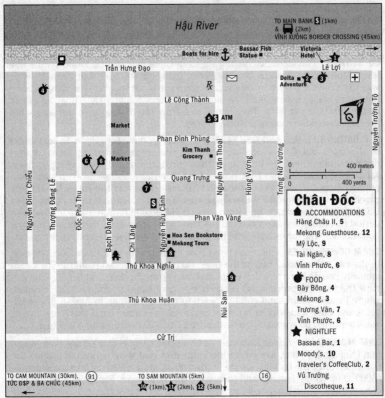

Châu Đốc

▲ ACCOMMODATIONS
Hàng Châu II, **5**
Mekong Guesthouse, **12**
Mỹ Lộc, **9**
Tài Ngân, **8**
Vĩnh Phước, **6**

🍎 FOOD
Bày Bông, **4**
Mékong, **3**
Trương Vân, **7**
Vĩnh Phước, **6**

★ NIGHTLIFE
Bassac Bar, **1**
Moody's, **10**
Traveler's CoffeeClub, **2**
Vũ Trường
Discotheque, **11**

overtake the city. **Hàng Châu II ❷**, 10 Nguyễn Văn Thoại, has spacious, well-maintained rooms, a friendly staff, and an ATM. (☎868 891. Rooms with fan US$6, with A/C US$8.) **Mekong Guesthouse ❶** is halfway up Sam Mountain, where you can spend your days watching the sun rise over the Mekong and set over Cambodia. All rooms have fans, and there's a DVD player and book rack in the lobby. (☎868 222; mekongtour-sag@yahoo.com. Rooms US$4-6.) The English-speaking proprietor of **Vĩnh Phước ❶**, 12-14 Quang Trưng, can provide a wealth of information on Châu Đốc and the sur-rounding area. (☎866 242. Rooms US$4-6.) **Tài Ngân ❶**, 11 Nguyễn Hữu Cảnh, is in the city's central square. Clean rooms, TVs, and plenty of natural light make this a nice budget deal. Receptionists speak English. (Rooms with fan US$5, with A/C US$10.) **Mỹ Lộc ❶**, 51B Nguyễn Văn Thoại, is another decent budget option, with clean, well-kept rooms. (☎866 455. Laundry 15,000Đ per kg. Rooms 60,000-120,000Đ.)

🔋 FOOD. Châu Đốc has surprisingly little to offer in terms of restaurants. The few places that do exist feel like haphazard but homey family kitchens. **Kim Thanh** grocery store is at 14 Nguyễn Văn Thoại. (☎866 529. Open daily 7am-10pm.) **Mékong ❷**, 41 Lê Lợi, is an outdoor eatery set in the lovely courtyard of an old French colonial villa. The entrance is through the gates across from the Victoria Hotel. (Most entrees 20,000-40,000Đ. Open daily 6am-10pm.) **Vĩnh Phước ❷**, 12-14 Quang Trưng, is on the first floor of the hotel. This standard Vietnamese kitchen is bustling all day with tourists in tran-sit, and it has the only significant vegetarian options in town. (Entrees 10,000-30,000. Open daily 6am-11pm.) **Bày Bông ❷**, 22 Thượng Đăng Lễ, draws crowds of tourists for its friendly service, flavorful fare, and make-your-own spring rolls. (Entrees 20,000-

30,000Đ. Open daily 9am-10pm.) The popular local joint **Tru'o'ng Vân ❷,** 15 Quang Trưng, specializes in hotpot and claypot dishes. If your timing is right, you can join the other customers crowded around the TV watching Vietnamese pop videos and competitive karaoke. (Most entrees 20,000-30,000Đ. Open daily 6am-9pm.)

⊙ SIGHTS. The most fascinating sights in Châu Đốc can be found on the **Hậu River.** Motorboat tours can be arranged at many guesthouses, but a much better way to cruise the river is by canoe, as it gives you more access to the sights. Canoe operators congregate around the pier at the end of Nguyễn Văn Thoại, and most charge 30,000Đ per hour. The chance to admire the technique of the somewhat precarious-looking rowers is worth the trip.

▧ FLOATING VILLAGES AND FISH FARMS. A whole community resides in **boathouses** of all shapes and sizes—some are complex, multi-room structures afloat on steel drums, while others are little more than corrugated-metal shacks atop canoes. Amazingly, most of these river homes have electricity, and some even have computers. There are more than a thousand fish farmers among the villages, and many catch fish in cages right underneath their floors. Each fish farm costs about US$50,000 to construct, and produces 60,000-80,000 fish in a single gestation period (8-10 months). You can tell the fish farms apart from the houses by their bottom half—the farms have wire mesh reaching down five meters into the water.

CHÀM COMMUNITIES. There are two Chàm communities near Châu Đốc, one next to the city and another across the river, each with about 400 families. The Chàm minority people here practice Islam and are known for their textiles. Visitors can view the weaving process, try on their signature sarongs, and visit the **mosques,** where locals worship and children learn to read the Qur'an in Arabic. These villages also have a history of flooding, and visitors can see each year's high-water mark scrawled on wooden posts—the mark for 2000 is almost nine feet high.

SAM MOUNTAIN. About 5km west of Châu Đốc's city center stands Sam Mountain (Núi Sam; 234m), named for the king crabs that were deposited around the mountain after the building of the border canal. Most travelers take a motorbike (5000Đ) up to the summit and then walk the 2km down. From the summit, you can see the Cambodian border amid wide stretches of rice fields. You might wonder about the loud noises echoing from atop the summit, but no fear, they're only monkeys—the noises don't, in fact, emanate from the bizarrely placed model T-Rex partway down the mountain. There is also a military post here; refrain from photographing the building and the soldiers.

PAGODAS NEAR SAM MOUNTAIN. Around the base of Sam Mountain are a number of pagodas. The most famous is the massive temple of **Bà Chúa Xứ,** which attracts throngs of pilgrims each year, particularly around the end of the fourth lunar month (late April). The pilgrims come from far and wide to shower the temple's leading lady, Chúa Xứ, with elaborate gifts such as colorful fruit platters and whole roast suckling pigs. Nearby, **Tây An Pagoda** is an ostentatiously neon structure with a number of architectural flourishes. **Cavern Pagoda** is set about halfway up the mountain on its opposite side. The legend of the pagoda maintains that the site was once threatened by two giant serpents, but when female worshipper and pagoda founder Lê Thị Thỏ arrived, they ceased to bother anybody. Talk about one bad-ass, diva snake charmer. Today the pagoda's highlight is a long dark cave lined on each side by a sinister fake serpent with glowing red eyes.

◪ NIGHTLIFE. There are a number of popular bars in town. **Bassac Bar,** at the Victoria Hotel, is the poshest place around to have a drink. The pool-side bar offers a sparkling view of the river. (Cocktails and beers US$2-5. Open daily 7am-11pm.) **Traveler's Coffee Club,** 53 Lê Lợi, draws a pretty diverse international crowd. Comfy couches grace the second floor, and there's a great city view from the third floor terrace. (Drinks 6000-10,000Đ; food 15,000-25,000Đ. Open daily 7:30am-9pm.) **Moody's,** a hopping local karaoke bar, is 1km outside of town on Nguyễn Văn Thoại. (Beer 6000-8000Đ. Open daily 8-11pm.) **Vũ Trường Discotheque** is 2km outside of town on Nguyễn Văn Thoại. Halfway between Châu Đốc and Sam Mountain, this is a popular weekend hangout for the locals. Look for the big neon signs. (Open F-Sa 7pm-midnight.)

■ HIKES. If you're starting to miss the mountain trekking of the Central Highlands or Northern Vietnam, **■Cam Mountain** can give you a short review of the country's natural wonders. The Mekong Delta's highest peak (1224m) offers what is arguably the best hike of the region. The mountain is full of surprises: a whole community of people lives along its slopes, so huts, temples, and even a post office grace its heights. The path upward begins as a series of stone steps (lined with food stalls and restaurants) and soon runs alongside rapids and small cascades. After the path turns to dirt and rock (about 45min.), there is a fork in the road: turn left and it is a straight shot (800m) to the **Cao Đài Temple.** But turn right for the longer, more rewarding trek to **Chùa Phật Lớn** (3km; follow the "chùa" sign, and take another left at the large T-junction). This truly breathtaking mountaintop pagoda takes hikers by surprise as its eight-story tower suddenly appears on the horizon. Cross the large red bridge and follow the stone path to the pagoda's entrance. During Buddhist holidays, the tower will be unlocked, and you can climb it to see a wonderful view of the Delta and its endless rivers and rice fields. The pagoda itself is small and tastefully ornate, its walls lined with white frescoes depicting scenes from the Buddha's life. In total, the trek is 7-8km, making for a 2½hr. ascent and a 1½hr. descent. Many detours along the way are fun to explore as well. The entire mountain is covered by jackfruit trees, and the fruit's pungent smell floods the air along most of the trail. (Open daily 7am-5pm. 5000Đ.)

■ BORDER CROSSING. Travelers can pass from Vietnam to Cambodia by boat at the **Vĩnh Xương** border crossing, about 40km from Châu Đốc. Cambodian visas can be obtained here for US$22. One passport photo is required. The trip can be arranged at many guesthouses in Châu Đốc or at tour offices in Hồ Chí Minh City.

■ DAYTRIPS FROM CHÂU ĐỐC. Tức Dụp and Ba Chúc are both located near Tri Tôn, 45km south of Châu Đốc. They are most easily reached by motorbike.

TỨC DỤP. A complicated cluster of huge boulders and deep caves, Tức Dụp served as a Việt Cộng base during the American War. Here the VC forces managed to hold off the US military against 3-to-20 odds between 1968 and 1976. Tức Dụp translates to "water runs at night" in Khmer, but the hill earned its nickname of "Two-Million-Dollar Hill" after the US spent that much money on weapons and still failed to capture it. Visitors can climb over the boulders and wander through the caves, which served as meeting rooms, living quarters, and hospitals. Letters painted on the hills' boulders indicate the location of various units during the war. The top of the hill provides great views of the surrounding countryside. Toward the bottom, there is a preserved B-52 bomb crater and a small museum with photographs of the soldiers, their munitions, and their camps. *(Open daily 7am-5pm. Museum open 7-11am and 1:30-5pm. 5000Đ.)*

BA CHÚC. Between 1975 and 1978, the area along the Cambodian border from Châu Đốc to Hà Tiên was routinely invaded by Khmer Rouge forces. Seeking to claim the territory as their own, the they marched into Vietnamese towns and slaughtered civilians. In April 1978, they massacred 3157 people at Ba Chúc. Today a glass case containing hundreds of victims' skulls (from infant to elderly) memorializes of the tragedy. Nearby, a collection of horrifying photographs documents the event in an all-too-visceral manner. There are also Khmer Rouge weapons on display. *(Open daily 7am-5pm. Free.)*

APPENDIX

LUNAR CALENDAR

While commercial Vietnam uses the secular calendar, holidays and festivals are often scheduled on the lunar calendar instead, and among ethnic minority communities, the lunar calendar is commonly used to determine market days. Here's a conversion chart for upcoming years:

LUNAR CALENDAR	2007	2008	2009 (LEAP YEAR)	2010
1st month, 1st day (Tết)	February 18th	February 7th	January 26th	February 14th
2nd month, 1st day	March 19th	March 8th	February 25th	March 16th
3rd month, 1st day	April 17th	April 6th	March 27th	April 14th
4th month, 1st day	May 17th	May 5th	April 25th	May 14th
5th month, 1st day	June 15th	June 4th	May 24th	June 12th
leap month, 1st day	n/a	n/a	June 23rd	n/a
6th month, 1st day	July 14th	July 3rd	July 22nd	July 12th
7th month, 1st day	August 13th	August 1st	August 20th	August 10th
8th month, 1st day	September 11th	August 31st	September 19th	September 8th
9th month, 1st day	October 11th	September 29th	October 18th	October 8th
10th month, 1st day	November 10th	October 29th	November 17th	November 6th
11th month, 1st day	December 10th	November 28th	December 16th	December 6th
12th month, 1st day	January 8th	December 27th	January 15th	January 4th

CLIMATE AND CONVERSIONS

Vietnam's climate is classified as "tropical monsoon," which roughly translates to a lot of rainfall, a lot of the time. In the south, temperatures stay roughly consistent; seasons are restricted to wet (May-Nov.) and dry (Dec.-Apr.). The farther north you go, the more temperature varies during the course of a year. For a rough conversion of Celsius to Fahrenheit, double the Celsius and add 30. For a more accurate conversion, multiply by the Celsius number by 1.8 and add 32. To convert in reverse, subtract 32 from the Fahrenheit number, multiply by 5, and divide by 9.

AVERAGE TEMPERATURES

Av. Temp. Precipitation	January			April			July			October		
	°C	°F	mm	°C	°F	mm	°C	°F	mm	°C	°F	mm
Hà Nội	14/19	58/66	18	22/30	71/80	81	27/32	80/90	323	23/28	73/82	99
Đà Nẵng	16/31	61/87	102	24/33	76/91	18	24/30	75/86	99	23/31	73/87	530
HCMC	22/31	72/88	15	26/34	79/93	43	25/32	77/89	315	24/31	76/87	269

MEASUREMENTS

Vietnam uses the metric system. The basic unit of length is the **meter (m),** which is divided into 100 **centimeters (cm),** or 1000 **millimeters (mm).** One thousand meters make up one **kilometer (km).** Fluids are measured in **liters (L),** each divided into

1000 **milliliters (ml).** A liter of pure water weighs one **kilogram (kg),** divided into 1000 **grams (g),** while 1000kg make up one metric **tons.**

1 in. = 25.4mm	1mm = 0.039 in.
1 ft.= 0.30m	1m = 3.28 ft.
1 yd. = 0.914m	1m = 1.09 yd.
1 mi. = 1.61km	1km = 0.62 mi.
1 oz. = 28.35g	1g = 0.035 oz.
1 lb. = 0.454kg	1kg = 2.202 lb.
1 fl. oz. = 29.57ml	1ml = 0.034 fl. oz.
1 gal. = 3.785L	1L = 0.264 gal.
1 square mile (sq. mi.) = 2.59 sq. km	1 square kilometer (sq. km) = 0.386 sq. mi.
1 sq. km = 100 hectares	1 hectare = 0.01 sq. km

LANGUAGE

VIETNAMESE PRONUNCIATION GUIDE

TONES

Vietnamese is a tonal language; the meaning of a word is determined by the pitch at which it's said. Each vowel assumes one of six different tones, which are indicated by the diacritical over the vowel.

a (no tone mark)	Spoken in a constant tone in one's upper range.
á (rising)	Spoken in a rising tone of voice, beginning in the middle of one's vocal range.
à (falling)	Spoken in a falling tone, beginning in one's lower range.
a (low glottal)	Very short, beginning in one's lower range and falling off abruptly.
ã (rising glottal)	Short, beginning mid-range, hitting a stop, and then rising abruptly.
â ("falling-rising")	Begins mid-range and falls quickly; if a final syllable, the vowel ends in a rising tone.

VOWEL AND CONSONANT SOUNDS

To further complicate things, some of the characters in written Vietnamese are pronounced differently than they would be in English, and certain vowels can be given additional diacriticals that change the vowel sound instead of the tone.

a	the vowel in "hat"	c	"k," but not aspirated; sounds a cross between "k" and "g"
ă	the vowel in "hat" with a schwa ("uh") on the end	d	northern dialect: "z," as in "zounds!"; southern/central dialect: "y," as in "yow!"
â	the vowel in "bun"	đ	"d," as in "darn"
e	the vowel in "bend"	gi	northern dialect: "z," as in "zounds!"; southern/central dialect: "y," as in "yow!"
ê	the second vowel in "cafe"	kh	"ch," as in a German person saying, "Ach!"
i	the vowel in "bee"	ng/ngh	"ng" with one's lips closed; sounds a cross between "ng" and "m"
o	the vowel in "law"	nh	"ni," as in "bunion"
ô	the vowel in "phone"	ph	"f," as in "fight"
o'	the vowel in "mud"	r	northern dialect: "z," as in "zounds"; southern/central dialect: "r" as in "rue"

u	the vowel in "boot"	t	"t," but not aspirated; sounds a cross between "t" and "d"
u'	the vowel in "cool" with a schwa at the end	th	"t," as in "terrible"
y	the vowel in "bee"	tr	northern dialect: "ch," as in "checkmate;" southern/central dialect: "tr," as in "trap"
yê/iê	the vowel combination in "the end"	x	"s," as in "salty"
uô	the vowel combination in "two one"	-ch	"ch," as in a German person saying "Ach!"
u'o'	the vowel combination in "you uh"	-nh	"ng" as in "bang"

PHRASEBOOK

Forms of address communicate levels of respect and are thus important to learn: don't address an older man as "friend" or a small child as "sir." Below we use the form of address *bạn* (friend); replace it wih other pronouns as circumstances dictate. Some vocabulary differs between northern and southern Vietnam.

FORM OF ADDRESS	VIETNAMESE	FORM OF ADDRESS	VIETNAMESE
friend, peer	bạn	child	em
younger man	anh	younger woman	chị
older man/male of higher status	ông	older woman/female of higher status	bà

THE BASICS	VIETNAMESE	THE BASICS	VIETNAMESE
hello	chào bạn	goodbye	chào bạn
What's your name?	Bạn tên gì	My name is...	Tôi tên là...
How are you?	Bạn khỏe không?	Excuse me.	Xin lỗi.
I don't speak Vietnamese.	Tôi không biết tiếng Việt.	Do you speak English?	Bạn biết nói tiếng Anh không?
please	làm ơn	Speak more slowly.	Xin nói chậm lại.
Thank you.	Cám ơn.	I don't understand.	Tôi không hiểu.
You're welcome.	Không có chi.	Please write it down.	Làm ơn viết nó ra.
Help!	Cứu với!	Do you have...?	Bạn có...?
I'm sorry.	Xin lỗi.	I want...	Tôi muốn...
yes	có	no	không
restroom	buồng tắm	toilet paper	giấy vệ sinh
Western toilet	cầu tiêu kiểu phương tây	squat toilet	cầu tiêu kiểu ngi chồm hổm
I'm lost.	Tôi lạc đường.	I don't know.	Tôi không biết.
I'm sick.	Tôi cảm thấy mệt.	doctor	bác sĩ
hospital	bệnh viện	police station	sở cảnh sát
hotel	khách sạn	guesthouse	nhà khách
room	phòng	air conditioning	điều hoà độ nhiệt (N)/ có máy lạnh (S)
passport	hộ chiếu	post office	bưu điện

NUMBERS	VIETNAMESE	NUMBERS	VIETNAMESE
0	không	11	mười một
half	nửa	12	mười hai
1	một	20	hai mươi

APPENDIX

NUMBERS	VIETNAMESE	NUMBERS	VIETNAMESE
2	hai	21	hai mươi mốt
3	ba	100	một trăm
4	bốn	200	hai trăm
5	năm	407	bốn trăm bảy
6	sáu	1000	một ngàn
7	bảy	10,000	mười ngàn
8	tám	11,000	mười một ngàn
9	chín	100,000	một trăm ngàn
10	mười	1,000,000	một triệu

DIRECTIONS	VIETNAMESE	DIRECTIONS	VIETNAMESE
Where is...?	...ở đâu?	I want to go to...	Tôi muốn đi đến...
How far is... from here?	... cách xa đây bao nhiêu?	How long does it take to get to...?	Đi bao lâu thì tới...?
close, near/nearby	gần	far, distant	xa
(to the) north	(phía) bắc	south	nam
east	đông	west	tây
left	bên trái	right	bên phải
kilometer	cây số	map	bản đồ

MONEY	VIETNAMESE	MONEY	VIETNAMESE
money	tiền	price	giá
US dollars	đô la	receipt	biên lai
credit card	thẻ tín dụng	How much does it cost?	Giá bao nhiêu?
bank	ngân hàng	inexpensive	rẻ
currency exchange	đổi tiền	expensive	đắt
ATM	máy lãy tiền/"ATM"	too expensive	đắt quá

FOOD	VIETNAMESE	FOOD	VIETNAMESE
to eat	ăn	I am a vegetarian.	Tôi ăn chay.
restaurant	tiệm ăn	I don't eat meat.	Tôi không ăn thịt.
I'm hungry.	Tôi đói.	I'm thirsty.	Tôi khát.
market	chợ	chopsticks	đôi đũa
hot	nóng	cold	lạnh
chicken	thịt gà	beef	thịt bò
pork	thịt lợn/thịt heo	fish	cá
tofu	đậu phụ	dog	thịt chó
eel	lươn	snake	rắn
rice	cơm	🍜 noodle soup	phở
spring rolls	nem rán	fish sauce	nước mắm
spicy	cay	not spicy	không cay
water	nước	bottled water	nước khoáng/nước chai
ice	đá	soup	xúp
fruit	hoa quả	vegetable	rau

FOOD	VIETNAMESE
beer	bia
coffee	cà phê
This is delicious!	Ngon lắm!
This could use more fish sauce.	Cần thêm nước mắm.

FOOD	VIETNAMESE
wine	rượu
tea	trà
This is not delicious!	Cái này không ngon!
Cheers!	Chúc!

TRANSPORT	VIETNAMESE
What time does the... leave?	Mấy giờ thì xe ... đi?
plane	maý bay
bus	xe buýt
bicycle	xe đạp
motorbike taxi	xe ôm
ticket	vé
train station	trạm xe lửa
airport	phi trường
Hey! This bus is filled with chickens!	Ê! Xe buýt này đầy những con gà!

TRANSPORT	VIETNAMESE
I would like to rent a...	Tôi muốn thuê một...
train	xe lửa
ferry	tàu
raft	xuồng
motorbike	xe máy/xe honda
stamp	tem
bus station	trạm xe buýt
luggage	hành lý
I am experiencing motion sickness.	Tôi đang bị say xe.

DAILY LIFE	VIETNAMESE
I already have a wife.	Tôi có vợ rồi.
Am I eating an endangered species?	Có phải tôi đang ăn một con thú sắp bị tuyệt chủng không?
Is there a problem, officer?	Có chuyện gì vậy chú?
How old are you?	Bạn bao nhiêu tuổi?
Zounds!	Chết rồi!
I am...	Tôi là...
... Australian	...người Úc
... English	...người Anh
... South African	...người Nam Phi

DAILY LIFE	VIETNAMESE
I already have a husband.	Tôi có chồng rồi.
Is that safe to eat?	Cái này ăn có an toàn không?
How is the road to...?	Con đường đi đến ... như thế nào?
I am... years old.	Tôi ... tuổi.
I love Vietnam.	Tôi yêu Việt Nam.
... American	...người Mỹ
... Canadian	...người Ca Na Đa
... European	...người Châu Âu
... Kiwi	...người Tân Tây Lan

GLOSSARY

Agent Orange: exfoliant used by the US during the American war; caused cancer, birth defects

ARVN: Army of the Republic of Vietnam; South Vietnam's armed forces during the American War

Bác Hồ: Uncle Ho; see "Hồ Chí Minh"

bãi biển: beach

bánh khoái: the "Huế pancake;" the best pork, mushroom, bean sprout, and onion omelette you've ever had

bánh xèo: shrimp-and-pork pancakes

Bahnar: an ethnic minority in the central highlands

bia ho'i: Vietnamese brew; nice and watered down

bò: beef

cá: fish

Cao Đài: an all-inclusive religion that started in the Mekong Delta

cao lẩu: specialty dish of Hội An

Chàm: an ethnic minority group in the southern and central regions of Vietnam; known for unique blending of Hindu, Buddhist, and Muslim traditions

Champa: kingdom of the Chàm minority group that dominated southern Vietnam from the 2nd-16th centuries

chè: popular street-side dessert; various kinds are made of coconut milk, grass jelly, and tapioca balls.

chó: dog

chợ: market

chúc: cheers!

cơm: rice; popular street-side dish

chữ nôm: Vietnamese language in Chinese characters

cyclo: a bike with a basket up front for you to sit in

Dao: an ethnic minority in northern Vietnam

Đại Việt: one of early Vietnam's names, utilized by the Lý and Trần dynasties; means "Great Việt"

đậu phụ/đậu hủ: tofu

đại lộ: less common word for street used in HCMC; also referred to as ĐL

Dau Quần Chẹt: ethnic minority in northwestern Vietnam

DMZ: Demilitarized Zone; the dividing line between North and South Vietnam

đổi mới: "renovation"; a set of economic reforms implemented in 1986 that essentially ushered in a market-based economy

đồng: Vietnamese currency

DRV: Democratic Republic of Vietnam; the full name given to North Vietnam after the country's split in 1954

đường: street

Êdê: an ethnic minority in the Central Highlands

gà: chicken

General Võ Nguyễn Giáp: famous general of the Việt Minh under Hồ Chí Minh

Geneva Convention: divided Vietnam and booted French troops; 1954

Giáy: an ethnic minority in northwestern Vietnam

grotto: a small cave

hẻm: alley

H'mông: an ethnic minority in northern Vietnam

Hồ Chí Minh: modern Vietnam's founding father; sole subject of many museums

Hoa: the largest minority group in Vietnam; descendants of the Han Chinese

Hòa Hảo: low-profile Vietnamese religion

Hùng kings: the earliest Vietnamese dynasty

Indochina Wars: a series of three wars between 1945 and 1979 fought against the French, Americans, and Chinese, respectively

Indochine: France's Southeast Asian colony

karst: dramatic limestone cliffs, caverns, and goodness

khách sạn: hotel

Khmer: an ethnic minority group in southern and central Vietnam

K'ho: an ethnic minority in the central highlands

Kinh: the ethnic Vietnamese majority

Lê Lợi: beloved national hero who began the Later Lê Dynasty; a friend of turtles

lợn/heo: pork

M'nong: an ethnic minority in the Central Highlands; elephant masters

Montagnards: French term for hill tribes

Mường: an ethnic minority in northern Vietnam

NLF: National Liberation Front, the army of Northern Vietnam during the American War

Ngô Đình Diệm: ruler of South Vietnam from 1954 until his assassination in 1963

Nông Dức Mạnh: Secretary-General of the Communist Party

Nùng: an ethnic minority in northern Vietnam

nước mắm: fish sauce

nước mía: sugarcane juice

Paris Peace Accords: the ceasefire signed by Vietnam and the US in 1973, calling for the withdrawl of American troops

phở: Vietnamese breakfast soup of choice made with beef broth, beef (most commonly), rice noodles, and a bunch of herbs

phố: street (used chiefly in Hà Nội)

Phu La: an ethnic minority in northwestern Vietnam

quán chay: vegetarian restaurant

quận: urban district; sometimes abbreviated Q

quốc ngữ: Latin-alphabet script invented during 17th century by French missionary Alexandre de Rhodes; still used today

rau: vegetables/herbs

RVN: Republic of Vietnam; the full name given to South Vietnam after the country's split in 1954

rượu: hard liquor

rượu đen: snake-blood vodka, a Vietnamese favorite

Saigon: the French name for Hồ Chí Minh City, officially used from 1862 to 1975

Shiva: a Hindu god, often pictured with more than one pair of arms

sinh tố: fruit shake shop

Tày: an ethnic minority in northern Vietnam

APPENDIX

Tết: Vietnamese New Year; cause for celebration

Thài: an ethnic minority in northern Vietnam

thịt bò: beef

triple religion: the term for what most Vietnamese practice; a combination of Confucianism, Mahayana Buddhism, and Taoism

tôm: shrimp

Uncle Ho: see "Hồ Chí Minh"

Việt Cộng: name given by the US for the National Front for the Liberation of South Vietnam (NLF), the northern Vietnamese guerrilla force active during the American War

Vietnamization: term for the slow removal of US troops from Vietnam initiated by President Richard Nixon that left the southern forces in the lurch

Việt Kiều: "overseas Vietnamese"; the Vietnamese diaspora

Việt Minh: guerrilla forces under the leadership of General Giap during WWII and First Indochina War; known officially as the Revolutionary League for the Independence of Vietnam

World Trade Organization (WTO): global organization that oversees trade between nations

xe máy: motorcycle

xe ôm: motorbike taxi; literally "hugging bike"

APPENDIX

INDEX

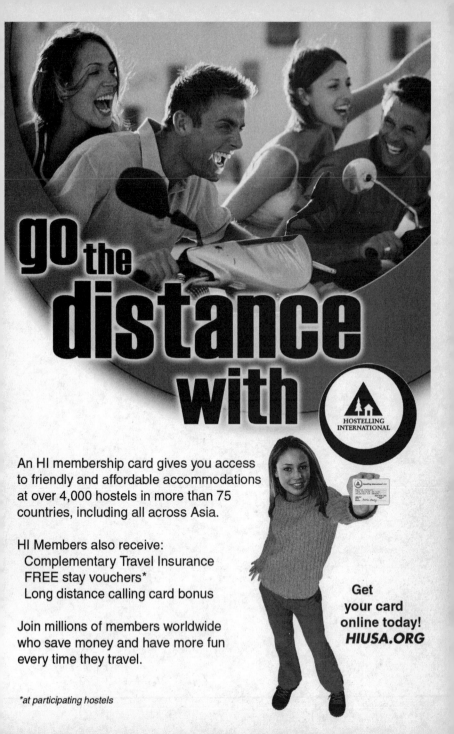

go the distance with

HOSTELLING INTERNATIONAL

An HI membership card gives you access to friendly and affordable accommodations at over 4,000 hostels in more than 75 countries, including all across Asia.

HI Members also receive:
  Complementary Travel Insurance
  FREE stay vouchers*
  Long distance calling card bonus

Join millions of members worldwide who save money and have more fun every time they travel.

Get your card online today! HIUSA.ORG

*at participating hostels

Visit www.orbitz.com today.

MAP INDEX

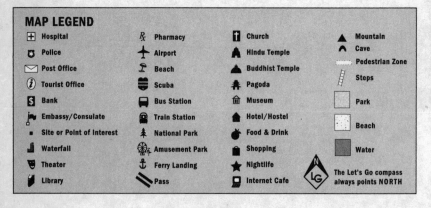

MAP LEGEND

Hospital
Police
Post Office
Tourist Office
Bank
Embassy/Consulate
Site or Point of Interest
Waterfall
Theater
Library

Pharmacy
Airport
Beach
Scuba
Bus Station
Train Station
National Park
Amusement Park
Ferry Landing
Pass

Church
Hindu Temple
Buddhist Temple
Pagoda
Museum
Hotel/Hostel
Food & Drink
Shopping
Nightlife
Internet Cafe

Mountain
Cave
Pedestrian Zone
Steps
Park
Beach
Water
The Let's Go compass always points NORTH